Double Jeopardy

A volume in the series

Adolescent Development and Legal Policy

EDITED BY FRANKLIN E. ZIMRING

Also in the series:

An American Travesty: Legal Responses to Adolescent Sexual Offending
by Franklin E. Zimring

Double Jeopardy

Adolescent Offenders with Mental Disorders

Thomas Grisso

Foreword by Franklin E. Zimring

University of Chicago Press | *Chicago & London*

Thomas Grisso, a clinical psychologist, is professor of psychiatry and coordinator of the Law and Psychiatry Program at the University of Massachusetts Medical School. He is the author or coauthor of several books, including *Youth on Trial,* also published by the University of Chicago Press.

The University of Chicago Press, Chicago 60637
The University of Chicago Press, Ltd., London
© 2004 by The University of Chicago
All rights reserved. Published 2004
Printed in the United States of America
13 12 11 10 09 08 07 06 05 04   1 2 3 4 5

ISBN: 0-226-30914-2 (cloth)

Library of Congress Cataloging-in-Publication Data

Grisso, Thomas.
    Double jeopardy : adolescent offenders with mental
    disorders / Thomas Grisso.
        p.   cm.—(Adolescent development and legal policy)
    Includes bibliographical references and index.
    ISBN 0-226-30914-2 (Cloth : alk. paper)
    1. Juvenile delinquents—Mental health—United States.
        2. Juvenile delinquents—Rehabilitation—United States.
        3. Juvenile delinquents—Mental health services—United
    States.   I. Title. II. Series.

    RJ506.J88 G75 2004
    364.36—dc22

                                        2003018271
♾ The paper used in this publication meets the minimum requirements of
the American National Standard for Information Sciences–Permanence of
Paper for Printed Library Materials, ANSI Z39.48-1992.

Contents

Foreword

At some point during adolescence, millions of young persons will be arrested by police or otherwise referred to the agencies of juvenile justice in the United States. Hundreds of thousands of young persons will suffer from serious emotional disorders during the transition to adulthood. The sheer arithmetic of American adolescence would guarantee that many thousands of those who are processed and adjudicated by institutions of juvenile justice suffer from serious emotional disabilities as well—even if there were no tendency for emotional problems to predispose adolescents to conflict and visible vulnerability. These are the children and adolescents at double disadvantage who are the subject of Thomas Grisso's important new study.

The conditions of double jeopardy that this book describes are important challenges to the quality of American juvenile justice. Youths who have serious emotional problems are more likely to be charged with serious acts of delinquency than nonafflicted youth. Every reform that reduces the number of kids who are locked up by diverting lower risk youths out of the system will probably increase the proportion of the institutional population that is at double jeopardy. Often, the further one goes in the system, the larger the overlap between emotional problems and custodial status in juvenile justice.

This study is organized around the special complications that the double-jeopardy population raises for the system's responses to their needs while in custody, to their potential incapacities to participate in the processes of juvenile justice, and to the assessment of their potential risk of harm to the community. In addition to organizing the growing body of research on emotional disorders among juvenile justice populations, this book provides a comprehensive structure for thinking about the double-jeopardy population. It uses a developmental perspective to inform its policy analysis, combining a command of the theoretical literature with practical insight in a most refreshing fashion.

Double Jeopardy is the first of a series of studies on adolescent development and legal policy that is supported by the John D. and Catherine T. MacArthur Foundation Research Network on Adolescent Development and Juvenile Justice. Our hope in launching the series is to commission monographs on specific topics that can be organized and addressed in ways that help researchers and policymakers alike. The model for this project is the series of monographs commissioned by Saleem Shah at the National Institute of Mental Health from the mid-1960s to the early 1980s. The board of editors for this series considered the overlap of emotional disorders and the institutions of juvenile justice to be an exemplary first topic for the project, and Thomas Grisso of the University of Massachusetts Medical School was an obvious choice as the author of a book on this topic.

This book vindicates the judgment of the editorial board. What Grisso provides for this important topic is a conceptual organization that serves as a structure for examining existing studies and as a framework for future work. In the immediate future, this book will serve as an up-to-date assessment of all that has been written in the field. But fifteen or twenty years from now, even as the literature on the topic will have expanded, the framework for analysis that Professor Grisso creates here will continue to provide assistance to the scholar and the practitioner.

Franklin E. Zimring

Acknowledgments

Writing this book required surveying the most recent works in a wide range of literature: developmental psychology, of course, but also child clinical psychology and psychiatry, developmental psychopathology, developmental criminology, juvenile justice policy, and mental health services research. Part of the journey took me to places I'd been before, but some expeditions led deep into unfamiliar territory. Finding the right information, assimilating it, and attempting synthesis across fields often proved perplexing.

It would have been a lonely trip indeed without friends, among whom I especially thank Elizabeth Cauffman, Dan Connor, Fran Lexcen, Bob Schwartz, Linda Teplin, and some of the best of colleagues associated with three organizations: members of the MacArthur Foundation Research Network on Adolescent Development and Juvenile Justice, faculty of the Center for Mental Health Services Research at the University of Massachusetts Medical School, and Joe Cocozza and Kathy Skowyra of the National Center for Mental Health and Juvenile Justice.

For stimulation of ideas during drafting and revision of the manuscript, I especially thank David Arredondo, Ed Mulvey, and Laurence Steinberg, as well as the Adolescent Development and Legal Policy series editor Frank Zimring—known affectionately during this process as "Sergeant Zimring of the Book Police"—who called almost weekly to ensure that I was neither delinquent in my duties nor without helpful encouragement to stay the course. Daily assistance in finding relevant texts was provided with resourceful efficiency by "Detective" Judith Quinlan. And thanks once again, Donna, for keeping the late-night coffeepot from running low.

Part 1

Examining Realities

Chapter 1

Reasons for Concern about Mental Disorders of Adolescent Offenders

Many agencies and advocates recently have urged that greater attention be given to the mental health needs of youths in the juvenile justice system (e.g., after an early warning by Cocozza, 1992: American Bar Association, 2001; Office of Juvenile Justice and Delinquency Prevention, 2000; National Council of Juvenile and Family Court Judges, 2000; National Mental Health Association, 2000; U.S. Surgeon General, 1999). They have pointed with alarm at an apparent increase in the proportion of youths with mental disorders in detention centers and juvenile correctional facilities, pressing the juvenile justice system to meet its obligation to provide them treatment.

This volume explores the basis for our obligations to identify and respond to adolescent offenders' mental disorders, examines the state of our knowledge about youths' mental disorders and their consequences, and charts a rational course for the juvenile justice system's response to the mental health needs of those who are in its custody. To set the stage, this chapter identifies why the question regarding mental health needs of juvenile offenders has arisen in recent years, the scope of the problem, and a foundation for examining the juvenile justice system's obligation to respond to youths' mental disorders.

How Delinquent Youths' Mental Disorders Got Our Attention

The juvenile justice system, now a little more than a century old, has weathered many storms in its first century. But it will probably require another two decades for it to recover from the tempests of the 1990s.

The barometer began to fall around 1987, when headlines and then

Justice Department statistics reported an increase in lethal violence by youth. The gathering clouds soon erupted and produced a growing flood of homicides and aggravated assaults committed by youths ages thirteen to seventeen, increasing year by year until the rates had more than doubled by 1994 (U.S. Department of Justice, 1980–1993, 1994, 1995–1996). Explanations ranged from notions that our country had spawned a generation of "super-predators" (DiIulio, 1995; Fox, 1996) to more reasonable interpretations of the confluence of changes in the drug market and the availability and use of guns by adolescents, especially in the cities (e.g., Blumstein, 1995; Zimring, 1998). Compounding the effect was an increase in school violence in suburbs and small towns nationwide, which, although contributing little to the crime rate, kindled intense public feelings of grief and vulnerability.

Out of the alarming words and images created by these events grew a "moral panic . . . an exaggerated perception of the seriousness of the threat and the number of offenders, and collective hostility toward the offenders, who [were] perceived as outsiders threatening the community" (Scott & Steinberg, 2003, p. 807). Reacting swiftly, legislators erected what were meant to be bulwarks against the rising flood of juvenile crime. Virtually every state modified its laws pertaining to juveniles in ways that resulted in more punitive sanctions for serious violent offenses by youths (U.S. General Accounting Office, 1995; Torbet et al., 1996; Snyder & Sickmund, 1999; Grisso, 1996). They lowered the age and broadened the offense criteria for trying adolescents in criminal court rather than juvenile court, more often required a transfer to criminal court for young people charged with serious offenses (reducing judicial discretion), and increased the penalties that were legally available or required for cases retained in juvenile court. Many states' legislatures made it clear that these changes constituted a fundamental reform in the purposes of the juvenile justice system, simultaneously revising the "purpose clause" of their juvenile codes to reflect a primary emphasis on public safety and only secondarily on rehabilitation (Grisso, 1996; Snyder & Sickmund, 1999). Momentum carried this trend in legal reform through the late 1990s, well beyond 1995 when Justice Department statistics began reporting a decrease in the volume of youths' violent offenses (Blumstein & Wallman, 2000). The bulwarks still stand; there has been little subsequent change to the more punitive sanctions that were put in place during those stormy years.

Concurrent with these events, juvenile justice personnel in the early 1990s began to report what they thought was an increasing proportion of youths with mental disorders entering the juvenile justice system

(Cocozza, 1992). In fact, reviews of epidemiologic studies seem to indicate that rates of mental disorders among adolescents in general (in the United States and European countries) were increasing during the past few decades compared to the first three-quarters of the twentieth century (e.g., Fombonne, 1998), possibly due to modern changes in the social context of adolescent development (Rutter & Smith, 1995). If the rates of mental disorder among youths in the juvenile justice system increased beyond that already-heightened base rate, there are several plausible explanations:

- The increase in youth violence itself produced traumatizing conditions in neighborhoods, elevating the prevalence of symptoms of mental disorders among youths in those neighborhoods.
- New laws reducing judicial discretion and assigning penalties based primarily on a youth's offense worked to decrease "screening" and "diversion" of mentally disordered youths from juvenile justice processing, allowing more of them to penetrate the juvenile justice system than had formerly been the case.
- Simultaneous with changes in crime rates and legal reforms, public mental health services for children were deteriorating in many states due to complex financial circumstances, creating a functional "diversion" of mentally disordered youths into juvenile justice facilities.

There is substantial evidence for the last of these explanations. During the 1990s, state after state experienced the collapse of public mental health services for children and adolescents (e.g., *New York Times*, 2001) and the closing of many—in some states, all—of their residential facilities for seriously disturbed youths (e.g., *Arizona Daily Star*, 2000; *Columbus Dispatch*, 2001). The juvenile justice system soon became the primary referral for youths with mental disorders. In California, the *Los Angeles Times* (November 21, 2000) reported that "absent adequate mental health services, the cop has become the clinician . . . the jail has become a crisis center," and quoted the chief of correctional services of the Los Angeles County Sheriff's Department as acknowledging that the Los Angeles County Jail was now the largest *de facto* mental health facility in the nation. Cases mounted in which parents gave up custody of their children to the juvenile justice system, or managed to have their children arrested, in order to obtain mental health services that they could no longer find in their communities (e.g., *Columbus Dispatch*, 2002; *Progressive*, 2001; *Omaha World-Herald*, 2002).

As the storm clouds of juvenile violence began to clear late in the 1990s, some surveyors of the wreckage—cited at the beginning of this chapter—began to call attention to the problem. They pointed to what appeared to be an alarming number of adolescents with mental disorders in juvenile justice custody, and they asserted the juvenile justice system's responsibility to identify them and to provide appropriate treatment.

But how big is the problem today? What is the nature of mental disorders among delinquent youths, and of what relevance are they for our nation's objectives for the juvenile justice system? Can we identify the young people about whom we are concerned? And above all, what types of intervention are needed? Can we chart a rational course for responding to their needs? The first step in answering these questions is to take a closer look at the scope of the problem, as described in studies of the prevalence of mental disorders among adolescent offenders in juvenile justice custody.

How Big Is the Problem?

We have no reliable data on the prevalence of mental disorders among juvenile justice youths prior to the 1990s (Otto et al., 1992). Therefore, an empirical estimate of the increase in prevalence does not exist. Nevertheless, the perception in the mid-1990s that the proportion was growing resulted in significant efforts by government agencies and social researchers to identify the prevalence of mental disorders among youths in juvenile detention and correction settings.

Studies of Prevalence in Juvenile Justice Settings

Several studies have identified a significant overlap between the populations of youths served by community public health agencies and youths in contact with a community's juvenile court (e.g., Rosenblatt, Rosenblatt, & Biggs, 2000; Vander Stoep, Evans, & Taub, 1997; Westendorp et al., 1986). In addition, some studies indicate that the prevalence of mental disorders among juvenile justice youths is higher than that among youths in other public health or educational settings (Stiffman et al., 1997), but about the same as those found among adolescents receiving services in community mental health programs and lower than those found in inpatient clinical services for youths (Atkins, Pumariega, & Rogers, 1999).

The specific scope of the problem, however, has been difficult to discern because of wide variations in estimates from study to study. (For a review of all such studies reported through 2002, see Cocozza & Skowyra, in press.) Research during the 1990s reported prevalence estimates for mental disorders in delinquent samples that varied from 50 to 100 percent. For example, prevalence for mental disorders among juvenile justice youth was reported as 53 percent in Maryland (Faenza, Siegfried, & Wood, 2000), about 60–70 percent for youths in Chicago (Teplin et al., 2002), 61 percent for youths in Georgia (Marsteller et al., 1997), and 76 percent in Texas (Pliszka et al., 2000). At the highest end of the spectrum, the prevalence of mental disorders for juvenile justice samples was reported to be 85 percent in Mississippi (Robertson & Husain, 2001) and 100 percent for youths in Ohio's juvenile justice facilities (Timmons-Mitchell et al., 1997).

The variability among these studies is considerable, but it is especially marked when one examines their reported prevalence rates for specific disorders. For example, a number of studies reported a prevalence of psychotic-spectrum disorders (e.g., schizophrenia) ranging from about 1 percent (Teplin et al., 2002) to 16 percent (Timmons-Mitchell et al., 1997) to 45 percent (Atkins, Pumariega, & Rogers, 1999). Mood disorders were listed as 10 percent (Wasserman et al., 2002), about 20 percent (Teplin et al., 2002), and 72 percent (Timmons-Mitchell et al., 1997); and anxiety disorders at 8 percent (Garland et al., 2001), 19 percent (Wasserman et al., 2002), 20–30 percent (Teplin et al, 2002), and 52 percent (Timmons-Mitchell et al., 1997). Attention-deficit/hyperactivity disorder (ADHD) was reported as low as 2 percent (Wasserman et al., 2002) and 18 percent (Pliszka et al., 2000) and as high as 76 percent (Timmons-Mitchell et al., 1997).

This troublesome variability may be related to many potential differences among studies in terms of their scope, framework, and measurement parameters. Moreover, often it is difficult to identify some of these study characteristics from their published reports. Generally, variation among studies has been along the following lines:

- Which mental disorders were included
- How "disorder" was defined (e.g., presence of symptoms versus a combination of their presence and their severity)
- Time frame for the presence of symptoms associated with the diagnosis (e.g., current, or past six or twelve months, or life-time prevalence)
- General methods for measuring disorders (e.g., unstructured clinical interviews, structured diagnostic interviews, paper-and-pencil measures, self-report, or multiple external sources of data)

- Specific instruments
- Use of criteria requiring a particular severity of disorder in order to qualify as a positive case
- Quality of the measures used
- Sample sizes (some being small)
- Contexts of youths' self-reports of symptoms (e.g., whether in the context of clinical care, the legal process, or research anonymity—which might influence youths' expectancies regarding use of the information and, thus, their motivations for reporting or concealing their symptoms)
- Types of facilities surveyed and thus the nature of the sample (e.g., youths on probation, in pretrial detention centers, or in postadjudication correctional facilities)
- Communities' uses of juvenile justice facilities (e.g., greater or lesser police diversion)
- Population characteristics, especially age, gender, and cultural or ethnic characteristics

Given the many ways studies can vary, it is not possible to sort out whether the differences in their results are due to actual differences in youths' characteristics from one study to another or due to methodological variation. The best we can do at present is examine a smaller set of studies that did have several methodological factors in common.

The DISC Studies

Three recent studies—Atkins, Pumariega, & Rogers (1999), Teplin et al. (2002), and Wasserman et al. (2002)—examined large samples of youths in secure juvenile justice facilities (with the proportions of youths by ethnicity being representative of the facilities) and used the Diagnostic Interview Schedule for Children (DISC) as their measure. As described in chapter 3, the DISC provides psychiatric diagnoses according to criteria established by the *Diagnostic and Statistical Manual of Mental Disorders* (DSM) (American Psychiatric Association, 1987, 1994). In addition, all three studies provided data for four major types of disorders, as well as overall prevalence (meeting criteria for one or more disorders). Prevalence was expressed two ways: youths meeting basic diagnostic criteria, and youths meeting those criteria as well as exceeding a level of impairment suggesting clinical significance. (This distinction is discussed in chapter 2.)

Table 1 compares the prevalence figures provided by these studies for boys (because not all studies included girls). The glass is half empty and

Table 1. Percent of Boys Meeting DSM Criteria for Mental Disorder
and Criteria for Mental Disorder Plus Significant Impairment

	Disruptive Disorders	Substance Use Disorders	Mood Disorders	Anxiety Disorders	One or More Disorders
Wasserman et al.					
Meets Criteria	32	50	10	20	62
Plus Impairment	25	30	2	12	NR
Teplin et al.					
Meets Criteria	41	51	19	21	66*
Plus Impairment	31	NR	16	20	63
Atkins et al.					
Meets Criteria	43	20	24	33	72
Plus Impairment	NR	NR	NR	NR	53

Notes: Atkins et al. sample includes a small proportion of girls; data were not reported separately by gender. Teplin et al. provide separate figures for girls as well, but they are omitted here in order to simplify the comparison to Wasserman et al.'s all-boy sample. Studies are from Wasserman et al. 2002; Teplin et al. 2002; and Atkins et al. 1999.
NR = not reported
*This figure was 74 percent for girls.

half full; there are some differences between studies, but overall, there are remarkable general similarities. The Wasserman et al. figures for specific disorders are somewhat lower than those of Teplin et al., which in turn are somewhat lower than those of Atkins, Pumariega, & Rogers. Wasserman et al. (2002) made this same comparison, noting that some of the discrepancies may be due to methodological differences between the studies:

- Wasserman used a newer version of the DISC (the DISC-IV) with somewhat different criteria than the one used by Teplin and Atkins (DISC-2.3) (described in chapter 3), and youths responded to questions via computer in Wasserman's administration in contrast to Teplin's and Atkin's use of interviewers.
- Wasserman's youths were in secure correctional facilities, while Teplin's were in a pretrial detention center. One might expect greater symptom severity for some psychological conditions among youths recently admitted to detention centers than among youths who have had time to "adjust" to confinement. Differences between results in these settings are

also possible because of differences in their willingness to report symptoms depending on their expectancies about people's responses to them.
• Wasserman measured current symptoms within the past month, while Teplin and Atkins measured symptoms during the past six months.
• The three studies used somewhat different measures of degree of impairment.

Despite these methodological differences, one sees considerable agreement at the broadest level of analysis; all three studies produced figures for "One or More Disorders" in roughly the 60–70 percent range. The discrepancies are more marked for specific levels of diagnostic classes, and they magnify further when one reaches a level of specificity beyond the classes shown in table 1. For example, for specific disorders associated with disruptive and impulsive behaviors, Wasserman and Teplin (respectively) reported 2 percent and 16 percent for ADHD, 3 percent and 14 percent for Oppositional Defiant Disorder, and 32 percent and 38 percent for Conduct Disorder. For disorders of mood, they reported (respectively) 7 percent and 13 percent for Major Depression, and 1 percent and 12 percent for Dysthymia. As noted earlier, these may be real differences associated with the different types of juvenile justice settings involved, or they might be related to one or more of the other methodological differences between the studies.

Thus, our best data suggest that the prevalence of disorders among juvenile justice youths is indeed quite high, but that either (a) we are uncertain about prevalence for specific disorders or (b) we should not expect to see similarities in prevalence of specific disorders across studies that sample from different types of facilities representing different "levels" of processing in the juvenile justice system.

The prevalence rates for almost all types of mental disorder are as high for girls in the juvenile justice system as for boys, and typically they are somewhat higher for girls, according to Teplin et al. (2002) and almost all other studies that have addressed the question. Very few studies have reported overall prevalence of mental disorders by ethnicity for juvenile justice youths. Teplin et al. (2002), however, reported a substantially higher prevalence (82 percent) among non-Hispanic white youths than among Hispanic (70 percent) or African American (65 percent) youths. I discuss these differences in greater detail later, but for the moment it is enough to note that the high prevalence rates in recent studies cut across gender and racial groups.

One would like to discuss these figures in the light of prevalence rates among adults in jails and prisons, but a meaningful comparison is not possible. The best data for adults in jails (Teplin, 1990, 1994) used an earlier version of the Diagnostic Interview Schedule designed for use with adults, so it did not identify the same disorders as in the adolescent studies (e.g., did not include attention deficit and disruptive behavior disorders). Moreover, it identified criteria for individuals' mental disorders only within the most recent two weeks (compared to one month for Wasserman et al. and six months for Teplin et al.). Where disorders themselves were more or less directly comparable (apart from the time factor), prevalence tended to be lower for adults in jail than for adolescents in detention. For example, Teplin et al. (2002) found that about 13 percent of detention boys (22 percent of girls) manifested Major Depressive Disorder, compared to about 4 percent of men in jail (10 percent of women) (Teplin, 1990, 1994). In the same studies, Substance Use Disorders were found for about 50 percent of boys and 46 percent of girls, compared to about 30 percent of men and 50 percent of women in jail. Similarly, prevalence of "serious mental disorders" for males in prisons has been reported to be in the area of 10–20 percent (Jemelka, Rahman, & Trupin, 1993; Pinta, 1999), figures that seem much lower than those found by Wasserman et al. (2002) for youths in juvenile correctional facilities. But method and measurement differences do not allow one to make much of the comparison.

Making a Best Estimate

Concluding just how high we believe the prevalence of mental disorder to be also requires taking into consideration choices in what we categorize as a mental disorder. Some choices would suggest adjustments downward from the figures in these studies, while others would suggest even higher rates.

For example, should we exclude Conduct Disorder from our definition of a "mental disorder," inasmuch as its diagnosis is based primarily on the presence of persistent delinquent behavior rather than symptoms of disturbed thought and emotion? While some might believe we should, others point to research that seems to identify neurological and psychological impairments of a "clinical" nature underlying the majority of cases of Conduct Disorder (see generally Barkley, 1996; Hinshaw & Anderson, 1996). Moreover, as we will see in later chapters, youths with Conduct

Disorder frequently meet criteria for one or more other mental disorders. In fact, Teplin et al. (2002) reported that excluding cases involving Conduct Disorder in the absence of any other disorder, the overall proportion of youths in their sample with mental disorders was reduced only from 66 to 61 percent for boys and from 74 to 70 percent for girls (with additional requirements for significant impairment: 59 percent for boys, 66 percent for girls). Thus excluding Conduct Disorder would only slightly lower our estimates of the proportion of youths with mental disorders.

We might say that our real concerns do not include all youths who can meet criteria for any mental disorder, but rather those who have serious and chronic mental disorders. "Seriously emotionally disturbed" or SED youths have chronic, persistent, and multiple disorders (Davis & Vander Stoep, 1997); and although they constitute a small proportion of adolescents meeting criteria for mental disorders, they consume an extraordinary proportion of mental health resources, and their mental health needs typically continue through their adolescent years into adulthood. Some efforts to estimate their numbers place the figure around 9–13 percent (e.g., Friedman et al., 1996), and one could presume that the figure might be twice as high among youths in the juvenile justice system (Cocozza & Skowyra, 2000). But we would not want to restrict the system's attention only to these youths without careful scrutiny, because it is not immediately apparent that other disorders of less severity or chronicity are irrelevant, and, as we shall see later, there are many ways to define the seriousness of mental disorders.

In contrast, there is a strong argument for raising the estimates above those provided by the studies we have been reviewing, because few of them examined the full range of disorders that we might choose to include. Most studies, for example, did not assess for Mental Retardation and other developmental disorders, and few examined Posttraumatic Stress Disorder. Including these might not greatly increase the general prevalence estimate (because many youths with such disorders might already have met criteria for other disorders within the existing studies), but it would certainly move the figure upward.

Where does this leave us? No study has ever reported prevalence rates in any juvenile justice sample that were similar to those reported for youths in the general population of the United States, usually estimated at 15–25 percent for six-month to one-year prevalence of mental disorders (Costello et al., 1996; Kazdin, 2000a; Roberts et al., 1998). At the level of secure pretrial detention or postadjudication secure corrections, the proportion of youths with mental disorders (although defined in diverse ways) is probably two to three times higher than the prevalence for youths in general in the community.

This estimate is believable on its face. If the prevalence estimate is 20 percent in the general population, it is likely to be higher than that for adolescents in the general population who live in lower socioeconomic communities in which some majority of delinquent youths reside. We may also assume that within that subsample, delinquent youths as a group are likely to be sufficiently *more* deviant (and disturbed) than their already high-risk peers in order to warrant referral to the juvenile justice system. Thus it is not surprising that they manifest substantially greater prevalence estimates of mental disorder than U.S. youths on average. Moreover, the figures provided in existing studies must be considered conservative estimates, because they typically do not include some disorders that are relevant for an analysis of youths' mental health needs, especially those related to mental retardation and a number of other developmental disorders that I identify later. This is enough to warrant our concern, even if we are uncertain where the prevalence figure falls in the 45–75 percent range.

The Relevance of Prevalence

As noted earlier, results from studies like those reviewed above have been part of the motivation for recent, urgent calls for widespread mental health screening and assessment of youths in the juvenile justice system, as well as appeals to provide appropriate services to all adolescents in the system with mental health needs. There is no doubt that our current prevalence figures offer a strong justification for increased attention to the problem. But of what kind, and with what scope? Must the juvenile justice system become the nation's mental health system for troubled adolescents?

As this analysis unfolds, we will see that our figures regarding youths who meet diagnostic criteria for mental disorders do not define the scope or nature of our obligation to respond to the mental health needs of adolescent offenders. Not all youths who meet diagnostic criteria need treatment. Some who do *not* meet diagnostic criteria nevertheless *do* need treatment. Others meet diagnostic criteria for which there is no reasonable treatment. Still other youths have multiple disorders that make it difficult to determine what type of treatment they need. And some treatments that are traditionally provided to youths are not effective and should not be provided at all.

We will later encounter all of these complexities as we explore the nature of psychopathology in adolescent offenders as it relates to the problem of deciding how the juvenile justice system should respond to their disorders. But first we must address a more basic question: Why should we respond to adolescent offenders' mental health needs? The question may seem superficial in light of the ease with which one can justify society's general obligation to provide treatment for youths suffering from mental disorders. Here, however, I suggest a broader perspective. There are three principal reasons why we should be concerned about adolescent offenders' mental disorders, reasons that provide a central structure for my analysis throughout this book:

- *Custodial treatment obligations:* Public agencies have a legal and moral responsibility to respond to the mental health needs of adolescents in their custody.
- *Due process protection in adjudicative proceedings:* Adults with mental disorders are afforded certain due process protections as defendants accused of criminal acts, and adolescents with mental disorders who are charged with crimes or with delinquencies in juvenile court must be assured equal protection.
- *Public safety:* To the extent that there is a relation between youths' mental disorders and their likelihood of future violent behaviors, obligations associated with the justice system's mandate to protect the public may require special provisions for the identification, management, and treatment of adolescents who manifest mental disorders.

These three areas of concern provide *sociolegal contexts* for our responses to young offenders with mental disorders. The following review of each context reveals primary questions regarding decisions about policy and practice in the juvenile justice system. They form the basic terrain for the later analyses in this book.

The Treatment Context: States' Obligations to Provide Mental Health Treatment for Adolescents in Justice System Custody

A moral argument can be made that individuals in the custody of criminal and juvenile justice systems are entitled to services that are designed to provide treatment for their mental disorders that result in significant distress or dysfunction. The rationale for this obligation resides in the condition of custody itself. Restrictions of liberty inherently reduce individuals' access to public health services ordinarily provided to individuals as a consequence of their eligibility as citizens. Confined persons in custody of the government should therefore be provided a way to obtain similar services. In the case of adolescents, an additional rationale is their dependence on adults for access to most health services (e.g., the need for parental or custodial consent to the treatment of children).

A full assessment of the degree to which this moral obligation is recognized in law would require reviewing federal and state statutes that define those obligations, case law in specific states, and federal or state regulations that have been developed to implement legal requirements—all of which are beyond the scope of the present work. Nevertheless, it is necessary to consider certain general features of this terrain if we are to understand the treatment context.

Courts have sometimes interpreted states' juvenile justice purpose clauses to require that juvenile justice systems have some degree of responsibility to identify, and provide treatment for, youths in juvenile justice custody who have special mental health problems (see, e.g., *State v. S.H.*, 877 P.2d 205 [Washington 1994]; *In re J.F.*, 787 P.2d 364 [Montana 1990]). Federal rules are consistent with this presumption. For example, section 223 of the Juvenile Justice and Delinquency Prevention Act, 42 U.S.C. § 5633, states with respect to state plans that "(a) . . . In accordance with regulations which the Administrator shall prescribe, such plans shall . . . (8)(D) contain . . . (i) an analysis of mental health services available to juveniles in the juvenile justice system . . . and (ii) a plan for providing needed mental health services to juveniles in the juvenile justice system."

What do regulations of this type mean when they refer to "mental health services"? Presumably they are not referring to the general rehabilitation efforts that apply to every youth in the juvenile justice system. For example, many detention or corrections facilities, as well as community probation services, operate on a day-to-day system of monitoring and correction, behavior modification principles, weekly individual and/or group counseling sessions involving discussions of problem behavior and problem solving, and special educational, occupational, and recreational activities. All of these are designed to "rehabilitate" youths, and sometimes they are even provided by mental health professionals. Yet, inasmuch as these types of general rehabilitative efforts are already provided in the majority of juvenile justice systems to some degree, exhortations and mandates for "mental health services" for youthful offenders must have some more specific meaning.

If we are not referring to routine "rehabilitation" services, and if "mental health services" are not defined simply by the profession of the person providing the services, what do we mean by "mental health services" in this context? Let us presume that our mandates refer to the need for special clinical services that are signaled in some way by the identification of certain underlying conditions that are considered to be "clinical" in nature. In that case, it is clear that a starting point for identifying the need for special mental health services beyond "routine" rehabilitative efforts would be signaled in part by the identification of youths who have diagnosable mental disorders that are frequently treated by psychiatric or psychological intervention. I review these disorders in chapter 2 in the course of examining the diagnostic categories within the DSM that are used by mental health professionals. Generally they include *anxiety, mood, attention deficit, psychotic, somatoform, dissociative, eating, sleeping,* and *substance use* disorders, as well as *disruptive behavior disorders (conduct disorder, oppositional defiant disorder).* These disorders are identified by strictly assessing the presence or absence of certain symptoms, on the basis of which adolescents are then classified as "having" one or more of these disorders. We could say that the mandates for mental health services call for the availability of interventions that are designed to treat those disorders.

This is a reasonable way to begin identifying young people who need treatment. As Jensen and Watanabe (1999) have observed, "few would dispute the necessity of (DSM) diagnostic labels. . . . For good or ill, [they] have become the benchmark by which the appropriateness of persons' access to services is judged" (p. 118). Obtaining third-party reimbursement that finances the provision of mental health services often requires the identification of "patients" according to their DSM diagnostic label. So DSM diagnosis must play a primary role in any effort to circumscribe the population of youths with which we are concerned.

But this does not mean that we should limit our notion of "disorder" to DSM diagnoses and our notion of treatment only to efforts to modify them. As we shall see in chapter 2, there are effective ways to identify the mental health needs of youths that do not involve diagnoses. And in chapter 4, I review some effective treatment approaches that do not base their definitions of success on the reduction of symptoms of DSM-diagnosed disorders. So we should not automatically restrict our definition of "mental health needs" to DSM-diagnosed disorders, or our definition of "mental health services" and "treatment" to interventions that define their success according to the remission of the disorders that DSM diagnoses represent.

Finally, no matter what system we use to identify the population of adolescent offenders who manifest mental disorder, having identified them will not necessarily define which of those youths are in need of special treatment. There are two reasons that we should resist the knee-jerk reaction to prescribe treatment for all youths manifesting a mental disorder.

First, enormous financial and professional resources would be required to identify each adolescent's mental disorder and to provide treatment for it. We would want to know what impact this would have on our financial ability to perform other important services that are expected of the juvenile justice system. A full analysis of this issue is far too complex to undertake here, but at least its dimensions will have to be explored. For example, do our mandates refer to every youth who comes into contact with the juvenile justice system, including those who are seen only momentarily before being diverted from the system? Or might our obligations vary with regard to youths who penetrate the juvenile justice system to various levels of case processing, and youths who manifest disorders of particular severity?

Second, beneficent interventions unrestrained can carry with them potential dangers to liberty and self-determination. Pleas for treatment of adolescent offenders' mental disorders have a laudable humanitarian intent, but history is replete with examples of beneficent public policies that have ended up serving less-than-beneficent ends. Current general appeals for mental health reforms in juvenile justice are rarely accompanied by careful analysis of the potential negative implications of the reforms that they propose. Among the dangers, discussed in greater detail in later chapters, are increases in delinquency referrals (e.g., by parents) merely in order to obtain mental health services, the potential overuse of medications to achieve behavioral control, increases in length of confinement for purposes of diagnosis and treatment, and the potential misuse of information gained in clinical diagnostic procedures (for instance, as evidence to secure convictions).

These practical considerations for placing some limiting constraints on our obligation to treat youthful offenders with mental disorders need not be seen as merely convenient ways to reduce our burden. Clinical treatment is not prescribed anywhere in the world of health care merely upon determining that a person has a diagnosable disorder. Some disorders are best left untreated, while others may or may not require treatment depending on the degree of severity of symptoms in a particular case and on what is known about the probable course of the disorder. For still other disorders there is no known treatment.

Refining our treatment obligation, therefore, requires consideration of the nature of psychopathology in adolescents, especially among youthful offenders. What is the state of the art in defining mental disorders of adolescence, their severity, and their effects on youths' functioning? Can they be defined discretely, and if so, can they be identified reliably, especially among adolescent offenders? Having been identified, what do we know about their course and their consequences that should inform our refinement of the mandate to provide treatment to young offenders with mental disorders? Do we even have treatments that will work, and if so, for what disorders? Subsequent chapters address these questions, examining definitions of mental disorders of adolescence, as well as our capacities to identify them, to anticipate their consequences, and to treat them. This will be necessary before we return (in chapter 5) to an analysis of how the juvenile justice system's mandate to provide treatment to young offenders can be interpreted and implemented.

The Adjudicative Context: Due Process Obligations in Legal Proceedings

A second reason for our concern about mental disorders among adolescent offenders is the potential relevance of mental disorder for due process guarantees in the adjudication of youths. Criminal law has long recognized the need for special protections of persons from potentially unfair consequences of their mental disorders during the adjudicative process. Three areas in which due process may be jeopardized by defendants' mental disorders include the waiver of *Miranda* rights during police interrogation, defendants' competence to stand trial, and exculpation or mitigation in the adjudication of alleged offenses (e.g., "not guilty by reason of insanity").

The first of these, waiver of *Miranda* rights, arises when there are questions about the admissibility of a defendant's confession at trial. Confessions are admissible if they have been made "knowingly, intelligently and voluntarily" after the defendant was informed of the rights to avoid self-incrimination and to obtain prior assistance of counsel (*Fare v. Michael C.*, 442 U.S. 707 [1979]). Defendants' mental disorders alone do not preclude a valid waiver of these rights (*Colorado v. Connelly*, 479 U.S. 157 [1986]). Yet the potential effects of mental disorder have long been considered relevant factors for judicial consideration when weighing the admissibility of a confession.

The second due process issue, competence to stand trial, requires that defendants must not be put to trial if they lack requisite abilities to participate meaningfully in their defense. Those abilities were broadly outlined in *Dusky v. United States*, 362 U.S. 402 (1960): whether the defendant has the capacity to assist counsel "with a reasonable degree of rational understanding" and has a "factual as well as rational understanding of the nature of the proceedings against him." These phrases typically have been interpreted to require the capacity to understand the nature and process of one's trial, to assist and work with counsel in one's defense, and to make important decisions that involve the potential waiver of constitutional rights—for example, accepting or refusing a pleas agreement (*Godinez v. Moran*, 113 S. Ct. 2680 [1993]). Deficits in these abilities typically must be due to mental illness or mental retardation, although not all states narrow the antecedent conditions in this way.

The insanity defense is a special plea of "not guilty by reason of insanity." It asserts that at the time of the alleged offense, due to mental illness or mental retardation, the defendant lacked the capacity to appreciate the wrongfulness of his or her conduct or lacked the capacity to control his or her behavior. The precise standard governing an insanity defense can vary from state to state, and the differences have important implications for the deficits that must be shown (Borum, 2003b). But over one-half of the states use some variation of the above definition, which is taken from the American Law Institute model standard (1962). In general, all of the standards require a showing of the effects of mental illness on the defendant's cognitions, motivations, emotions, or behavior at the time of the offense, with the potential that the defendant receive a "not guilty by reason of insanity" verdict, avoiding the usual sentence that would accompany a guilty verdict.

Over time, the evolution of modern law has created a functional approach to all three of these issues of due process (Grisso, 2003). It is not the mere presence of mental disorder that creates conditions of invalid waiver of rights, incompetence to stand trial, or insanity. They require sufficient evidence that an individual's mental disorder actually impairs functioning in a way that is legally relevant (for competence, actually impairs one's ability to participate in a defense, or for insanity, impairs a person's ability to appreciate wrongfulness or to control one's behavior at the time of an offense). Thus, among defendants with serious mental disorders, some may be found competent and some incompetent, and some may be found fully culpable and others not. The consequence of the disorder in the individual case—whether and how it actually impaired one's functioning—is the fact that matters for deciding the legal issue. In addition, laws in this area typically exclude certain mental disorders (e.g., personality disorders and substance abuse/dependence disorders) from consideration as a basis for insanity (Melton et al., 1997). Laws pertaining to competence to stand trial generally have been less restrictive regarding the types of disorders that might form a basis for dysfunction related to participation in one's defense.

How do these laws apply to youths with mental disorders? Criminal law (pertaining to adolescents tried in criminal court), juvenile law, and social science treatises provide little guidance (Grisso, 1998; Woolard, Reppucci, & Redding, 1996). Even recent treatises on the application of *Miranda* waiver (Feld, 2000), competence to stand trial (Bonnie & Grisso, 2000), and culpability laws (Scott, 2000) in adolescent cases say little about their application to youths with mental disorders in either criminal or juvenile court, focusing their arguments instead on youths' immaturity. Similarly, there is little case law on the application of the insanity defense in juvenile court (Woolard et al., 1996), and few cases (and no research) have addressed the potential relevance of psychopathology for the insanity defense among adolescents tried in criminal court. Concerning youths' capacities to waive *Miranda* rights, the most comprehensive study (Grisso, 1981) did not examine their relation to youths' mental disorders.

Why is there so little information on the relevance of mental disorder among adolescents for their capacities associated with adjudicative matters? The reason in part is historical; not until recent decades have the issues of adolescents' due process rights been seriously tested in the law.

In *criminal* court, for example, the issue of youths' competence to stand trial was not raised with any frequency until the 1990s. Before then, most youths tried in criminal court were older adolescents, and most had arrived there through a screening process that depended on judicial discretion, retaining those with serious mental disorders for juvenile court adjudication. Changing laws in the 1990s, however, took this screening process away from judges by transferring youths to criminal court based on the nature of their offenses alone, increasing the likelihood that criminal courts would have to deal with mentally disordered adolescents.

In *juvenile* court, the legal concepts of "incompetence" and "insanity" were rarely applied in delinquency cases prior to the 1990s (Scott, 1992). The potential for their application was set in the 1960s when the U.S. Supreme Court established that many constitutional protections for defendants in criminal courts were to be afforded to youths in delinquency cases in juvenile court (*Kent v. United States,* 383 U.S. 541 [1966]; *In re Gault,* 387 U.S. 1 [1967]). Among these were the right to avoid self-incrimination, the right to representation by counsel, and the right to an adjudicative process that mirrored many of the due process protections of criminal court proceedings. Yet the concepts of incompetence to participate in one's defense and exculpation due to insanity were slow to evolve in juvenile courts, partly because of their "civil" history and their continued mandate to provide rehabilitation.

Legislative reforms of the 1990s, however, made the concept of competence to stand trial very much a part of the picture in juvenile courts (see generally Grisso & Schwartz, 2000). Among these changes were the recognition of public protection as the primary purpose of the juvenile court (relegating rehabilitation to a secondary purpose), an increase in penalties and determinate sentences, and dispositional schemes that allowed for corrections jurisdiction of the juvenile justice system to extend well into the adult years in some circumstances. These conditions greatly reduced the salience of a "best interest" rationale for avoiding a "strong" interpretation of the place of defendant's rights in juvenile court. Confessions by adolescents now had more long-ranging implications, and a fair trial seemed now to require a "competent" defendant. By the end of the 1990s, over one-half of the states formally recognized the application of the concept of competence to stand trial in juvenile courts (Redding & Frost, 2002). Similarly, the trend to hold youths responsible for their offenses in ways that created significant punitive consequences began to draw some attention to the need to scrutinize the potential effects of mental disorder on their offending, such that serious mental disorder might warrant exculpation for reasons of insanity as in criminal cases.

As these issues were raised more frequently for adolescents in both criminal and juvenile courts, there was a tendency toward simple downward extensions of relevant legal definitions and procedures that had evolved in criminal law. Little attention was given to potential difficulties in their application created by adolescents' developmental status and the nature of mental disorders in adolescence. For example, the majority of adults who are found incompetent to stand trial for reasons of mental illness carry diagnoses of serious mental disorders, usually schizophrenia (Nicholson & Kugler, 1991). The typical age of onset for a first psychotic episode of schizophrenia is in the early twenties (for men) to late twenties (for women) (American Psychiatric Association, 1994). Does this mean that adolescents could rarely be found incompetent to stand trial due to mental illness? Or is it possible that other disorders of childhood and adolescence, different in form or kind from those seen in adults, might create functional deficits amounting to incompetence to stand trial?

Further analysis of these due process issues requires an examination of what we know about adolescent psychopathology that might relate to capacities associated with trial participation and culpability of defendants. Given the types of abilities that are relevant for these legal concepts, what are the relations between mental disorders of adolescence and those abilities? And how well can we identify those conditions in individual cases in order to ensure equitable application of due process protections for youths with mental disorders? I undertake this examination in subsequent chapters.

The Public Safety Context: The Obligation to Reduce the Risk of Harm to Others

A third reason for concern about mental disorders among adolescent offenders is the potential relation between mental disorders and aggressive, harmful behavior. Although the system's mandate to reduce aggression may be interpreted broadly to refer to all forms of aggression, harm to others (in contrast to harm to property) has been the primary focus of public concern. The justice system's mandate to reduce the likelihood of harm to others creates two types of obligations, pertaining to (a) assessment and security, and (b) treatment to reduce risk of violence.

Concerning assessment and security, the justice system has an obligation to identify youths in its custody who present increased potential for future physical harm to others (hereinafter, "risk of harm") and to take reasonable steps to reduce the likelihood of harm. This responsibility arises at various points in juvenile case processing. "Danger to others" is one of the legal criteria justifying secure pretrial detention (*Schall v. Martin,* 467 U.S. 253 [1984]). Criteria applied to the question of judicial transfer (waiver) of an adolescent for trial in criminal court often requires a finding that the youth presents too great a danger to the public to be dealt with in juvenile justice programs (Dawson, 2000; Grisso, Tomkins, & Casey, 1988). For youthful offenders who remain in juvenile court, risk of harm arises as an important consideration in arranging for dispositional placements (e.g., secure correctional options) that will ensure the protection of the public.

Not all risk-of-harm questions are the same (Grisso, 1998). Detention cases focus on imminent likelihood of harm, whereas courts weighing posttrial disposition options will want to consider the risk of potential harm over a longer period of time—for example, the next year or two. In a juvenile court hearing on the question of an adolescent's transfer to criminal court, inquiring about future risk of harm may require considering an even more distant future, asking whether the youth is likely to continue to be a threat to the community many years later in adulthood.

The second public safety obligation—treatment to reduce risk of harm—is related to the more general mandate for the juvenile justice system to "rehabilitate" young offenders. The purpose of justice system rehabilitation is to change behavior in order to reduce recidivism and maximize public safety. Virtually all delinquency cases involve a judgment (if not a formal assessment) regarding the rehabilitative option that is most likely to decrease recidivism and therefore best serve public safety (and the interests of the youth).

Like questions about risk of harm, questions concerning rehabilitative disposition occur throughout juvenile case processing. They arise informally at early stages of processing where diversion from the full adjudicative process may be considered by probation officers. They occur formally in relation to the question of transfer to criminal court, asking whether the youth is "unamenable to rehabilitation" in the juvenile justice system (that is, whether in light of the characteristics of the youth and the potential interventions available to the juvenile justice system, there is little or no prospect for rehabilitation prior to the end of juvenile court jurisdiction) (Dawson, 2000; Grisso, Tomkins & Casey, 1988). They arise again, of course, in all cases with a delinquency finding, requiring a dispositional decision by the court regarding placement or services that will best serve the public interest in safety and reduced recidivism.

Questions of risk of harm and rehabilitation potential are brought together when raised in transfer and disposition hearings. The higher the risk of harm, the more restricted the range of intervention options that can be considered for potential rehabilitation plans. And the more resistant to rehabilitation influence the youth is perceived to be, the greater the likelihood that he may present both a short-term and a long-term risk of harm.

In all such questions, personnel in the juvenile justice system—from intake probation officers to judges—endeavor to weigh a youth's likelihood of future aggressive or violent behavior. How do adolescents' mental disorders enter into these judgments? First, mental disorders can effect the likelihood that a youth will engage in aggressive behavior. Some disorders might increase the risk and others decrease it, though still others may have no relation to future violence. If such relationships exist, then mental disorders—their type, chronicity, and expected course—would be factors to consider in an assessment and judicial weighing of the risk of harm. Second, if mental disorders play a role in risk of harm or recidivism, then their treatment becomes part of the juvenile justice system's rehabilitative obligation to reduce that risk. The likelihood that treatment will help to reduce risk, however, may vary for different disorders. Thus the nature and relative effectiveness of treatments for relevant mental disorders among delinquent youths becomes important information in assessing future risk of harm as well as likelihood of rehabilitation success.

Therefore, to improve policy and practice in meeting public safety obligations in cases involving youths with mental disorders, it is necessary that we examine our knowledge about (a) the relation between mental disorder and violence among youthful offenders, (b) our capacities to assess the likelihood of future violence in individual cases, and (c) the effects of various treatments for reducing aggression associated with mental disorders.

Research on the risk of violence among adults with mental disorders has progressed remarkably in the past decade (e.g., Link & Steuve, 1994; Monahan et al., 2001; Quinsey et al., 1998; Steadman et al., 1998). The findings suggest that simply knowing that people have a mental disorder does not always tell us much about their likelihood of engaging in future violence. Some disorders have a substantial relation to future violence (e.g., psychopathy: e.g., Hare, 1999), others have no relations or small to modest relations to future violence, and still others have small *negative* relations to violence (e.g., schizophrenia: e.g., Steadman et al., 1998). All disorders present increased potential for violence in combination with substance abuse (e.g., Swanson et al., 1997; Steadman et al., 1998). Many of the studies cited above have developed relatively sophisticated assessment methods for identifying which adults, with and without mental disorders, are more or less likely to be violent in the future, over both the short and the long term.

Unfortunately, research on the relation of violence and mental disorders among adolescent offenders lags far behind these advances with regard to adult patients and offenders. In chapter 4 I review some of the progress that has been made in identifying the antecedents of future violence in adolescents generally, as well as advances in understanding aggression among youths with mental disorders. What is needed, however, is information on the relevance of mental disorders for future aggression specifically among young offenders, as well as reliable ways to assess both their disorders and their risk of future harm. Later I examine the state of our knowledge and art in this regard, in preparation for considering what is needed to fulfill the juvenile justice system's responsibilities for public safety in cases of adolescent offenders with mental disorders.

Laying a Foundation

I have outlined three reasons for concern about justice system responses to young offenders with mental disorders: (a) the custodial obligation to provide for their treatment, (b) the obligation to provide due process that protects defendants from the consequences of their disorders at trial and in relation to culpability for their offenses, and (c) the systems' obligation to provide for public safety. These form three sociolegal contexts within which we must examine how best to fulfill our obligations to respond to the mental disorders of adolescent offenders.

The description of each of these contexts raised questions about the nature of youths' mental disorders, their identification, and their consequences, all of which must be answered before we can form a coherent set of policies and practices for meeting our obligations in these three contexts. The following three chapters review the state of our knowledge in those areas, as evidenced in the basic research and clinical literature on developmental psychopathology (chapter 2), the clinical assessment of adolescents (chapter 3), and the potential ways in which youths' mental disorders are related to the purposes embedded in each of our three sociolegal contexts (chapter 4). After laying this foundation regarding current knowledge in these areas, we can return to the three sociolegal contexts (chapters 5, 6, and 7), applying that information to determine what we can and cannot confidently conclude—and what more we need to know—in order to shape policy and practice in the interests of society and of adolescent offenders with mental disorders.

In order to get our bearings, here is a brief preview of the questions explored in subsequent chapters:

- Chapter 2: What conditions should be included under the category of "mental disorders" for purposes of identifying the prevalence of mental disorders among adolescent offenders and our appropriate legal responses to them? To what extent is mental disorder stable or transient during adolescence? To what extent is it predictive of mental disorder in adulthood? The answers to these questions will have a substantial impact on how we can fulfill our treatment, due process, and public safety obligations.
- Chapter 3: How reliably can we identify mental disorders and their

symptoms among adolescent offenders? The nature of mental disorders among adolescents presents special challenges for accurately measuring them. Youths' mental disorders often are fluid and confounded by general developmental processes, setting a sort of ceiling on the degree to which they can be identified clearly. Other limitations arise because of the state of the art in measurement technology, as well as difficulties in its application in the context of juvenile justice programs.

- Chapter 4: What do we know about the relation between adolescent offenders' mental disorders and the purposes for which we want to identify them? All of our sociolegal contexts require attention to the relation between mental disorders of youthful offenders and matters of practical future consequence. The treatment context raises questions about our knowledge of a youth's specific mental disorder as a guide to the selection of a specific treatment modality in the fulfillment of our treatment obligation. The due process context requires asking about the actual relations between youths' mental disorders and capacities related to competence to stand trial and criminal responsibility. And the public safety context requires knowing whether and how youths' mental disorders are related to risk of short-range and longer-range future offending, as well as the degree to which their treatment is likely to reduce that risk. Given the nature of mental disorders in adolescence, can we even expect to find consistent relations between disorders and future offending, or predictable outcomes of treatment to reduce risk of harm?

- Chapters 5–7: Having established those foundations, we use them to address each of the three sociolegal contexts themselves, forming tentative policy and practice recommendations where we can—and where we cannot, pointing out what types of reliable information are needed to improve policy and practice in the future.

Chapter 2

Defining Mental Disorders in Adolescents

The first step in determining the juvenile justice system's obligations to respond to youths' mental disorders is to define "mental disorder." We must approach the definition in three ways, each of which is the subject of a section of this chapter.

First, how do clinicians and developmental psychopathologists define *types* of mental disorder? What is the predominant approach to the taxonomy of mental disorders among adolescents? How are they classified?

Second, how do we define the *severity* of mental disorders and their actual impact on youths' activities of daily living? Simply identifying a mental disorder does not tell us all we want to know in our search for adequate responses to adolescent's disorders. For reasons explained later, we also need to know the seriousness of the disorder as it arises in specific cases. What concepts are available to do that?

Third, how does juvenile justice system *context* influence what is defined as a mental disorder for purposes of fulfilling the three sociolegal obligations? What we call "mental disorder" for purposes of policy is not necessarily determined only by clinical condition or even clinical necessity. The relevance of a clinical condition for specific areas of policy will be determined in part by legal and social objectives. In fact, some conditions might be defined as mental disorders for purposes of one sociolegal objective and not another.

Classification of Mental Disorder

As noted in chapter 1, laws and policies that call for responses to youths' mental disorders usually do not define the disorders to which they apply.

They defer to the experts, presuming that psychiatry and clinical psychology have a consensual definition of child and adolescent psychopathology. This suggests a sense of assurance that the clinical sciences classify and conceptualize adolescent disorders in relatively clear-cut ways, which can then be applied to questions of treatment obligations, due process concerns, and public safety issues.

Yet this is not the message to be gleaned in the current literature by experts in psychopathology of children and adolescents. They tell us that "there is little professional consensus on how to define psychopathology [in adolescence]" (Ingram & Price, 2001, p. 6). Mash and Dozois (1996) identify the situation well: "Although it may appear that efforts to categorize mental disorders [of children and adolescents] are carving 'nature at the joints,' whether or not such 'joints' actually exist is open to debate (p. 15) . . . any classification system represents a construction rather than a reality" (p. 32).

This is not good news, given that eventually, when we analyze our obligations to respond to the mental health needs of juvenile offenders, we will need a way to define and conceptualize those needs and distinguish their varieties. So it is important to understand the controversies and limitations associated with current definitions of adolescent psychopathology, and how they manifest themselves in several important categories of disorder among young offenders.

Until fairly recently, the study of psychopathology in adolescence was dominated by conceptual systems and logical assumptions borrowed from the study of adult psychopathology. This tradition, largely medical in origin, uses sets of symptoms as criteria for categories of psychopathology. It presumes that each category of disorder may lead to the discovery of common causes, is likely to have a predictable course, and will facilitate the choice of effective treatment. Proper diagnosis of people in order to place them within this conceptual and empirical field is achieved by applying objective rules for their classification, such as those described in the *Diagnostic and Statistical Manual of Mental Disorders* (DSM-IV) (American Psychiatric Association, 1994).

This classification tradition, developed in the context of clinical psychiatry as applied to adults, has long been—and is currently—our primary way of defining disorders of children and adolescents. It is not the only way, however. Psychological research on child psychopathology has provided alternatives that describe disorder on various conceptual dimensions using a continuum rather than all-or-none diagnostic categories. One of the most fruitful examples is the description of child psychopathology along dimensions of "externalizing" and "internalizing" symptoms (e.g., Achenbach & Edelbrock, 1989). I later return to this approach after examining the traditional psychiatric classification of disorders, which clearly predominates in all current discussions of policy regarding child and adolescent disorders.

DSM-IV Disorders of Adolescence

The DSM-IV system deals with the classification of disorders of children and adolescents in two broad ways. First, it offers a number of "Disorders Usually First Diagnosed in Infancy, Childhood, or Adolescence," organized under the following categories:

- mental retardation
- learning, motor skill, and communication disorders
- pervasive developmental disorders
- attention-deficit and disruptive behavior disorders (including oppositional defiant and conduct disorders)
- feeding and eating, tic, and elimination disorders
- "other disorders of infancy, childhood and adolescence"

Second, the system offers hundreds of categories (diagnoses) for other conditions that do not have separate criteria for children, adolescents, and adults (with a few exceptions that are noted later). These are grouped in such a way that each contains a large number of specific categories or diagnoses (e.g., the substance-related disorders group alone has over a hundred specific diagnostic categories). A partial list of these groupings includes:

- delirium, dementia, and amnestic and other cognitive disorders
- substance-related disorders
- schizophrenia and other psychotic disorders
- mood disorders (e.g., depressive disorders, bipolar disorders)
- anxiety disorders
- somatoform disorders
- personality disorders (except for antisocial personality disorder, which cannot be employed as a diagnosis for youths under eighteen)

Successive versions of the DSM system have continuously sought to improve the application of the criteria to children and adolescents.

Nevertheless, mental health professionals and researchers who study, diagnose, and treat children claim that the paradigmatic assumptions at the heart of the DSM classification system continue to bedevil its application to adolescents. The model is substantially a downward extension of disorders of adulthood, treating disorders of adolescents simply as pre-adult forms of disabilities—buds that will reach full flower in adulthood. In so doing, child specialists have claimed, the system fails to conceptualize and classify what they see in practice and in empirical studies of children's and adolescents' psychological problems.

These discontents have become increasingly more articulate since the evolution of a conceptual approach called "developmental psychopathology." This perspective crystallized in the 1980s (Cicchetti, 1984, 1990; Rutter & Garmezy, 1983; Sroufe & Rutter, 1984) and matured in the 1990s (Cicchetti & Cohen, 1995; Cicchetti & Rogosch, 2002). Developmental psychopathology is not merely the study of psychopathology in childhood and adolescence. It is the study of how psychopathology emerges and changes in a developmental context, structured and guided by what is known about normal biological, cognitive, emotional, and social development during childhood, adolescence, and adulthood. Pertaining to adolescence, the developmental psychopathology perspective is "a shift away from seeing psychological disturbance during adolescence as either the grown-up version of childhood disorder or the immature or prodromal counterpart of adult pathology . . . to *the study of clinical phenomena in the context of adolescence as a developmental period*" (Steinberg, 2002, p. 124).

This perspective provides some concepts and general empirical findings that help us understand why we will encounter problems when we try to apply our traditional diagnostic concepts to the three sociolegal contexts for responding to young offenders' mental health needs. They include issues of (a) age relativity, (b) discontinuity, (c) comorbidity, and (d) racial, cultural, and gender-related factors.

Age Relativity

Entering the first-grade classroom on the first day of school, the six-year-old begins to sob, lingers by the door, and will not come in without special encouragement from the teacher. We watch and smile, remembering our own first day in school. But when the twelve-year-old does the same on the first day of middle school, we wonder what is wrong.

The fourteen-year-old carefully arranges drawing materials in a neat row in preparation for an art assignment, and we are impressed. The four-year-old does the same, refusing to begin drawing until each crayon is perfectly aligned just above the top edge of the drawing paper, and we consider for a moment that this is odd and perhaps significant regarding some underlying insecurity.

Few specific behaviors or reported emotions can be considered "symptoms" of mental disorder across the developmental span. Virtually every observed behavior or emotion that can be called a "symptom" is seen in almost all children or adolescents sometime during their development, with or without psychopathology (Mash & Dozois, 1996). Behaviors that are adaptive and "normal" at one age may be maladaptive and "abnormal" at another. And, of course, some behaviors and emotional conditions that signal psychopathology in adulthood are relatively normal at various pre-adult ages or developmental stages. As a consequence, most developmental psychopathologists emphasize that behaviors can be considered "symptoms" of disorder only to the extent that they deviate from normative behavior of one's own developmental peers, and that they are maladaptive only within the context of one's developmental period (e.g., Cicchetti & Rogosch, 2002).

In contrast, the DSM-IV system for classifying mental disorders provides little to distinguish the developmental relevance of various criteria that define certain disorders. For example, the system provides one set of behavioral and emotional criteria for diagnosing Major Depressive Disorder and Dysthymia in children, adolescents, and adults alike, with only brief notations concerning possible additional considerations for pre-adults (e.g., that "depressed mood," one of nine symptoms to be considered, might be expressed in children and adolescents as "irritable mood").

Another example outside the DSM-IV system is provided by recent research efforts to discover psychopathy in children and adolescents (e.g., Forth, Hart, & Hare, 1990; Frick et al., 1994; Lynam, 1997). Psychopathy is a concept that has been well defined in adult research for many years as a personality disorder involving callous, antisocial behavior (Hart & Hare, 1997). Recently the construct and its diagnostic criteria have been extended downward by researchers and clinicians for application to children and adolescents (as I discuss in chapter 4). In doing so, researchers have made few or no adjustments in the personal characteristics that are used to define it. Yet several "psychopathic" characteristics (e.g., impulsiveness, egocentricity) are both theoretically and empirically common, if not normative, at various stages of child or adolescent development (e.g., Edens et al., 2001; Seagrave & Grisso, 2002).

The concept of "age relativity," therefore, warns us that *adolescents' behaviors that appear as "symptoms" of mental disorders in DSM-IV are not always symptoms of mental disorder.* As in the case of psychopathy, this increases the risk that we will label as "disordered" certain classes of youths whose "symptoms" may simply be normative behavior for certain developmental transitions of adolescence. This is important when we are trying to locate mental disorders, and youths who have them, for purposes of identifying the juvenile justice system's treatment obligations.

Discontinuity

Upon reaching a diagnosis for a disordered youth, there is a tendency to presume that his or her disorder is likely to manifest itself across time, especially if it goes untreated. That assumption generally is true for adults. In contrast, clinical developmental researchers tell us that some disorders identified in adolescence will tend to persist into adulthood while others will not, and still others are quite variable.

Continuity is more predictable for some disorders of childhood than for others. For example, childhood mental retardation and disorders with a basis in brain dysfunction are likely to continue across the developmental life span, while disorders of mood (Hammen & Rudolph, 1996) and anxiety (Albano et al., 1995) are more variable. For most disorders involving behavioral dysfunction or emotional distress, merely obtaining a diagnosis for a particular disorder in adolescence may not tell us much about its development or implications for the adolescent's diagnostic condition later in adulthood.

Some principles based on empirical findings help us to deal with this question. For example, research concerning some disorders suggests that if they appear early in childhood they are more likely to persist to later developmental periods. Yet the picture is complicated by the fact that among children or adolescents who are symptomatic and who *continue* to be symptomatic into adolescence or adulthood, their subsequent disorder may not be the *same* as their earlier one (for reviews, see Kazdin & Johnson, 1994; Pennington & Ozonoff, 1991).

While investigating these variations, child psychopathology researchers have developed the concepts of "equifinality" (different paths to a single disorder) and "multifinality" (one disorder taking multiple paths to different disorders) to express the complex pathways they discover in search of patterns of disorder (and remission) among children and adolescents (e.g., Loeber, 1991). There may be *general* consistencies behind these processes; for example, youths who have developed an inhibited, introversive personality style early in life may progress to certain types of disorders during their developmental life span that are less aggressive than for youths who are generally less inhibited (Kagan et al., 1984). But youths with either personality style may manifest a variety of disorders compatible with it.

As a consequence, it is difficult to infer cause or course of a youth's condition based simply on a diagnosis at a particular point during the youth's adolescence. There will be greater variability among adolescents than among adults in the projected meaning of the diagnosis for the future. Among youths given that diagnosis, some will not persist in the disorder while others will, and still others may follow a course to a different disorder. This warns us that we must be less confident about the long-range consequences of many disorders in adolescents, a fact that will be important later in deciding whether and how we should respond to young offenders' mental disorders.

Comorbidity

A good auto mechanic knows that one problem in an automotive system often coexists with another. A worn set of spark plugs used too long will eventually result in damage elsewhere in the system, so that replacing the plugs will only partly solve the problem.

In addition to finding that two-thirds of the youths in Cook County's detention center met criteria for mental disorders, Teplin et al. (in press) discovered that about one-half of the youths met criteria for *two or more* mental disorders. (See also Marstellar et al., 1997: 44 percent.) Clinicians sometimes refer to the *presence* of two or more disorders as "comorbidity." But the term is often used by researchers to refer to a *relationship* between two or more disorders, such that across cases they tend to occur together at a greater-than-chance expectancy (Achenbach, 1995; Caron & Rutter, 1991), suggesting that they may have some causal relation.

Comorbidity is found among various disorders in persons across the developmental life span, but it is especially evident among children and adolescents. For purposes of our later discussions, some of the most important disorders for which comorbidity is high among adolescents are disorders of mood (e.g., Major Depression and Dysthymia), anxiety, attention-deficit/hyperactivity, disruptive behavior (e.g., Conduct Disorder), and substance use.

Examples are numerous. One review found that the presence of depression among community youths increased the likelihood of receiving some additional diagnosis by twenty times (Angold & Costello, 1993), and another found comorbidity rates of depression with anxiety disorders in the range of 30–75 percent (Kovacs, 1990). Depression and disruptive disorders have high comorbidity among adolescents (see Hammen & Rudolph, 1996, for a review). About 30–50 percent of adolescents with Attention-Deficit/Hyperactivity Disorder (ADHD) meet criteria for Oppositional Defiant or Conduct Disorder in adolescence (Barkley, 1990), and as many as 40–50 percent meet criteria for a mood disorder at some time in childhood or adolescence (Biederman, Newcorn, & Sprich, 1991). Finally, disruptive, anxiety, and depressive disorders have been found in increased proportions among delinquent youths with substance abuse diagnoses (e.g., Neighbors, Kempton, & Forehand, 1992; Richards, 1996). Teplin et al. (in press) found that about one-third of boys and girls in juvenile detention met criteria for both a substance use disorder and a disruptive behavior disorder or ADHD. Moreover, about half of the youths with that comorbid combination also met criteria for an anxiety disorder, an affective disorder, or both.

In policy or clinical discussions, one sometimes hears the claim that young offenders do not have "real" mental disorders, but are "mostly just conduct disordered" and therefore in need of offender rehabilitative services other than mental health interventions. (I discuss this assumption in greater detail at the end of this chapter.) Current data suggest that this view is usually wrong. Teplin et al. (in press) did not report separate figures for Conduct Disorder in their article on comorbidity, but they can be extrapolated from their original report of prevalence (Teplin et al., 2002). There they noted that 66 percent of their boys in detention ($n = 1,170$) met criteria for some mental disorder, and that the exclusion of Conduct Disorder reduced that figure only to 61 percent. In other words, only 5 percent of the male sample manifested Conduct Disorder alone. Those 5 percent constituted 13 percent of the boys diagnosed with Conduct Disorder, with 87 percent of boys with Conduct Disorder meeting criteria for at least one other psychiatric disorder. This finding is not unique. In an earlier review of the literature, Offord, Alder, and Boyle (1986) concluded that a majority of youths diagnosed with Conduct Disorder meet criteria for one or more additional diagnostic categories, and more recent studies continue to find the same (e.g., Angold, Costello, & Erkanli, 1999; Lambert et al., 2001). In light of these findings, when a clinician informs the court that a particular youth meets criteria for Conduct Disorder, the court routinely ought to reply, "And what else?"

Why is comorbidity so high among adolescents? One possible reason is that the development of symptoms of mental disorder, like the development of other cognitive and emotional conditions, tends to proceed during childhood and adolescence from global to more differentiated forms. Thus children and adolescents might manifest distinct and separate forms of disorder less often than is seen in adults. For example, among adults, the concepts of "depression" and "anxiety" are sufficiently different from each other to be of value in defining distinct emotional experiences. In contrast, developmental psychopathologists are not sure that depression and anxiety represent entirely separate conditions in children or adolescents (Hinden et al., 1997). They overlap so greatly in measures of adolescent dysfunction that often test developers have combined them in one "anxious-depressed" scale (e.g., Achenbach, 1991b; Grisso & Barnum, 2003). Similarly, some theorists have proposed that the overlap between conduct problems and attention-deficit/hyperactivity is so great that it questions the existence of separate entities (Hinshaw & Anderson, 1996).

High comorbidity rates among youth have led some theorists to propose that symptoms manifested in children and adolescents may reflect a "general psychopathology," consistent with immature development and consequent lack of differentiation of disorder into discrete categories (e.g., Lilienfeld, Waldman, & Israel, 1994; Rutter, 1994). Others have noted that the evidence for comorbidity might be due to patterns in the development of psychopathology in which some disorders naturally precede and "phase into" (and thus "overlap") others in childhood and adolescence. It is possible that more discrete ways to describe adolescent disorders could be found, but that our search has been obscured by the tendency to try to describe them with concepts developed in clinical studies of adults.

Discovering rates and patterns of comorbidity is further complicated by the fact that they are likely to be different depending on the settings and populations in which studies are performed. For example, youths with more severe disturbance more often have comorbid disorders, and they are more often clinically referred or arrested. Therefore, clinically referred or arrested samples of youths are likely to manifest greater comorbidity than would be found in random samples of youths with a particular disorder. Such conditions would produce inaccurate rates of comorbidity. But, of course, it would not change the fact that the published rates are applicable *within* the clinical and juvenile justice settings from which the results were obtained, and with which we are most concerned.

Comorbidity will play an important role in our analysis of the juvenile justice system's obligations to respond to mental disorders of adolescents. Identifying a diagnosis does not necessarily provide a meaningful guide to a youth's mental health needs, if youths receiving that diagnosis tend to manifest any of a variety of other disorders. Moreover, as we shall see later, the considerable overlap of disorders among youths challenges our ability to define discretely different treatment or rehabilitation responses for those with particular diagnoses.

Race and Gender

The nature of psychopathology in adolescents is likely to be different for boys and girls, and for youths of different racial and ethnic backgrounds. The emergence of mental health problems and the form they take may be influenced by social context interacting with developmental processes (Mash & Dozois, 1996). Boys and girls develop in different social contexts that might contribute to gender-based differences in prevalence or types of disorders. Similarly, during normal development, youths of different ethnicities may develop somewhat different personality characteristics because of the social contexts in which they grow up, leading to different mental disorders or to differences in the way disorders are manifested (Murray, Smith, & West, 1989).

Gender differences in psychiatric diagnoses of adolescents are fairly well documented. Conduct Disorder and ADHD, for example, are less prevalent among girls than boys (e.g., Szatmari, Boyle, & Offord, 1989), rates of depression are higher among girls (e.g., Offord et al., 1987), and girls are more likely to develop comorbid disorders (Loeber & Keenan, 1994). Until recently, very little was known about the relative prevalence of mental disorders among girls in the juvenile justice system, in part because their smaller numbers failed to attract research interest. More recent studies in juvenile detention centers, however, consistently find higher rates of almost all types of mental disorders and mental health problems (including anger and aggression) among girls than among boys (e.g., Cocozza & Skowyra, in press; Grisso et al., 2001; Teplin et al., 2002).

While ethnic differences in rates of mental disorder have been documented for adults (e.g., Warner et al., 1995), there have been few epidemiological surveys of the mental health problems of African American, Latino, or Asian adolescents in the general population (Isaacs, 1992; Cauffman & Grisso, in press). A recent exception is a study of diagnoses (using the Child and Adolescent Psychiatric Assessment, an interview structured to provide DSM-IV diagnoses) among a random sample of over 1,000 youths in rural North Carolina (Angold et al., 2002). About 20 percent of both non-Hispanic white and African American youths met criteria for one or more disorder. There were no ethnic differences for ADHD, Conduct Disorder, Substance Abuse Disorder, or Anxiety Disorders. But non-Hispanic white youths had higher rates of "any depressive disorder," Oppositional Defiant Disorder, and "any affective or anxiety disorder" than did African American youths.

For juvenile justice samples, very few studies of mental disorders have reported their data in ways that allow one to examine racial or ethnic differences. The Cook County Detention Center study by Teplin et al. (2002) is an exception. Higher rates were reported among non-Hispanic white males than among African American males for most disorders and Latino males for some disorders. Non-Hispanic white males were more likely than African American males to present with substance abuse and anger symptoms, whereas Latino males were more likely to exhibit signs of depressed-anxious mood as compared to African American males. Among girls, non-Latino white females presented with more substance abuse and trauma when compared to African American females, whereas Latino females were more likely to endorse somatic complaints and suicidal ideation when compared to African American females.

More research in a greater range of juvenile justice settings eventually may give us greater confidence when applying Teplin's findings beyond Cook County. But if they do, how are they to be explained? Are the differences due to actual tendencies for certain disorders to be more or less prevalent for certain ethnic groups? Or are they the result of differences in arrest patterns—for example, that mental disorder greatly increases the likelihood of arrests for non-Hispanic white youths but that a greater range of African American youths are arrested? Most important, is it possible that our DSM-IV system for classifying mental disorders does not work the same when applied to youths of different ethnic backgrounds? (For a review of concerns about application of the DSM system with African American youths, see Johnson, 1993). Just as certain behaviors and emotional conditions may be normal at one age and not another, they may also be differentially normal or abnormal for boys and girls, or for youths of different ethnic backgrounds, at different ages and stages of development. But our present research base does not allow us to address such possibilities.

Alternatives to Diagnostic Categories

Thus far, we have encountered evidence that the predominant system for identifying and classifying mental disorders—the DSM-IV—has serious limitations for describing disorders of adolescence because it is rooted in adult psychopathology. It is less useful for adolescents than for adults in describing the cause and course of mental disorders, and it manifests substantial comorbidity of disorders when applied to adolescents, creating diagnostic groups with considerable heterogeneity. Finally, we have found that strict reliance on the DSM-IV diagnostic scheme may not take into account the contextual differences in the development of psychopathology among girls and boys, and among youths of different ethnicities. Therefore, in this search for responses to the mental health needs of adolescents in the juvenile justice system, we begin our journey on very unsteady ground. The field's predominant classification system has been the basis for the prevalence estimates of mental disorder among juvenile justice youths. While it might be trusted to provide gross estimates of the extent of the need, it is less clear that we can rely on it to describe the specific nature of those needs. In this light, it makes sense to consider alternatives to the DSM-IV classification system for identifying youths' psychopathology. Developmental psychopathology offers two general approaches that do not use diagnostic classification.

The first alternative describes youths according to *conceptual dimensions of psychopathology* that are expressed on scales, rather than placing them into diagnostic groups. The prototype for this approach in child and adolescent psychopathology is a system developed by Achenbach (1993; Achenbach & Edelbrock, 1984), which comprises a family of measures called the Child Behavior Checklist (Achenbach, 1991a, 1991b, 1991c; see chapter 3 for further discussion of the CBCL). The system uses a number of dimensions (e.g., "anxious-depressed," "attention problems") that were determined by statistical methods for grouping together symptoms and behaviors in ways that best fit their appearance across large samples of youths. The eight dimensions in Achenbach's system can be further grouped into more global syndromes representing "externalizing" problems (undercontrolled, outward expression) and "internalizing" problems (overcontrolled, inner-directed). Adolescents are not classified into categories in this system. Instead their psychopathology is identified according to the elevation or depression of their scores on the various dimensions or the two syndromes. Their scores may even by high on both the externalizing and internalizing syndromes. Dimensional systems like Achenbach's identify degrees and types of disturbance, as well as patterns of their manifestation, without the use of discrete categories and without presumptions regarding an underlying disease process.

The second alternative is a *problem-oriented approach* that identifies how well or poorly youths have adapted within various personal and social contexts (e.g., Rahdert, 1991; others are described in chapter 3). Frequently these contexts correspond to the everyday social milieus of family relations, peer relations, school functioning, work, leisure activities, and so forth. Whatever the methods used to identify strengths and weaknesses in these areas, they are typically expressed on scales that indicate degree of maladjustment or dysfunction relative to one's age peers.

Both of these alternatives have advantages and disadvantages compared to DSM-IV classification, and we will explore those differences later. But it is not necessary that we choose among them—they all have something important to contribute—although we may have to decide which ways of describing youths' psychopathology are best suited for various contexts and purposes that arise in juvenile justice custody. One strength of these two alternatives, however, is their dimensional quality, which can be very useful for describing degrees of psychopathology (and can even be converted to classify youths into groups by identifying "cut-off scores" on their dimensions). The importance of this is explained later.

The Clinical Significance of Mental Disorders

Recall from chapter 1 the very high prevalence rates of mental disorders among juvenile justice youths, as well as our conclusion that even these high estimates might be conservative. If meeting criteria for a mental disorder was the deciding factor for requiring some special clinical response to youths in the juvenile justice system, then almost all those entering the system would need clinical attention. In chapter 1, we anticipated that accepting "clinical treatment for all youthful offenders" as the juvenile justice system's mandate required scrutiny and probable refinement of such a mandate.

Discriminating between various types of disorder will provide part of this analysis. In addition, we can seek to identify the relative seriousness of cases involving mental disorders, as well as their potential consequences, for purposes of determining their clinical significance. Not all mental disorders, and not all cases that meet criteria for a particular disorder, necessarily present the same degree of suffering, disability, dysfunction, or short-term and long-term consequences. Therefore, it is important to consider ways to conceptualize *degrees of impairment,* as these might supplement and refine our use of data to classify youths according to specific disorders. What can guide us in conceptualizing seriousness of symptoms, and their functional consequences, when determining the need for a clinical response by the juvenile justice system?

Classifying "Clinically Significant" Severity of Symptoms

Chapter 3 examines various measures of child and adolescent psychopathology that express *symptom severity* on a continuum, when symptoms are measured according to the dimensional perspective discussed in the previous section. Classification of symptom severity requires some definition of "high" scores warranting special attention. There are three ways to conceptualize a "clinically significant" level of symptom severity.

THE PEER-NORM APPROACH. We may identify high symptom severity according to statistical deviation from the norm of one's peers (as employed, for instance, in the CBCL: Achenbach, 1991b). This requires the collection of symptom severity data from large general samples of children or adolescents, establishing the distribution of scores on a scale, and finding the score that exceeds a particular standard deviation or *t-*score above the mean, or that identifies a particular percentage of youths (e.g., top one-third, one-quarter, or one-tenth). This approach clearly assists in identifying groups of youths (or cases) in which symptom severity can be considered "high" relative to one's peers. The difficulty here is in determining where to place the cut-off. It can be done arbitrarily, as when a test developer decides to call scores "significant" when they are above +2 standard deviations from the mean, or above a *t-*score of 70. No one would doubt that this is high, but it is possible that what we call "high" might vary for different purposes. This can be remedied by research that demonstrates the value of the cut-off for specific purposes (which is the starting point for another approach described below). But without that refinement, there is no particular reason to believe that scoring high relative to one's peers necessarily signifies the need for treatment.

THE CLINICAL CRITERION GROUP APPROACH. A second approach compares an adolescent to groups of youths who have required clinical care. This requires empirical identification of the level of symptom severity manifested by those who have met eligibility criteria for treatment. Typically the criterion sample includes youths currently receiving inpatient or outpatient mental health services, and who therefore have been judged by clinicians (in the course of routine intake activities) to need psychiatric care. A "clinically significant" level of symptom severity, then, is defined as any score that is well within the range of the symptom severity scores of the clinical criterion group. This is the approach taken by Millon, Millon, and Davis (1993) in development of the "clinically significant" cut-off scores for the Millon Adolescent Clinical Inventory.

This empirical approach to conceptualizing severity of symptoms has considerable value, but in practice it requires careful scrutiny. For example, in specific studies using this approach, the level of symptom severity that it identifies as "clinically significant" is heavily dependent on intake or eligibility criteria for the particular mental health programs in which the criterion data were collected. The level of severity of symptoms required in order to obtain treatment in a particular community may vary, for example, as a function of the resources of mental health programs in that community. If resources are very limited in the criterion sample location, so that only youths with extremely severe symptoms receive treatment, research in that setting might lead to higher cut-off scores (a more restrictive definition of "clinical significance") than would be found in other communities. Application of the results to later cases, therefore, would tend to exclude from "clinical significance" some youths who would indeed be considered eligible for mental health services in their own communities. For this reason, the approach is of value only if the cut-off score has been based on data collection in a diverse set of clinical treatment programs, or in a treatment setting that closely matches the one in which we want to apply it.

THE EMPIRICAL CONSEQUENCE APPROACH. A third approach is to set cut-off scores on the basis of empirical evidence of the relation between scores and actual functional consequences of concern. For example, the development of a scale with items that are designed to identify suicidal behavior might include collecting research evidence on whether youths subsequently did or did not attempt suicide. Then statistical procedures can be used to find the right cut-off score, defined as the score that optimally divides youths so that as many as possible who attempted suicide scored above the cut-off score (the method's "sensitivity") and as many as possible who did not attempt suicide scored below the cut-off score ("specificity").

Chronicity or Multiplicity of Symptoms or Disorders

All three of the approaches just described focus on *intensity* of symptoms in identifying "clinically significant" psychopathology. But this may not be sufficient to identify the seriousness of disorder for purposes of making some decisions about youths' mental health treatment. Two additional considerations are often helpful.

CHRONICITY. We may distinguish between acute and chronic conditions. Some youths may manifest acute symptoms that are not part of a chronic or persistent disorder, but that suggest the need for some type of clinical intervention in order to avoid relatively imminent consequences (such as prevention of suicidal behavior). Others may have chronic and persistent disorders yet manifest a relatively lower intensity of symptoms at a given point in time. This is especially true for some mental disorders that are episodic, waxing and waning in intensity of symptoms across time, so that high symptom levels sometimes are not presented at the particular time of assessment. Moreover, adolescents are more prone to lability and instability in presentation than are adults, especially for mood disorders and anxiety disorders. The fact that their immediate presentation is not acute does not necessarily mean that they are not in need of a clinical response, especially if their disorder may have important longer-term negative consequences.

As we will see in later chapters, the importance of chronicity in understanding the relevance of mental disorder for youths' delinquent behaviors cannot be overstated. For example, one of the best-documented indicators of whether delinquent behaviors will persist through adolescence and into adulthood is whether the behaviors had an onset in the primary school years (Moffitt, 1993). Similarly, in general, the likelihood that adolescents will persist in manifesting mental disturbances of some kind is increased if they manifested mental disorders before the adolescent years (for a review, see Connor, 2002).

MULTIPLICITY. Earlier we noted that many youths in juvenile justice settings meet criteria for two, three, and even four mental disorders. It is commonly observed that adolescents who require the greatest extent of mental health services across the longest period also manifest a large number of symptoms and multiple disorders (Davis & Vander Stoep, 1997). Thus there is some overlap between chronicity and multiplicity of symptoms. But it is helpful to retain both of these ways of identifying seriousness of mental health needs, because some youths have chronic disorders that are relatively specific in their symptom presentation rather than involving a wide array of symptoms and multiple diagnoses.

Later we will examine methods for expressing chronicity and multiplicity of symptoms and disorders among adolescents. The important point for now is that we must consider both of these indexes, as well as symptom severity, when making policy and clinical decisions about our response to youths' mental health needs.

Conceptualizing Functional Consequences of Mental Disorders

Instead of focusing on symptom severity or chronicity and multiplicity of symptoms, one can identify the clinical significance of youths' psychopathology by examining the *nature and degree of an individual's functional impairment.* This approach measures clinical significance by evidence of the *effects* of disorder and symptoms on the individual's functioning in everyday matters of life, such as social relations with family and peers or meeting obligations regarding school or work. Impaired functioning is expressed in degrees, depending on the extent to which the individual's behavior—as a consequence of mental disorder—departs from developmental and culturally normal behaviors of age peers within one's everyday social setting.

Chapter 3 describes a number of ways to assess functional impairment, some for use specifically with children and adolescents. The "problem-oriented" methods mentioned earlier for describing youths' maladaptive behaviors are primarily focused on functional impairment in various social spheres, using this alone as a measure of psychopathology and need for treatment.

Several developments have promoted increased attention to the concept and use of functional impairment in describing youths' disorders. It is consistent with modern definitions of disorder in developmental psychopathology, which focus less on classification of disorders and more on identifying psychopathology as maladaptative behaviors, deviating from age-peer norms, that represent failures in negotiating developmental tasks in social contexts (Cicchetti & Cohen, 1995; Mash, 1989; Sroufe & Rutter, 1984; Wakefield, 1992). In addition, as discussed later, federal and state agencies have adopted functional impairment as a way to measure eligibility for various public mental health services.

The potential importance of identifying clinically significant disorder according to functional criteria cannot be overstated for purposes of our analysis of the juvenile justice system's treatment obligations. The reason is that many studies find that DSM-IV diagnostic disorder maps imperfectly onto functional impairment. In some cases, youths who meet criteria for *no* mental disorders appear to be at considerable risk of (Jensen & Watanabe, 1999) or actually manifest (Angold et al., 1999) functional impairment requiring treatment. Conversely, many studies (reviewed by

Canino, Costello, & Angold, 1999) have found that "a substantial proportion of children and adolescents who meet criteria for a diagnosis according to the DSM are functioning within the normal range" (p. 95).
For example, in one study of a Puerto Rican community, while almost
half the children and adolescents met criteria for some DSM disorder, only
17 percent of the sample (about one-third of youths with DSM disorders)
manifested moderate or severe impairment on a measure of the effects of
the disorder in impairing their everyday functioning (Bird et al., 1988).
Similarly, in a juvenile justice sample (Virginia Policy Design Team,
1994), researchers found that about 80 percent of youths in Virginia secure
detention facilities met diagnostic criteria, but only 9 percent were considered to be in *immediate* need (would deteriorate while in detention if not
served), and another 40 percent might need mental health services at some
time in the future.

A Note on DSM-IV and Clinically Significant Disorder

Before leaving this discussion of definitions of clinically significant mental
disorder, it is worth noting that all three of the approaches that I have
described—severity of symptoms, their chronicity, and level of maladaptive functioning—are employed in the DSM-IV system for describing
mental disorders. That system, however, includes them in ways that have
important limitations.

Specifically, the criteria for some DSM disorders allow for "specifiers"
that require the clinician to classify the patient's current condition as
"mild, moderate, or severe." This judgment is based on the clinician's
assessment of the level of the patient's distress as well as the patient's
degree of functional impairment. Criteria for these specifications, however, are not standardized and therefore allow for differences in judgment
among clinicians. For example, there are no guides for defining what
might be considered mild, moderate, or severe "distress."

Concerning functional impairment, the DSM multi-axial system includes an Axis V designation of "Global Assessment of Functioning" (GAF:
see pp. 30–32 of DSM-IV), using a rating scale that requires the clinician
to focus on the effects of a disorder on the patient's psychological, social,
and occupational functioning. The system has anchors for a 0–100 rating,
providing brief phrases to assist the clinician in deciding how to express
the extent of the patient's functional impairment (e.g., in DSM-IV, p. 32,
scores of 61–70: "Some mild symptoms . . . some difficulty in social, occupational or school functioning . . . but generally functioning pretty well").

The same GAF anchoring phrases are used for adults, adolescents, and children alike. (Not part of the DSM system, the Children's Global Assessment Scale has been developed for use with children and adolescents: Schaffer et al., 1983). The GAF may have value as a repeated measure by a single clinician with a particular patient, thus documenting relative improvements in functioning as a course of treatment. Its value as a tool for identifying clinical significance of disorder and treatment needs, however, has not been substantiated, especially for children and adolescents.

Concerning chronicity, the DSM calls for many diagnoses to be accompanied by a specifier to indicate whether the condition is "chronic," although it provides only vague instructions for how this is applied to children and adolescents. Some disorders, most notably Conduct Disorder, may be specified as "Childhood-Onset Type" or "Adolescent-Onset Type." But these do not necessarily signify chronicity; for example, one does not know the chronicity of childhood-onset Conduct Disorder at the time that it is diagnosed in a ten-year-old.

Summary

What we call "mental disorder" for purposes of responding to youths' mental health needs is determined not only by the type of disorder, but also by the level of its clinical significance. This can be expressed as severity of symptoms, their persistence (chronicity) or number (multiplicity), and the degree to which the youth's condition results in functional impairment. We will employ all of these definitions at various times in the later analyses of our juvenile justice system's obligations. But we must now consider one more way to define mental disorder for these purposes.

Defining Mental Disorder within Sociolegal Contexts

The fact that disorder can be clinically classified, and that a person's condition is considered clinically significant, does not necessarily define the condition or its severity as a mental disorder for the three sociolegal contexts. This is because *the context itself* may prescribe or limit what will "qualify" as a mental disorder for purposes of fulfilling society's objectives associated with that context.

For example, there are many areas of criminal and civil law in which certain forms of psychopathology, regardless of their severity in specific cases, are not deemed "mental disabilities" for purposes of the legal obligations or protections that apply in that legal context (see generally

Gutheil & Appelbaum, 2000; Melton et al., 1997). One legal definition of mental disability may be used for purposes of regulating the involuntary psychiatric hospitalization of individuals, while another may be used for defining employment disability, and yet another for questions of insanity in criminal cases. Differences in what is considered a "qualifying" mental disorder in these disparate areas of law reflect society's underlying purposes for the functions of civil, employment disability, and criminal law. Similarly, many sociological perspectives have conceptualized mental disorder not as a medical or psychological "given," but as a culturally shared inferential conclusion (varying from one culture to another) about the nature of individuals' socially deviant behavior (e.g., Mechanic, 1973; Scheff, 1973). Cultures call certain behaviors deviant—and define them as illness, evil, or harmless—in order to justify a particular social response that is believed to be in the individual's interests and/or the interests of society.

Applying this perspective to our present analysis, we must anticipate that different disorders might be relevant for different sociolegal contexts, even though all of them exist within the broader context of juvenile law and policy. This is because the purposes of these contexts—beneficent treatment, due process, and public safety—are themselves quite different. In the final chapters of this book, I seek to define which mental disorders are relevant for the social purposes about which the question of mental disorder is being raised in each of these three sociolegal contexts. In preparation, let us consider briefly the elements of each context that will structure that inquiry.

Custodial Obligations regarding Treatment

LEGAL DEFINITIONS. All state statutes provide definitions of mental illness, but typically their terms refer to broad conditions of thought, mood, and behavior (not specific diagnoses) that create some level of impairment (e.g., "grossly impairs functioning"). Specific disorders are sometimes noted with regard to Substance Abuse and Mental Retardation, excluding them from the definition of mental disorder (Woolard et al., 1996). The main reason for this is to define conditions under which persons may be committed involuntarily to state mental hospitals, and most states have separate provisions for care and treatment of persons with substance disorders or mental retardation.

Other laws provide definitions of persons who are eligible for mental health services for purposes other than civil commitment. An examination of these, however, shows that they will not take us far in our analysis. For example, Public Law No. 102-321 (establishing the Substance Abuse and Mental Health Services Administration) mandated block grants to fund mental health services for patients who met criteria for "serious mental illness" (SMI), which it defined as any DSM disorder, substance use disorder, or developmental disorder leading to substantial interference with one or more major life activities. According to PL 102-321, "life activities" include "basic daily living skills such as eating and bathing, instrumental living skills (e.g., managing money . . .), and functioning in social, family, and vocational/education contexts."

Concerning children and adolescents, various federal entities (e.g., the U.S. Department of Education and the U.S. Administration on Developmental Disabilities) employ a category of "serious emotional disturbance" (SED) to identify adolescents and young adults whose disorders are sufficiently chronic and severe to identify them as a special, core target population and establish their service eligibility (Bazelon Center for Mental Health Law, 1993). Yet these agencies use different definitions, refer to "significant functional impairment" without operationalizing the term, and specify no particular psychiatric diagnoses (Davis & Vander Stoep, 1997).

Thus, legal concepts such as state definitions of mental illness and federal definitions of SMI and SED provide only vague guidance in determining the responsibilities of the juvenile justice system for responding to youths with mental disorders. Their inclusion of all (or undefined) DSM disorders does little to differentiate among adolescent offenders, most of whom can be classified according to some DSM disorder.

Legal definitions, however, do allow us to make two important points for our future analysis. First, once a youth meets criteria for some DSM disorder, whether it is called a "mental disorder" for purposes of state definitions or federal obligations to provide treatment depends on the *degree of functional impairment* manifested in the youth's behavior. This also means that clinical diagnosis itself is at best a threshold issue for defining the scope of the juvenile justice system's treatment mandate.

Second, the definitions do not disqualify some disorders that one might otherwise assume would be outside the scope of psychiatric treatment for mental health needs. For example, in discussions of treatment for mental health needs in juvenile justice settings, typically little attention is given to functional deficits associated with developmental disabilities, such as mental retardation and the learning and communication disorders. Moreover, both the juvenile justice system and the child mental health system have long seen Conduct Disorder as a target for correctional rehabilitation rather than clinical treatment provided by mental health professionals. Conduct Disorder is diagnosed not with reference to symptoms of an emotional or mental nature, but on the basis of a "repetitive and persistent pattern of behavior in which the basic rights of others . . . are violated" (American Psychiatric Association, 1994, p. 85). Yet the standards noted earlier do not exclude any of these disorders from treatment eligibility, as long as they create significant functional impairment.

The question of the inclusion or exclusion of these disorders, however, is largely moot in light of our earlier discussion of comorbidity. The great majority of youths in the juvenile justice system with Conduct Disorder or Mental Retardation are comorbid for other psychiatric disorders as well (Teplin et al., in press). Thus, even if these disorders *were* excluded from eligibility, this would alter the reason but not the case-by-case obligation for treatment of adolescent offenders.

THE CONTEXTS WITHIN THE CONTEXT. Within the sociolegal context of custodial care, definitions of disorder and impairment for purposes of defining our treatment obligations may not be the same throughout a youth's custody. They may differ during various stages of juvenile justice processing. By "stages," I mean steps in the process, beginning with arrest, referral to the juvenile court, intake processing, secure detention if it is warranted, diversion or full adjudicative processing, waiver (transfer) to criminal court, decisions about disposition for adjudicated youths, and implementation of dispositional options ranging from community-based interventions to secure correctional facilities. For general discussion, these stages can be divided into pretrial and posttrial contexts.

Analysis of the custodial obligations of the system must take into account that the relation between the state and the youth is not the same across pretrial and posttrial legal contexts. Inherent in this relation are two primary factors: (a) the state's obligation to meet adolescents' developmental and psychological needs, and (b) the state's obligation to avoid intrusions that may jeopardize the constitutional rights of persons who are (or may be) deprived of liberty. A youth in pretrial detention is both a temporary ward of the state and a defendant in a legal proceeding that challenges that custodial arrangement. The duality of this relationship places pretrial limits on the juvenile justice system's responses to the youthful defendant's mental health needs, to the extent that unbridled assessment and treatment might jeopardize the youth's legal defense regarding the alleged delinquency. Once the delinquency is proven (adjudicated), the posttrial balance shifts to favor the state's custodial obligation.

I suggest that what is called a "mental disorder" or "functional impairment" that triggers the system's custodial obligation to provide treatment may be different in these two "contexts within the context." After adjudication, the system's custodial obligation might be triggered by any disorder or degree of functional impairment that would apply (according to public mental health regulations) in considering eligibility for services in the public health system generally. At the pre-adjudication stage, however, the types of mental disorder and the degrees of functional impairment that require a treatment response is not solely a clinical matter. They must be weighed against the system's competing obligation to respect the constitutional rights of autonomy and protection against state powers that are afforded defendants not yet adjudicated. This assertion takes into account the fact that assessment and treatment may produce self-incriminating information that would jeopardize the youth's defense, and it can involve increased restrictions on liberty and procedural delays in adjudication.

In later chapters I examine how this principle should be applied for various disorders, levels of symptom severity, and degrees of functional impairment. By way of example, however, this might mean that the state is justified—indeed, might be obligated—to seek pretrial treatment in an inpatient psychiatric facility for a youth in pretrial detention who is experiencing an acute psychotic episode. But in the same pretrial context, the system might be obligated *to refrain* from comprehensive assessment and treatment of a youth's dysthymic (depressed) condition, even if it is producing important emotional distress and impairment of certain everyday functions. In contrast, the same dysthymic condition might trigger an obligation to treat the youth after adjudication and placement in custody of the state's juvenile corrections authority.

The consequences of this principle will be greatest, therefore, at the pretrial stage. Policy regarding how the competing interests should be weighed can be guided by at least two dimensions: (a) the severity of disorder or functional impairment (representing the degree of necessity for immediate treatment), and (b) the seriousness of the alleged offense (representing the degree of liberty that might be lost by inadequate protection of the defendant's rights). We will return to these dimensions in chapter 5.

Due Process Obligation

Chapter 1 introduced the justice system's obligation to identify and respond to youths' mental disorders to the extent that those disorders might jeopardize their defense. I described three areas of law relevant for this obligation: waiver of *Miranda* rights to avoid self-incrimination and advice of counsel, competence to stand trial, and questions of culpability such as the insanity defense.

Determining the relevance of various mental disorders for each of these purposes must begin with modern law's functional approach in all three of these areas (Grisso, 2003). It is not the mere presence of mental disorder that creates conditions of invalid waiver of rights, incompetence to stand trial, or insanity, but rather sufficient evidence that an individual's mental disorder actually impairs functioning in a way that is legally relevant. For example, pertaining to the validity of youths' waiver of *Miranda* rights, the U.S. Supreme Court in *Fare v. Michael C.*, 442 U.S. 707 (1979), affirmed that no single factor (such as age, intelligence, or mental disorder) was ever dispositive of the question, but that each case must be weighed in light of the "totality of the circumstances" that might be relevant for judging whether the waiver was made "voluntarily, knowingly and intelligently."

Case law on the relevance of mental disorders for adolescents' competence to stand trial and criminal responsibility is virtually nonexistent. Statutes in many states, however, have recently been modified to apply these concepts in juvenile court as they are defined for adults in criminal court (Redding & Frost, 2002), so our analysis can begin there.

With regard to competence to stand trial, statutes and case decisions in criminal law make it abundantly clear that while mental illness or mental retardation are predicates to incompetence in most states, neither their presence in general, nor any specific disorder, is dispositive of the question of competence (Grisso, 2003; Melton et al., 1997). The question focuses on whether the functional consequences of the disorder for this defendant are such that his or her degree of deficit in ability to understand the nature of the proceedings or to participate with counsel in the defense (*Dusky v. United States*, 362 U.S. 402 [1960]) creates a substantial risk of an unfair trial.

With regard to criminal responsibility (the insanity defense), the question before the court is whether, due to "mental disease or defect" at the time of the alleged offense, the defendant could not appreciate (or know) the wrongfulness (or illegality) of the act or could not conform his or her conduct to the requirements of law. (The precise wording varies from state to state, but most approximate the formulation above. For variations, see Borum, 2003b; Melton et al., 1997). Thus mental disorder or mental retardation are predicates, but they are not determinative of the legal question. Many states, however, exclude disorders "manifested only by repeated criminal or otherwise antisocial conduct" (American Bar Association, 1989), thus avoiding the risk of excusing the illegal behaviors of persons whose "inability to appreciate" the wrongfulness of their acts may be related merely to antisocial character. This has generally been interpreted as excluding Antisocial Personality Disorder as defined in DSM-IV as a predicate for insanity (Melton et al., 1997).

Chapter 4 considers which mental disorders might make a difference in youths' capacities in ways that are relevant for analyzing the juvenile justice system's obligations regarding due process for mentally disordered adolescents. Two concerns will guide that analysis.

First, we must look for disorders that are most likely to produce the functional deficits about which the law is concerned in each of the three legal questions involving due process protections. The only disorders excluded *per se* in law are in the area of insanity, where diagnoses based simply on repetitive antisocial behavior do not qualify. When applied to youths, this could lead us to conclude that Conduct Disorder would not apply, because that diagnosis is based largely on repetitive illegal behaviors. However, as we have noted frequently already, this would exclude only a small percentage of youths in the juvenile justice system, because most youths with Conduct Disorder also manifest other mental disorders.

Second, the functional deficits that need attention are narrower than in a custodial treatment context, which is concerned with general functional impairment in everyday life. All three due process areas are concerned primarily with cognitive or motivational deficits, as well as their influence on performance within relatively narrow contexts. Thus we seek mental disorders that are more likely to impair attention, comprehension, and appreciation of matters with legal relevance for avoiding self-incrimination (waiver of interrogation rights), participating in a defense (competence), and knowing and appreciating the consequences of what one is about to do (criminal responsibility).

The law's focus on functional deficits means that one is not limited to the use of disorders in adult criminal cases as a guide for identifying disorders relevant to the due process obligation in juvenile cases. This is important, because such limitations would be prejudicial, in light of the substantial differences between psychopathology of adults and adolescents. For example, Schizophrenia—the most frequent diagnosis among adults found incompetent to stand trial—typically does not develop until young adulthood (American Psychiatric Association, 1994).

But possibly of greater importance, the consequences of mental disorders with regard to cognitive capacities relevant in these areas of law may be different for youths than for adults. The capacities to which these three areas of law refer generally can be translated into functions that behavioral and neuropsychological researchers call by such names as "attention," "comprehension," "reasoning," "problem-solving," "deciding," and "planning." Collectively these are often called "executive functions," and, as discussed in chapter 4, there is ample evidence that they are still developing during adolescence, not having reached average, adult levels of maturity. Maturation of these capacities in part requires experience in exercising them in increasingly adult-like contexts of responsibility. But maturation of executive functions is also limited by the pace of normal neurological development. Thus normally developing adolescents are at some greater risk of deficits (compared to average adults) in the types of capacities that are involved in these areas of due process.

To the extent that many mental disorders may delay normal development, it is likely that a wider range of mental disorders among youths than among adults may have an impact on their cognitive capacities associated with these due process areas of concern. The task of identifying which disorders among youths are most salient with regard to the cognitive capacities in question is undertaken in chapters 4 and 6. The point here is that the developmental context in which adolescents' mental disorders are manifested may lead to different conclusions about their relevance for due process obligations than we would reach in similar analyses for adult defendants.

Public Safety Obligations

As described in chapter 1, the public safety obligation has two primary objectives: (a) to assess risk of violence in order to provide adequate security, and (b) to provide rehabilitation and treatment in order to reduce dangerous recidivism. How should mental disorders be defined for these purposes?

If there are particular mental disorders of adolescence that are empirically associated with a substantially higher degree of risk of harm to others, then those disorders will determine the focus of the system's assessment and treatment efforts in fulfilling the public safety obligation. In chapter 4 we will examine whether such a set of disorders can be found, but we should not expect a highly satisfying conclusion. For example, some disorders may be related to aggression in adolescent *clinical* populations, but they might "wash out" when one is working with a *juvenile justice* population. The fact that some majority of juvenile justice youths have been referred because of their impulsive, angry, and aggressive behaviors could reduce the likelihood that differences between diagnostic groups will emerge.

We will almost certainly find no differences in aggressive potential between youths with or without mental disorders (or between disorders) if we frame the question in terms of "whether youths will engage in aggressive or assaultive behaviors." Much research tells us that most boys engage in assaults (that is, get into physical fights) that are serious enough to do harm at some time during their adolescent years (e.g., Elliott, Huizinga, & Morse, 1986). However, differences between diagnostic groups in juvenile justice populations still might arise if we frame the question another way: "Do some mental disorders increase the risk of specific *types* of aggression, more *frequent or repetitive* aggression, and long-range *persistence* of aggressive behavior?" It is here that we might look with guarded optimism.

Framed in that way, the question is most appropriate for pursuing the system's objective to identify youths who require special security for public protection. As described in chapter 1, there are many points in juvenile justice processing that require assessments of risk of harm to others, and the nature of the risk that needs to be predicted is not the same at all of these points. Pretrial detention questions focus on the likelihood of harm to others in the next few days if the youth is not detained; at the other extreme, hearings regarding potential waiver of a juvenile offender for trial in criminal court ask whether the youth is likely to continue to be a danger as an adult. Thus knowledge of how particular mental disorders or dimensions of psychopathology might increase or decrease immediate risks, long-range risks, and types of harmful behavior will be more relevant than global relationships between psychopathology and aggression.

Concerning the system's obligation to treat mental disorders in order to reduce recidivism, we must both broaden and narrow our search for relevant mental disorders in an important way. Specifically, we need to recognize that *we are looking for (a) disorders with (b) symptoms that are (c) associated with future aggression and (d) are within the domain of clinical intervention*. Factors (a) and (b) in this formula broaden our perspective, recognizing that the relation between mental disorder and aggression, when it exists, may be due to symptoms (e.g., depressed mood, anger, impulsivity) that are characteristic of many mental disorders of adolescence. Factors (c) and (d) narrow our perspective. Recall the distinction in chapter 1 between "rehabilitation" and "clinical treatment." The juvenile justice system has an obligation to provide *rehabilitative services* to all youths in their care, whatever their psychological conditions, in order to reduce recidivism. It has a public safety mandate to provide *clinical treatment* for mental health needs, however, only to the extent that specialized clinical services are also necessary in order to reduce dangerous recidivism.

Thus, the mere fact that an adolescent has a DSM diagnostic condition and is assaultive does not create a public safety obligation to provide clinical treatment. There must be a connection between the symptoms of the condition and the youth's aggression. Moreover, there must be a reason to believe that clinical treatment can alter the relevant symptoms. A clinical intervention cannot be "necessary" if it does not have a history of altering—at least sometimes—the symptom condition that is related to aggression.

Therefore, for purposes of the mandate to provide treatment in the interest of public safety, this formula further limits our search to those disorders and symptoms associated with aggression that one can reasonably expect to modify with clinical care. As we will see in chapters 4 and 7, this may place some mental disorders outside the treatment-for-safety obligation, even though they may be related to future aggression.

Postscript: Is Conduct Disorder a "Disorder"?

Before concluding this chapter, it is important to consider a significant question that earlier discussions have skipped: Should Conduct Disorder be considered a mental disorder? The question arises in part because Conduct Disorder (CD) is diagnosed solely on the basis of a youth's persistent and repetitive manifestation of any three of fifteen behaviors involving aggression, destruction of property, theft, or "serious violation of rules." The "symptoms" of this "disorder," therefore, are solely behaviors punishable by authority, rather than the types of phenomena—cognitive, affective, and other psychological conditions—that are part of the criteria for most other DSM disorders.

One purpose of a classification system for disorders is to assist in the construction and discovery of underlying causal processes associated with a disorder. Richters (1996), for one, has argued that no such underlying process has ever been found for CD. It is true that research has found relations between CD and many factors that can increase aggression, such as impulsivity, poor learning and problem-solving skills, and biochemical and neurobiological deficits associated with disinhibition and harmfully maladaptive outcomes. But a correlation does not indicate cause; often it is not clear whether studies of these factors among CD youths are identifying causes, spurious correlates, or perhaps even consequences of aggression (Richters, 1996).

Lambert et al. (2001) explained this in a different way in an article titled "Looking for the Disorder in Conduct Disorder." They found that youths diagnosed with CD showed a very wide range of pervasive impairments. They attributed this in part to the fact that the CD criteria (doing any three of fifteen bad or antisocial things persistently) are so varied that a wide variety of youths are drawn into the diagnosis. Imagine, Lambert et al. proposed, that one flipped through the DSM-IV manual picking symptoms at random, then called this meaningless collection of symptoms a "disorder." The internal logic and psychometric value of employing those symptoms to identify youths who manifest "random symptom disorder" would not be too different, they suggest, from the internal logic of using DSM-IV criteria for CD to identify youths as having a "conduct disorder."

Finally, there is little reason to believe that engaging in repetitive and persistent illegal and disobedient behavior is the consequence of a particular underlying causal condition. As we will see in chapter 4, persistent delinquency is associated with *many* disorders of adolescence (e.g., ADHD, depressive disorders, learning disorders, and anxiety disorders, especially Posttraumatic Stress Disorder). Moreover, in contrast to CD, research on these other disorders has revealed a number of plausible underlying causal processes. Since the majority of youths with CD have one or more of those diagnoses as well, is it not possible that a CD diagnosis—like a juvenile detention center—simply acts as a collection point for a lot of adolescents who engage in aggressive and illegal behaviors for reasons best explained by a range of other disorders?

Nevertheless, it would be premature to completely reject CD as a potentially useful category. Its status as a mental disorder needs to be questioned, but it may yet have a limited role to play in research and clinical considerations.

Conclusion

This chapter has taken stock of ways to define mental disorders as a first step on our path toward an analysis of the juvenile justice system's obligations to respond to mental disorders among young offenders. The chapter described classifications of disorders, their clinical significance, and their relevance for various contexts. This has raised many warnings about difficulties that we will confront in later chapters when we apply these concepts in the process of defining the obligations. Many of these difficulties are related to the fact that psychopathology in adolescence cannot be understood outside of the context of adolescent development. This makes the terrain entirely different and more complex than the territory of adult psychopathology and its relation to legal questions. Moreover, the chapter has pointed out that diagnoses alone do not define the juvenile justice system's obligation to meet adolescents' needs for mental health services. We must also take into account the severity, chronicity, multiplicity, and functional significance of youths' disorders, as well as the fact that what qualifies as a mental disorder requiring treatment may vary across sociolegal contexts.

The focus has been on conceptual definitions of mental disorders. But to arrive at a complete picture of the juvenile justice system's obligations, we must now explore two further issues. First, any prospect for meeting the obligations we have discussed here will require that the system identify mental disorders in youths reliably and efficiently. Chapter 3 examines that proposition. Second, the final section of this chapter identified the need to know the relation between various mental disorders of adolescence and the functional abilities, impairments, and characteristics that are relevant for our three sociolegal contexts. Chapter 4 takes stock of those characteristics.

Chapter 3

Assessing Mental Disorders in Adolescents

The juvenile justice system's ability to respond to young offenders with mental disorders depends substantially on its ability to identify them. This chapter examines the potentials and challenges facing the system when identifying youths with disorders relevant for the three sociolegal contexts of custodial treatment, adjudication, and public safety. This requires attention to three broad assessment issues: (a) *availability* (what methods are available, and what do they claim to do?); (b) *reliability* (to what extent can we depend on their results?); and (c) *applicability* (what are the practical implications of their use in the three sociolegal contexts?).

The discussion bypasses the question of clinicians' abilities to make diagnoses based on unstructured interviews and clinical intuition. The days when society depends on the diagnostic judgment of clinicians are rapidly drawing to a close. Reliance on their art has been replaced by demands for "evidence-based methods" (objective, data-based accountability) in a world in which managed care and state budget regulatory offices control the availability of treatment resources and require more proof of need for care than a clinician's general impression. Moreover, we know little about the abilities of clinicians—unaided by assessment tools—to make reliable diagnoses with children and adolescents. Structured tools and instruments are the focus of this chapter.

The range of options for assessing youths' mental disorders is extensive, and it is not possible here to provide detailed guidance to clinicians regarding the values and limits of all of these methods. A number of sources can be consulted to obtain reviews of (and references to) the wider range of interview methods, screening tools, rating scales, and psychological tests that are available for use with adolescents in the juvenile justice system (e.g., Hoge & Andrews, 1996; Grisso & Underwood, in press).

What Methods Are Available?

A method is "available," for present purposes, if it (a) assesses characteristics of youths related to mental disorders, (b) has been developed for, or has a history of use with, boys and girls in the juvenile justice system, ages twelve to seventeen, and (c) is published in English and Spanish. Here I discuss four categories of measures that meet these requirements and briefly describe some representatives of those categories. This provides a general notion of the available options, which will aid later discussion of issues in identifying adolescents' disorders.

DSM Diagnostic Interviews

A number of well-researched tools use structured or semistructured interviews employing standardized questions to determine whether youths meet criteria for various diagnostic categories of the *Diagnostic and Statistical Manual of Mental Disorders* (DSM-IV) (American Psychiatric Association, 1994). There are, for example, the Diagnostic Interview for Children and Adolescents (Herjanic & Reich, 1983) and the Schedule for Affective Disorders and Schizophrenia for school-aged children, also known as the Kiddie-SADS (Puig-Antich & Chambers, 1978). But the Diagnostic Interview Schedule for Children (DISC) is the most comprehensively developed tool and serves as a prototype for this class of instrument. The DISC grew out of research conducted under the aegis of the National Institute of Mental Health and benefits from a history of various versions dating back to 1979. The most recent is the DISC-IV (Shaffer et al., 2000), which uses diagnostic criteria consistent with the current DSM-IV. The version it replaced, the DISC-2.3 (Shaffer et al., 1996), corresponded to criteria in an earlier version of the DSM (DSM-III-R). As noted in chapter 1, both of these versions have been used in important research on the prevalence of mental disorders among adolescent offenders.

The procedure for the DISC-IV involves asking questions of respondents, exactly as they are written and in a specific sequence, with branching sequences depending on the respondent's answers. Examiners have the choice of asking questions that will provide a current (past four weeks) diagnosis, diagnoses for status during the past twelve months, and diagnoses during the youth's lifetime. Examiners also may ask questions related only to select diagnoses. The DISC-IV includes an assessment of significance of impairment (consistent with DSM-IV levels of mild, moderate, and severe) for diagnoses made for a given individual.

Shaffer et al. (2000) report a DISC-IV administration time with youths of one to two hours, and they recommend about three to six days of training for DISC-IV administration. Processing the answers to achieve diagnoses typically must be accomplished with a computerized algorithm. The DISC-IV usually is administered in a face-to-face interview format, but it is available on CD, including a version that verbally asks the youths questions that they answer at a computer keyboard. Wasserman et al. (2002) have tested this computer-assisted "Voice DISC-IV" in juvenile correctional facilities.

Personality and Behavioral/Emotional Problems Inventories

Several important paper-and-pencil inventories for clinical use with adolescents measure their characteristics on certain personality dimensions or on constructs that identify behavioral and emotional problems. Three of these instruments, developed in the early 1990s, have been used with some frequency in juvenile justice settings. They are the Minnesota Multiphasic Personality Inventory-Adolescent (MMPI-A: Butcher et al., 1992), the Millon Adolescent Clinical Inventory (MACI: Millon, Millon, & Davis, 1993), and a "family" of instruments under the name Child Behavior Checklist (CBCL: there are several manuals and guides for these various instruments—for a description of all of them, see Achenbach & McConaughy, 1997). There have been recent, comprehensive reviews of each of these three instruments (MMPI-A: Archer, 1999; Forbey & Ben-Porath, 2001; MACI: McCann, 1999; CBCL: Achenbach, 1999).

The MMPI-A uses dimensions that were derived from the adult MMPI, in use since the 1950s (and used with adolescents as well as adults until the development of the MMPI-A in 1992). It consists of 474 true–false items (reading level approximately sixth grade) that can be administered in paper form or with computer or audiotape. These items contribute scores to ten clinical scales (e.g., "Depression," "Paranoia") that represent personality and behavioral tendencies, not DSM diagnostic conditions. Other scales on the instrument assist in detecting problematic response styles, such as overreporting or underreporting of clinical abnormalities. A youth's scores are compared to norms based on results of administration of the instrument to a large number of adolescents, allowing one to identify the age-relative degree of pathology on each of the scales. The MACI is much the same type of instrument, but its 331 items contribute to seven "Clinical Syndromes" (e.g., Anxious Feelings, Impulsive Propensity), several personality characteristics (e.g., Inhibited, Conforming), several "Expressed Problems" scales (e.g., Identity Diffusion, Family Discord), and several scales examining response styles. Both instruments require from one to two hours to administer.

The CBCL comes in Parent, Teacher, and Youth Self-Report forms. Shorter (112 items) than the other two inventories, it focuses on eight behavioral and problem dimensions (e.g., Withdrawn, Anxious/Depressed, Aggressive Behavior) that can be grouped into two broader types or styles of pathology, called "externalizing" (outward expression) and "internalizing" (inward feelings and thoughts). The CBCL also has a "competencies" section that is intended to identify specific social capacities and problems in everyday life. Youths are compared to age-peer norms. Administration requires about thirty to forty-five minutes. There is an enormous research literature on the reliability and validity of the CBCL, less with the MMPI-A, and least for the MACI.

Symptom Inventories

A number of instruments assess specific symptoms without providing diagnostic classifications (see Grisso & Underwood, in press, for a comprehensive list). Two that have gained substantial use in juvenile justice settings are the Brief Symptom Inventory (BSI: Derogatis, 1993; Derogatis & Melisaratos, 1983) and the Massachusetts Youth Screening Instrument-Second Version (MAYSI-2: Grisso & Barnum, 2003; Grisso et al., 2001). These instruments are designed to obtain information about symptom conditions or mental/emotional distress—nine for the BSI (e.g., Paranoid Ideation, Psychoticism) and six for the MAYSI-2 (e.g., Angry/Irritable, Depressed/Anxious, Suicide Ideation). Both are designed for quick administration and scoring (BSI: fifty-three items, ten minutes; MAYSI-2: fifty-two items, ten minutes). The BSI was originally developed for adults but has been used with adolescents. The MAYSI-2 was developed and normed specifically for adolescents in the juvenile justice system.

Measures of Functional Impairment

Functional impairment instruments seek to measure the degree to which psychopathology is actually interfering with a youth's everyday functioning. They therefore typically focus on evidence of the individual's current performance, behavior, and interpersonal relations at home, at school, and with peers. (For a review of many measures of this type, as well as their purposes, see Canino, Costello, & Angold, 1999).

The Children's Global Assessment Scale (CGAS: Shaffer et al., 1983) is patterned after the DSM-IV Global Assessment of Functioning in that it uses a 0–100 rating scale with verbal case anchors, but the CGAS provides anchors that are more appropriate for children and adolescents than in the DSM-IV's method. Two others, though, are more often seen in juvenile justice settings. The Child and Adolescent Functional Assessment Scale (CAFAS: Hodges & Wong, 1996; Hodges, 1997; for recent reviews, see Bates, 2001; Hodges, 1999) is a quick method for clinicians to rate youths (based on whatever case information is available) on adequacy and deficits in functioning within various life domains (e.g., home, school) and with regard to various potential problem areas (substance use or self-harmful behavior, for instance). It was developed specifically to assist in identifying those with "serious emotional disturbances" (SED) for purposes of determining services eligibility and assessing performance outcome (e.g., identifying functioning before and after services are provided). It is said to be used statewide in child mental health systems in about one-half of the states (Hodges, 1999), many of them by legislative authority in order to document eligibility for services. The extent of its use specifically in juvenile justice facilities in those states, however, has not been reported. The Problem-Oriented Screening Instrument for Teenagers (POSIT: Rahdert, 1991; McLaney, Del Boca, & Babor, 1994; Dembo et al., 1996), a 139-item questionnaire, was developed by the National Institute on Drug Abuse as a quick method for identifying youths whose level of impairment in ten areas might require further evaluation and services. The POSIT is used extensively in juvenile justice intake assessment programs in a number of states (e.g., Dembo et al., 1998).

Another class of problem-oriented instruments developed specifically for use with adolescents identifies the potential for suicidal or self-injurious behavior, or the history, frequency, and consequences of substance use. Scales to assess suicide potential, of which there a considerable number, typically are brief and rely on self-report. (For reviews, see American Academy of Child and Adolescent Psychiatry, 2001; Grisso & Underwood, in press). Some of them have undergone research to establish their ability to identify suicidal youths. A very large number of instruments are available for use specifically with adolescents to assess extent of alcohol and drug involvement and psychosocial factors associated with substance use. (For surveys of these instruments, see Center for Substance Abuse Treatment,

1999; Winters, 2001). Some of them are embedded in other problem-oriented instruments (such as the POSIT), but most are free standing, and many of them have been adequately researched and found to have acceptable psychometric qualities.

About the Instruments

As mentioned earlier, the methods noted here are only representatives of a much larger field of instruments—certainly at least several hundred—that have been developed for assessing youths' clinical conditions. However, most of this larger field of tools has been used only in research or only occasionally in applied clinical settings. As one explores the adolescent mental health and juvenile justice programs across the country, the dozen instruments identified here are the ones that repeatedly arise in actual practice.

The BSI is the only instrument among them that was originally developed for adults and has been pressed into service with youths without modification. What limited data are available suggest caution in its use with age groups (children or adolescents) for which it was not designed (e.g., Broday & Mason, 1991; Piersma, Boes, & Reaume, 1994).

The other instruments developed specifically for use with adolescents have appeared mostly within the past ten years; a few were based on earlier prototypes, but most are first-generation instruments. Their recent evolution is probably related to several factors. Many advances in the field of developmental psychopathology during the 1980s stimulated interest in developing instruments in this area, prompting at the same time an increase in the conceptual capacity necessary for carrying out this work. In addition, a sea change in the economics of mental health care during the 1980s and 1990s, involving managed care and cost containment (Young, 1998), created the need for assessment tools to meet the accountability requirements for evidenced-based practice (hard data on case-by-case mental health needs and treatment outcome). This produced a market incentive for the development of child mental health assessment tools. The market is substantial, because the states' juvenile justice systems recently have begun adopting assessment practices that screen every youth entering their systems for mental health needs.

Two implications of the recent history of these instruments are relevant. First, they have not had much time to establish their research or applied track record. Most of them can provide some evidence for their reliability and validity, but often the evidence is based on the initial studies performed by the test authors themselves during the tests' development with initial samples of youths. Moreover, often the research has examined an instrument's utility and meaning only in the context of clinics or in-patient psychiatric programs. For example, no studies have reported the reliability and validity of the BSI, MMPI-A, and MACI specifically with youths in juvenile justice custody. Initial assessments of a method's reliability and validity may or may not hold up when later compared with results obtained from testing adolescents in different clinical and delinquent settings, geographic areas, or ethnic groups.

Second, these instruments are in active competition for the child mental health and juvenile justice assessment market. Buyers must beware, because sellers (and consumers, too) might be tempted to implement the instruments for purposes that exceed their design. As seen in their description, these instruments are not generally interchangeable. One should not use a symptom screening device to make diagnoses, and a comprehensive diagnostic tool like the DISC-IV does not produce a picture of specific areas of functional impairment in everyday life. The choice of an instrument for a juvenile justice program must be informed by the program's specific purposes in wanting a tool. We will return to this issue later when examining the assessment objectives associated with each of our three sociolegal contexts.

How Reliable Are the Methods?

"Reliability" has a variety of technical meanings in the field of psychometrics, some of which we will encounter in a moment. For this discussion, however, I use the term in the broader sense, asking to what extent we can depend on instruments of the type described earlier to inform us with some degree of accuracy about the mental disorders and mental health needs of youths in the juvenile justice system. The discussion focuses especially on the way that the developmental status and circumstances of youths raise extraordinary challenges for these instruments.

Measuring Imperfect Concepts Well

Chapter 2 described the difficulties encountered by developmental psychopathologists in defining discrete mental disorders and their symptoms. Their frustration is most evident in the problem of comorbidity of disorders, as well as the degree to which various symptoms of disorder in adolescence (e.g., depression, anxiety, anger) are shared across current diagnostic categories. In terms that were quoted earlier, there do not seem to be any natural "joints" at which to carve the beast. Yet that is precisely where the test developer must start—first with the process of determining which diagnostic concepts and symptoms to measure, and then with the task of turning them into items and scales.

Sometimes the test developer's process can contribute to the refinement of the original concepts. For example, efforts like Achenbach's statistical procedures for developing the CBCL sometimes introduce a degree of order into chaos, showing us more coherent arrangements of symptoms into categories and clusters than were evident in clinical practice. (Achenbach's work has provided support for the notion of grouping youths' problems within "externalizing" and "internalizing" concepts, which have gained wide acceptance in child psychopathology.)

Typically, though, tests developed on the basis of current diagnostic structures will reflect the comorbidity and symptom nonspecificity of the structures that they operationalize. In other words, the scales that the tests measure will have considerable overlap. Youths scoring high on Conduct Disorder are likely to score high on various other diagnostic categories, and youths who report depressed mood often will also report being troubled by other negative emotions such as anger and anxiety. This is seen empirically when one examines the correlations between scales within any personality instrument (e.g., the MMPI-A or MACI), behavioral/emotional problem tool (e.g., the CBCL), or symptom inventory (e.g., MAYSI-2), many of which have average interscale correlations of about .35 to .50. (These figures are considered rather higher than one would wish, and higher than is generally found in adult measures of psychopathology.)

In other words, our instruments tend not to divide youths "cleanly" into those who are conduct disordered on the one hand and dysthymic on the other, or depressed youths here and angry youths there. Instead, they reflect accurately what we know about adolescents' disorders from developmental theory and clinical experience. As chapter 2 explained, distinct types of disorders are more a feature of adult psychopathology than childhood or adolescent psychopathology, which have more comorbid variations. Ironically, then, if a tool for assessing youths' mental disorders is well developed, it will have limited ability to identify one disorder from another (or will show considerable overlap among disorders), because that appears to be the way that psychopathology really is in adolescence.

Dealing with Moving Targets

There are several things about adolescent development that make youths "moving targets" when it comes to identifying their mental disorders and their implications. Some of these we discussed in chapter 2, especially the matter of discontinuity of disorders in adolescence. This means that there is some chance—greater in adolescents than in adults—that the disorder one discovers today when testing a youth will not be the youth's disorder for the longer-range future (even if it goes untreated), and may indeed be a precursor for some other disturbance at a later time.

In addition, the normal course of change during adolescent years creates the possibility that some youths may manifest disorders at one point in their adolescence that simply do not persist. For example, their disorder as it appeared at a particular time arose in response to their difficulty in mastering a particular developmental task (like managing increasing independence in early adolescence) for which they finally find a solution. Or their behavior regressed to an earlier form of adaptation (temper tantrums that are no longer appropriate at their age) in reaction to a difficult change in their life (their parents' divorce, for example), but regained a normal developmental course when they subsequently received adequate parental support. Finally, basic studies of adolescents' emotional lives indicate that their thoughts and feelings tend to be more labile than those of adults (Steinberg & Cauffman, 1996). From day to day, youths are more susceptible to brief but dramatic changes in mood, so that they might honestly report some current thoughts or feelings that we would not consider typical for them if we were able to assess them repeatedly at random intervals.

Thus, when a clinician sees, or a youth reports, substantial evidence for "anger," it could represent (a) an uncharacteristic reaction to a current circumstance or situation in the youth's life, (b) a currently characteristic response of the youth that may endure through a developmental phase but not longer, or (c) a characteristic that will transcend his developmental phases, perhaps even continuing into adulthood. This has significant consequences for the identification of disorders in adolescence with data obtained at a given point in time, and for grasping their longer-range significance. First, some of the data that one might be seeing at any given point are "states" rather than "traits," related to momentary emotions or temporary developmental phases, rather than enduring characteristics. They should not be ignored; indeed, they might have great significance in signaling the need for immediate clinical attention. For example, serious depressed mood and suicidal thoughts are not insignificant simply because they are momentary. But the data are less dependable for making longer-term predictions or extended treatment plans. Second, even if what one sees is not temporary, the overall results still are likely to have a shorter "shelf life" than for adults. With adolescents, one should not presume the current validity of a diagnosis made more than a few months earlier, or that last year's diagnosis necessarily explains a youth's current clinical episode.

Some sense of the magnitude of this "moving-target problem" is provided by the results of a major, longitudinal study of 4,000 inner-city youths in Pittsburgh, Denver, and Rochester, in which youths' serious delinquency, drug use, and mental health problems (externalizing and internalizing indexes on the CBCL) were assessed annually for three years (Huizinga et al., 2000). Among all youths who were identified as "having mental health problems" at the start (that is, were in the top 10 percent of the sample on the CBCL), about 75–80 percent did *not* meet those criteria when retested after one year, and only 5–10 percent of them continued to score high on the measure after two years. Interestingly, delinquency followed the same pattern; among youths meeting criteria for a serious delinquent behavior in the starting year, only about 20–25 percent "persisted"—continued to engage in serious delinquency yearly—over a two-year period.

It is not surprising, therefore, that when test developers examine the relation between diagnoses or symptom scores for the same youths at two different points in time, their "test–retest reliability" (the correspondence of the two scores) is only modestly good for most disorders and quite inadequate for others. Test–retest research procedures typically minimize the time between testing, usually two to three weeks, because the objective is to examine the stability of the test, not to document changes in youths' conditions that might normally occur over longer periods of time. Even so, the average test–retest reliability correlations are in the area of .65 to .85 for various scales in instruments like the MMPI-A, the MACI, the MAYSI-2, and the DISC-IV, and they are in the range of .35 to .60 for at least some scales in each of these instruments. Test–retest correlations in the former range are acceptable but do not bring a gleam of satisfaction to the psychometrist's eye, and those in the latter range are considered troubling.

The relevance of these observations depends on what a test intends to measure. Test–retest reliability is more important for tests that claim to measure characteristics that should endure more than a few weeks (most diagnostic conditions) and less important if they claim to measure thoughts and emotions that might be expected to change over that amount of time among many youths.

Relying on Youth and Parent Reports

Most of the instruments described earlier rely either on youths' reports of their thoughts, feelings, and behaviors in response to standardized questions, or on the reports of others—usually parents—who have observed the youth over time. Thus, the reliability of the data on which standardized diagnoses and symptom descriptions are based depends on the abilities and inclinations of informants to provide accurate and relevant information. This is a matter that requires some caution and must be taken into account when reviewing the options for assessing mental disorders in juvenile justice contexts.

YOUTH OR PARENT? One might expect that it would be better to ask parents about their children rather than to expect youths to be able or will ing to provide reliable information in the context of their arrests and adjudications. But this expectation has its limits. Every experienced examiner in a juvenile court clinic has observed the fear, embarrassment, or barely contained rage on the part of parents as they react to the recent arrests of their children. It should not be surprising that their observations are often quite different than those offered by parents who are seeking help for their children at mental health clinics.

In addition, parents sometimes cannot report things that youths can report about themselves. Child diagnosticians used to rely primarily on parents' reports of their children's conditions, believing that children and adolescents were incapable of providing reliable information. Several important studies (e.g., Lapouse & Monk, 1958; Rutter & Graham, 1968), however, altered this view. The weight of the evidence suggested that mothers reported the *observable behaviors* of their children somewhat more reliably, but that children reported more *"internalized" difficulties* (fears, disturbed thoughts and emotions), and they reported them more reliably (test–retest) than did their mothers. Over the years, therefore, practice has evolved to virtually require youth-reported information in clinical assessments, as well as caretaker information whenever the matter being assessed goes beyond the youth's thoughts and feelings. (Grills and Ollendick [2002] provide a very readable, complete review of the research on this issue.)

Several instruments—the DISC-IV, the CBCL, and the CAFAS (in its use of records that often contain others' reports of children's behaviors)—employ both adolescent- and parent-reported data. What is one to do with discrepant data obtained from these two sources? There are methods for integrating discrepant information (Grills & Ollendick, 2002). But typically one either believes one informant more than the other or one relies on both informants for different types of information, depending on which type (behaviors or internal states) they are more likely to report reliably.

Sometimes, though, one has no choice but to rely on youths themselves as the only source of information. Parents usually are not available, for example, when youths are first detained after arrest, a point at which assessment to determine emergency or immediate treatment needs may be critical. The information instruments can provide at that point is almost entirely based on the reliability of the youth's own self-report.

YOUTHS' RESPONSE BIASES. Youths (and adults) do not always report their thoughts, feelings, and behaviors as they actually are. This may result from the emotional circumstances in which juvenile justice assessments sometimes occur, as well as from youths' awareness of the implications of admitting to various thoughts, feelings, and behaviors in the context of custody.

As an illustration, imagine a youth who has been arrested by police officers in his home in the middle of the night, taken from his own bed to the police station, booked, threatened explicitly or implicitly with being removed from friends and family for a period of anywhere from a week to several years, and taken in shackles to a detention center, strip-searched, and led to a small room with a cot and locked door and told that he would have to stay there "for a while." The next morning, after being roused at 6:00 A.M. and fed along with fifty other youths whom he does not know, he is led to a room where a staff member proceeds to ask him questions to identify where he lives and attends school, then gives him a test booklet to complete that asks, among other things, the following questions:

- Have you been feeling lonely much of the time?
- Have you felt angry a lot?
- Have you been bothered by worried and nervous feelings?

  Other questions ask:

- Have you thought a lot about getting back at someone you have been angry at?
- Have you used alcohol and drugs at the same time?

  How a person answers such questions so soon after being admitted to detention may well be quite different than one's answers given under different circumstances. For the first three questions, the youth might endorse these "feelings" because of the painful experience of the past forty-eight hours, reflecting his transient rather than typical characteristics.

As for the last two questions, one would not be surprised to find that a youth was disinclined to admit to aggressive and illegal acts when faced with an authority figure representing the legal system that will decide his fate. In fact, the last time the youth was arrested, his attorney might have cautioned against responding too openly to questions that might get one in trouble. There is some comfort in the very consistent report of clinicians in the juvenile justice system that youths more often than not will report negative information about themselves more readily than one might expect. But Wasserman et al. (2002) observed that in their study in juvenile justice settings, as in other studies (e.g., Atkins, Pumariega, & Rogers, 1999; Randall et al., 1999; Teplin et al., 2002), the rate of identified Attention-Deficit/Hyperactivity Disorder cases has been so low that it is likely that youths in juvenile justice custody are underreporting the aggressive and impulsive symptoms that are often associated with that disorder.

When instruments have been developed specifically with youths in juvenile justice circumstances, it is possible for the test's norms to compensate somewhat for these sources of situational bias in responding. But most of the instruments we considered earlier were developed in community mental health and inpatient psychiatric settings for clinical populations of adolescents and their parents. In these settings, children and parents are there to be helped, and their relation to doctors is typically collaborative and hopeful when doctors ask them questions about their thoughts and feelings. Unlike youths in pretrial detention, typically they are going home at the end of the day and have been promised confidentiality when they were given assessment instruments.

Youths' possible inclination to conceal their thoughts or feelings is not always the problem. Clinicians frequently report that girls in the juvenile justice system often tend to *overreport* their negative emotions and thoughts, either because of social role differences that make the expression of feelings more acceptable to girls than to boys, or because they have learned that doing so may elicit greater attention and support. There is little research to substantiate these observations. As chapter 1 explained, girls in the juvenile justice system do have higher average scores than boys on almost every measure of mental or emotional disturbances. But it is not clear whether this reflects overreporting or simply greater psychopathology among girls than boys in juvenile justice settings. Some studies, though, have found poorer agreement for girls than for boys when their self-reports are compared to information obtained from parents (e.g., Angold et al., 1987; Rapee et al., 1994).

Virtually absent from the research on this issue are data regarding the reporting of symptoms by youths of varying ethnic and cultural backgrounds. There are intuitive reasons to suspect that ethnicity, and differences in ethnicity between youth and examiner, may make a difference in the reporting of symptoms and problems. Some of the instruments described earlier have examined ethnic group differences in scores (which we will consider later), but those data do not address reliability of reporting.

Most tools for assessing mental disorders and problems of youths are vulnerable to these reporting biases of adolescents. The MACI and MMPI-A have indicators built into their instruments meant to detect under- or overreporting of symptoms and problems. But this does not resolve the issue, because they were not developed with populations of youths in juvenile justice custody at the time of testing.

Despite these cautions, there is no reason to believe that the problem is so great that it invalidates the use of youth self-reports (or parent reports) in adolescent assessment. But it is a source of error that must be weighed in practice, and it must be given greater attention in many situations in the juvenile justice process, depending on the likelihood that the results of the assessment may be interpreted by youths or parents as representing substantial gains or losses.

Validity

The "validity" of an instrument is the degree to which it measures what it purports to measure—in this case, whether it identifies the mental disorders, symptoms, or impairments that it is intended to identify. There is no single way to establish an instrument's validity, and no single study can do so. Indeed, there is no rule regarding the number and kinds of studies it takes to conclude that a test is "valid." Moreover, a test may be valid for some purposes (e.g., identifying depressive disorders) and invalid for others (e.g., identifying which youths with depressive disorders are in need of treatment).

There are many methods for testing an instrument's validity, and they go by many names—face, internal, concurrent, construct, predictive, and so forth (see, e.g., Anastazi, 1988). But they can all be categorized as representing one of two broad approaches: *theoretical* and *concurrent*.

Theoretical approaches examine whether the instrument has a record of finding results that are consistent with our theoretical notions of mental disorders. By analogy, imagine we came across historical records that we had good reason to believe accurately pointed to the location of a buried treasure. We use a device at that location that is said to detect precious metals. If it registers, we have indirect evidence that the device does what it is supposed to do, even if we are not immediately able to dig up the treasure. Similarly, if theory tells us that youths with Major Depression are more likely than other youths to have parents who manifested Major Depression, and if the measure we use to form our depressed and nondepressed groups helps us to substantiate that prediction, the measure moves up a notch in our belief in its validity for identifying Major Depression. If a disorder is expected to produce a high suicide risk, and if our measure of suicide potential achieves higher scores with the group diagnosed with that disorder than with youths in general, our confidence that the measure assesses what it is supposed to assess increases.

Concurrent approaches to validity examine the degree to which the instrument produces scores or diagnostic groups that comport with results obtained with other methods for determining those groups. For example, if a measure of Major Depression usually identifies the same youths that are identified by a panel of highly expert clinicians, the measure gains a degree of recognition regarding its validity for measuring the disorder.

When examining an instrument's validity, a difficulty inherent in both of these approaches is that the instrument is always being compared to something else (theoretical expectancy, or some other definition of the "right" answer). Therefore, whether the results are positive or negative, one's conclusions about validity can only be as good as the validity of that to which the instrument is being compared. Typically, the validity of the thing to which it is being compared is either unknown, or what is known about it is based on past studies that compared *that* thing to something else (which, of course, is of unknown validity or is considered valid because *it* was once compared to something else).

The logic seems circular, yet a substantially reliable field of clinical assessment has been built under these conditions. But it is important to understand that to declare an instrument "valid" establishes no firm anchor and, indeed, has meaning only in a particular psychometric sense. Moreover, tests too often are declared to be "valid" without specifying that they are valid only for some specific purpose. For example, we might prove that a test identifies 90 percent of youths who later manifest suicide attempts and, in doing so, falsely identifies as suicidal only 30 percent of youths who do not attempt suicide. In general, this might be considered a highly valid test; it certainly establishes a strong relationship between the test and the thing it intends to measure. Now imagine that you operate a detention center where, out of every 1,000 youths admitted, 100 have actual suicide tendencies and 900 do not. The test will identify 360 of these 1,000 youths as potentially suicidal: that is, 90 percent of 100 youths who actually are (90), and 30 percent of 900 youths who are not (270). Therefore, if you provide suicide precautions or hospitalization to all those scoring positive, you will be doing so for almost all youths who need it, but 75 percent of those to whom you provide it (270 out of the 360) do not need it. Would you still consider the test "valid?" Or is it valid for some purposes, but not for yours?

Norms

The manuals of most instruments provide norms with which one can compare a youth's scores. Norms are developed by administering the instrument to large samples of adolescents (often including clinical and non-clinical samples) in order to determine the range of scores and consequently what is considered high and low relative to one's peers, and to provide ways to identify where a particular youth falls in that range.

It is important for norms to be age-appropriate for the youths one is assessing, and many instruments do provide separate norms for younger and older adolescents. But one of the nagging problems with many measures of psychopathology reviewed earlier is the questionable use of their norms with various ethnic subgroups in juvenile justice settings.

According to federal statistics (Snyder & Sickmund, 1995), the ethnic proportions of those in juvenile pretrial detention centers nationally are as follows: 43 percent African American, 35 percent White (non-Hispanic), 19 percent Hispanic, and 3 percent other ethnicities (e.g., Asian, Native American). In contrast, the norming samples for the MACI, MMPI-A, CBCL, BSI, and DISC-IV range from 58 to 89 percent White (non-Hispanic), with African American youths comprising less than 15 percent of the samples for the MACI, the CBCL, and the MMPI-A. Figures are not available for the proportion of Hispanic youths in some test norms, but they were less than 12 percent for the MMPI-A and 6 percent for the MACI. Moreover, none of these instruments' manuals contain separate tables showing the average scores of youths by ethnicity on the instrument's various scales. None publish statistics (such as scale alpha coefficients) to show whether the scales as constructed have adequate internal consistency for each ethnic group, and none have employed special statistical methods that determine whether individual items in the instruments are consistently interpreted the same or differently by various ethnic groups taking the test. This is important because, without that information, one does not know whether youths of different ethnic backgrounds approach the test questions differently, thus perhaps nullifying the intended meaning of the scale for certain ethnic groups.

Similarly, when researchers have compared an instrument's scores to some other criterion to test the validity of the instrument, almost never (with the exception of the CBCL) have those comparisons been made separately for youths of different ethnicities. Thus one does not know whether the evidence for the validity of the instrument applies equally well to African American, Hispanic, and Asian youths as to White (non-Hispanic) youths.

Why such limitations of these instruments have not been resolved is not clear. Correcting them would not be impossible. For example, almost all of the types of information noted above have been provided for the MAYSI-2 (Cauffman & McIntosh, in press; Grisso et al., 2001). The difference might be in their starting points. The MAYSI-2 was developed and normed in juvenile justice settings, with minority ethnic youths comprising 56 percent and 85 percent of its Massachusetts and California samples, respectively. Similarly, the use of the DISC-2.3 by Teplin et al. (2002) and the DISC-IV by Wasserman et al. (2002) in juvenile justice samples both have ethnic minorities in high proportions, and Teplin et al. (but not Wasserman et al.) reported separate prevalence rates for youths of different ethnicity. In contrast, most developers of measures of adolescent psychopathology have begun with outpatient and/or inpatient clinical samples, drawn from settings where the greatest proportion of youths are non-Hispanic White. This produces fairly small samples of ethnic minority youths, discouraging separate analyses because of the potential instability of the results.

The fact that most child psychopathology instruments have not been studied within juvenile justice settings raises other concerns as well, and we will return to those in the next section.

Summary

The field offers a reasonable number of adequately developed instruments from which to choose when trying to identify youths with mental health needs. Moreover, there are several instruments to accomplish the several objectives—for example, arriving at diagnoses, estimating degree of functional impairment—that will arise in various contexts within the juvenile justice system.

But the degree to which they provide reliable case-by-case information about youths is limited in several ways, including inherent difficulties in classifying youths' disorders, error associated with the temporal meaning of child clinical data obtained at any given point in a youth's life, and error associated with reliance on youths' and parents' reports of youths' behaviors and feelings. In addition to these sources of error associated with the developmental status of adolescents, we are currently faced with inadequate information about the reliability or meaning of performance on these instruments specifically in juvenile justice settings, and especially with the multi-ethnic population of adolescents whose mental disorders and impairments we are attempting to assess.

This does not mean that the juvenile justice system cannot use the instruments described earlier. But there is a need for caution, as well as for substantial future research to identify the meaning of scores on these instruments for youths of various ethnic backgrounds.

Applicability: Instruments in Context

Ultimately, one's choice of methods to assess disorders among adolescents will depend also on their compatibility with the demands of the juvenile justice context in which they are used. This requires four types of considerations:

- *Justice Processing:* Where and when is information needed in the processing of delinquency cases?
- *Feasibility:* Do instruments meet the practical demands of the system?
- *Relevance:* Do instruments tell us what the system needs to know, given its purposes for wanting to know?
- *Resilience:* Can instruments endure the conditions under which they will be used?

Justice Processing: Where and When Mental Health Information Is Needed

INTAKE. Soon after arrest, juvenile justice personnel must make decisions about which youths will be referred to outpatient or inpatient mental health services in the community. Often these decisions are made by intake probation staff or intake assessment centers. Screening procedures may help to identify those who are most likely to need more careful evaluation for making these decisions (Cocozza & Skowyra, in press; Grisso & Underwood, in press).

PRETRIAL DETENTION. Some youths are placed in secure pretrial detention centers soon after their arrest. Typically decisions must be made within a few days regarding the need for continued detention, requiring some information about their mental status to the extent that it is relevant for the question of risk of harm to self or others (one of the criteria justifying continued detention). In addition, staff of detention centers frequently are expected to make decisions about youths' immediate needs, especially as they relate to potential suicide risk, risk of harm to other youths in the facility, and possible acute mental disorder that would require professional consultation or a petition for immediate inpatient commitment.

PRE-ADJUDICATIVE LEGAL QUESTIONS. Questions are raised in some cases that require information about adolescents' clinical status as it pertains to specific legal decisions prior to trial (see generally Grisso, 1998). Among these are questions concerning a youth's potential transfer to criminal court for trial, which require making a judgment about likelihood of rehabilitation and degree of danger posed if the youth were retained in the juvenile justice system. Any evidence of mental disorders might be relevant for this decision. In addition, questions of a youth's competence to stand trial and of criminal responsibility (related to the insanity defense) often hinge specifically on the presence and effect of mental disorders.

DISPOSITION AFTER ADJUDICATION. If youths are found guilty (delinquent), courts frequently require information about their needs when deciding on their placement, in light of the need for services or the danger posed to the community. Typically this information is collected prior to trial to provide its timely use if the youth is adjudicated delinquent. Courts' disposition options fall generally into various types of community programs with probation contact or referral to the state's juvenile corrections authority that also has various placement options (although typically focused on more secure placements). Community options include the possibility of court-ordered clinical services, and juvenile authority secure placements may include options for clinical treatment.

CORRECTIONS. When someone is referred by the court for placement with state correctional programs for youth, the corrections authority of many states provides for an intake assessment to determine, among other things, whether the youth has special mental health needs that require services while in the custody of the youth authority or that suggest the need for more or less secure placement. These results are used for rehabilitation, treatment, and placement planning. Some progressive youth authorities also provide for mental health assessments near the time of program completion, especially when the youth has been in secure facilities and is being considered for return to the community where services might be provided through community agencies during continued custody under the youth authority.

Feasibility: The Practical Demands on Mental Health Assessment Methods

Recommendations for the use of particular types of assessment methods must take into account the costs of their use, as well as the need for special expertise in administering the methods. Cost is a multifaceted factor. Specific costs include testing materials, the expense of training and maintaining expertise of personnel, the personnel time required for administration of the instrument, costs involved in processing the assessment information and documenting results, and financial compensation associated with the time and level of professional expertise involved. Secondary financial considerations include the possibility of delays in case processing (e.g., reduction in cases-per-day due to longer processing time, longer bed-days in detention or assessment centers), as well as expenses of increased consultations, comprehensive evaluations, and referrals that might be generated by the results of screening procedures.

The instruments described earlier vary widely in these costs for relatively obvious reasons. Some test developers require a per-case fee for administering certain psychological tests, while other tests may be used without cost for materials. Various instruments require more or less time per case and may or may not require administration and interpretation by more costly doctoral-level examiners.

The level of expertise required for various assessment methods must be weighed against the availability of specialized examiners at various points in juvenile justice processing, as well as the volume of cases at those points. At the intake stage, general observation suggests that intake probation information is collected by social work probation officers, and detention intake assessments are performed by nonprofessional detention staff at the time of the youth's admission, with doctoral-level professionals performing more in-depth evaluations in a minority of cases. The number of intake evaluations in a given year is enormous. In 1996, about 1.75 million youths were processed through the juvenile justice system in the

United States on delinquency charges, and about 320,000 youths were admitted to pretrial detention centers (Snyder & Sickmund, 1999). For jurisdictions that have routine screening (every-admission) evaluations at their intake probation and detention intake levels, this represents a very large number of youths annually in most metropolitan areas, even with the increased availability of technology in recent years for processing intake information. For example, Miami/Dade County intake assessment centers (which screen all youths soon after arrest) performed over 120,000 screening evaluations during a recent eighteen-month period.

Mental health professionals (psychiatrists and psychologists) are more likely to be involved in evaluating adolescents' mental health needs related to pre-adjudicative legal questions like competence to stand trial. The number of youths evaluated for questions of competence or criminal responsibility is not known, although some states (Florida and Virginia, for instance) perform several hundred competence-to-stand-trial evaluations annually for children and adolescents.

Typically court probation officers are required to provide some type of disposition-related behavioral and mental health information to judges in virtually every case that is adjudicated. In only a minority of these cases will psychologists and psychiatrists perform comprehensive evaluations. Similarly, evaluations of youths entering juvenile correctional programs after adjudication will be performed by specialized social workers, with occasional assistance from psychologists and psychiatrists in special cases.

Fiscal responsibility and management of scarce resources requires that cost and required level of expertise must be taken into account when deciding what assessment methods should be used. Indeed, very high assessment costs may actually subtract from available resources for providing treatment to youths who are identified as having mental health needs. On the other hand, costs must not be reduced at the expense of selecting methods that provide reliable information that we need in order to meet our obligations. Brief screening devices for identifying symptoms should not be used throughout the juvenile justice process merely because they are cheaper. Cost must be weighed against a method's ability to tell us what we need to know at a particular point in the process.

Relevance: Telling Us What We Need to Know When We Need to Know It

Our consideration of what methods to use in order to identify youths' mental health needs must take stock of what juvenile justice personnel need to know about youths' mental disorders, at various stages in the adjudicative process and for various purposes related to our three socio-legal contexts. I do not attempt that here, except to describe a general template for the later analyses of this issue (chapters 5–7).

The type and depth of mental health information that the system needs varies considerably from one step in the adjudication process to another. For example, we must ask whether probation intake staff really need to know specific diagnoses for every youth who comes through the door. Alternatively, might a brief screening instrument that provides a rough index of symptoms such as depressed mood and anger be sufficient? Do detention staff need to know an adolescent's diagnosis, or is it sufficient for them to learn that the youth is or is not a suicide or assaultive risk? Is it sufficient for staff who are preparing to make disposition recommendations to only know about symptoms provided by a brief screening instrument, or is something more needed?

The point of these questions, although prosaic, must be kept clearly in mind. *No instrument will serve all purposes for mental health evaluation at all points in the juvenile justice process.* Earlier I noted that the instruments we reviewed were in competition for the juvenile justice market. They should not be, because most of them are not interchangeable in light of the differences across juvenile justice contexts in what the system needs to know. A final analysis of the system's obligations to identify youths' mental health needs will suggest different types of instruments for different points in juvenile justice case processing, tailored to the type of information relevant for objectives at each of those points.

Resilience: Meeting Challenges to Validity and Ethical Use

Like all products of science and industry, assessment tools are at the mercy of their users. They may be deployed with care and sensitivity or with ignorance, and occasionally their misuse suggests less than appropriate motives of the users. Some instruments may be more resilient than others when used roughly, but none are immune from being misused. Wonderful plans for screening and assessing youths' mental disorders in the juvenile justice system can easily go awry in practice.

UNSTANDARDIZED ADMINISTRATION. Students of psychological assessment are accustomed to hearing their professors intone the oft-repeated adage, "A test is no more valid than its administration." Standardized tools are immediately unstandardized if they are introduced and administered to youth in a different manner than was intended, and having been unstandardized, the results the test produces are invalid, even when the instrument itself enjoys impressive evidence for its validity.

The point here is not about professional expertise. Many of the instruments described earlier have been developed to allow non-Ph.D. and non-M.D. juvenile justice personnel—with various degrees of inservice training—to administer the instruments competently, score them, and translate the scores into diagnostic categories, levels of distress, or degrees of impairment. But the care with which they will do this cannot be guaranteed by the instrument. Often the degree to which instruments will be administered as intended depends on staff motivation. My own team of trainers (for the MAYSI-2) has conducted staff trainings of juvenile justice personnel who quickly embraced the instrument with enthusiasm, an attitude that is often seen among public sector workers who are committed to the youths in their charge. We have also conducted staff trainings of juvenile justice personnel who stubbornly resisted anything having to do with the instrument, fully intending to subvert its use with half-hearted implementation, an attitude that is often seen among public sector workers who are committed to minimizing changes in their established routine.

MISUSE OF THE RESULTS. Tests may be misused in many ways, but in the present context it is especially important to attend to misuses that are related to the two-sided relationship between youths and their juvenile justice custodians. The system is obligated to provide for youths' needs in a manner that is humane and beneficent, which in some states is still interpreted as requiring a rehabilitative and therapeutic objective. But the system has many other objectives, including "moving cases along," maximizing adjudications, and getting kids off the streets. Ironically, increased assessment of youths' mental disorders offers opportunities to further these latter, less-beneficent objectives.

For example, one way to reduce crowding in a juvenile justice system's pretrial detention center is to set the cut-off scores on mental health screens low enough to increase the number of cases that "need" to be transferred to inpatient psychiatric beds, thus freeing more beds in detention. Youths who admit to drug use or angry feelings in pretrial mental health screens may find that their answers get into the hands of prosecutors, thus influencing court decisions about their guilt (or more likely, strengthening the prosecutor's hand in a plea bargain).

There is not much that test developers can do about such misuses. But knowing that they can happen suggests the need for two precautions. First, we should recognize that more assessment is not necessarily better assessment. In fact, one should probably err on the conservative side, concluding that *the state should do no more by way of assessment than that which is essential to meet its treatment, due process, and public safety obligation.* Nonessential assessment increases the risk of unjustified intrusion on privacy, multiplies the opportunities for information to be misused, wastes public funds that could be allocated to other purposes (e.g., treatment of youths' mental disorders), and sets up youths and parents to expect benefits that too often are unfulfilled. Second, recommendations for particular assessment methods or tools should be accompanied by requirements for the conditions in which they should be used. This means attending to the assessment process, not merely the tool, and providing assurances that the results will be used in ways that are appropriate from both clinical and legal perspectives.

Conclusion

Many good tools have been designed to provide the types of information that the juvenile justice system needs in order to identify youths with mental disorders and functional impairments. Their capacity to assist the system, however, is limited for a number of reasons. Some of these reasons are inherent in psychopathology in the context of child and adolescent development, which produces conceptual and measurement issues of great complexity. Other are related to the development of the tools in clinical and general community samples, raising questions about the meaning of their scores when we rely on youths' and parents' reports in a very different juvenile justice context. And one must be concerned about the utility of norms that often do not reflect the ethnic composition of youths in juvenile justice settings.

Ultimately the value of assessment tools for meeting the system's objectives will depend also on their ability to fit within the juvenile justice system's financial constraints and need for efficiency. In addition, tools must be chosen with regard to specific decision objectives at various stages in case processing, because classes of tools will vary in their value for different purposes. Finally, the potential for misuse of assessment data requires that the practice of identifying youths' mental disorders and impairments should be targeted, efficient, and bounded by requirements that limit the uses of data obtained from assessments of youths' mental health needs.

Chapter 4

The Consequences of Mental Disorders in Adolescence

The mere fact that youths have been identified as having mental disorders and functional impairments is not enough to determine how we should respond to their disorders. We also need to know the relation of those disorders to the objectives of our three sociolegal contexts.

- What does the treatment literature tell us about the *prospects for treating youths' mental disorders* and mental health problems?
- What mental disorders of youths are *relevant for protection of the due process rights* of youths during their adjudication?
- What do we know about the *relation between mental disorders and aggression* for purposes of attending to public safety?

These questions form the three sections of this chapter. Our later analyses of how the juvenile justice system should be responding to young offenders' mental disorders depend substantially on our answers to these questions.

The Treatment Context: What Are the Prospects for Treatment?

An extensive body of scientific literature describes research on treatments for child and adolescent psychopathology, and makes recommendations for clinical application of treatment methods. It focuses on treatments for specific DSM diagnostic disorders (e.g., Attention-Deficit/Hyperactivity Disorder [ADHD], anxiety disorders), for general symptom conditions (for instance, depressed mood, anger and aggression), and for specific disorder-related outcomes (e.g., suicide). It addresses preventive interventions, emergency interventions, and long-term management of chronic conditions. It describes inpatient and community-based interventions. It identifies the value of psychopharmacological treatment, forms of individual psychotherapy, group therapies, and psychosocial approaches involving systematic interventions in the lives of youths, their parents, and other relevant people in their social networks. It analyses systems of mental health service delivery, including referral processes, networks of service provision, and economic schemes for managing the costs of mental health care for children and adolescents.

This literature is vast and complex. Yet, until the past decade, most treatment of youths' mental disorders was guided by theory and clinical art. Only recently has the field of child and adolescent psychopathology begun to *demonstrate* the value of clinical treatments for youths' mental disorders. This new era has been stimulated in part by advances in scientific methods for examining treatment effects, and in part by a managed care health system in which reimbursement for care requires a demonstration that the treatment to be provided has some value (Weisz & Jensen, 1999).

The lexical icon for this movement, found in the introduction of virtually every recent review of treatment methods, is "evidence-based practice." Treatment is no longer defined simply as anything that a mental health professional provides. Especially if it is to be reimbursed by insurers, *"treatment" is an intervention for which there is research evidence of an effect that is appreciably more beneficial than no intervention.*

This section takes stock of what is known about evidence-based benefits of treatments for young offenders with mental disorders. It addresses three questions:

- *Dimensions of Treatment:* How can we organize the topic of "treatment" so that it helps us to think through the system's obligations?
- *Values of Treatment:* What does research say about the benefits of various treatments for mental disorders, so that we can begin to identify what the system should be required to provide, and what it should *not* be required to provide because of lack of value?
- *Systems for Treatment Delivery:* Treatment is not simply something one goes out and orders; it requires a plan for its administration. What do we know from mental health services research regarding the juvenile justice system's options for managing the delivery of necessary treatment services to youths?

Dimensions of Treatment in a Juvenile Justice System Context

The term "treatment" is often used in a monolithic way in juvenile justice rhetoric to refer to anything that is intended to modify youths' behavior. Chapter 1 proposed a distinction, however, between juvenile justice systems' "rehabilitative interventions"—the behavior modification, special and occupational education, monitoring, and group counseling activities around which many corrections programs are based—and "treatment" interventions designed to address youths' mental disorders. The meaning of "treatment" in the juvenile justice context can be further refined by considering several concepts related to its implementation: (a) objectives of mental health care, (b) modes of treatment, (c) clinical targets, and (d) definitions of treatment success.

OBJECTIVES OF MENTAL HEALTH CARE. The objectives of clinical treatment vary depending on the course of disorder at the time of clinical intervention. For example, a man develops chest pains and rushes to a hospital's emergency room. Cardiac arrest is diagnosed and treatment is provided with the goal of averting the immediate life-threatening consequences. When the crisis is over, the man is moved to the hospital's recovery area for several days to receive treatment with a different objective—namely, monitoring and stabilization to ensure that the underlying disease process is in remission. For some diseases, this period of treatment may continue for weeks or months, even after the patient has returned home. Once in remission, a third type of treatment frequently occurs, focused on health maintenance to avoid relapse in a patient who is now known to be at risk of the disease that has been successfully treated at the crisis and stabilization levels.

Similarly, treatment may mean all of these things when applied to potential obligations of the juvenile justice system with reference to youths' mental health needs. I refer to these three objectives of treatment as *crisis-related* or *emergency treatment, stabilization,* and *maintenance.*

Crisis-related treatment may be required for some youths on admission to detention facilities or sometime during pretrial detention, community probation, or a stay in a correctional facility. This emergency intervention often is in response to behaviors—such as suicide threats, "out-of-control" aggressive behaviors, psychotic-like episodes, or drug withdrawal reactions—that require rapid response with the sole objective of reducing the immediate harm associated with the behavior. Effective crisis-related treatment depends on a system's ability to identify an impending crisis, to obtain clinical assistance quickly, and to have in place procedures for transporting a youth to facilities with specialized treatment resources for dealing with the crisis.

Mental health service directed toward *stabilizing* a youth's condition is often necessary following a crisis, and focuses on achieving a condition that allows the youth to function with less distress and greater effectiveness when returned to the routine of the detention center, correctional facility, or community-based program. This level of care is also needed, however, in many cases that do not involve a preceding crisis. For example, a youth may manifest significant anxiety causing considerable distress and greatly reducing the ability to function in rehabilitation programs or in the community, but without that anxiety involving a highly disruptive episode that would be labeled a "crisis." Treatment for stabilization typically requires the availability of treatment services within juvenile justice facilities or, if the youth is not in a secure setting, in community justice or mental health programs.

Finally, treatment for juvenile justice youths might involve *maintenance* services that ensure continuity of care after maximal functioning had been achieved, to prevent relapses and perpetuate the benefits of stabilization treatment. This level of care might arise during the "rehabilitation" phase of juvenile justice custody, but most importantly after custody has been relinquished.

I use this three-part treatment scheme in chapter 5, when considering the system's custodial treatment obligations. It is also useful in gauging the relevance of our review of treatment effects later in this section.

MODES OF INTERVENTION. There are at least three fundamental modes of treatment that are available to mental health and juvenile justice systems. They are (a) *psychopharmacological* agents, (b) *psychotherapies,* and (c) *psychosocial* interventions. In theory, all three may be applied in any of the health service contexts dedicated to one of the treatment goals just described.

Psychopharmacological treatment of mental disorders involves administration of medications that chemically alter mood, cognition, or behavior, their effect typically being achieved by altering the process of brain neurotransmission. (These are reviewed in more detail later.) The distinction between psychotherapies and psychosocial interventions is not a bright line; indeed, one can view them as ranging across a spectrum. At one end of this spectrum is any mode of treatment primarily involving a therapist and patient in conversation, for any theoretical or practical reason, focused on changing the patient's behavior, thinking, or emotional condition. At the other end is an intervention that seeks these changes by altering the environmental circumstances in which the patient is expected to function in everyday life. Midway along this spectrum are a variety of methods that involve direct work with the patient in the context of people and social systems that are important in the patient's life.

Examples of interventions that may be arrayed along such a spectrum are listed below. (The methods described here are not necessarily "preferred" methods—a notion dealt with later—but are used simply to exemplify what the spectrum may include.) Thus, moving along the spectrum from one pole to the other, one might encounter the following methodologies:

- Youth-focused—Kendall's (1994) individual cognitive-behavioral therapy for youths with anxiety disorders, as well as Assertiveness Training (Huey & Rank, 1994) and Problem-Solving Skills Training (Kazdin, 1996), together with various psychodynamic approaches to assist youths in developing insight into their behavior, typically through the patient-therapist relationship carried out in individual therapy sessions
- Youth in Group—Cognitive-behavioral group treatment for adolescents with depression (Clarke et al., 1999), as well as a variety of peer group methods for treating drug abuse and dependency (Jarvis, Tebbutt, & Mattick, 1995)
- Youth and Family—Functional Family Therapy (Alexander et al., 1988) that focuses on reducing youths' clinical problems by improving interpersonal functioning and communication within the family, with all members participating in the therapy
- Youth and Systems—Multisystemic Therapy (Henggeler et al., 1986; Borduin et al., 1995), in which the therapist works on a daily basis with the youth by intervening directly in the youth's social systems (e.g., family, school, work place) while the youth is involved in them
- Systems—Therapies that train parents (e.g., the Oregon Social Learning Center program: Patterson, 1975, and McMahon & Wells, 1998; also Barkley, 1997), teachers (e.g., Gittelman et al., 1980), or others in the youth's social spheres of interaction to alter the behaviors of youths with disruptive behavior disorders or ADHD by altering their own behaviors in response to the youth (typically without the youth's involvement in the treatment)

All of these approaches may be called "psychotherapy." But it is of value to distinguish them as increasingly "psychosocial" in nature as they move further along the spectrum away from the traditional mode of individual therapy involving the youth alone.

The degree to which one can proceed toward the psychosocial end of the spectrum typically is inversely related to the degree of security surrounding a youth's incarceration. Treatments in secure detention and correctional facilities are confined almost entirely to methods in the less psychosocial part of the spectrum, because the people and social situations that would be needed to employ more psychosocial modes of treatment typically are not available in those settings. Psychopharmacological interventions also involve special requirements that need to be considered when implementing treatment. For example, prescribing must be done by child psychiatrists, who typically are not full-time employees of juvenile justice facilities and sometimes are not even to be found in the communities in which juvenile justice facilities are located. Other implications of various treatments will become clearer when we review the research on the effectiveness of psychopharmacology and psychosocial interventions with adolescents.

CLINICAL TARGETS. All forms of treatment seek to reduce symptoms and problem behaviors associated with some disorder. Some treatments, however, seek to do this by targeting the *disorder,* while other treatments aim at *specific symptoms.* (See Connor, 2002, for a discussion regarding these two strategies in adolescent psychopharmacology.) For example, for a youth who is both seriously depressed and prone to aggressive outbursts, some medications for the treatment of depression will reduce depressed affect as well as the aggression associated with the youth's condition. In addition, though, some medications (e.g., risperidone, an atypical antipsychotic drug: e.g., Simeon et al., 1995) appear to be effective in reducing aggression among youths regardless of their psychiatric diagnosis, so that the medication may be used to target aggression apart from the underlying disorder. Similarly, a psychotherapy for depression may reduce the youth's aggression if it successfully treats the depression (and if the aggression is related to the disorder). But treatment for a similar youth might target a reduction in aggression by assignment to a group anger-management therapy that is not designed to treat depression.

Whether one treats the disorder or the symptom is, of course, a clinical question that has no single answer for all cases. What one must consider, however, is that clinical questions in correctional settings may not always be the same as clinical questions in clinical settings. Imagine a medication targeted for reducing aggression that works more quickly, efficiently, or cheaply than one that treats the disorder. Treating the disorder, however, may offer a more fundamental and lasting change in the conditions giving rise to the youth's aggression. Whichever of these approaches is chosen may be influenced by the way one balances objectives. The first is more aligned with immediate public safety obligations and the second with general treatment obligations and longer-range concerns. There need not be a conflict between these two approaches, but the potential for conflict is present if either obligation is one-sidedly paramount over the other.

DEFINING TREATMENTS OF VALUE. Researchers who study the potential benefits of methods of treatment examine their value in terms of "efficacy" and "effectiveness" (e.g., Hoagwood et al., 1995). To examine a method's *efficacy*, therapy researchers employ the treatment mode under highly controlled conditions. As an analogy, imagine the test of a new pesticide in which it is applied in exactly the same carefully measured and uniform amount per square foot of lawn as is a pesticide already in use. A significant advantage in weed control for the new pesticide demonstrates its efficacy. For tests of therapies, study patients must be selected according to rigorous specifications to ensure that they have the disorder for which the method is intended to be of benefit. The method itself is carefully designed and systematically documented, and the "research doctors" who will be providing the treatment undergo special training in the method to ensure that they will always follow its procedures in a standardized way. The group to which the study patients are compared—the control group—is also carefully chosen to ensure its members have the same diagnosis as the study group, but they receive some other (or no) intervention. Efficacy is expressed as the proportion of patients in the experimental group, compared to the proportion in the control group, who demonstrate a specific beneficial outcome (as measured with standardized instruments).

In contrast, a method's *effectiveness* refers to its value in the real world where researchers cannot control the quality of its application. Using the same analogy as above, we may test the new pesticide's effectiveness by giving it to a number of homeowners, along with instructions for its use, but with no further intervention by the researchers other than their measurement of weed control in the homeowners' yards as the summer proceeds. Similarly, the effectiveness of a method of therapy refers to its value when ordinary clinicians in actual clinical settings provide it to whatever patients obtain their services. Presuming that the method has been shown to be efficacious, will it be of benefit where it really counts—in the real world, complete with its time pressures, individual differences between doctors, and patterns of referral determined simply by whoever (with a specific type of disorder) comes through the clinic door? And if it is of benefit, what real-world circumstances make a difference in increasing or decreasing the likelihood of that benefit?

I later use the distinction between efficacy and effectiveness when examining research on the beneficial effects of various treatments. But two caveats should be noted in the context of that distinction's more general use. First, it does no good to simply require that the juvenile justice system provide "treatment" unless the *efficacy* of that treatment is "evidence-based." Second, the mere fact that the juvenile justice system employs an efficacious treatment does not mean that it will be effective. *Wherever we require treatment, we must also require that the system provide the means— the personnel, training, and quality-control monitoring—that will allow the efficacy of the treatment to be translated into effective practice.* Treatment without efficacy *and* effectiveness is at risk of offering little benefit, at the possible cost of resources that could meet other important objectives of the juvenile justice system.

What Treatments Have Value?

During the 1970s and 1980s, "Nothing Works" was the bumper-sticker message from those who summarized what we knew about interventions in juvenile justice (e.g., Martinson, 1974). Today we know that some interventions with juvenile justice youths are of value (Greenwood, 1996; Lipsey, 1992). But those findings must be distinguished from our present concern. The Martinson and Lipsey reviews focused on "what works" to reduce recidivism among delinquent youths in general, not "what works" in the treatment of delinquent youths with mental disorders. In fact, the message regarding the value of clinical treatment of delinquent youths typically has been, "We don't know whether anything does or doesn't work." Very recently, however, we have begun to get some answers, and the news is both good and bad.

Kazdin (1988) claimed that he found over 200 types of child and adolescent psychotherapy in the literature, most of which have never been examined in controlled research. Reviews of research on child and adolescent treatment methods, however, have included well over 300 outcome studies (Weisz & Jensen, 1999). There have been many excellent, comprehensive reviews of research on the efficacy and effectiveness of psychopharmacological, psychotherapy, and psychosocial interventions for adolescents' mental disorders. The discussion here is based on general conclusions that can be drawn from commonalities across the results of those reviews.

Some of the best recent reviews covering a broad range of disorders and treatments include Burns, Hoagwood, and Mrazek (1999), Hughes, La Greca, and Conoley (2001), Mash and Barkley (1998), Weisz and Jensen (1999), Weisz et al. (1987), and Weisz et al., (1995). Especially important is a series of reviews initiated by the National Institute of Mental Health assessing the research on the beneficial effects of psychotropic medications (antipsychotic agents: Campbell, Rapoport, & Simpson, 1999; selective serotonin reuptake inhibitors: Emslie et al., 1999; tricyclic antidepressants: Geller et al., 1999; psychostimulants: Greenhill, Halperin, & Abikoff, 1999; mood stabilizers: Ryan, Bhatara, & Perel, 1999), as well as a recent review by Connor (2002) focused on psychopharmacological treatments for aggression in adolescents. (See also Connor et al., 2002, for a meta-analytic study of the value of stimulants in the treatment of aggression in youths with ADHD.) Other reviews that cover research on a specific type of treatment, or for treatments of a single disorder, are cited later.

PSYCHOPHARMACOLOGICAL TREATMENT. One cannot expect a single, bottom-line answer to the question whether psychopharmacological agents "work." The results of research on this question will vary when one examines efficacy or effectiveness with various types of medication, some of them disorder-targeted and some symptom-targeted (e.g., to reduce aggression), and employed across a number of different diagnostic groups. But some generalizations within these subdivisions are now possible.

Looking first at *efficacy* (well-controlled research studies in the "lab"), more psychopharmacological research has focused on *ADHD* than on any other childhood/adolescent disorder. There is considerable, reliable evidence for the efficacy of stimulants such as methylphenidate (Ritalin) in reducing aggression in ADHD youths (review by Connor et al., 2002), as well as general improvement in the condition as manifested in better school achievement and problem-solving (review by Weisz & Jensen, 1999). This does not necessarily mean that ADHD youths on Ritalin become like youths who have never had ADHD (Elia et al., 1991), and the effects generally have been studied only over periods of a few months rather than involving long-term follow-ups. But symptom reduction across studies has been relatively consistent, especially when used in conjunction with behavioral interventions.

Studies of the psychopharmacological treatment of *depression* in youths (Geller et al., 1999) have focused on tricyclic antidepressants, with little evidence of benefit for youths past puberty. More recently, selective serotonin reuptake inhibitors (SSRIs, newer antidepressants with safer side effects than tricyclics) have received "tentative support" (Weisz & Jensen, 1999) for the treatment of Major Depression. Interestingly, the value of antidepressants (even the older tricyclics) has been more clearly demonstrated for the reduction of aggressive behaviors in youths with disruptive behavior disorders (e.g., Conduct Disorder), especially in the context of ADHD (Connor, 2002).

Mood stabilizers (e.g., lithium) have been used increasingly in the treatment of adolescents with *Bipolar Disorder,* which often is manifested in manic-like symptoms involving extreme emotionality and impulsiveness. The results have been mixed, both for reduction in general symptoms of Bipolar Disorder (Ryan, Bhatara, & Perel, 1999) and with regard to reduction in aggression specifically (Connor, 2002). Concerning youths with *Schizophrenia,* several studies have demonstrated the relative efficacy of antipsychotic medications for reducing thought disturbance, although with mixed results with regard to degree of improvement, as well as serious cautions regarding the side effects of available medications (Campbell, Rapoport, & Simpson, 1999). Interestingly, few studies have examined the effects of psychopharmacological treatments for *anxiety disorders.* Those that have been conducted offer "no convincing evidence of benefit from any agents for childhood anxiety disorders" (Weisz & Jensen, 1999, p. 143), except for the well-studied efficacy of SSRIs for youths with Obsessive Compulsive Disorder.

It is worth noting that the use of even efficacious psychopharmacological agents with youths has its risks in the form of side effects, which range from minor discomforts (e.g., dry mouth) that are experienced in many cases to serious and even irreversible conditions in a smaller percentage of cases. Often these more serious side effects, such as tardive dyskinesia (uncontrollable twitching of hands or facial muscles), are associated with prolonged use.

Turning to the *effectiveness* of these psychopharmacological agents (when applied in actual practice in the real world of clinical care), Weisz and Jensen (1999) concluded that such studies "are noticeably absent from the research literature" (p. 145). This is especially important because some medications are not used in the disorder-targeted fashion when applied in actual clinical programs for youths. For example, in clinical settings treating youths with episodic acute aggressive behaviors, it is quite common for medications to be used for sedation—simply to stop the current aggressive outburst—by administering them on a p.r.n. basis (*pro re nata,* or "as needed") (Vitiello, Ricciuti, & Behar, 1987). There has been almost no research "to support the use of p.r.n. medications for acute aggression in psychiatrically-referred youth" (Connor, 2002).

The mere fact that psychiatrists may report, or experience, that such practices are of value is not evidence for the effectiveness of sedatives. For example, Vitiello et al. (1991) examined the effects of a sedative medication, compared to a placebo, on acute disruptive behaviors in children and younger adolescents. Further, some youths received the sedative or placebo in oral doses and some in intramuscular injections. Aggressive behavior was more greatly reduced by intramuscular than by oral administration, regardless of whether youths received the sedative or the placebo, while the mere fact of sedative or placebo condition had no different effect. In other words, the results suggested that decreases in youths' aggression were explained better by their desire to avoid the needle than by whatever the needle was delivering.

PSYCHOTHERAPY AND PSYCHOSOCIAL INTERVENTIONS. There has been far more research on the beneficial effects of psychotherapy and psychosocial interventions than on psychopharmacological interventions. Primary reviews of the general child and adolescent clinical literature in this area were noted earlier, to which may be added reviews of treatment effects specific to youths with aggressive behaviors that resulted in their adjudication (e.g., Frick, 1998; Greenwood, 1996; Schoenwald, Scherer, & Brondino, 1997; see also reviews of treatment programs for adolescents produced by a project called Blueprints for Violence Prevention at the Center for the Study and Prevention of Violence, 2002). Generally, both the efficacy and the effectiveness of such interventions increase as one moves from the youth-focused forms of intervention to the psychosocial forms.

Least beneficial are various modes of *individual psychotherapy* focused on developing the client's "insight" through the therapist–patient relationship; on average they have resulted in no significant benefit compared to nontreatment controls (Weiss et al., 1999). In his meta-analysis of treatments for juvenile justice youths, Lipsey (1992) found that individual counseling provided outside the juvenile justice system—for example, by community providers during probation—actually had a negative effect (that is, was worse than nothing, with recidivism as the outcome variable). (See also Kazdin, 2000b, reviewing traditional individual psychotherapy with conduct-disordered youths.) This is not to say that delinquent youths never benefit from individual psychotherapy or counseling based on a one-to-one therapist–client relationship, and it is possible that counselors who work within the juvenile justice system may be more capable of adapting psychotherapeutic methods to the capacities of delinquent youths. But such therapies typically depend on verbal abilities and conceptual processing of problems (e.g., thinking about things in the abstract), both of which are strengths for only a minority of delinquent youths.

Appreciably better results have been demonstrated for interventions that use a *cognitive-behavioral approach.* These therapies typically focus on cognitive restructuring—changing one's awareness of social cues and interpretation of what one encounters, and promoting strategies for delay, reflection, problem-solving, and responding. Thus the focus is on increasing one's interpersonal skills, self-control, and problem-solving in social contexts. Efficacy studies leave no doubt about the value of cognitive-behavioral therapies, either in individual or group therapy, in treating youths with conduct problems (e.g., Kazdin, 1996, 1997; Kendall et al., 1990; Lochman et al., 1987; Lochman & Wells, 1996) as well as depression (as reviewed by Kaslow & Thompson, 1998) and anxiety disorders (e.g., Kendall, 1994).

Connor (2002), however, has described three factors that may lower the degree of benefit of these therapies in actual practice. First, cognitive-behavioral therapies tend to have less beneficial outcomes when conducted by less experienced clinicians (Kazdin, 2000b). This is significant for our purposes, since the structured nature of these therapies, together with the limited financial resources available to the juvenile justice system for hiring staff, may encourage the system to use clinicians who are less trained than those who conducted therapies in the studies demonstrating the efficacy of the methods. Second, these therapies are likely to be somewhat less effective for youths who are significantly delayed in their cognitive development (Durlak, Fuhrman, & Lampman, 1991), as are many youths in the juvenile justice system, and who therefore might not bring as much cognitive capacity to the therapy process. Third, the benefit is reduced for youths who are facing severe family dysfunction, which often may undo whatever the therapy has achieved (Kazdin, 1997).

Recognition of the latter point—that youths are significantly influenced by dysfunction within their families—has resulted in considerable development of treatment methods that include the *family in therapy with adolescents.* These approaches, many of which have demonstrated efficacy with a broad range of diagnoses among adolescents, conceptualize adolescents' disorders as representative of maladaptive interactions within the family and therefore take the family, not the individual youth, as the identified unit for treatment. In their various forms, they focus on teaching parents to manage their children's behavior (e.g., Barkley, 1997;

McMahon & Wells, 1998) and on reconstructing expectations and interpersonal interactions of family members (e.g., Functional Family Therapy:
Alexander et al., 1988).

Reaching the very psychosocial end of the psychotherapy spectrum,
Multisystemic Therapy (MST) (Borduin et al., 1995; Henggeler, Melton, &
Smith, 1992; Schoenwald, 1998) has set the standard for efficacy among
treatments targeted for delinquent adolescents. The therapy is nonspecific
regarding types of youth disorders. It involves a "therapist" who is actually
a social engineer, virtually living alongside the youth and family as they
carry out their daily activities, negotiating events that arise between the
youth and anyone in any "systems" within which the youth functions—
family, school, work, and peer groups. The method has been clearly demonstrated to be cost effective and to achieve its objectives of improved
functioning, increased family cohesion, and reduced recidivism with lasting effects (e.g., Henggeler, Melton, & Smith, 1992; Henggeler et al.,
1993). For our purposes, it is most relevant for treating Conduct Disorder,
and it is significant that the treatment outcome studies have involved
youths with significant impairments and serious prior offenses.

Until recently there has been little quality research on the value of
treatment of adolescents for substance use disorders (Kaminer, 2001). That
picture is changing, with several new reports of successful interventions
with substance-abusing and substance-dependent adolescents using MST
(Hengeller, Pickrel, & Brondino, 2000), Functional Family Therapy
(Waldron, Brody, & Slesnick, 2001), the Twelve-Step Approach (Winters,
Stinchfield, & Opland, 2000), and cognitive-behavioral therapy (Kaminer, Burleson, & Goldberger, 2000). (See generally Monti, Colby, &
O'Leary, 2001.)

Most of the studies on psychotherapy and psychosocial interventions
for adolescents with mental and substance use disorders have been controlled efficacy studies. But what about the effectiveness of these methods
in the real world? Unfortunately, effectiveness studies have been rare, and
the few that have been done show little evidence for positive effects compared to control groups (Weisz et al., 1995). In what has perhaps been
the largest test of the value of real-world mental health treatment services
for children, the Fort Bragg Project (Bickman, 1996) involved an investment of $80 million for a well-designed study of the value of an enriched,
state-of-the-art system of mental health care and treatment for all children
in a catchment area in North Carolina during a period of several years.
Compared to another "services as usual" site, the Fort Bragg Program
produced far better access to treatment and greater user satisfaction, but

no better clinical or functional outcomes. Bickman's own conclusion was consistent with the title of his 1996 article, "A Continuum of Care: More Is Not Always Better." He concluded, in part, that merely providing a lot of treatment is not the answer; we must look for ways to teach clinicians how to provide efficacious treatments well.

REDEFINING THE "EVIDENCE-BASED PRACTICE" REQUIREMENT. In summary, *efficacy* studies provide substantial evidence that various psychopharmacological and psychotherapeutic interventions have beneficial effects for youths' mental disorders and aggressive behaviors. This is very good news. After several decades of knowing little about the value of treatment for adolescent offenders, we now know that some treatments can make a positive difference—not just for youths with mental disorders, but for youths with mental disorders *and* consequent delinquent behaviors. These treatments can reduce symptoms as well as delinquency recidivism. And studies have even begun to show us what kinds of treatment are more or less likely to be beneficial with what kinds of youths.

The bad news is that we have little evidence that these treatments are *effective,* that is, that they achieve their capacity (as demonstrated in controlled efficacy studies) when they are put in place in everyday practice. Therefore, few treatments are "evidence-based" as we defined that term at the outset of this section on the treatment context; many pass the efficacy test, but for most their effectiveness is not known. And what evidence does exist suggests that treatments that are promising in the lab are much less satisfying in the chaotic real world of clinical care.

This presents a dilemma. If we insist that treatments be evidence-based before the system is allowed or obligated to provide them, no treatment will be forthcoming if this guideline requires demonstrations of both efficacy and effectiveness. Clearly we must lighten our requirement, allowing treatments to be applied on the basis of efficacy demonstrations even when we are not sure that they will work (be effective) when put into everyday clinical practice. After all, we cannot obtain evidence for effectiveness until we do provide (and study) efficacious treatments in the real world.

What also emerges from this review, however, is that merely "trying out" efficacious treatments in real-world clinical circumstances is not likely to result in effective treatment. Something must be done in practice to maximize fidelity to the concepts and methods that contributed to their success in controlled efficacy studies. Asking how that might be achieved brings us to our final consideration—the systemic context in which treatments are provided.

Systems of Service Delivery

Whether efficacious treatments will work in practice depends significantly on conditions that are outside the theory and formal procedures of the treatments themselves. There are at least four perspectives to consider in this regard, all of them related to the context in which treatment services might be delivered to youths in the juvenile justice system: (a) quality control, (b) professional availability, (c) consumer issues, and (d) systemic contexts for service delivery.

QUALITY CONTROL. As we decide on the system's treatment obligations, we must recognize the need for quality control that will ensure that a treatment with known efficacy is implemented in a manner that maximizes its effectiveness in practice. Among other things, this requires adequate staff and professional training, as well as periodic monitoring to ensure that the procedure is implemented according to the manual.

In addition, the effectiveness of a treatment may depend on other procedural and administrative details that are not in the treatment manual. Determining whether a treatment with known efficacy will be effective, desirable, or even possible in juvenile justice practice typically requires a more detailed look at the actual procedures involved in its implementation. Cost-benefit and quality-control analysts, for example, are not content with defining a treatment merely by repeating its description given in the treatment manual. They typically need to examine the microlevel clinical procedures that are actually required to implement and complete the treatment with a given patient (Yates, 1996). Often these are not manualized.

For example, the obligation to provide psychopharmacological services to detention center youths with mental disorders is not as simple as asking the on-call psychiatrist to drive to the detention center, interview the youth, make a diagnosis, and prescribe an efficacious medication. The psychiatrist first is faced with the fact that many youths will present with more than one diagnosis, requiring a decision to focus on one of them or to focus instead on a particular symptom (e.g., aggression). In any of those cases, several medications may be considered for use, although the range may be restricted by the institution's formulary (availability and restrictions for specific types of medications). Sound judgment is involved in making that decision, sometimes requiring information about the family (e.g., the family's history of psychopathology). It is potentially dangerous to begin medicating without knowing whether the youth has already been taking prescribed (or illegal) drugs, the youth's reactions to past attempts at medication, and a general medical history (e.g., allergies, past medical and psychiatric diagnoses). Such information typically must be obtained from some reliable source before venturing too far.

Considerations also must be given to the length of time before one can expect to see the effects of the medication, especially when the behaviors associated with the disorder are dangerous and in need of a rapid response. Dosage should start at a level that is low enough to be safe yet potentially effective. A reliable mechanism for administering the medication across the next few days or weeks (e.g., trained and reliable front-line staff or nursing) will be necessary, and the actions of that person or those persons must be included in the procedural analysis. Once the medication procedure begins, the youth's condition must be monitored daily for the possible need to increase dosage in order to obtain the desirable effect or decrease it to reduce undesirable side effects—a process called "titration"—or to abandon the first choice and try another medication altogether. Once a desired effect has been obtained, decisions must be made about maintenance medication as well as the possibility of additional medication to reduce side effects.

This example allows us to make two points based on clinical considerations for any treatment that is contemplated when making recommendations for the care of adolescents in the juvenile justice system. First, an analysis of the actual microlevel procedures required to implement a treatment is crucial in order to know specifically what is being required when we obligate the juvenile justice system to be responsible for various treatments. Moreover, understanding procedures at this level of detail may be important for maintaining quality control. It is at this level of procedural detail that the difference between adequate efficacy and poor effectiveness may occur. Unstandardized implementation at the microlevel of clinical practice may be the source of reduced effectiveness when a treatment with known efficacy is put into practice. *Thus, to do it right, we must ensure that practitioners are not only "providing the service," but that they are abiding by the macrolevel procedures of the manual and effectively managing the microlevel clinical and administrative procedures embedded in the service.*

Second, if we do *not* require that treatment must be done right, no amount of good intentions will absolve us of the harm that results. Without the precautions described in the preceding description, prescribing medications for youths would be so dangerous as to justify the conclusion that it would be better for them to receive no treatment at all—and the same may be said for virtually all forms of psychotherapy and psychosocial interventions. Administered outside of protocol, treatments are likely to be ineffective, wasteful of precious resources, and open to abuses and perversions that can make them destructive of the welfare of youths. *Treatment without attention to clinical quality is not treatment and is likely to have worse consequences than if no intervention at all were provided.* Obligating the system to provide a treatment also obligates the system to ensure that it is competently provided.

PROFESSIONAL AVAILABILITY. Treatment requires qualified people to administer it. Depending on the type of treatment, this will mean people with a medical degree, a Ph.D. in psychology, a master's degree in psychology, or specialized training in psychiatric nursing or psychiatric social work. Having the degree, however, is not enough; most persons in those professions will not be qualified for our purposes, because only a minority of them have training in services for adolescents. Moreover, among those who are trained to work with adolescents and families, only some will be trained specifically to provide the treatments reviewed earlier.

Contrast this requirement with the fact that many areas of the United States have no psychiatrist—much less a child psychiatrist—within several hours drive of the local detention center. When we require that properly licensed social workers must provide particular psychosocial interventions, we must recognize that in many communities, clinical social workers leave detention centers for more fulfilling and financially rewarding positions the day that they obtain their licenses. Paying psychiatrists and psychologists one-quarter to one-third of their standard hourly fee for providing services to juvenile justice agencies—as is the case in some jurisdictions—tends to attract the very best (who accept the loss of income because they genuinely care about kids) and the less competent (who for various reasons cannot obtain better employment elsewhere).

As one formulates obligations for the juvenile justice system to provide treatment, one must recognize that how these obligations are fulfilled will require attention to the availability of professionals to administer them, as well as mechanisms to train them and monitor their performance.

CONSUMER ISSUES. Although youths are the "patients" in clinical relationships, parents typically are the "clients" or consumers of mental health services for children. In general child clinical practice, youths do not present themselves for treatment; they are brought by their parents or schools. Youths cannot independently consent to most treatments without their parents' consent, and in some jurisdictions the juvenile justice system may not medicate a youth without the parent's consent. In aftercare planning, the system often must depend on parents to ensure that their children continue to go to their psychotherapy appointments or maintain their medication schedules. And, as noted earlier, parents themselves often are the "patients" in some of the more efficacious psychosocial interventions. The roles of parents in youths' treatment are pervasive and important.

This is not to say that parents should always be involved in their children's treatment. Juvenile justice personnel are well aware of cases in which a parent's abusive or neglectful behaviors so endanger the child that direct parental involvement in the child's treatment is not desirable. But short of these circumstances, parental involvement should be the norm.

The juvenile justice system faces various obstacles in its enlistment of parents to facilitate treatment for youths' mental health needs. The parents of some delinquent youths are caring and concerned, but many struggle with their own personal and financial difficulties or mental illnesses. Early in the adjudicative process, a parent is often angry at their child because of his or her behavior that precipitated arrest; they might not always have their child's best interest at heart when making decisions or abiding by commitments regarding their youth's treatment. Youths sometimes are housed in pretrial detention or correction facilities that are several hours from their homes, and many parents of delinquent youths have no personal means of transportation to maintain therapeutic contact with the child or treatment staff. Obligations to provide treatment to youths in the juvenile justice system require meeting all of these challenges, because the most efficacious treatments for adolescents are predicated on some type of parental involvement.

SYSTEMIC CONTEXTS FOR SERVICE DELIVERY. Discussing treatment without considering systems of service delivery is like building a ship in the desert; it won't get far without the right medium to convey it. Efficacious treatments without a mechanism for their delivery are—like the ship without water—pretty, but useless.

During the 1990s, as evidence mounted regarding the efficacy of some treatments for adolescents' disorders, applied researchers turned their attention to the development of better models and practices for systems to deliver those mental health services to children, adolescents, and families (see, e.g., Bickman & Rog, 1995; Burns, 1999; Burns & Hoagwood, 2002; Nixon & Northrup, 1997; Stroul, 1996). "Better" generally means decreasing the use of inpatient care, increasing community-based service, improving coordination between services in the community, creating continuity of services across the child and adolescent years into young adulthood, promoting involvement of families and schools, and maximizing limited resources in a world of health care in which the true driving forces are managed care, Medicaid, and privatization of services with public funds (together with expenses associated with malpractice and civil rights litigation). Some models for service delivery, such as the "wraparound approach" (Burchard, Bruns, & Burchard, 2002), have achieved a level of articulation and acceptance that qualifies them as interventions themselves rather than simply ways to deliver services.

Most of this research has not yet focused on models of the delivery of treatment service within the juvenile justice system. It has, however, documented the nature and scope of the population of youths whose lives are spent in and out of both the state's mental health and juvenile justice systems. Youths who have juvenile justice referrals in a given year are several times more likely than their neighborhood peers to have come to the attention of the community mental health and social service agencies (Rosenblatt, Rosenblatt, & Biggs, 2000; Stiffman et al., 1997; Vander Stoep, Evans, & Taub, 1997; Westendorp et al., 1986). Moreover, among clients of child mental health services with "serious emotional disturbances"—the 10 percent who use a vastly greater proportion of child mental health services—well over one-half of males and only a somewhat lower proportion of females have juvenile justice or, in adulthood, criminal justice records (Davis & Vander Stoep, 1997).

Traditionally this overlap population of seriously delinquent and seriously mentally ill youths is labeled "not ours" by whichever system they happen to be in at a given moment. In recent years, however, some jurisdictions have witnessed collaborative efforts between juvenile justice and mental health systems to provide mental health services to those youths for whom they "share" responsibilities. At least some states have found ways to pool mental health and juvenile justice funds to create consultation and referral services for young offenders in juvenile justice custody who need mental health services (e.g., McMackin & Fulwiler, 2001). Medicaid will not pay for the treatment of those in secure juvenile justice institutions after having been found delinquent. In some jurisdictions, however, Medicaid is available for services provided to youths in pretrial detention, offering the potential for juvenile justice programs to develop arrangements with private providers who can bill Medicaid for services rendered to mentally disordered youths in detention centers.

As we think about the juvenile justice system's obligation to provide treatment to those with mental disorders, we must consider the fact that it cannot afford to become a mental health system for delinquent youths.

Certainly there are some types of treatment services that it must take the responsibility to provide. There are other treatments that it could not provide without duplicating the functions of a community's public mental health system, but which it might obtain through collaboration and coordination with mental health agencies. These systemic issues of service delivery will play a significant role in our later analysis of the juvenile justice system's implementation of its treatment obligations.

Summary

The various ways to describe treatments provide different dimensions for analyzing the juvenile justice system's obligations, including objectives and modes of treatment, disorder- and symptom-targeted treatment, and the value of treatment as judged by studies of efficacy and effectiveness. While research has demonstrated the efficacy (value in controlled laboratory studies) of many types of treatment—psychopharmacological, psychotherapeutic, and psychosocial—with many types of adolescent disorders, far fewer studies have demonstrated the effectiveness of those treatments in real-world clinical circumstances. The juvenile justice system may be able to go forward in the implementation of apparently efficacious modes of treatment despite a lack of evidence of their effectiveness in application. But in doing so, it must implement those treatments with fidelity, because it is likely that merely providing efficacious treatments, without attention to quality, will be no better (and perhaps worse) than providing no treatment at all. Finally, the success or failure of even the best treatments will depend on a variety of clinical, professional, and consumer issues in service delivery, as well as the development of model systems for funding and delivering mental health services.

The Adjudicative Context: How Are Mental Disorders Related to Legally Relevant Capacities?

James, fourteen years old, has been charged with assault with a deadly weapon and attempted murder. He was running from the scene—a street corner—with three older youths. The evidence against him gives the prosecutor some chance to make the charges stick. It's not at all certain, however, because the other youths are not providing evidence about each other, there was only one shooter, and there isn't substantial evidence to identify conclusively who among them it was.

James's three friends are one year short of being adults under criminal law. The prosecutor has filed for transfer hearings on all four cases, asking the judge to allow the state to prosecute the youths in criminal court as adults. James's transfer hearing is today. He and his attorney are sitting in the holding cell when the prosecutor calls the attorney out to talk. The attorney returns to the cell to find James's mother there, sitting on a bench in the corner, sobbing uncontrollably. James, as usual, looks blank. It's the look that his mother has gotten used to seeing since about a year ago when he suddenly became depressed and moody and would sometimes hit the wall with his fist. He'll talk to you, look at you, but it's almost like he isn't there—the psychologist said he was trying to control some terrible feelings inside him by distancing himself from everything around him, more or less denying the importance of whatever is going on.

"Look, I've got to talk to both of you right now," the attorney says to James and his mother. "The prosecutor just offered us a deal. He'll call off the transfer hearing this afternoon, James, if you'll admit you were there—not that you were the shooter, just that you went there with them. And you need to tell him who held the gun and pulled the trigger. Now you've got to think carefully about this. If you get transferred—which is likely—and you are found guilty even of just being an accomplice—which is a 50-50 thing—you can get anywhere from ten to twenty-five years, at least some of it in prison. But if you take this deal, there's no transfer—you stay a juvenile, maybe two or three years in DYS custody, probably at juvenile secure over in Plymouth. After a year or two I might be able to get you out, and back home. Now I know you're going to be worried about the other guys' friends on the street—that they might try to get you. But who knows, maybe they won't even be friends anymore— or maybe you could leave your mom, go stay with your aunt in Virginia. . . . Hey, buddy, pay attention here! You listening to me? This is your life, man. What you and your Mom decide in the next couple of minutes is going to make all the difference in what kind of life you are going to have from now until you're forty years old."

James's case is fictional, but most juvenile defense attorneys can recount several stories with the same dilemma. It might be a youth's decision to waive the right to silence and confess (sometimes to things the youth didn't do) at a police interrogation, or to be of no help to the attorney in reconstructing the crime event when preparing a defense, or to decide against accepting a plea bargain that any lawyer would consider an excellent deal. Sometimes it's the attorney's feeling that the youth's "mental problems" didn't even allow him to really grasp what was going on at the time of the crime.

In all of these cases, though, the critical issue is the youth's ability to make decisions. From the time of police interrogation through the trial, law requires that the defendant must be the sole decisionmaker in matters that pertain to waiver or assertion of important constitutional rights. Parents can help their children at these times, of course, as can attorneys. But they cannot "stand in" for the youth to offer the court decisions on his or her behalf. Moreover, as in James's case, parents frequently are in no condition even to offer advice, and attorneys can only advise, not make the decision on behalf of their client. Thus youthful defendants—whom, as adolescents, society considers too young to be making decisions about smoking, drinking, driving, contracting for major financial commitments, voting, or marrying—are the only people authorized to make trial-related decisions that can seal their fate for the rest of their lives.

Are youths as capable as adults of making these decisions? The question especially raises doubts in cases like James's that involve a double jeopardy, with the effects of mental disorder potentially compounding the effects of immaturity on one's decisions as a defendant. What does knowledge of youths' mental disorders tell us, if anything, about potential deficits in their abilities to do things that are important for protection of their rights during adjudication? As a first step in addressing this question, one must (a) *identify abilities that are legally relevant,* especially for waiving rights in interrogation, participating in one's trial (competence to stand trial), and judging defendants' culpability within the framework of the insanity defense. The second step is to (b) *examine what is known about the development of those abilities in youths in general.* This will provide a developmental background against which to (c) *determine whether and how research on mental disorders of adolescence provides us any more specific guidance.*

What Abilities Are Relevant?

The abilities associated legally and psychologically with decisionmaking about the exercise of constitutional rights have been categorized and described in considerable detail (e.g., Appelbaum & Grisso, 1988, 1995), especially in the context of waiver of *Miranda* rights (Grisso, 1981, 2003), defendants' participation in their defense (competence to stand trial, including pleading decisions: e.g., Bonnie, 1992; Grisso, 2000, 2003; Hoge et al., 1992; Melton et al., 1997), and concepts associated with criminal responsibility and the insanity defense (Melton et al., 1997). At the broadest level, most of these analyses focus on sets of abilities that have been labeled "understanding," "reasoning," and "appreciating the significance of information." To these have been added "judgment" in decisionmaking, although it stands somewhat outside the mainstream with regard to analyses of abilities associated with legal competence to make decisions.

At the most basic level are defendants' abilities to *understand* information that is critically relevant for their decision. If offered the right to consult an attorney, do defendants grasp what an attorney is and what protections an attorney is supposed to provide? When pleading guilty, do they know what the consequences might be? When they engaged in the act for which they are charged, did they know that it was illegal?

Reasoning refers to the process of working with information that is understood in order to reach a decision. When defendants weigh their choices in a plea bargain, for example, are they at least capable of focusing on, imagining, thinking about, and comparing the positive and negative consequences of the options they are provided?

The concept of *appreciation* arises especially in some cases involving persons with mental disorders. It recognizes that some defendants may be able to tell you the facts (they understand) and may have the ability to compare and weigh their options (they can reason), but nevertheless have a distorted view—as a consequence of their mental disorder—regarding how the facts apply to them. For example, imagine that a defendant understands that a defense attorney is supposed to try to prove the defendant's innocence, but that her paranoid delusion about her own attorney causes her to believe that he is collaborating with the prosecutor. She may understand what an attorney is for, and may be able to reason about her options. But her decision to reject everything that her attorney tells her will be based on a false belief created by her mental disorder. Thus we might have such serious doubts concerning the "validity" of her decisionmaking that we instead find her legally incompetent to decide. Similarly, her paranoid disorder might also have influenced her beliefs about the victim at the time of her offense, rendering it questionable that she should be held responsible for the crime.

Finally, recent theories have been advanced regarding "immaturity of judgment" as a factor to be considered when weighing the legal capacities of children and adolescents (e.g., Scott, 1992; Scott, Reppucci, & Woolard, 1995; Steinberg & Cauffman, 1996; Woolard, Fried, & Reppucci, 2001). Currently there are few legal references that formally recognize the concept when considering youths' capacities to make decisions as defendants, but the concept is compelling and seems implicit in the legal reasoning of some courts. Below some age, the perspective of young people on the meaning of time (future orientation), their susceptibility to influence by peers (autonomy of choice), and their perceptions of the likelihood of risky outcomes (risk perception) are still developing and are not like those of the average adult. In this sense, they are not the decisionmakers that they will be when they attain whatever level of perspective they will have during their own adult years. While these matters might be true in general for children and younger adolescents, they might be true for at least some older adolescents as well who are slower to develop than their peers.

These developing perspectives are important in decisionmaking because they influence how one perceives the consequences of one's decisions. Time perspective is a good example. How heavily would you weigh the potential consequences of a two-year period of confinement? You have a grasp of what two years feels like and what it is worth. Now consider the eight-year-old who was asked (in a competence-to-stand-trial evaluation) to explain what he meant when he said he understood that he could be "put in juvenile jail for a long, long time." He likened it to "a *really* long time, like when my Mom sends me to my room for the whole weekend." Or the explanation of a twelve-year-old who, when offered a hypothetical plea agreement in a research situation, accepted it when he learned that to do otherwise would risk a six-year sentence; as he explained it, "That's half my life!"

Neither of these is a wrong answer. The youths' understanding and reasoning abilities might be fine, and neither had a mental disorder. In fact, many adults might choose the same option as these youths. But adolescents are probably not making such choices based on the same reasons—nor are their time-related perspectives about these decisions the same—as they would be if they were asked the question after they were eighteen or twenty-five. We are not confident that the weight they will give to the factors in their options—their "judgment" involved in the decision—is "mature." We doubt that the bright fifteen-year-old girl who pleads guilty to a crime that could get her twenty years in prison is exercising the same judgment as she would if she were older, when she tells us that she is doing it so that "when my boyfriend [already sentenced for the same crime] gets out, he'll know that I loved him enough to do the same time."

Where Do Youths Stand on These Legally Relevant Abilities?

Let us set aside for a moment questions about mental disorder, delinquency, and even individual differences in development among same-age youths. What do we know about youths of various ages, on average, regarding the abilities we are discussing? There are two broad kinds of scientific information to consider.

DEVELOPMENT OF COGNITIVE ABILITIES. For over 100 years, when measuring absolute levels of performance of intellectual functions associated with the global concept of "intelligence," developmental psychologists have found age curves that continue to rise through adolescence. These abilities include what youths know about the world, their reasoning abilities, and their capacities to think abstractly ("What if . . . ?" and "How are these things alike?"), all of which increase year by year until they begin to reach an "adult-like" level around age sixteen or seventeen. Experimental studies of specific abilities within this domain find somewhat different rates or patterns of development, depending on exactly which ability is being examined. But their sum supports two general conclusions. First, on average, youths tend not to have adult-like *capacities* for understanding and reasoning until sometime in early to mid adolescence. Second, achieving those capacities does not mean that adolescents can necessarily *employ* them with the efficiency or dependability that one associates with adult performance. In other words, on average, youths of fourteen years of age might have some of the tools, but they need a few more years to make them work sufficiently well to match average adult performance.

Explaining why and how adolescents' cognitive abilities require some time to mature to a level that approximates adult performance is a bit more complex than saying that they simply need experience and practice. Recent studies that point to other factors range from research on brain development to evidence of noncognitive, social-psychological aspects of development. For example, recent advances in magnetic resonance imaging of the brain have allowed neuroscientists to study changes in brain activity while youths or adults are viewing objects or performing cognitive tasks. This allows one to locate specific areas of the brain that appear to manage certain cognitive and emotional functions. Moreover, by performing these examinations repeatedly over time as youths develop, or by comparing youths and adults of different ages, neuroscientists are plotting the course of development of those brain areas and functions across childhood and adolescence.

Studies using these methods are discovering that much is taking place in normal brain development in the early to middle adolescent years. For example, the growth of myelin—sheaths on neurons that improve their conductive efficiency—continues through childhood and is not completed for certain areas of the brain until well into adolescence (Giedd et al., 1999). Whereas early childhood is characterized by rapid growth in the number of synaptic connections available in the brain, late childhood and early adolescence involves a "pruning" process (e.g., Huttenlocher, 1990) in which neural connections are gradually reduced so that transmissions become more efficient and less random. (Picture a city developing across centuries, its chaos of early footpaths gradually evolving into a more orderly and efficient set of streets and highways.)

One of the areas of the brain in which this activity is particularly apparent in early and middle adolescence is the prefrontal cortex. This area is especially important for "executive cognitive functions," a term that neuroscientists give to a set of functions that are critical for abstract reasoning, planning, and organizing information so that individuals can respond in an adaptive, goal-directed way to whatever they encounter in their environment (Foster, Eskes, & Stuss, 1994). An important related function of this area is "affect regulation"—the capacity to inhibit or delay one's impulsive and emotional reactions to incoming stimuli so that more effective responses have time to take shape through prefrontal activity (Giancola et al., 1996; Price et al., 1990). A number of studies have demonstrated that development of the prefrontal cortex and its connections with emotion centers in the brain continue well into adolescence (e.g., Casey et al., 1997; Giedd et al., 1999; Luna et al., 2001; Paus et al., 1999).

The significance of the relatively late completion of neural development related to executive cognitive functions is relevant for our discussion because these functions—for example, delaying one's response in order to consider and plan, and integrating information to foresee the consequences of one's possible choice—are all involved in adolescents' decisionmaking about the legal options with which we are concerned. They suggest that youths who are making choices with far-reaching consequences (e.g., about plea bargains, or about how to react to a threatening event on the street) may not be functioning with the same neurological capacities that they will have when they reach adulthood.

Additional evidence that adolescents' problem-solving and decisional abilities have not reached adult levels comes from other studies far removed from neuroscience. For example, on average, adolescents perceive everyday risks somewhat differently than do adults (Benthin, Slovik, & Severson, 1993; Furby & Beyth-Marom, 1990) and have a shorter future time orientation (Greene, 1986; Nurmi, 1991). Maturation of these social and psychological functions as they apply to everyday problems of life continues through adolescence (Cauffman & Steinberg, 2000), a scientific finding that almost no parent would be surprised to hear. What the neurological studies tell us is that this is not merely a matter of youthful in-experience, but rather a more complex mix of neurological and social maturation.

DEVELOPMENT OF PERFORMANCE IN LEGALLY RELEVANT CONTEXTS. A second significant body of research has examined youths' performance in tasks that involve the capacities of understanding, reason-ing, and appreciation when they are faced with decisions as defendants. In general, the results are much as one would expect from the prior review of basic scientific studies of adolescents' cognitive development (for reviews, see Grisso, 1997, 2000b). These studies have examined youths' abilities to understand and reason about *Miranda* warnings and the op-tions to talk or remain silent (e.g., Abramovitch, Peterson-Badali, & Rohan, 1995; Grisso, 1981), as well as their abilities to grasp and process information (e.g., about the trial process, attorneys, and making plea agreements) that is considered important for competence to stand trial (e.g., Peterson-Badali & Abramovitch, 1993; Peterson-Badali, Abramo-vitch, & Duda, 1997).

The findings of these studies are generally consistent with those of the recent MacArthur Juvenile Adjudicative Competence Study, currently the most comprehensive investigation of youths' capacities as trial defendants (Grisso et al., 2003). The study used objective measures of how well juve-nile offenders grasped trial-relevant matters, and involved over 900 youths and 450 adults, some in juvenile or criminal custody and some with little court involvement. The results indicated that those fifteen years old and younger were three times more likely than young adults to have serious deficiencies in their understanding or reasoning about trial processes and defendant decisions. The risk of incompetence to stand trial was greatest for youths younger than fourteen and for adolescents with IQ scores below 80. The effects were similar across genders and ethnic groups. On addi-tional methods requiring hypothetical decisions about waiving rights and dealing with plea bargains, adolescents' choices and their manner of arriv-ing at them also manifested differences from adults, tending to be less focused on essentials and more strongly influenced by concerns about compliance with authority.

Does Mental Disorder Make a Difference?

A significant body of research has confirmed the effects of mental disorders on adult defendants' legally relevant capacities. The most common disor-der found in cases of incompetent adult defendants is Schizophrenia, followed by other psychotic disorders and Mental Retardation (Nicholson & Kugler, 1991). Similarly, acquittal due to insanity among adults typically involves disorders in the psychotic spectrum, although defendants in only a minority of cases involving psychotic disorders are acquitted due to insanity (Cirincione, Steadman, & McGreevy, 1995). In contrast, there have been no studies that examine whether youths with specific mental disorders perform more poorly than other adolescents (or adults) in tasks of understanding, reasoning, or appreciation in legal contexts, and no studies of the mental condition of youths found not guilty by reason of insanity.

In a study of the capacities of delinquent youths to understand and appreciate *Miranda* rights as given by police officers, Grisso (1981) found that these abilities were significantly poorer for younger adolescents than for older adolescents and adults, as well as for youths with general deficits in intelligence (especially youths with IQ scores in the mental retardation range). But the study did not examine the relation of *Miranda* comprehension to youths' mental disorders.

A few studies have examined relations between youths' capacities associated with competence to stand trial and their mental disabilities. Cowden and McKee (1995) found that clinicians judged youths to be incompetent to stand trial significantly more frequently when they had serious psychiatric diagnoses or remedial educational histories. The types of disorders, however, were not specified. McGaha et al. (2001) reported that among youths in Florida who were found incompetent to stand trial and were remanded to programs to "restore" their competence, functional deficits related to their incompetence were due to mental retardation in about one-half of the cases, with serious emotional disturbance as the cause in most of the remaining cases.

Grisso et al. (2003) found that youths with levels of intelligence associated with mental retardation clearly performed more poorly than youths with average intelligence on abilities related to competence to stand trial. But the study did not include identification of youths' mental disorders, and no significant differences were found between those who reported more symptoms of mental or emotional distress and those who reported fewer.

In fact, virtually no published studies have examined the relation between adolescents' mental disorders and their decisionmaking abilities in *any* realm of practical, everyday life. The closest approximation, perhaps, is a study (Cauffman, 2002) in which youths with significant mental disorders obtained lower scores on measures of psychosocial maturity than did youths without diagnostic disorders, and they made less mature decisions about avoiding dangerous risk than did nondisordered same-age peers or adults.

While we do not know the specific effects of symptoms of mental disorders on youths' actual decisionmaking, we do know that they influence cognitive abilities that are important for basic understanding and reasoning functions on which decisionmaking depends. Kazdin (2000a) has reviewed cognitive deficits associated with various mental disorders of adolescence that can influence decisionmaking. For example, the symptoms of psychotic disorders often include gross disorganization of thought, sometimes involving delusions that distort reality during problem-solving. Anxiety disorders and ADHD are likely to impair attention and focus in decisionmaking situations, as well as increase the risk of impulsive decisions. Depression is associated with distortions in information processing, as well as reduced motivation to take hold of a problem sufficiently to fully consider its implications (Kazdin, 2000a).

One of the most important policy questions raised by these observations is whether the nature of disorders that create antecedent conditions relevant for due process concerns is, or should be, different for youths than for adults. As noted earlier, incompetence to stand trial in adults typically has been found in cases involving Schizophrenia. Rarely will an adult be found incompetent as a consequence of mood or anxiety disorders or the adult variant of ADHD. Yet due to developmental differences between adolescents and adults, the latter disorders may have an effect on youths' decisionmaking capacities that is no less detrimental than that of more serious psychotic disorders for adults. This is an important possibility that plays a significant role in the analysis in chapter 6 of the juvenile justice system's obligation to ensure due process for adolescent defendants with mental disorders.

In summary, there is substantial evidence that youths in general are still developing capacities that are relevant for making decisions as defendants and for our considerations regarding their responsibility for their illegal behaviors. Youths with mental disorders, therefore, may begin with a lower baseline of ability than adults, and any effects of mental disorders simply compound the risks of immature decisionmaking. Moreover, a greater range of disorders, not only serious psychotic disorders, may be relevant in juvenile than in adult cases. But the specific nature of the effects of various mental disorders on legally relevant abilities is not yet known empirically, in the absence of decisionmaking research with delinquent or nondelinquent samples of youths with mental disorders. This will necessarily limit how definitive we can be in our recommendations in chapter 6, where the focus is on identifying youths with mental disorders that could influence their decisionmaking as defendants or their criminal responsibility.

The Public Safety Context: How Are Mental Disorders Related to Aggression?

Imagine that you are a legislator sitting in a hearing to gather information that will help you decide a matter of policy regarding youths with mental disorders and their likelihood of doing harm to others. The committee has invited two experts to testify about this matter. The first provides the following information (the expert's supporting research citations have been inserted):

> There is substantial evidence that youths with mental disorders present a greater risk to public safety than do youths without mental disorders. About seven in ten youthful offenders in the juvenile justice system have at least one mental disorder (Teplin et al., 2002), compared to only two in ten in the general population of adolescents (Kazdin, 2000a). Moreover, aggression has been associated with almost all forms of adolescent psychopathology, both clinically and empirically (Connor, 2002), but especially with ADHD—which is one of the better predictors of physical aggression (Loeber et al., 1998)—and Conduct Disorder (numerous studies). Moreover, Conduct Disorder does not go away; 87 percent of youths with this diagnosis in adolescence continue to have it three years later (Lahey et al., 1995), and 67 percent of them go on to have criminal records in adulthood (Kratzer & Hodgins, 1997). About two-thirds of youths with psychotic disorders have been found to have violent histories (Inamdar et al., 1982), and juveniles who commit murder are more likely to show psychotic symptoms than other violent (non-homicidal) youth with conduct disorders (Lewis et al., 1988; Myers et al., 1995).

As you frown and make a note to schedule your teenager for a psychological evaluation, the next expert takes the microphone:

> The evidence that youths with mental disorders are likely to commit acts of violence is weak at best. Little is known about hostile aggres-

sion and youths' depressive or anxiety disorders; one study found that depression slightly raises the risk, but no more so for physical aggression than for nonviolent and minor offenses (Huizinga & Jakob-Chien, 1998). Most youths with ADHD do not commit violent crimes; in fact, ADHD is found in juvenile justice settings no more frequently (2.3 percent: Wasserman et al., 2002) than in the general population (3–6 percent: Barkley, 1996), is related to delinquency mainly when it coexists with Conduct Disorder (Frick, 1998), and usually does not continue into adulthood (10–15 percent: Mannuzza & Klein, 1992). While Conduct Disorder applies for many youths in juvenile justice settings, it is unrelated to recidivism in some studies (Wierson & Forehand, 1995). Moreover, Conduct Disorder symptoms tend to diminish across time in 60–80 percent of cases (Cohen et al., 1993; Huizinga et al., 2000), and fewer than one-third of such youths graduate to adult Antisocial Personality Disorder (Robins, 1966). Youths who commit murder are no more likely to have mental disorders—psychotic or otherwise—than high school students in general or youths with other violent and nonviolent offenses (Benedek & Cornell, 1989; Katz & Marquette, 1996).

The experts, of course, have reported selectively from the literature to support their respective advocacy positions. But they have not reported falsely. The reason why their mutually contradictory testimony—and all of their assertions—can be true is related to the bewildering complexity of differences in what is being studied by each of the authorities that they cite. The differences between studies that create the most chaos in cross-study comparisons are the following:

- *Definitions of the target behavior,* which include, for example, "aggressive behavior," "delinquent behavior," "physically harmful behavior," "serious violent and serious nonviolent behavior," "persistently delinquent behavior," and "arrest for physically harmful behavior." Moreover, each of these terms may be operationalized differently across studies.
- *Definitions of significance of results,* which include tests of differences between mean scores, tests of differences between proportions (percents), bivariate correlations, regression analyses, odds ratios, effect sizes, and receiver operating characteristic analyses (to name a few). All of these statistics are important for certain purposes, but they are instructive for *different* purposes. A given data set can produce a substantially signifi-

cant relation of a disorder to aggressive behaviors with an analysis of variance, but at the same time might show only a modest correlation, a large odds ratio, and inadequate predictive power according to an "area under the curve" analysis.

- *Different population sampling fields,* which include random community samples, public school samples, community mental health clinic samples, inpatient clinical samples, inpatient forensic clinical samples, juvenile justice system samples, juvenile pretrial detention samples, and juvenile corrections samples. For example, any relation between physical violence and depression will be relatively low in a sample of youths drawn from the general population, relatively higher in a juvenile detention sample, and possibly higher still if drawn from an inpatient psychiatric facility (where civil commitment often requires a finding that youths are mentally ill and dangerous).
- *Differences in reference groups,* for example, when discussing the relation between delinquency and ADHD, stating the proportion of delinquent youths who have ADHD will suggest a smaller relation between the two than stating the proportion of ADHD youths who are delinquent.
- *Differences in the time frame,* for example, studies differ in whether they examine the relation of mental disorder to lifetime aggressive tendencies, to aggressive tendencies recently, to a recent aggressive act (e.g., the reason for present arrest), or aggression prospectively—which may be within the next few months, a year, subsequently at any time during the adolescent years, or into adulthood.

It is helpful to begin the review of mental disorders and aggression in this way, because it shows that efforts to force a general conclusion about their relation based on current research will probably produce an oversimplified and distorted message. While looking at this research, one should also keep in mind that the objective is to assist juvenile justice decisionmakers at three points in the juvenile justice process: (a) *the pretrial detention decision* (likelihood of harm to others if not detained), (b) *the disposition decision* (degree of security and nature of treatment that is necessary to protect the public from harm during the youth's rehabilitation), and (c) *the waiver of jurisdiction and extension of jurisdiction decisions* (likelihood of continued harm to others in the future when the youth ages into adulthood).

These decisions are all about future aggression, but they place different demands on decisionmakers. For example, detention decisions are made about a much more varied set of youths than are disposition or waiver decisions, because various types of youths (first-time offenders, minor offenders, very young offenders) are less likely to reach the latter decision points. The three decisions also focus on somewhat different time frames for anticipated aggression, ranging from immediate (within the next few weeks if not detained) to very long range (several years from now in adulthood). In all cases, though, we are interested in whatever research can tell us about *the risk of (a) physical harm to others (b) in the future (c) among youths with mental disorders (d) identified at time of contact with the juvenile justice system.*

In the three subsections that follow, I briefly review some relevant and important "principles" in the development of aggressive behavior in childhood and adolescence, as well as what is known clinically about the relation of aggression to specific psychiatric diagnoses of adolescents. I then reflect on the value of these perspectives for identifying and responding to youths' potential aggressive behaviors related to their mental disorders.

Aggression from a Developmental Perspective

Aggression is normal as an evolutionary, biologically based response to one's environment. The capacity for hostile and harmful behavior ordinarily is shaped and channeled by society as the person develops, so that it fits society's needs (e.g., for soldiers and police officers) and is exercised in socially appropriate ways (e.g., self-defense, sports). The shaping process involves complex social responses that are intended to teach self-restraint and inhibition. This process is more or less successful partly as a function of variations in psychosocial (e.g., family) and environmental (e.g., neighborhood) factors, and partly as a result of biological and psychological differences among youths. There is substantial evidence, for example, that hormonal, neurological, and psychophysiological differences among children make self-restraint and inhibition more difficult and more resistant to social influences for some youths than for others (e.g., Raine, 1996). Moreover, a child's history of stressful or traumatic experiences can itself influence the development of neurotransmitter systems in the brain or the development of neuroanatomical areas of the brain involved in inhibition or disinhibition of aggression (for a review, see Ferris & Grisso, 1996).

If we think of childhood and adolescence as a journey, there are predictable changes in the terrain on which the path to self-restraint is traveled.

Typically these different terrains are viewed as three broad phases of the journey: infancy, the elementary school years, and the adolescent years. The developing infant is gradually taught not to express internal impulses spontaneously in socially annoying or harmful ways. New demands for self-restraint arise in the preschool and elementary years in the context of developing relations with other children, and again in early adolescence in relation to new capacities brought about by biological changes, increasing opportunity for independent (unsupervised) activities, and peer group demands.

The initiation of each of these phases and its new demands seems to be characterized by a "surge" of aggressive behavior—not for each youth, but as an average for youths at a given phase—that then declines somewhat (on average) across that phase. For example, Tremblay (2002) documented that mothers report a surge of aggressive activity (frustration and rage reactions) in their infants when they are about two to three months of age, with an overall decline during the next few years. Similarly, an increase and decline in seriously harmful behaviors toward others has been well documented during adolescence (e.g., Elliott, 1994).

Beyond that, the nature of the general terrain is not the issue so much as the search for the various pathways taken by youths as they traverse it. Some youths display no aggressive tendencies early in a given phase of the journey. Others do so for a period of time before apparently adjusting successfully (some rapidly, others gradually) to new self-restraint demands of that phase. And, of course, a proportion continue aggressive behaviors throughout that phase (in infancy and toddler years, about 10 percent: Tremblay, 2002; in elementary school years, about 8 percent: Haapasalo & Tremblay, 1994; and in the adolescent years, 10–20 percent: e.g., Elliott, 1994). There is a tendency for youths who have manifested greater hostile aggression throughout one phase of the journey to continue to do so during the subsequent phase as they enter new terrain. But researchers have also found subgroups whose prior-phase behavior does not predict their behavior in the next phase, especially youths who were seen as nonaggressive earlier but for whom aggressive behavior arises "unexpectedly" as they move on.

The search for order in these pathways has encountered increasingly complex patterns during the past fifteen years of criminological and developmental investigation (Loeber & Hay, 1994; Loeber & Stouthamer-Loeber, 1998; Moffitt, 1993; Moffit et al., 1996; Tolan & Gorman-Smith, 1998). But a few general principles have evolved to guide our thinking about aggression and serious harmful behavior in adolescence.

First is the principle of *desistance*. Most youths who engage in or are arrested for physically harmful behaviors do not continue to present a significant risk for those behaviors as they age into late adolescence and early adulthood (e.g., Elliott, 1994; Huizinga, 1995; Loeber & Hay, 1996). For most youths who engage in physical harm to others at some time in adolescence, their behavior is "adolescent-limited" (Moffitt, 1993). Ironically, this does not mean that total arrests for serious violent behaviors are lower for young adults than for adolescents; violent arrest rates per age group peak at about ages eighteen to twenty-three and then decline (Zimring, 1998). This peak appears to be a surge of increasingly serious and repetitive violence among a minority of delinquent youths who do persist in violent behavior past adolescence (Loeber & Stouthamer-Loeber, 1998).

The second principle pertains to *age of onset*. In general, if physically aggressive behavior is apparent in the preschool and early elementary school years and persists well into adolescence, there is an increased likelihood that it will persist into adulthood as well (called "life-course-persistent" aggressors by Moffitt, 1993). This is not always true (Magnusson, Stattin, & Duner, 1983), of course, but the odds are much greater that early-onset aggressors will graduate to adult violent offending.

The third principle is that *the first and second principles do not necessarily hold for women and ethnic minorities*. Several studies and reviews (e.g., Loeber & Stouthamer-Loeber, 1998; Moffitt et al., 2001; Silverthorn & Frick, 1999; Zoccolillo, 1993) find that a "delayed-onset" pathway, in which hostile aggression first becomes evident in adolescence, is more typical than early childhood onset for girls whose aggression in adolescence continues into adulthood. Regarding ethnic minority youths, the applicability of the early-onset pathway to African American and Latino youths, especially those in high-risk inner-city environments, is still being sorted out. Tolan and Gorman-Smith (1998), for example, found the expected relation between early onset of aggression and violent delinquency in adolescence when examining a group of youths who represented ethnic proportions for U.S. adolescents, but not among a sample of African American and Latino youths from poor, high-crime neighborhoods in Chicago. As with many "race" differences in criminological studies, these findings may be related to socioeconomic rather than specific ethnic differences, reflecting special risk factors associated with growing up in harmful surroundings (Hawkins, Laub, & Lauritsen, 1998). Nevertheless, the results do suggest that caution be used in applying the general developmental principles of aggression to low-socioeconomic minority youths.

Aggression from a Clinical Perspective

When we consider the relation of mental disorder to violent behavior among delinquent youths, we must combine what we know about the development of aggression in general with what we know about the relation of mental disorders in adolescence to anger, impulsivity, and other mental states that promote aggression. There is a good deal of evidence for such connections.

AFFECTIVE DISORDERS. So pervasive is irritability and hostility among youths with Major Depression and Dysthymia that DSM-IV criteria allow "irritable mood" to be substituted for "depressed mood" in identifying depressive disorders among children and adolescents (e.g., pp. 327 and 349, American Psychiatric Association, 1994). The relation between adolescent depressive disorders and anger, irritability, and hostility is thoroughly documented (Biederman & Spencer, 1999; Goodyer & Cooper, 1993; Knox et al., 2000). The significance of anger as a motivator for aggression is well known (Novaco, 1994). The role of depression-related irritability as a forerunner of aggression lies in its implications in social contexts. Youths who clearly manifest a sullen, angry, and belligerent attitude are more likely to get angry responses from other youths (and adults), thus increasing the risk of events that escalate to physical aggression. And an irritable adolescent is more likely to interpret ordinary annoyances by others as direct threats, increasing the risk that the youth will respond with defensive aggression.

ANXIETY DISORDERS. Clinicians (and some clinical researchers: Connor, 2002; Walker et al., 1991) find that most adolescents with anxiety disorders are shy, withdrawn, and tend to avoid fearful situations, resulting in less aggressive behavior than is normal for youths of their age. The exception is Posttraumatic Stress Disorder (PTSD), which involves (a) exposure to a traumatizing event, (b) persistent reexperiencing of distress about the event through recollections or dreams, (c) avoidance or numbing regarding the related emotions, and (d) being "on edge" as manifested in startle responses, outbursts of anger, or hypersensitivity to possible harm (American Psychiatric Association, 1994). The relation between PTSD and youths' aggressive reactions has been well documented (for a review, see Connor, 2002). It appears to be related to the conditioning of neurobiological fear responses that underlie our natural tendencies to react aggressively and self-protectively when events occur that remind us of the original trauma (Charney et al., 1993; Fletcher, 1996). Most youths with PTSD do not engage in serious harmful acts, but their risk for such behaviors is increased. For example, in juvenile justice samples, both boys (Steiner, Garcia, & Matthews, 1997) and girls (Cauffman et al., 1998) with Conduct Disorder and PTSD have been found to be more impulsive and aggressive than youths with Conduct Disorder alone.

PSYCHOTIC DISORDERS. Serious psychotic disorders like Schizophrenia are rare prior to early adulthood. The presence of delusional beliefs among persons with Schizophrenia, often including paranoid notions about harm from others, might suggest an increased risk of aggression. Yet research on adults indicates that they present less risk of violence than persons with other serious mental illnesses (indeed, no greater risk than persons with no mental disorders: Monahan et al., 2001), and the evidence for increased risk among youths with Schizophrenia is weak (Connor, 2002).

DISRUPTIVE BEHAVIOR DISORDERS. Attention-Deficit/Hyperactivity Disorder (ADHD), Oppositional Defiant Disorder (ODD), and Conduct Disorder (CD) form a cluster of disorders the DSM-IV calls "Attention-Deficit and Disruptive Behavior Disorders." They are clustered for good reasons:

- ODD tends to precede CD, with about 80–90 percent of CD youths having been diagnosed ODD at an earlier age; but ODD does not predict CD well, because only about 25 percent of ODD youths are later diagnosed CD.
- About one-half of youths diagnosed with ADHD will eventually be diagnosed CD, and more than two-thirds of CD youths also carry a diagnosis of ADHD.

(For reviews, see Barkley, 1996; Biederman, Newcorn, & Sprich, 1991; Connor, 2002; Frick, 1998; Loeber et al., 1998). Extrapolating from these statistics, if one were to randomly choose from the files of a clinical treatment facility a group of 100 youths with ADHD and/or CD diagnoses, one could expect roughly forty of them to be ADHD only, about twenty CD only, and about forty diagnosed as having both disorders.

Substantially higher rates of physically aggressive behavior are found for youths with ODD, CD, or ADHD disorders than for youths in general or with other mental disorders (Connor, 2002). This is not surprising, of course, since impulsive and/or aggressive behaviors form a substantial part of the criteria for obtaining these diagnoses in the first place. But it is significant because these disorders, especially CD, identify youths who are at greater risk for *continued* illegal and aggressive behaviors in adulthood. For example, about two-thirds of adolescents with CD diagnoses have criminal records as adults (Kratzer & Hodgins, 1997), although only some of these will be arrested in adulthood on offenses involving physical harm to others. While only about 30 percent of youths with CD diagnoses develop Antisocial Personality Disorder in adulthood (among which are our most serious adult offenders) (Robins, 1966), this is a far greater proportion than for youths with other non-comorbid affective, anxiety, or psychotic disorders.

Recently special attention has focused on the long-range consequences among youths who meet criteria for *both* ADHD and CD (especially if they manifested ODD earlier in childhood). Studies have suggested that these youths have a substantially greater rate of delinquency in adolescence, of harmful behavior to others as their adolescence proceeds, and of continued harmful aggression and offending as they enter adulthood (e.g., Barkley, 1996; Biederman et al., 2001; Frick, 1998; Fischer et al., 1993; Loeber, 1990; Mannuzza et al., 1993). This does *not* mean that most or even the majority of youths who are comorbid for these disorders are eventually arrested for violent crimes in adulthood. Moreover, some evidence suggests that other characteristics, especially a callous and unemotional personality style together with substance use, may be better indicators than ADHD when attempting to identify which CD adolescents will continue their aggression into adulthood (Loeber, Burke, & Lahey, 2002).

Youths with CD have also been in the spotlight as a result of a significant movement among clinical delinquency researchers to find the "fledgling psychopath." Psychopathy is a personality type (not currently part of DSM-IV) that, in adults, has been related to repeated, long-term criminal behavior (Hart & Hare, 1997). Measures of psychopathy in adulthood are more powerfully related to future illegal aggression than any other single characteristic investigated by violence-prediction researchers (Quinsey et al., 1998; Monahan et al., 2001). The psychopathic personality is high on antisocial characteristics (e.g., impulsiveness and irresponsibility) found in Antisocial Personality Disorder (APD), but differs from APD in combining these with several characteristics suggesting a selfish, callous, and remorseless life-style. These characteristics are durable (relatively resistant to change) and quite likely to have been developing during childhood and adolescence. So it is not surprising that intense interest has developed in recent years in determining whether psychopathy (or some early form of it) can be identified among youths (e.g., Brandt et al., 1997; Christian et al., 1997; Frick et al., 1994; Lynam, 1998; Rogers et al., 1997). The search has narrowed to the group of youths with hyperactive and early-onset disruptive symptoms, assisted by special tools intended to assess child/adolescent variants of adult characteristics of psychopathy (Forth, Kosson, & Hare, 1997; Frick et al., 1994; Lynam, 1997).

While evidence is mounting that disruptive disorders comorbid with other disorders (e.g., ADHD, depression, or substance use) raise the risk of future violence, currently the research does not allow one to call this group psychopathic or even pre-psychopathic (Edens, Skeem, Cruise & Cauffman, 2001; Hart, Watt, & Vincent, 2002; Salekin, Rogers, & Machin, 2001; Seagrave & Grisso, 2002). As yet there is no evidence that youths with high scores on the junior psychopathy scales during adolescence actually manifest psychopathy in adulthood. Moreover, the mere fact that adolescents manifest characteristics associated with the construct of psychopathy—for example, grandiose, manipulative, irresponsible, impulsive—does not mean that they are psychopathic. Notice that one or more of these characteristics is very likely to be named when one asks almost any parent "Please describe the teenager in your family." As explained in chapter 2, a great many youths manifest these tendencies as transient features of normal developmental tasks (Edens et al., 2001; Seagrave & Grisso, 2002). Thus it is impossible at present to say whether hyperactive/disruptive youths manifesting psychopathic-like characteristics are tomorrow's adults with psychopathy and violent behavior.

SUBSTANCE USE DISORDERS. A significant body of research tells us what is perhaps obvious: there is a strong relation among adolescents' substance use and aggression, seriousness of delinquent behavior (for reviews: Brady, Myrick, & McElroy, 1998; Huizinga & Jakob-Chien, 1998; Loeber & Dishion, 1983), and continuity of aggression among CD youths as they transition to adulthood (Loeber, Burke, & Lahey, 2002). For example, in one general community sample of adolescents, prevalence of problem alcohol use was 15 percent for nondelinquent youths, 38 percent for minor delinquent youths, and over 50 percent for youths with serious violent and nonviolent offenses (Loeber et al., 1991).

Note, however, that while these statistics show that the risk of serious offending is far greater among youths who have problems of alcohol use, about one-half of serious offenders do not. Moreover, the difference in substance use between youths who engage in serious violent versus serious nonviolent behavior is not substantially different, and the rates themselves differ considerably across studies from various sites (Huizinga & Jakob-Chien, 1998). Finally, the relation of Substance Use Disorders to delinquent behaviors appears to vary depending on their presence with comorbid conditions. For example, the seriousness of delinquent behavior is related more strongly to Substance Use Disorder among youths with Conduct Disorders alone than among those with "internalizing" disorders alone (e.g., depressive disorders) (Randall et al., 1999). This is an area, however, in which there are substantial differences among ethnic groups. Prevalence studies (e.g., Teplin et al., 2002) consistently report lower rates of disorders related to substance use among delinquent African American youths than among delinquent non-Hispanic white youths.

Using the Data in the Public Safety Context

Developmental criminology and developmental psychopathology have made significant progress toward understanding the relations between adolescent mental disorder and aggressive offenses. What guidance can they give us to address policy (see chapter 7) regarding youths' mental disorders and public safety? At least one lesson is that modesty and caution are necessary when translating the results for policy considerations. The following review of some of the pertinent caveats that are required does not criticize the existing scientific research on mental disorders and aggression; indeed, most of it is useful. But we must recognize inherent limits for interpreting and applying their results in order to avoid turning good science into bad practice.

MENTAL DISORDER, DELINQUENCY, AND AGGRESSION. Clearly there is some relation between mental disorder and aggression. But this will not necessarily help juvenile justice personnel to separate delinquent youths into those who are more or less likely to be harmful to others. A good illustration of the reason for this caution is found in Huizinga and Jakob-Chien's (1998) description of a general community sample of youths who self-reported (a) violent, (b) serious nonviolent, or (c) minor illegal behaviors, and youths who reported (d) none of the above behaviors in the past year. When there were differences among these four groups on a measure of mental health problems (e.g., depression, hyperactivity) in the Child Behavior Checklist the differences most often were found between youths who report *none* of these behaviors and the other three groups. Most of the scales showed no significant differences in mental health problems between youths at the various levels of offense—for example, between serious violent offenders (serious physical harm) and serious nonviolent offenders (delinquent but not physically harmful to others).

This is important because all of the youths in the juvenile justice system are in those three groups that show few differences among them in mental disorders. Even if mental disorder is greater among seriously aggressive delinquent youths than among nondelinquent youths, identifying mental disorder *among* a group of delinquent youths might not take us very far in identifying which of them will be more aggressive in the future.

FIGURE AND GROUND REVERSAL. Relations between youths' mental disorders and physically harmful behavior can be expressed two ways: the proportion of violent youths who are mentally disordered, and the proportion of mentally disordered youths who are violent. The proportions are substantially different depending on the reference group. For example, Huizinga et al. (2000) offered a helpful set of analyses pertaining to persistent serious delinquent youths and youths with persistent mental health problems (not including those with drug use problems alone). "Persistent" meant continued evidence for at least two years. *Among all persistent delinquents,* about 13–20 percent (different rates in different cities) had persistent mental health problems. But *among all youths with persistent mental health problems,* about 30–45 percent were persistently delinquent. This is not a problem of science, but it can be a source of confusion when one is *translating* science for policy implications. The relationship between mental disorders and violent behavior "looks" quite different when the figures from either source are quoted simply as a "violence and mental disorder overlap" without specifying the reference group from which the figures are obtained.

COMMUNITY/CLINICAL DATA AND JUVENILE JUSTICE DATA. Our knowledge of the relation of mental disorders to youths' harmful aggression is based substantially on the study of youths selected from the general community or encountered in clinical (psychiatric) settings. Far fewer studies have begun with a group of youths, all of whom were referred to the juvenile justice system where their mental disorders or mental health problems were identified, who were then followed for comparison regarding their future aggression. This is important for at least two reasons.

First, as noted in chapter 3, some error in identification of mental disorders is associated with the context in which assessment is performed. Adolescents assessed at the time of referral to juvenile justice are in circumstances that can increase (for some) or decrease (for others) the appearance of particular symptoms, and measurement at one point may identify some youths whose mental health problems are transitory rather than persistent (Huizinga et al., 2000). As a consequence, we must be careful about how much we say about the relation of mental disorders and aggression for youths encountered in juvenile justice settings, based on data that were collected in very different community or clinical settings.

Second, the aggression outcome measures used in community and clinical studies often do not represent the outcomes with which we are concerned in juvenile justice contexts associated with public safety. No studies, for example, have examined specifically what courts want clinicians to consider for the pretrial detention question—namely, the degree to which mental disorder is related to harmful aggression *during the next few weeks or months* before adjudication. On the other hand, several studies have examined outcomes representing what the courts want to know in longer-term dispositional questions—namely, the degree to which youths with mental disorders are more or less likely to continue to engage in aggressive behaviors during and beyond their adolescent years.

STATISTICAL RELATIONS AND CLINICAL PREDICTIONS. The fact that a relation between two things has been demonstrated—even a strong relation—does not necessarily mean that the relation has practical importance. For example, many researchers state that "mental disorder predicts aggression" when describing these relations. When they say this, they simply mean that mental disorder offers something of value in our attempt to understand or account for aggression. They usually do *not* mean that they would be willing to bet large sums of money on the application of this knowledge in specific clinical cases.

For example, if we were told that 20 percent of youths with a particular disorder engage in future violence, compared to 5 percent of youths without it, we would certainly say that this disorder should be considered when we are trying to grasp the relevance of mental disorder for aggression. After all, the odds for future violence in the group with this disorder are four times greater than in the group without it. Yet if we used these figures in a clinical or legal context to predict that all youths with that disorder would be violent, we would be wrong 80 percent of the time, because only 20 percent of youths with that disorder eventually engage in violent behavior.

The day may come when collecting a combination of personality and historical facts about youths will provide decisionmakers with probability statements about future violence in individual juvenile cases. That day has, in fact, arrived for adults. Clinicians can now collect specific pieces of information about a mentally disordered felon (Quinsey et al., 1998,) or a civilly committed adult with a mental disorder (Monahan et al., 2001) and, with proper algorithms, identify within acceptable limits the percentage probability of risk that the individual will commit a violent act upon release from prison or hospital. But this technology is some way off for adolescents.

When it arrives, it is questionable whether mental disorders as such will even be included among the factors in these predictive equations, even though we trust the research that says there is a "relation" between some mental disorders and violent behavior. DSM-IV diagnoses typically play little or no role in the adult prediction schemes cited above, because the researchers who developed the tools found that they contributed too little to the predictive power of the instruments after other factors were taken into account. Some "risk assessment" tools are now in development for use with adolescents, including the Structured Assessment of Violence Risk in Youth (SAVRY: Borum, Bartel, & Forth, 2002) and the Early Assessment Risk List for Boys (EARL-20B: Augimeri et al., 2001). The developers reviewed the best information available in the field before selecting "risk factors" that would maximize the likelihood of validity (which is still under study). Thus it is interesting that both instruments make very limited use of mental disorders to guide clinical judgments about risks of future violence among youths. Both tools include hyperactivity and attention deficit disorder, and one urges consideration of Conduct Disorder when rating a factor called "antisocial attitudes." Beyond this, experts who develop such tools appear to have concluded that *traits or affective states* associated with some mental disorders—for example, impulsivity, anger, psychopathic characteristics, or substance use difficulties—offer better potential for prediction than specific diagnoses of mental disorders themselves.

In summary, we reach the frustrating conclusion that (a) there is a substantial relation between adolescents' mental disorders and their future aggression, and (b) there are serious limitations in the degree to which this relation can be used to advance the juvenile justice system's obligations regarding public safety. Chapter 7 explores how the relation between mental disorders and the risk of harm to others can be used with less equivocation in forming general *policy* regarding public protection, while the state of our current knowledge will limit more seriously our ability to apply it to *predict* future aggression in individual cases.

Part II

Discovering the Obligations

Chapter 5

Refining the Custodial Obligation to Provide Treatment

Using reliable methods, researchers have established that considerably more than one-half of the youths processed through the juvenile justice system meet criteria for various DSM-IV mental disorders (chapter 1). The juvenile justice system should attend to their needs clinically as a matter of custodial obligation. But what is the nature of that obligation? How can it be translated into objectives that are potentially beneficial to youths, families, and society?

Previous chapters provide a number of insights that can help us refine the mandate to provide treatment to youths with mental disorders, and those are summarized in the first section of this chapter. Then, in the three sections that follow—on crisis-related treatment, stabilization treatment, and maintenance treatment—I sketch the juvenile justice system's obligations with regard to these three treatment contexts. The final two sections examine systemic implications, as well as unanswered research and policy questions, for implementing the mandate.

Charting a Treatment Mandate

It is rare that any social agency can do everything that it might wish to do, largely because financial resources, time, and energy are not limitless. Formulating the treatment mandate begins by considering a number of ways in which the scope of the mandate might be limited in order to better ensure its feasibility. The first four chapters reached conclusions that we now can use to limit the juvenile justice system's obligation in a rational manner:

- Diagnosis does not define the obligation.
- Not all treatment is worthwhile.
- Clinical care is sometimes harmful.
- Justice systems are not ideal settings for clinical care.

Diagnosis Does Not Define the Obligation

Assuming that youths' mental disorders can be identified with an acceptable degree of reliability, we learned in chapter 2 that this still does not tell us whom the system should treat. Not all mental disorders require clinical care. The earlier reviews focused on disorders that are more likely to require treatment, but there are hundreds of other disorders in the DSM-IV system. Many of them are minor in their effects on youths' functioning, such that clinical care would not be prescribed even in the context of community mental health programming. Moreover, even for youths with the more troubling mental disorders, not all have equal needs for clinical care or equal urgency regarding its implementation. Cases within any category of mental disorder vary with regard to severity and degree of actual functional impairment (chapter 2). Some cases present a degree of impairment for which clinical care may not be necessary, or that allows one to delay treatment without serious suffering or social consequence.

Not All Treatment Is Worthwhile

As concluded in chapter 4, whatever treatment is required must have a clear purpose and a reasonable promise. For many mental disorders, treatment may be of benefit with regard to some objectives but not others. For example, for some disorders, there may be ways to reduce acute symptoms that constitute conditions of emergency, but little evidence that clinical intervention will produce remission, improve everyday functioning, or avoid reemergence of the disorder. *Some treatments actually have no known efficacy* (no proven value in controlled research studies), and often it is unclear that those with efficacy can be implemented effectively in ordinary clinical or juvenile justice services. Sometimes this might argue for the necessity to increase the system's capacity to implement efficacious and necessary treatment. But at other times this would be fruitless, as when the relevant conditions for treatment simply cannot be met (e.g., implementing a treatment that requires a long time to show progress in cases in which the system will loose jurisdiction of the youth in the near future).

Providing treatment that does not have a clear purpose and a reasonable promise of benefit is wasteful. All clinical interventions have a financial cost, and the cost of some interventions is considerable, including professional time and infrastructure (e.g., hospital beds, transportation, program staff for special mental health treatment units in juvenile justice facilities). Funds spent on treatments of little value are better spent on meeting other basic health and rehabilitative needs of youths.

I do not provide in this chapter a cost-benefit analysis to determine whether the expenses required to obtain benefits through treatment are greater than the financial costs to society of failing to provide treatment. The point here is more basic. *Providing treatment of mental disorders for juvenile justice youths can only be worthwhile if provided with integrity, and integrity (quality) will have a considerable financial cost.* Our review has shown that clinical treatment of youths, like many good things in life, is of little value unless it is applied selectively and with attention to quality as outlined in efficacy research and standardized practice. Integrity and quality of services cannot be obtained without incurring expenses sufficient to implement a treatment as it was intended when first developed and studied for its efficacy.

Clinical Care Is Sometimes Harmful

Financial cost is not the only reason that clinical care should be limited to treatment that has a clear purpose and sufficient quality to provide a promise of real benefit. *Every treatment intervention runs the risk of harming youths or society.* Those risks are acceptable only to the extent that they are justified by the purpose and probable benefit of the treatment.

Some risks are obvious. Psychopharmacological interventions involve risks of unpleasant and sometimes dangerous side effects, and medical care provided incompetently or under thoughtless conditions increases the probability of those risks. Some treatments can be antitherapeutic; for example, some group therapies are potentially effective but, if not properly implemented, run the risk of negative peer influences that promote delinquency.

Other negative risks are not so obvious. Cases for which treatment has no effect are not merely failed cases; the record or experience of "no effect" can have important negative consequences. A judge, reviewing the record of a youth who was "in treatment" but has again been arrested, notes that the youth "failed to respond to treatment." It is common for courts to presume that this "failure to respond" reflects the youth's lack of amenability to rehabilitation, without examining whether there is any reason to question the efficacy of the treatment itself. Youths and parents themselves may draw similar conclusions. When an initial treatment effort is unsuccessful because it had no known value, was ill chosen for the case, or was poorly executed, the willingness of youths and their parents to engage in future clinical interventions might be seriously curtailed by their conclusions that "therapy is just a waste of time."

Finally, a potential side effect of clinical interventions is the abuse of state's powers. Assessment and treatment in juvenile and criminal justice settings always require attention to risks associated with loss of privacy, autonomy, and due process protections for youths as defendants in legal proceedings and state custody. The content of screening instruments, psychological tests, and diagnostic interviews typically involve the report of behaviors, thoughts, feelings, and inferred personality characteristics that are "legally sensitive." These data can increase the state's ability to adjudicate youths when used at the pretrial stage of legal proceedings, and to seriously restrict their liberty after adjudication. A variety of protections—discussed later in this chapter—can allow beneficial assessment and treatment to go forward while minimizing these risks, but the risks cannot be eliminated. Once again, the point is that assessment and treatment should not be implemented simply because they sound helpful. *Providing any screening, assessment, or clinical treatment that does not have a clear necessity, purpose, and potential benefit incurs risks of harm without adequate justification.*

Justice Systems Are Not Ideal Settings for Clinical Care

How the mandate for treatment is constructed must be limited also by certain systemic realities. As others have long observed (e.g., Melton, 1989; Mulvey, 1989), the juvenile justice system is not and cannot be a mental health system, and its mandates sometimes are at cross-purposes.

First, some evidence suggests that treatment performed in milieus involving primarily youths at high risk of aggressive behaviors may actually be antitherapeutic. Especially in group therapies involving antisocial youths, negative peer influences on group members sometimes overcome the potential positive benefits, especially for those with relatively less risk in the first place (e.g., Dishion, McCord, & Poulin, 1999). This produces a disadvantage, in terms of treatment outcome, for treatment programs within parts of the juvenile justice system that collect the more aggressive youths who come before the courts.

Second, treatment within the juvenile justice system must recognize certain limits imposed by the legal relation between the state and persons accused of delinquencies. *The state does not have unlimited authority to intervene clinically in youths' lives, especially at certain stages of juvenile justice processing.* For example, the system typically cannot require youths in pretrial detention centers to participate in a variety of therapeutic or rehabilitative activities. Their immediate needs, especially in crisis, must be met during that process. But they are being held for trial, and there is much that the juvenile justice system cannot require by way of a youth's participation in clinical treatment until its authority to do so is established by a trial that finds that the youth has indeed committed an offense allowing the state to take custody.

Finally, from a practical perspective, some clinical interventions are difficult or impossible to implement at certain stages of juvenile justice processing. Group therapies for youths in pretrial detention, for example, would be largely a waste of time, given that most of them do not remain in detention centers for more than a week or two. Therapies designed to encourage discussions of intimate thoughts and feelings related to psychopathology would make little sense at a pre-adjudicative stage, when the adversarial and accusatory nature of the state's relation to the youth are antithetical to the trusting, nonjudgmental therapeutic relationship that such therapies require.

Fortunately, the mandate to provide clinical care to youths with mental disorders need not mean that the juvenile justice system must administer that care. The system can provide treatment in two broad ways. It can administer treatment (or contract with private providers to do it), or it can obtain treatment from other government agencies (such as public mental health services). Its moral or legal obligation is the same in either case, as long as it fulfills its responsibility to ensure that the mental health needs of eligible youths are met.

These conclusions gleaned from earlier chapters will help to refine and qualify the juvenile justice system's custodial treatment obligation. The discussion in the following three sections structure that obligation with regard to the three general objectives of custodial treatment described in chapter 4: *crisis-related treatment, stabilization treatment,* and *maintenance treatment.* In the course of our discussion, it is convenient from time to time to refer to stages of juvenile justice processing when identifying the system's obligations. The terms used for those stages are "intake" (probation intake, pretrial detention intake), "adjudicative processing" (for cases that proceed beyond intake and are awaiting trial on delinquency charges), and "postadjudicative rehabilitation" (after adjudication and under custody of the youth authority, rehabilitation in the community or in juvenile secure corrections facilities).

Crisis-Related Treatment

Intervention should be available at all points in the juvenile justice system (intake, adjudicative processing, and postadjudicative rehabilitation) for mental health problems that present an *imminent threat of serious physical or psychological harm to youths*. There are two key terms in this definition. "Imminence" refers to the urgency to provide an immediate response in the face of deteriorating mental conditions that may lead quickly to outcomes of a type that will constitute serious damage and sometimes death. "Threat" refers to the obligation not merely to respond when the "physical or psychological harm" occurs, but to anticipate the emergency in order to prevent its potential outcome. Thus the obligation includes the *detection* of a threatened harm, a response to *prevent* it, and the ability to *respond to the consequences* in cases in which detection and prevention efforts have failed.

To examine the obligation to intervene and provide crisis treatment, we must (a) specify a set of *crisis conditions* that trigger this obligation, (b) specify the *interventions* needed to respond to them, (c) determine ways to *identify* youths who need those interventions on a case-by-case basis, and (d) *divert* some youths from the juvenile justice system when their continued mental health care is justified.

Crisis Conditions

Several organizations concerned about standards for mental health services during juvenile justice custody have offered definitions of crisis conditions requiring intervention services (e.g., American Correctional Association, 1991; Council of State Governments, 2002; Office of Juvenile Justice and Delinquency Prevention, 1994; American Association for Correctional Psychology, 2000; National Commission on Correctional Health Care, 1999). Their recommendations vary in certain respects, but they are generally consistent in their attention to the following conditions:

- Risk of self-injurious behavior, including risk of suicide
- Risk of substance use consequences
- Acute mental and emotional distress

- Risk of discontinued medication
- Risk of imminent harm to others

The first four of these conditions are explored in the subsections that follow, while chapter 7 provides an examination of obligations regarding the risk of imminent harm to others.

SELF-INJURIOUS BEHAVIOR AND SUICIDE. The annual rate of suicide among adolescents in the general population has been estimated (Centers for Disease Control and Prevention, 1998, 1999) to be:

- 1.6 per 100,000 for ten- to fourteen-year-olds
- 9.5 per 100,000 for fifteen- to nineteen-year-olds
- Four times higher among boys than among girls (although girls are twice as likely to engage in suicide "attempts" that are not successful)
- Higher among Hispanic youths than among other ethnic groups

The rate of suicide among youths in juvenile justice facilities has been reported as less than 1 in 100,000 admissions for pretrial detention centers, and about 5 in 100,000 admissions for postadjudication (correctional) facilities (Snyder & Sickmund, 1995). (One cannot compare these rates to those in the general population, of course, because the suicide rates for youths in general are based on whether youths have made attempts during a given year.) Equally important, however, is the rate of suicide attempts, gestures, and self-mutilations that endanger adolescents' lives but do not result in suicide; these occur in about 2,500 cases per 100,000 detention admissions (Snyder & Sickmund, 1995).

Youths engage in self-injurious behaviors (resulting, e.g., in bleeding, poisoning, asphyxiation) for a variety of reasons. Sometimes they intend to kill themselves, but other motives include punishing themselves, expressing anger at others, or gaining attention. Most of them do not die as a result of these behaviors, but death is not the only consequence with which we are concerned. Other damages are considerable, such as the life-long consequences of self-mutilation or brain damage from prolonged oxygen deprivation. This helps focus the objective not only on avoiding suicide (a rare consequence of self-harm), but also on identifying and responding to the imminent risk of serious self-injury for whatever reason and with whatever suicidal or nonsuicidal consequences.

The obligation to identify and respond to the risk of self-injurious behavior is relevant at all points in juvenile justice custody, from intake through postadjudicative rehabilitation. But suicidal thoughts and self-injurious behaviors are often precipitated by moments of high emotional stress and by feelings of loss (Hollinger et al., 1994). This suggests two points of contact during which the system's concern should be especially great: at intake and at the time of the postadjudication dispositional decision.

Concerning juvenile justice intake, because periods of high stress often are precipitants for delinquent acts, youths at intake are quite likely to experience levels of stress that are higher than their own "baseline" across time. Whether the intake contact is between a probation officer and a youth living at home or between a detention staff member and a youth recently admitted to detention, adolescents at intake are only moments removed from stressful family conflicts and street dangers in the community. Moreover, intake through detention can engender a feeling of loss of family or peer support, and intake involving meetings with a probation officer represents a threat of that loss. The second point of heightened stress is when youths learn the outcomes of their adjudication and the court's dispositional decision. When the disposition decision signals their imminent removal from the community for long periods of time, many youths experience the decision itself as representing a significant loss.

Suicidal and self-injurious behavior is most commonly associated with Major Depression or other mood disorders. But consistent with discussions in chapter 2, the presence of those disorders alone should not define the need for crisis intervention to avoid suicide and self-injury. It is true that many youths who are at high risk for self-injury will meet criteria for some depressive disorder, but only a minor proportion of adolescents with depressive disorders engage in self-injury. Moreover, the comorbidity of mood, anxiety, conduct, and attention disorders is such that cases involving suicidal and other self-injurious behaviors are very heterogeneous; suicidal youths are found in almost every diagnostic category.

RISK OF SUBSTANCE USE CONSEQUENCES. At the crisis intervention level of treatment, substance use is of concern in order to avert the consequences of current high levels of intoxication or the immediate dangers of withdrawal from substance addiction. The danger may arise especially for youths who are residing in their communities (intake probation, postdispositional community placement) or are being admitted to pretrial detention centers "off the street." For example, at detention admission, youths who are currently intoxicated may be at higher risk of harming themselves (or others). Those who have been maintaining habitual and daily use may undergo painful and dangerous withdrawal symptoms when faced with the unavailability of substances.

Crises associated with substance use are most likely to arise in cases in which youths meet criteria for DSM-IV disorders of Substance Abuse and Substance Dependence. Substance Dependence involves prolonged, chronic (often daily) use to the extent that the youth has built up a tolerance and strong need for continued use of the substance. Substance Abuse refers to frequent substance use that is maladaptive (endangers the youth or others in various ways), but falls short of physiological or psychological dependence. Both refer to degrees of substance use that seriously impair the youth's functioning.

Most youths who present substance-related crisis conditions will meet the criteria for one or the other of these diagnostic classifications. But the diagnosis alone does not call for emergency intervention. Many youths diagnosed with Substance Abuse Disorder will not present an immediate danger due to current intoxication, and the majority of those with Substance Dependence Disorder will not manifest acute withdrawal symptoms on admission to detention centers. Moreover, occasionally a young person may enter a detention center in a state of intoxication but without a history that would qualify for Substance Abuse or Dependence.

ACUTE MENTAL OR EMOTIONAL DISTRESS. This condition concerns youths who currently are experiencing intense psychological and emotional distress associated with acute symptoms of mental disorders. In the typical cases, their distress has been "building" in recent hours or days and they are in the midst of an episode or eruption of symptoms. Their state is such that delay in responding to their disorder (e.g., until after adjudication) is likely to have serious psychological consequences. Often their pain represents a process of rapid deterioration that may quickly result in increasingly impaired functioning and maladaptive behavior if something is not done immediately to alter its course by reducing the intensity of the symptoms.

For example, a youth who cannot sleep because he sees human forms coming and going through the walls of his detention room may be in need of intervention to deal with an acute, mounting psychotic episode. An adolescent who, over the course of a few days in detention, becomes increasingly withdrawn, isolative, emotionally distant, and unapproachable may be experiencing such intense anxiety that she is trying to protect herself from being overwhelmed by her emotions. Another youth who does not have these psychological defenses at his disposal manifests frequent outbursts, striking out at staff and youths whom he perceives as threats despite an absence of provocation. The intensity of a youth's mental or emotional distress, and the appearance of a condition that is worsening, obligates the system to respond in order to relieve that distress and reverse a process of escalating symptoms and functional impairment.

Youths for whom these episodic crisis conditions occur may meet criteria for any of a number of disorders, such as Schizophrenia, Bipolar Disorder, Major Depressive Disorder, and certain anxiety disorders. Only a minority of those who meet these criteria, however, will be experiencing acute mental or emotional distress of the type described here as engendering a crisis. Youths in these diagnostic groups present with various degrees of symptom severity, so that only some will manifest a level of severity and escalating pattern that requires immediate crisis-related intervention.

RISK OF DISCONTINUED MEDICATION. Some youths with mental disorders are on psychoactive medications at the time that they enter the juvenile justice system. Sometimes they do not mention this to probation and detention staff, and parents often are not available to inform them. Therefore, there is a risk—especially at detention intake—that youths' medications will be discontinued, resulting in relapse and the potential consequences of escalating symptoms of their disorders. Crisis avoidance requires that staff be aware of cases in which this might occur. A wide range of diagnoses are relevant here, consistent with the use of psychopharmacological treatment for many disorders, although they are probably most likely in cases involving mood disorders, psychotic disorders, and youths with Attention-Deficit/Hyperactivity Disorder (ADHD).

Intervention for Crisis Conditions

Given these four potential crisis conditions related to mental and emotional disturbances of youths, two general interventions are required of the system: the conditions must be identified, and cases thus identified must be provided access to psychiatric and other medical services. Here we discuss the second obligation—necessary services—followed by a discussion of the obligation to identify youths experiencing crises.

MANAGEMENT OF SUICIDE AND SUBSTANCE USE RISK. When probation or facility staff become aware that a youth is at substantial risk of self-injury, crisis intervention must focus on (a) *providing conditions to increase immediate safety* and (b) *altering the psychological condition that elevates the risk.*

Providing safe conditions typically involves creating the physical and psychological environment in which the youth may be monitored and assisted to avoid self-injury. For those being seen in intake probation or on postdisposition probation, this is likely to mean referral to a mental health facility that can provide this environment. Some juvenile detention and corrections facilities may be able to provide safe conditions within the facility if they can ensure separation of the youth from others in a way that allows for staff "in-sight" monitoring and psychological support. Where this cannot be provided, the alternative is referral to a mental health facility that can ensure such conditions. Cases involving withdrawal related to substance dependence will usually require hospitalization or residence in a specialized facility for substance use crises, due to the medical dangers inherent in the process.

In addition to managing the youth's safety, the juvenile justice system is obligated to take steps to alter the psychological condition that is elevating the risk of self-harm or the crisis substance use condition. Typically the type of care required in these cases cannot be handled solely by intake probation officers, detention or corrections facility front-line staff, social workers operating as mental health counselors, or psychologists. Any of these professionals might provide important case management, one-on-one emotional support for the youth, and monitoring of the youth's condition. But self-harm and substance use crisis conditions are substantially medical in nature, and systems must have a method for obtaining psychiatric consultation services to fulfill additional and essential objectives. The psychiatrist's consultation typically will involve interviewing the youth, discussing the case with staff, and making essential medical decisions about the youth's care. Pharmacological interventions with demonstrated efficacy are available for responding to these crises (chapter 4), and often they will be needed. Other alternatives for professional intervention are brief emergency counseling and/or referral to an inpatient mental health facility for at least brief hospitalization until the crisis subsides.

If medication occurs outside a mental health facility—whether on intake probation status or in a detention or corrections facility—a method must be in place for continuous monitoring of the youth's response to the medication over a period of days. This monitoring is necessary in order to observe the effectiveness of the medication and the possible emergence of unwanted side effects. Lack of effectiveness or the presence of serious side effects may require adjustments of dosage or the trial of a different medication. Mental health counselors may provide some of these day-to-day monitoring functions. But nurse qualifications typically are needed for medication management, with periodic reviews by a consulting psychiatrist.

RESPONDING TO ACUTE MENTAL AND EMOTIONAL DISTRESS. The level of crisis described earlier as "acute mental and emotional distress" will sometimes require brief inpatient psychiatric hospitalization to reduce symptoms below a crisis level. All detention centers and intake probation departments should have referral procedures available for implementing hospitalization for such cases. Attempting to treat active and acute psychotic or major depressive episodes on an outpatient basis or in juvenile detention and corrections facilities runs substantial risks, unless the correctional facility in which the youth resides is specialized to do so.

Other cases of intense emotional distress may not require hospitalization, but need psychiatric or psychological consultation within a day or two. Some detention centers are equipped, staffed, and managed in a way that allows some youths with serious but less disruptive symptoms of depression or anxiety to be treated by a consulting mental health professional, especially when medication may be prescribed and monitored within the detention center.

Identification of Crisis Conditions: A Two-Tiered Approach

Methods to identify crisis conditions should be in place at every initial contact with a youth (e.g., first interview with a new probation officer, admission to a rehabilitation program). But the most critical identification points are at probation intake and detention intake, when youths are entering the system from the general community. These same points, however, are among the most difficult for evaluating adolescents' mental conditions. Often no record of past behavior or past mental health service history is available, and parents frequently are not present to offer reliable information.

The nature of the obligation requires that every youth be evaluated at this point for the crisis conditions of concern. The cost of intake evaluation of every youth by psychiatrists or psychologists typically is prohibitive, so whatever methods are used must be employed by intake probation officers and detention intake staff. The volume of cases does not allow them to spend more than a brief time to evaluate every person.

Under these circumstances, a two-tiered standardized intake screening process is suggested for identification of critical mental health problems associated with our crisis conditions. This process is intended to sort youths into progressively smaller groups representing greater risk and therefore the greater potential need for immediate intervention.

FIRST-LEVEL SCREENING. The first level of intake screening should involve a brief screening tool that asks standardized questions about various behaviors, thoughts, and feelings related specifically to suicide and self-injurious behavior, extent of recent substance use, and symptoms relevant for depressed mood, anxiety, and thought disturbance. All of these factors can be assessed with existing screening tools that have some degree of known reliability and validity, as well as a track-record of application in juvenile justice intake settings by nonclinical staff (see chapter 3). These methods use a relatively small number of items to screen for recent thoughts of self-harm and feelings of hopelessness and worthlessness, as well as recent substance use. Items regarding depression, anxiety, and thought disturbance also focus on thoughts and feelings associated with mental disorders, although they do not address all criteria that would be required to establish formal diagnoses.

Large numbers of youths in juvenile justice intake are likely to endorse at least some questions within each or all of these areas. Thus the tool should identify levels of severity or frequency of these symptoms and provide cut-off scores that represent "clinical significant" or "abnormally high" levels of endorsement of the screening questions for a given dimension. Youths scoring "high" are then considered potentially at risk for the related crisis condition.

Some of the available mental health screening instruments do not ask specifically about recent use of medication for a mental or emotional disorder. This could be accomplished, however, with one or two interview items to that effect.

The instrument used in first-level screening should have known reliability and validity. Given the nature of brief symptom screening instruments (chapter 3), however, the first-level screening will at best have good sensitivity—that is, will identify most youths who actually present substantial risks in the crisis conditions in question—while manifesting only modest specificity—that is, will misidentify as "high risk" a significant number of youths who do not actually present substantial risks ("false positive" cases). This raises the need for additional screening.

SECOND-LEVEL SCREENING. The second level of intake screening should be applied to all youths scoring above the cut-off threshold on first-level screening. Its purpose is simply to reduce obvious false positives and maximize the obvious true positives. In this sense, the second-level screening is a "triage" system that separates those youths who are "screened in" during the first-level screening into three categories: (a) those clearly not in need of crisis intervention, (b) those who clearly are in need (and for whom crisis intervention is begun immediately), and (c) those whose status remains questionable.

Second-level screening can be accomplished in different ways for the various potential crisis conditions, typically involving standardized interview tools that have been developed to screen for specific problems or disorders. For *suicide, self-injury, and substance use conditions,* one might suppose that second-level screening would involve examination for formal diagnoses of mental disorders often associated with these conditions. But the discussion in chapter 2 suggests that this is not necessarily the most effective approach in these cases. For example, while mood disorders are common among youths with self-injurious tendencies, most youths with mood disorders are not self-injurious, and some without mood disorders are self-injurious. The objective of second-level screening for self-injury and substance use risks can be accomplished better with any of a number of specialized screening tools that establish directly what we want to know, rather than providing diagnoses from which we have to make inferences about what we want to know. Several of these tools, described in chapter 3, ask a limited number of standardized interview questions about suicide potential of substance use requiring only a few minutes. They can be used in a brief "discussion" format, indicating to the youth that the staff member wants to further explore some issues because of the youth's endorsement of a high number of first-level screening items.

For suicide potential, for example, these tools typically focus on whether youths were reporting their present feelings in the first-level screening (versus thoughts and feelings that they have had recently but not currently), whether the feelings have been momentary or continuous, whether they themselves believe that they might harm themselves in the next few days and, if so, whether the youth has a plan and whether there are means and the opportunity to carry it out. The use of these screening tools will raise some cases to an "obvious" level of concern and suggest a low level of concern for others, while some will remain "questionable."

Second-level screening with tools that focus specifically on substance use can identify conditions that would make the risk of immediate effects of intoxication or of withdrawal symptoms highly likely or unlikely. For example, is the youth currently under the influence of a substance that was ingested in the hours prior to intake (without which the immediate effects of substance use are unlikely)? Has the youth been under the influence of any substance every day for a period of several days (raising the likelihood of Substance Dependence and the risk of withdrawal symptoms)? A number of substance use screens are available that focus on such questions (chapter 3), allowing one to identify obviously low-risk cases and obviously high-risk cases with relatively little time commitment.

For youths with high first-level screening scores on *mood, anxiety, or thought disturbance symptoms,* and who have not already been identified for crisis intervention related to imminent self-injury or substance use problems, deciding on the nature of second-level screening is a bit more complex. Let us consider three approaches.

First, one might imagine that second-level screening related to these conditions should involve determining a formal diagnosis, on the theory that a crisis case related to these types of symptoms should at least rise to the level of meeting criteria for a DSM-IV disorder. This could include administration of a structured interview tool (see chapter 3) that determines whether the youth meets DSM-IV criteria for a mood, anxiety, or psychotic disorder. This approach seems important, but what we have learned in chapters 2 and 3 raises concerns about its adequacy. Some youths in crisis may not meet formal criteria for a DSM-IV diagnosis. For example, an adolescent may present with a number of serious symptoms usually associated with Dysthymic Disorder yet fail to meet criteria for the disorder because their condition is newly developed and the complete symptom picture has not yet emerged. Most youths in significant distress associated with a crisis condition will meet criteria for some mental disorder, but some will not. For this reason, using diagnosis as a threshold for crisis intervention runs a risk, whatever its magnitude, of overlooking some of those who need crisis intervention.

Alternatively, second-level screening for youths scoring high on symptoms associated with mood, anxiety, or thought disturbances could focus on discovering the extent and magnitude of impaired functioning that may place them in danger in the community (if screening is occurring at intake) or in pretrial detention. In other words, questions of diagnosis could be set aside, using instead instruments that assess severity of functional impairment (see chapter 3) as our second screen for identifying cases that need attention immediately. This may seem appropriate in light of the limited objectives of crisis intervention, but it has its liabilities. DSM-IV is the language of the mental health system and of mental health professionals from whom the juvenile justice system may be seeking assistance in responding to youths' mental health crises. While an accurate diagnosis under crisis conditions often will not say what to do to respond to the crisis, it does provide important clinical information. Moreover, some evidence that a formal disorder exists may be required before third-party payers will reimburse providers for psychiatric services. In addition, mental health professionals will certainly need a diagnostic impression before they implement treatment. For example, some youths may describe bizarre ideas or apparent hallucinations without having Schizophrenia or other psychotic disorders. Administering antipsychotic medication would not be appropriate in those cases, but could be mistakenly provided if no effort was made to determine whether the youth's report of bizarre ideas was part of a more systematic set of symptoms suggesting a formal psychotic disorder.

The obvious third choice for second screening of these cases is to employ both a structured diagnostic tool and a measure of functional impairment. This, too, is not an easy choice, because it requires more time than either of the other two options alone. But the use of both types of tools clearly creates the best second-level screening to distinguish between youths who create the greatest concern and those about whom there is less pressing worry.

IMPLEMENTING SCREENING. The instruments described for first-level screening typically can be administered and scored by probation officers and front-line detention and juvenile corrections staff with only a few hours of in-service training on the instrument. Second-level screening, however, requires greater experience with interviewing young people. While standardized interview questions can be used for second-level screening (and can even be accomplished by computer with the Voice DISC-IV: see chapter 3), interviewers need practiced skill in communicating with youths to explore their intent when they answered first-level screening questions positively. This process can be taught to a wide range of juvenile justice personnel, but it is best conducted by social workers or bachelor's degree mental health counselors who have had some training in the concepts of mental and emotional disturbances among youths.

Mental health screening is likely to occur in the context of staff members' routine process of gathering a broader range of intake information from each youth. Typically staff must spend some time interviewing a person at intake to obtain information about birth date and place of residence, parents' names and phone numbers, name of school, and information about medical conditions and recent medical contacts.

Precisely when mental health intake screening should occur in detention, however, is a matter of some uncertainty. As described in chapter 3, youths' self-reports may be influenced by momentary emotions, so that screening them within the first hour after admission risks obtaining reports of thoughts and feelings that are very transient. Allowing for at least a brief delay so that youths may become oriented to their new surroundings seems warranted. On the other hand, delaying the screening for many hours might cause one to miss the crisis condition one wishes to identify, risking a suicide attempt or drug-use reaction before the potential is known. The proper time is probably between one and twelve hours after admission, but there is no authoritative answer to the best time within that span. A safe policy would include two administrations of the screening tool, the first one within an hour or two after admission to detention and the second one about twenty-four hours later. For the screening tools identified in chapter 3, there is no reason to believe that a second administration soon after the first would interfere appreciably with the accuracy of the results.

Probation intake and detention facilities employing mental health screening must have in place a set of effective rules to prevent the potential for the unfair use of screening data in subsequent adjudicative processes. Staff must be able to tell youths, at the time of screening, that their answers to mental health screening questions will not be used at their trials. Without this assurance, at least some youths who would otherwise be forthcoming might withhold information, thus defeating the purpose of screening for mental health problems. Jurisdictions that do not have such protections in place should follow the examples of other jurisdictions that have prohibited the use of screening data from use in subsequent legal hearings. Legal mechanisms for ensuring such protections range from legislation to agency regulations or judicial orders pertaining to a specific juvenile court.

OUTCOMES OF SCREENING. Clear-cut cases of high risk may need no further evaluation prior to referral to inpatient mental health or substance-related crisis facilities. Others may present clear risks and require some clinical intervention, but fall short of the need for hospitalization. A request for psychiatric consultation will be appropriate in many of the latter cases, as well as those in which the risk is not clearly apparent but is still questionable after screening.

But what is meant by a "clear-cut case of high risk," or "those in which the risk is not clearly apparent?" While we may be tempted to answer that "we know it when we see it," that is not sufficient for purposes of defining screening outcomes for crisis intervention. The instruments themselves will give us an indication of the degree of severity of various types of symptoms. For example, the Massachusetts Youth Screening Instrument (see chapter 3) provides scores on six types of clinical symptoms, as well as two kinds of cut-off scores for identifying "high" scorers. But instruments will not tell the user specifically which cut-off scores, on what scales, signal the need for hospitalization, referral for psychiatric consultation, or simply close monitoring.

These decisions are matters of policy. Juvenile justice agencies themselves must determine how screening results will be translated into staff directives for the emergency interventions described earlier. Unfortunately, the state of the art provides juvenile justice administrators little structure for deciding how to make policy decisions that turn screening results into staff responses. It would be helpful, of course, if we could tell the administrators that their cut-off criteria for intervention should identify some specific percentage of youths because current evidence tells us that this is approximately the proportion of youths that needs crisis intervention. Were we to attempt this for detention centers, the following sets of data would be relevant.

First, the figure cited earlier regarding suicide attempts and gestures—about one in forty admissions—is our best estimate regarding cases that might need intervention related to self-harm. The ratio would be considerably higher for girls' facilities, perhaps one in twenty admissions. But there are no data with which to make estimates for youths seen at intake probation or during postdisposition probation in the community.

Second, the actual proportion of youths entering juvenile justice detention and corrections facilities who meet criteria for Substance Abuse or Substance Dependence disorders is relatively high (chapter 1)—between one-third and one-half of admissions. But there are no data with which to estimate the proportion that presents crisis conditions.

Third, as observed in chapter 1, it is difficult to estimate the proportion of youths in juvenile justice facilities meeting criteria for disorders with a higher risk of serious mental or emotional disturbance (e.g., Schizophrenia, Bipolar Disorder, Major Depressive Disorder, and more serious anxiety disorders). Conservative estimates might calculate the proportion at about 20 percent (Cocozza & Skowyra, 2000). Recall, however, that only some of these cases will manifest symptoms of sufficient severity to require emergency attention. For example, the Virginia study cited in chapter 2 found that only 9 percent of youths (in a detention center in which 80 percent met criteria for some mental disorder) required immediate intervention.

These data are the best we can offer, but they are not of much value to the juvenile justice administrator who wishes to set a cut-off score at a level that identifies about the "right" proportion of youths as crisis cases. As can be seen, the data barely address this question, much less answer it. Moreover, any estimates are likely to be enormously misleading for some detention centers, because patterns of referral of youthful offenders with and without mental disorders vary greatly from one detention center to another. A particular detention center's actual proportion of youths with serious mental disorders (or crisis conditions) may be far above or far below any estimates based on studies of specific facilities or national averages. Thus juvenile justice administrators have little guidance for deciding that specific screening scores should translate into "positive" cases requiring specific crisis interventions.

Diversion

The process of diversion typically refers to the juvenile justice system's option not to pursue adjudication of certain youths at intake, but instead to refer them to community programs early in the juvenile justice process. Diversion may be implemented by juvenile courts for various purposes (e.g., to avoid stigmatization of young first-time, minor offenders who might never again offend if they are left alone). In the case of youths with mental disorders, diversion may be employed to maximize the youth's opportunity for obtaining necessary treatment. Adolescents in need of treatment for their mental disorders, it is argued, should be diverted from the juvenile justice system when the system's interest in their treatment, especially for purposes of reducing their future delinquency, outweighs the value of their adjudication. This circumstance is most likely to arise in two types of cases: (a) misdemeanor cases involving first-time offenders with mental disorders, and (b) misdemeanor or felony cases involving youths with serious and chronic mental disorders (see the discussion later in this chapter of youths with "serious emotional disturbances" [SED]). The number of such cases in the average juvenile court is not known, but it is substantial.

The range of methods and programs for diverting youths with mental disorders from ordinary delinquency processing during the intake process has not been documented. In one sense, diversion is probably part of most juvenile intake probation systems, since almost all intake probation officers exercise some discretion (at least in cases involving nonserious charges) in determining whether a youth's case will be filed for adjudication or "adjusted informally"—for example, by an agreement with the parents for the youth to obtain community services. At the other extreme are highly programmatic efforts for the diversion of seriously emotionally disturbed adolescents from traditional delinquency processing. One recent example is the "juvenile mental health court." In Santa Clara County (California), the Court for the Individualized Treatment of Adolescents (CITA: Arredondo et al., 2001), for example, targets the 10–15 percent of delinquency cases involving youths with chronic and serious mental disorders. It uses a screening and assessment process to identify such youths for special legal processing by a team of clinical and legal professionals (including prosecutor and defense counsel), all of whom have special knowledge of and sensitivity to adolescent mental disorders. Cases adjudicated through this process are heard by a specially designated CITA judge. The process fashions case outcomes that hold youths accountable for their offenses while focusing the disposition on the use of community and juvenile justice resources to provide treatment for the offenders and their families.

Special programs for diversion may have the potential to target treatment efforts for young offenders with mental disorders. But it is important to recognize that neither generalized or programmatic diversion efforts can do much good if there are inadequate services awaiting diverted youths. Diversion programs might be helpful when effective community mental health services actually are available to youths, and when there is sufficient follow-through to ensure that young offenders and families actually become involved in those services. But if that part of the diversion process is not given adequate attention, or if the community mental health services are nonexistent, "diversion" simply becomes the juvenile justice system's way of avoiding its responsibility. Diversion without services or follow-through throws youths back on the street without help at a time that is critical for responding to their symptoms and potentially avoiding their development of more chronic delinquency.

Stabilization Treatment

Beyond treatment for crisis conditions, the juvenile justice system should *identify youths in need of clinical interventions because of mental disorders that seriously impair their future functioning, and the system should make clinical interventions available, consistent with legal limits, to the extent that they have known efficacy for improving functioning sufficiently to facilitate rehabilitative objectives.* The complexity of this definition is related to a number of issues reviewed in previous chapters, and they need to be further explained here.

What Stabilization Treatment Means

"MENTAL DISORDERS THAT SERIOUSLY IMPAIR FUTURE FUNCTIONING." This definition identifies stabilization treatment not as treatment for every youth with a mental disorder, but as treatment in cases in which symptoms of disorder seriously impair functioning in a way that matters for overall rehabilitative objectives. This proposition recognizes that not all youths with mental disorders need treatment insofar as symptom severity and its functional consequences vary among those with any given mental disorder (chapter 2). Meeting criteria for a mental disorder is a threshold prerequisite, and the definition does not limit the obligation to any particular subset of DSM-IV disorders. But the definition does not necessarily obligate the juvenile justice system to provide treatment for all of the 60–70 percent of youths who meet criteria for a mental disorder. It limits the obligation to those whose functioning is seriously impaired by the symptoms of their disorders. The degree of impairment that may be called "serious," however, is not limited to the acute, crisis conditions reviewed earlier.

"IMPROVING FUNCTIONING SUFFICIENTLY TO FACILITATE REHABILITATIVE OBJECTIVES." This concept defines the objective of stabilization treatment in the juvenile justice system. The goal of clinical intervention of this type is *not* the remission of disorders or even "adequate functioning" in general. The objective is to improve functioning incrementally by reducing the severity of symptoms of mental disorder, so that other rehabilitation efforts have a better chance of succeeding.

"KNOWN EFFICACY." The system should provide treatment that evidence has shown to be of benefit when applied to youths with psychiatric and demographic characteristics similar to those of the youth in question. This requirement is two-pronged. The system is obligated to provide treatments for which there is evidence of efficacy. By the same token, the system is not obligated to provide—indeed, should be *required not* to provide—treatments for which there is no known efficacy for the type of youths in question. To do otherwise is wasteful of resources and potentially detrimental to youths, caretakers, and the interests of society (see the first section of this chapter, as well as chapter 4).

By implication, this concept also requires that when the juvenile justice system seeks to meet its obligation to implement a treatment for which efficacy is known, it must do so in accordance with the specifications associated with the evidence for the treatment's efficacy. For example, if evidence of efficacy was established with procedures administered by mental health professionals with a certain level or type of training, the treatment must be provided by that type of professional. If evidence for efficacy was established with youths who were seen on an outpatient basis, then the treatment must be implemented in that context, not with youths in secure juvenile justice facilities.

"MAKE CLINICAL INSTRUMENTS AVAILABLE." The juvenile justice system's custodial obligation should not hold the system responsible
for treating youths, but for providing the opportunity for treatment to
occur. Two qualifying points are embedded in this concept. First, while
the juvenile justice system might implement treatments for a variety of
disorders, it might instead find ways to provide access to some treatments
provided by other agencies, such as a state's mental health system for
children and adolescents. Thus the juvenile justice system's obligation to
make certain treatments "available" does not require that it administer all
of those treatments.

Second, the "availability" concept recognizes that *youths and their caretakers should have the opportunity to accept or forgo treatment* that is made
available *as a custodial obligation* of the juvenile justice system. The system
does not neglect its obligation by not providing treatment if youths and
their caretakers choose not to take advantage of the appropriate treatment
that the system offers. As we shall see later, this does not mean that the
system must receive consent from caretakers in all cases. For example,
chapter 7 proposes that when clinical treatment will be beneficial for the
youth and is *necessary in order to ensure public safety,* the system may have
an independent authority to engage the youth in that treatment. But when
potential beneficial clinical treatment is not essential to reduce risk of
harm to others (and is not covered under the system's crisis-related treatment obligations), the system should obtain caretaker's or guardian's consent. Note that the same is not true for the broad range of methods employed in *rehabilitation* efforts of the juvenile justice system, which may
be implemented without parental consent. It applies to psychopharmacological and psychotherapeutic activities that are designed to alter impaired
functioning associated with the symptoms of mental disorder.

"IDENTIFY YOUTHS IN NEED." The system must discover which
youths are in need of stabilization treatment (as defined in the foregoing
paragraphs). This implies that there be in place a system of assessment,
which will be discussed later.

"CONSISTENT WITH LEGAL LIMITS." This qualifier recognizes
that law might prohibit certain types of interventions at certain stages of
juvenile justice processing. For example, some states (or courts) will allow defense attorneys to bar pre-adjudication psychological assessment
or treatment of their young clients (except for purposes of mandated
screening and crisis intervention). This practice is based on due process
considerations that protect one against providing self-incriminating evidence during the adjudicative process.

What Treatments Are Required for Which Youths?

PSYCHOPHARMACOLOGIC INTERVENTION. There is considerable evidence (chapter 4) for the efficacy of medication for youths with ADHD and youths with mood disorders, and more equivocally for those with anxiety disorders. Some of these youths will not have received psychopharmacological interventions—indeed, will not have been diagnosed—prior to their entrance into the juvenile justice system. The system should make medications for these disorders available to those in juvenile justice custody.

Our definition of stabilization treatment, however, suggests some limits to the use of medications. First, medication should be confined to cases in which the symptoms of the disorders seriously impair functioning in ways that produce an impediment to rehabilitative objectives. All youths with ADHD manifest impulsiveness or attention problems to some degree, and all adolescents with mood disorders manifest problems in motivation, self-esteem, and irritability. But their effects in terms of functional impairment vary across cases, so that not all persons with these diagnoses will require medication.

Second, caretaker (e.g., parental) consent should be required for pharmacological interventions related to stabilization treatment. There are legal and moral reasons to impose this limit on the use of medications by the justice system. A compelling clinical reason, however, is the importance of involving parents in the treatment of their children. Youths' compliance with medication while they are being rehabilitated in the community, or after they return to the community from secure rehabilitation programs, often depends heavily on their parents' efforts. Failing to engage parents in the treatment process decreases the likelihood that they will play this role.

PSYCHOTHERAPIES AND PSYCHOSOCIAL INTERVENTIONS. Juvenile justice planners might suppose that the custodial treatment obligation includes the need to provide a different type of psychotherapy or psychosocial intervention for each different type of mental disorder encountered among youths. But our review of treatment efficacy in chapter 4 does not suggest this. Certainly there are diagnosis-specific psychotherapies, and sometimes they are important to provide. But many of the methods with known efficacy are not designed for one diagnostic type alone. Cognitive-behavioral therapies, family therapies, and Multisystemic Therapy focus on building skills, problem-solving, and learning new cognitive and social responses, or on modifying the relations between youths and others in their world, especially family members. Their intent is to alter conditions that underlie or exacerbate the symptoms of mental disorder, and many of these conditions apply across various mood and anxiety disorders, as well as substance use disorders (chapter 4). Given that this is so, it suggests that the juvenile justice system is not necessarily obligated to arrange for specific types of psychotherapies for specific types of disorders.

Indeed, almost all youths in juvenile justice custody might benefit from these methods, and ideally they would be widely available to delinquent youths. In the present context, however, our definition of stabilization treatment creates a special obligation to make them available to youths with mental disorders, when their disorders are responsible for serious functional impairments that must be remedied to meet the system's rehabilitative objectives.

Some of the more efficacious psychosocial treatment methods described in chapter 4 involve the family in therapy or work with youths to develop new behavioral and social patterns within various systems in the community (e.g., school, work, and peer groups). Depending on the specific method, these forms of therapy typically are difficult to implement in secure juvenile facilities, because the youth's incarceration restricts access to the psychosocial interactions that are needed in order to implement the therapy. If the obligation to provide these treatments to youths with mental disorders is taken seriously, it means that the juvenile justice system must not only make these methods available, but it must also reduce to a minimum the mentally disordered youths it incarcerates and therefore deprives of the opportunity to benefit from the methods.

SPECIAL NEEDS YOUTHS. In this review of treatment methods, I have thus far not mentioned specifically the need for certain treatment services that do not fall neatly into either psychopharmacological or psychosocial therapy categories. These special services pertain to (a) young offenders with Schizophrenia and SEDs—a special category of youths with "serious emotional disturbances" (described in chapters 2 and 4)—and (b) youths with developmental disabilities. Their needs require not merely discrete forms of therapy, but broader and more complex systems of care.

Youths with Schizophrenia rarely are seen in the juvenile justice system, partly because Schizophrenia itself is rare in adolescence. When they are encountered, typically their treatment requires expert psychiatric care, often involving periodic inpatient services, transitional services, and continuity of outpatient services. Similarly, the category of youths called SEDs typically have chronic, multiple, and serious emotional disorders that require special care. Among clients of child mental health services outside the juvenile justice system, approximately 10 percent are SED youths who require nearly one-half or more of the resources of the child mental health system (Davis & Vander Stoep, 1997). Young offenders in these categories need specialized treatment, transitional services, and continuity of care after community reentry that the juvenile justice system not only cannot provide but also should not attempt on its own. Its obligation to these youths is to ensure that the mental health system, ideally in collaboration with the juvenile justice system (as discussed later in this chapter), provides the treatment and continuity of care that they need.

Youths with *developmental disabilities,* especially those with mental retardation, have a variety of special educational needs that fall outside our definition of clinical treatment. When they also have other types of mental disorders, though, the system's obligation to treat those disorders applies to them as to other youths. Having said this, one must recognize that the efficacy of the psychotherapies and psychosocial interventions reviewed earlier often is not known when applied to youths with mental retardation. Youths with intelligence test scores well below 70 and whose everyday functioning is seriously compromised by their intellectual deficits typically are not included in research studies of the efficacy of treatments for other mental disorders (e.g., mood or anxiety disorders). While cognitive-behavioral modes of therapy often are helpful for youths with these disorders, those with mental retardation frequently do not bring to therapy the necessary cognitive abilities to engage in this type of therapy process. Their treatment is best managed by public or private agencies charged with treating those with mental retardation, which have the specialized professionals and programs necessary to meet the needs of developmentally disabled youths.

Assessment for Stabilization Treatment

The obligation to provide stabilization treatment to youths whose symptoms of mental disorder seriously impair their functioning includes an obligation to identify those youths. How is this best accomplished?

THE ASSESSMENT PROCESS. The screening procedures described earlier provide a reasonable way to identify the minority of youths who may be in need of more comprehensive assessment in order to determine their specific stabilization treatment needs. Screening methods, however, will almost never provide the necessary information to formulate stabilization treatment needs and objectives. That requires a more careful, individualized, and extensive assessment.

There are two points in the juvenile justice process where comprehensive assessments to plan stabilization treatment are especially important. One is during the process of intake, and involves youths for whom it is unclear whether they will be processed for adjudication or will instead be referred to community services. The other is for youths during adjudicative processing, involving those who are scheduled for court hearings to adjudicate their charges, which usually will be followed by a dispositional hearing to determine their placement and the type of rehabilitative and clinical services they will be provided. In both circumstances, when screening suggests the possibility of serious mental and emotional problems, the system should be able to provide to this relatively select group of youths a comprehensive assessment by a child psychologist or child psychiatrist. This assessment can be of critical assistance to probation and the court in identifying the nature of a youth's mental disorder and stabilization treatment needs. The assessment should produce the following:

- A developmental and psychological profile of the youth
- A diagnosis if disorder is present
- If disorder is present, an indication of the severity of symptoms and their actual effects on the youth's functioning
- A treatment recommendation
- An explanation concerning how the treatment is expected to improve the youth's functioning in ways that are important for the court's overall rehabilitative objectives

A formal diagnosis, as well as a measure of the level of impairment of functioning, typically is necessary not only to guide the treatment recommendation, but also because treatment may require reimbursement from third-party payers who will not pay without this information.

The nature of assessments for juvenile courts regarding the need for treatment and rehabilitation has been described elsewhere (e.g., Grisso, 1998). Typically such an assessment requires clinical interviews with the youth and the youth's parents, and obtaining detailed information from past records regarding the youth's functioning in various settings throughout his or her development (especially school records, past medical and mental health records, and law enforcement and court records). Psychological testing may be required, especially in complex cases (e.g., when there are substantial difficulties in determining among several psychiatric diagnoses), as well as special medical tests in some circumstances (e.g., when a youth's difficulties suggest the possibility of medical disease or neurological impairment).

IMPLEMENTING THE ASSESSMENT FOR STABILIZATION TREAT-MENT NEEDS. For cases involving youths with serious mental disorders, some juvenile courts obtain their treatment-planning assessments from mental health professionals who are employed full-time or part-time in "juvenile court clinics." Other juvenile courts obtain these assessments from public mental health agencies or professionals in private practice (Grisso, 1998), and psychopharmacological assessments may sometimes be provided by general physicians rather than mental health professionals.

Whatever arrangement is used, the system should rely on professionals who have training and experience in working with young people. Psychological or psychiatric examiners charged with making assessments for stabilization treatment must understand, for example, the concepts of developmental psychopathology described in chapter 2, such as age-relativity of symptoms, comorbidity, and continuity/discontinuity of mental disorders among children and adolescents. Most clinical psychologists and psychiatrists have had some exposure to developmental concepts, as well as assessment and treatment of adolescents, sometime during their training. Only some of them, however, subsequently go on to specialize in the area. Some juvenile justice systems face a dilemma in this regard, in that child-specialized clinicians are few or nonexistent in some jurisdictions (especially in some rural areas). Thus, while professionals who specialize in child and adolescent development issues are preferred when they are available, to require them would risk some jurisdictions having no services at all. Nevertheless, the risk of inappropriate assessment and treatment when employing non-child-specialized professionals must be recognized.

Juvenile courts should have in place policies and practices that restrict the use of information from assessments during adjudicative processing, allowing it to be used only after the youth has been found delinquent and the court is ready to consider the disposition—that is, the youth's placement and the nature of services that are deemed to be needed. Results of assessments for treatment planning should not be available during the adjudicative hearing at which allegations of delinquency are tried. Whether a youth has a mental disorder is usually irrelevant for determining whether he or she did what was charged. Moreover, the availability of information at trial based on a compulsory evaluation could constitute a violation of the right to avoid self-incrimination.

One way to ensure this protection is to require that all assessments for treatment planning be conducted after adjudication. But the delay that this creates between adjudication and disposition has prompted many jurisdictions to allow examiners to perform their assessments prior to adjudication, so that the results will be readily available at the time of the dispositional hearing (which usually occurs very soon—ranging from minutes to a few days—after adjudication of the charges). When this is so, pertinent state law or regulations must be in place to prevent the use of the results as evidence at trial.

Maintenance Treatment

The term "maintenance treatment" refers to clinical services that are provided after the objectives of crisis and stabilization treatment have been accomplished. The goal of maintenance treatment is to prevent the recurrence of serious functional impairment as a result of relapse. In the context of juvenile justice custody, maintenance treatment typically involves care that continues beyond the time that the system has custody of the youth. Its objective in that regard is "preventive," insofar as it seeks to decrease the likelihood that youths will return to the juvenile justice system at some future time as a consequence of behaviors related to recurrent symptoms of mental disorder. Examples include the youth with ADHD who needs to continue stimulant medication, SED adolescents with chronic and multiple mental disorders that make them especially prone to relapse, and those whose functioning is especially associated with family dysfunctions that may need continued attention beyond the juvenile justice system's period of custody.

The system's responsibility for maintenance treatment, of course, does not require direct provision of clinical services after custody has been relinquished. Its obligation is to take reasonable steps to facilitate youths' and families' continued access to mental health services outside the juvenile justice system, as needed in order to maintain the youths' adequate functioning. (One might also argue that the system has an obligation to exercise influence on mental health agencies to provide the types of maintenance treatment that young offenders with mental disorders require.) Continued access to services typically begins by ensuring that referral to appropriate community mental health resources routinely occurs at termination of juvenile justice custody. In most cases it will not be sufficient merely to "inform" youths and parents of potential sources of services. The referral process usually should be deliberate and systematic—for example, arranging for initial appointments and providing relevant information to the service provider regarding the youth's and family's needs.

Unanswered Questions for Policy and Research

This perspective on the juvenile justice system's obligations to provide custodial treatment raises several challenges for which there are no ready answers. Some of them could be addressed if adequate empirical information were available. Others will never be answered with better data, because they are essentially matters of policy that require weighing competing values. They can be described as (a) *issues of measurement and criteria*, (b) *dilemmas associated with the "efficacy" of treatment*, and (c) *systemic and intersystemic modes of service delivery*.

Can Our Measures of Psychopathology Be Improved?

Our ability to identify youths with significant functional impairments due to mental disorders relies heavily on the quality of our screening and assessment methods. How well those instruments can do their jobs is seriously limited by problems in conceptualizing and defining mental disorders of children and adolescents (chapter 2). The field of developmental psychopathology does not appear to be on the verge of finding better ways to define discrete disorders among adolescents or to project their course. Indeed, the fact that youths are still developing biologically and psychologically suggests that the comorbidity, symptom overlap, and discontinuity seen in youths' mental disturbances are not due to our inability to find the true order hidden beneath the chaos, but rather constitute the true, chaotic nature of psychopathology in adolescence.

If this is so, we can never expect our screening and diagnostic tools to be highly efficient in identifying various types of mental disorders or discrete symptoms among adolescents; they cannot find what is not there. Our current tools may be doing as well as can be expected. But three issues need special attention.

THE VALIDITY OF SCREENING INSTRUMENTS. A very significant part of the system's custodial treatment obligation lies in its screening of every young offender for symptoms associated with mental disorder. The best screening tools we now have for this purpose in juvenile justice settings (see chapter 3: the BSI, CAFAS, MAYSI-2, and POSIT) provide adequate standardization and good evidence of reliability, as does the

Voice DISC-IV for diagnoses. But evidence for their validity—their ability to measure what they say they measure—is barely sufficient to support their use. This is not because current research challenges their validity, but because not enough research has been done. This research must receive high priority, because almost everything else in the juvenile justice system's mandate for treatment flows from this starting point.

THE UTILITY OF SCREENING INSTRUMENTS. Good screening and assessment methods are useful to the extent that they are implemented and used competently, and they are useless if they are not. If they are not administered and used appropriately by juvenile justice staff, screening tools are little more than window dressing implemented only for purposes of meeting requirements rather than trying to accomplish the purposes that those requirements represent. Yet we know little about the actual use of screening tools in detention centers and intake probation offices. Moreover, there is no literature that systematically guides the juvenile justice system in developing and maintaining the quality of mental health screening.

The type of research that is needed to provide this guidance is not likely to be done by researchers who develop screening tools. Their interests and skills are focused on the fine points of translating psychological concepts into test items and refining them psychometrically. Studying real-world uses and consequences of those tools requires special research methods associated with the field of evaluation research, aimed at describing the performance, outcome, costs, and benefits of programs as they use the tools that psychometrists have produced. In part, the difference between these research endeavors is captured in terms we have encountered earlier when discussing the value of treatment methods. Test developers study the "efficacy" of tools to measure what was intended when they were designed. But evaluation research is required to determine whether those tools are "effective" when used in actual practice. Moreover, evaluation research can help us determine whether a program's use of tools to identify youths who need mental health services has an impact on the actual provision of services.

THE INTERPRETATION OF SCREENING AND ASSESSMENT RESULTS. The purpose of screening and assessment is to provide reliable case-by-case data that can express a youth's degree of symptoms, diagnoses, or functional impairments. Tools can also provide cut-off scores that signal when a case manifests critically high degrees of these characteristics compared to other youths. But none of the instruments can tell juvenile justice personnel how high is "high enough" to warrant the need for crisis intervention or special stabilization treatment. When are symptoms *severe,* and how much is required to make a mental disorder *serious?* Is it sufficient for the youth's level of depression to be higher than for 70 percent of her peers? 85 percent? 90 percent? There are no empirical answers to these questions. Their answers lie primarily in judgments about the degree of suffering we are not willing to tolerate.

This question is of enormous importance, because it goes to the heart of the definition for our custodial obligation to provide treatment. Where the cut-off is set will determine which youths, and how many youths, we must provide clinical care. Without policies that offer guidance for setting a standard, juvenile justice systems may set the level for "seriousness" so high that many of those who should receive treatment will not, or so low that the large number of adolescents referred for treatment will abuse our resources and reduce the quality of care for the ones who are truly in need.

How Can We Best Apply the "Known Efficacy" Requirement?

The system's obligation to implement only treatments with known efficacy presents certain dilemmas for stabilization treatment that must be recognized, but for which no ideal resolution is immediately apparent. These include (a) questions about the generalizability of efficacy, and (b) costs of the obligation to implement efficacious treatments with fidelity.

EFFICACY, GENDER, AND ETHNICITY. Girls in the juvenile justice system have special needs compared to boys in the system and to girls outside it. As noted in chapter 2, a greater proportion of girls than boys in juvenile justice facilities meet criteria for mental disorders, and the severity and comorbidity of their disorders on average are greater than for boys. Girls often have been included in the studies that established the efficacy of various types of treatment, but few of those studies focused on juvenile justice samples of girls. As a consequence, we are less certain that the efficacy of certain psychotherapies and psychosocial interventions extends to girls in juvenile justice custody.

Minority youths often have been included in tests of the efficacy of various treatments for adolescents. Unfortunately, treatment efficacy studies rarely report separate outcome data by ethnicity, and some of the psychopharmacological studies have been in clinical settings in which the majority were not ethnic minority youths. More encouraging, efficacy studies of several of the psychosocial interventions have been performed with samples containing substantial proportions of ethnic minority youths.

Where there are questions about the efficacy of treatments by gender and ethnicity, our mandate to provide treatments with known efficacy presents a dilemma. Failure to provide those interventions for girls and ethnic minority youths seems clearly and unfairly discriminatory. Yet when we include them in treatment, we do so with some degree of uncertainty regarding the value of the treatment for them.

The proper empirical approach to this dilemma is to stimulate a great deal more research on the efficacy of various treatments for girls and ethnic minority youths, and if necessary, to develop special treatment methods for girls who are young offenders with mental disorders. The proper policy while we wait for those results is less certain, but on balance it would seem to require that we apply treatments with known efficacy without distinction for gender or ethnicity, while taking extra care to monitor the potential risks and value of treatment for those categories of youths as treatment proceeds.

MAKING EFFICACIOUS TREATMENTS EFFECTIVE. In chapter 4 we noted that few treatments with efficacy have been studied for their effectiveness when implemented in real-world settings—that is, with self-referred cases in ordinary practice, outside of clinical research studies that controlled the samples and conditions of treatment experimentally. Therefore, were we to require that treatments must have known efficacy *and* effectiveness before using them to fulfill obligations to provide treatment, the system would have little to offer youths with mental disorders. Under these circumstances, providing efficacious treatments without evidence for their effectiveness seems the best course, rather than denying services until researchers can provide the information.

The ultimate answer to this dilemma, of course, is to engage in as much research as possible to test the effectiveness of treatments while they are being provided to young offenders with mental disorders. In the meantime, policy should require that efficacious treatments of unknown effectiveness must be implemented with fidelity. The manner in which a treatment is executed must be true to the fundamentals that were employed when the treatment was tested and found to be of value. For example, the treatment must be administered according to the manualized directions for the method. The level of training of therapists who administer a particular type of treatment must be the same as the training of therapists in the efficacy studies that demonstrated the treatment's potential. Moreover, that level of expertise must be maintained over time to avoid changes in the procedure as a consequence of staff turnover or the tendency for therapists to "drift" away from the method's specific procedures. This attention to quality will justify the use of efficacious treatments for which actual effectiveness in practice is uncertain.

What Systemic Arrangements Can Best Fulfill the Mandate?

As noted earlier, the juvenile justice system is not a mental health system. It has a variety of responsibilities that may conflict with the provision of diverse methods of clinical care that are needed by youths with mental disorders. But the system need not always administer the treatments that it is obligated to make available. Some things it must do itself, especially the identification of youths who should be receiving treatment. Some of that treatment can be provided by the system, but as noted earlier in this chapter, much of it probably must be obtained from other sources.

Exactly how that can best be accomplished is a complex and unresolved question. Barnum and Keilitz (1992) offered one of the better descriptions of some of the options for "models of service delivery" involving various degrees and types of interaction between the juvenile justice system and other child welfare agencies. In brief, they described four models, three of which are relevant for our consideration:

- *Agency-Centered Interaction:* The juvenile justice system provides as much clinical service as it can, then purchases services in the community from local providers (child mental health centers, independent clinicians) when a youth's clinical service needs are beyond the system's capacity.
- *Collaborative Interaction:* The juvenile justice system and the child mental health system together operate specific programs, facilities, or community services for young offenders who need mental health services. The two systems recognize their joint responsibility for subsets of youths whose behaviors and needs are associated with the responsibilities of both systems, and their funds are pooled for purposes of providing the specific programs or running the special facilities for these "overlap" youths.
- *Child-Centered Interaction:* Instead of developing specific intersystem programs or facilities, the juvenile justice and mental health systems take joint responsibility for obtaining whatever broad range of services a youth might need. Typically cases are managed by multi-agency teams, so that system boundaries are almost invisible, at least for purposes of finding clinical and rehabilitative services for young offenders with mental disorders.

In the years since this formulation of models of delivery of mental health services to young offenders, a number of communities have implemented variations on these three themes (e.g., Cocozza & Skowyra, in press), and research is underway to evaluate their effectiveness. There is no reason to believe that any one of these models is inherently superior to the others. What works for a particular community may depend on complex factors associated with its systems' budgets, histories, flexibility, and particular constellation of service providers.

Juvenile justice and mental health system interactions have a chance to work well in meeting the juvenile justice system's custodial treatment obligations, because the youths in question and the traditional objectives of both systems present a maximum opportunity for alignment of their interests. This does not necessarily mean, however, that the same will be true with regard to the juvenile justice system's obligations in the other two sociolegal contexts. Due process for adolescent defendants with mental disorders, and the management of public safety risks associated with them, are more closely aligned to juvenile justice objectives than those of the mental health system. We will confront those issues in the two chapters that follow.

Chapter 6

Locating the Due Process Obligation

As the juvenile justice system of the 1990s moved progressively toward a model of just deserts patterned after the criminal justice system, it was necessary that juvenile courts pay increasing attention to due process in the adjudication of youths (chapter 1). Moreover, increases in the transfer (waiver) of youths to criminal court for trial "as adults" put the spotlight on developmental factors and mental disorders that might place them in special jeopardy in the adjudicative process. Special due process concerns focusing on adolescents and mental disorder have been raised regarding the following:

- Competence to waive *Miranda* rights "voluntarily, knowingly and intelligently"
- Capacities to participate meaningfully in their trials (competence to stand trial)
- Criminal responsibility (questions of "not guilty by reason of insanity")

What is the juvenile justice system's obligation to protect youths from unfair adjudicative consequences associated with their mental disorders? The legal, procedural, and clinical circumstances of each of these three due process issues are so different that they must be considered individually. Therefore, they form the three primary sections of this chapter, followed by a summary of policy and research questions that must be answered in order to fulfill the system's due process obligations to youths with mental disorders.

Mental Disorder and the Waiver of *Miranda* Rights

Context

Recall that the legal question about the waiver of *Miranda* rights is whether a youth, when making a statement to police officers, has waived the rights "voluntarily, knowingly and intelligently." When courts are required to weigh the validity of such prior waivers of *Miranda* rights, they are instructed to consider the "totality of the circumstances" (*Fare v. Michael C.*, 442 U.S. 707 [1979]). This includes (a) the circumstances surrounding police questioning, such as the actions of police officers when giving the *Miranda* warnings or eliciting a confession, as well as (b) characteristics of the youth that might have reduced his or her capacities to understand and weigh the nature of the waiver decision. An invalid waiver excludes the youth's statement (usually a confession) as evidence at trial. This applies in juvenile court and in criminal court if the youth is to be tried as an adult.

Although our focus is on the capacities of adolescents to make decisions about the waiver of their legal rights, a second question often raised regarding police interrogations of youths is the reliability or truthfulness of their confessions after they have waived their *Miranda* rights. There is mounting evidence of cases in which youths have confessed to police officers things that they did not do (e.g., Drizin, 2003). Whereas immaturity may increase the risks of false confessions (e.g., Gudjonsson, 1992), there is no systematic evidence about the relation of mental disorders to the truthfulness of youths' confessions, and theories that would provide a foundation for discussing the relation have yet to be explored. So our focus here is exclusively on the validity of waiver of rights, not the reliability of statements made thereafter.

At the time of *Miranda* waiver, some police officers might be concerned that a youth's waiver could be invalid due to his immaturity or mental disorder. After all, they have a prosecutorial interest in obtaining a confession that will stick. Little is known empirically, however, about whether or how often police officers consider these matters, and how it may affect their behavior.

A youth's obvious intoxication at the time of questioning probably suggests to some officers that they should delay the process if they want to use the confession in court. And in some jurisdictions suspects of a certain young age may not be asked to waive rights and make statements without parental involvement (Grisso, 1981). (Even so, parents may not waive or assert the rights for youths; only defendants may waive their constitutional rights in delinquency or criminal proceedings.) But in most jurisdictions, no particular procedures or requirements are in place urging police officers to investigate whether a youth might have a mental disorder that could invalidate the youth's waiver of *Miranda* rights.

Questions about the validity of waiver typically occur long after the period of police interrogation, several weeks or months into the adjudicative process. The question arises as a motion to the court by the youth's attorney for excluding the confession on the grounds that it was obtained improperly. In principle, the question could be raised by the judge, but in practice it arises only if the defense decides to make it an issue. No one has studied the practices of defense lawyers in this regard, but experience suggests that there are a number of factors that influence whether a youth's attorney will raise the *Miranda* waiver question:

- The attorney's competence, awareness of the legal issue, and assertiveness
- The nature of other evidence in the case (for example, other facts that substantiate the charges even without the youth's confession, reducing the importance of a challenge on the basis of invalid waiver)
- The seriousness of the charges and the costs of challenging the validity of the waiver (for example, whether the process and time required to argue the motion—sometimes prolonging pretrial detention—might not be in the best interest of the youth in a case involving very minor charges)
- Attorney, judicial, and legal uncertainty regarding the relevance of nonpsychotic mental disorders for abilities associated with the invalidation of waiver of rights

If the waiver is challenged due to a youth's mental disorder (or on any other basis such as immaturity), typically defense counsel will need a forensic mental health evaluation by a clinical psychologist or psychiatrist to provide evidence regarding the youth's mental or emotional state at the time the police interrogation, as well as the effects this may have had on the youth's abilities to provide a valid waiver of rights. A few studies have provided procedural guidance for clinicians when performing these evaluations (e.g., Frumkin, 2000; Fulero & Everington, 1995; Grisso, 1998, 2003; Oberlander & Goldstein, 2001; Oberlander, Goldstein, & Goldstein, 2003), although little is known about typical practices. In general, the evaluation requires paying attention to the specific circumstances of the interrogation and to the characteristics of the youth (including mental disorder), and obtaining information to address whether and to what degree those characteristics are likely to have had a negative influence on the youth's understanding and reasoning at the time of the waiver. Most important for our purposes, this evaluation will require an examination of (a) the youth's relevant cognitive abilities and developmental status, (b) the presence of mental disorder and, if it is found, (c) the nature and degree to which it existed at the time of police questioning and, if it did, (d) the degree to which it might have impaired the youth's functioning in a way that is relevant for the legal question.

The forensic mental health evaluation may be sought independently by defense counsel or ordered by the court (on petition by defense counsel) and paid for with public funds. In the latter case, the evaluation may be performed by a mental health professional who typically performs court-ordered evaluations, or the courts in some jurisdictions allow defense counsel to use public funds to obtain an "independent" examiner.

Given this general context, our interest in the juvenile justice system's obligations to protect youths from the consequences of invalid waiver of *Miranda* rights boils down to two questions:

- Does the juvenile justice system have an obligation to impose special due process protections for youths with mental disorders *at the time of police questioning?*
- What are the system's obligations to youths with mental disorders to ensure that the question of the validity of the waiver is *properly raised during the adjudicative process* and, when raised, results in a proper clinical assessment and adjudication of the question?

The analysis here focuses primarily on special protections for adolescents with mental disorders. But it cannot be divorced from the broader issue of special protections that may be due to youths simply because of their developmental immaturity compared to adults.

Police Interrogation

Law and policy concerning the need for special protections for youths in general at the time of police interrogation (Feld, 2000; Grisso, 1981) have focused primarily on the questioning of those under the age of fourteen, calling for a requirement to provide parental or attorney assistance prior to any request for a waiver of rights. Many jurisdictions have adopted rules of this type, and some of them require adult assistance for youths ages fourteen and older as well. But none go beyond age or intoxication when specifying any other characteristics requiring special caution.

Should police officers be required to delay interrogation of youths with mental disorders until legal counsel or parents are present to advise the youth? If so, two approaches to implementing the requirement are possible. Under the first approach, the assumption is made that most youths interrogated for suspected crimes have a mental disorder (based on current data on the prevalence of mental disorders among young offenders: chapter 1). Thus legal counsel or parental assistance would be required in the questioning of *every* juvenile suspect, with possible exceptions (e.g., questioning to stop crimes in progress). This approach is neither practically nor clinically satisfying. It could create considerable interference with effective law enforcement, prosecution, and public safety interests. It also presumes that we know the prevalence of mental disorders among youths questioned by police officers, which we do not since our data are based on the smaller proportion of youths who penetrate to the detained and adjudicated level of the system. Even if the prevalence rates could be applied, this approach presumes that all youths who meet criteria for mental disorders are sufficiently impaired in their functioning to warrant this protection. This probably is not the case (chapter 2), although in fact we simply do not know (chapter 4).

The second approach requires pre-interrogation judgments in each case regarding the presence and seriousness of mental disorder. But there is no reasonable way to fulfill this requirement. Given the circumstances, police officers could not obtain mental health records on the spot. Expecting them to administer a screening instrument for mental health needs to provide a reliable index of mental disorder would be absurd in such a high-stress context, as would inferences based on an interview by a mental health examiner (even provided that some system could be devised to make examiners available routinely for "prewaiver evaluations").

The only interrogation-level protection for youths with mental disorders that makes sense is to enhance the review of cases later in the adjudicative process. If the system is to exercise a special obligation to protect mentally disordered youths from invalid waiver of rights, that can best be done by focusing on postinterrogation review—the process whereby the validity of waivers is challenged—rather than on attempts to control the interrogation process itself.

Postinterrogation Review

The juvenile justice system should offer special protections to ensure that the potential for an invalid waiver due to the effects of mental disorder is reviewed early in the adjudication process. Two approaches can be taken for special protections with this purpose.

First, the system might require that judges review the waivers of all youths with mental disorders as they approach their trial dates. This could begin with some mechanism for identifying that a youth has a serious mental disorder with symptoms of sufficient severity that they seriously impair the youth's cognitive or social functioning. Mental health screening in intake probation and pretrial detention programs (see chapter 5) might provide a starting point for identifying such youths. When identified as potentially meeting some criterion for degree of disorder, youths who have waived rights and made confessions without assistance of parents or legal counsel could be scheduled automatically for forensic mental health evaluation and judicial review. The difficulty with this approach is deciding whether the costs are warranted by the protections it provides. For example, putting a youth through the ordeal of an additional forensic evaluation, and consuming valuable court evaluation resources, may be insensitive and wasteful when the prosecution's case is heavily based on evidence other than the youth's confession. In other cases it may actually be in the youth's interest to plead delinquent rather than challenge the allegation.

A good argument, therefore, can be made for a second approach that relies on defense counsel's discretion concerning whether to refer the question to the court. That request would trigger an assessment by a forensic mental health professional for an opinion about the nature of the youth's disorder and what effect, if any, it is likely to have had on his of her capacities to understand and decide at the time of waiver of the rights. In addition to allowing defense counsel to avoid *Miranda* evaluations where they are not in the youth's legal interest, it encourages counsel to raise the question in some cases that would not have met the "serious mental disorder" screen-in criteria of an automatic review approach. For example, attorneys might have an obligation to make every possible challenge in cases in which youths' might be transferred for trial in criminal court, where their confessions could be used to obtain substantial sentences "as adults." Thus, the judgment about whether to set in motion an assessment and a complete review of the validity of waiver is so closely tied to the task of building a defense that it is best left to defense counsel, not to automatic rules for routine review.

If this approach is accepted, then the system's obligation is twofold. *First,* it should develop a mechanism for routinely providing relevant information to defense counsel—for example, data from mental health screening, intake probation officer's knowledge of past mental health history—for purposes of considering the potential invalidity of *Miranda* waiver due to symptoms of mental disorder. *Second,* the court should make available adequate forensic mental health assessment services on the question of mental disorder and the youth's waiver when reasonably requested by defense counsel.

This approach hinges heavily on the quality of defense counsel. The system has an obligation to provide youths with attorneys who are aware of the importance of the question of waiver of *Miranda* rights, as well as the potential relation of mental disorder to abilities that are relevant for rights waiver decisions. Toward the end of this chapter I further explore the problem of ensuring the quality of forensic assessments and legal counsel for youths with mental disorders.

Mental Disorder and Youths' Competence to Stand Trial

The legal label for this due process question can be misleading because it suggests that we are concerned about defendants' abilities to participate in the hearing at which they "stand trial." In fact, however, at issue is the defendant's ability to participate in the *process of adjudication,* which extends from arraignment through the hearings at which guilt or innocence and disposition are decided. In some jurisdictions, many youths— probably 80 percent or more—plead guilty and never actually have to participate in a formal courtroom argument about their cases. The adjudication process may go on for several weeks or months, and it includes the youth's participation with legal counsel in building a defense and considering options about pleading and plea bargaining. In some cases the amount of time during which they must participate in the adjudicative process can be quite long—one or two years for youths who are charged in juvenile court, participate in hearings regarding their transfer to criminal court and, if transferred, participate in the process of criminal adjudication. So our concern is not merely with the effects of mental disorder on adolescents' understanding and participation in the courtroom (although those are relevant). Our concern extends also to their understanding and decisionmaking throughout the process as they work with counsel in the development of a defense and consideration of legal options. Abilities relevant for these purposes are described in chapter 4.

Context

As noted in chapter 1, about two-thirds of the states have laws explicitly acknowledging that the protections of competence to stand trial apply in delinquency hearings, and only one state (Oklahoma) has rejected the application of the concept in juvenile court (Bonnie & Grisso, 2000). Judges are required to address the question of competence whenever it is raised, even if the evidence for concern is slight (*Drope v. Missouri*, 420 U.S. 162 [1975]; Grisso, 2003). In virtually every jurisdiction, any party—defense, prosecution, or the judge—may raise the question of the defendant's competence to stand trial at any time during the adjudication process (Melton et al., 1997). Nevertheless, in practice it will almost always be defense counsel that raises the question.

We have little information to suggest when or why defense counsel raises the question of competence to stand trial for their juvenile clients, but we know that they do not raise it in most cases involving youths with mental disorders. This is borne out by qualitative evidence (case examples) (Tobey, Grisso, & Schwartz, 2000), although it is easily inferred when one compares the small number of competence cases to the prevalence of mental disorder in studies of juvenile defendants. (This observation does *not* imply that the question should be raised for all youths with mental disorders; that question is addressed later.)

Many factors might influence whether defense counsel will raise the question in cases involving youths with mental disorders. They are similar to those suggested in the previous discussion of waiver of *Miranda* rights: (a) attorney competence and awareness of the legal issue; (b) clarity or uncertainty about the standard for competence when applied to youths, especially the degree to which the variety of mental disorders among them are legally and clinically relevant for questions of trial-relevant abilities; and (c) costs of raising the question weighed against the consequences.

The cost-benefit analysis is particularly pertinent in deciding whether to raise the question of competence to stand trial. Some attorneys will petition the court to address the question not so much because they are concerned about their clients' incompetence as because they believe the consequences may have secondary benefits for them (Barnum, 2000; Grisso, Miller, & Sales, 1987). For example, pretrial treatment or mental health evaluations for mentally disordered youths may be very hard to obtain in some jurisdictions. If those jurisdictions also provide for inpatient hospitalization during evaluation of a youth's competence to stand trial, this motivates some attorneys to raise the competency question, without actual concern about competence, primarily to obtain a mental health evaluation and immediate inpatient treatment that they believe their clients need.

Conversely, some attorneys will decide *not* to raise the question even if they believe their mentally disordered clients lack substantial abilities associated with competence to stand trial, because they wish to protect them from the secondary consequences. Will a hearing on the competency question itself require a delay in the process so that my client, already burdened with a mental disorder, must endure the stresses of pretrial detention even longer? If she is found incompetent to stand trial, might the disposition—treatment to restore competence so that the trial process can be resumed—involve a secure facility, where she will be further deprived of family contact and educational or mental health services she might otherwise have received in the community? Might it be better for her to avoid the competency question, plead guilty, and get things over with so that she can start the process of longer-range treatment?

Attorneys in these situations walk a tightrope between two ethical obligations. In the first instance (calling for a forensic evaluation without an interest in its intended purpose), they misuse the legal process in order to fulfill their obligation to meet the mental health needs of their clients. In the second instance, they choose to go forward at trial with potentially incompetent clients who may not be able to make decisions with the autonomy that due process requires, in order to fulfill their obligation to protect their clients from the consequences of a competency inquiry that may be detrimental to their longer-term welfare.

Jurisdictions vary regarding the procedures they employ for obtaining forensic mental health evaluations when the question of a youth's competence is raised. Some require evaluations in inpatient child psychiatric hospital units, while others allow for evaluations wherever the youth is residing (pretrial detention or at home). Models for the clinical process for evaluating an adolescent's competence to stand trial have been created (e.g., Barnum, 2000; Grisso, 1998). Typically they include a psychological description of the youth, an evaluation of type and severity of mental disorder, the youth's actual understanding and reasoning abilities relevant for participation (as defined in legal standards for competence), and the relation between the mental disorder and deficits in those abilities. The degree to which forensic examiners actually assess and provide information related to all of these conditions in juvenile cases is not known.

As noted in chapter 4, we have little empirical evidence regarding the actual relation between youths' mental disorders and their abilities associated with competence to stand trial. Moreover, case law itself has not yet provided appellate decisions that clearly define the ways in which immaturity or specific mental disorders of youths should be interpreted when applying the concept of competence to stand trial in juvenile court (Bonnie & Grisso, 2000; Redding & Frost, 2002).

When youths are found incompetent to stand trial due to the effects of mental disorders, the law typically provides that the trials be placed on hold while they receive treatment for "restoration of competence." Little is known about the nature of this treatment in most jurisdictions, although a few states have developed special competency restoration programs for juveniles (e.g., inpatient in Florida: McGaha et al., 2001; outpatient in Virginia: Virginia Department of Mental Health, Mental Retardation, and Substance Abuse Services, 2001). A juvenile's treatment progress must be assessed periodically to determine whether he or she has achieved competence (e.g., every three months or six months in some jurisdictions), and the trial process resumes whenever they have attained competence. Following well-established legal requirements in the criminal courts, the charges against juvenile defendants typically must be dismissed if competency is deemed incapable of being accomplished or if they do not attain competence within a specific period of time (within one year in some jurisdictions).

The circumstances of evaluations for youths' competence to stand trial if they are being tried in *criminal* court have never been described. Law provides them the same protections as for any other criminal defendant, of course. But the relevance of immaturity or specific developmental forms of psychopathology for competence to stand trial in criminal court is almost entirely unexplored and unspecified in most jurisdictions (Bonnie & Grisso, 2000; Redding & Frost, 2002). Moreover, forensic mental health examiners in criminal courts may or may not have an adequate knowledge of developmental psychopathology and special expertise in evaluating youths.

Given this context, a number of points in the adjudicative process warrant concern in view of the juvenile justice system's obligation to protect the right of youths with mental disorders to be competent to stand trial:

- Does the system have a special obligation to identify youths with mental disorders for whom the question of competence should be raised?
- What are the system's obligations regarding the assessment of mentally disordered youths for whom the question is raised?

- What are the system's obligations for treatment in cases in which youths with mental disorders are found incompetent?

Raising the Question of Competence

As in criminal proceedings, all parties in delinquency proceedings are charged with ensuring the fairness of the trial process. This means that all bear some responsibility for raising the issue of a youth's potential incompetence to stand trial when they have evidence to suggest it. It is reasonable, however, to let most of that responsibility rest on defense counsel, who has the greatest opportunity to observe and interact with the youth while beginning the process of building a defense. Ideally there would be screening guidelines to assist counsel in identifying youths who are at greater risk of incompetence due to mental disorder. Grisso, Miller, and Sales (1987), for example, suggested that attorneys at least should consider the competence question for youths who have any one of the following characteristics:

- Twelve years of age or younger (more recent evidence suggests fourteen or younger: Grisso et al., 2003)
- Past mental health records indicate earlier diagnosis and/or treatment for a serious mental illness or mental retardation
- Past educational records suggest very low IQ or indicate that schools have identified a "learning disability"
- Pretrial behaviors suggest deficits in memory, attention, or interpretation of reality when compared to other youths of similar age in similar legal circumstances

These sorts of guidelines, however, should not be used to infer incompetence, nor should attorneys necessarily be required to raise the issue in every case in which these criteria are met. Not all youths with mental disorders of the type suggested in these guidelines manifest important deficits in competency abilities. The system should rely on the attorney's own observations of a youth who meets any of these criteria to suggest whether the question needs to be raised—for example, the attorney's own experience of talking to a youth who is so distracted that he does not seem to be able to grasp what the attorney is saying, or the suicidal youth who seems to have no interest in working with her attorney. Of course, this presumes a level of competence among juvenile defense attorneys to actually make such observations and recognize their potential importance. I further explore this issue in the final section of this chapter.

Bonnie and Grisso (2000) have suggested an exception to attorney discretion for one circumstance. They propose that the juvenile justice system consider a requirement to obtain an assessment and a judicial decision about competence to stand trial in *all* cases in which youths are being considered for transfer to criminal court for trial, and for all youths in criminal court in states that automatically charge juveniles as adults for certain offenses. This obligation rests on evidence that the risk of incompetence is greater for youths in general than for adults (see studies in chapter 4), and that the potential consequences of criminal prosecution warrant added protection. Its importance is even greater for youths with serious mental disorders. The proposal is not without difficulties. States that automatically transfer large numbers of youths (e.g., Florida, with several thousand a year) would find this number of competence evaluations a considerable burden. Moreover, in some states, the consequences of criminal court conviction after transfer are not necessarily substantially different from those in juvenile court, with many youths simply being placed on adult probation. So a desire to protect youths from unfair adjudications is only a starting point for deciding whether a state should require competency evaluations for all youths facing transfer. The decision must also be based on costs (to the state and to youths) and on the degree to which the protection seems to be needed in light of actual dispositions facing transferred youths in various types of transferred cases (e.g., seriousness of offenses) in the state in question.

Assessments for Competence to Stand Trial

The system has an obligation to provide forensic mental health evaluations for competence to stand trial upon counsel's request. Evaluations should be timely and should not require inpatient hospitalization except in cases in which this is necessary for the youth's welfare. Evaluations related to trial competence require intimate knowledge of the developmental context for mental disorders that might impair the capacities of juveniles for trial participation (chapter 4). Thus competency evaluations should be performed by clinicians with specialization in both child/adolescent clinical conditions and a clear knowledge of the forensic issues involved. To avoid the possibility of providing information that would assist in prosecution, the evaluation should focus fairly narrowly on questions of competence to participate in future legal proceedings, not on matters pertaining to reasons for the juvenile's past or present offending. Laws or regulations should be in place—as they are in almost all criminal courts for adult defendants (Melton et al., 1997)—to prohibit the use of any information from this evaluation in adjudication hearings.

Treatment for Incompetence

Laws of most jurisdictions will require that youths found incompetent due to mental disorder must be provided treatment in order to remediate their deficits. The specific purpose of treatment in such cases is to reduce symptoms sufficiently to allow competence abilities to improve (Barnum, 2000). When the symptoms responsible for those impairments are related to disorders such as depression, psychotic conditions, Posttraumatic Stress Disorder (PTSD) or Attention-Deficit/Hyperactivity Disorder (ADHD), treatment should include psychopharmacological or psychosocial methods that have been shown to have efficacy for those disorders (chapter 4). The system's primary obligation at this point is not only to provide effective treatment, but to do so in a context that avoids unnecessary restriction of liberty. Hospitalization should be avoided in favor of treatment in the community whenever possible, and reevaluation should be frequent and result in quick notification of the court when substantial gains have been made.

The system must recognize that the relevant abilities of some youths with mental disorders will not improve within a reasonable period of time—for example, cases that simply do not respond to otherwise effective treatments, youths whose mental disorders are comorbid with mental retardation that limits the cognitive gains that can be made, or those who manifest some improvement but who are limited by their immaturity associated with their very young age or developmental delays. When treatment does not achieve competence within a reasonable period of time (one year in the criminal laws of many states), the juvenile justice system must dismiss the charges and ensure that the youth continues to obtain necessary treatment services within the broader context of the state's child welfare system. While dismissing charges in such cases may seem insensitive to values associated with victim empathy and just deserts, the rule has been applied routinely in all jurisdictions in criminal courts for many decades (Melton et al., 1997). It is based on the principle that one may not use criminal charges as a justification for continued treatment and confinement in order to "restore" competence when there is little or no prospect that restoration can ever occur (*Jackson v. Indiana,* 406 U.S. 715 [1972]).

An Insanity Defense in Juvenile Court?

The insanity defense constitutes admission to the alleged illegal act but a claim that the mental state that is required to hold an individual responsible for a criminal act was absent due to mental disorder, rendering the defendant "not guilty by reason of insanity" (NGRI). Among the more common definitions of the mental states in question is whether the defendant, due to mental disorder, was unable to "appreciate the wrongfulness" of the act or to "conform his conduct to the requirements of law" (Melton et al., 1997).

The relevance of the insanity defense as a legal concept in juvenile court is highly questionable. Even the most zealous juvenile advocates almost never raise the insanity defense in states that provide it for delinquency cases. Cases are rare in criminal court as well, where the defense is raised in less than 1 percent of adult felony cases (and is unsuccessful in three out of four) (for a review, see Borum, 2003b). But most juvenile justice jurisdictions have never seen an insanity defense raised in juvenile court, and many others may have seen only one or two in recent history. Either the relevance of the insanity defense has not been discovered by the juvenile court, or it has simply been deemed unnecessary.

One can offer reasons why the insanity defense *could* apply to delinquency cases as well as criminal cases. United States constitutional law has extended most of the protections of criminal court to defendants in juvenile court, and adolescents may sometimes have serious mental disorders that, at the time of the alleged offense, severely impair their "appreciation" of what they are doing or the type of self-control to which the insanity definition refers.

But from a clinical perspective, it is difficult to argue that the juvenile justice system should be obligated to consider the insanity defense in delinquency cases in juvenile court except in exceptional circumstances. In most delinquency cases, the outcome of a finding of not guilty by reason of insanity for a youth with serious mental disorder has no different consequence than if the youth were found delinquent. In either case, the system would be obligated to ensure the provision of whatever mental health treatment was needed in light of the youth's mental disorder and level of impairment. The only time that an NGRI defense in juvenile court might be of any different consequence would be in cases involving potential penalties that extended beyond the juvenile court's usual jurisdictional age. For example, for some of the most serious offenses, some states allow juvenile courts to retain custody of delinquent youths well beyond age eighteen, and some may sentence youths to periods of time extending to their twenty-fifth birthdays. In these cases, one might consider the juvenile justice system's obligation to provide the insanity defense for this small minority of youths with serious mental disorders, in that it is provided for adult defendants who face similar punitive consequences.

Having said this, it is difficult to imagine how the concept would be applied. After 150 years of experience with the insanity defense in criminal court, neither the law nor legal and mental health scholars have been able to agree on just what is meant by a "substantial lack of appreciation of the wrongfulness of one's act" or an "inability to conform one's conduct to the requirements of law" (Finkel, 1988; Melton et al., 1997). Some experts in forensic psychiatry have concluded that there is no way for mental health professionals to determine whether people, with or without mental disorder, were able to control their behavior at the time of an alleged offense, and law expressly forbids clinicians to offer such conclusions in federal cases (American Bar Association, 1989). In contrast to the concept of competence to stand trial, no empirical evidence exists to show that forensic psychiatrists or psychologists can make reliable judgments about the relation between defendants' mental disorders and these legal concepts. Given this history of the insanity defense, one can only imagine the chaos that would ensue if it were applied to youths with mental disorders that are far more complex, comorbid, fluid, and idiosyncratic than adult Schizophrenia, the disorder that has most commonly been involved in adult insanity cases.

In summary, the juvenile justice system should not be obligated to "protect" youths with mental disorders by offering them the insanity defense in delinquency cases, except in rare circumstances in which youths with mental disorders are being considered for transfer to criminal court. The meaning of the NGRI concept is vague, its application to adolescents with developmental forms of mental disorders is completely uncharted, and its legal and clinical consequences are of dubious value.

Unanswered Questions for Policy and Research

Several challenges stand between the juvenile justice system's due process obligations to youths with mental disorders and its ability to meet those obligations. They include the need for (a) *legal clarity* regarding the system's application of due process concepts to cases involving youths with mental disorders, and (b) *competent professionals* to recognize and handle cases involving adolescents whose mental disorders require special attention.

*Discovering How Due Process Concepts Should Apply
in Juvenile Cases*

The legal concepts of trial competence and valid waiver of rights have developed in the context of criminal law applied to adults. As a consequence, the relation of mental disorders to these concepts has been heavily influenced by the nature of psychopathology in adults. For example, disorders such as Schizophrenia, Major Depression, and profound Mental Retardation are typical of almost all adult cases in which the question of competence to stand trial is raised. It can be argued that a wider range of disorders is relevant for questions of legal competence among adolescents. Many mood, anxiety, and attention deficit disorders create cognitive and emotional impairments in youths that are the equivalent of those seen in more serious disorders of adulthood (chapter 2), especially when they add to already deficient abilities associated with "normal" immaturity of adolescents.

It is imperative that the system make substantial efforts to clarify the application of competence criteria to mentally disordered youths in delinquency cases, as well as youths who are tried in criminal court. Those clarifications should not require the specific types of disorders that have dominated the application of the concepts in criminal law. In fact, they should not even define specific childhood disorders that "qualify" for meeting the legal criteria. They should focus instead on the nature of a youth's actual functional impairments—due to mental disorder—that are relevant for the competency concept. The focus should be on identifying the abilities that are relevant for defining a "competent defendant" in juvenile court, allowing for a broad recognition of the types of mental disorders that might impair those abilities.

This approach will be more easily adopted in juvenile courts than in criminal courts that try adolescents as adults. For example, few criminal courts will ever have seen cases in which the question of competence to stand trial was raised because of the adult defendant's ADHD or anxiety disorder. But those disorders in adolescents should not be considered irrelevant for the question of competence. (Of course, they should not be considered dispositive either; usually ADHD will not create disabilities that are so serious as to require a finding of incompetence.) Imagine an extreme case in which ADHD is responsible for an adolescent's inability to focus on decisions or the trial process. This consequence is as relevant for the legal question as if the same inability was due to the distractions of psychotic delusions. And it may be more relevant for an adolescent than for an adult, given the youth's lesser maturity (chapter 4).

Clarifying the application of legal standards requires either the modification of statutes or the establishment of new interpretations through case law. The justice system has a long way to go in modifying its laws regarding mental disorder and due process for adolescents through either of these mechanisms. For example, the laws of most states have yet to recognize "immaturity" as a potential reason for incompetence to stand trial, much less the implications of child and adolescent forms of psychopathology or severe learning disabilities for applying the concept in juvenile or criminal court.

Can We Improve the Quality of Legal and Clinical Professionals?

If there is a single most important obligation of the system for protecting the legal interests of youths with mental disorders, it is *the obligation to provide them competent defense attorneys and competent forensic mental health professionals who perform evaluations related to waiver of rights and competence to stand trial.* Fulfilling this obligation requires solving problems related to both availability and competence of these professionals.

DEFENSE COUNSEL. The story regarding legal representation of youths in delinquency proceedings is told candidly and painfully by an American Bar Association document entitled "A Call for Justice" (Puritz et al., 1995: for all quotations in this paragraph). The vast majority of youths must rely on defense attorneys appointed by the court and paid by public funds. While many excellent and dedicated juvenile defense attorneys accept this role, juvenile bar advocates say that this is not the norm. Many public defenders for youths are "neophytes who receive less training than their prosecutorial counterparts" and who are "more concerned with maintaining ongoing relationships with the judges who appoint them than with protecting interests of their clients" (p. 22). Too frequent are views like that of one attorney who, when talking about representing youths, suggested that "It's better for my clients if I don't make a stink about their cases . . . judges don't like it when you file motions" (p. 32). In one study reviewed by Puritz et al. (1995), over one-half of public defenders of youths said they had little interest in juvenile law itself, most had no special preparation for representing youths, and only 15 percent thought of their role as being like that of a true defense attorney. It is the norm—not the exception—for youths in our nation's juvenile courts to have spoken to their defense attorneys only for a few minutes prior to trial, often in the hallway or holding cell just before entering the courtroom to offer their "defense" (which is often a guilty plea).

If these prospects for youths' representation are not sufficiently disturbing, one must recognize that in some jurisdictions adolescents in delinquency cases are not represented by counsel at all. They are guaranteed the constitutional right to legal representation by U.S. Supreme Court cases such as *In re Gault*, 387 U.S. 1 (1967). But in some juvenile courts they are asked to waive their right to counsel early in the pretrial process, and many youths do so before a defense attorney has ever been appointed (and thus, of course, without advice of counsel). This practice is particularly troubling in light of evidence that many youths are not competent to know what they are waiving (chapter 4). And their waiver of counsel typically means that no one will raise the question of their incompetence.

Thus it is clearly naïve to believe that our obligations to protect the rights of due process for youths with mental disorders are resolved by assigning the task to defense counsel. Ultimately something must be done to improve the average quality of lawyering for juveniles before we can expect any meaningful improvement in legal protections for young defendants with mental disorders. Puritz et al. (1995) prescribed a wide range of initiatives to begin to remedy the situation, including changes in law, comprehensive training efforts, certification standards, and monitoring of practice. An important part of this effort must include in-service training that improves juvenile defense attorneys' understanding of youths' developmental capacities, mental disorders, and their relation to legal questions about their competence and waiver of rights (e.g., Schwartz & Rosado, 2001).

Defense attorneys are not the only ones who need this education. Indeed, their heightened awareness of competency issues among juveniles may only increase their frustration if juvenile prosecutors and juvenile court judges with whom they work are unclear about the issues. Judges who are well informed about issues of juveniles' competency can communicate to defense attorneys the expectation that counsel attend to their clients' legal interests, and they can promote judicial education for attorneys and other juvenile court judges within their jurisdictions. Moreover, a fair use of criteria for competence in juvenile court will depend substantially on prosecutors' abilities to address the issues that defense attorneys raise in juvenile competence cases. Prosecutors and chief juvenile court judges can also have a significant influence on juvenile justice policy at a state or national level. But education of the defense bar is key to the solution, because it is up to defense counsel to know when to raise the issue of juveniles' competence.

FORENSIC MENTAL HEALTH PROFESSIONALS. Very little is known about the mental health professionals who are asked to perform evaluations for the courts in juvenile *Miranda* waiver and competence-to-stand-trial cases (Grisso, 1998). Examination of early data from a study in progress in urban areas of the United States (Grisso, Quinlan, & Vincent, 2003) indicates that most examiners who perform these evaluations are clinical psychologists, and most of them have some child and adolescent clinical training. Fewer, however, have specialized training in evaluations for forensic issues like competence to stand trial or *Miranda* waiver. Requests for competency evaluations in delinquency cases are rare (zero to ten per year) in about one-half of large juvenile courts and are frequent (over fifty per year) in a minority of them. One suspects that requests are far less frequent, and the assessment abilities of the examiners less forensically specialized, in smaller jurisdictions where the courts rely primarily on local child mental health agencies or private practitioners for occasional evaluations rather than on clinicians whose primary, everyday practice is service to the court. Currently little information is available, though, on the quality of competence evaluations in juvenile courts, either nationally or in specific jurisdictions.

The good news is that the issue of forensic evaluations for youthful offenders recently has gained national attention in the professional organizations and literature to which court examiners turn for guidance (chapter 4). Most clinicians whose practice substantially involves forensic evaluations for juvenile courts probably are at least aware of the fundamental issues involved in these evaluations. But they have not yet been provided reliable information with which to address those issues. They have not yet been given specialized tools and strategies for assessing competence in juvenile cases, and no national standards for those evaluations have emerged. Developmental psychology has provided *some* information on the development of decisionmaking abilities among adolescents compared to adults (see chapter 4), *a little* information about their decisionmaking in specific legal contexts (e.g., participation in one's trial: Grisso et al., 2003), and *almost no* information on the relevance of mental disorders for decisionmaking among adolescents in any context. These are priority areas for future research and development, and the field will be limited in its ability to improve due process protections for youths until researchers can provide information of this type.

Chapter 7

Fulfilling the Public Safety Obligation

Chapter 1 identified the juvenile justice system's mandate to reduce the likelihood of harm to others by youths in its custody. This creates three types of obligations: (a) to assess and identify youths who pose significant risk to the public in order to provide necessary security, (b) to reduce the risk through proper management to avoid current harm to others, and (c) through rehabilitation to reduce the risk of future violence by youths. Assessment, security, and rehabilitation issues arise at various points in juvenile case processing, and the relevant questions are asked (in principle) about every juvenile who passes through the system.

This chapter does not seek to develop comprehensive standards or strategies with which the juvenile justice system can fulfill these obligations in general. It addresses a narrower question. What role should *mental disorder* play in the system's process of assessing and identifying youths with high risks of violence, and thus in exercising greater security (e.g., pretrial detention, long-term secure rehabilitation) and special interventions when high-risk adolescents are encountered? Is mental disorder relevant and, if so, how is it relevant and what is the proper response?

This chapter first examines the various points in juvenile justice case processing where the assessment of risk arises, and reviews briefly some of the important lessons of chapter 4 regarding the relation between youths' mental disorders and their aggressive and violent behavior. Then these lessons are used to chart the system's public safety obligations regarding *short-range, medium-range,* and *long-range* risks of violence.

When Does the Public Safety Obligation Arise?

There are three general points in the processing of delinquency cases when the identification of potentially violent juvenile behavior is most critical. One is at the *point of entry* soon after arrest and referral to the juvenile court. The second is at the *dispositional stage* of the process, when judgments are made about the placement of delinquent youths. The third is at the *point of exit from secure facilities or juvenile justice custody,* often requiring a judgment about the degree to which it is safe to release youths to the community.

Judging Aggression Risk Going In

Soon after an adolescent is taken into custody by police officers, a decision must be made whether to allow the youth to live at home during further processing of the referral or whether he or she needs the security of a pretrial juvenile detention facility. Typically youths may be held in "emergency detention" at the discretion of police or probation officers and detention staff for a day or two (jurisdictions vary regarding the allowable time), but judicial review is required in most states to hold them beyond that brief period. The review decides in each case whether criteria (usually statutory) are met that justify continued detention. These legal criteria typically focus on the likelihood that the youth otherwise will be endangered, is likely to run away from home, or will endanger others in the community if not detained (Grisso, Tomkins, & Casey, 1988). Thus, while our discussion here is on the potential for harmful acts committed by juveniles against others, some youths will be held in detention because they themselves need protection—for example, when there is no parent or guardian available to provide the youth a place of residence. Once a juvenile offender is in detention, staff are expected to make judgments concerning whether he or she is likely to present a risk of harm to other youths or staff, so that they can exercise appropriate precautions to safeguard residents and themselves.

At this point in the process, the focus is on estimating the "short-range" risk of harm to others (or harm to the youth)—whether the person would be likely to harm others within the next few days, weeks, or months if not detained. Continued pretrial detention because of risk of harm to others is almost *pro forma* in many jurisdictions for youths charged with serious assaultive offenses. In other cases the judgment is often based on past offenses, observations of present behavior, and home conditions, as judged by the intake or supervisory probation officer. Many jurisdictions have developed their own sets of checklists and rating forms to assist in this judgment, typically employing "risk factors" that are believed to be important in identifying high-risk youths. Occasionally clinicians are asked to do brief evaluations to assist the court in the detention decision.

Judging Aggression Risk at Disposition

There are three decision points at which the question of the risk of future harm to others affects disposition decisions: judicial transfer hearings, postadjudication disposition hearings, and state youth authority decisions about placement after commitment.

JUDICIAL TRANSFER (WAIVER) TO CRIMINAL COURT. Sending youths to criminal court for trial occurs in two broad ways. (Some states use both mechanisms, while some use one or the other: see Snyder & Sickmund, 1995; Fagan & Zimring, 2000). One approach requires that certain serious offenses by youths above a particular age (most often twelve or fourteen) are filed in criminal court automatically (typically called "statutory exclusion") or at the prosecutor's discretion. Many states have added this approach to their statutes during the past twenty years. The second approach, employed in most states since the earliest days of juvenile courts, makes youths' trial in criminal court a matter of juvenile court discretion, rather than automatic on the basis of the offense alone. In those states, prosecutors may petition the juvenile court for a judicial hearing to consider the transfer of a youth to the jurisdiction of the criminal court for trial as an adult (in some states, "waiver of jurisdiction," "certification," or "bindover").

These two general forms of transfer appear to have different motivations and purposes. The use of statutory exclusion—that is, automatic transfer based on the nature of the offense—is primarily a statement about the public's desire to "teach kids a lesson," or to make sure that youths get what the public perceives as appropriate punishment for serious offenses, or to deter them from committing transferable offenses in the first place. Transfer by judicial discretion, on the other hand, is governed by criteria that judges are supposed to weigh to determine whether the *youth*—not only the youth's offense—is of a "type" that should be tried under criminal law applied to adults.

In this second form of transfer, the "real" factors that go into judicial decisions to transfer youths are difficult to identify. Cases involving sensational or particularly heinous offenses sometimes create considerable public pressure on judges to transfer youths simply for retributive reasons. The legal criteria, however, specify that transfer requires evidence at a special hearing supporting the conclusion that the youth is "not amenable to rehabilitation" in the juvenile justice system and presents a significant "danger to others" (Grisso, Tomkins, & Casey, 1988). Paraphrased, these criteria are aimed at identifying those about whom the juvenile justice system concludes, "This is a youth who is a serious danger to others, and will continue to be a danger to others beyond adolescence, because there is a very low likelihood that this adolescent will respond to any rehabilitation or treatment efforts available to the juvenile justice system." In effect, the juvenile justice system is giving up on the youth, who is believed to be dangerous, unsalvageable, and a continuing threat to public safety.

The focus of these judicial transfer criteria is on estimating "long-range" risk of harm to others, in that the transfer question asks about risk not only during adolescence but also into adulthood. Forensic clinicians often are asked to evaluate adolescents scheduled for transfer hearings, so they can advise the court about the youth's characteristics that bear on the "amenability" and "dangerousness" criteria.

POSTADJUDICATION DISPOSITION HEARINGS. Disposition hearings follow courts' findings of delinquency. They focus in large part on whether a youth can be rehabilitated in the community while on juvenile court probation or should be committed to the state's youth authority (the juvenile equivalent of a state's department of corrections for adults). Most states' youth authorities have a range of program options, including greater levels of security than can be provided by most juvenile court probation departments. Thus the court's disposition decision is in part a judgment about the degree of security a youth is likely to need in order to ensure public safety during the period of rehabilitation or correction.

This requires an estimate of "middle-range" risk of harm to others— the likelihood of serious aggression during a period of months or years between the adjudication and the time that the youth will reach the end of a prescribed period of custody associated with the offense that was committed or the state's maximum age for juvenile justice custody. Typically judicial decisions are based on information provided by intake probation officers, and sometimes clinicians, who make rehabilitation and security recommendations to the court at the disposition hearing.

STATE YOUTH AUTHORITY PLACEMENT. In many states, when a juvenile court commits a juveniles to the state's youth authority, the youth authority itself decides whether it will work with them on probation in the community (at home, at community residential facilities) or in juvenile corrections facilities with varying degrees of security. That decision is based in part on judgments about the adolescent's likelihood of harm to others in the community if he or she were not incarcerated. These, too, are "middle-range" judgments about risk of harm to others during the person's remaining adolescent years. Often such decisions are made on the basis of prior offense record and other historical variables that locate the youth on a multidimensional table (sometimes called a "grid"). This assigns a level of risk to the youth, with the level itself determining his or her eligibility for community services or correctional facility placements with various degrees of security.

Judging Aggression Risk Going Out

Finally, the system is obligated to make judgments about level of risk of harm to others when it considers transitioning the youth from more to less secure placements, and when it considers terminating probation or juvenile justice custody. One particularly important judgment may be made for some adolescents when they reach the age limit of the juvenile justice system (sixteen, seventeen, or eighteen, depending on the state). Many states have laws that allow the juvenile justice system to extend its jurisdiction over a youth beyond the maximum age under certain circumstances, sometimes to the age of twenty-one. Some states provide for this on the basis of a finding of continued danger to the community, while others require a finding of danger as well as continued need for treatment services that the system has been providing, or the need for a period of transition from a secure facility to the community in which the youth must establish contacts for the future.

These judgments generally focus on "short-range" and "middle-range" risks of harm, since they are concerned with transition and stabilization after custody. Judgments about long-range risk (likelihood of engaging in violent behavior during adulthood) usually are not relevant, because at this point the juvenile justice system typically would have no authority to retain jurisdiction beyond age seventeen or eighteen (or beyond age twenty-one if jurisdiction were extended), even if the youth were a high risk to society in the long run.

A Summary of What We Know

These are the contexts in which the system might consider an adolescent's mental disorder to be a factor related to short-range, middle-range, or long-range risk of aggression. But, as reviewed in chapter 4, our actual use of mental disorders as factors in judging and responding to youths' aggressive behaviors is promoted and limited in the following ways.

There is evidence that adolescents' mental disorders may have some influence on their future aggression. When measured at a given point in time, some symptoms of mental disorders increase the likelihood of aggression in the short-range sense. But data on mental disorders often will not be of great use for longer-range judgments of risk. Symptom states may change considerably in response to further maturation or changes in stressful conditions in a youth's life, and because of the general discontinuity of some disorders during the adolescent years. Estimates of longer-range risk require evidence that a disorder (as well as aggressive tendencies) has persisted for some time—for example, that it began earlier in the youth's development and has continued across several years. Even so, the relation is not strong enough to be predictive. For example, youths with persistent symptoms of Attention-Deficit/Hyperactivity Disorder (ADHD) and Conduct Disorder (CD) are at greater risk of aggression in the long-range sense than youths with other mental disorders, yet only some of them actually continue to be aggressive threats beyond adolescence. The norm of desistance from aggression as adolescents age into adulthood holds even for this group.

The literature on mental disorders and aggression in youth (chapter 4) provides a number of other cautions to keep in mind:

- Research is discovering a number of "pathways" to (and out of) aggressive patterns of behavior, creating complexity in efforts to estimate or predict continuity of aggression in individual cases.
- The few "principles" that are arising in research cannot necessarily be applied to girls and to ethnic minority youths, whose patterns of development and relations between mental disorder and aggression might be different than for boys and non-Hispanic white youths.
- The fact of comorbidity of disorders among adolescents complicates the relation between mental disorder and aggression (as when Substance Use Disorders are related to increased aggression when comorbid with ADHD or CD but far less so when comorbid with internalizing disorders)
- Adolescents with mental disorders are more likely to have juvenile justice system involvement than youths without them, but mental disorder is far less helpful in distinguishing between more or less aggressive youths *within* the juvenile justice system.

Regarding the relation between treatment of mental disorders and aggression, there is evidence (chapter 4) that some forms of treatment reduce symptoms of mental disorder and reduce both aggression and delinquency recidivism. However, most of these studies assess outcomes over a relatively short-range or medium-range period of time. Little research has addressed whether treatment creates a longer-range benefit—for example, whether aggressive youths with mental disorders who obtain treatment during adolescence are less likely to engage in violent behaviors as they mature into adulthood than similar youths who do not receive treatment.

Given what is currently known about these matters, what are the juvenile justice system's obligations to identify and respond to youths' mental disorders in the interest of public safety? Separate analyses are needed for measuring the short-range risks at intake, the medium-range risks during treatment, and the long-range risks to society as adolescents age into adulthood.

Mental Disorders and Risks of Harm at Intake

Assessing Mental State at Intake

Mental and emotional states that may be symptoms of mental disorders should be identified for public safety purposes at probation and detention intake, and should be available when decisions are made regarding the need to continue detention beyond an emergency period. There is sufficient theoretical and empirical evidence (chapter 4) to believe that certain symptoms of some mental disorders among youths warrant an increase in concern about their short-range potential for aggression. When current mental states of adolescents are assessed at the detention decision point and found to include potentially important symptoms of mental disorder associated with aggression—for example, anger associated with depression, anxiety associated with trauma, or hyperactive impulsiveness—these conditions do not "predict" imminent aggression. But they increase the risk of it, especially if the youth is expected to be in an environment that may include provocation or stressful situations if not detained.

More than the mere "existence" of anger or anxiety would be necessary, of course, even to warrant short-range concern. Many youths are angry or anxious from time to time without posing a risk of harm. And the period of time involving arrest and detention is likely to engender some degree of these emotions for most adolescents. As measured, the mental or emotional states in question would need to be high or intense in relation to one's peers in order to warrant increased concern—that is, high in comparison to other same-age youths (consistent with a developmental perspective on psychopathology: chapter 2) under similar circumstances (for example, at time of arrest).

This assessment obligation can be met with mental health screening measures (see chapter 3) that provide triage regarding mental and emotional states, including anger or hostility. None of these methods can predict aggression, of course, but they are capable of indicating the presence and severity of various thought, emotional, and behavioral symptoms of mental disorder associated with risk of aggression.

Across time, however, the value of a single moment-in-time measurement of a youth's symptoms will decrease. Changes in mood and affect are more the rule than the exception for most adolescents. And evidence in chapter 4 suggested that a majority of youths who manifest mental health problems at one point in time do not manifest them persistently across a year or two. A single measure does not help us to distinguish whether a persons anger, sadness, anxiety, or impulsiveness (or the lack of them) is transient or whether it is characteristic of that person across time. A symptom may be relevant for short-range concerns even if it is transient. But brief measures alone cannot tell us whether it will have continued significance as the time since the measurement increases by several weeks or months.

This suggests two cautions. First, to ensure the safety of other juveniles and the public, *evaluation for mental states related to aggression should be repeated periodically* while youths are in detention. This would, in fact, be routine for youths who initially showed severe symptoms, if detention centers sought more comprehensive assessments for them as recommended under the custodial treatment obligation outlined in chapter 5. Second, the information obtained from brief screening instruments at this point *should not be used to make any guesses about middle-range or long-range risk.* Information from front-door assessments of depression, anger, or impulsiveness should not follow youths into the courtroom several weeks or months later. The information often will be obsolete or irrelevant regarding middle-range concerns at the disposition hearing. Moreover, pretrial screening and assessment data should be prohibited from use in adjudication hearings (see chapter 5).

Of course, symptom information when determining whether a youth needs secure pretrial detention for public safety should be only one piece of information among several. Typically some information is available regarding any aggressive incidents in the adolescent's immediate past (that is, the past few days), and sometimes detention staff or probation officers are aware of family, community, and peer stressors (or positive family support) that represent the environment to which the youth would be returning if not detained. Many of these factors are used in the Structured Assessment of Violence Risk in Youth (SAVRY: Borum, Bartel, & Forth, 2002), a tool that offers good potential as a second screen for youths whose characteristics raise concern on the first brief screening of mental and emotional states. Symptoms of mental disorders may take on more or less significance in light of these additional observations (Grisso, 1998).

Managing Risks of Harm at Intake

The system also has an obligation, of course, to do something to reduce the risk of harm to others when a youth's symptoms suggest a substantial risk. Placement in pretrial detention is one response, but it is not the end of the system's obligation. Once detained, some juveniles manifest conditions that threaten other adolescents or staff in the detention facility itself. When these conditions are potentially related to symptoms of serious mental disorders, merely exercising staff members' usual disciplinary options to control youths' behavior often will not reduce the risk. Anger resulting from depression, irritability associated with anxiety, and delusional thinking that includes the notion that other people are a threat to oneself usually cannot be "disciplined away." As in the custodial treatment obligation at the pretrial detention stage, the public safety obligation also requires that the juvenile justice system seek psychiatric consultation in such cases, and emergency inpatient mental health services when necessary, in order to reduce the severity of the symptoms that are behind the risk to others in the immediate environment. Psychopharmacological interventions that have been found efficacious in reducing symptoms associated with aggression (chapter 4) will often play some role in this response.

Detention, however, is not the only response to a risk of harm to the public. Other possible responses include allowing the youth to return home with arrangements for accepting voluntary services from community mental health programs while awaiting trial, finding the youth a temporary community placement (e.g., temporary foster home), or foregoing detention altogether in favor of immediate treatment in an adolescent inpatient psychiatric program.

But why would a juvenile justice system even consider nondetention options when youths present a risk of harm to others? The answer lies in two considerations. First, *there is no absolute level of risk that determines whether youths should be placed in secure detention prior to trial.* "Risk" is encountered in degrees across cases. No bright-line of risk clearly defines when adolescents should be detained and when they should not. Some clearly are high risk, some are little or no risk, and some present more equivocal degrees of risk for which the need for detention is less certain. And courts themselves will differ in the degree of risk that they are willing to tolerate when making the detention decision. Thus some youths may not be detained although they present a "moderate" level of risk in relation to their peers. When this is so, and when symptoms of mental disorders are part of the condition creating the risk, the system should be obligated to ensure that youths obtain and accept mental health services in the community to safeguard against the escalation of symptoms—and an increase in risk of harm—during the immediate future.

The second consideration is that *detention may not be the best place to ensure public safety in some cases involving very disruptive mental disorders.* For those with psychotic-like symptoms that seriously impair their functioning and self-control, placing them in detention to determine whether they might "settle down" in a few days not only runs serious risks of increasing their suffering, but also may exacerbate their symptoms, increase the likelihood of violence, and create undue risks of harm to others in the detention facility. In such cases, detention should be bypassed for immediate hospitalization.

Mental Disorders and Risks of Harm during Treatment

The focus in this section is on the relation of mental disorder to risk of harm at the dispositional stage of legal processing and during the period of time when the juvenile justice system has custody of the youth for rehabilitation and treatment purposes. Two public safety concerns are raised at this point for adolescents with mental disorders: (a) whether their mental disorders contribute to increased risk requiring security measures during their custody, and (b) the degree to which their mental disorders require special treatment that will reduce future risk of aggression. Both of these are issues for medium-range judgments about risk of aggression. Does the youth's mental disorder contribute to increased risk during the expected period of custody (typically several months to a year or two)? And should the dispositional plan, and the ensuing period of custody, include treatment for the youth's disorder because of a prospect for decreased risk of aggression at least during the adolescent years? Because attending to medium-range risk is also involved in deciding whether to release youths from secure placements or from custody itself, I examine special obligations associated with those decisions as well.

Making Dispositional Recommendations about Risk of Harm

Chapter 5 identified the system's obligation to perform comprehensive mental health evaluations for use in disposition hearings, when information from mental health screening or other sources suggests that the youth's functioning may be impaired by symptoms of mental disorder. Chapter 5 also described the process and content of those disposition evaluations. The public safety obligation simply adds to that recommendation the need for the evaluation to include data and careful interpretation regarding the implications of the youth's mental disorder for risk of harm to others during the future custody and rehabilitation, as well as the role that treatment for mental disorder should play in reducing the postcustodial risk of aggression.

Such an evaluation obviously will require a thorough diagnostic assessment, involving both structured methods and clinical interviewing by a professional with child clinical expertise. But our limited ability to make estimates of the risk of aggression beyond a few weeks or months suggests that the evaluation cannot rely solely on a clear picture of the youth's *current* status. As judgments about risk of harm focus on periods of time increasingly removed from the present, they require ever more detailed historical information about the past—about the youth's course of development, both normal and pathological, as well as information about the family and environmental context in which that development has occurred.

This information must also include data to build a picture of the adolescent's pattern of past aggressive behavior. This requires going far beyond "arrest records" and general descriptions of "unruliness." For example, some aggressive youths are aggressive wherever they go, but most are more or less aggressive depending on the social contexts they encounter. Thus one youth may get into fights while on the street, but show few signs of aggression in structured, supervised settings like school. Another may only exhibit aggression when confronted by authority. Some aggressive adolescents frequently exhibit aggressive behavior, while others are usually quiet until they suddenly "explode." (For a more detailed discussion of these variables in child clinical assessments of risk of harm, see Borum, 2000; Grisso, 1998.) As a consequence, examiners have an obligation to obtain information from past school and mental health records, as well interviews with parents and other third parties with frequent contact with the youth.

Only in this way can they acquire the types of information that will augment diagnostic results when trying to describe levels, types, and probable conditions of future risk.

This needs to be stressed because it must be taken into consideration when juvenile courts construct their expectancies for disposition assessments involving youths with serious mental disorders. Courts cannot expect examiners to perform these evaluations adequately by giving the youth a paper-and-pencil test and asking a few diagnostic questions. At least two to three weeks are required—sometimes more—to request and obtain relevant records from various agencies, arrange and conduct interviews, give and score various tests, process the information, and write a report for the court. Part of the juvenile justice system's obligation is to provide the resources and time to allow this process to happen in a manner that fulfills the public safety objective with integrity.

Having said this, we must acknowledge that even dispositional assessments of the best quality cannot be expected to provide courts with empirically validated probability statements regarding the degree of risk if a youth were not placed in a secure facility. Instruments designed to approximate that level of certainty for juvenile offenders are only now being developed (chapter 3). In the meantime, the obligation is fulfilled if courts are provided reliable and complete information about adolescents' mental disorders, as well as logical interpretation that characterizes youths as presenting lower, higher, or similar levels of risk compared to their peers who come before the court. Even if this is all that is achieved, it will be more than is normally found in current juvenile court practices.

Deciding to Provide Treatment to Reduce Risk

Disposition assessments should describe, and the juvenile justice system should make available, treatment that will reduce the risk of future harm associated with mental disorders of aggressive youths. Typically the treatments identified in chapter 4 and discussed for the custodial treatment obligation in chapter 5 are those that are needed to satisfy the public safety obligation. By and large, treatments that have been found to reduce symptoms of mental disorder in aggressive youths have also reduced aggression and recidivism (chapter 4), at least for periods that might be called middle range (during adolescent years). Whether they reduce the long-range risk of aggression (behavior later in adulthood) has not been determined for most treatments.

Clinical debates about the treatment of aggression in delinquent youths sometimes ask whether treatment for mental disorders can actually be expected to make a dent in the public safety issue, given that youths with mental disorders may have underlying antisocial personalities—represented, for example, by comorbid Conduct Disorder—that are the "real" source of their aggression. If this is so, isn't treating symptoms of mental disorder irrelevant for many youths from a public safety perspective?

Undoubtedly, adolescents with both antisocial characteristics and mental disorders do exist, and for them, treatment of their disorder might not provide the ultimate "success" that we seek. But two considerations suggest that the treatment of Conduct Disorder youths for their comorbid psychiatric disorders is worth the effort. First, even in antisocial youths, it is likely that reducing symptoms of anxiety- or depression-related anger also reduces the risk of short-range and medium-range aggressive incidents, in that it lessens the likelihood that they will react emotionally to potential triggering events. Second, diagnosis of Conduct Disorder is made on the basis of repetitive and illegal behavior over a significant period of time (chapter 2). It is likely that in many youths, the diagnosis itself was made on the basis of behavior that was the consequence of their other mental disorders. In other words, the label "Conduct Disorder" is not necessarily a sign that a youth has an "antisocial personality" that will continue to threaten society even if other symptoms are successfully reduced. In this light, it would seem unwise to forgo treatment of young Conduct Disorder offenders to reduce their aggression risk, based solely on the notion that "treatment might change symptoms, but it won't change their underlying antisocial character."

Mental Disorders and Long-Range Risks of Harm

As noted earlier in this chapter, all states provide for the transfer (waiver) of some young offenders to be tried in criminal court. Statutes typically require that the offense charged must be serious (often assaultive), and that the youth must be above a certain minimum age (typically twelve, thirteen, or fourteen). We reviewed two types of transfer. One of these—judicial transfer—requires a court hearing and a judgment about the youth's "dangerousness" and "amenability to treatment," both of which focus primarily on the risk of long-range (adulthood) aggression if the youth is retained in the juvenile justice system. Two other mechanisms—statutory exclusion and prosecutor discretion—transfer youths based primarily on their age and the nature or frequency of their offenses, without a judicial consideration regarding their psychological characteristics or mental conditions. What is the juvenile justice system's obligation to consider adolescents' mental disorders in relation to these two types of transfer, given the system's interest in reducing long-range risks of harm to others when youths reach their adult years?

Judicial Transfer

In cases in which juvenile courts are considering the transfer of young offenders to criminal court for trial, the system should be obligated to provide the court a thorough and comprehensive developmental and mental health evaluation. This follows from the presumption that the history and course of some mental disorders of adolescence bear some relation to the risk of long-range aggression. In addition, the prospect for treatment of those disorders is relevant for the question of their long-range risk of aggression, and thus relevant for the "danger" and "amenability to rehabilitation" questions that drive the judicial transfer decision.

But can mental health professionals actually provide that information? Standards recently have been proposed for performing mental health evaluations specifically to address the questions raised in transfer hearings (Grisso, 1998, 2000a), as well as questions of future aggression (e.g., Borum, 2000). But can mental health examiners determine whether an adolescent's prior offending has been in part a function of his mental disorder? And can they project which youths with mental disorders are more and less likely to respond to treatment for their disorders, thus reducing or augmenting the long-range risk of danger to others in their adult years?

These questions are extraordinarily complex. From the general literature on prediction of future violent behavior (chapter 4), we know that the mere presence of current symptoms or aggressive behaviors at a point in time in adolescence has little value for long-range predictions of risk of violence during adulthood. From the field of juvenile criminology (chapter 4), we know that (a) most youths who engage in delinquent behaviors in adolescence desist from serious illegal behaviors as they age into adulthood, and that (b) youths with certain patterns of development of mental disorders and aggressive behavior are less likely to desist in the long run. Yet even among those in the latter "high-risk" group, only a minority manifest serious aggression persisting into adulthood, and we have yet to develop good ways to distinguish among them in a predictive sense. From the field of developmental psychopathology (chapter 2), we know that the continuity of youths' mental disorders—whether they will persist throughout adolescence and into adulthood—differs from one disorder to another and is difficult to predict from case to case. There are some treatments that will decrease the persistence of their disorders (chapter 4). But there is little information to distinguish between youths for whom this is more or less likely to happen given that they are provided treatment—that is, which of them are more or less "amenable" to efficacious treatments that the system might offer them. In short, our current state of knowledge based on empirical research about adolescent offenders' mental disorders provides only very limited guidance for projecting their long-range risk of harm to others.

Why, then, should a mental health evaluation be mandatory for transfer hearings involving the question of treatment responsiveness and long-range risk of harm? If clinicians cannot provide courts with opinions—based on sound research evidence—regarding the relation of youths' current mental disorders to their long-range risk of harm, should they be providing any judicial input at all? The answer is yes, but the answer itself reveals a serious risk in the use of clinical information in transfer cases.

The legal criteria for transfer mandates that a judge must decide whether a youth will be a danger to others beyond the adolescent years. Neither law nor science provides any clear guidance for judges in making this decision. But few would deny that the decision, however it is to be made, requires knowledge of the life circumstances of the youth thus far. If those circumstances include a mental disorder, it would be strange to conclude that information about it should go undiscovered or ignored by the court, even if its relation to future, long-range violence is empirically uncertain. In many cases the information at least helps provide a context for the youth's past and current aggressive behavior, and it is reasonable to expect judges to want to make inferences about the nature of a youth's current aggression when attempting the task of estimating the risk of future aggression. Moreover, imagine that a youth has a particular mental disorder for which there is a psychopharmacological or psychosocial treatment with known efficacy, he has yet to receive that treatment, and his characteristics are similar to those of youths who have benefited from it in the past. Would one wish to exclude that information from judicial consideration because (a) one is not sure that the mental disorder caused the youth's past aggression, and (b) there is no evidence that this would necessarily reduce this particular youth's likelihood of future aggression in adulthood?

From this perspective, it seems clear that mental health evaluations should be a part of the process of transfer hearings. The information they can provide about the past and current status of adolescents with mental disorders would seem to be necessary for any logical consideration of their future treatment response and long-range aggression, even if there is little scientific evidence to make those predictions.

But note that this explanation for the relevance of mental health evaluations in transfer cases also identifies their risks. The judge is required to make a decision with great uncertainties and little guidance. The clinician can provide information that is relevant for the decision, but without a scientific basis for reducing the uncertainties about how the information should be used. In these circumstances, judges often want more from clinicians than they can provide—an "answer" to the questions of long-range aggression and amenability—and clinicians will want to be helpful. This dynamic can draw clinicians well beyond the boundaries within which they can legitimately provide information about an adolescent's disorder, its relation to current and past offending, and the potential value of particular types of treatment. They often expect—and are expected—to conclude their evaluations by offering opinions and testimony about the "answer" to the "future dangerousness" and "amenability to treatment" criteria, the very conclusions for which they do not have an empirical foundation.

One might say that clinicians are in no poorer position than judges, and are possibly in a better one, to draw such conclusions (an argument the U.S. Supreme Court itself made for admitting mental health experts' predictions of future aggression as evidence: *Barefoot v. Estelle*, 463 U.S. 880 [1983]). But that very status as "expert" means that judges are likely to place more weight on clinicians' opinions than their science can support. The better use of mental health evaluations in transfer cases is to ensure that judges understand the role of mental disorder in a youth's offending, as well as the treatment prospects, without expecting that clinicians have a scientific basis for answering the bottom-line questions with which the court is faced.

Nonjudicial Transfer (Statutory Exclusion, Prosecutor Discretion)

When charges against juvenile offenders are filed in criminal court by statutory exclusion or prosecutor discretion (based largely on offense and age), one would think that little could be said about the juvenile justice system's obligations to those youths. After all, after transfer they are not in the juvenile justice system's jurisdiction, and no juvenile court had any hand in transferring them. *But the juvenile court is not only a system for processing youths. It is also a political force with some influence in the making of laws that affect them.* Therefore, it is worthwhile to consider what obligation the juvenile court might have regarding youths with mental disorders whose charges are automatically filed in criminal court.

A majority of young people who offend meet criteria for at least one mental disorder, and in some of those cases their mental disorders seriously impair their functioning and play some role in their offending. Only some of the latter cases present a substantial risk of long-range persistence of either mental illness or aggressive behavior in adulthood. Yet statutory exclusion brings all of these youths into criminal court as long as they are over a certain age and are charged with a serious offense. Statutory exclusion makes no distinction among adolescents regarding those who have mental disorders, those who have persistent patterns of development of disorders and aggressive behaviors, or those whose mental disorders may respond to treatment that would reduce long-range risks to public safety.

What happens when these disordered adolescents arrive at the doorstep of the criminal justice system? We have virtually no reliable information describing young defendants with mental disorders who appear in criminal courts, much less reliable information about their fate. But on its face, the nature of most criminal courts offers no reason to believe that they are equipped to identify adolescents' mental disorders. Many adult defendants have mental disorders, but this does not prepare criminal courts to recognize developmental forms of psychopathology, given their many differences and complexities compared to adult psychopathology (chapter 2). Even if a criminal court were to call for a mental health evaluation (and there is no evidence concerning whether or how often this is done for adolescents in criminal court), the criminal justice system's forensic mental health examiners often are not qualified to evaluate children, and the court itself is unprepared to grasp the significance of youths' disorders for their offending. Moreover, if youths' mental disorders are identified while they are in the criminal justice system, the system's laws and procedures do not ensure that careful attention will be paid to them. And even if they did, the likelihood that the system could provide or arrange for appropriate mental health treatment of adolescents is probably small.

Therefore, transferring youths with mental disorders to the criminal justice system is almost certain to produce some volume of cases in which the justice system fails to provide treatment in the interest of long-range public safety. The risk is compounded by the fact that many youths tried in criminal court will not receive lengthy sentences, but will be returned to the community on probation, usually under the loose supervision of criminal court probation officers who have no knowledge of adolescent development, developmental psychopathology, or community mental health resources for adolescents.

Not all young offenders with mental disorders need treatment for public safety purposes, and not all young offenders with mental disorders should necessarily be retained in the juvenile justice system. But statutory exclusion as a mechanism for transfer provides no way to potentially identify those youths for whom the long-range risk might be reduced with treatment—adolescents for whom public safety interests would be better served by retaining them in the juvenile justice system where they might be provided treatment.

Given these circumstances, one might propose that the juvenile justice system, as part of its public safety obligation, should actively seek the development of laws and procedures that make special provisions for avoiding inappropriate prosecution of youths with mental disorders who are charged with offenses in criminal court. The proposal would urge this obligation because of the risk to public safety when the criminal justice system does not provide treatment to youths whose further development of aggressive patterns of behavior might be avoided. This obligation can be advanced even though we do not know specifically which adolescents, with what types of mental disorders and aggression histories, will be long-range risks. The fact that statutory exclusion is indiscriminate means that the criminal justice system is receiving but failing to respond to at least some youths with mental disorders whose treatment could enhance public safety.

If the juvenile justice system has a public safety obligation to attend to this issue, what alternatives could it seek in the form of "special provisions for avoiding inappropriate criminal court prosecution of youths with mental disorders?" Two broad options are possible, but both meet with substantial objections.

One option is to provide for hearings prior to arraignment for those transferred to criminal court through statutory exclusion. In each case, the hearing would determine whether criminal court prosecution is appropriate in light of the adolescent's developmental and mental health status. Mental health evaluations would be performed in preparation for the hearing. A variation on this theme would create routine assessment, perhaps including a diagnostic tool like the Voice DISC-IV (see chapter 3) that could determine the need for a more comprehensive evaluation.

Some states already provide for a "reverse transfer" hearing of this type (Snyder & Sickmund, 1995), although little is known about the nature of the hearings or the criteria that criminal courts apply to make their decisions. There is no evidence that the identification and consideration of mental disorders receive any special attention in current reverse transfer hearings.

A proposal for the routine evaluation and judicial review of mental disorders for statutorily transferred youths raises many questions and problems:

- Who would perform the evaluations? The criminal courts' usual mental health examiners typically would not be competent to diagnose and describe the consequences of adolescents' mental disorders.
- What would be the consequences of procedural delay? The proposed evaluations would further prolong the adjudication of youths, with some consequence for their development and the courts' dockets.
- What would be the costs? They would be negligible in some states (statutory exclusion transfers a few cases annually in Massachusetts, where it is limited to first-degree murder charges) and enormous in others (Florida transfers for a wide range of offenses, resulting in 2,000 transferred youths annually in recent years).
- What legal standards would be applied? Various standards are possible, requiring a focus on medium-range or long-range risks, definitions of applicable mental disorders, and standards and burdens of proof.
- What empirical guidance could be offered? As noted earlier, the state of knowledge regarding the relation between youths' mental disorders, aggressive behaviors, predictions and trajectories for future aggression, and effects of treatment on those trajectories is frustratingly limited.

Many of these obstacles are created by society's decision to subject children to a system of criminal law designed for adults. But adolescents are not adults. The criminal justice system cannot provide a meaningful solution to public safety questions pertaining to youths with mental disorders any more than clinical diagnostic systems developed for adult psychopathology can provide a meaningful structure for understanding child psychopathology (chapter 2). Legal, social, diagnostic, forensic, and treatment systems developed for adults do not work for young offenders with mental disorders. Attempts to "fix" the criminal justice process so that it can better respond to adolescents with mental disorders probably would be a wasted effort.

The second alternative, therefore, is to abolish statutory exclusion laws, providing for transfers to criminal court only by juvenile court discretion based on evidence provided at judicial transfer hearings. This would offer the best review of cases to determine those in which treatment for mental disorders in the juvenile justice system, rather than incarceration in adult prisons, might best serve the public's long-range safety interest, as well as those cases in which patterns of development suggest little benefit of continued care by the juvenile justice system.

This proposal would meet with substantial resistance from those who argue that statutory exclusion is an important tool in dealing with juvenile crime. Moreover, an argument can be made for retention of statutory exclusion laws by asserting that intentions to abolish it in the interests of youths with mental disorders are bogus. The sentiment against statutory exclusion presumes that those persons retained in the juvenile justice system for treatment to reduce the risk of future aggression will actually receive that treatment, and that the treatment they receive will have known efficacy. As matters stand today, few if any juvenile courts can make that claim. Better solutions for ensuring public safety through treatment of young offenders with mental disorders will first require that the system live up to the proposed custodial treatment mandate.

Unanswered Questions for Policy and Research

The juvenile justice system's public safety obligation raises some of the most pressing and difficult questions one encounters when addressing the problems associated with young offenders and their mental disorders. A few of the more salient issues include (a) the need for research to provide information relevant to public safety decisions about young offenders with mental disorders, (b) the need to resolve a conflict between the objectives of short-range and long-range public safety, and (c) the absence in the juvenile justice system of an adequate response to young offenders with chronic and persistent mental disorders.

Research to Improve Decisionmaking about Risk of Harm

Cautions about what we do not know regarding the relation of mental disorders and future aggression among adolescents have been offered at every turn in this chapter. Glancing back over the section in chapter 4 that explores issues related to the public safety context will bring into focus a host of unanswered questions in this area that require attention by researchers. Among these, a few are especially pressing in light of the juvenile justice system's policy and practice needs:

- *Developing Risk Assessment Tools and Strategies.* Clinicians are greatly in need of empirically validated measures and strategies for assessing risk of future aggression among youths. Prototypes are now available (e.g., EARL-20B and SAVRY: see chapter 3), and current research to develop their validity should also provide new information on the relation between mental disorders and future aggression among young offenders.

- *"Pathway" Research on Aggression and Mental Disorders.* Some of the most important studies of delinquency in the past ten years have investigated developmental pathways to persistent delinquency and to desistance in aggression during the transition from adolescence to adulthood (chapter 4). Parallel to these studies, the field of developmental psychopathology has increased its investigation of continuity and discontinuity in the development and course of various types of mental disorders in children and adolescents. The field needs a marriage of these two strands of research, examining the developmental trajectories of aggressive behavior in the context of the development of mental disorders (not merely Conduct Disorder and ADHD) across childhood and adolescence.
- *Variations in Principles for Girls and Ethnic Minorities.* Research on adolescents' mental disorders and aggression must address the relative lack of information on variations in general principles associated with gender and ethnicity. There is a small but growing literature for girls, but separate data for various ethnic minority groups in juvenile justice settings is more the exception than routine practice.
- *Discovering Whether Treatment Matters.* This chapter frequently acknowledges that policy and practice regarding public safety are difficult to determine in the absence of actual evidence that treating young offenders' mental disorders alters their long-range trajectory—for example, reduces the likelihood that their aggression would continue into adulthood. Addressing this question is an ambitious research undertaking, but it is necessary if we ever want to advance the ultimate public-safety justification for providing treatment to young and aggressive offenders with mental disorders.

The research that we need most urgently often requires the most time to carry out. Such is the case here, but it is some consolation that studies have already begun in each of these areas.

A Conflict between Short-Range and Long-Range Obligations

There are a number of difficult policy issues to resolve if juvenile court dispositions are to make available worthwhile treatment for adolescents' mental disorders in the interest of reducing future aggression. One of these issues deserves special discussion, because it is created by a conflict between two obligations that are both part of the public safety mandate.

The juvenile justice system has an obligation to identify youths who need secure residential placement to protect the public. Having identified the risk and the disorder in a particular case, the system also has an obligation to make available treatment that will reduce the risk of aggression when the youth is released from secure custody. Yet satisfying one of these obligations often frustrates the system's ability to satisfy the other. The secure facility that is required often will not be the best place for the youth to receive the treatment that is required. Psychopharmacological treatments, as well as some individual and peer group methods, can be employed in secure facilities. But as noted in chapter 4, the known efficacy of treatments for young offenders is almost in inverse relation to their capacity to be administered in secure youth authority programs. The two most promising treatments, Functional Family Therapy and Multisystemic Therapy, both require intervention with the youth in conjunction with entities—the family, and the community—to which youths in secure facilities typically have little or no access. The latest authoritative reviews aimed at maximizing the system's ability to reduce future aggression among high-risk delinquent youths clearly point to community interventions (e.g., Borum, 2003a).

There is little that can be done about this dilemma if the public truly needs to be protected from the immediate risk of violent behavior. But "truly needs to be protected" may be the key to reducing the weight of the dilemma. Given that the most efficacious treatments for reducing aggression related to mental disorders must be implemented outside secure facilities, might the system be obligated to avoid secure incarceration of youths with mental disorders whenever possible?

How could this be done? One way is to employ a realistic and responsible threshold for risk in discretionary decisions about secure placement. There will always be some whose risk of harm to others is so great that it cannot be tolerated without secure placement. There are others, however, for whom the risk is modest, vague, or questionable, yet who are sent to secure placements simply because it is "safer" for the immediate future. Erring on the side of safety cannot be faulted. But it can be challenged when there are competing social interests in reducing medium-range and longer-range risks. *The advantage of efficacious community-based treatment to reduce later risk might outweigh incarcerating youths in order to err on the side of caution, in cases involving ambiguous or only moderate risk.* Moreover, the fact that a youth might be receiving a treatment such as Multisystemic Therapy reduces the immediate risk because of the high degree of structure and support provided by this form of treatment.

A second way to deal with the dilemma is to ensure that youths placed in secure facilities do not remain there longer than is necessary to reduce risk sufficiently to warrant community reentry. This requires a twist in policy perspective for some juvenile justice programs. Typically community release is predicated on evidence that a youth has been "rehabilitated" or "successfully treated." The policy perspective I propose here is that community release should sometimes occur when risk has been sufficiently lowered to *begin* the system's primary intervention—occurring after the youth's release—to reduce middle- and long-range risk.

This perspective, of course, flies in the face of determinate sentences, just deserts, and "holding kids responsible." That is a conflict with which the system should struggle. It was a rather one-sided argument when everyone knew that "nothing" was the answer to questions about what worked in the treatment of aggressive behaviors, and "very little" described what was known about the value of treatments for mental disorders among youths. These circumstances have somewhat improved (chapter 4). It is time to talk about modifying sentencing policies that deprive youths of community-based treatments that might better serve the public safety mandate.

For those who would take up this struggle, be forewarned that your armor is thin and your swords are not yet well honed. When arguing for discretionary and often "early" release from secure facilities in order to allow community treatment of mental disorders, here are some of the thrusts that you will have to parry:

- "So, in your system, when two boys rob a woman at gunpoint, the one who has a mental disorder would do less hard time?"
- "Does the victim of an assault by a neighborhood boy feel more safe knowing that the boy—who's next door again getting his community-based Multisystemic Therapy—might be less harmful in a year or two?"
- "Since mental disorders are more frequent among white than minority kids in juvenile secure facilities, doesn't your proposal mean that white kids will tend to get community treatment while black kids will more often be locked up?"
- "Do you remember *why* the juvenile justice system turned to determinate sentencing in the 1980s? It was because juvenile *advocates* thought it was better than the inconsistent, biased discretion of courts whose dis-

position decisions often resulted in disproportionately long confinement for minorities. How will you protect against abuses of discretion when the system is deciding who will be released for community treatment and who will not?"

- "That book, *Double Jeopardy*, says it over and over again—things related to development in childhood and adolescence make diagnoses and risk estimates far more difficult in young offender cases than in adult cases. Given that state of the art, how are you going to weigh the costs of potential misdiagnoses and miscalculations of risk against the potential value of the treatment that will be provided?"

These questions are not unanswerable, but they deserve more than a superficial, ideological response. They represent real and important problems that need to be resolved regarding the risks the system can take in moving toward better community-based treatment for young offenders with mental disorders.

A Basis for Collaboration

Surfacing from time to time throughout this book has been a group of youths that constitute an important but relatively small minority within the juvenile justice system. They are the "seriously emotionally disturbed"—SED youths with chronic, persistent, and multiple mental disorders who constitute a small proportion of the consumers of public mental health services but who consume an extraordinary proportion of its resources. As described by Davis and Vander Stoep (1997), their mental health needs are extreme and continue through their adolescent years into adulthood. They experience episodic, acute distress periodically, often in response to stressful life circumstances that push them beyond their fragile capacities to cope. In those moments, if their reaction includes aggressive behavior, their destination—a psychiatric or a correctional facility—often will depend on a police officer's interpretation of the momentary act as "crazy" or criminal.

When SED youths arrive at detention centers or juvenile correctional facilities, staff typically feel ill-equipped to deal with the depth and complexity of their disorders and their degree of functional impairment. Their occasional acute episodes of disorder while in detention or secure corrections often require their repeated transportation to inpatient mental health units, where they are treated for a few days until their episode begins to subside, allowing them to be returned to the juvenile justice facility.

Eventually they return to the community for some period of time, where the juvenile justice system again places them in the hands of community mental health programs that often feel ill-equipped to deal with their needs. For example, in most communities, acceptance of mental health services is voluntary. Individuals may not be coerced into taking medications that stabilize their conditions or engaging in psychosocial therapies. Given many SED youths' limited capacities to recognize their own needs, together with motivations that are driven by "normal" adolescent impulses and oppositional tendencies and, too often, with parents who fail to guide them, often these youths avail themselves of mental health services inconsistently or lose touch with them altogether. When SED youths with serious problems with aggression require psychiatric hospitalization, often their behaviors stretch the capacities of hospital staff to ensure the safety of others in the unit.

The needs and behaviors of many SED youths are such that they belong to both the mental health and the juvenile justice system. But neither system is equipped to provide what they need in order to manage their disorders and protect them and society from their occasionally dangerous behaviors. The irony of this situation is that both systems embody some of the parts that are needed for effective functioning. Broken as it is in some communities, the child public health system is the primary mechanism for appropriate mental health services for youths. The juvenile justice system, in turn, has the legal authority to provide the structure that can ensure that SED youths with problems of aggression use those services in the consistent manner that is necessary for their welfare and public safety interests.

These objectives would best be served by collaboration on the parts of the two systems. By collaboration I mean a joint venture in which the systems share specially trained personnel and joint-agency funding for specific programs, targeting youths whose lives typically require the attention of both agencies (such as SED youths with frequent delinquent behaviors). An outpatient program of this type would use the legal authority of probation and the clinical skill of mental health professionals and child welfare managers to ensure continuity of care for the youths involved. Most states of moderate size would benefit also from a collaborative secure inpatient psychiatric unit, devoted exclusively to SED youths with frequent juvenile justice system involvement, and accessible from both the community and the juvenile justice system's detention and corrections facilities.

The notion of collaborative programs involving state mental health and juvenile justice agencies is not new (see Barnum & Keilitz, 1992; chapter 5). But it has been slow to develop, despite the recent emergence of models for mental health service delivery that try in part to overcome difficulties created by boundaries between various child public welfare agencies (for example, "wraparound" programs: Burchard, Bruns, & Burchard, 2002).

Collaborations that are less comprehensive than the type that I have suggested have begun to appear. For example, "treatment foster care" programs have experienced the values of close collaboration with juvenile probation officers "as team members . . . to provide a law enforcement presence," "assist in problem situations," and serve as "a backup if the youth becomes highly noncompliant" (Chamberlain, 2002, p. 132). Another example is offered by the new "juvenile mental health courts" (see discussion of "diversion" in chapter 5 in the section on crisis-related treatment; Arredondo et al., 2001), in which multidisciplinary teams of mental health professionals and attorneys fashion special dispositions for SED delinquent youths that integrate community mental health services and the juvenile court's public safety concerns. These descriptions of innovative, collaborative programs have the feel of the benefits that might accrue if mental health and juvenile justice systems engaged in limited, joint-agency ventures targeted for specific subsamples of youths that currently "belong" to both agencies.

Chapter 1 reviewed evidence for the substantial proportion of youths in juvenile justice custody meeting criteria for mental disorders, as well as recent calls for greater attention to their needs. It then posed the question "Are we calling for the juvenile justice system to become the nation's mental health system for troubled adolescents?" The answer throughout this volume is "no." But almost every obligation we have encountered has pointed to the need for the juvenile justice system to consider more effective collaborations with the child mental health system. And some conceptual tools to guide the invention of innovative policies and agency structures are available (e.g., Barnum & Kielitz, 1992; Friedman, 2003).

The most extreme collaboration, of course, would entail that the juvenile justice system lose its identity in a total restructuring of state agencies, creating one child welfare agency that responds to youths' mental health needs as well as their aggressive and other illegal behaviors. There are many reasons why this "ultimate" collaboration probably is not desirable. But cosmetic fixes at the other end of the spectrum weakly proposing "better communication between agencies" will fall far short of what is needed. Somewhere between these extremes are the creative collaborations that the two systems must develop if the juvenile justice system is ever to fulfill its public safety, adjudicative, and custodial treatment obligations to society and to young offenders with mental disorders.

References

Abramovitch, R., Peterson-Badali, J., & Rohan, M. (1995). Young people's understanding and assertion of their rights to silence and legal counsel. *Canadian Journal of Criminology, 37,* 1–18.

Achenbach, T. (1991a). *Manual for the Youth Self-Report and 1991 profile.* Burlington, VT: University of Vermont, Department of Psychiatry.

Achenbach, T. (1991b). *Manual for the Child Behavior Checklist/4-18 and 1991 profiles.* Burlington, VT: University of Vermont, Department of Psychiatry.

Achenbach, T. (1991c). *Manual for the Teacher's Report Form and 1991 profile.* Burlington, VT: University of Vermont, Department of Psychiatry.

Achenbach, T. (1993). *Empirically based taxonomy: How to use syndromes and profile types derived from the CHCL/4-18, TRF, and YSR.* Burlington, VT: University of Vermont, Department of Psychiatry.

Achenbach T. (1995). Diagnosis, assessment, and comorbidity in psychosocial treatment research. *Journal of Abnormal Psychology, 23,* 45–65.

Achenbach, T. (1999). The Child Behavior Checklist and related instruments. In M. Maruish (Ed.), *The use of psychological testing for treatment planning and outcomes assessment* (2nd ed., pp. 429–466). Mahwah, NJ: Lawrence Earlbaum.

Achenbach, T., & Edelbrock, C. (1984). Psychopathology of childhood. *Annual Review of Psychology, 35,* 227–256.

Achenbach, T., & Edelbrock, C. (1989). Diagnostic, taxonomic, and assessment issues. In T. Ollendick & M. Hersen (Eds.), *Handbook of child psychopathology* (pp. 53–73). New York: Plenum Press.

Achenbach, T., & McConaughy, S. (1997). *Empirically based assessment of child and adolescent psychopathology: Practical applications* (2nd ed.). Thousand Oaks, CA: Sage.

Albano, A., DiBartolo, P., Heimberg, R., & Barlow, D. (1995). Children and adolescents: Assessment and treatment. In R. Heimberg, M. Liebowitz, D. Hope, & F. Schneier (Eds.), *Social phobia: Diagnosis, assessment, and treatment* (pp. 387–425). New York: Guilford.

Alexander, J., Waldron, H., Newberry, A., & Liddle, N. (1988). Family approaches to treating delinquents. In E. Nunnally, C. Chilman, & F. Cox (Eds.), *Mental illness, delinquency, addictions, and neglect* (pp. 128–146). Newbury Park, CA: Sage.

American Academy of Child and Adolescent Psychiatry. (2001). Practice parameter for the assessment and treatment of children and adolescents with suicidal behavior. *Journal of the American Academy of Child and Adolescent Psychiatry, 40*, 24/S–51/S.

American Association for Correctional Psychology. (2000). Standards for psychological services in jails, prisons, correctional facilities, and agencies. *Criminal Justice and Behavior, 27*, 433–494.

American Bar Association. (1989). ABA *criminal justice mental health standards.* Washington, DC: American Bar Association.

American Bar Association. (2001). *Youth in the criminal justice system: Guidelines for policymakers and practitioners.* Washington, DC: ABA.

American Correctional Association. (1991). *Standards for juvenile detention facilities.* Lanham, MD.

American Law Institute. (1962). *Model penal code.* Washington, DC: ALI.

American Psychiatric Association. (1994). *Diagnostic and statistical manual of mental disorders* (4th ed.). Washington, DC: American Psychiatric Association.

Anastasi, A. (1988). *Psychological testing* (6th ed.). New York: Macmillan.

Angold, A., & Costello, E. (1993). Depressive comorbidity in children and adolescents: Empirical, theoretical, and methodological issues. *American Journal of Psychiatry, 150*, 1779–1791.

Angold, A., Costello, E., & Erkanli, A. (1999). Comorbidity. *Journal of Child Psychology and Psychiatry, 40*, 57–87.

Angold, A., Costello, E., Farmer, E., Burns, B., & Erkanli, A. (1999). Impaired but undiagnosed. *Journal of the American Academy of Child and Adolescent Psychiatry, 38*, 129–137.

Angold, A., Erkanli, A., Farmer, E., Fairbank, J., Burns, B., Keeler, G., & Costello, E. (2002). Psychiatric disorder, impairment, and service use in rural African American and white youth. *Archives of General Psychiatry, 59*, 893–901.

Angold, A., Weissman, J., John, K., Merikangas, K., Prusoff, B., & Wickramaratne, P. (1987). Parent and child reports of depressive symptoms in children at low and high risk for depression. *Journal of Child Psychology and Psychiatry, 28,* 901–915.

Appelbaum, P., & Grisso, T. (1988). Assessing patients' capacities to consent to treatment. *New England Journal of Medicine, 319,* 1635–1638.

Appelbaum, P. S., & Grisso, T. (1995). The MacArthur Treatment Competence Study, I: Mental illness and competence to consent to treatment. *Law and Human Behavior, 19,* 105–126.

Archer, R. (1999). Overview of the Minnesota Multiphasic Personality Inventory—Adolescent (MMPI-A). In M. Maruish (Ed.), *The use of psychological testing for treatment planning and outcomes assessment* (2nd ed., pp. 341–380). Mahwah, NJ: Lawrence Earlbaum.

Arizona Daily Star (2000, November 13). "Mental Health Care: Too Many Teens, Too Few Beds: Financial Woes Have Forced Nearly All Long-Term Residential Facilities in Tucson to Close."

Arredondo, M., Kumli, J., Soto, L., Colin, E., Ornellas, J., Davilla, R., Edwards, L., & Hymn, E. (2001). Juvenile mental health court: Rationale and protocols. *Juvenile and Family Court Journal, 52,* 1–20.

Atkins, D., Pumariega, W., & Rogers, K. (1999). Mental health and incarcerated youth, I: Prevalence and nature of psychopathology. *Journal of Child and Family Studies, 8,* 193–204.

Augimeri, L., Koegl, C., Webster, C., & Levene, K. (2001). *Early Assessment Risk List for Boys (EARL-20B):* Version 2. Toronto, Canada: Earlscourt Child and Family Centre.

Barkley, R. (1996). Attention-Deficit/Hyperactivity disorder. In E. Mash & R. Barkley (Eds.), *Child psychopathology* (pp. 63–112). New York: Guilford.

Barkley, R. (1997). *Defiant children: A clinician's manual for assessment and parent training* (2nd ed.). New York: Guilford.

Barkley, R. (1990). *Attention-deficit hyperactivity disorder: A handbook for diagnosis and treatment.* New York: Guilford.

Barnum, R. (2000). Clinical and forensic evaluation of competence to stand trial in juvenile defendants. In T. Grisso & R. Schwartz (Eds.), *Youth on trial: A developmental perspective on juvenile justice* (pp. 193–224). Chicago: University of Chicago Press.

Barnum, R., & Keilitz, I. (1992). Issues in systems interactions affecting mentally disordered juvenile offenders. In J. Cocozza (Ed.), *Responding to the mental health needs of youth in the juvenile justice system* (pp. 49–87). Seattle, WA: National Coalition for the Mentally Ill in the Criminal Justice System.

Bates, M. (2001). The Child and Adolescent Functional Assessment Scale (CA-FAS): Review and current status. *Clinical Child and Family Psychology Review, 4,* 63–84.

Bazelon Center for Mental Health Law. (1993). *Federal definitions of children with emotional disorders.* Washington, DC: Bazelon Center for Mental Health Law.

Benedek, L., & Cornell, D. (Eds.). (1989). *Juvenile homicide.* Washington, DC: American Psychiatric Press.

Benthin, A., Slovic, P., & Severson, H. (1993). A psychometric study of adolescent risk perception. *Journal of Adolescence, 16,* 153–168.

Bickman, L. (1996). A continuum of care: More is not always better. *American Psychologist, 51,* 689–701.

Bickman, L., & Rog, D. (Eds.). (1995). *Creating a children's mental health service system: Policy, research and evaluation.* Beverly Hills, CA: Sage.

Biederman, J., Mick, E., Faraone, S., & Burback, M. (2001). Patterns of remission and symptom decline in conduct disorder: A four-year prospective study of an ADHD sample. *Journal of the American Academy of Child and Adolescent Psychiatry, 40,* 290–298.

Biederman, J., Newcorn, J., & Sprich, S. (1991). Comorbidity of attention deficit hyperactivity disorder with conduct, depressive, anxiety, and other disorders. *American Journal of Psychiatry, 148,* 564–577.

Biederman, J., & Spencer, T. (1999). Depressive disorders in childhood and adolescence: A clinical perspective. *Journal of Child and Adolescent Psychopharmacology, 9,* 233–237.

Bird, H., Canino, G., Rubio-Stipec, M., Gould, M., Ribera, J., Sesman, M., Woodbury, J., Huertas-Goldman, S., Pagan, A., Sanchez-Lacay, A., & Moscoso, M., (1988). Estimates of the prevalence of childhood maladjustment in a community survey of Puerto Rico: The use of combined measures. *Archives of General Psychiatry, 45,* 1120–1126.

Blumstein, A. (1995). Youth violence, guns, and the illicit drug industry. *Journal of Criminal Law and Criminology, 86,* 10–36.

Blumstein, A., & Wallman, J. (Eds.). (2000). *The crime drop in America.* Cambridge: Cambridge University Press.

Bonnie, R. (1992). The competence of criminal defendants: A theoretical reformulation. *Behavioral Sciences and the Law, 10,* 291–316.

Bonnie, R., & Grisso, T. (2000). Adjudicative competence and youthful offenders. In T. Grisso & R. Schwartz (Eds.), *Youth on trial: A developmental perspective on juvenile justice* (pp. 73–103). Chicago: University of Chicago Press.

Borduin, C., Mann, H., Cone, L., Hengeller, S., Fucci, B., Blaske, D., & Williams, R. (1995). Multisystemic treatment of serious juvenile offenders: Long-term prevention of criminality and violence. *Journal of Consulting and Clinical Psychology, 63,* 569–578.

Borum, R. (2000). Assessing violence risk among youth. *Journal of Clinical Psychology, 56,* 1263–1288.

Borum, R. (2003a). Managing at-risk juvenile offenders in the community. *Journal of Contemporary Criminal Justice, 19,* 114–137.

Borum, R. (2003b). Not guilty by reason of insanity. In T. Grisso, *Evaluating competencies: Forensic assessments and instruments* (2nd ed., pp. 193–227). New York: Kluwer Academic/Plenum Publishers.

Borum, R., Bartel, P., & Forth, A. (2002). *Manual for the Structured Assessment of Violence Risk in Youth (SAVRY): Version I, Consultation Edition.* Tampa, FL: Florida Mental Health Institute, University of South Florida. Online information available at http://www.fmhi.usf.edu/mhlp/savry/statement.htm.

Brady, K., Myrick, H., & McElroy, S. (1998). The relationship between substance use disorders, impulse control disorders, and pathological aggression. *American Journal on Addictions, 7,* 221–230.

Brandt, J., Kennedy, W., Patrick, C., & Curtin, J. (1997). Assessment of psychopathy in a population of incarcerated adolescent offenders. *Psychological Assessment, 9,* 429–435.

Broday, S., & Mason, J. (1991). Internal consistency of the Brief Symptom Inventory. *Psychological Reports, 68,* 94–101.

Burchard, J., Bruns, E., & Burchard, S. (2002). The wraparound approach. In B. Burns & K. Hoagwood (Eds.), *Community treatment for youth* (pp. 69–90). New York: Oxford University Press.

Burns, B. (1999). A call for a mental health services research agenda for youth with serious emotional disturbance. *Mental Health Services Research, 1,* 5–20.

Burns, B., & Hoagwood, K. (Eds.). (2002). *Community treatment for youth: Evidence-based interventions for severe emotional and behavioral disorders.* New York: Oxford University Press.

Burns, B., Hoagwood, K., & Mrazek, P. (1999). Effective treatment for mental disorders in children and adolescents. *Clinical Child and Family Psychology Review, 2,* 199–254.

Butcher, J., Williams, C., Graham, J., Archer, R., Tellegen, A., Ben-Porath, Y., & Kaemmer, B. (1992). *Minnesota Multiphasic Personality Inventory— Adolescent (MMPI-A): Manual for administration, scoring and interpretation.* Minneapolis, MN: University of Minnesota Press.

Campbell, M., Rapoport, J., & Simpson, G. (1999). Antipsychotics in children and adolescents. *Journal of the American Academy of Child and Adolescent Psychiatry, 38,* 537–545.

Canino, G., Costello, E., & Angold, A. (1999). Assessing functional impairment and social adaptation for child mental health services research: A review of measures. *Mental Health Services Research,* 1, 93–108.

Caron, C., & Rutter, M. (1991). Comorbidity in child psychopathology: Concepts, issues and research strategies. *Journal of Child Psychology and Psychiatry,* 32, 1063–1080.

Casey, H., Trainor, R., Orendi, J., Schubert, A., Nystrom, L., Giedd, J., Astellanos, F., Haxby, J., Noll, D., Cohen, J., Forman, S., Dahl, R., & Rapaport, J. (1997). A developmental functional MRI study of prefrontal activation during performance of a go-no-go task. *Journal of Cognitive Neuroscience,* 9, 835–847.

Cauffman, E. (2002, October). *Development and diagnosis: Developmental considerations for mentally ill juvenile offenders.* Paper presented at the annual meeting of the American Academy of Child & Adolescent Psychiatry, San Francisco, CA.

Cauffman, E., Feldman, S., Waterman, J., & Steiner, H. (1998). Posttraumatic stress disorder among female juvenile offenders. *Journal of the American Academy of Child and Adolescent Psychiatry,* 37, 1209–1216.

Cauffman, E., & Grisso, T. (in press). Mental health issues among minority offenders in the juvenile justice system. In D. Hawkins and K. Leonard (Eds.), *Our children, their children: Confronting race and ethnic differences in American criminal justice.* Chicago: University of Chicago Press.

Cauffman, E., & MacIntosh, R. (in press). The measurement validity of the Massachusetts Youth Screening Instrument (MAYSI-2): An assessment of race and gender item bias among juvenile offenders. *Journal of Personality and Social Psychology.*

Cauffman, E., & Steinberg, L. (2000). (Im)maturity of judgment in adolescence: Why adolescents may be less culpable than adults. *Behavioral Sciences & the Law,* 18, 741–760.

Center for the Study and Prevention of Violence. (2002). *Blueprints for Violence Prevention: Blueprints model programs overview.* Boulder, CO: University of Colorado. Available at http://www.colorado.edu/cspv/blueprints.html.

Center for Substance Abuse Treatment. (1999). *Screening and assessing adolescents for substance use disorders.* Rockville, MD: Substance Abuse Mental Health Services Administration.

Centers for Disease Control and Prevention. (1998). *Youth risk behavior surveil-*

lance—United States, 1997. CDC Surveillance Summaries, August 14, 1998.

Centers for Disease Control and Prevention. (1999). *Suicide deaths and rates per* 100,000. Available at http://www.cdc.gov/ncipc/data/us9794/suic/htm.

Chamberlain, P. (2002). Treatment foster care. In B. Burns & K. Hoagwood (Eds.), *Community treatment for youth* (pp. 117–138). New York: Oxford University Press.

Charney, D., Deutch, A., Krystal, J., Southwick, S., & Davis, M. (1993). Psychobiological mechanisms of posttraumatic stress disorder. *Archives of General Psychiatry,* 50, 294–305.

Christian, R., Frick, P., Hill, N., Tyler, L., & Frazer, D. (1997). Psychopathy and conduct problems in children: II. Subtyping children with conduct problems based on their interpersonal and affective style. *Journal of the American Academy of Child and Adolescent Psychiatry,* 36, 233–241.

Cicchetti, D. (1984). The emergence of developmental psychopathology. *Child Development,* 55, 1–7.

Cicchetti, D. (1990). An historical perspective on the discipline of developmental psychopathology. In J. Rolf, A. Master, D. Cicchetti, K. Nuechterlien, & S. Weintraub (Eds.), *Risk and protective factors in the development of psychopathology* (pp. 2–28). New York: Cambridge University Press.

Cicchetti, D., & Cohen, D. (1995). *Developmental psychopathology.* New York: Wiley.

Cicchetti, D., & Rogosch, F. (2002). A developmental psychopathology perspective on adolescence. *Journal of Consulting and Clinical Psychology,* 70, 6–20.

Cirincione, C., Steadman, H., & McGreevy, M. (1995). Rates of insanity acquittals and the factors associated with successful insanity please. *Bulletin of the American Academy of Psychiatry and Law,* 23, 399–409.

Clarke, G., Rohde, P., Lewinson, P., Hops, H., & Seeley, J. (1999). Cognitive-behavioral treatment of adolescent depression: Efficacy of acute group treatment and booster sessions. *Journal of the American Academy of Child and Adolescent Psychiatry,* 38, 272–279.

Cocozza, J. (Ed.). (1992). *Responding to the mental health needs of youth in the juvenile justice system.* Seattle, WA: National Coalition for the Mentally Ill in the Criminal Justice System.

Cocozza, J., & Skowyra, K. (2000). Youth with mental health disorders: Issues and emerging responses. *Juvenile Justice Journal,* 8(1), Washington, DC: U.S. Department of Justice, Office of Justice Programs, Office of Juvenile Justice and Delinquency Prevention.

Cocozza, J., & Skowyra, K. (Eds.) (in press). *Mental health needs of juvenile offenders: A comprehensive review.* Washington, DC: U.S. Department of Justice, Office of Justice Programs, Office of Juvenile Justice and Delinquency Prevention.

Cohen, P., Cohen, J., & Brook, J. (1993). An epidemiological study of disorders in late childhood and adolescence: II. Persistence of disorders. *Journal of Child Psychology and Psychiatry,* 34, 869–877.

Columbus Dispatch (2001, April 8). "Broken System: Latest Closing Weakens an Overwhelmed Mental Health Network" (reporting the closing of adolescent and children's psychiatric care at Riverside Methodist Hospitals).

Columbus Dispatch (2002, July 28). "Families Face Torturous Trade-off: Parents Give Up Children to Ensure Treatment for Mental Illnesses."

Connor, D. (2002). *Aggression and antisocial behavior in children and adolescents: Research and treatment.* New York: Guilford.

Connor, D., Glatt, S., Lopez, I., Jackson, D., & Melloni, R. (2002). Psychopharmacology and aggression. I: A meta-analysis of stimulant effects on overt/covert aggression-related behaviors in ADHD. *Journal of the American Academy of Child and Adolescent Psychiatry,* 41, 253–261.

Costello, E., Angold, A., Burns, H., Stangle, D., Tweed, D., Erkanli, A., & Worthman, C. (1996). The Great Smoky Mountains Study of Youth: Goals, design, methods and the prevalence of DSM-III-R disorders. *Archives of General Psychiatry,* 53, 1129–1136.

Council of Juvenile Correctional Administrators. (2001). *Performance-based standards for juvenile correction and detention facilities.* Available at http://www.performance.standards.org.

Council of State Governments. (2002). *Criminal justice/mental health consensus project.* Washington, DC: Council of State Governments

Cowden, V., & McKee, G. (1995). Competency to stand trial in juvenile delinquency proceedings: Cognitive maturity and the attorney-client relationship. *Journal of Family Law,* 33, 629–660.

Davis, M., & Vander Stoep, A. (1997). The transition to adulthood for youth who have serious emotional disturbance: Developmental transition and young adult outcomes. *Journal of Mental Health Administration,* 24, 400–427.

Dawson, R. (2000). Judicial waiver in theory and practice. In J. Fagan & F. Zimring (Eds.), *The changing borders of juvenile justice: Transfer of adolescents to the criminal court* (pp. 45–81). Chicago: University of Chicago Press.

Dembo, R., Schmeidler, J., Borden, P., Turner, G., Sue, C., & Manning, D. (1996). Examination of the reliability of the Problem Oriented Screening

Instrument for Teenagers (POSIT) among arrested youths entering a juvenile assessment center. *Substance Use and Misuse,* 31, 785–824.

Dembo, R., Schmeidler, J., Sue, C., Borden, P., Manning, D., & Rollie, M. (1998). Psychosocial, substance use, and delinquency differences among Anglo, Hispanic White, and African-American male youths entering a juvenile assessment center. *Substance Use and Misuse,* 33, 1481–1510.

Derogatis, L. (1993). *Brief Symptom Inventory: Administration, scoring and procedures manual.* Minneapolis, MN: National Computer Systems.

Derogatis, L., & Melisaratos, N. (1983). The Brief Symptom Inventory: An introductory report. *Psychological Medicine,* 13, 595–605.

DiIulio, J. (1995, November 27). The coming of the super-predators. *Weekly Standard,* p. 23.

Dishion, T., McCord, J., & Poulin, F. (1999). When interventions harm: Peer groups and problem behavior. *American Psychologist,* 54, 755–764.

Drizin, S. (2003). The problem of false confessions in Illinois: A report of the Northwestern University Legal Clinic's Children and Family Justice Center. Available at http://www.law.nwu.edu/depts/clinic/news/index.htm.

Durlak, J., Furman, T., & Lampman, C. (1991). Effectiveness of cognitive-behavior therapy for maladapting children: A meta-analysis. *Psychological Bulletin,* 110, 204 –214.

Edens, J., Skeem, J., Cruise, K., & Cauffman, E. (2001). Assessment of "juvenile psychopathy" and its association with violence: A critical review. *Behavioral Sciences and the Law,* 19, 53–80.

Elia, J., Borcherding, B., Rapoport, J., & Keysor, C. (1991). Methylphenidate and dextroamphetamine treatments of hyperactivity: Are there true responders? *Psychiatry Research,* 36, 141–155.

Elliott, D. (1994). Serious, violent offenders: Onset, developmental course, and termination—The American Society of Criminology 1993 Presidential Address. *Criminology,* 32, 1–21.

Elliott, D., Huizinga, D., & Morse, B. (1986). Self-reported violent offending. *Journal of Interpersonal Violence,* 1, 472–514.

Emslie, G., Walkup, J., Pliszka, S., & Ernst, M. (1999). Nontricyclic antidepressants: Current trends in children and adolescents. *Journal of the American Academy of Child and Adolescent Psychiatry,* 38, 517–528.

Faenza, M., Siegfried, C., & Wood, J. (2000). *Community perspectives: On the mental health and substance abuse treatment needs of youth involved in the juvenile justice system.* Washington DC: National Mental Health Association and Office of Juvenile Justice and Delinquency Prevention.

Fagan, J., & Zimring, F. (eds.) (2000). *The changing borders of juvenile justice.* Chicago: University of Chicago Press.

Feld, B. (2000). Juveniles' waiver of legal rights: Confessions, *Miranda,* and the right to counsel. In T. Grisso & R. Schwartz (Eds.), *Youth on trial: A developmental perspective on juvenile justice* (pp. 105–138). Chicago: University of Chicago Press.

Ferris, C., & Grisso, T. (Eds.). (1996). *Understanding aggressive behavior in children.* New York: New York Academy of Sciences.

Finkel, N. (1988). *Insanity on trial.* New York: Plenum.

Fischer, M., Barkley, R., Fletcher, K., & Smallish, L. (1993). The stability of dimensions of behavior in ADHD and normal children over an 8-year follow-up. *Journal of Abnormal Child Psychology, 21,* 315–337.

Fletcher, K. (1996). Childhood posttraumatic stress disorder. In E. Mash & R. Barkley (Eds.), *Child psychopathology* (pp. 242–276). New York: Guilford.

Fombonne, E. (1998). Increased rates of psychosocial disorders in youth. *European Archives of Psychiatry and Clinical Neuroscience, 248,* 14–21.

Forbey, J., & Ben-Porath, Y. (2001). Minnesota Multiphasic Personality Inventory—Adolescent (MMPI-A). In W. Dorfman & M. Hersen (Eds.), *Understanding psychological assessment* (pp. 313–334). New York: Kluwer Academic/Plenum.

Forth, A., Hart, S., & Hare, R. (1990). Assessment of psychopathy in male young offenders. *Psychological Assessment, 2,* 342–344.

Forth, A., Kosson, D., & Hare, R. (1997). *The Hare Psychopathy Checklist: Youth Version (PCL-YV)—Rating Guide.* Toronto, Ontario: Multi-Health Systems.

Foster, J., Eskes, G., & Stuss, D. (1994). The cognitive neuropsychology of attention: A frontal lobe perspective. *Cognitive Neuropsychology, 11,* 133–147.

Fox, J. (1996). *Trends in juvenile violence: A report to the United States Attorney General on current and future rates of juvenile offending.* Boston: Northeastern University Press.

Frick, P. (1998). *Conduct disorders and severe antisocial behavior.* New York: Plenum.

Frick, P., O'Brien, B., Wootton, J., & McBurnett, K. (1994). Psychopathy and conduct problems in children. *Journal of Abnormal Psychology, 103,* 700–707.

Friedman, R. (2003). A conceptual framework for developing and implementing effective policy in children's mental health. *Journal of Emotional and Behavioral Disorders, 11,* 11–18.

Friedman, R., Katz-Levy, J., Manderscheid, R., & Sondheimer, D. (1996). Prevalence of serious emotional disturbance in children and adolescents.

In R. Manderscheid & M. Sonnenschein (Eds.), *Mental health in the United States* (pp. 71–89). Rockville, MD: U.S. Department of Health and Human Services.

Frumkin, H. (2000). Competency to waive *Miranda* rights: Clinical and legal issues. *Mental and Physical Disability Law Reporter*, 24, 326–331.

Fulero, S., & Everington, C. (1995). Assessing competence to waive *Miranda* rights in defendants with mental retardation. *Law and Human Behavior*, 19, 533–543.

Furby, L., & Beyth-Marom, R. (1990). *Risk taking in adolescence: A decision-making perspective.* Washington, DC: Office of Technology Assessment.

Garland, A., Hough, R., McCabe, K., Yeh, M., Wood, P., & Aarons, G. (2001). Prevalence of psychiatric disorders in youths across five sectors of care. *Journal of the American Academy of Child and Adolescent Psychiatry*, 40, 409–418.

Geller, H., Reising, D., Leonard, H., Riddle, M., & Walsh, B. (1999). Critical review of tricyclic antidepressant use in children and adolescents. *Journal of the American Academy of Child and Adolescent Psychiatry*, 38, 513–516.

Giancolo, P., Martin, C., Tarter, R., Pelham, W., & Moss, H. (1996). Executive cognitive functioning and aggressive behavior in preadolescent boys at high risk for substance abuse/dependence. *Journal of Studies on Alcohol*, 57, 352–359.

Giedd, J., Blumenthal, J., Jeffries, N., Castellanos, F., Liu, H., Zikdenbos, A., Paus, T., Evans, A., & Rapaport, J. (1999). Brain development during childhood and adolescence: A longitudinal MRI study. *Nature Neuroscience*, 2, 861–863.

Gittelman, R., Abikoff, H., Pollack, E., Klein, D., Katz, S., & Mattes, J. (1980). A controlled trial of behavior modification and metholphenidate in hyperactive children. In C. Whalen & B. Henker (Eds.), *Hyperactive children: The social ecology of identification and treatment* (pp. 221–243). New York: Academic Press.

Goodyer, I., & Cooper, P. (1993). A community study of depression in adolescent girls: II. The clinical features of identified disorder. *British Journal of Psychiatry*, 163, 374–380.

Greene, A. (1986). Future-time perspective in adolescence: The present of things future revisited. *Journal of Youth and Adolescence*, 15, 99–113.

Greenhill, L., Halperin, J., & Abikoff, H. (1999). Stimulant medications. *Journal of the American Academy of Child and Adolescent Psychiatry*, 38, 503–512.

Greenwood, P. (1996). Responding to juvenile crime: Lessons learned. *Juvenile Court*, 6, 75–85.

Grills, A., & Ollendick, T. (2002). Issues in parent-child agreement: The case of structured diagnostic interviews. *Clinical Child and Family Psychology Review, 5,* 57–83.

Grisso, T. (1981). *Juveniles' waiver of rights: Legal and psychological competence.* New York: Plenum.

Grisso, T. (1996). Society's retributive response to juvenile violence: A developmental perspective. *Law and Human Behavior, 20,* 229–247.

Grisso, T. (1997). The competence of adolescents as trial defendants. *Psychology, Public Policy, and Law, 3,* 3–32.

Grisso, T. (1998). *Forensic evaluation of juveniles.* Sarasota, FL: Professional Resource Press.

Grisso, T. (2000a). Forensic clinical evaluations related to waiver of jurisdiction. In J. Fagan & F. Zimring (Eds.), *The changing borders of juvenile justice* (pp. 321–352). Chicago: University of Chicago Press.

Grisso, T. (2000b). What we know about youths' capacities as trial defendants. In T. Grisso & R. Schwartz (Eds.), *Youth on trial: A developmental perspective on juvenile justice* (pp. 139–172). Chicago: University of Chicago Press.

Grisso, T. (2003). *Evaluating competencies: Forensic assessments and instruments* (2nd ed.). New York: Kluwer Academic/Plenum Press.

Grisso, T., & Barnum, R. (2003). *Massachusetts Youth Screening Instrument— Second Version: User's manual and technical report.* Sarasota, FL: Professional Resource Press. For information online, see http://www. umassmed.edu/nysap.

Grisso, T., Barnum, R., Fletcher, K., Cauffman, E., & Peuschold, D. (2001). Massachusetts Youth Screening Instrument for mental health needs of juvenile justice youths. *Journal of the American Academy of Child and Adolescent Psychiatry, 40,* 541–548.

Grisso, T., Miller, M., & Sales, B. (1987). Competency to stand trial in juvenile court. *International Journal of Law and Psychiatry, 10,* 1–20.

Grisso, T., Quinlan, J., & Vincent, G. (2003). *Organization, structure and functions of juvenile court forensic evaluation services: A national survey.* Worcester, MA: University of Massachusetts Medical School.

Grisso, T., Steinberg, L., Woolard, J., Cauffman, E., Scott, E., Graham, S., Lexcen, F., Reppucci, N., & Schwartz, R. (2003). Juveniles' competence to stand trial: A comparison of adolescents' and adults' capacities as trial defendants. *Law and Human Behavior, 27,* 333–363.

Grisso, T., & Schwartz, R. (Eds.). (2000). *Youth on trial: A developmental perspective on juvenile justice.* Chicago: University of Chicago Press.

Grisso, T., Tomkins, A., & Casey, P. (1988). Psychosocial concepts in juvenile law. *Law and Human Behavior, 12,* 403–437.

Grisso, T., & Underwood, L. (in press). *Screening and assessing mental health and substance use disorders among youth in the juvenile justice system: A resource guide for practitioners.* Washington, DC: Office of Juvenile Justice and Delinquency Prevention.

Gudjonsson, G. (1992). *The psychology of interrogations, confessions and testimony.* London: Wiley.

Gutheil, T., & Appelbaum, P. (2000). *Clinical handbook of psychiatry and the law* (3rd ed.). Baltimore: Williams and Wilkins.

Haapasalo, J., & Tremblay, R. (1994). Physically aggressive boys from age 6 to 12: Family background, parenting behavior, and prediction of delinquency. *Journal of Consulting and Clinical Psychology, 62,* 1044–1052.

Hammen, C., & Rudolph, K. (1996). Childhood depression. In E. Mash & R. Barkley (Eds.), *Child psychopathology* (pp. 153–195). New York: Guilford.

Hare, R. (1999). Psychopathy as a risk factor for violence. *Psychiatric Quarterly, 70,* 181–197.

Hart, S., & Hare, R. (1997). Psychopathy: Assessment and association with criminal conduct. In D. Stoff, J. Breiling & J. Maser (Eds.), *Handbook of antisocial behavior* (pp. 22–35). New York: Wiley.

Hart, S., Watt, K., & Vincent, G. (2002). Commentary on Seagrave and Grisso: Impressions of the state of the art. *Law and Human Behavior, 26,* 241–245.

Hawkins, D., Laub, J., & Lauritsen, J. (1998). Race, ethnicity, and serious juvenile offending. In R. Loeber & D. Farrington (Eds.), *Serious and violent juvenile offenders* (pp. 30–46). Thousand Oaks, CA: Sage.

Hayes, L. (1999), *Suicide prevention in juvenile correction and detention facilities: A resource guide for performance-based standards for juvenile correction and detention facilities.* Washington, DC: Council of Juvenile Correctional Administrators.

Henggeler, S., Melton, G., & Smith, L. (1992). Family preservation using multisystemic therapy: An effective alternative to incarcerating serious juvenile offenders. *Journal of Consulting and Clinical Psychology, 60,* 953–961.

Henggeler, S., Melton, G., Smith, L., Schoenwald, S., & Hanley, J. (1993). Family preservation using multisystemic treatment: Long-term followup to a clinical trial with serious juvenile offenders. *Journal of Child and Family Studies, 4,* 283–293.

Henggeler, S., Pickrel, S., & Brondino, J. (2000). Multisystemic treatment of substance- abusing and -dependent delinquents: Outcomes, treatment fidelity, and transportability. *Mental health Services Research, 1,* 171–184.

Henggeler, S., Rodick, J., Bordoin, C., Hanson, C., Watson, S., & Urey, J. (1986). Multisystemic treatment of juvenile offenders: Effects on adolescent behavior and family interaction. *Developmental Psychology*, 22, 132–141.

Herjanic, B., & Reich, W. (1983). *Diagnostic Interview for Children and Adolescents: Child version.* St. Louis, MO: Washington University School of Medicine.

Herjanic, H., & Campbell, W. (1977). Differentiating psychiatrically disturbed children on the basis of a structured interview. *Journal of Abnormal Child Psychology*, 5, 127–134.

Hinden, B. R., Compas, B. E., Achenbach, T. M. & Howell, D. (1997). Covariation of the anxious/depressed syndrome: Separating fact from artifact. *Journal of Consulting and Clinical Psychology*, 65, 6–14.

Hinshaw, S., & Anderson, C. (1996). Conduct and oppositional defiant disorders. In E. Mash & R. Barkley (Eds.), *Child psychopathology* (pp. 113–149). New York: Guilford.

Hoagwood, K., Hibbs, E., Brent, D., & Jensen, P. (1995). Introduction to the special section: Efficacy and effectiveness in studies of child and adolescent psychotherapy. *Journal of Consulting and Clinical Psychology*, 63, 683–687.

Hodges, K. (1997). *CAFAS manual for training coordinators, clinical administrators, and data managers.* Ann Arbor, MI: Author.

Hodges, K. (1999). Child and Adolescent Functional Assessment Scale (CAFAS). In M. Maruish (Ed.), *The use of psychological testing for treatment planning and outcomes assessment* (2nd ed., pp. 631–664). Mahwah, NJ: Lawrence Earlbaum.

Hodges, K., & Wong, M. (1996). Psychometric characteristics of a multidimensional measure to assess impairment: The Child and Adolescent Functional Assessment Scale. *Journal of Child and Family Studies*, 5, 445–467.

Hoge, R., & Andrews, D. (1996). *Assessing the youthful offender.* New York: Plenum.

Hoge, S., Bonnie, R., Poythress, N., & Monahan, J. (1992). Attorney-client decision making in criminal cases: Client competence and participation as perceived by their attorneys. *Behavioral Sciences and the Law*, 10, 385–394.

Hollinger, P., Offer, D., Barter, J., & Bell, C. (1994). *Suicide and homicide among adolescents.* New York: Guilford.

Huey, W., & Rank, R. (1994). Effects of counselor and peer-led group assertiveness training on black adolescent aggression. *Journal of Counseling Psychology*, 31, 95–98.

Hughes, J., La Greca, A., & Conoley, J. (Eds.). (2001). *Handbook of psychologi-*

cal services for children and adolescents. New York: Oxford University Press.

Huizinga, D. (1995). Developmental sequences in delinquency. In L. Crockett & N. Crowder (Eds.), *Pathways through adolescence: Individual development in context* (pp. 15–34). Hillsdale, NJ: Lawrence Erlbaum Associates.

Huizinga, D., & Jakob-Chien, C. (1998). The contemporaneous co-occurrence of serious and violent juvenile offending and other problem behaviors. In R. Loeber & D. Farrington (Eds.), *Serious and violent juvenile offenders: Risk factors and successful interventions* (pp. 47–67). Thousand Oaks, CA: Sage Publications.

Huizinga, D., Loeber, R., Thornberry, T., & Cothern, L. (2000). *Co-occurrence of delinquency and other problem behaviors.* Washington, DC: Office of Juvenile Justice and Delinquency Prevention.

Huttenlocher, P. (1990). Morphometric study of human cerebral cortex development. *Neuropsychologia, 28,* 517–527.

Inamdar, S., Lewis, D., Siomopoulos, G., Shanok, S., & Lamela, M. (1982). Violent and suicidal behavior in psychotic adolescents. *American Journal of Psychiatry, 139,* 932–935.

Ingram, R., & Price, J. (Eds.). (2001). *Vulnerability to psychopathology: Risk across the lifespan.* New York: Guilford.

Isaacs, M. (1992). Assessing the mental health needs of children and adolescents of color in the juvenile justice system: Overcoming institutionalized perceptions and barriers. In J. Cocozza (Ed.), *Responding to the mental health needs of youth in the juvenile justice system* (pp. 143–163). Seattle, WA: National Coalition for the Mentally Ill in the Criminal Justice System.

Jarvis, T., Tebbutt, J., & Mattick, R. (1995). *Treatment approaches for alcohol and drug dependence: An introductory guide.* Chichester, UK: Wiley.

Jemelka, R., Rahman, S., & Trupin, E. (1993). Prison mental health: An overview. In H. Steadman & J. Cocozza (Eds.), *Mental illness in America's prisons.* Seattle, WA: National Coalition of the Mentally Ill in the Criminal Justice System.

Jensen, P., & Watanabe, H. (1999). Sherlock Holmes and child psychopathology assessment approaches: The case of the false-positive. *Journal of the American Academy of Child and Adolescent Psychiatry, 38,* 138–146.

Johnson, R. (1993). Clinical issues in the use of the DSM-III-R with African American Children: A diagnostic paradigm. *Journal of Black Psychology, 19,* 447–460.

Kagan, J., Resnick, J., Clark, C., Snidman, N., & Garcia-Coll, C. (1984). Behavioral inhibition to the unfamiliar. *Child Development, 55,* 2212–2225.

Kaminar, Y. (2001). Adolescent substance abuse treatment: Where do we go from here? *Psychiatric Services,* 52, 147–149.

Kaminar, Y., Burleson, J., & Goldberger, R. (2000). *Cognitive-behavioral versus psychoeducational therapy: 3- and 9-month treatment outcomes for adolescent substance abusers.* Presented at the Ninth International Conference on Treatment of Addictive Behaviors.

Kaslow, N., & Thompson, M. (1998). Applying the criteria for empirically supported treatments to studies of psychosocial interventions for child and adolescent depression. *Journal of Clinical Child Psychology,* 27, 146–155.

Katz, R., & Marquette, J. (1996). Psychosocial characteristics of young violent offenders: A comparative study. *Criminal Behaviour and Mental Health,* 6, 339–348.

Kazdin, A. (1988). *Child psychotherapy: Developing and identifying effective treatments.* Elmsford, NY: Pergamon.

Kazdin, A. (1996). Problem solving and parent management in treatment for aggressive and antisocial behavior. In E. Hibbs & P. Jensen (Eds.), *Psychological treatments for child and adolescent disorders: Empirically based strategies for clinical practice* (pp. 377–408). Washington, DC: American Psychological Association.

Kazdin, A. (1997). Practitioner review: Psychosocial treatments for conduct disorder in children. *Journal of Child Psychology and Psychiatry,* 38, 161–178.

Kazdin, A. (2000a). Adolescent development, mental disorders, and decision making of delinquent youths. In T. Grisso & R. Schwartz (Eds.), *Youth on trial: A developmental perspective on juvenile justice* (pp. 33–65). Chicago: University of Chicago Press.

Kazdin, A. (2000b). *Psychotherapy for children and adolescents: Directions for research and practice.* New York: Oxford University Press.

Kazdin, A., & Johnson, H. (1994). Advances in psychotherapy for children and adolescents: Interrelations of adjustment, development and intervention. *Journal of School Psychology,* 32, 217–246.

Kendall, P. (1994). Treating anxiety disorders in children: Results of a randomized clinical trial. *Journal of Consulting and Clinical Psychology,* 62, 100–110.

Kendall, P., Reber, J., McLeer, S., Epps, J., & Ronan, K. (1990). Cognitive-behavioral treatment of conduct-disordered children. *Cognitive Therapy and Research,* 14, 279–297.

Knox, M., King, C., Hanna, G., Logan, D., & Ghaziuddin, N. (2000). Aggressive behavior in clinically depressed adolescents. *Journal of the American Academy of Child and Adolescent Psychiatry,* 39, 611–618.

Kovacs, M. (1990). Comorbid anxiety disorders in childhood-onset depressions. In J. Maser & C. Cloninger (Eds.), *Comorbidity of mood and anxiety disorders* (pp. 272–281). Washington, DC: American Psychiatric Press.

Kratzer, L., & Hodgins, S. (1997). Adult outcomes of child conduct problems: A cohort study. *Journal of Abnormal Child Psychology, 25,* 65–81.

Lambert, E., Wahler, R., Andrade, A., & Bickman, L. (2001). Looking for the disorder in conduct disorder. *Journal of Abnormal Psychology, 110,* 110–123.

Lahey, B., Loeber, R., Hart, E., Frick, P., Applegate, B., Zhang, Q., Green, S., & Russo, J. (1995). Four-year longitudinal study of conduct disorder in boys: Patterns of predictors of persistence. *Journal of Abnormal Psychology, 104,* 83–93.

Lapouse, R., & Monk, A. (1958). An epidemiologic study of behavior characteristics of children. *American Journal of Public Health, 48,* 1134–1144.

Lewis, D., Lovely, R., Yeager, C., Ferguson, G., Friedman, M., Sloane, G., Friedman, H., & Pincus, J. (1988). Intrinsic and environmental characteristics of juvenile murderers. *Journal of the American Academy of Child and Adolescent Psychiatry, 27,* 582–587.

Lilienfeld, S., Waldman, I., & Israel, A. (1994). A critical examination of the use of the term and concept of comorbidity in psychopathology research. *Clinical Psychology: Science and Practice, 1,* 71–83.

Link, B., & Steuve, A. (1994). Psychotic symptoms and the violent/illegal behavior of mental patients compared to community controls. In J. Monahan & H. Steadman (Eds.), *Violence and mental disorder: Developments in risk assessment* (pp. 137–159). Chicago: University of Chicago Press.

Lipsey, M. (1992). Juvenile delinquency treatment: A meta-analytic inquiry into the variability of effects. In T. Cook, H. Cooper, & D. Cordray (Eds.), *Meta-analysis for explanation* (pp. 83–126). New York: Russell Sage Foundation.

Lochman, J., Lampron, L., Gemmer, T., & Harris, S. (1987). Anger coping intervention with aggressive children: A guide to implementation in school settings. In P. Keller & S. Heyman (Eds.), *Innovations in clinical practice: A source book* (pp. 339–356). Sarasota, FL: Professional Resource Exchange.

Lochman, J., & Wells, K. (1996). A social-cognitive intervention with aggressive children: Prevention effects and contextual implementation issues. In R. Peters & R. McMahon (Eds.)., *Preventing childhood disorders, substance abuse, and delinquency* (pp. 111–143). Thousand Oaks, CA: Sage.

Loeber, R. (1990). Developmental and risk factors of juvenile antisocial behavior and delinquency. *Clinical Psychology Review, 10,* 1–41.

Loeber, R. (1991). Questions and advances in the study of developmental pathways. In D. Cicchetti & S. Toth (Eds.), *Rochester symposium on developmental psychopathology: Vol. 3. Models and integrations* (pp. 97–116). New York: University of Rochester Press.

Loeber, R., Burke, J., & Lahey, B. (2002). What are adolescent antecedents to an antisocial personality disorder? *Criminal Behavior and Mental Health,* 12, 24–36.

Loeber, R., & Dishion, T. (1983). Early predictors of male delinquency: A review. *Psychological Bulletin,* 94, 68–99.

Loeber, R., Farrington, D., Stouthamer-Loeber, M., & Van Kammen, W. (1998). *Antisocial behavior and mental health problems: Explanatory factors in childhood and adolescence.* Mahwah, NJ: Lawrence Erlbaum Associates.

Loeber, R., & Hay, D. (1994). Developmental approaches to aggression and conduct problems. In M. Rutter & D. Hay (Eds.), *Development through life: A handbook for clinicians* (pp.488–515). Oxford: Blackwell.

Loeber, R., & Hay, D. (1996). Key issues in the development of aggression and violence from childhood to early adulthood. *Annual Review of Psychology,* 48, 371–410.

Loeber, R., & Keenan, K. (1994). Interaction between conduct disorder and its comorbid conditions: Effects of age and gender. *Clinical Psychology Review,* 14, 497–523.

Loeber, R., & Stouthamer-Loeber, M. (1998). Development of juvenile aggression and violence: Some common misconceptions and controversies. *American Psychologist,* 53, 242–259.

Loeber, R., Van Kammen, W., Krohn, M., & Huizinga, D. (1991). The crime-substance use nexus in young people. In D. Huizinga, R. Loeber, & T. Thornberry (Eds.), *Urban delinquency and substance abuse.* Washington, DC: Office of Juvenile Justice and Delinquency Prevention.

Los Angeles Times (2000, November 21). "California's Mental Health System Woefully Inadequate, Report Says."

Luna, H., Thulborn, K., Monoz, D., Merriam, E., Garver, K., Minshew, N., Keshavan, M., Genovese, C., Eddy, W., & Sweeney, J. (2001). *Maturation of widely distributed brain function subserves cognitive development.* Available at http://www.idealibrary.com.

Lynam, D. (1997). Pursuing the psychopath: Capturing the fledgling psychopath in a nomological net. *Journal of Abnormal Psychology,* 106, 425–438.

Lynam, D. (1998). Early identification of the fledgling psychopath: Locating the psychopathic child in the current nomenclature. *Journal of Abnormal Psychology,* 107, 566–575.

Magnusson, D., Stattin, H., & Duner, A. (1983). Aggression and criminality in a longitudinal perspective. In K. Van Dusen & S. Mednick (Eds.), *An-*

tecedents of aggression and antisocial behavior (pp. 277–301). Boston: Kluwer-Nijhoff.

Mannuzza, S., & Klein, R. (1992). Predictors of outcome of children with attention-deficit hyperactivity disorder. In G. Weiss (Ed.), *Child and adolescent psychiatric clinics of North America: Attention-deficit hyperactivity disorder* (pp. 567–578). Philadelphia: Saunders.

Mannuzza, S., Klein, R., Bessler, A., Mally, P., & LaPadula, M. (1993). Adult outcome of hyperactive boys: Educational achievement, occupational rank, and psychiatric status. *Archives of General Psychiatry, 50,* 565–576.

Marsteller, F., Brogan, D., Smith, I., Ash, P., Daniels, D., Rolka, D., & Falek, A. (1997). *The prevalence of substance use disorders among juveniles admitted to regional youth detention centers operated by the Georgia Department of Children and Youth Services.* Rockville, MD: Department of Health and Human Services, Substance Abuse and Mental health Services Administration, Center for Substance Abuse Treatment.

Martinson, R. (1974). What works? Questions and answers about prison reform. *Public Interest, 10,* 22–54.

Mash, E. (1989). Treatment of child and family disturbance: A behavioral-systems perspective. In E. Mash & R. Barkley (Eds.), *Treatment of childhood disorders* (pp. 3–38). New York: Guilford Press.

Mash, E., & Barkley, R. (Eds.) (1998). *Treatment of childhood disorders* (2nd ed.). New York: Guilford.

Mash, E., & Dozois, D. (1996). Child psychopathology: A developmental-systems perspective. In E. Mash & R. Barkley (Eds.), *Child Psychopathology* (pp. 3–60). New York: Guilford.

McCann, J. (1999). *Assessing adolescents with the MACI: Using the Millon Adolescent Clinical Inventory.* New York: John Wiley.

McGaha, A., Otto, R., McClaren, M., & Petrila, J. (2001). Juveniles adjudicated incompetent to proceed: A descriptive study of Florida's competence restoration program. *Journal of the American Academy of Psychiatry and the Law, 29,* 427–437.

McLaney, M., Del Boca, F., & Babor, T. (1994). A validation study of the Problem Oriented Screening Instrument for Teenagers (POSIT). *Journal of Mental Health, 3,* 363–376.

McMackin, R., & Fulwiler, C. (2001). A public health-juvenile justice collaboration to address the psychiatric needs of incarcerated youth. *Organizational Response to Social Problems, 8,* 335–361.

McMahon, R., & Wells, K. (1998). Conduct problems. In E. Mash & R. Barkley (Eds.), *Treatment of childhood disorders* (2nd ed., pp. 111–207). New York: Guilford.

Mechanic, D. (1973). Some factors in identifying and defining mental illness. In R. Price & B. Denner (Eds.), *The making of a mental patient* (pp. 19–31). New York: Holt, Rinehart and Winston.

Melton, G. (1989). Taking *Gault* seriously: Toward a new juvenile court. *Nebraska Law Review, 68*, 146–181.

Melton, G., Petrila, J., Poythress, N., & Slobogin, C. (1997). *Psychological evaluations for the courts* (2nd ed.). New York: Guilford.

Millon, T., Millon, C., &Davis, R. (1993). *Millon Adolescent Clinical Inventory manual.* Minneapolis, MN: National Computer Systems.

Moffitt, T. (1993). Adolescence-limited and life-course-persistent antisocial behavior: A developmental taxonomy. *Psychological Review, 100*, 674–701.

Moffitt, T., Caspi, A., Dickson, N., Silva, P., & Stanton, W. (1996). Childhood-onset versus adolescent-onset antisocial conduct problems in males: Natural history from ages 3 to 18 years. *Development and Psychopathology, 8*, 399–424.

Moffitt, T., Caspi, A., Rutter, M., & Silva, P. (2001). *Sex differences in antisocial behavior.* Cambridge: Cambridge University Press.

Monahan, J., Steadman, H., Silver, E., Appelbaum, P., Robbins, P., Mulvey, E., Roth, L., Grisso, T., & Banks, S. (2001). *Rethinking risk assessment: The MacArthur study of mental disorder and violence.* New York: Oxford University Press.

Monti, P., Colby, S., & O'Leary, T. (Eds.). (2001). *Adolescents, alcohol, and substance abuse: Reaching teens through brief interventions.* New York: Guilford.

Mulvey, E. (1989). Scenes from a marriage: How can juvenile justice and mental health go on together? *Forensic Reports, 2*, 9–24.

Murray, C., Smith, S., & West, E. (1989). Comparative personality development in adolescence: A critique. In R. Jones (Ed.), *Black adolescents* (pp. 49–62). Berkeley, CA: Cobb and Henry.

Myers, W., Scott, K., & Burgess, A. (1995). Psychopathology, biopsychosocial factors, crime characteristics, and classification of 25 homicidal youths. *Journal of the American Academy of Child and Adolescent Psychiatry, 34*, 1483–1489.

National Commission on Correctional Health Care. (1999). *Standards for health services in juvenile detention and confinement facilities.* Chicago, IL: National Commission on Correctional Health Care.

National Council of Juvenile and Family Court Judges. (2000). *Enhancing the mental health and well being of infants, children and youth in the juvenile and family courts: A judicial challenge.* Reno, NV: National Council of Juvenile and Family Court Judges.

National Mental Health Association. (2000). *Community perspectives on the mental health and substance abuse treatment needs of youth involved in the juvenile justice system.* Washington, DC: Office of Juvenile Justice and Delinquency Prevention.

Neighbors, H., Kempton, T., & Forehand, R. (1992). Co-occurrence of substance abuse with conduct, anxiety and depression disorders in juvenile delinquents. *Addictive Behaviors,* 17, 379–386.

New York Times (2001, July 9). "Mentally Ill Children Trapped in Hospitals."

Nicholson, R., & Kugler, K. (1991). Competent and incompetent criminal defendants: A quantitative review of comparative research. *Psychological Bulletin,* 109, 355–370.

Nixon, T., & Northrup, A. (Eds.) (1997). *Children's mental health services: Research, policy and evaluation.* Thousand Oaks, CA: Sage.

Novaco, R. (1994). Anger as a risk factor for violence among the mentally disordered. In J. Monahan & H. Steadman (Eds.), *Violence and mental disorder* (pp. 21–59). Chicago: University of Chicago Press.

Nurmi, J. (1991). How do adolescents see their future? A review of the development of future orientation and planning. *Developmental Review,* 11, 1–59.

Oberlander, L., & Goldstein, N. (2001). A review and update of the practice of evaluating *Miranda* comprehension. *Behavioral Sciences and the Law,* 19, 453–471.

Oberlander, L., Goldstein, N., & Goldstein, A. (2003). Competence to confess. In A. Goldstein (Ed.), *Handbook of psychology: Vol. 11. Forensic psychology* (pp. 335–357). New York: John Wiley.

Office of Juvenile Justice and Delinquency Prevention. (1994). *Conditions of confinement: Juvenile detention and corrections facilities* (Report No. 145793). Washington, DC: Office of Juvenile Justice and Delinquency Prevention.

Office of Juvenile Justice and Delinquency Prevention. (2000). *Juvenile Justice Journal, Vol. VII*(1). Washington, DC: U.S. Department of Justice, Office of Justice Programs, Office of Juvenile Justice and Delinquency Prevention.

Offord, D., Alder, R., & Boyle, M. (1986). Prevalence and sociodemographic correlates of conduct disorder. *American Journal of Social Psychiatry,* 4, 272–278.

Offord, D., Boyle, M., Szatmari, P., Rae-Grant, N., Links, P., Cadman, D., Byles, J., Crawford, J., Blum, C., Thomas, H., & Woodward, C. (1987). Ontario Child Health Study, II: Six-month prevalence of disorder and rates of service utilization. *Archives of General Psychiatry,* 44, 832–836.

Omaha World-Herald (2002, January 14). "Nebraska Mental Health System for Children in 'Sorry Condition.'"

Otto, R., Greenstein, J., Johnson, M., & Friedman, R. (1992). Prevalence of mental disorders among youth in the juvenile justice system. In J. Cocozza (Ed.), *Responding to the mental health needs of youth in the juvenile justice system* (pp. 7–48). Seattle, WA: National Coalition for the Mentally Ill in the Criminal Justice System.

Patterson, G. (1975). *Families: Applications of social learning to family life.* Champaign, IL: Research Press.

Paus, T., Zijdenbos, A., Worsley, K., Collins, D., Blumental, J., & Evans, A. (1999). Structural maturation of neural pathways in children and adolescents: In vivo study. *Science, 283,* 1908–1911.

Pennington, B., & Ozonoff, S. (1991). A neuroscientific perspective on continuity and discontinuity in developmental psychopathology. In D. Cicchetti & S. Toth (Eds.), *Rochester symposium on developmental psychopathology: Vol. 3.* Models and integrations (pp. 117–159). New York: University of Rochester Press.

Peterson-Badali, M., & Abramovitch, R. (1993). Grade related changes in young people's reasoning about plea decisions. *Law and Human Behavior, 17,* 537–552.

Peterson-Badali, M., & Abramovitch, R., & Duda, J. (1997). Young children's legal knowledge and reasoning ability. *Canadian Journal of Criminology, 39,* 145–170.

Piersma, H., Boes, J., & Reaume, W. (1994). Unidimensionality of the Brief Symptom Inventory (BSI) in adult and adolescent inpatients. *Journal of Personality Assessment, 63,* 338–344.

Pinta, E. (1999). The prevalence of serious mental disorders among U.S. prisoners. *Correctional Mental Health Report, 1,* 33–34, 44–47.

Pliszka, S., Sherman, J., Barrow, M., & Irick, S. (2000). Affective disorder in juvenile offenders: A preliminary study. *American Journal of Psychiatry, 157,* 130–132.

Price, H., Daffner, K., Stowe, R., & Mesulam, M. (1990). The comportmental learning disabilities of early frontal lobe damage. *Brain, 113,* 1383–1393.

Progressive (2001, July). "Arrest My Kid: He Needs Mental Health Care."

Puig-Antich, J., & Chambers, W. (1978). *The Schedule for Affective Disorders and Schizophrenia for School-Aged Children.* New York: State Psychiatric Institute of New York.

Puritz, P., Burrell, S., Schwartz, R., Soler, M., & Warboys, L. (1995). *A call for justice: An assessment of access to counsel and quality of representation in delinquency proceedings.* Washington, DC: American Bar Association Juvenile Justice Center.

Quinsey, V., Harris, G., Rice, M., & Cormier, C. (1998). *Violent offenders: Appraising and managing risk.* Washington, DC: American Psychological Association.

Rahdert, E. (1991). *The Adolescent Assessment/Referral System: Manual.* Rockville, MD: Alcohol, Drug Abuse, and Mental Health Administration.

Raine, A. (1996). Autonomic nervous system factors underlying disinhibited, antisocial and violent behavior: Biosocial perspectives and treatment implications. In C. Ferris & T. Grisso (Eds.), *Understanding aggressive behavior in children* (pp. 46–59). New York: New York Academy of Sciences.

Randall, J., Henggler, S., Pickrel, S., & Brondini, M. (1999). Psychiatric comorbidity and the 16-month trajectory of substance-abusing and substance-dependent juvenile offenders. *Journal of the American Academy of Child and Adolescent Psychiatry,* 38, 1118–1124.

Rapee, R., Barrett, P., Dadds, M., & Evans, L. (1994). Reliability of the DSM-III-R childhood and anxiety disorders using structured interview: Interrater and parent-child agreement. *Journal of the American Academy of child and Adolescent Psychiatry,* 33, 984–992.

Redding, R., & Frost, J. (2002). Adjudicative competence in the modern juvenile court. *Virginia Journal of Social Policy and Law,* 9, 353–410.

Richards, I. (1996). Psychiatric disorder among adolescents in custody. *Australian and New Zealand Journal of Psychiatry,* 30, 788–793.

Richters, J. (1996). Disordered views of aggressive children: A late twentieth century perspective. In C. Ferris & T. Grisso (Eds.), *Understanding aggressive behavior in children* (pp. 208–223). New York: New York Academy of Sciences.

Roberts, R., Attkinson, C., & Rosenblatt, A. (1998). Prevalence of psychopathology among children and adolescents. *American Journal of Psychiatry,* 155, 715–725.

Robertson, A., & Husain, J. (2001). *Prevalence of mental illness and substance abuse disorders among incarcerated juvenile offenders.* Mississippi State, MS: Mississippi State University Social Science Research Center.

Robins, L. (1966). *Deviant children grown up.* Baltimore: Williams & Wilkins.

Rogers, R., Johansen, J., Chang, J., & Salekin, R. (1997). Predictors of adolescent psychopathy: Oppositional and conduct-disordered symptoms. *Journal of the American Academy of Psychiatry and the Law,* 25, 261–271.

Rosenblatt, J., Rosenblatt, A., & Biggs, E. (2000). Criminal behavior and emotional disorder: Comparing youth served by the mental health and juvenile justice systems. *Journal of Behavioral Health Services and Research,* 27, 227–237.

Rutter, M. (1994). Comorbidity: Meanings and mechanisms. *Clinical Psychology: Science and Practice,* 1, 100–103.

Rutter, M., & Garmezy, H. (1983). Developmental psychopathology. In P. Mussen & E. Hetherington (Eds.), *Handbook of child psychology: Vol. 4. Socialization, personality and social development* (pp. 775–911). New York: Wiley.

Rutter, M., & Graham, P. (1968). The reliability and validity of the psychiatric assessment of the child: I. Interview with the child. *British Journal of Psychiatry*, 114, 563–579.

Rutter, M., & Smith, D. (Eds.). (1995). *Psychosocial disorders in young people: Time trends and their cases.* Chichester, UK: Wiley.

Ryan, N., Bhatara, V., & Perel, J. (1999). Mood stabilizers in children and adolescents. *Journal of the American Academy of Child and Adolescent Psychiatry*, 38, 529–536.

Salekin, R., Rogers, R., & Machin, D. (2001). Psychopathy in youth: Pursuing diagnostic clarity. *Journal of Youth and Adolescence*, 30, 173–194.

Scheff, T. (1973). The societal reaction to deviance: Ascriptive elements in psychiatric screening of mental patients in a midwestern state. In R. Price & B. Denner (Eds.), *The making of a mental patient* (pp. 100–119). New York: Holt, Rinehart and Winston.

Schoenwald, S. (1998). *Multisystemic therapy consultation manual.* Charleston, SC: MST Institute.

Schoenwald, S., Scherer, D., & Brondino, M. (1997). Effective community-based treatments for serious juvenile offenders. In S. Henggeler & A. Santos (Eds.), *Innovative approaches for difficult to treat populations* (pp. 65–82). Washington, DC: American Psychiatric Press.

Schwartz, R., & Rosado, L. (Eds.). (2000). *Evaluating youth competence in the justice system.* (Series, "Understanding adolescents: A juvenile court training curriculum.") Washington, DC: American Bar Association Juvenile Justice Center.

Scott, E. (1992). Judgment and reasoning in adolescent decision making. *Villanova Law Review*, 37, 1607–1669).

Scott, E. (2000). Criminal responsibility in adolescence: Lessons from developmental psychology. In T. Grisso & R. Schwartz (Eds.), *Youth on trial: A developmental perspective on juvenile justice* (pp. 291–324). Chicago: University of Chicago Press.

Scott, E., Reppucci, N., & Woolard, J. (1995). Evaluating adolescent decision-making in legal contexts. *Law and Human Behavior*, 19, 221–244.

Scott, E., & Steinberg, L. (2003). Blaming youth. *Texas Law Review*, 81, 799–840.

Seagrave, D., & Grisso, T. (2002). Adolescent development and the measurement of juvenile psychopathy. *Law and Human Behavior*, 26, 219–239.

Shaffer, D., Fisher, P., Dulcan, M., Davies, M., Piacentini, J., Schwab-Stone, M., Lahey, B., Bourdon, K., Jensen, P., Bird, H., Canino, G., & Regier, D. (1996). The NIMH Diagnostic Interview Schedule for Children Version 2.3 (DISC-2.3): Description, acceptability, prevalence rates, and performance in the MECA study. *Journal of the American Academy of Child and Adolescent Psychiatry, 35,* 865–877.

Shaffer, D., Fisher, P., Lucas, C., Dulcan, M., & Schwab-Stone, M. (2000). NIMH Diagnostic Interview Schedule for Children Version IV (NIMH DISC-IV): Description, differences from previous versions, and reliability of some common diagnoses. *Journal of the American Academy of Child and Adolescent Psychiatry, 39,* 28–37.

Shaffer, D., Gould, M., Brasic, J., Ambrosini, P., Fisher, P., Bird, H., & Aluwahlia, S. (1983). A Children's Global Assessment Scale (C-GAS). *Archives of General Psychiatry, 40,* 1228–1231.

Silverthorn, P., & Frick, P. (1999). Developmental pathways to antisocial behavior: The delayed-onset pathway in girls. *Development and Psychopathology, 11,* 101–126.

Simeon, J., Carrey, N., Wiggins, D., Milin, R., & Hosenbocus, S. (1995). Risperidone effects in treatment-resistant adolescents: Preliminary case reports. *Journal of Child and Adolescent Psychopharmacology, 5,* 69–79.

Snyder, H., & Sickmund, M. (1995). *Juvenile offenders and victims: A national report.* Washington, DC: Office of Juvenile Justice and Delinquency Prevention.

Snyder, H., & Sickmund, M. (1999). *Juvenile offenders and victims: 1999 national report.* Washington, DC: Office of Juvenile Justice and Delinquency Prevention.

Sroufe, L., & Rutter, M. (1984). The domain of developmental psychopathology. *Child Development, 55,* 17–29.

Steadman, H., Mulvey, E., Monahan, J., Robbins, P., Appelbaum, P., Grisso, T., Roth, L., & Silver, E. (1998). Violence by people discharged from acute psychiatric facilities and by others in the same neighborhoods. *Archives of General Psychiatry, 55,* 393–401.

Steinberg, L. (2002). Clinical adolescent psychology: What it is, and what it needs to be. *Journal of Consulting and Clinical Psychology, 70,* 124–128.

Steinberg, L., & Cauffman, E. (1996). Maturity of judgment in adolescence: Psychosocial factors in adolescent decision-making. *Law and Human Behavior, 20,* 249–272.

Steiner, H., Garcia, I., & Matthews, X. (1997). Posttraumatic stress disorder in incarcerated juvenile delinquents. *Journal of the American Academy of Child and Adolescent Psychiatry, 36,* 357–365.

Stiffman, A., Chen, Y., Elze, D., & Dore, P. (1997). Adolescents' and providers' perspectives on the need for and use of mental health services. *Journal of Adolescent Health,* 21, 335–342.

Stroul, B. (Ed.). (1996). *Children's mental health: Creating systems of care in a changing society.* Baltimore, MD: Paul H. Brookes Publishing.

Swanson, J., Estroff, S., Swartz, M., Borum, R., Lachicotte, W., Zimmer, C., & Wagner, R. (1997). Violence and severe mental disorder in clinical and community populations: The effects of psychotic symptoms, comorbidity, and lack of treatment. *Psychiatry,* 60, 1–22.

Szatmari, P., Boyle, M.,& Offord, D. (1989). ADHD and CD: Degree of diagnostic overlap and differences among correlates. *Journal of the American Academy of Child and Adolescent Psychiatry,* 31, 1036–1040.

Teplin, L. (1990). The prevalence of severe mental disorder among urban male detainees: Comparison with the Epidemiologic Catchment Area Program. *American Journal of Public Health,* 80, 663–669.

Teplin, L. (1994). Psychiatric and substance abuse disorders among urban male detainees. *American Journal of Public Health,* 84, 290–293.

Teplin, L., Abram, K., McClelland, G., & Dulcan, M. (in press). Comorbid psychiatric disorders in youth in juvenile detention. *Archives of General Psychiatry.*

Teplin, L., Abram, K., McClelland, G., Dulcan, M., & Mericle, A. (2002). Psychiatric disorders in youth in juvenile detention. *Archives of General Psychiatry,* 59, 1133–1143.

Timmons-Mitchell, J., Brown, C., Schulz, C., Webster, S., Underwood, L., & Semple, W. (1997). Comparing the mental health needs of female and male incarcerated juvenile delinquents. *Behavioral Sciences and the Law,* 15, 195–202.

Tobey, A., Grisso, T., & Schwartz, R. (2000). Youths' trial participation as seen by youths and their attorneys: An exploration of competence-based issues. In T. Grisso & R. Schwartz (Eds.), *Youth on trial: A developmental perspective on juvenile justice* (pp. 225–242). Chicago: University of Chicago Press.

Tolan, P., & Gorman-Smith, D. (1998). Development of serious and violent juvenile offending careers. In R. Loeber & D. Farrington (Eds.), *Serious and violent juvenile offenders* (pp. 68–85). Thousand Oaks, CA: Sage.

Torbet, P., Gable, R., Hurst, H., Montgomery, I., Szymanski, L., & Thomas, D. (1996). *State responses to serious and violent juvenile crime.* Washington, DC: Office of Juvenile Justice and Delinquency Prevention.

Tremblay, R. (2002). *Patterns of development of aggression in childhood.* Paper presented at the convention of the Society for Research on Adolescence, New Orleans, LA.

U.S. Department of Justice, Federal Bureau of Investigation. (1976–1993, 1994a, 1995–1996). *Crime in the United States.* Washington, DC: Government Printing Office.

U.S. General Accounting Office. (1995). *Juvenile justice: Juveniles processed in criminal court and case dispositions.* Washington, DC: U.S. General Accounting Office (Document # GAO/VVD-95-170).

U.S. Surgeon General. (1999). *Mental health: A report of the Surgeon General.* Rockville, MD: U.S. Public Health Service.

Vander Stoep, A., Evens, C., & Taub, J. (1997). Risk of juvenile justice system referral among children in a public mental health system. *Journal of Mental Health Administration, 24,* 428–441.

Virginia Department of Mental Health, Mental Retardation, and Substance Abuse Services. (2001, September 17). *Memorandum: New contract for the provision of restoration services to juveniles pursuant to the Code of Virginia 16.1-356 through 16.1-361.* Availability: J. Duval, Director of Juvenile Competency Services, DMHMRSAS, Richmond, VA.

Virginia Policy Design Team. (1994). *Mental health needs of youth in Virginia's juvenile detention center.* Richmond, VA: Virginia Policy Design Team.

Vitiello, B., Hill, J., Elia, J., Cuningham, E., McLeer, S., & Behar, D. (1991). P.R.N. medications in child psychiatric patients: A pilot placebo-controlled study. *Journal of Clinical Psychiatry, 52,* 499–501.

Vitiello, B., Ricciuti, A., & Behar, D. (1987). P.R.N. medications in child state hospital inpatients. *Journal of Clinical Psychiatry, 48,* 351–354.

Wakefield, J. (1992). The concept of mental disorder: On the boundary between biological facts and social values. *American Psychologist, 47,* 373–388.

Waldron, H., Brody, J., & Slesnick, N. (2001). Integrative behavioral and family therapy for adolescent substance abuse. In P. Monti, S. Colby, & T. O'Leary (Eds.), *Adolescents, alcohol, and substance abuse: Reaching teens through brief interventions* (pp. 216–243). New York: Guilford.

Walker, J., Lahey, B., Russo, M., Frick, P., Christ, M., McBurnett, K., Loeher, R., Stouthamer-Loeber, M., & Green, S. (1991). Anxiety, inhibition, and conduct disorder in children: I. Relations to social impairment. *Journal of the American Academy of Child and Adolescent Psychiatry, 30,* 187–191.

Warner, L., Kessler, R., Hughes, M., Anthony, J., & Nelson, C. (1995). Relevance and correlates of drug use and dependence in the United States:

Results from the National Comorbidity Survey. *Archives of General Psychiatry, 52,* 219–229.

Wasserman, G., McReynolds, L., Lucas, C., Fisher, P., & Santos, L. (2002). The Voice DISC-IV with incarcerated male youths: Prevalence of disorder. *Journal of the American Academy of Child and Adolescent Psychiatry, 41,* 314–321.

Weiss, B., Catron, T., Harris, V., & Phung, T. (1999). The effectiveness of traditional child psychotherapy. *Journal of Consulting and Clinical Psychology, 67,* 82–94.

Weisz, J., & Jensen, P. (1999). Efficacy and effectiveness of child and adolescent psychotherapy and pharmacotherapy. *Mental Health Services Research, 1,* 125–157.

Weisz, J., Weiss, B., Alicke, M., & Klotz, M. (1987). Effectiveness of psychotherapy with children and adolescents: A meta-analysis for clinicians. *Journal of Consulting and Clinical Psychology, 55,* 542–549.

Weisz, J., Weiss, B., Han, S., Granger, D., & Morton, T. (1995). Effects of psychotherapy with children and adolescents revisited: A meta-analysis of treatment outcome studies. *Psychological Bulletin, 117,* 450–468.

Westendorp, F., Brink, K., Roberson, M., & Ortiz, I. (1986). Variables which differentiate placement of adolescents in juvenile justice or mental health systems. *Adolescence, 21,* 23–37.

Wierson, M., & Forehand, R. (1995). Predicting recidivism in juvenile delinquents: The role of mental health diagnoses and the qualification of conclusions by race. *Behavioral Research and Therapy, 33,* 63–67.

Winters, K. (2001). Assessing adolescent substance use problems and other areas of functioning: State of the art. In P. Monti, S. Colby, & T. O'Leary (Eds.), *Adolescents, alcohol, and substance abuse* (pp. 80–108). New York: Guilford.

Winters, K., Stinchfield, R., & Opland, E. (2000). The effectiveness of the Minnesota model approach in the treatment of adolescent drug abusers. *Addiction, 95,* 601–612.

Woolard, J., Fried, C., & Reppucci, N. (2001). Toward an expanded definition of adolescent competence in legal situations. In R. Roesch, R. Corrado, & R. Dempster (Eds.), *Psychology in the courts: International advances in knowledge* (pp. 21–40). London: Routledge.

Woolard, J., Reppucci, N., & Redding, R. (1996). Theoretical and methodological issues in studying children's capacities in legal contexts. *Law and Human Behavior, 20,* 219–228.

Yates, B. (1996). *Analyzing costs, procedures, processes, and outcomes in human services.* Thousand Oaks, CA: Sage.

Young, J. (1998). Trends in cost management for healthcare services: Managed care in the 1990s. In J. Young & P. Ferrari (Eds.), *Designing mental health services and systems for children and adolescents: A shrewd investment* (pp. 25–41). Philadelphia: Brunner/Mazel.

Zimring, F. (1998). *American youth violence.* New York: Oxford University Press.

Zoccolillo, M. (1993). Gender and the development of conduct disorder. *Development and Psychopathology, 5,* 65–78.

Index

A

Study of Hawthorne.

BY

GEORGE PARSONS LATHROP.

AMS PRESS
NEW YORK

Reprinted from a copy in the collections of the
Harvard College Library
From the edition of 1876, Boston
First AMS EDITION published 1969
Manufactured in the United States of America

Library of Congress Catalogue Card Number: 70-86168

AMS PRESS, INC.
New York, N.Y. 10003

CONTENTS.

vi CONTENTS.

A STUDY OF HAWTHORNE.

I.

POINT OF VIEW.

THIS book was not designed as a biography, but is rather a portrait. And, to speak more carefully still, it is not so much this, as my conception of what a portrait of Hawthorne should be. For I cannot write with the authority of one who had known him and had been formally intrusted with the task of describing his life. On the other hand, I do not enter upon this attempt as a mere literary performance, but have been assisted in it by an inward impulse, a consciousness of sympathy with the subject, which I may perhaps consider a sort of inspiration. My guide has been intuition, confirmed and seldom confuted by research. Perhaps it is even a favoring fact that I should never have seen Mr. Hawthorne; a personality so elusive as his may possibly yield its traits more readily to one who can never obtrude actual intercourse between himself and the mind he is meditating upon. An honest report upon personal contact always has a value denied to the reviews of after-comers, yet the best criticism and biography is not always that of contemporaries.

Our first studies will have a biographical scope, because a certain grouping of facts is essential, to give point to the view which I am endeavoring to present; and as Hawthorne's early life has hitherto been but little explored, much of the material used in the earlier chapters is now for the first time made public. The latter portion of the career may be treated more sketchily, being already better known; though passages will be found throughout the essay which have been developed with some fulness, in order to maintain a correct atmosphere, compensating any errors which mere opinions might lead to. Special emphasis, then, must not be held to show neglect of points which my space and scope prevent my commenting on. But the first outline requiring our attention involves a distant retrospect.

The history of Hawthorne's genius is in some sense a summary of all New England history.

From amid a simple, practical, energetic community, remarkable for its activity in affairs of state and religion, but by no means given to dreaming, this fair flower of American genius rose up unexpectedly enough, breaking the cold New England sod for the emission of a light and fragrance as pure and pensive as that of the arbutus in our woods, in spring. The flower, however, sprang from seed that rooted in the old colonial life of the sternly imaginative pilgrims and Puritans. Thrusting itself up into view through the drift of a later day, it must not be confounded with other growths nourished only by that more recent deposit; though the surface-drift had of course its own weighty influence in the nourishment of it. The artistic results of a period of action must sometimes be looked for at a point of time long subsequent, and this was especially sure to be so in the first phases of New England civilization. The settlers in this region, in addition to the burdens and obstacles proper to pioneers, had to deal with the cares of forming a model state and of laying out for posterity a straight and solid path in which it might walk with due rectitude. All this was in itself an ample enough subject to occupy their powerful imaginations. They were enacting a kind of sacred epic, the dangers and the dignity and exaltation of which they felt most fervently. The Bible, the Bay Psalm Book, Bunyan, and Milton, the poems of George Wither, Baxter's Saint's Rest, and some controversial pamphlets, would suffice to appease whatever yearnings the immense experiment of their lives failed to satisfy. Gradually, of course, the native press and new-comers from England multiplied books in a community which held letters in unusual reverence. But the continuous work of subduing a new country, the dependence upon the mother-land for general literature, and finally the excitements of the Revolutionary period, deferred the opportunity for any æsthetic expression of the forces that had been at work here ever since Winthrop stepped from the Arbella on to the shore of the New World, with noble manliness and sturdy statesmanship enough in him to uphold the whole future of a great people. When Hawthorne came, therefore, his utterance was a culmination of the two preceding centuries. An entire side of the richly endowed human nature to which we owe the high qualities of New England, — a nature which is often so easily disposed of as meagre, cold, narrow, and austere, — this side, long suppressed and thrown into shade by the more active front, found expression at last in these pages so curiously compounded of various elements, answering to those traits of the past which Hawthorne's genius revived.   The sensuous substance of the early New England character had piously surrendered to the severe maxims which religion and prudence imposed; and so complete was its suppression, that all this part of Puritan nature missed recording itself, except by chance glimpses through the history of the times.   For this voluntary oblivion it has been rarely compensated in the immortality it meets with through Hawthorne.   Not that he set himself with forethought to the illustration of it; but, in studying as poet and dramatist the past from which he himself had issued, he sought, naturally, to light it up from the interior, to possess himself of the very fire which burned in men's breasts and set their minds in movement at that epoch.   In his own person and his own blood the same elements, the same capabilities still existed, however modified or differently ordered.   The records of Massachusetts Bay are full of suggestive incongruities between the ideal, single-souled life which its founders hoped to lead, and the jealousies, the opposing opinions, or the intervolved passions of individuals and of parties, which sometimes unwittingly cloaked themselves in religious tenets.   Placing himself in the position of these beings, then, and conscious of all the strong and various potencies of emotion which his own nature, inherited from them, held in curb, it was natural that Hawthorne should give weight to this contrast between the intense, prisoned life of shut sensibilities and the formal outward appearance to which it was moulded. This, indeed, is the source of motive in much of his writing; notably so in "The Scarlet Letter."   It is thus that his figures get their tremendous and often terrible relief. They are seen as close as we see our faces in a glass, and brought so intimately into our consciousness that the throbbing of their passions sounds like the mysterious, internal beating of our own hearts in our own ears. And even when he is not dealing directly with themes or situations closely related to that life, there may be felt in his style, I think, — particularly in that of the "Twice-Told Tales," — a union of vigorous freedom, and graceful, shy restraint, a mingling of guardedness which verges on severity with a quick and delicately thrilled sensibility for all that is rich and beautiful and generous, which is his by right of inheritance from the race of Non-conformist colonizers. How subtile and various this sympathy is, between himself and the past of his people, we shall see more clearly as we go on.

Salem was, in fact, Hawthorne's native soil, in all senses; as intimately and perfectly so as Florence was the only soil in which Dante and Michael Angelo could have had their growth. It is endlessly suggestive, this way that historic cities have of expressing themselves for all time in the persons of one or two men. Silently and with mysterious precision, the genius comes to birth and ripens — sometimes despite all sorts of discouragement — into a full bloom which we afterward see could not have reached its maturity at any other time, and would surely have missed its most peculiar and cherished qualities if reared in any other place. The Ionian intellect of Athens culminates in Plato; Florence runs into the mould of Dante's verse, like fluid bronze; Paris secures remembrance of her wide curiosity in Voltaire's settled expression; and Samuel Johnson holds fast for us that London of the eighteenth century which has passed out of sight, in giving place to the capital of the Anglo-Saxon race today. In like manner the sober little New England town which has played a so much more obscure, though in its way hardly less significant part, sits quietly enshrined and preserved in Hawthorne's singularly imperishable prose.

Of course, Salem is not to be compared with Florence otherwise than remotely or partially. Florence was naturally the City of Flowers, in a figurative sense as well as in the common meaning. Its splendid, various, and full-pulsed life found spontaneous issue in magnificent works of art, in architecture, painting, poetry, and sculpture, — things in which New England was quite sterile. Salem evolved the artistic spirit indirectly, and embodied itself in Hawthorne by the force of contrast: the weariness of unadorned life which must have oppressed many a silent soul before him at last gathered force for a revolt in his person, and the very dearth which had previously reigned was made to contribute to the beauty of his achievement. The unique and delicate perfume of surprise with which his genius issued from its crevice still haunts his romances. A quality of homeliness dwells in their very strangeness and rarity which endears them to us unspeakably, and captivates the foreign sense as well; so that one of Hawthorne's chief and most enduring charms is in a measure due to that very barrenness of his native earth which would at first seem to offer only denial to his development. It is in this direction that we catch sight of the analogy between his intellectual unfolding and that of the great Florentines. It consists in his drawing up into himself the nourishment furnished by the ground upon which he was born, and making the more and the less productive elements reach a climax of characteristic beauty. One marked difference, however, is that there was no abundant and inspiriting municipal life of his own time which could enter into his genius: it was the consciousness of the past of the place that affected him. He himself has expressed as much: "This old town of Salem — my native place, though I have dwelt much away from it, both in boyhood and maturer years — possesses, or did possess, a hold on my affections, the force of which I have never realized during my seasons of actual residence here. . . . . And yet, though invariably happiest elsewhere, there is within me a feeling for old Salem, which, in lack of a better phrase, I must be content to call affection. . . . . But the sentiment has likewise its moral quality. The figure of that first ancestor, invested by family tradition with a dim and dusky grandeur, was present to my boyish imagination as far back as I can remember. It still haunts me, and induces a kind of home-feeling with the past, which I scarcely claim in reference to the present phase of the town."

It is by briefly reviewing that past, then trying to reproduce in imagination the immediate atmosphere of Hawthorne's youth, and comparing the two, that we shall best arrive at the completion of our proposed portrait. We have first to study the dim perspective and the suggestive coloring of that historic background from which the author emerges, and then to define clearly his own individual traits as they appear in his published works and Note-Books.

The eagerness which admirers of such a genius show, to learn all permissible details of his personal history, is, when freed from the vulgar and imbecile curiosity which often mars it, a sort of homage that it is right to satisfy. It is a respect apt to be paid only to men whose winning personal qualities have reached through their writing, and touched a number of grateful and appreciative hearts. But two objections may be urged against giving such details here : one is, that Hawthorne especially disapproved the writing of a Life of himself; the other, that the history of Salem and the works of Hawthorne are easily accessible to any one, without intervention.

Of the first it may frankly be said, indeed, that Hawthorne alone could have adequately portrayed his life for us ; though in the same breath it should be added that the idea of his undertaking to do it is almost preposterous. To such a spirit as his, the plan would have had an exquisite absurdity about it, that might even have savored of imposition. The mass of trivial details essential to the accurate and consecutive account of an entire life could never have gained his serious attention : his modesty would have made as little of them as of boyish slate-scribblings, full of significance, fun, and character to observers, but subjected to the sponge without a pang by their producer. There is something natural and fine in this. I confess that to me the spectacle presented by Goethe when dwelling on the minutest incidents of his childhood with senile vanity and persistence, and fashioning with avaricious care the silver shrine and crystal case in which — like a very different sort of Saint Charles Borromeo — he hopes to have the reverent ages view him, is one which increases my sense of his defective though splendid personality. And yet I cannot suppress the opposite feeling, that the man of note who lets his riches of reminiscence be buried with him inflicts a loss on the world which it is hard to take resignedly. In the Note-Books of Hawthorne this want is to a large extent made good. His shrinking sensitiveness in regard to the embalming process of biography is in these somewhat abated, so that they have been of incalculable use in assisting the popular eye to see him as he really was. Other material for illustration of his daily life is somewhat meagre ; and yet, on one account, this is perhaps a cause for rejoicing. There is a halo about every man of large poetic genius which it is difficult for the world to wholly miss seeing, while he is alive. Afterward, when the biographer comes, we find the actual dimensions, the physical outline, more insisted upon. That is the biographer's business; and it is not altogether his fault, though partly so, that the public regard is thus turned away from the peculiar but impalpable sign that floats above the poet's actual stature. But, under this subtile influence, forgetting that old, luminous hallucination (if it be one), we suddenly feel the want of it, are dissatisfied; and, not perceiving that the cause lies largely with us, we fall to detracting from the subject. Thus it is fortunate that we have no regular biography of Shakespere authoritative enough to fade our own private conceptions of him; and it is not an unmixed ill that some degree of similar mystery should soften and give tone to the life of Hawthorne. Not that Hawthorne could ever be seriously disadvantaged by a complete record; for behind the greatness of the writer, in this case, there stands a person eminent for strength and loveliness as few men are eminent in their private lives. But it is with dead authors somewhat as it proved with those Etruscan warriors, who, seen through an eyehole lying in perfect state within their tombs, crumbled to a powder when the sepulchres were opened. The contact of life and death is too unsympathetic. Whatever stuff the writer be made of, it seems inevitable that he should suffer injury from exposure to the busy and prying light of subsequent life, after his so deep repose in death.

"Would you have me a damned author?" exclaims Oberon, in "The Devil in Manuscript," * "to undergo sneers, taunts, abuse, and cold neglect, and faint praise

---

* See The Snow Image, and other Twice-Told Tales.

bestowed against the giver's conscience ! . . . . An out-
law from the protection of the grave, — one whose ashes
every careless foot might spurn, unhonored in life, and
remembered scornfully in death!" This, to be sure, is
a heated statement, in the mouth of a young author who
is about to cast his unpublished works into the fire;
but the dread expressed here is by no means unfounded.
Even the publication of Hawthorne's Note-Books has
put it in the power of various writers of the day to
assume an omniscience not altogether just, and far from
acceptable. Why, then, should further risk of this be
incurred, by issuing the present work ?

It is precisely to put a limit to misconstructions, as
well as to meet — however imperfectly — the desire of
genuine appreciators, that it has been written. If this
study for a portrait fulfils its aim, it will at least furnish an outline, fix a definite shape, within which whatever is observed by others may find its place with a truer
effect and more fitting relation. The mistakes that have
been made, indeed, are in no wise alarming ones ; and
it would be difficult to find any author who has been
more carefully considered, on the whole, or with such
generally fair conclusions, as Hawthorne. Still, if one
sees even minor distortions current, it can do no harm
to correct them. Besides, there has as yet been no
thorough attempt at a consistent synthetic portraiture ;
and the differences of different critics' estimates need
some common ground to meet and be harmonized upon.
If this can be supplied, there will be less waste of time
in future studies of the same subject.

It will be seen, therefore, that my book makes no pre-
tension to the character of a Life. The wish of Hawthorne on this point would alone be enough to prevent
that. If such a work is to be undertaken, it should be

by another hand, in which the right to set aside this wish is much more certainly vested than in mine. But I have thought that an earnest sympathy with the subject might sanction the present essay. Sympathy, after all, is the talisman which may preserve even the formal biographer from giving that injury to his theme just spoken of. And if the insight which guides me has any worth, it will present whatever material has already been made public with a selection and shaping which all researchers might not have time to bestow.

Still, I am quite alive to the difficulties of my task; and I am conscious that the work may to some appear supererogatory. Stricture and praise are, it will perhaps be said, equally impertinent to a fame so well established. Neither have I any rash hope of adding a single ray to the light of Hawthorne's high standing. But I do not fear the charge of presumption. Time, if not the present reader, will supply the right perspective and proportion.

On the ground of critical duty there is surely defence enough for such an attempt as the one now offered; the relative rank of Hawthorne, and other distinctions touching him, seem to call for a fuller discussion than has been given them. I hope to prove, however, that my aim is in no wise a partisan one. Criticism is appreciative estimation. It is inevitable that the judgments of competent and cultivated persons should flatly contradict each other, as well as those of incompetent persons; and this whether they are coeval or of different dates. At the last, it is in many respects matter of simple individual impression; and there will always be persons of high intelligence whom it will be impossible to make coincide with us entirely, touching even a single author. So that the best we can do is to set about giving rational explanation of our diverse admirations. Others will explain

B

theirs; and in this way, everything good having a fit showing, taste finds it easier to become catholic.

Whoever reverences something has a meaning. Shall he not record it ? But there are two ways in which he may express himself, — through speech and through silence, — both of them sacred alike. Which of these we will use on any given occasion is a question much too subtile, too surely fraught with intuitions that cannot be formulated, to admit of arbitrary prescription. In preferring, here, the form of speech, I feel that I have adopted only another kind of silence.

II.

SALEM.

LET us now look more closely at the local setting. To understand Hawthorne's youth and his following development, we must at once transport ourselves into another period, and imagine a very different kind of life from the one we know best. It hardly occurs to readers, that an effort should be made to imagine the influences surrounding a man who has so recently passed away as Hawthorne. It was in 1864 that he died, — little more than a decade since. But he was born sixty years before, which places his boyhood and early youth in the first quarter of the century. The lapse since then has been a long one in its effects; almost portentously so. The alterations in manners, relations, opportunities, have been great. Restless and rapid in their action, these changes have multiplied the mystery of distance a hundred-fold between us and that earlier time; so that there is really a considerable space to be traversed before we can stand in thought where Hawthorne then stood in fact. Goldsmith says, in that passage of the Life of Parnell which Irving so aptly quotes in his biography of the writer: "A poet while living is seldom an object sufficiently great to attract much atten-

tion. . . . . When his fame is increased by time, it is
then too late to investigate the peculiarities of his disposition ; the dews of morning are past, and we vainly try
to continue the chase by the meridian splendor." The
bustle of American life certainly does away with "the
dews of morning" very promptly ; and it is not quite a
simple matter to reproduce the first growth of a life
which began almost with the century. But there are
resources for doing so. To begin with, we shall view
Salem as it is. Vigorous and thriving still, the place
has fortunately not drifted so far from its moorings of
seventy years since as to take us out of our bearings, in
considering its present aspect. Pace its quiet thoroughfares awhile, and you will find them leading softly and
easily into the past.

You arrive in the ordinary way, by railroad, and at
first the place wears a disappointingly commonplace aspect. It does not seem impressively venerable ; hacks
and horse-cars rattle and tinkle along the streets, people
go about their affairs in the usual way, without any due
understanding that they ought to be picturesque and
should devote themselves to falling into effective groups
posed in vistas of historic events. Is antiquity, then,
afraid to assert itself, even here in this stronghold, so
far as to appear upon the street ? No. But one must
approach these old towns with reverence, to get at their
secrets. They will not yield inspiration or meaning save
to an imaginative effort. Under the influence of that,
the faded past, traced in sympathetic ink, as it were, re-
vives and starts into distinctness. Passing down Essex
Street, or striking off from its modest bustle a little
way, we come upon shy, ungainly relics of other times.
Gray gambrel-roofed houses stand out here and there,
with thick-throated chimneys that seem to hold the whole

together. Again you pass buildings of a statelier cast,
with carved pilasters on the front and arched doorways
bordered with some simple, dainty line of carving; old
plaster-covered urns, perhaps, stand on the brick garden-
wall, and the plaster is peeling off in flakes that hang
long and reluctant before falling to the ground. There
are quaint gardens everywhere, with sometimes an entrance arched with iron gracefully wrought by some
forgotten colonial Quentin Matsys, and always with their
paths bordered by prim and fragrant box, and grass that
keeps rich and green in an Old World way, by virtue of
some secret of growth caught from fresher centuries than
ours. If your steps have the right magic in them, you
will encounter presently one of the ancient pumps like to
the Town Pump from which Hawthorne drew that clear
and sparkling little stream of revery and picture which
has flowed into so many and such distant nooks, though
the pump itself has now disappeared, having been directly
in the line of the railroad. But, best of all, by ascending
Witch Hill you may get a good historic outlook over the
past and the present of the place. Looking down from
here you behold the ancient city spread before you, rich in
chimneys and overshadowed by soft elms. At one point
a dark, strong steeple lifts itself like a huge gravestone
above the surrounding houses, terminating in a square top
or a blunt dome; and yonder is another, more ideal in its
look, rising slight and fine, and with many ascents and alter-
nating pauses, to reach a delicate pinnacle at great height
in the air. It is lighted at intervals with many-paned and
glittering windows, and wears a probable aspect of being
the one which the young dreamer would have chosen for
the standpoint of his " Sights from a Steeple "; and the
two kinds of spire seem to typify well the Puritan gloom
and the Puritan aspiration that alike found expression on

this soil. Off beyond the gray and sober-tinted town is
the sea, which in this perspective seems to rise above it
and to dominate the place with its dim, half-threatening
blue; as indeed it has always ruled its destinies in great
measure, bringing first the persecuted hither and then
inviting so many successive generations forth to warlike expedition, or Revolutionary privateering or distant
commercial enterprise. With the sea, too, Hawthorne's
name again is connected, as we shall presently notice.
Then, quitting the brimming blue, our eyes return over
the " flat, unvaried surface covered chiefly with wooden
houses, few or none of which pretend to architectural
beauty," with its " irregularity which is neither picturesque nor quaint, but only tame "; and retracing the
line upon which Hawthorne has crowded the whole history of Salem, in " Main Street," * we fall to pondering
upon the deeds that gave this hill its name. At its foot
a number of tanneries and mills are grouped, from which
there are exhalations of smoke and steam. The mists of
superstition that once overhung the spot seem at last to
have taken on that form. Behind it the land opens out
and falls away in a barren tract known from the earliest
period as the Great Pastures, where a solitude reigns almost as complete as that of the primitive settlement, and
where, swinging cabalistic webs from one to another of the
arbor-vitæ and dwarf-pine trees that grow upon it, spiders
enough still abide to furnish familiars for a world full of
witches. But here on the hill there is no special suggestion of the dark memory that broods upon it when
seen in history. An obliging Irish population has re-
lieved the descendants of both the witches and their
exterminators from an awkward task, by covering with
their own barren little dwellings the three sides of the

* See The Snow Image, and other Twice-Told Tales.

height facing the town. Still, they have not ventured beyond a certain line. One small area at the summit is wholly unencroached upon. Whether or not through fear of some evil influence resting upon the spot, no house as yet disturbs this space, though the thin turf has been somewhat picked away by desultory sod-diggers. There is nothing save this squalid, lonely desolation to commemorate the fact that such unhappy and needless deaths were here endured. It is enough. Mere human sympathy takes us back with awful vividness to that time when the poor victims looked their last from this, upon the bleak boundary-hills of the inland horizon and that hopeless semicircle of the sea on the other side. A terrible and fitting place for execution, indeed! It looms up visible for many miles of lower country around; and as you stand upon the top, earth seems to fall away with such a fatal ease around it!

The stranger is naturally drawn hence to the Court House, where, by calling a clerk from his routine in a room fairly lined and stuccoed with bundles of legal papers, he may get a glimpse of the famous "witch-pins." These are the identical little instruments which the afflicted children drew from different parts of their dress, in the trial-room, declaring that some one of the accused had just caused them to be sharply inserted into their persons. The pins are kept in a small glass bottle, and are thin and rudely made; and as one looks at the curious, homely little relics, it is hard to know whether to laugh at the absurdly insignificant sight, or shudder at the thought of what deadly harm they worked in the hands of the bewitched. So, while one is hesitating, one gives the bottle back to the clerk, who locks it up speedily, and at the next instant is absorbed in the drawing up of some document; leaving the intruder free to

pursue his search for antiquities elsewhere. But the
monuments and remains of the past are nowhere large
enough, in our American towns, to furnish the pilgrim a
complete shelter and make an atmosphere of their own.
The old Curwin Mansion, or " Witch House," to be sure,
with its jutting upper story, and its dark and grimy room
where witch-trials are rumored to have been held, is a
solid scrap of antique gloom ; but an ephemeral drug-
gist's shop has been fastened on to a corner of the old
building, and clings there like a wasp's nest, — as sub-
versive, too, of quiet contemplation.   The descendants of the first settlers have with pious care preserved
the remains of the First Church of Salem, and the plain
little temple may still be seen, though hidden away in
the rear of the solid, brick-built Essex Institute.   Yet,
after all, it is only the skeleton of the thing, the original framework set into a modern covering for protection, — the whole church being about as large as a
small drawing-room only.   Into this little space a few
dumb and shrinking witnesses of the past have been
huddled : the old communion-table, two ancient harpsichords, a single pew-door, a wooden samp-mortar,
and a huge, half-ruinous loom ; and some engraved
portraits of ancient ministers hang upon the walls.
When I visited the place, a party of young men and
women were there, who hopelessly scattered any slight
dust of revery that might have settled on me from
the ancient beams, and sent the ghosts fleeing before
their light laughter.   The young women fingered the old
harpsichords, and incontinently thrummed upon them ;
and one cried, " Play a waltz ! "   She was a pretty
creature ; and, as her gay tone mingled with the rattle
of protesting strings in the worn-out instrument, one
might easily have divined how dire a fate would have

been hers, in the days when men not only believed in
bewitchment, but made it punishable.   Then a young
man who had clung for guidance amid her spells to
the little printed pamphlet that describes the church,
read aloud from its pages, seriously: " ' Nowhere else
in this land may one find so ancient and worshipful a
shrine.   Within these walls, silent with the remembered
presence of Endicott, Skelton, Higginson, Roger Williams, and their grave compeers, the very day seems
haunted, and the sunshine falls but soberly in.' "

"O don't!" besought the siren, again.   "We're not
in a solemn state."

And, whether it was the spell of her voice or not, I
confess the sunshine did not seem to me either haunted
or sober.

Thus, all through Salem, you encounter a perverse fate
which will not let you be alone with the elusive spirit of
the past.   Yet, on reflection, why should it?   This perverse fate is simply the life of to-day, which has certainly an equal right to the soil with that of our dreams
and memories.   And before long the conflict of past and
present thus occasioned leads to a discovery.

In the first place, it transpires that the atmosphere is
more favorable than at first appears for backward-reach-
ing revery.   The town holds its history in reverence, and
a good many slight traces of antiquity, with the quiet
respect maintained for them in the minds of the inhabitants, finally make a strong cumulative attack on the
imagination.   The very meagreness and minuteness of
the physical witnesses to a former condition of things
cease to discourage, and actually become an incitement
more effective than bulkier relics might impart.   The
delicacy of suggestion lends a zest to your dream; and the
sober streets open out before you into vistas of austere

2

reminiscence. The first night that I passed in Salem, I heard a church-bell ringing loudly, and asked what it was. It was the nine-o'clock bell; and it had been appointed to ring thus every night, a hundred years ago or more. How it reverberated through my mind, till every brain-cell seemed like the empty chamber of a vanished year! Then, in the room where I slept, there was rich and ponderous furniture of the fashion of eld; the bed was draped and canopied with hangings that seemed full of spells and dreamery; and there was a mirror, tall, and swung between stately mahogany posts spreading their feet out on the floor, which recalled that fancy of Hawthorne's, in the tale of " Old Esther Dudley," * about perished dames and grandees made to sweep in procession through " the inner world " of a glass. Such small matters as these engage the fancy, and lead it back through a systematic review of local history with unlooked-for nimbleness. Gradually the mind gets to roving among scenes imaged as if by memory, and bearing some strangely intimate relation to the actual scenes before one. The drift of clouds, the sifting of sudden light from the sky, acquire the import of historic changes of adversity and prosperity. The spires of Salem, seen one day through a semi-shrouding rain, appeared to loom up through the mist of centuries; and the real antiquity of sunlight shone out upon me, at other times, with cunning quietude, from the weather-worn wood of old, unpainted houses. Every hour was full of yesterdays. Something of primitive strangeness and adventure seemed to settle into my mood, and the air teemed with anticipation of a startling event; as if the deeds of the past were continually on the eve of returning. With all this, too,

* See also American Note-Books, Vol. I.; and the first chapter of The House of the Seven Gables.

a certain gray shadow of unreality stole over everything.

Then one becomes aware that this frame of mind,
produced by actual contact with Salem, is subtly akin to
the mood from which so many of Hawthorne's visions
were projected. A flickering semblance, perhaps, of what
to him must have been a constant though subdued and
dreamy flame summoning him to potent incantation over
the abyss of time; but from this it was easy to conceive
it deepened and intensified in him a hundred-fold. Moreover, in his youth and growing-time, the influence itself
was stronger, the suggestive aspect of the town more
salient. If you read even now, on the ground itself, the
story of the settlement and the first century's life of
Salem and the surrounding places, a delicate suffusion of
the marvellous will insensibly steal over the severe facts
of the record, giving them a half-legendary color. This
arises partly from the imaginative and symbolic way of
looking at things of the founders themselves.

John White, the English Puritan divine, who, with the
"Dorchester Adventurers," established the first colony
at Cape Ann, was moved to this by the wish to establish
in Massachusetts Bay a resting-place for the fishermen
who came over from Dorchester in England, so that they
might be kept under religious influences. This was the
origin of Salem; for the emigrants moved, three years
later, to this spot, then called Naumkeag. In the Indian
name they afterward found a proof, as they supposed,
that the Indians were an offshoot of the Jews, because
it "proves to be perfect Hebrew, being called Nahum
Keike; by interpretation, the bosom of consolation."
Later, they named it Salem, " for the peace," as Cotton
Mather says, "which they had and hoped in it "; and
when Hugh Peters on one occasion preached at Great

Pond, now Wenham, he took as his text, "At Enon, near
to Salim, because there was much water there." This
playing with names is a mere surface indication of the
ever-present scriptural analogy which these men were
constantly tracing in all their acts. Cut off by their
intellectual asceticism from any exertion of the imagination in literature, and denying themselves all that side
of life which at once develops and rhythmically restrains
the sense of earthly beauty, they compensated themselves
by running parallels between their own mission and that
of the apostles, — a likeness which was interchangeable
at pleasure with the fancied resemblance of their condition to that of the Israelites. When one considers the
remoteness of the field from their native shores, the
enormous energy needful to collect the proper elements
for a population, and to provide artificers with the means
of work; the almost impassable wildness of the woods;
the repeated leagues of hostile Indians; the depletions by
sickness; and the internal dissensions with which they
had to struggle, — one cannot wonder that they invested
their own unsurpassed fortitude, and their genius for
government and war, with the quality of a special Providence. But their faith was inwoven in the most singular
way with a treacherous strand of credulity and superstition. Sometimes one is impressed with a sense that
the prodigious force by which they subdued the knotty
and forest-fettered land, and overcame so many other
more dangerous difficulties, was the ecstasy of men made
morbidly strong by excessive gloom and indifference to
the present life. "When we are in our graves," wrote
Higginson, "it will be all one whether we have lived
in plenty or penury, whether we have died in a bed of
downe or lockes of straw." And Hawthorne speaks of
the Puritan temperament as "accomplishing so much,

precisely because it imagined and hoped so little." Yet, though they were not, as Winthrop says, " of those that dreame of perfection in this world," they surely had vast hopes at heart, and the fire of repressed imagination played around them and before them as a vital and guiding gleam, of untold value to them, and using a mysterious power in their affairs. They were something morbid in their imaginings, but that this morbid habit was a chief source of their power is a mistaken theory. It is true that their errors of imagination were so closely knit up with real insight, that they could not themselves distinguish between the two. Their religious faith, their outlook into another life, though tinged by unhealthy terrorism, was a solid, energetic act of imagination ; but when it had to deal with intricate tangles of mind and heart, it became credulity. That lurking unhealthiness spread from the centre, and soon overcame their judgment entirely. The bodeful glare of the witchcraft delusion makes this fearfully clear. Mr. Upham, in his " Salem Witchcraft," — one of the most vigorous, true, and thorough of American histories, without which no one can possess himself of the subject it treats, — has shown conclusively the admirable character of the community in which that delusion broke out, its energy, common-sense, and varied activity ; but he points out for us also the perilous state of the Puritan imagination in a matter where religion, physiology, and affairs touched each other so closely as in the witchcraft episode. The persecution at Salem did not come from such deep degeneration as has been assumed for its source, and it was not at the time at all a result of uncommon bigotry. In the persecution in England in 1645 – 46, Matthew Hopkins, the " witch-finder-general," procured the death, " in one year and in one county, of more than

three times as many as suffered in Salem during the
whole delusion"; several persons were tried by water
ordeal, and drowned, in Suffolk, Essex, and Cambridge-
shire, at the same time with the Salem executions; and
capital punishments took place there some years after the
end of the trouble here. It is well known, also, that
persons were put to death for witchcraft in two other
American colonies. The excess in Salem was heightened
by a well-planned imposture, but found quick sustenance
because "the imagination, called necessarily into extraordinary action in the absence of scientific certainty,
was . . . . exercised in vain attempts to discover, unassisted by observation and experiment, the elements and
first principles of nature," * and "had reached a monstrous growth," nourished by a copious literature of magic and demonology, and by the opinions of the most
eminent and humane preachers and poets.

The imagination which makes beauty out of evil, and
that which accumulates from it the utmost intensity of
terror, are well exemplified in Milton and Bunyan.
Doubtless Milton's richly cultured faith, clothed in lustrous language as in princely silks that overhang his
chain-mail of ample learning and argument, was as intense as the unlettered belief of Bunyan; and perhaps he
shared the prevalent opinions about witchcraft; yet when
he touches upon the superstitious element, the material
used is so transfused with the pictorial and poetic quality which Milton has distilled from the common belief,
and then poured into this *image* of the common belief,
that I am not sure he cared for any other quality in it.

> " Nor uglier follow the night-hag, when, call'd
> In secret, riding through the air she comes,
> Lured by the smell of infant blood, to dance

* Upham, I. 382.

With Lapland witches, while the laboring moon
Eclipses at their charms."
Paradise Lost, II. 662.

Again, in Comus : —

" Some say, no evil thing that walks by night,
  Blue meagre hag, or stubborn, unlaid ghost
  That breaks his magic chains at curfew time,
  No goblin, or swart faery of the mine,
  Hath hurtful power o'er true virginity."

How near these passages come to Shakespere, where
he touches the same string! And is it not clear that
both poets exulted so in the *beauty* born among dark,
earthy depths of fear, that they would have rejected any
and every horror which failed to contribute something
to the beautiful? Indeed, it may easily be that such
high spirits accept awful traditions and cruel theologies,
merely because they possess a transmuting touch which
gives these things a secret and relative value not in-
trinsically theirs ; because they find here something to
satisfy an inward demand for immense expansions of
thought, a desire for all sorts of proportioned and balanced extremes. This is no superficial suggestion,
though it may seem so. But in such cases it is not
the positive horror and its direct effect which attract
the poet : a deeper symbolism and an effect both æsthetic
and moral recommend the element to him. With Milton, however, there follows a curious result. He produces his manufactured myth of Sin and Death and his
ludicrous Limbo of Vanity with a gravity and earnestness as convincing as those which urge home any part
of his theme ; yet we are aware that he is only making
poetic pretence of belief ; so that a certain distrust of his
sincerity throughout creeps in, as we read. How much,
we ask, is allegory in the poet's own estimation, and

how much real belief ? Now in Bunyan there is nothing
of this doubt. Though the author declares his narrative
to be the relation of a dream, the figment becomes absolute fact to us; and the homely realism of Giant Despair
gives him a firmer hold upon me as an actual existence,
than all the splendid characterization of Milton's Beelzebub can gain. Even Apollyon is more real. Milton assumes the historic air of the epic poet, Bunyan admits
that he is giving an allegory ; yet of the two the humble
recorder of Christian's progress seems the more worthy
of credit. Something of this effect is doubtless due to art :
the "Pilgrim's Progress" is more adequately couched
in a single and consistent strain than the "Paradise Lost."
Milton, by implying veracity and then vaporing off into
allegory, challenges dispute ; but Bunyan, in humbly
confessing himself a dreamer, disarms his reader and
traps him into entire assent. Certainly Bunyan was
not the greater artist : that supposition will not even
bear a moment's contemplation ; but, as it happened, his
weakness was his strength. He had but one chance.
His work would have been nothing without allegory,
and the simple device of the dream — which is the refuge
of a man unskilled in composition, who feels that his
figures cannot quite stand as self-sufficient entities —
happens to be as valuable to him as it was necessary ;
for the plea of unreality brings out, in the strong light
of surprise, a contrast between the sincere substance of
the story and its assumed insubstantiality. Milton had
many chances, many resources of power to rely on ; but
by grasping boldly at the effect of authenticity he loses
that one among the several prizes within his reach. I
do not know that I am right, but all this seems to me
to argue a certain dividing and weakening influence exerted by the imagination which uses religious or super-

stitious dread for the purposes of beauty; while that which discourses confidently of the passage from this to another life, with all the several stages clearly marked, and floods the whole scene with a vivid and inartificial light from "the powers and terrors of what is yet unseen," affects the mind with every atom of energy economized and concentred.

Leaving the literary question, we may bring this conclusion to bear upon the Puritans and Salem, as their history affected Hawthorne. I have said that a gradual suffusion of the marvellous overspreads the comparatively arid annals of the town, if one reviews them amid the proper influences; and I have touched upon the two phases of imagination which, playing over the facts, give them this atmosphere. Now if what I guess from the contrast between Milton and Bunyan be true, the lower kind of imagination — that is, imagination deformed to credulity — would be likely to be the more impressive. This uncanny quality of superstition, then, is the one which insensibly exudes from the pages of New England's and perhaps especially of Salem's colonial history, as Hawthorne turns them. This is the dank effluence that, mingling with the sweeter and freer air of his own reveries, has made so many people shudder on entering the great romancer's shadowy but serene domain.

And just here it is advisable to triangulate our ground, by bringing Milton, Bunyan, and Hawthorne together in a simultaneous view. Wide apart as the first two stand, they seem to effect a kind of union in this modern genius; or, rather, their influence here conjoins, as the rays from two far-separated stars meet in the eye of him who watches the heavens for inspiration. Something of the peculiar virtue of each of these Puritan writers seems to

2 *   C

have given tone to Hawthorne's no less individual nature. In Bunyan, who very early laid his hand on Hawthorne's intellectual history, we find a very fountain-head of allegory. His impulse, of course, was supremely didactic, only so much of mere narrative interest mixing itself with his work as was inseparable from his native relish for the matter of fact; while in Milton's poetry the clear æsthetic pleasure held at least an exact balance with the moral inspiration, and, as we have just seen, perhaps outweighed it at times. The same powerful, unrelaxing grasp of allegory is found in the American genius as in Bunyan, and there likewise comes to light in his mind the same delight in art for art's sake that added such a grace to Milton's sinewy and large-limbed port. In special cases the allegorical motive has distinctly got the upper hand, in Hawthorne's work; yet even in those the artistic integument, that marvellous verbal style, those exquisite fancies, are not absent: on the contrary, in the very instances where Hawthorne has most constantly and clearly held to the illustration of a single idea, and made his fiction fit itself most absolutely to the jewelled truth it holds, — in these very causes, I say, the command of his genius over literary resources is generally shown by an unusual splendor of means applied to the ideal end in view. It is here that, while resembling Bunyan, he is so unlike him. But more commonly we find in Hawthorne the two moods, the ethical and the æsthetic, exerted in full force simultaneously; and the result seems to be a perfection of unity. The opposing forces, like centripetal and centrifugal attractions, produce a finished sphere. And in this, again, though recalling Milton, he differs from him also. In Milton's epic the tendency is to alternate these moods; and one works against the other. In short, the

two elder writers undergo a good deal of refinement
and proportioning, before mixing their qualities in Hawthorne's veins. However great a controversialist Milton
may be held, too, the very fact of his engaging in the
particular discussions and in the manner he chose, while
never to be deplored, may have something to do with
the want of fusion of the different qualities present in
his poetry. We may say, and doubtless it is so, that
Hawthorne could never have written such magnificent
pamphlets as the "Eikonoklastes," the "Apology," the
"Tetrachordon": I grant that his refinement, though
bringing him something which Milton did not have, has
cost him something else which Milton possessed. But, for
all that, the more deep-lying and inclusive truths which
he constantly entertained, and which barred him from the
temporary exertion of controversy, formed the sources of
his completer harmony. There is a kind of analogy, too,
between the omnipresence of Milton in his work, and
that of Hawthorne in his. The great Puritan singer
cannot create persons : his Satan is Milton himself in
singing-robes, assuming for mere argument's and epic's
sake that side of a debate which he does not believe, yet
carrying it out in the most masterly way ; his angels and
archangels are discriminated, but still they are not divested of his informing quality ; and "Comus" and
"Samson Agonistes," howsoever diverse, are illustrations
of the athletic prime and the autumnal strength of the poet
himself, rather than anywise dramatic evolutions of his
themes. Bunyan, with much less faculty for any subtle
discrimination of characters, also fails to give his persons
individuality, though they stand very distinctly for a
variety of traits : it is with Bunyan as if he had taken
an average human being, and, separating his impulses,
good and evil, had tried to make a new man or woman

out of each; so that there is hardly life-blood enough to
go round among them.   Milton's creatures are in a certain way more vital, though less real.   Bunyan's characters being traits, the other's are moods.   Yet both
groups seem to have been cast in a large, elemental
mould.   Now, Hawthorne is vastly more an adept than
either Milton or Bunyan in keeping the creatures of his
spirit separate, while maintaining amongst them the
bond of a common nature; but besides this bond they
are joined by another, by something which continually
brings us back to the author himself.   It is like a family
resemblance between widely separated relatives, which
suggests in the most opposite quarters the original type
of feature of some strong, far-back progenitor.   These
characters, with far more vivid presence and clear definition than those of the other two writers, are at the
same time based on large and elementary forces, like
theirs.   They are for the most part embodied moods, or
emotions expanded to the stature of an entire human
being, and made to endure unchanged for years together.
Thus, while Hawthorne, as we shall see more fully further on, is essentially a dramatic genius, Bunyan a simple allegorist, and Milton an odic poet of unparalleled
strength, — who, taking dramatic and epic subjects and
failing to fill them, makes us blame not *his* size and
shape, but the too minute intricacies of the theme, —
there is still a sort of underground connection between all
three.   It is curious to note, further, the relation of Milton's majestic and multitudinous speech, the chancellor-
like stateliness of his wit, in prose, to Hawthorne's resonant periods, and dignity that is never weakened though
admirably modified by humor.   Altogether, if one could
compound Bunyan and Milton, combine the realistic imagination of the one with the other's passion for ideas,

pour the ebullient undulating prose style of the poet into the veins of the allegorist's firm, leather-jerkined English, and make a modern man and author of the whole, the result would not be alien to Hawthorne.

Yet that native love of historic murkiness and mossy tradition which we have been learning to associate with Salem would have to be present in this compound being, to make the likeness complete. And this, with the trains of revery and the cast of imagination which it must naturally breed, would be the one thing not easily supplied, for it is the predisposition which gives to all encircling qualities in Hawthorne their peculiar coloring and charm. That predisposition did not find its sustenance only in the atmosphere of sadness and mystery that hangs over the story of Salem; bygone generations have left in the town a whole legacy of legend and shudder-rousing passages of family tradition, with many well-supported tales of supernatural hauntings; and it is worth while to notice how frequent and forcible a use Hawthorne makes of this enginery of local gossip and traditional horror, in preparing the way for some catastrophe that is to come, or in overshooting the mark with some exaggerated rumor which, by pretending to disbelieve it, he causes to have just the right effect upon the reader's mind. Some of the old houses that stand endwise to the street, looking askant at the passer, — especially if he is a stranger in town, — might be veritable treasuries of this sort of material. Gray, close-shuttered, and retiring, they have not so much the look of death; it is more that they are poor, widowed homes that have mournfully long outlived their lords. One would not have them perish; and yet there is something drearily sad about them. One almost feels that the present tenants must be in danger of being crowded out by ghosts, or at least that

they must encounter strange obstacles to living there.
Are not their windows darkened by the light of other
days ? An old mansion of brick or stone has more
character of its own, and is less easily overshadowed
by its own antiquity; but these impressible wooden
abiding-places, that have managed to cling to the soil
through so many generations, seem rife with the inspirations of mortality. They have a depressing influence,
and must often mould the occupants and leave a peculiar impress on them. We are all odd enough in our
way, whatever our origin or habitation ; but is it not
possible that in a town of given size, placed under specified conditions, there should be a greater proportion
of oddities produced than in another differently circum-
stanced ? Certainly, if this be so, it has its advantages
as well as its drawbacks; a stability of surrounding and
of association, which perhaps affects individuals in the
extreme, is still a source of continuity in town character. And Salem is certainly remarkable for strong,
persistent, and yet unexhausted individuality, as a town,
no less than for a peculiar dignity of character which
has become a pronounced trait in many of its children. But, on the other hand, it is fecund of eccen-
tricities. Though many absorb the atmosphere of age
to their great advantage, there must be other temperaments among the descendants of so unique and so
impressionable a body of men as the early settlers of
this region, which would succumb to the awesome and
depressing influences that also lurk in the air; and
these may easily pass from piquant personality into
mere errant grotesqueness. Whether from instinctive
recognition of this or not, it has never seemed to
me remarkable that people here should see appari-
tions of themselves, and die within the year; it did

not strike me as strange when I was told of persons
who had gone mad with no other cause than that of
inherited insanity, — as if, having tried every species of
sane activity for two or three hundred years, a family
should take to madness from sheer disgust with the
monotony of being healthy; nor could any case of
warped idiosyncrasy, or any account of half-maniacal
genius be instanced that seemed at all out of keeping.
One day I passed a house where a crazy man, of harmless temper, habitually amused himself with sitting at a
window near the ground, and entering into talk, from
between the half-closed shutters, with any one on the
sidewalk who would listen to him. Such a thing, to be
sure, might easily be met with in twenty other places;
but here it seemed natural and fitting. It was not a
preposterous thought, that any number of other men in
the neighborhood might quietly drop into a similar vein
of decrepitude, and also attempt to palm off their dis-
jointed fancies upon the orderly foot-passengers. I
do not by this mean to insinuate any excessive leaning toward mental derangement on the part of the inhabitants; but it is as if the town, having lived long
enough according to ordinary rules to be justified in
sinking into superannuation, and yet not availing itself
of the privilege, but on the contrary maintaining a life of
great activity, had compensated itself in the persons
of a few individuals. But when one has reached this
mood, one remembers that it is all embodied in "The
House of the Seven Gables." Though Hawthorne, in
the Preface to that romance, takes precautions against
injuring local sentiment, by the assurance that he has
not meant "to describe local manners, nor in any way
to meddle with the characteristics of a community for
whom he cherishes a proper respect and a natural re-

gard," the book is not the less a genuine outgrowth of
Salem.   Perhaps the aspect under which Salem presents
itself to me is tinged with fancy, though Hawthorne in
the same story has called it " a town noted for its frugal,
discreet, well-ordered, and home-loving inhabitants, ...
but in which, be it said, there are odder individuals, and
now and then stranger occurrences, than one meets with
almost anywhere else."   But it is certain that poor
Hepzibah Pyncheon, and the pathetic Clifford, and quaint
Uncle Venner, are types which inevitably present themselves as belonging pre-eminently to this place.   Not less
subtle is the connection with it of the old wizard Maule,
and the manner of his death at the witchcraft epoch ; for
it is hinted in the romance that old Colonel Pyncheon
joined in denouncing the poor man, urged by designs on
a piece of land owned by Maule ; and Mr. Upham's careful research has shown that various private piques were
undoubtedly mixed up in the witchcraft excitement,
and swelled the list of accusations.   Young Holgrave,
the photographer, also, represents in a characteristic way
the young life of the place, the germ that keeps it fresh,
and even dreams at times of throwing off entirely the
visible remains of the past.

It may be mentioned, at this point, as a coincidence,
even if not showing how Hawthorne insensibly drew
together from a hundred nooks and crannies, and formulated and embodied his impressions of this his native
place in " The House of the Seven Gables," that the
name of Thomas Maule (the builder of the house, and
son of the Matthew brought to his death by Colonel
Pyncheon) appears in Felt's " Annals of Salem " as that
of a sympathizer with the Quakers.   He was also author
of a book called " Truth Held Forth," published in
1695 ; and of a later one, the title of which, " The

Mauler Mauled," shows that he had humor in him as well as pluck. He seems to have led a long career of independent opinion, not altogether in comfort, however, for in 1669 he was ordered to be whipped for saying that Mr. Higginson preached lies, and that his instruction was "the doctrine of devils"; and his book of "Truth Held Forth," which contained severe reflections on the government for its treatment of the Quakers, was seized and suppressed. It is not improbable that at some time Hawthorne may have read of this person. At all events, he serves as a plausible suggestion of the Maule who so early in the romance utters his prophecy of ill against Colonel Pyncheon, that he "shall have blood to drink."

Another minor coincidence, and yet proper to be noted, is that of the laboring-man Dixey, who appears in the opening of the story with some comments upon Aunt Hepzibah's scheme of the cent-shop, and only comes in once afterward, at the close, to touch upon the subject in a different strain. At first, unseen, but overheard by Miss Pyncheon, he prophesies to a companion, "in a tone as if he were shaking his head," that the cent-shop will fail; and when Clifford and Hepzibah drive off in their carriage, at the end, he remarks sagaciously, "Good business, — good business." It certainly is odd that this subordinate in the romance should find a counterpart in one William Dixy, appointed ensign of the Salem military company which John Hawthorne commanded, in 1645.

The name Pyncheon, also, on which the imaginary Colonel and Judge cast such a doubtful light, was a well-known name in old New England, and became the source of some annoyance to Hawthorne, after he had written the "Seven Gables"; but of this we shall hear more, further on. It is enough, now, to recall these coincidences. I do not suppose that he searched the names out and founded his use of them upon some suggestion already connected with them; indeed, he expressly declared, when remonstrated with on his use of the Pyncheons, that he did not know of any person of that title connected with Salem history of that time; but the circumstance of his using the other names is interesting as showing that many minute facts must have gone to make up the atmosphere of that half-historic and half-imaginative area whereon so many of his short tales and two of the romances were enacted. Maule and Dixey were very likely absorbed into his mind and forgotten; but suddenly when he chanced to need these characters for the "Seven Gables," they revived and took shape with something of the historic impress still upon them. That their very names should have been reproduced finds explanation in the statement once made by Hawthorne to a friend, that the most vexatious detail of romance-writing, to him, was the finding of suitable names for the *dramatis personæ*. Balzac used to look long among the shop-signs of Paris for the precise name needed by a preconceived character, and the absolute invention of such titles is doubtless very rare; few fictionists are gifted with Dickens's fertility in the discovering of names bearing the most forcible and occult relations to the fleshless owners of them. And it is interesting to find that Hawthorne — somewhat as Scott drew from the local repertory of his countrymen's nomenclature — found many of his surnames among those of the settlers of New England. Hooper, Prynne, Felton, Dolliver, Hunnewell, and others belong specially to these and to their descendants. Roger Chillingworth, by the by, recalls the celebrated English divine and controversialist, William ; and Bishop Miles Coverdale's name has been transferred, in "Blithedale," from the reign of Edward VI. to the experimental era of Brook Farm.

It has been urged as a singular deficiency of Hawthorne's, that he could not glorify the moral strength and the sweeter qualities of the Puritans and of their lives. But there was nothing in the direction of his genius that called him to this. As well urge against him that he did not write philanthropic pamphlets, or give himself to the inditing of biographies of benevolent men, or compose fictions on the plan of Sir Charles Grandison, devoted to the illumination of praiseworthy characters. It is the same criticism which condemns Dickens for ridiculing certain preachers, and neglecting to provide the antidote in form of a model apostle, contrasted in the same book. This is the criticism which would reduce all fiction to the pattern of the religious tract. Certain men have certain things before them to do; they cannot devote a lifetime to proving in their published works that they appreciate the excellence of other things which they have no time and no supreme command to do. Nothing, then, is more unsafe, than to imply from their silence that they are deficient in particular phases of sympathy. The exposition of the merits of the New England founders has been steadily in progress from their own time to the present; and they have found a worthy monument in the profound and detailed history of Palfrey. All the more reason, why the only man yet born who could fill the darker spaces of our early history with palpitating light of that wide-eyed truth and eternal human consciousness which cast their deep blaze through Hawthorne's books, should not forego his immortal privilege ! The eulogy is the least many-sided and perpetual of literary forms, and

unless Hawthorne had made himself the eulogist of the
Puritans, he would still have had to turn to our gaze the
wrongs that, for good or ill, were worked into the tissue
of their infant state.   But as it is, he has been able to
suggest a profounder view than is permitted either to
the race of historians or that of philosophers.   It does
not profess to be a satisfactory statement of the whole,
nor is there the least ground for assuming that it does
so.   Its very absorption in certain phases constitutes its
value, — a value unspeakably greater than that of any
other presentation of the Puritan life, because it rests
upon the insight of a poet who has sounded the darkest
depths of human nature.   Had Hawthorne passed mutely
through life, these gloomy-grounded pictures of Puritan-
ism might have faded from the air like the spectres of
things seen in dazzling light, which flit vividly before the
eye for a time, then vanish forever.

But in order to his distinctive coloring, no distortion
had to be practised ; and I do not see why Hawthorne
should be reckoned to have had no sight for that which
he did not record.   With his unique and penetrating
touch he marked certain salient and solemn features
which had sunk deep into his sensitive imagination, and
then filled in the surface with his own profound dramatic
emanations.   But in his subtle and strong moral insight,
his insatiable passion for truth, he surely represented his
Puritan ancestry in the most worthy and obviously sympathetic way.   No New-Englander, moreover, with any
depth of feeling in him, can be entirely wanting in reverence for the nobler traits of his stern forefathers, or in
some sort of love for the whole body of which his own
progenitors formed a group.   Partly for his romantic
purposes, and merely as an expedient of art, Hawthorne
chose to treat this life at its most picturesque points ;

and to heighten the elements of terror which he found
there was an æsthetic obligation with him. But there
is even a subtler cause at work toward this end. The
touches of assumed repugnance toward his Puritan forefathers, which appear here and there in his writings, are
not only related to his ingrained shyness, which would
be cautious of betraying his deeper and truer sentiment
about them, but are the ensigns of a proper modesty in
discoursing of his own race, his own family, as it were.
He shields an actual veneration and a sort of personal
attachment for those brave earlier generations under a
harmless pretence that he does not think at all too
tenderly of them. It is a device frequently and freely
practised, and so characteristically American, and especially Hawthornesque, that it should not have been overlooked for even a moment. By these means, too, he
takes the attitude of admitting the ancestral errors, and
throws himself into an understanding with those who
look at New England and the Puritans merely from the
outside. Here is a profound resort of art, to prepare a
better reception for what he is about to present, by not
seeming to insist on an open recognition from his readers
of the reigning dignity and the noble qualities in the
Puritan colony, which he himself, nevertheless, is always
quietly conscious of. And in this way he really secures
a broader truth, while reserving the pride of locality and
race intact; a broader truth, because to the world at
large the most pronounced feature of the Puritans is their
austerity.

But if other reason were wanted to account for his
dwelling on the shadows and severities of the Puritans
so intently, it might be found in his family history and
its aspects to his brooding mind. His own genealogy
was the gate which most nearly conducted him into the

still and haunted fields of time which those brave but stern religious exiles peopled.

The head of the American branch of the Hathorne, or Hawthorne family, was Major William Hathorne, of Wigcastle, Wilton, Wiltshire,* in England, a younger son, who came to America with Winthrop and his company, by the Arbella, arriving in Salem Bay June 12, 1630. He probably went first to Dorchester, having grants of land there, and was made a freeman about 1634, and representative, or one of "the ten men," in 1635. Although a man of note, his name is not affixed to the address sent by Governor Winthrop and several others from Yarmouth, before sailing, to their brethren in the English Church ; but this is easily accounted for by the fact that Hathorne was a determined Separatist, while the major part of his fellow-pilgrims still clung to Episcopacy. In 1636, Salem tendered him grants of land if he would remove hither, considering that "it was a public benefit that he should become an inhabitant of that town." He removed accordingly, and, in 1638, he had additional lands granted to him "in consideration of his many employments for towne and countrie." Some of these lands were situated on a pleasant rising ground by the South River, then held to be the most desirable part of the town ; and a street running through that portion bears the name of Hathorne to this day. In 1645, he petitioned the General Court that he might be allowed, with others, to form a "company of adventurers" for

---

* This name appears in the American Note-Books (August 22, 1837) as Wigcastle, Wigton. I cannot find any but the Scotch Wigton, and have substituted the Wilton of Wiltshire as being more probable. Memorials of the family exist in the adjoining county of Somerset. (A. N. B., October, 1836.)

trading among the French; and in the same year he was appointed captain of a military company, the first regular troop organized in Salem to "advance the military art." From 1636 to 1643 he had been a representative of the people, from Dorchester and Salem; and from 1662 to 1679 he filled the higher office of an assistant. It was in 1667 that he was empowered to receive for the town a tax of twenty pounds of powder per ton for every foreign vessel over twenty tons trading to Salem and Marblehead, thus forestalling his famous descendant in sitting at the receipt of customs. Besides these various activities, he officiated frequently as an attorney at law; and in the Indian campaign of 1676, in Maine, he left no doubt of his efficiency as a military commander. He led a portion of the army of twelve hundred men which the colony had raised, and in September of this year he surprised four hundred Indians at Cocheco. Two hundred of these "were found to have been perfidious," and were sent to Boston, to be sold as slaves, after seven or eight had been put to death. A couple of weeks later, Captain Hathorne sent a despatch: "We catched an Indian Sagamore of Pegwackick and the gun of another; we found him in many lies, and so ordered him to be put to death, and the Cocheco Indians to be his executioners." There was some reason for this severity, for in crossing a river the English had been ambuscaded by the savages. The captain adds: "We have no bread these three days." This early ancestor was always prominent. He had been one of a committee in 1661, who reported concerning the "patent, laws, and privileges and duties to his Majesty" of the colonists, opposing all appeals to the crown as inconsistent with their charter, and maintained the right of their government to defend itself against all attempts at overthrow. Two years later he was charged by Charles's commissioners with seditious words, and apologized for certain "unadvised" expressions; but the committee of 1661 reported at a critical time, and it needed a good deal of stout-heartedness to make the declarations which it did; and on the whole William Hathorne may stand as a sturdy member of the community. He is perhaps the only man of the time who has left a special reputation for eloquence. Eliot speaks of him as " the most eloquent man of the Assembly, a friend of Winthrop, but often opposed to Endicott, who glided with the popular stream; as reputable for his piety as for his political integrity." And Johnson, in his " Wonder-Working Providence," naming the chief props of the state, says: " Yet through the Lord's mercy we still retain among our Democracy the godly Captaine William Hathorn, whom the Lord hath indued with a quick apprehension, strong memory, and Rhetorick, volubility of speech, which hath caused the people to make use of him often in Publick Service, especially when they have had to do with any foreign government." It is instructive to find what ground he took during the Quaker persecutions of 1657 to 1662. Endicott was a forward figure in that long-sustained horror; and if Hathorne naturally gravitated to the other extreme from Endicott, he would be likely, one supposes, to have sympathized with the persecuted. The state was divided in sentiment during those years; but James Cudworth wrote that " he that will not whip and lash, persecute, and punish men that differ in matters of religion, must not sit on the bench nor sustain any office in the commonwealth." Cudworth himself was deposed; and it happens that Hathorne's terms of service, as recorded, seem at first to leave a gap barely wide enough to include this troublesome period. But, in fact, he resumed power as a magistrate just in time to add at least one to the copious list of bloody and distinguishing atrocities that so disfigure New England history.

Sewel relates * that "Anne Coleman and four of her friends were whipped through Salem, Boston, and Dedham by order of Wm. Hawthorn, who before he was a magistrate had opposed compulsion for conscience; and when under the government of Cromwell it was proposed to make a law that none shall preach without license, he publicly said at Salem that if ever such a law took place in New England he should look upon it as one of the most abominable actions that were ever committed there, and that it would be as eminent a Token of God's having forsaken New England, as any could be." His famous descendant, alluding to this passage,† says that the account of this incident " will last longer, it is to be feared, than any record of his better deeds, though these were many." Yet it should not be overlooked that Hathorne is the only one among the New England persecutors whom Sewel presents to us with any qualifying remark as to a previous more humane temper. Sole, too, in escaping the doom of sudden death which the historian solemnly records in the cases of the rest. So that even if we had not the eminent example of Marcus Aurelius and Sir Thomas More, we might still infer from this that it is no less possible for the man of enlightened ability and culture, than for the ignorant bigot, to find himself, almost of necessity, a chief instrument of religious coercion. Doubtless this energetic Puritan denouncer of persecution never conceived of a fanaticism like that of the Friends, which should so systematically

* History of the Quakers, I. 411, 412.

† See "The Custom House," introductory to "The Scarlet Letter."

outrage all his deepest sense of decency, order, and piety, and — not content with banishment — should lead its subjects to return and force their deaths, as it, were, on the commonwealth; as if a neighbor, under some mistaken zeal, were to repeatedly mix poison with our porridge, until his arrest and death should seem our only defence against murder. Perhaps he was even on the dissenting side, for a time, though there is no record of his saying, like one Edward Wharton of Salem, that the blood of the Quakers was too heavy upon him, and he could not bear it. Wharton received twenty lashes for his sensitiveness, and was fined twenty pounds, and subjected to more torture afterward. But, whatever Hathorne's first feeling, after five years of disturbance, exasperation was added to the responsibility of taking office, and he persecuted. It is easy to see his various justifications, now; yet one cannot wonder that his descendant was oppressed by the act. That he was so cannot be regretted, if only because of the authentic fact that his reading of Sewel inspired one of his most exquisite tales, "The Gentle Boy."

William Hathorne, however, — whatever his taste in persecution, — makes his will peacefully and piously in 1679 – 80 : "*Imprimis*, I give my soul into the hands of Jesus Christ, in whom I hope to bind forevermore my body to the earth in hope of a glorious resurrection with him, whom this vile body shall be made like unto his glorious body; and for the estate God hath given me in this world . . . . I do dispose of as followeth." Then he bequeaths various sums of money to divers persons, followed by "all my housing and land, orchard and appurtenances lying in Salem," to his son John. Among other items, there is one devising his "farm at Groton" to "Gervice Holwyse my gr. ch. [grandchild] if he can come over and enjoy it." Here, by the way, is another bit of coincidence for the curious. *Gervase Helwyse* is the name of the young man who appears in "Lady Eleanor's Mantle," * bereft of reason by his love for the proud and fatal heroine of that tale.† Captain Hathorne must have been well advanced in years when he led his troops against the Indians at Cocheco in 1676; for it was only five years later that he disappeared from history and from this life forever.

His son John inherited, together with housing and land, a good deal of the first Hathorne's various energy and eminence. He was a freeman in 1677, representative from 1683 to 1686, and assistant or counsellor, from 1684 to 1712, except the years of Andros's government. After the deposition of Andros, he was called to join Bradstreet's Council of Safety pending the accession of William of Orange; a magistrate for some years; quartermaster of the Essex companies at first, and afterward, in 1696, the commander of Church's

* Twice-Told Tales, Vol. II.

† In the English Note-Books, May 20, 1854, will be found some facts connected with this name, unearthed by Mr. Hawthorne himself. He there tells of the marriage of one *Gevase Elwes*, son of Sir Gervase Elwes, Baronet of Stoke, in Suffolk. This Gervase died before his father; his son died without issue; and thus John Maggott Twining, grandson of the second Gervase through a daughter, came into the baronetcy. This Twining assumed the name of Elwes. "He was the famous miser, and must have had Hawthorne blood in him," says Mr. Hawthorne, "through his grandfather Gervase, whose mother was a Hawthorne." He then refers to William's devise, and says: "My ancestor calls him his *nephew*." The will says, "gr. ch."; and I suppose the mistake occurred through Mr. Hawthorne's not having that document at hand, for reference.

troops, whom he led against St. John.   He attacked the
enemy's fort there, but, finding his force too weak, drew
off, and embarked for Boston.   As his father's captaincy
had somehow developed into the dignity of major, so
John found himself a colonel in 1711.   But in 1717 he,
too, died.   And now there came a change in the fortunes of the Hathorne line.   Colonel John, during his
magistracy, had presided at the witchcraft trials, and had
shown himself severe, bigoted, and unrelenting in his
spirit toward the accused persons.   Something of this
may be seen in Upham's volumes.   One woman was
brought before him, whose husband has left a pathetic
record of her suffering.   "She was forced to stand with
her arms stretched out.   I requested that I might hold
one of her hands, but it was declined me ; then she desired me to wipe the tears from her eyes, and the sweat
from her face, which I did; then she desired that she
might lean herself on me, saying she should faint.   Justice Hathorne replied she had strength enough to tor-
ment these persons, and she should have strength enough
to stand.   I repeating something against their cruel proceedings, they commanded me to be silent, or else I
should be turned out of the room." *   It is not strange
that this husband should have exclaimed, that God would
take revenge upon his wife's persecutors ; and perhaps
he was the very man whose curse was said to have fallen
upon the justice's posterity.

From this time, at all events, the family lost its commanding position in Salem affairs.   Justice Hathorne's
son Joseph subsided into the quiet of farm-life.   The only
notable association with his name is, that he married
Sarah Bowditch, a sister of the grandfather of the distinguished mathematician, Nathaniel Bowditch.   But it

* Chandler's American Criminal Trials, I. p. 85.

is in the beginning of the eighteenth century that the Hathornes begin to appear as mariners. In the very year of the justice's death, one Captain Ebenezer Hathorne earned the gloomy celebrity attendant on bringing small-pox to Salem, in his brig just arrived from the Barbadoes. Possibly, Justice John may have died from this very infection; and if so, the curse would seem to have worked with a peculiarly malign appropriateness, by making a member of his own family the unwilling instrument of his end. By and by a Captain Benjamin Hathorne is cast away and drowned on the coast, with four other men. Perhaps it was his son, another Benjamin, who, in 1782, being one of the crew of an American privateer, "The Chase," captured by the British, escaped from a prison-ship in the harbor of Charleston, S. C., with six comrades, one of whom was drowned. Thus, gradually, originated the traditional career of the men of this family, — "a gray-headed shipmaster in each generation," as the often-quoted passage puts it, "retiring from the quarter-deck to the homestead, while a boy of fourteen took the hereditary place before the mast." But the most eminent among these hardy skippers is Daniel, the son of farmer Joseph, and grandfather of the author.

Daniel Hathorne lived to be eighty-five, and expired only on April 18, 1796, eight years and a little more before his famous grandson came into the world. Something of the old prowess revived in him, and being a stout seafarer, and by inheritance a lover of independence, he became commander of a privateer during our Revolution; indeed, it is said he commanded several. His guns have made no great noise in history, but their reverberation has left in the air a general tradition of his bravery. The only actual account of his achievements which I

have met with is the following ballad, written by the
surgeon of his ship, who was perhaps better able than
any one else to gauge the valor of his countryman and
commander, by the amount of bloodshed on his piratical
craft: —

BRIG "FAIR AMERICAN": DANIEL HATHORNE, COMMANDER.

The twenty-second of August, before the close of day,
All hands on board our privateer, we got her under weigh.
We kept the Eastern shore on board for forty leagues or more,
When our departure took for sea, from the Isle of Monhegan
      shore.

Bold Hathorne was commander, a man of real worth,
Old England's cruel tyranny induced him to go forth;
She with relentless fury was plundering all the coast,
And thought because her strength was great, our glorious cause
      was lost.

Now farewell to America, — farewell our friends and wives,
We trust in Heaven's peculiar care, for to protect their lives,
To prosper our intended cruise upon the raging main,
And to preserve our dearest friends till we return again.

The wind it being leading and bore us on our way,
As far unto the Eastward as the Gulf of Florida,
When we fell in with a British ship bound homeward from the
      main;
We gave her two bow-chasers, and she returned the same.

We hauled up our courses and prepared for fight;
The contest held four glasses,* until the dusk of night;
Then having sprung our mainmast, and had so large a sea,
We dropped astern, and left our chase till the returning day.

* The time consumed in the emptying of a half-hour glass four times,
— two hours.

Next day we fished our mainmast, the ship still being nigh,
All hands was for engaging, our chance once more to try;
But wind and sea being boisterous, our cannon would not bear;
We thought it quite imprudent, and so we left her there.

We cruised to the Eastward, near the coast of Portuigale:
In longitude of twenty-seven we saw a lofty sail.
We gave her chase, and soon perceived she was a Bristish scow
Standing for fair America with troops for General Howe.

Our captain did inspect her with glasses, and he said: —
" My boys, she means to fight us, but be you not afraid;
All hands repair to quarters, see everything is clear;
We 'll give him a broadside, my boys, as soon as she comes near."

She was prepared with nettings, and her men were well secured,
And bore directly for us, and put us close on board,
When the cannons roared like thunder, and the muskets fired
      amain;
But soon we were alongside, and grappled to her chain.

And now the scene is altered, — the cannon ceased to roar;
We fought with swords and boarding-pikes one glass and some-
      thing more;
The British pride and glory no longer dared to stay,
But cut the Yankee grappling, and quickly bore away.

Our case was not so desperate, as plainly might appear,
Yet sudden death did enter on board our privateer;
Mahany, Clew, and Clemmans, the valiant and the brave,
Fell glorious in the contest, and met a watery grave!

Ten other men were wounded, among our warlike crew,
With them our noble captain, to whom all praise is due.
To him and all our officers let 's give a hearty cheer!
Success to fair America and our good privateer!

This ballad is as long as the cruise, and the rhythm of it seems to show that the writer had not quite got his sea-legs on, in boarding the poetic craft. Especially is he to be commiserated on that unhappy necessity to which the length of the verse compels him, of keeping "the Eastern shore on board for forty leagues," in the first stanza; but it was due to its historic and associative value to give it entire.

Perhaps, after all, it was a shrewd insight that caused the Hathornes to take to the sea. Salem's greatest glory was destined for a term to lie in that direction. Many of these old New England seaports have magnificent recollections of a commercial grandeur hardly to be guessed from their aspect to-day. Castine, Portsmouth, Wiscasset, Newburyport, and the rest, — they controlled the carrying of vast regions, and fortune's wheel whirled amid their wharves and warehouses with a merry and reassuring sound. Each town had its special trade, and kept the monopoly. Portsmouth and Newburyport ruled the trade with Martinique, Guadaloupe, and Porto Rico, sending out fish and bringing back sugar; Gloucester bargained with the West Indies for rum, and brought coffee and dye-stuffs from Surinam; Marblehead had the Bilboa business; and Salem, most opulent of all, usurped the Sumatra, African, East Indian, Brazilian, and Cayenne commerce. By these new avenues over the ocean many men brought home wealth that literally made princes of them, and has left permanent traces in the solid and stately homes they built, still crowded with precious heirlooms, as well as in the refinement nurtured therein, and the thrifty yet generous character they gave to the town. Among these successful merchants was Simon Forrester, who married Nathaniel Hawthorne's great-aunt Rachel, and died in 1817, leaving an immense

property. Him Hawthorne speaks of in "The Custom
House"; alluding to "old King Derby, old Billy Gray,
old Simon Forrester, and many another magnate of his
day; whose powdered head, however, was scarcely in
the tomb, before his mountain-pile of wealth began to
dwindle." But Nathaniel's family neither helped to un-
dermine the heap, nor accumulated a rival one. However good the forecast that his immediate ancestors had
made, as to the quickest and broadest road to wealth,
they travelled long in the wake of success without ever
winning it, themselves. The malediction that fell on
Justice Hathorne's head might with some reason have
been thought to still hang over his race, as Hawthorne
suggests that its "dreary and unprosperous condition
. . . . for many a long year back" would show. Indeed,
the tradition of such a curse was kept alive in his family,
and perhaps it had its share in developing that sadness
and reticence which seem to have belonged to his
father.

It is plain from these circumstances how the idea of
"The House of the Seven Gables" evolved itself from
the history of his own family, with important differences. The person who is cursed, in the romance, uses
a special spite toward a single victim, in order to get
hold of a property which he bequeaths to his own heirs.
Thus a double and treble wrong is done, and the notion
of a curse working upon successive generations is subordinate to the conception of the injury which a man en-
tails to his own descendants by forcing on them a stately
house founded upon a sin. The parallel of the Hathorne
decline in fortune is carried out; but it must be observed
that the peculiar separateness and shyness, which doubtless came to be in some degree a trait of all the Hathornes, is transferred in the book from the family of the

3 *

accursed to that of Maule, the utterer of the evil prophecy. "As for Matthew Maule's posterity," says the romancer, "to all appearance they were a quiet, honest, well-meaning race of people"; but "they were generally poverty-stricken; always plebeian and obscure; working with unsuccessful diligence at handicrafts; laboring on the wharves, or following the sea as sailors before the mast"; and "so long as any of the race were to be found, they had been marked out from other men — not strikingly, nor as with a sharp line, but with an effect that was felt, rather than spoken of — by an hereditary character of reserve. Their companions, or those who endeavored to become such, grew conscious of a circle round about the Maules, within the sanctity or the spell of which, in spite of an exterior of sufficient frankness and good-fellowship, it was impossible for any man to step." The points of resemblance here may be easily distinguished. In the "American Note-Books" occurs an anecdote which recalls the climax of the romance. It concerns Philip English, who had been tried for witchcraft by John Hathorne, and became his bitter enemy. On his death-bed, he consented to forgive him; "But if I get well," said he, "I'll be damned if I forgive him!" One of English's daughters (he had no sons) afterward married a son of John Hathorne. How masterly is the touch of the artist's crayon in this imaginative creation, based upon the mental and moral anatomy of actual beings! It is a delicate study of the true creative art to follow out this romantic shape, and contrast it with the real creatures and incidents to which it has a sort of likeness. With perfect choice, the artist selects, probably not consciously, but through association, whatever he likes from the real, and deviates from it precisely where he feels this to be fitting; adds a trait here, and transfers

another there ; and thus completes something having a
unity and inspiration of its own, neither a simple reproduction nor an unmixed invention, the most subtile and
harmonious product of the creative power. It is in this
way that "The House of the Seven Gables" comes to be
not merely fancifully a romance typical of Salem, but in
the most essentially true way representative of it. Surely
no one could have better right to thus embody the characteristics of the town than Hawthorne, whose early
ancestors had helped to magnify it and defend it, and
whose nearer progenitors had in their fallen fortunes almost foreshadowed the mercantile decline of the long-
lived capital. Surely no one can be less open to criticism
for illustrating various phases of his townsmen's character
and exposing in this book, as elsewhere, though always
mildly, the gloomier traits of the founders, than this deep-
eyed and gentle man, whose forefathers notably possessed
"all the Puritanic traits, both good and evil," and who
uses what is as much to the disadvantage of his own
blood as to that of others, with such absolute, admirable
impartiality.

III.

BOYHOOD. — COLLEGE DAYS. — FANSHAWE.

1804–1828.

ITH such antecedents behind him, and such associations awaiting him, Nathaniel Hawthorne was born, July 4, 1804.

His father, the captain of a trading-vessel, was one of three sons of the privateersman Daniel, and was born in 1776; so that both father and son, it happens, are associated by time of birth with the year and the day that American independence has made honorable and immemorial. The elder Nathaniel wore his surname in one of several fashions that his predecessors had provided, — for they had some eight different ways of writing, though presumably but one of pronouncing it, — and called himself Hathorne. It was not long after the birth of his only boy, second of his three children, however, that he left the name to this male successor, with whom it underwent a restoration to the more picturesque and flowered form of Hawthorne. Nathaniel, the son of Daniel, died in Surinam, in the spring of 1808, of a fever, it is thought, and left his widow stricken with a lifelong grief, his family suddenly overwhelmed with sorrow and solitude. I think I cannot convey the sadness of this more fully than by simply saying it. Yet sombre as the event is, it seems a fit overture to the opening life of this spirit so nobly sad whom we are about to study. The tradition seems to have become established that Captain Nathaniel was inclined to melancholy, and very reticent ; also, that though he was an admirable shipmaster, he had a vigorous appetite for reading, and carried many books with him on his long voyages. Those who know the inheritances that come with the Puritan blood will easily understand the sort of dark, underlying deposit of unutterable sadness that often reminds such persons of their austere ancestry ; but, in addition to this, the Hathornes had now firmly imbibed the belief that their family was under a retributive ban for its share in the awful severities of the Quaker and the witchcraft periods. It was not to them the symbolic and picturesque thing that it is to us, but a real overhanging, intermittent oppressiveness, that must often have struck across their actions in a chilling and disastrous way. Their ingrained reticence was in itself, when contrasted with Major Hathorne's fame in oratory, a sort of corroboration of the idea that fate was making reprisals upon them. The captain's children felt this ; and the son, when grown to manhood, was said to greatly resemble his father in appearance, as well. Of the Endicotts, who also figured largely in the maritime history of Salem, it is told that in the West Indies the name grew so familiar as being that of the captain of a vessel, that it became generic ; and when a new ship arrived, the natives would ask, " Who is the Endicott ? " Very likely the Hathornes had as fixed a fame in the ports where they traded. At all events, some forty years after the captain's death at Surinam, a sailor one day stopped Mr. Surveyor Hawthorne on the steps of the Salem Custom House, and asked him if he had

not once a relative — an uncle or a father — who died
in Surinam at the date given above. He had recognized
him by his likeness to the father, of whom Nathaniel
probably had no memory at all.

But he inherited much from his mother, too. She has
been described by a gentleman who saw her in Maine,
as very reserved, " a very pious woman, and a very minute observer of religious festivals," of " feasts, fasts,
new moons, and Sabbaths," and perhaps a little inclined
to superstition. Such an influence as hers would inevitably foster in the son that strain of reverence, and that
especial purity and holiness of thought, which pervade all
that he has written. Those who knew her have said
also, that the luminous, gray, magnificent eyes that so
impressed people in Hawthorne were like hers. She
had been Miss Elizabeth Clarke Manning, the daughter
of Richard Manning, whose ancestors came to New England about 1680, and sister of Richard and of Robert Manning, a well-known pomologist of the same place. After
the death of her husband, this brother Robert came to
her assistance, Captain Hathorne having left but little
property : he was only thirty-two when he died.

Nathaniel had been born in a solid, old-fashioned little
house on Union Street, which very appropriately faced
the old shipyard of the town in 1760 ; and it appears
that in the year before his birth, the Custom House of
that time had been removed to a spot " opposite the long
brick building owned by W. S. Gray, and Benjamin H.
Hathorne," — as if the future Surveyor's association with
the revenue were already drawing nearer to him. The
widow now moved with her little family to the house of
her father, in Herbert Street, the next one eastward
from Union. The land belonging to this ran through
to Union Street, adjoining the house they had left ; and

from his top-floor study here, in later years, Hawthorne could look down on the less lofty roof under which he was born. The Herbert Street house, however, was spoken of as being on Union Street, and it is that one which is meant in a passage of the "American Note-Books" (October 25, 1838), which says, "In this dismal chamber FAME was won," as likewise in the longer revery in the same volume, dated October 4, 1840.

"Certainly," the sister of Hawthorne writes to me of him, "no man ever needed less a formal biography." But the earlier portion of his life, of which so little record has been made public, must needs bear so interesting a relation to his later career, that I shall examine it with as much care as I may.

Very few details of his early boyhood have been preserved; but these go to show that his individuality soon appeared. "He was a pleasant child, quite handsome, with golden curls," is almost the first news we have of him; but his mastering sense of beauty soon made itself known. While quite a little fellow, he is reported to have said of a woman who was trying to be kind to him, "Take her away! She is ugly and fat, and has a loud voice!" When still a very young school-boy, he was fond of taking long walks entirely by himself; was seldom or never known to have a companion; and in especial, haunted Legg's Hill, a place some miles from his home. The impression of his mother's loss and loneliness must have taken deep and irremovable hold upon his heart; the wide, bleak, uncomprehended fact that his father would never return, that he should never see him, seems to have sunk into his childish reveries like a cabalistic spell, turning thought and feeling and imagination toward mournful and mysterious things. Before he had passed from his mother's care to that of the schoolmaster,

it is known that he would break out from the midst of
childish broodings, and exclaim, "There, mother!   I
is going away to sea, some time"; then, with an ominous shaking of the head, "and I'll never come back
again!" The same refrain lurked in his mind when, a
little older, he would tell his sisters fantastic tales, and
give them imaginary accounts of long journeys, which he
should take in future, in the course of which he flew at
will through the air; on these occasions he always ended
with the same hopeless prophecy of his failing to return.
No doubt, also, there was a little spice of boyish mischief in this; and something of the fictionist, for it enabled him to make a strong impression on his audience.
He brought out the *dénouement* in such a way as to
seem — so one of those who heard him has written
— to enjoin upon them "the advice to value him the
more while he stayed with" them.   This choice of the
lugubrious, however, seems to have been native to him;
for almost before he could speak distinctly he is reported
to have caught up certain lines of " Richard III." which
he had heard read; and his favorite among them, always
declaimed on the most unexpected occasions and in his
loudest tone, was, —

    " Stand back, my Lord, and let the coffin pass! "

Though he has nowhere made allusion to the distant
and sudden death of his father, Hawthorne has mentioned an uncle lost at sea, in the " English Notes," * —
a startling passage.   " If it is not known how and when
a man dies," he says " it makes a ghost of him for many
years thereafter, perhaps for centuries.   King Arthur is
an example; also the Emperor Frederic [Barbarossa] and

* June 30, 1854.

other famous men who were thought to be alive ages
after their disappearance. So with private individuals.
I had an uncle John, who went a voyage to sea about
the beginning of the War of 1812, and has never returned to this hour. But as long as his mother lived, as
many as twenty years, she never gave up the hope of
his return, and was constantly hearing stories of persons
whose descriptions answered to his. Some people actually affirmed that they had seen him in various parts of
the world. Thus, so far as her belief was concerned, he
still walked the earth. And even to this day I never
see his name, which is no very uncommon one, without
thinking that this may be the lost uncle." At the time
of that loss Hawthorne was but eight years old; he
wrote this memorandum at fifty; and all that time the
early impression had remained intact, and the old semi-
hallucination about the uncle's being still alive hung
about his mind through forty years. When we change
the case, and replace the uncle in whom he had no very
distinct interest with the father whose decease had so
overclouded his mother's life, and thwarted the deep
yearnings of his own young heart, we may begin to
guess the depth and persistence of the emotions which
must have been awakened in him by this awful silence
and absence of death, so early thrown across the track
of his childish life. I conceive those lonely school-boy
walks, overblown by shadow-freighting murmurs of the
pine and accompanied by the far-off, muffled roll of the
sea, to have been full of questionings too deep for words,
too sacred for other companionship than that of unin-
quisitive Nature; — questionings not even shaped and
articulated to his own inner sense.

Yet, whatever half-created, formless world of profound
and tender speculations and sad reflections the boy was

E

moulding within himself, this did not master him. The seed, as time went on, came to miraculous issue; but as yet the boy remained, healthily and for the most part happily, a boy still. A lady who, as a child, lived in a house which looked upon the garden of the widow's new abiding-place, used to see him at play there with his sisters, a graceful but sturdy little figure; and a little incident of his school-days, at the same time that it shows how soon he began to take a philosophical view of things, gives a hint of his physical powers. He was put to study under Dr. J. E. Worcester, the famous lexicographer, (who, on graduating at Yale, in 1811, had come to Salem and taken a school there for a few years;) and it is told of him at this time, on the best authority, that he frequently came home with accounts of having fought with a comrade named John Knights.

"But why do you fight with him so often?" asked one of his sisters.

"I can't help it," he said. "John Knights is a boy of very quarrelsome disposition."

Something in the judicial, reproving tone of the reply seems to hint that Hawthorne had taken the measure of his rival, physically as well as mentally, and had found himself more than a match for the poor fellow. All that is known of his bodily strength in maturer boyhood and at college weighs on this side; and Horatio Bridge,* his classmate and most intimate friend at Bowdoin College, tells me that, though remarkably calm-tempered, any suspicion of disrespect roused him into readiness to give the sort of punishment that his athletic frame warranted.

But one of the most powerful influences acting on this healthy, unsuspected, un-self-suspecting genius must have

* See Prefatory Note to The Snow Image.

been that of books. The house in Herbert Street was
well provided with them, and he was allowed to make
free choice. His selection was seldom, if ever, questioned; and this was well, for he thus drew to himself
the mysterious aliment on which his genius throve.
Shakespere, Milton, Pope, and Thomson are mentioned
among the first authors with whom he made acquaintance
on first beginning to read; and "The Castle of Indolence" seems to have been one of his favorite poems
while a boy. He is also known to have read, before
fourteen, more or less of Rousseau's works, and to have
gone through, with great diligence, the whole of "The
Newgate Calendar," which latter selection excited a good
deal of comment among his family and relatives, but no
decisive opposition. A remark of his has come down
from that time, that he cared " very little for the history
of the world before the fourteenth century"; and he
had a judicious shyness of what was considered useful
reading. Of the four poets there is of course but little
trace in his works; Rousseau, with his love of nature
and impressive abundance of emotion, seems to stand
more directly related to the future author's development, and "The Newgate Calendar" must have supplied
him with the most weighty suggestions for those deep
ponderings on sin and crime which almost from the first
tinged the pellucid current of his imagination. There is
another book, however, early and familiarly known to
him, which indisputably affected the bent of his genius
in an important degree. This is Bunyan's "Pilgrim's
Progress."

Being a healthy boy, with strong out-of-door instincts
planted in him by inheritance from his seafaring sire, it
might have been that he would not have been brought
so early to an intimacy with books, but for an accident

similar to that which played a part in the boyhoods of Scott and Dickens. When he was nine years old he was struck on the foot by a ball, and made seriously lame. The earliest fragment of his writing now extant is a letter to his uncle Robert Manning, at that time in Raymond, Maine, written from Salem, December 9, 1813. It announces that his foot is no better, and that a new doctor is to be sent for. " May be," the boy writes, " he will do me some good, for Dr. B—— has not, and I don't know as Dr. K—— will." He adds that it is now four weeks since he has been to school, " and I don't know but it will be four weeks longer." This weighing of possibilities, and this sense of the uncertain future, already quaintly show the disposition of the man he is to grow into; though the writing is as characterless as extreme youth, exaggerated distinctness, and copy-books could make it. The little invalid has not yet quite succumbed, however, for the same letter details that he has hopped out into the street once since his lameness began, and been " out in the office and had four cakes." But the trouble was destined to last much longer than even the young seer had projected his gaze. There was some threat of deformity, and it was not until he was nearly twelve that he became quite well. Meantime, his kind schoolmaster, Dr. Worcester (at whose sessions it may have been that Hawthorne read Enfield's " Speaker," the name of which had " a classical sound in his ears," long, long afterward, when he saw the author's tombstone in Liverpool), came to hear him his lessons at home. The good pedagogue does not figure after this in Hawthorne's boyish history; but a copy of Worcester's Dictionary still exists and is in present use, which bears in a tremulous writing on the fly-leaf the legend: " Nathaniel Hawthorne, Esq., with the respects of J. E.

Worcester." For a long time, in the worst of his lameness, the gentle boy was forced to lie prostrate, and choosing the floor for his couch, he would read there all day long. He was extremely fond of cats, — a taste which he kept through life; and during this illness, forced to odd resorts for amusement, he knitted a pair of stockings for the cat who reigned in the household at the time. When tired of reading, he diverted himself with constructing houses of books for the same feline pet, building walls for her to leap, and perhaps erecting triumphal arches for her to pass under. In this period he must have taken a considerable range in literature, for his age; and one would almost say that Nature, seeing so rare a spirit in a sound body that kept him sporting and away from reading, had devised a seemingly harsh plan of luring him into his proper element.

It was more likely after this episode than before, that Bunyan took that hold upon him so fraught with consequences. He went every Sunday to his grandmother Hathorne's, and every Sunday he would lay hands upon the book; then, going to a particular three-cornered chair in a particular corner of the room, "he would read it by the hour, without once speaking." I have already suggested the relations of the three minds, Milton, Bunyan, and Hawthorne. The more obvious effect of this reading is the allegorical turn which it gave the boy's thoughts, manifest in many of his shorter productions while a young man; the most curious and complete issue being that of "The Celestial Railroad," in the "Mosses," where Christian's pilgrimage is so deftly parodied in a railroad route to the heavenly goal. Full of keen satire, it does not, as it might at first seem, tend to diminish Bunyan's dignity, but inspires one with a novel sense of it, as one is made to gradually pierce the shams of certain modern cant. But a more profound consequence was the direction of Hawthorne's expanding thought toward sin and its various and occult manifestations. Imagine the impression upon a mind so fine, so exquisitely responsive, and so well prepared for grave revery as Hawthorne's, which a passage like the following would make. In his discourse with Talkative, Faithful says: "A man may cry out against sin, of policy; but he cannot abhor it but by virtue of a godly antipathy. I have heard many cry out against sin in the pulpit, who can abide it well enough in the heart, house, and conversation."

Here is almost the motive and the moral of "The Scarlet Letter." But Hawthorne refined upon it unspeakably, and probed many fathoms deeper, when he perceived that there might be motives far more complex than that of policy, a condition much more subtly counterfeiting the mien of goodness and spirituality. Talkative replies, "You lie at a catch, I perceive," — meaning that he is sophistical. "No, not I," says Faithful; "I am only for setting things right." Did not this desire of setting things right stir ever afterward in Hawthorne's consciousness? It is not a little singular to trace in Bunyan two or three much more direct links with some of Hawthorne's work. When Christiana at the Palace Beautiful is shown one of the apples that Eve ate of, and Jacob's ladder with some angels ascending upon it, it incites one to turn to that marvellously complete "Virtuoso's Collection," * where Hawthorne has preserved Shelley's skylark and the steed Rosinante, with Hebe's cup and many another impalpable marvel, in the wardenship of the Wandering Jew. So, too, when we read

* Mosses from an Old Manse, Vol. II.

Great-Heart's analysis of Mr. Fearing, this expression, "He had, I think, a Slough of Despond in his mind, a slough that he carried everywhere with him," we can detect the root of symbolical conceptions like that of "The Bosom Serpent." * I cannot refrain from copying here some passages from this same portion which recall in an exceptional way some of the traits of Hawthorne, enough, at least, to have given them a partially prophetic power over his character. Mr. Great-Heart says of Mr. Fearing: "He desired much to be alone; yet he always loved good talk, and often would get behind the screen to hear it." (So Hawthorne screened himself behind his genial reserve.) "He also loved much to see ancient things, and to be pondering them in his mind." What follows is not so strictly analogous throughout. Mr. Honest asks Great-Heart why so good a man as Fearing "should be all his days so much in the dark." And he answers, "There are two sorts of reasons for it. One is, the wise God will have it so: some must pipe, and some must weep. . . . . And for my part, I care not at all for that profession which begins not in heaviness of mind. The first string that the musician usually touches is the bass, when he intends to put all in tune. God also plays upon this string first, when he sets the soul in tune for himself. Only there was the imperfection of Mr. Fearing; he could play upon no other music but this, till towards his latter end." Let the reader by no means imagine a moral comparison between Hawthorne and Bunyan's Mr. Fearing. The latter, as his creator says, "was a good man, though much down in spirit"; and Hawthorne, eminent in uprightness, was also overcast by a behest to look for

* Mosses from an Old Manse, Vol. II.

the most part at the darker phases of human thinking
and feeling; yet there could not have been the slightest
real similarity between him and the excellent but weak-
kneed Mr. Fearing, whose life is made heavy by the
doubt of his inheritance in the next world. Still, though
the causes differ, it could be said of Hawthorne, as of
Master Fearing, "Difficulties, lions, or Vanity Fair, he
feared not at all; it was only sin, death, and hell that
were to him a terror." I mean merely that Hawthorne
may have found in this character-sketch — Bunyan's most
elaborate one, for the typical subject of which he shows
an evident fondness and leniency — something peculiarly
fascinating, which may not have been without its shaping
influence for him. But the intimate, affectionate, and
lasting relation between Bunyan's allegory and our romancer is something to be perfectly assured of. The
affinity at once suggests itself, and there are allusions in
the "Note-Books" and the works of Hawthorne which
recall and sustain it. So late as 1854, he notes that
"an American would never understand the passage in
Bunyan about Christian and Hopeful going astray along
a by-path into the grounds of Giant Despair, from
there being no stiles and by-paths in our country."
Rarely, too, as Hawthorne quotes from or alludes to
other authors, there is a reference to Bunyan in "The
Blithedale Romance," and several are found in "The Scarlet Letter": it is in that romance that the most powerful
suggestion of kinship between the two imaginations occurs. After Mr. Dimmesdale's interview with Hester,
in the wood, he suffers the most freakish temptations to
various blasphemy on returning to the town: he meets
a deacon, and desires to utter evil suggestions concerning the communion-supper; then a pious and exemplary
old dame, fortunately deaf, into whose ear a mad impulse

urges him to whisper what then seemed to him an
"unanswerable argument against the immortality of the
soul," and after muttering some incoherent words, he
sees "an expression of divine gratitude and ecstasy
that seemed like the *shine of the celestial city* on her
face." Then comes the most frightful temptation of all,
as he sees approaching him a maiden newly won into
his flock. "She was fair and pure as a lily that had
bloomed in Paradise. The minister knew well that he
himself was enshrined within the stainless sanctity of her
heart, which hung its snowy curtains about his image,
imparting to religion the warmth of love, and to love a
religious purity. Satan, that afternoon, had surely led
the poor young girl away from her mother's side, and
thrown her into the pathway of this sorely tempted, or —
shall we not rather say? — this lost and desperate man.
As she drew nigh, the arch-fiend whispered to him to
condense into small compass and drop into her tender
bosom a germ of evil that would be sure to blossom
darkly soon, and bear black fruit betimes." Now, in
the Valley of the Shadow of Death, " poor Christian was
so confounded, that he did not know his own voice. . . .
Just when he was come over against the mouth of the
burning pit, one of the wicked ones got behind him
and stepped up softly to him, and, whisperingly, suggested many grievous blasphemies to him, which he verily
thought had proceeded from his own mind." I need not
enlarge upon the similar drift of these two extracts; still
less mark the matured, detailed, and vividly human and
dramatic superiority of Hawthorne's use of the element
common to both.

For other reading in early boyhood he had Spenser
(it is said that the first book which he bought with his
own money was "The Faëry Queen," for which he kept

4

a fondness all his life), Froissart's "Chronicles," and Clarendon's "History of the Rebellion." The incident of Dr. Johnson's penance in Uttoxeter Market dwelt so intimately in Hawthorne's mind (he has treated it in the "True Stories," and touches very tenderly upon it in "Our Old Home," where he says that he "has always been profoundly impressed" by it), that I fancy a childish impression must have endeared it to him; and Boswell may have been one of his acquisitions at this time. Perhaps Dr. Worcester made the book known to him; and he would not be at a loss to find endless entertainment there.

It was in November, 1813, that the accident at ball disabled him. In June of the same year an event had taken place which must have entered strongly into his heart, as into that of many another Salem boy. Young Lawrence, of the American navy, — who had won honors for himself at Tripoli and in the then prevailing war with Great Britain, — had just been promoted, for gallant achievements off the coast of Brazil, to a captaincy, and put in command of the frigate "Chesapeake," at Boston. A British frigate, the "Shannon," had been cruising for some time in the neighborhood, seeking an encounter with the "Chesapeake," and the valiant Lawrence felt compelled to go out and meet her, though he had only just assumed command, had had no time to discipline his crew (some of whom were disaffected), and was without the proper complement of commissioned officers. Americans know the result; how the "Chesapeake" was shattered and taken in a fifteen minutes' fight off Marblehead, and how Lawrence fell with a mortal wound, uttering those unforgotten words, "Don't give up the ship." The battle was watched by crowds of people from Salem, who swarmed upon the hillsides to get a glimpse of the result.

When the details at last reached the town, many days afterward, Captain George Crowninshield fitted out a flag of truce, sailed for Halifax with ten shipmasters on board, and obtained the bodies of Lawrence and his lieutenant, Ludlow. Late in August they returned, and the city gave itself to solemnities in honor of the lost heroes, with the martial dignity of processions and the sorrowing sound of dirges. Cannon reverberated around them, and flags drooped above them at half-mast, shorn of their splendor. Joseph Story delivered an eloquent oration over them, and there was mourning in the hearts of every one, mixed with that spiritualized sense of national grandeur and human worth that comes at hours like this. Among the throngs upon the streets that day must have stood the boy Nathaniel Hawthorne; not too young to understand, and imbibing from this spectacle, as from many other sources, that profound love of country, that ingrained, ineradicable American quality, which marked his whole maturity.

I have not found any distinct corroboration of the report that Nathaniel again lost the use of his limbs, before going to Maine to live. In another brief, boyish letter dated " Salem, Monday, July 21, 1818 " (all these documents are short, and allude to the writer's inability to find anything more to say), he speaks of wanting to " go to dancing-school a little longer " before removing with his mother to the house which his uncle is building at Raymond. He has also, he says, been to Nahant, which he likes, because " fish are very thick there " ; both items seeming to show a proper degree of activity. There has been a tendency among persons who have found nothing to obstruct the play of their fancies, to establish a notion of almost ill-balanced mental precocity in this powerful young genius, who seems to have advanced as well in muscular as in intellectual development.

It was in October, 1818, that Mrs. Hathorne carried her family to Raymond, to occupy the new house, a dwelling so ambitious, gauged by the primitive community thereabouts, that it gained the title of "Manning's Folly." Raymond is in Cumberland County, a little east of Sebago Lake, and the house, which is still standing, mossy and dismantled, is near what has since been called Radoux's Mills. Though built by Robert Manning, it was purchased afterward by his brother Richard, whose widow married Mr. Radoux, the owner of these mills. Richard Manning's will provided for the establishing of a meeting-house in the neighborhood, and his widow transformed the Folly into a Tabernacle; but, the community ceasing to use it after a few years, it has remained untenanted and decaying ever since, enjoying now the fame of being haunted. Lonely as was the region then, it perhaps had a more lively aspect than at present. A clearing probably gave the inmates of the Folly a clear sweep of vision to the lake; and to the northwest, beyond the open fields that still lie there, frown dark pine slopes, ranging and rising away into "forest-crowned hills; while in the far distance every hue of rock and tree, of field and grove, melts into the soft blue of Mount Washington." This weird and woodsy ground of Cumberland became the nurturing soil of Hawthorne for some years. He stayed only one twelve-month at Sebago Lake, returning to Salem after that for college preparation. But Brunswick, where his academic years were passed, lies less than thirty miles from the home in the woods, and within the same county : doubtless, also, he spent some of his summer vacations at Raymond. The brooding spell of his mother's sorrow was perhaps even deepened in this favorable solitude. I know not whether the faith of women's hearts really finds an easier avenue to such consecration as this of Mrs. Hathorne's, in Salem, than elsewhere. I happen lately to have heard of a widow in that same neighborhood who has remained bereaved and uncomforted for more than seventeen years. With pathetic energy she spends the long days of summer, in long, incessant walks, sorrow-pursued, away from the dwellings of men. But, however this be, I think this divine and pure devotion to a first love, though it may have impregnated Hawthorne's mind too keenly with the mournfulness of mortality, was yet one of the most cogent means of entirely clarifying the fine spirit which he inherited, and that he in part owes to this exquisite example his marvellous, unsurpassed spirituality. A woman thus true to her highest experience and her purest memories, by living in a sacred communion with the dead, annihilates time and is already set in an atmosphere of eternity. Ah, strong and simple soul that knew not how to hide your grief under specious self-comfortings and maxims of convenience, and so bowed in lifelong prostration before the knowledge of your first, unsullied love, be sure the world will sooner or later know how much it owes to such as you!

More than once has Nathaniel Hawthorne touched the delicate fibres of the heart that thrill again in this memorial grief of his mother's; and, incongruous as is the connection of the following passage out of one of the Twice-Told Tales, it is not hard to trace the origin of the sensibility and insight which prompted it: "It is more probably the fact," so it runs, "that while men are able to reflect upon their lost companions as remembrances apart from themselves, women, on the other hand, are *conscious that a portion of their being has gone with the departed, whithersoever he has gone."* But the most perfect example of his sympathy with this sorrow of widowhood is that brief, concentrated, and seemingly slight tale, "The Wives of the Dead," † than which I know of nothing more touching and true, more exquisitely proportioned and dramatically wrought out among all English tales of the same scope and length. It pictures the emotions of "two young and comely women," the "recent brides of two brothers, a sailor and a landsman; and two successive days had brought tidings of the death of each, by the chances of Canadian warfare and the tempestuous Atlantic." The action occupies the night after the news, and turns upon the fact that each sister is roused, unknown to the other, at different hours, to be told that the report about her husband is false. One cannot give its beauty without the whole, more than one can separate the dewdrop from the morning-glory without losing the effect they make together. It is a complete presentment, in little, of all that dwells in widowhood. One sentence I may remind the reader of, nevertheless: "Her face was turned partly inward to the pillow, and had been hidden there to weep; but a look of motionless contentment was now visible upon it, as if her heart, like a deep lake, had grown calm because its dead had sunk down so far within it." Even as his widowed mother's face looked, to the true-souled boy, when they dwelt there together in the forest of pines, beside the placid lake!

Yet clear and searching as must then have been his perceptions, he had not always formulated them or

---

* "Chippings with a Chisel," in Vol. II. of the Twice-Told Tales.

† See The Snow Image, and other Twice-Told Tales.

made them his chief concern. On May 16, 1819 (the first spring after coming to the new abode), he writes to his uncle Robert that "we are all very well"; and "the grass and some of the trees look very green, the roads are very good, there is no snow on Lymington mountains. The fences are all finished, and the garden is laid out and planted. . . . . I have shot a partridge and a henhawk, and caught eighteen large trout out of our brooke. I am sorry you intend to send me to school again." Happy boy! he thinks he has found his vocation: it is, to shoot henhawks and catch trout. But his uncle, fortunately, is otherwise minded, though Nathaniel writes, in the same note: "Mother says she can hardly spare me." The sway of outdoor life must have been very strong over this stalwart boy's temperament. One who saw a great deal of him has related how in the very last year of his life Hawthorne reverted with fondness, perhaps with something of a sick and sinking man's longing for youthful scenes, to these early days at Sebago Lake; "Though it was there," he confessed, "I first got my cursed habits of solitude." "'I lived in Maine,' he said, 'like a bird of the air, so perfect was the freedom I enjoyed.' During the moonlight nights of winter he would skate until midnight all alone upon Sebago Lake, with the deep shadows of the icy hills on either hand. When he found himself far away from his home and weary with the exercise of skating, he would sometimes take refuge in a log-cabin, where half a tree would be burning on the broad hearth. He would sit in the ample chimney, and look at the stars through the great aperture through which the flames went roaring up. 'Ah,' he said, 'how well I recall the summer days, also, when with my gun I roamed at will through the woods of Maine! . . . . Everything is beautiful in youth, for all things are allowed to it then!" The same writer mentions the author's passion for the sea, telling how, on the return from England in 1860, Hawthorne was constantly saying in his quiet, earnest way : "I should like to sail on and on forever, and never touch the shore again." I have it from his sister that he used to declare that, had he not been sent to college, he should have become a mariner, like his predecessors. Indeed, he had the fresh air and the salt spray in his blood.

Still it is difficult to believe that by any chance he could have missed carrying out his inborn disposition toward literature. After we have explained all the fostering influences and formative forces that surround and stamp a genius of this sort, we come at last to the inexplicable mystery of that interior impulse which, if it does not find the right influences at first, presses forth, breaks out to right and left and keeps on pushing, until it feels itself at ease. It cannot wholly *make* its own influences, but it fights to the death before it will give up the effort to lay itself open to these; that is, to get into a proper surrounding. The surrounding may be as far as possible from what we should prescribe as the fit one; but the being in whom perception and receptivity exist in that active state which we call genius will adapt itself, and will instinctively discern whether the conditions of life around it can yield a bare nourishment, or whether it must seek other and more fertile conditions. Hawthorne had an ancestry behind him connected with a singular and impressive history, had remarkable parents, and especially a mother pure and lofty in spirit; lived in a suggestive atmosphere of private sorrow and amid a community of much quaintness; he was also enabled to know books at an early age; yet these things only helped, and not produced, his genius. Sometimes they helped by repression, for there was much that was uncongenial in his early life; yet the clairvoyance, the unconscious wisdom, of that interior quality, *genius*, made him feel that the adjustment of his outer and his inner life was such as to give him a chance of unfolding. Had he gone to sea, his awaking power would have come violently into contact with the hostile conditions of sailor-life : he would have revolted against them, and have made his way into literature against head-wind or reluctant tiller-rope alike. It may, of course, be said that this prediction is too easy. But there are evidences of the mastering bent of Hawthorne's mind, which show that it would have ruled in any case.

As we have seen, he returned to Salem in 1819, to school; and on March 7, 1820, he wrote thus to his mother : —

" I have left school, and have begun to fit for College under Benjm. L. Oliver, Lawyer. So you are in great danger of having one learned man in your family. Mr. Oliver thought I could enter College next commencement, but Uncle Robert is afraid I should have to study too hard. I get my lessons at home, and recite them to him [Mr. Oliver] at 7 o'clock in the morning. . . . . Shall you want me to be a Minister, Doctor, or Lawyer ? A minister I will not be." This is the first dawn of the question of a career, apparently. Yet he still has a yearning to escape the solution. " I am extremely homesick," he says, in one part of the letter ; and at the close he gives way to the sentiment entirely : " O how I wish I was again with you, with nothing to do but to go a gunning. But the happiest days of my life are gone. . . . . After I have got through college, I will come down to learn E—— Latin and Greek." (Is it too fanciful to note that at this stage of the epistle " college "

4 *   F

is no longer spelt with a large C?) The signature to
this letter shows the boy so amiably that I append it.
" I remain," he says,

 " Your
   Affectionate
   and
    Dutiful
     son,
      and
       Most
        Obedient
       and
       Most
       Humble
        Servant,
       and
       Most
        Respectful
       and
       Most
        Hearty
         Well-wisher,
     NATHANIEL HATHORNE."

A jesting device this, which the writer, were he now
living, would perhaps think too trivial to make known;
yet why should we not recall with pleasure the fact that
in his boyish days he could make this harmless little
play, to throw an unexpected ray of humor and gladness
into the lonely heart of his mother, far away in the Maine
woods? And with this pleasure, let there be something
of honor and reverence for his pure young heart.

In another letter of this period * he had made a long

---

* This letter, long in the possession of Miss E. P. Peabody,
Mr. Hawthorne's sister-in-law, unfortunately does not exist any

stride towards the final choice, as witness this extract : —

" I do not want to be a doctor and live by men's diseases, nor a minister to live by their sins, nor a lawyer and live by their quarrels. So, I don't see that there is anything left for me but to be an author. How would you like some day to see a whole shelf full of books, written by your son, with ' Hawthorne's Works ' printed on their backs ? "

But, before going further, it will be well to look at certain " Early Notes," purporting to be Hawthorne's, and published in the Portland " Transcript " at different times in 1871 and 1873. A mystery overhangs them ;* and it has been impossible, up to this time, to procure proof of their genuineness. Most of the persons named in them have, nevertheless, been identified by residents of Cumberland County, who knew them in boyhood, and the internal evidence of authorship seems to make at least some of them Hawthorne's. On the first leaf of the manuscript book, said to contain them, was written (as reported by the discoverer) an inscription, to the effect that the book had been given to Nathaniel Hawthorne by his uncle Richard Manning, " with the advice that he write out his thoughts, some every day, in as good words as he can, upon any and all subjects, as it is one of the best means of his securing for mature years command of thought and language " ; and this was dated at Raymond, June 1, 1816. This account, if true, puts the book into the boy's hands at the age of twelve. He did not go to Raymond to live until two years later, but had certainly been there, before, and his Uncle Richard

longer. The date has thus been forgotten, but the passage is clear in Miss Peabody's recollection.

* See Appendix I.

was already living there in 1816. So that the entries may have begun soon after June, of that year, though their mature character makes this improbable. In this case, they must cover more than a year's time. The dates were not given by the furnisher of the extracts, and only one item can be definitely provided with a date. This must have been penned in or after 1819; and yet it seems also probable that the whole series was written before the author's college days. If genuine, then, they hint the scope and quality of Hawthorne's perceptions during a few years antecedent to his college-course, and — whether his own work or not — they picture the sort of life which he must have seen at Raymond.

"Two kingbirds have built their nest between our house and the mill-pond. The male is more courageous than any creature that I know about. He seems to have taken possession of the territory from the great pond to the small one, and goes out to war with every fish-hawk that flies from one to the other, over his dominion. The fish-hawks must be miserable cowards, to be driven by such a speck of a bird. I have not yet seen one turn to defend himself.

"Swapped pocket-knives with Robinson Cook yesterday. Jacob Dingley says that he cheated me, but I think not, for I cut a fishing-pole this morning, and did it well; besides, he is a Quaker, and they never cheat."

Richard Manning had married Susan Dingley; this Jacob was probably her nephew. In this allusion to Quakers one might fancy a germ of tolerance which ripened into "The Gentle Boy."

"Captain Britton from Otisfield was at Uncle Richard's to-day. Not long ago, uncle brought here from Salem a new kind of potatoes called 'Long Reds.' Captain Britton had some for seed, and uncle asked how he liked them. He answered, 'They yield well, grow very long, — one end is very poor, and the other good for nothing.' I laughed about it after he was gone, but uncle looked sour and said there was no wit in his answer, and that the saying was 'stale.' It was new to me, and his way of saying it very funny. Perhaps uncle did not like to hear his favorite potato spoken of in that way, and that if the captain had praised it he would have been called witty."

" Captain Britton promised to bring 'Gulliver's Travels' for me to read, the next time he comes this way, which is every time he goes to Portland. Uncle Richard has not the book in his library.

" This morning the bucket got off the chain, and dropped back into the well. I wanted to go down on the stones and get it. Mother would not consent, for fear the wall might cave in, but hired Samuel Shane to go down. In the goodness of her heart, she thought the son of old Mrs. Shane not quite so valuable as the son of the Widow Hawthorne. God bless her for all her love for me, though it may be some selfish. We are to have a pump in the well, after this mishap.

" Washington Longley has been taking lessons of a drumming master. He was in the grist-mill to-day, and practised with two sticks on the half-bushel. I was astonished at the great number of strokes in a second, and if I had not seen that he had but two sticks, should have supposed that he was drumming with twenty."

" Major Berry went past our house with a large drove of sheep yesterday. One, a last spring's lamb, gave out; could go no farther. I saw him down near the bridge. The poor dumb creature looked into my eyes, and I thought I knew just what he would say if he could speak, and so asked Mr. Berry what he would sell him for. 'Just the price of his pelt, and that will bring sixty-five cents,' was the answer. I ran and petitioned mother for the money, which she soon gave me, saying with a smile that she tried to make severe, but could not, that I was 'a great spendthrift.' The lamb is in our orchard now, and he made a bow (without taking off his hat) and thanked me this morning for saving him from the butcher.

"Went yesterday in a sail-boat on the Great Pond, with Mr. Peter White of Windham. He sailed up here from White's Bridge to see Captain Dingley, and invited Joseph Dingley and Mr. Ring to take a boat-ride out to the Dingley Islands and to the Images. He was also kind enough to say that I might go (with my mother's consent), which she gave after much coaxing. Since the loss of my father she dreads to have any one belonging to her go upon the water. It is strange that this beautiful body of water is called a 'Pond.' The geography tells of many in Scotland and Ireland not near so large that are called 'Lakes.' It is not respectful to speak of so noble, deep, and broad a collection of clear water as a 'Pond'; it makes a stranger think of geese, and then of goose-pond. Mr. White, who knows all this region, told us that the streams from thirty-five ponds, large and small, flow into this, and he calls it Great Basin. We landed on one of the small islands that Captain Dingley cleared for a sheep pasture when he first came to Raymond. Mr. Ring said that he had to do it to keep his sheep from the bears and wolves. A growth of trees has started on the island, and makes a grove so fine and pleasant, that I wish almost that our house was there. On the way from the island to the Images Mr. Ring caught a black spotted trout that was almost a whale, and weighed before it was cut open, after we got back to Uncle Richard's store, eighteen and a half pounds. The men said that if it had been weighed as soon as it came out of the water it would have been nineteen pounds. This trout had a droll-looking hooked nose, and they tried to make me believe, that if the line had been in my hands, that I should have been obliged to let go, or have been pulled out of the boat. They were men, and had a right to say so. I am a boy, and have a right to think differently. We landed at the Images, when I crept into the cave and got a drink of cool water. In coming home we sailed over a place, not far from the Images, where Mr. White has, at some time, let down a line four hundred feet without finding bottom. This seems strange, for he told us, too, that his boat, as it floated, was only two hundred and fifty feet higher than the boats in Portland Harbor, and that if the Great Pond was pumped dry, a man standing on its bottom, just under where we then were, would be more than one hundred and fifty feet lower than the surface of the water at the Portland wharves. Coming up the Dingley Bay, had a good view of Rattlesnake Mountain, and it seemed to me wonderfully beautiful as the almost setting sun threw over its western crags streams of fiery light. If the Indians were very fond of this part of the country, it is easy to see why; beavers, otters, and the finest fish were abundant, and the hills and streams furnished constant variety. I should have made a good Indian, if I had been born in a wigwam. To talk like sailors, we made the old hemlock-stub at the mouth of the Dingley Mill Brook just before sunset, and sent a *boy* ashore with a hawser, and was soon safely moored to a bunch of alders. After we got ashore Mr. White allowed me to fire his long gun at a mark. I did not hit the mark, and am not sure that I saw it at the time the gun went off, but believe, rather, that I was watching for the noise that I was about to make. Mr. Ring said that with practice I could be a gunner, and that now, with a very heavy charge, he thought I could kill a horse at eight paces. Mr. White went to Uncle Richard's for the night, and I went home and amused my mother with telling how pleasantly the day had passed. When I told her what Mr. Ring said about my killing a horse, she said he was making fun of me. I had found that out before.

"Mr. March Gay killed a rattlesnake yesterday not far from his house, that was more than six feet long and had twelve rattles. This morning Mr. Jacob Mitchell killed another near the same place, almost as long. It is supposed that they were a pair, and that the second one was on the track of its mate. If every rattle counts a year, the first one was twelve years old. Eliak. Maxfield came down to mill to-day and told me about the snakes.

" Mr. Henry Turner of Otisfield took his axe and went out between Saturday and Moose ponds to look at some pine-trees. A rain had just taken off enough of the snow to lay bare the roots of a part of the trees. Under a large root there seemed to be a cavity, and on examining closely something was exposed very much like long black hair. He cut off the root, saw the nose of a bear, and killed him, pulled out the body; saw another, killed that, and dragged out its carcass, when he found that there was a third one in the den, and that he was thoroughly awake, too; but as soon as the head came in sight it was split open with the axe, so that Mr. Turner, alone with only an axe, killed three bears in less than half an hour, the youngest being a good-sized one, and what hunters call a yearling. This is a pretty great bear story, but probably true, and happened only a few weeks ago; for John Patch, who was here with his father Captain Levi Patch, who lives within two miles of the Saturday Pond, told me so yesterday.

" A young man named Henry Jackson, Jr., was drowned two days ago, up in Crooked River. He and one of his friends were trying which could swim the faster. Jackson was behind but gaining; his friend kicked at him in fun, thinking to hit his shoulder and push him back, but missed, and hit his chin, which caused him to take in water and strangle, and before his friend could help or get help, poor Jackson was (Elder Leach says) beyond the reach of mercy. I read one of the Psalms to my mother this morning, and it plainly declares twenty-six times that ' God's mercy endureth forever.' I never saw Henry Jackson; he was a young man just married. Mother is sad, says that she shall not consent to my swimming any more in the mill-pond with the boys, fearing that in sport my mouth might get kicked open, and then sorrow for a dead son be added to that for a dead father, which she says would break her heart. I love to swim, but I shall not disobey my mother.

" Fishing from the bridge to-day, I caught an eel two thirds as long as myself. Mr. Watkins tried to make me believe that he thought it a water moccasin snake. Old Mr. Shane said that it was a ' young sea-sarpint sure.' Mr. Ficket, the black-smith, begged it to take home for its skin, as he said for buskin-strings and flail-strings. So ends my day's fishing.

" Went over to-day to see Watkins make bricks. I have always thought there was some mystery about it, but I can make them myself. Why did the Israelites complain so much at having to make bricks without straw? I should not use straw if I was a brick-maker; besides, when they are burned in the kiln, the straw will burn out and leave the bricks full of holes.

" I can, from my chamber window, look across into Aunt Manning's garden, this morning, and see little Betty Tarbox, flitting among the rose-bushes, and in and out of the arbor, like a tiny witch. She will never realize the calamity that came upon her brothers and sisters that terrible night when her father and mother lay within a few rods of each other, in the snow, freezing to death. I love the elf, because of her loss ; and still my aunt is much more to her than her own mother, in her poverty, could have been."

This little girl was the child of some poor people of the neighborhood who were frozen to death one March night, in 1819. In a letter to his uncle Robert, March 24, 1819, Nathaniel says : " I suppose you have not heard of the death of Mr. Tarbox and his wife, who were froze to death last Wednesday. They were brought out from the Cape on Saturday, and buried from Captain Dingley's on Sunday." This determines the time of writing the last-quoted extract from the journal.

"This morning I saw at the grist-mill a solemn-faced old horse, hitched to the trough. He had brought for his owner some bags of corn to be ground, who, after carrying them into the mill, walked up to Uncle Richard's store, leaving his half-starved animal in the cold wind with nothing to eat, while the corn was being turned to meal. I felt sorry, and nobody being near, thought it best to have a talk with the old nag, and said, ' Good morning, Mr. Horse, how are you to-day ? ' ' Good morning, youngster,' said he, just as plain as a horse can speak, and then said, ' I am almost dead, and I wish I was quite. I am hungry, have had no breakfast, and must stand here tied by the head while they are grinding the corn, and until master drinks two or three glasses of rum at the store, then drag him and the meal up the Ben Ham Hill, and home, and am now so weak that I can hardly stand. O dear, I am in a bad way '; and the old creature cried. I almost cried myself. Just then the miller went down stairs to the meal-trough; I heard his feet on the steps, and not thinking much what I was doing, ran into the mill, and taking the four-quart toll-dish nearly full of corn out of the hopper, carried it out and poured it into the trough before the horse, and placed the dish back before the miller came up from below. When I got out, the horse was laughing, but he had to eat slowly, because the bits were in his mouth. I told him that I was sorry, but did not know how to take them out, and should not dare to if I did, for his master might come out and see what I was about. ' Thank you,' said he, ' a luncheon of corn with the bits in is much better than none. The worst of it is, I have to munch so slowly, that master may come before I finish it, and thrash me for eating his corn, and you for the kindness.' I sat down on a stone out of the wind, and waited in trouble, for fear that the miller and the owner of the corn would come and find out what I had done. At last the horse winked and stuck out his upper lip ever so far, and then said, 'The last kernel is gone'; then he laughed a little, then shook one ear, then the other, then shut his eyes as if to take a nap. I jumped up and said: 'How do you feel, old fellow; any better?' He opened his eyes, and looking at me kindly, answered 'very much,' and then blew his nose exceedingly loud, but he did not wipe it. Perhaps he had no wiper. I then asked if his master whipped him much. He opened his eyes, and looking at me kindly, answered, 'Not much lately; he used to till my hide got hardened, but now he has a white-oak goad-stick with an iron brad in its end, with which he jabs my hind quarters and hurts me awfully.' I asked him why he did not kick up, and knock his tormentor out of the wagon. 'I did try once,' said he, 'but am old and was weak, and could only get my heels high enough to break the whiffletree, and besides lost my balance and fell down flat. Master then jumped down, and getting a cudgel struck me over the head, and I thought my troubles were over. This happened just before Mr. Ben Ham's house, and I should have been finished and ready for the crows, if he had not stepped out and told master not to strike again, if he did he would shake his liver out. That saved my life, but I was sorry, though Mr. Ham meant good.' The goad with the iron brad was in the wagon, and snatching it out I struck the end against a stone, and the stabber flew into the mill-pond. 'There,' says I, 'old colt,' as I threw the goad back into the wagon, 'he won't harpoon you again with *that* iron.' The poor old brute knew well enough what I said, for I looked him in the eye and spoke horse language. At that moment the brute that owned the horse came out of the store, and down the hill towards us. I slipped behind a pile of slabs. The meal was put in the wagon, the horse unhitched, the wagon mounted, the goad picked up and a thrust made, but dobbin was in no hurry. Looking at the end of the stick, the man bawled, 'What little devil has had my goad?' and then began striking with all his strength; but his steed only walked, shaking his head as he

went across the bridge; and I thought I heard the ancient
Equus say as he went, 'Thrash as much as you please, for
once you cannot stab.' I went home a little uneasy, not feeling sure that the feeding the man's corn to his horse was not
stealing, and thinking that if the miller found it out, he would
have me taken down before Squire Longley.

"Polly Maxfield came riding to mill to-day on horseback.
She rode as gracefully as a Trooper. I wish with all my heart
that I was as daring a rider, or half so graceful.

"This morning walked down to the Pulpit Rock Hill, and
climbed up into the pulpit. It looks like a rough place to
preach from, and does not seem so much like a pulpit when one
is in it, as when viewing it from the road below. It is a
wild place, and really a curiosity. I brought a book and sat
in the rocky recess, and read for nearly an hour. This is
a point on the road known to all teamsters. They have a
string of names for reference by which they tell each other
where they met fellow-teamsters and where their loads got
stuck, and I have learned them from those who stop for drinks
at the store. One meets another near our house, and says,
'Where did you meet Bill?' 'Just this side of Small's
Brook,' or 'At the top of Gray's Pinch,' 'At the Dry Mill-
Pond,' 'Just the other side of Lemmy Jones's,' 'On the
long causeway,' 'At Jeems Gowen's,' 'Coming down the
Pulpit Rock Hill,' 'Coming down Tarkill Hill.' I have heard
these answers till I have them by heart, without having any
idea where any of the places are, excepting the one I have
seen to-day. While on the bridge near the Pulpit, Mr. West,
who lives not far away, came along and asked where I had
been. On my telling him, he said that no money would hire
him to go up to that pulpit; that the Devil used to preach from
it long and long ago; that on a time when hundreds of them
were listening to one of his sermons, a great chief laughed in
the Devil's face, upon which he stamped his foot, and the ground

to the southwest, where they were standing, sunk fifty feet, and every Indian went down out of sight, leaving a swamp to this day. He declared that he once stuck a pole in there, which went down easily several feet, but then struck the skull-bone of an Indian, when instantly all the hassocks and flags began to shake; he heard a yell as from fifty overgrown Pequots; that he left the pole and ran for life. Mr. West also said that no Indian had ever been known to go near that swamp since, but that whenever one came that way, he turned out of the road near the house of Mr. West, and went straight to Thomas Pond, keeping to the eastward of Pulpit Rock, giving it a wide berth. Mr. West talked as though he believed what he said.

" A pedler named Dominicus Jordan was to-day in Uncle Richard's store, telling a ghost-story. I listened intently, but tried not to seem interested. The story was of a house, the owner of which was suddenly killed. Since his death the west garret-window cannot be kept closed; though the shutters be hasped and nailed at night, they are invariably found open the next morning, and no one can tell when or how the nails were drawn. There is also on the farm an apple-tree, the fruit of which the owner was particularly fond of, but since his death no one has been able to get one of the apples. The tree hangs full nearly every year, but whenever any individual tries to get one, stones come in all directions as if from some secret infernal battery, or hidden catapult, and more than once have those making the attempts been struck. What is more strange, the tree stands in an open field, there being no shelter near from which tricks can be played without exposure. Jordan says that it seems odd to strangers to see that tree loaded with apples when the snow is four feet deep; and, what is a mystery, there are no apples in the spring; no one ever sees the wind blow one off, none are seen on the snow, nor even the vestige of one on the grass under the tree; and that children may play on the grass under and around it while it is in the blossom, and until the fruit is large enough to tempt them, with perfect safety ; but the moment one of the apples is sought for, the air is full of flying stones.   He further says, that late one starlight night he was passing the house, and looking up saw the phantom walk out of the garret window with cane in hand, making all the motions as if walking on *terra firma*, although what appeared to be his feet were at least six yards from the ground ; and so he went walking away on nothing, and when nearly out of sight there was a great flash and an explosion as of twenty field-pieces, then — nothing.   This story was told with seeming earnestness, and listened to as though it was believed.   How strange it is that almost all persons, old or young, are fond of hearing about the supernatural, though it produces nervousness and fear !   I should not be willing to sleep in that garret, though I do not believe a word of the story.

" The lumbermen from Saccarappa are getting their logs across the Great Pond.   Yesterday a strong northwest wind blew a great raft of many thousands over almost to the mouth of the Dingley Brook.   Their anchor dragged for more than a mile, but when the boom was within twenty or thirty rods of the shore, it brought up, and held, as I heard some men say who are familiar with such business.   All the men and boys went from the mill down to the pond to see the great raft, and I among them.   They have a string of logs fastened end to end and surrounding the great body, which keeps them from scattering, and the string is called a boom.   A small, strong raft, it may be forty feet square, with an upright windlass in its centre, called a capstan, is fastened to some part of the boom.   The small raft is called ' Head Works,' and from it in a yawl-boat is carried the anchor, to which is attached a strong rope half a mile long.   The boat is rowed out the whole length of the rope, the anchor thrown over, and the men on the headworks wind up the capstan and so draw along the acres of logs.   After we went down to the shore, several of the men came out on the boom nearest to us, and, striking a single log, pushed it under and outside; then one man with a gallon jug slung to his back, taking a pickpole, pushed himself ashore on the small single log, — a feat that seemed almost miraculous to me. This man's name was Reuben Murch, and he seemed to be in no fear of getting soused. This masterly kind of navigation he calls 'cuffing the rigging'; nobody could tell me why he gave it that name. Murch went up to the store, had the jug filled with rum (the supply having run out on the headworks), and made the voyage back the way he came. His comrades received him with cheers, and after sinking the log and drawing it back under the boom, proceeded to try the contents of the jug, seeming to be well satisfied with the result of his expedition. It turned out that Murch only rode the single log ashore to show his adroitness, for the yawl-boat came round from the headworks, and brought near a dozen men in red shirts to where we were. I was interested listening to their conversation mixed with sharp jokes. Nearly every man had a nickname. Murch was called 'Captain Snarl'; a tall, fierce-looking man, who just filled my idea of a Spanish freebooter, was 'Dr. Coddle.' I think his real name was Wood. The rum seems to make them crazy, for one, who was called 'Rub-a-dub,' pitched 'Dr. Coddle' head and heels into the water. A gentlemanly man named Thompson, who acted as master of ceremonies, or Grand Turk, interfered and put a stop to what was becoming something like a fight. Mr. Thompson said that the wind would go down with the sun, and that they must get ready to start. This morning I went down to look for them, and the raft was almost to Frye's Island.

"I have read 'Gulliver's Travels,' but do not agree with Captain Britton that it is a witty and uncommonly interesting book; the wit is obscene, and the *lies* too *false*."

The next and last piece of this note-book was printed two years later than the preceding items, and after the death of the person who professed to own the manuscript, but still with the same degree of mystery, except in the matter of date.

"Day before yesterday Mr. Thomas Little from Windham, Mr. M. P. Sawyer of Portland, Mr. Thomas A. Deblois, a lawyer, Mr. Hanson of Windham, and Enoch White, a boy of about my own age, from White's Bridge, came up to the Dingley Brook in a sail-boat. They were on the way to Muddy River Bog, for a day's sport, fishing, and shooting ducks. Enoch proposed that I should go with them. I needed no urging, but knew how unwillingly my mother would consent. They could wait but a few minutes, and Uncle Richard kindly wrote a note, asking her to be willing to gratify me *this* time.

"She said, 'Yes,' but I was almost sorry, knowing that my day's pleasure would cost *her* one of anxiety. However, I gathered up hooks and lines, with some white salted pork for bait, and with a fabulous number of biscuit, split in the middle, the insides well buttered, then skilfully put together again, and all stowed in sister's large work-bag, and slung over my shoulder. I started, making a wager with Enoch White, as we walked down to the boat, as to which would catch the largest number of fish.

"The air was clear, with just breeze enough to shoot us along pleasantly, without making rough waves. The wind was not exactly after us, though we made but two tacks to reach the mouth of Muddy River. The men praised the grand view, after we got into the Great Bay. We could see the White Hills to the northwest, though Mr. Little said they were eighty miles from us; and grand old Rattlesnake, to the northeast, in its immense jacket of green oak, looked more inviting than I had ever seen it; while Frye's Island, with its close growth of great trees, growing to the very edge of the water, looked like a monstrous green raft, floating to the southeastward. Whichever way the eye turned, something charming appeared.

"Mr. Little seems to be familiar with every book that has ever been written, and must have a great memory. Among other things, he said : —

" ' Gentlemen, do you know that this should be called the sea, instead of the Great Pond; that ships should be built here and navigate this water? The surface of the Sea of Galilee, of which we hear so much in the New Testament, was just about equal to the surface of our sea to-day.'

" And then he went on to give a geographical description of the country about the Sea of Galilee, and draw parallels between places named in the Testament and points in sight. His talk stole my attention until we were fairly at Muddy River mouth.

" Muddy River Bog is quite a curiosity. The river empties into the pond between two small sandy capes or points, only a short distance apart; but after running up a little between them we found the bog to widen to fifty or sixty rods in some places, and to be between two or three miles long. People say that it has no bottom, and that the longest poles that ever grew may be run down into the mud and then pushed down with another a little longer, and this may be repeated until the long poles are all gone.

" Coarse, tall water-grass grows up from the mud over every part, with the exception of a place five or six rods wide, running its whole length, and nearly in the middle, which is called the Channel. One can tell at first sight that it is the place for pickerel and water-snakes.

" Mr. Deblois stated something that I never heard before as a fact in natural history, that the pickerel wages war upon all fish, except the trout, who is too active for him; that he is a piscatorial cannibal; but that under all circumstances and in all places, he lives on good terms with the water-snake.

" We saw a great many ducks, but they seemed to know that Mr. Sawyer had a gun, and flew on slight notice. At last, as four were flying and seemed to be entirely out of gunshot, he fired, saying he would frighten them, if no more; when, to our surprise, he brought one down. The gun was loaded with ball, and Mr. Deblois told him he could not do it again in a million shots. Mr. Sawyer laughed, saying that he had always been a

5   G

votary of Chance, and that, as a general thing, she had treated him handsomely.

"We sailed more than a mile up the bog, fishing and trolling for pickerel; and though we saw a great many, not one offered to be caught, but horned pouts were willing, and we caught them till it was no sport. We found a man there who had taken nearly two bushels of pouts. He was on a raft, and had walked from near the foot of Long Pond, in Otisfield. Mr. Little knew him, and, intending to have some fun, said, 'The next time you come to Portland I want half a dozen of your best jewsharps; leave them at my store at Windham Hill. I need them very badly.'

"The man deliberately took from the hook a large pout that he had just pulled up, and, laying his fishing-pole down, began solemnly to explore in his pockets, and brought out six quaint jewsharps carefully tied to pieces of corn-cobs; then he tossed them into our boat to Mr. Little, saying, 'There they are, Tom, and they are as good ones as I ever made; I shall charge you fifty cents for them.' Mr. Little had the worst of the joke; but as the other men began to rally him, he took out the silver and paid the half-dollar; but they laughed at him till he told them, if they would say no more about it, he would give them all the brandy they could drink when they got home.

"Mr. Deblois said he would not be bribed; that he must tell Peter White when he got to Windham Hill.

"Mr. Little said he would not have Peter White know it for a yoke of steers.

"After fishing till all were tired, we landed on a small dry knoll that made out into the bog, to take our luncheon. The men had a variety of eatables, and several bottles that held no eatables. The question was started whether Enoch and I should be invited to drink, and they concluded not to urge us, as we were boys, and under their care. So Mr. Deblois said, 'Boys, anything to eat that is in our baskets is as much yours as ours; help yourselves; but we shall not invite you to drink spirits.'

" We thanked them, and said that we had plenty of our own to eat, and had no relish for spirits, but were very thirsty for water. Mr. Little had been there before, and directed us to a spring of the best of water, that boiled up like a pot from the ground, just at the margin of the bog.

" Before starting to return, the bet between Enoch and myself had to be settled. By its conditions, the one who caught the largest number of fish was to have all the hooks and lines of the other. I counted my string and found twenty-five. Enoch made twenty-six on his; so I was about turning over the spoils, when Mr. Sawyer said that my string was the largest, and that there was a mistake. So he counted, and made twenty-six on mine, and twenty-five on Enoch's. We counted again, and found it was as he said, and Enoch prepared to pay the bet, when Mr. Sawyer again interfered, saying that Enoch's string was certainly larger than mine, and proposed to count again. This time I had but twenty-four, and Enoch twenty-seven. All the men counted them several times over, until we could not tell which was which, and they never came out twice alike.

" At length Mr. Deblois said solemnly, ' Stop this, Sawyer, you have turned these fish into a pack of cards, and are fooling us all.' The men laughed heartily, and so should I if I had known what the point of the joke was.

" Mr. Deblois said the decision as to our bet would have to go over to the next term. After starting for home, while running down the bog, Mr. Sawyer killed three noble black ducks at one shot, but the gun was not loaded this time with ball. Mr. Hanson struck with his fishing-pole, and killed a monstrous water-snake. Mr. Little measured a stick with his hands, and using it as a rule, declared him to be five feet long. If I thought any such snakes ever went over to Dingley Bay, I never would go into the water there again.

" When we got out of the bog into the open water, we found a lively breeze from the northwest, and they landed me at the Dingley Brook in less than an hour, and then kept on like a great white bird down towards the Cape, and for the outlet. I stood and watched the boat until it was nearly half-way to Frye's Island, loath to lose sight of what had helped me to enjoy the day so much. Taking my fish I walked home, and greeted mother just as the sun went out of sight behind the hills in Baldwin. The fish were worthless, but I thought I must have something to show for the day spent. After exhibiting them to mother and sister, and hearing the comments as to their ugliness, and much speculation as to what their horns were for, I gave them to Mr. Lambard, who said that pouts were the best of fish after they were skinned.

" I have made this account of the expedition to please Uncle Richard, who is an invalid and cannot get out to enjoy such sport, and wished me to describe everything just as it had happened, whether witty or silly, and give my own impressions. He has read my diary, and says that it interested him, which is all the reward I desire. And now I add these lines to keep in remembrance the peculiar satisfaction I received in hearing the conversation, especially of Mr. Deblois and Mr. Little. August, 1818, Raymond."

These extracts from the Raymond Journal, if they be genuine, as in most respects I believe they must be, will furnish a clew, otherwise wanting, to the distinct turn which the boy's mind took toward authorship after his return to Salem, and on passing the propylon of classical culture. We can also see in them, I think, the beginning of that painstaking accumulation of fact, the effort to be first of all accurate, which is a characteristic of his maturer and authenticated note-books; very significant, too, is the dash of the supernatural and his tone concerning it. A habit of thus preserving impressions, and of communing with himself through the pen, so constant and assiduous as we know it to have been in his later years, — even when mind and time were preoccupied, —

must have been formed early, to retain so strong a hold upon him. But there is another reason for supposing that he had begun to compose with care before coming from Raymond to Salem ; and this is found in the fact that, in 1820, he began issuing (probably to a very small and intimate circle of subscribers) a neat little weekly paper printed with the pen on sheets of a much-curtailed note size, and written in an excellent style.

The first number, dated Monday, August 21, 1820, opens with the Editor's Address : —

" Our feelings upon sending into the world the first number of the Spectator may be compared to those of a fond Parent, when he beholds a beloved child about to embark on the troubled Ocean of public Life. Perhaps the iron hand of Criticism may crush our humble undertaking, ere it is strengthened by time. Or it may pine in obscurity neglected and forgotten by those, with whose assistance it might become the Pride and Ornament of our Country. . . . . We beg leave farther to remark that in order to carry on any enterprise with spirit MONEY is absolutely necessary. Money, although it is the root of all evil, is also the foundation of everything great and good, and therefore our Subscribers . . . . will please carefully to remember that the terms are two cents per month."

A little further on there is this allusion to the Scriptural proverb cited above : " We have been informed that this expression is incorrect, and that it is the love of Money which is the ' Root of all Evil.' But money is certainly the cause of the love of Money. Therefore, Money is the deepest ' Root of Evil.' " (Observe, here, the young student's pride of reason, and the consciousness of a gift for casuistry !) Under the head of " Domestic News " occur some remarks on the sea-serpent, the deduction from various rumors about the monster being that "he seems to possess a strange and we think rather unusual faculty of appearing in different shapes to different eyes, so that where one person sees a shark, another beholds a nameless dragon." (Here, too, is the humorously veiled distrust that always lurked beneath his dealings with the marvellous.) In the next columns there is found an advertisement of the Pin Society, which "will commence lending pins to any creditable person, on Wednesday, the 23d instant. No numbers except ten, twenty, and thirty will be lent"; and the rate of interest is to be one pin on every ten per day. This bold financial scheme is also carried on by the editor in person, — a combination which in these days would lay him open to suspicions of unfair dealing. I have seen a little manuscript book containing the remarkable constitution and by-laws of this society, in which there were but two members; and it is really a curious study of whimsical intricacy, the work of a mind perfectly accustomed to solitude and fertile in resources for making monotony various and delightful. It does not surprise one to meet with the characteristic announcement from this editor that he has "concluded not to insert deaths and marriages (except of very distinguished persons) in the Spectator. We can see but little use in thus giving to the world the names of the crowd who are tying the marriage knot, and going down to the silent tomb." There is some poetry at the end of the paper, excellent for a boy, but without the easy inspiration of the really witty prose.

It would seem that this weekly once made a beginning, which was also an end, before flourishing up into the series of which I have synopsized the first issue; for there is another Number One without date, but apparently earlier. This contains some exemplary sentiments

"On Solitude," with a touch of what was real profundity in so inexperienced a writer. "Man is naturally a sociable being," he says; "and apart from the world there are no incitements to the pursuit of excellence; there are no rivals to contend with; and therefore there is no improvement. . . . . The heart may be more pure and uncorrupted in solitude than when exposed to the influences of the depravity of the world; but the benefit of virtuous examples is equal to the detriment of vicious ones, and both are equally lost." The "Domestic Intelligence" of this number is as follows: "The lady of Dr. Winthrop Brown, a son and Heir. Mrs. Hathorne's cat, Seven Kittens. We hear that both of the above ladies are in a state of convalescence." Also, "Intentions of Marriage. The beautiful and accomplished Miss Keziah Dingley will shortly be united to Dominicus Jordan Esq." (The young author appears to have allowed himself in this paragraph the stimulus of a little fiction respecting real persons. Dominicus Jordan is the pedler of the Raymond notes. Who Miss Keziah was I do not know, but from the name I guess her to have been a relative, by appellation at least, through Richard Manning's wife. If Hawthorne did not himself call Miss Dingley aunt, he may very likely have heard her commonly spoken of by that title. Did the old, boyish association perhaps unconsciously supply him with a name for the Indian aunt of "Septimius Felton"?) The next item is "DEATHS. We are sorry to be under the necessity of informing our readers that no deaths of importance have taken place, except that of the publisher of this Paper, who died of Starvation, owing to the slenderness of his patronage." Notwithstanding this discouraging incident, one of the advertisements declares that "Employment will be given to any number of indigent

Poets and Authors at this office." But shortly afterward
is inserted the announcement that "Nathaniel Hathorne
proposes to publish by subscription a new edition of the
Miseries of Authors, to which will be added a sequel,
containing Facts and Remarks drawn from his own experience."

In Number Two of the new series, the editor speaks of
a discourse by Dr. Stoughton, "on Tuesday evening. . . . .
With the amount of the contribution which was taken
up . . . . we are unacquainted, as, having no money in
our pockets, we departed before it commenced." This
issue takes a despondent view of the difficulties that beset editors. There is a clever paragraph of "Domestic
News" again. "As we know of no News," it says,
"we hope our readers will excuse us for not inserting
any. The law which prohibits paying debts when a person has no money will apply in this case." Next we
have a very arch dissertation "On Industry": "It has
somewhere been remarked that an Author does not write
the worse for knowing little or nothing of his subject.
We hope the truth of this saying will be manifest in the
present article. With the benefits of Industry we are
not personally acquainted." The desperate editor winds
up his week's budget with a warning to all persons who
may be displeased by observations in the Spectator,
that he is going to take fencing lessons and practise
shooting at a mark. "We also," he adds, "think it
advisable to procure a stout oaken cudgel to be the constant companion of our peregrinations." The assumption of idleness in the essay on Industry, just quoted,
breaks down entirely in a later number, when the editor
— in apologizing for inaccuracies in the printing of his
paper — enumerates his different occupations: "In the
first place we study Latin and Greek. Secondly we

write in the employment of William Manning Esq., [at that time proprietor of an extensive line of stage-coaches]. Thirdly, we are Secretary, Treasurer, and Manager of the 'Pin Society'; Fourthly, we are editor of the Spectator; fifthly, sixthly, and lastly, our own Printers, Printing Press and Types." But the young journalist carried on his labors unabatedly, for the term of some five weeks, and managed to make himself very entertaining. I take from an essay "On Benevolence" a fragment which has a touch of poetry out of his own life. Benevolence, he says, is "to protect the fatherless, and to make the Widow's heart sing for joy." One of the most cherishable effusions is that "On Wealth," in which the venerable writer drops into a charmingly confidential and reminiscent vein. "All men," he begins, "from the highest to the lowest, desire to pursue wealth. . . . . In process of time if we obtain possession" of a sum at first fixed as the ultimatum, "we generally find ourselves as far from being contented as at first. . . . . When I was a boy, I one day made an inroad into a closet, to the secret recesses of which I had often wished to penetrate. I there discovered a quantity of very fine apples. At first I determined to take only one, which I put in my pocket. But those which remained were so very inviting that it was against my conscience to leave them, and I filled my pockets and departed, wishing that they would hold more. But alas! an apple which was unable to find space enough among its companions bounced down upon the floor before all the Family. I was immediately searched, and forced, very unwillingly, to deliver up all my booty." In the same number which contains this composition appears the token of what was doubtless Hawthorne's first recognition in literature. It is a " Communication," of tenor following : —

5 *

"MR. EDITOR : I have observed in some of your last papers, Essays on Various subjects, and am very much pleased with them, and wish you to continue them. If you will do this, you will oblige

"MARIA LOUISA HATHORNE."

"We hail the above communication," writes the editor with exaggerated gratitude, "as the dawn of a happy day for us." In his next and final issue, though (September, 18, 1820), he satirically evinces his dissatisfaction at the want of a literary fraternity in his native land, through this "Request" : —

"As it is part of the plan of the Spectator to criticise home-manufactured publications, we most earnestly desire some of our benevolent Readers to write a book for our special benefit. At present we feel as we were wont to do in the days of our Boyhood, when we possessed a Hatchet, without anything to exercise it upon. We engage to execute the Printing and Binding, and to procure the Paper for the Work, free of all expense to the Author. If this request should be denied us, we must infallibly turn our arms against our own writings, which, as they will not stand the test of criticism, we feel very unwilling to do. We do not wish that the proposed work should be too perfect; the Author will please to make a few blunders for us to exercise our Talents upon."

In these quotations one sees very clearly the increased maturity (though it be only by a year or two) of the lad, since the engrossing of his records at Raymond. We get in these his entire mood, catch gleams of a steady fire of ambition under the light, self-possessed air of assumed indifference, and see how easily already his humor began to play, with that clear and sweet ripeness that warms some of his more famous pages, like late sunshine striking through clusters of mellow and translucent grapes. Yet our grasp of his mental situation at this point would not be complete, without recognition of the graver emotions that sometimes throbbed beneath the surface. The doubt, the hesitancy that sometimes must have weighed upon his lonely, self-reliant spirit with weary movelessness, and all the pain of awakening ambition and departing boyhood, seem to find a symbol in this stanza from the fourth "Spectator" : —

> " Days of my youth, ye fleet away,
>   As fades the bright sun's cheering ray,
>   And scarce my infant hours are gone,
>   Ere manhood's troubled step comes on.
>   My infant hours return no more,
>   And all their happiness is o'er ;
>   The stormy sea of life appears,
>   A scene of tumult and of tears."

Of the vexations of unfledged manhood the boy of sixteen did not speak without knowledge. Various sorts of pressure from uncongenial sources were now and then brought to bear upon him ; there was present always the galling consciousness of depending on others for support, and of being less self-sustaining than approaching manhood made him wish to be. Allusion has been made to his doing writing for his uncle William. "I still continue," he says in a letter of October, 1820, to his mother at Raymond, "to write for Uncle William, and find my salary quite convenient for many purposes." This, to be sure, was a first approach to self-support, and flattering to his sense of proper dignity. But Hawthorne, in character as in genius, had a passion for maturity. An outpouring of his thoughts on this and other matters, directed to his sister, accompanies the letter just cited. Let us read it here as he wrote it more than a half-century ago : —

DEAR SISTER : — I am very angry with you for not sending me some of your poetry, which I consider a great piece of ingratitude. You will not see one line of mine until you return the confidence which I have placed in you. I have bought the ' Lord of the Isles,' and intend either to send or to bring it to you. I like it as well as any of Scott's other poems. I have read Hogg's " Tales," " Caleb Williams," " St. Leon," and " Mandeville." I admire Godwin's novels, and intend to read them all. I shall read the " Abbot," by the author of " Waverley," as soon as I can hire it. I have read all Scott's novels except that. I wish I had not, that I might have the pleasure of reading them again. Next to these I like " Caleb Williams." I have almost given up writing poetry. No man can be a Poet and a book-keeper at the same time. I do find this place most " dismal," and have taken to chewing tobacco with all my might, which, I think, raises my spirits. Say nothing of it in your letters, nor of the " Lord of the Isles." . . . . I do not think I shall ever go to college. I can scarcely bear the thought of living upon Uncle Robert for four years longer. How happy I should be to be able to say, " I am Lord of myself ! " You may cut off this part of my letter, and show the other to Uncle Richard. Do write me some letters in skimmed milk. [The shy spirit finds it thus hard, even thus early, to be under possible surveillance in his epistolary musings, and wants to write invisibly.] I must conclude, as I am in a " monstrous hurry ! "

Your affectionate brother,   NATH. HATHORNE.

P. S. The most beautiful poetry I think I ever saw begins : —

> " She's gone to dwell in Heaven, my lassie,
> She's gone to dwell in Heaven :
> Ye're ow're pure quo' a voice aboon
> For dwalling out of Heaven."

It is not the words, but the thoughts. I hope you have read it, as I know you would admire it.

As to the allusion to college, it is but a single ray let into the obscurity of a season when the sensitive, sturdy, proud young heart must have borne many a vigil of vexatious and bitter revery. And this must not be left out in reckoning the grains and scruples that were compounding themselves into his inner consciousness. But at last he struck a balance, wisely, among his doubts; and in the fall of 1821 he went to Bowdoin to become one of the famous class with Longfellow and Cheever, the memory of which has been enwreathed with the gentle verse of " Morituri Salutamus," — a fadeless garland. In " Fanshawe," an anonymous work of his youth, Hawthorne has pictured some aspects of the college at Brunswick, under a very slight veil of fiction.

" From the exterior of the collegians," he says, " an accurate observer might pretty safely judge how long they had been inmates of those classic walls. The brown cheeks and the rustic dress of some would inform him that they had but recently left the plough, to labor in a not less toilsome field. The grave look and the intermingling of garments of a more classic cut would distinguish those who had begun to acquire the polish of their new residence ; and the air of superiority, the paler cheek, the less robust form, the spectacles of green, and the dress in general of threadbare black, would designate the highest class, who were understood to have acquired nearly all the science their Alma Mater could bestow, and to be on the point of assuming their stations in the world. There were, it is true, exceptions to this general description. A few young men had found their way hither from the distant seaports ; and these were the models of fashion to their rustic companions, over whom they asserted a superiority in exterior accomplishments, which the fresh, though unpolished intellect of the sons of the forest denied them in their literary competitions. A third class, differing widely from both the former, consisted of a few young descendants of the aborigines, to whom an impracticable philanthropy was endeavoring to impart the benefits of civilization.

"If this institution did not offer all the advantages of elder and prouder seminaries, its deficiencies were compensated to its students by the inculcation of regular habits, and of a deep and awful sense of religion, which seldom deserted them in their course through life. The mild and gentle rule . . . . was more destructive to vice than a sterner sway ; and though youth is never without its follies, they have seldom been more harmless than they were here. The students, indeed, ignorant of their own bliss, sometimes wished to hasten the time of their entrance on the business of life ; but they found, in after years, that many of their happiest remembrances, many of the scenes which they would with least reluctance live over again, referred to the seat of their early studies."

He here divides the honors pleasantly between the forest-bred and city-trained youth, having, from his own experience, an interest in each class. Yet I think he must have sided, in fact, with the country boys. Horatio Bridge, his classmate, and throughout life a more confidential friend than Pierce, was brought up on his father's estate at Bridgton, north of Sebago Lake ; and Franklin Pierce, in the class above him, his only other frequent companion, was a native of the New Hampshire hill-lands. He himself, in his outward bearing, perhaps gathered to his person something the look of both the seaport lads and the sturdy mountaineers and woodsmen. He was large and strong (in a letter to his uncle Robert, just before entering college, he gives the measure of his foot, for some new shoes that are to be sent ; it is ten inches), but an interior and ruling grace removed all suspicion of heaviness. Being a sea-captain's son, he would naturally make his connections at college with men who had the out-of-doors glow about them; the simple and severe life at Raymond, too, had put him in sympathy with the people rather than with the patricians (although I see that the reminiscences of some of the old dwellers near Raymond describe the widow and her brother Richard as being exclusive and what was there thought "aristocratic"). Hawthorne, Pierce, and Bridge came together in the Athenæan Society, the newer club of the two college literary unions, and the more democratic; and the trio preserved their cordial relations intact for forty years, sometimes amid confusions and misconstructions, or between cross-fires of troublous counter-considerations, with a rare fidelity. Hawthorne held eminent scholarship easily within his grasp, but he and his two cronies seem to have taken their curriculum very easily, though they all came off well in the graduation. Hawthorne was a good Latinist. The venerable Professor Packard has said that his Latin compositions, even in the Freshman year, were remarkable; and Mr. Longfellow tells me that he recalls the graceful and poetic translations which his classmate used to give from the Roman authors. He got no celebrity in Greek, I believe, but he always kept up his liking for the Latin writers. Some years since a Latin theme of his was found, which had been delivered at an exhibition of the Athenæan Society, in December, 1823.* It shows some niceties of selection, and the style is neat; I even fancy something individual in the choice of the words *sanctior nec beatior*, as applied to the republic, and a distinctly Hawthornesque distinction in the *fulgor tantum fuit sine fervore;* though a relic of this kind should not be examined too closely, and claims the same exemption that one gives to Shelley's school-compelled verses, *In Horologium.*

* See Appendix II.

His English compositions also excited notice. Professor Newman gave them high commendation, and Mr. Bridge speaks of their superiority. But none of them have survived; whether owing to the author's vigilant suppression, or to the accidents of time. It was Hawthorne's habit as a young man to destroy all of his own letters that he could find, on returning home after an absence; and few records of his college life remain. Here is a brief note, however.

BRUNSWICK, August 12, 1823.

MY DEAR UNCLE : — I received your letter in due time, and should have answered it in due season, if I had not been prevented, as L—— conjectures, by laziness. The money was very acceptable to me, and will last me till the end of the term, which is three weeks from next Wednesday. I shall then have finished one half of my college life. . . . . I suppose your farm prospers, and I hope you will have abundance of fruit, and that I shall come home time enough to eat some of it, which I should prefer to all the pleasure of cultivating it. I have heard that there is a steamboat which runs twice a week between Portland and Boston. If this be the case I should like to come home that way, if mother has no apprehension of the boiler's bursting.

I really have had a great deal to do this term, as, in addition to the usual exercises, we have to write a theme or essay of three or four pages, every fortnight, which employs nearly all my time, so that I hope you will not impute my neglect of writing wholly to laziness. . . . .

Your affectionate nephew,

NATH. HATHORNE.

This letter, as well as the others here given, shows how much of boyish simplicity surrounded and protected the rare and distinct personality already unfolded in this youth of eighteen. The mixture makes the charm of

Hawthorne's youth, as the union of genius and common-sense kept his maturity alive with a steady and whole-some light. I fancy that obligatory culture irked him then, as always, and that he chose his own green lanes toward the advancement of learning. His later writings vouchsafe only two slight glimpses of the college days. In his Life of Franklin Pierce, he recalls Pierce's chairmanship of the Athenæan Society, on the committee of which he himself held a place. "I remember, likewise," he says, "that the only military service of my life was as a private soldier in a college company, of which Pierce was one of the officers. He entered into this latter business, or pastime, with an earnestness with which I could not pretend to compete, and at which, perhaps, he would now be inclined to smile." But much more intimate and delightful is the reminiscence which, in the dedicatory preface of "The Snow Image," addressed to his friend Bridge, he thus calls up. "If anybody is responsible for my being at this day an author, it is yourself. I know not whence your faith came: but, while we were lads together at a country college, gathering blueberries in study hours under those tall academic pines; or watching the great logs as they tumbled along the current of the Androscoggin; or shooting pigeons and gray squirrels in the woods; or bat-fowling in the summer twilight; or catching trouts in that shadowy little stream, which, I suppose, is still wandering riverward through the forest, — though you and I will never cast a line in it again, — two idle lads, in short (as we need not fear to acknowledge now), doing a hundred things that the Faculty never heard of, or else it had been the worse for us, — still it was your prognostic of your friend's destiny, that he was to be a writer of fiction." I have asked Mr. Bridge what gave him this impression of Hawthorne,

H

and he tells me that it was an indescribable conviction, aroused by the whole drift of his friend's mind as he saw it. Exquisite indeed must have been that first fleeting aroma of genius; and I would that it might have been then and there imprisoned and perpetuated for our delight. But we must be satisfied with the quick and sympathetic insight with which Hawthorne's friend discovered his true bent. The world owes more, probably, to this early encouragement from a college companion than it can ever estimate.

Nothing in human intercourse, I think, has a more peculiar and unchanging value than the mutual impressions of young men at college : they meet at a moment when the full meaning of life just begins to unfold itself to them, and their fresh imaginations build upon two or three traits the whole character of a comrade, where a maturer man weighs and waits, doubts and trusts, and ends after all with a like or dislike that is only lukewarm. Far on toward the close of life, Hawthorne, in speaking of something told him by an English gentleman respecting a former classmate of the latter's, wrote : "It seemed to be one of those early impressions which a collegian gets of his fellow-students, and which he never gets rid of, whatever the character of the person may turn out to be in after years. I have judged several persons in this way, and still judge them so, though the world has come to very different opinions. Which is right, — the world, which has the man's whole mature life on its side ; or his early companion, who has nothing for it but some idle passages of his youth ? " The world, doubtless, measures more accurately the intrinsic worth of the man's mature actions ; but his essential characteristics, creditable or otherwise, are very likely to be better understood by his classmates. In

this, then, we perceive one of the formative effects on
Hawthorne's mind of his stay at Brunswick. Those
four years of student life gave him a thousand eyes for
observing and analyzing character. He learned then,
also, to choose men on principles of his own. Always
afterward he was singularly independent in selecting
friends; often finding them even in unpopular and
out-of-the-way persons. The affinity between himself
and Bridge was ratified by forty years of close confidence; and Hawthorne never swerved from his early loyalty to Pierce, though his faithfulness gave him severe
trials, both public and private, afterward. I am not
of those who explain this steadfastness by a theory
of early prepossession on Hawthorne's part, blinding
him to Pierce's errors or defects. There is ample proof
in the correspondence between Bridge and himself, which
I have seen, that he constantly and closely scanned his
distinguished friend the President's character with his
impartial and searching eye for human character, what-
soever its relations to himself. I believe if he had
ever found that the original nucleus of honor and of a
certain candor which had charmed him in Pierce was
gone, he would, provided it seemed his duty, have rejected the friendship. As it was, he saw his old friend and
comrade undergoing changes which he himself thought
hazardous, saw him criticised in a post where no one
ever escaped the severest criticism, and beheld him return to private life amid unpopularity, founded, as he
thought, upon misinterpretation of what was perhaps error, but not dishonesty. Meanwhile he felt that the old
"Frank," his brother through Alma Mater, dwelt still
within the person of the public man; and though to
claim that brotherhood exposed Hawthorne, under the
circumstances, to cruel and vulgar insinuations, he saw

that duty led him to the side of his friend, not to that of the harsh multitude.

Perhaps his very earliest contribution to light literature was an apocryphal article which he is said to have written when about eighteen or nineteen. Just then there came into notice a voracious insect, gifted with peculiar powers against pear-trees. Knowing that his uncle was especially concerned in fruit culture, Hawthorne wrote, and sent from college to a Boston paper, a careful description of the new destroyer, his habits, and the proper mode of combating him, all drawn from his own imagination. It was printed, so the tale runs; and a package of the papers containing it arrived in Salem just as the author reached there for a brief vacation. Mr. Manning is said to have accepted in good faith the knowledge which the article supplied, but Hawthorne's amusement was not unmixed with consternation at the success of his first essay.

In the two or three letters from him at college which still survive, there is no open avowal of the inner life, which was then the supplier of events for his outwardly monotonous days; not a breath of that strain of revery and fancy which impressed Bridge's mind! One allusion shows that he systematically omitted declamation; and an old term bill of 1824 (the last year of his course) charges him with a fine of twenty cents for neglect of theme! Spur to authorship : — the Faculty surely did its best to develop his genius, and cannot be blamed for any shortcomings.* Logically, these tendencies away

---

* The amount of this bill, for the term ending May 21, 1824, is but $ 19.62, of which $ 2.36 is made up of fines. The figures give a backward glimpse at the epoch of cheap living, but show that the disinclination of students to comply with college rules was even then expensive. The " average of damages " is only thirty-three cents, from which I infer that the class was not a destructive one.

from essay and oratory are alien to minds destined to produce literature; but empirically, they are otherwise. Meantime, we get a sudden light on some of the solid points of character, apart from genius, in this note from the college president, and the student's parallel epistles.

May 29, 1822.

MRS. ELIZABETH C. HATHORNE.

MADAM: — By note of the Executive Government of this college, it is made my duty to request your co-operation with us in the attempt to induce your son faithfully to observe the laws of this institution. He was this day fined fifty cents for playing cards for money, last term. He played at different times. Perhaps he might not have gamed, were it not for the influence of a student whom we have dismissed from college. It does not appear that your son has very recently played cards; yet your advice may be beneficial to him. I am, madam,

Very respectfully,

Your obedient, humble servant,

WILLIAM ALLEN, *President.*

The next day after this note was written (on May 30, 1822) the subject of it wrote thus: —

" MY DEAR MOTHER: — I hope you have safely arrived in Salem. I have nothing particular to inform you of, except that all the card-players in college have been found out, and my unfortunate self among the number. One has been dismissed from college, two suspended, and the rest, with myself, have been fined fifty cents each. I believe the President intends to write to the friends of all the delinquents. Should that be the case, you must show the letter to nobody. If I am again detected, I shall have the honor of being suspended; when the President asked what we played for, I thought it proper to inform him it was fifty cents, although it happened to be a quart of wine; but if I had told him of that, he would probably have fined me for having a blow. [It appears that the mild dissipation of wine-drinking in vogue at Bowdoin at that time was called having a " blow " ; probably an abbreviation for the common term "blow-out," applied to entertainments.] There was no untruth in the case, as the wine cost fifty cents. I have not played at all this term. I have not drank any kind of spirits or wine this term, and shall not till the last week."

But in a letter to one of his sisters (dated August 5, 1822) a few months afterward, he touches the matter much more vigorously : —

"To quiet your suspicions, I can assure you that I am nei-ther ' dead, absconded, or anything worse.' [The allusion is to some reproach for a long silence on his part.] I have involved myself in no ' foolish scrape,' as you say all my friends sup-pose ; but ever since my misfortune I have been as steady as a sign-post, and as sober as a deacon, have been in no ' blows ' this term, nor drank any kind of ' wine or strong drink.' So that your comparison of me to the ' prodigious son ' will hold good in nothing, except that I shall proba-bly return penniless, for I have had no money this six weeks. . . . . The President's message is not so severe as I expected. I perceive that he thinks I have been led away by the wicked ones, in which, however, he is greatly mistaken. I was full as willing to play as the person he suspects of having enticed me, and would have been influenced by no one. I have a great mind to commence playing again, merely to show him that I scorn to be seduced by another into anything wrong."

I cannot but emphasize with my own words the manly, clear-headed attitude of the young student in these re-marks. He has evidently made up his mind to test the value of card-playing for wine, and thinks himself — as his will be the injury, if any — the best judge of the wisdom of that experiment. A weaker spirit, too, a person who knew himself less thoroughly, would have taken shelter under the President's charitable theory with thanksgiving; but Hawthorne's perfectly simple moral sense and ingrained manhood would not let him forget that self-respect lives by truth alone. In this same letter he touches lesser affairs : —

"I have not read the two novels you mention. I began some time ago to read Hume's ' History of England,' but found it so abominably dull that I have given up the undertaking until some future time. I can procure books of all sorts from the library of the Athenæan Society, of which I am a member. The library consists of about eight hundred volumes, among which is Rees's Cyclopædia [this work was completed in 1819], and many other valuable works. . . . . Our class will be examined on Tuesday for admittance to our Sophomore year. If any of us are found deficient, we shall be degraded to the Freshman class again; from which misfortune may Heaven defend me."

But the young Freshman's trepidation, if he really felt any, was soon soothed ; he passed on successfully through his course. Not only did he graduate well, but he had also, as we shall see, begun to prepare himself for his career. Here is a letter which gives, in a fragmentary way, his mood at graduation : —

"BRUNSWICK, July 14, 1825.

"MY DEAR SISTER : — . . . . I am not very well pleased with Mr. Dike's report of me. The family had before conceived much too high an opinion of my talents, and had probably formed expectations which I shall never realize. I have thought much upon the subject, and have finally come to the conclusion that I shall never make a distinguished figure in the world, and all

I hope or wish is to plod along with the multitude. I do not say this for the purpose of drawing any flattery from you, but merely to set mother and the rest of you right upon a point where your partiality has led you astray. I did hope that Uncle Robert's opinion of me was nearer to the truth, as his deportment toward me never expressed a very high estimation of my abilities."

Mr. Dike was a relative, who had probably gone back to Salem, after seeing the young man at Brunswick, with a eulogy on his lips. Hawthorne's modesty held too delicate a poise to bear a hint of praise, before he had yet been put to the test or accomplished anything decisive. In some ways this modesty and shyness may have postponed his success as an author; yet it was this same delicate admixture which precipitated and made perfect the mysterious solution in which his genius lay. The wish " to plod along with the multitude," seemingly unambitious, is only a veil. The hearts that burn most undyingly with hope of achievement in art, often throw off this vapor of discontent; they feel a prophetic thrill of that nameless suffering through which every seeker of truth must pass, and they long beforehand for rest, for the sweet obscurity of the ungifted.

Another part of this letter shows the writer's standing at college : —

"Did the President write to you about my part? He called me to his study, and informed me that, though my rank in the class entitled me to a part, yet it was contrary to the law to give me one, on account of my neglect of declamation. As he inquired mother's name and residence, I suppose that he intended to write to her on the subject. If so, you will send me a copy of the letter. I am perfectly satisfied with this arrangement, as it is a sufficient testimonial to my scholarship,

while it saves me the mortification of making my appearance
in public at Commencement. Perhaps the family may not be
so much pleased by it. Tell me what are their sentiments on
the subject.

"I shall return home in three weeks from next Wednesday."

Here the dim record of his collegiate days ceases, leaving him on the threshold of the world, a fair scholar, a
budding genius, strong, young, and true, yet hesitant;
halting for years, as if gathering all his shy-souled cour-
age, before entering that arena that was to echo such
long applause of him. Yet doubt not that the purpose
to do some great thing was already a part of his life,
together with that longing for recognition which every
young poet, in the sweet uncertain certainty of beginning,
feels that he must some day deserve. Were not these
words, which I find in "Fanshawe," drawn from the
author's knowledge of his own heart?

"He called up the years that, even at his early age, he had
spent in solitary study, — in conversation with the dead, — while
he had scorned to mingle with the living world, or to be actu-
ated by any of its motives. Fanshawe had hitherto deemed
himself unconnected with the world, unconcerned in its feelings,
and uninfluenced by it in any of his pursuits. In this respect
he probably deceived himself. If his inmost heart could have
been laid open, there would have been discovered that dream of
undying fame, which, dream as it is, is more powerful than a
thousand realities."

Already, while at Bowdoin, Hawthorne had begun to
write verses, and perhaps to print some of them anony-
mously in the newspapers. From some forgotten poem
of his on the sea, a single stanza has drifted down to us,
like a bit of beach-wood, the relic of a bark too frail to
last. It is this : —

6

> " The ocean hath its silent caves,
>   Deep, quiet, and alone ;
> Though there be fury on the waves,
>   Beneath them there is none."

If one lets the lines ring in his ears a little, the true Hawthornesque murmur and half-mournful cadence become clear. I am told, by the way, that when the Atlantic cable was to be laid, some one quoted this to a near relative of the writer's, not remembering the name of the author, but thinking it conclusive proof that the ocean depths would receive the cable securely. Another piece is preserved complete, and much more nearly does the writer justice : —

"MOONLIGHT.

> " We are beneath the dark blue sky,
>   And the moon is shining bright ;
> O, what can lift the soul so high
>   As the glow of a summer night ;
> When all the gay are hushed to sleep
> And they that mourn forget to weep,
>   Beneath that gentle light !

> " Is there no holier, happier land
>   Among those distant spheres,
> Where we may meet that shadow band,
>   The dead of other years ?
> Where all the day the moonbeams rest,
> And where at length the souls are blest
>   Of those who dwell in tears ?

> " O, if the happy ever leave
>   The bowers of bliss on high,
> To cheer the hearts of those that grieve,

And wipe the tear-drop dry ;
It is when moonlight sheds its ray,
More pure and beautiful than day,
And earth is like the sky."

At a time when the taste and manner of Pope in poetry still held such strong rule over readers as it did in the first quarter of the century, these simple stanzas would not have been unworthy of praise for a certain independence ; but there is something besides in the refined touch and the plaintive undertone that belong to Hawthorne's individuality. This gentle and musical poem, it is curious to remember, was written at the very period when Longfellow was singing his first fresh carols, full of a vigorous pleasure in the beauty and inspiration of nature, with a rising and a dying fall for April and Autumn, and the Winter Woods. One can easily fancy that in these two lines from " Sunrise on the Hills " : —

" Where, answering to the sudden shot, thin smoke
Through thick-leaved branches from the dingle broke,"

it was the fire of Hawthorne's fowling-piece in the woods that attracted the young poet, from his lookout above. But Longfellow had felt in the rhythm of these earliest poems the tide-flow of his future, and Hawthorne had as yet hardly found his appropriate element.

In 1828, however, three years after graduating, he published an anonymous prose romance called " Fanshawe," much more nearly approaching a novel than his later books. It was issued at Boston, by Marsh and Capen ; but so successful was Hawthorne in his attempt to exterminate the edition, that not half a dozen copies are now known to be extant. We have seen that he read and admired Godwin and Scott, as a boy. " Kenilworth," " The Pirate," " The Fortunes of Nigel," " Peveril of the Peak," " Quentin Durward," and others of Scott's novels had appeared while Hawthorne was at Bowdoin; and the author of " Waverley " had become the autocrat of fiction.   In addition to this, there is an inbred analogy between New England and Scotland.   In the history and character of the people of each country are seen the influence of Calvin, and of a common-school system.   Popular education was ingrafted upon the policy of both states at about the same period, and in both it has had the same result, making of the farming-class a body of energetic, thrifty, intelligent, and aspiring people.   Scotland and New England alike owe some of their best as well as their least attractive traits to bitter climate and a parsimonious soil; and the rural population of either is pushed into emigration by the scanty harvests at home.   It is not a little singular that the Yankee and the canny Scot should each stand as a butt for the wit of his neighbors, while each has a shrewdness all his own.   The Scotch, it is true, are said to be unusually impervious to a joke, while our Down-Easters are perhaps the most recondite and many-sided of American humorists.   And, though many of the conditions of the two regions are alike, the temperaments of the two races are of course largely dissimilar.   The most salient distinction, perhaps, is that of the Scotch being a musical and dancing nation ; something from which the New-Englanders are fatally far removed.   As if to link him with his Puritan ancestry and stamp him beyond mistake as a Pilgrim and not a Covenanter, Hawthorne was by nature formed with little ear for music. It seems strange that a man who could inform the verses on " Moonlight," just quoted, with so delicate a melody, and never admitted an ill-timed strain or jarring cadence into his pure, symphonious prose, should scarcely be able to distinguish one tune from another.   Yet such was the case. But this was owing merely to the absence of the *musical* instinct.   He would listen with rapture to the unaccompanied voice ; and I have been always much touched by a little incident recorded in the " English Note-Books " : " There is a woman who has several times passed through this Hanover Street in which we live, stopping occasionally to sing songs under the windows ; and last evening . . . she came and sang ' Kathleen O'Moore ' richly and sweetly.   Her voice rose up out of the dim, chill street, and made our hearts throb in unison with it as we sat in our comfortable drawing-room.   I never heard a voice that touched me more deeply.   Somebody told her to go away, and she stopped like a nightingale suddenly shot."   Hawthorne goes on to speak with wonder of the waste of such a voice, " making even an unsusceptible heart vibrate like a harp-string " ; and it is pleasant to know that Mrs. Hawthorne had the woman called within, from the street.   So that his soul was open to sound.   But the unmusicalness of New England, less marked now than formerly, is only a symbol, perhaps, — grievous that it should be so ! — of the superior temperance of our race.   For, by one of those strange oversights that human nature is guilty of, Scotland, in opening the door for song and dance and all the merry crew of mirth, seems to admit quite freely two vagabonds that have no business there, Squalor and Drunkenness.   Yet notwithstanding this grave unlikeness between the two peoples, Hawthorne seems to have found a connecting clew, albeit unwittingly, when he remarked, as he did, on his first visit to Glasgow, that in spite of the poorer classes there excelling even those of Liverpool in filth and drunkenness, " they are a better looking people than the English (and this is true of all classes), more intelligent of aspect, with more regular. features." There is certainly one quality linking the two nations together which has not yet been commented on, in relation to Hawthorne; and this is the natural growth of the weird in the popular mind, both here and in Scotland. It is not needful to enter into this at all at length. In the chapter on Salem I have suggested some of the immediate factors of the weird element in Hawthorne's fiction; but it deserves remark that only Scott and Hawthorne, besides George Sand, among modern novelists, have used the supernatural with real skill and force; and Hawthorne has certainly infused it into his work by a more subtle and sympathetic gift than even the magic-loving Scotch romancer owned. After this digressive prelude, the reader will be ready to hear me announce that "Fanshawe" was a faint reflection from the young Salem recluse's mind of certain rays thrown across the Atlantic from Abbotsford. But this needs qualification.

Hawthorne indeed admired Scott, when a youth; and after he had returned from abroad, in 1860, he fulfilled a tender purpose, formed on a visit to Abbotsford, of re-reading all the Waverley novels. Yet he had long before arrived at a ripe, unprejudiced judgment concerning him. The exact impression of his feeling appears in that delightfully humorous whimsey, " P.'s Correspondence," which contains the essence of the best criticism.* In allusion to Abbotsford, Scott, he says, " whether in verse, prose, or architecture, could achieve but one thing, although that one in infinite variety." And he adds : " For my part, I can hardly regret that Sir Walter Scott had lost his consciousness of outward things before his works

* See Mosses from an Old Manse, Vol. II.

went out of vogue. It was good that he should forget his fame, rather than that fame should first have forgotten him. Were he still a writer, and as brilliant a one as ever, he could no longer maintain anything like the same position in literature. The world, nowadays, requires a more earnest purpose, a deeper moral, and a closer and homelier truth than he was qualified to supply it with. Yet who can be to the present generation even what Scott has been to the past?" Now, in "Fanshawe" there is something that reminds one of Sir Walter; but the very resemblance makes the essential unlikeness more apparent.

The scene of the tale is laid at Harley College, " in an ancient, though not very populous settlement in a retired corner of one of the New England States." This, no doubt, is a reproduction of Bowdoin. Mr. Longfellow tells me that the descriptions of the seminary and of the country around it strongly suggest the Brunswick College. The President of Harley is a Dr. Melmoth, an amiable and simple old delver in learning, in a general way recalling Dominie Sampson, whose vigorous spouse rules him somewhat severely : their little bickerings supply a strain of farce indigenous to Scott's fictions, but quite unlike anything in Hawthorne's later work. A young lady, named Ellen Langton, daughter of an old friend of Dr. Melmoth's, is sent to Harley, to stay under his guardianship. Ellen is somewhat vaguely sketched, in the style of Scott's heroines ; but this sentence ends with a trace of the young writer's quality : "If pen could give an adequate idea of Ellen Langton's beauty, it would achieve what pencil . . . . never could ; for though the dark eyes might be painted, the pure and pleasant thoughts that peeped through them could only be seen and felt." This maiden the doctor once took into his study, to begin a course of modern languages with her; but she " having discovered an old romance among his heavy folios, contrived by the sweet charm of her voice to engage his attention," and quite beguiled him from severer studies. Naturally, she inthralls two young students at the college: one of whom is Edward Wolcott, a wealthy, handsome, generous, healthy young fellow from one of the seaport towns; and the other, Fanshawe, the hero, who is a poor but ambitious recluse, already passing into a decline through overmuch devotion to books and meditation. Fanshawe, though the deeper nature of the two, and intensely moved by his new passion, perceiving that a union between himself and Ellen could not be a happy one, resigns the hope of it from the beginning. But circumstances bring him into intimate relation with her. The real action of the book, after the preliminaries, takes up only some three days, and turns upon the attempt of a man named Butler to entice Ellen away under his protection, then marry her, and secure the fortune to which she is heiress. This scheme is partly frustrated by circumstances, and Butler's purpose towards Ellen then becomes a much more sinister one. From this she is rescued by Fanshawe; and, knowing that he loves her, but is concealing his passion, she gives him the opportunity and the right to claim her hand. For a moment, the rush of desire and hope is so great that he hesitates; then he refuses to take advantage of her generosity, and parts with her for the last time. Ellen becomes engaged to Wolcott, who had won her heart from the first; and Fanshawe, sinking into rapid consumption, dies before his class graduates. It is easy to see how the sources of emotion thus opened attracted Hawthorne. The noble and refined nature of Fanshawe, and the mingled craftiness, remorse, and ferocity of Butler, are crude embodiments of the same characteristics which he afterward treated in modified forms. They are the two poles, the extremes, — both of them remote and chilly, — of good and evil, from which the writer withdrew, after exploring them, into more temperate regions. The movement of these persons is visionary, and their personality faint. But I have marked a few characteristic portions of the book which suggest its tone.

When the young lady's flight with the stranger actually takes place, young Wolcott and President Melmoth ride together in the pursuit, and at this point there occurs a dialogue which is certainly as laughable and is better condensed than most similar passages in Scott, whom it strongly recalls. A hint of Cervantes appears in it, too, which makes it not out of place to mention that Hawthorne studied " Don Quixote " in the original, soon after leaving college.

" ' Alas, youth ! these are strange times,' observed the President, ' when a doctor of divinity and an undergraduate set forth like a knight-errant and his squire, in search of a stray damsel. Methinks I am an epitome of the church militant, or a new species of polemical divinity. Pray Heaven, however, there be no encounter in store for us ; for I utterly forgot to provide myself with weapons.'

" ' I took some thought for that matter, reverend knight,' replied Edward, whose imagination was highly tickled by Dr. Melmoth's chivalrous comparison.

" ' Ay, I see that you have girded on a sword,' said the divine. ' But wherewith shall I defend myself ? — my hand being empty except of this golden-headed staff, the gift of Mr. Langton.'

" ' One of those, if you will accept it,' answered Edward, exhibiting a brace of pistols, ' will serve to begin the conflict, before you join the battle hand to hand.'

6 *   I

" ' Nay, I shall find little safety in meddling with that deadly instrument, since I know not accurately from which end proceeds the bullet,' said Dr. Melmoth. ' But were it not better, seeing we are so well provided with artillery, to betake ourselves, in the event of an encounter, to some stone-wall or other place of strength ? '

" ' If I may presume to advise,' said the squire, ' you, as being most valiant and experienced, should ride forward, lance in hand (your long staff serving for a lance), while I annoy the enemy from afar.'

" ' Like Teucer behind the shield of Ajax,' interrupted Dr. Melmoth, ' or David with his stone and sling. No, no, young man ; I have left unfinished in my study a learned treatise, important not only to the present age, but to posterity, for whose sakes I must take heed to my safety. But lo ! who rides yonder ? ' "

In one place only does the author give full rein to his tragic power ; but this is a vigorous burst, and remarkable also for its sure and trenchant analysis. During his escape with Ellen, Butler is moved to stop at a lonely hut inhabited by his mother, where he finds her dying ; and, torn by the sight of her suffering while she raves and yearns for his presence, he makes himself known to her.

" At that unforgotten voice, the darkness burst away at once from her soul. She arose in bed, her eyes and her whole countenance beaming with joy, and threw her arms about his neck. A multitude of words seem struggling for utterance ; but they gave place to a low moaning sound, and then to the silence of death. The one moment of happiness, that recompensed years of sorrow, had been her last. . . . . As he [Butler] looked, the expression of enthusiastic joy that parting life had left upon the features faded gradually away, and the countenance, though no longer wild, assumed the sadness which it had worn through a long course of grief and pain. On beholding this natural consequence of death, the thought perhaps occurred to him that her soul, no longer dependent on the imperfect means of intercourse possessed by mortals, had communed with his own, and become acquainted with all its guilt and misery. He started from the bedside and covered his face with his hands, as if to hide it from those dead eyes. . . . . But his deep repentance for the misery he had brought upon his parent did not produce in him a resolution to do wrong no more. The sudden consciousness of accumulated guilt made him desperate. He felt as if no one had thenceforth a claim to justice or compassion at his hands, when his neglect and cruelty had poisoned his mother's life, and hastened her death."

What separates this story from the rest of Hawthorne's works is an intricate plot, with passages of open humor, and a rather melodramatic tone in the conclusion. These are the result in part of the prevalent fashion of romance, and in part of a desire to produce effects not quite consonant with his native bent. The choice of the title, "Fanshawe," too, seems to show a deference to the then prevalent taste for brief and quaint-sounding names; and the motto, "Wilt thou go on with me?" from Southey, placed on his title-page, together with quotations at the heads of chapters, belongs to a past fashion. Fanshawe and Butler are powerful conceptions, but they are so purely embodiments of passion as to assume an air of unreality. Butler is like an evil wraith, and Fanshawe is as evanescent as a sad cloud in the sky, touched with the first pale light of morning. Fanshawe, with his pure heart and high resolves, represents that constant aspiration toward lofty moral truth which marked Hawthorne's own mind, and Butler is a crude example of the sinful spirit which he afterward analyzed under many forms. The verbal style has few marks of the maturer mould afterward impressed on it, except that there is the

preference always noticeable in Hawthorne for Latin wording.   Two or three phrases, however, show all the lim-
pidness and ease for which he gained fame subsequently.
For instance, when Fanshawe is first surprised by his love
for Ellen, he returns to his room to study : "The books
were around him which had hitherto been to him like
those fabled volumes of magic, from which the reader
could not turn away his eye, till death were the consequence of his studies."   This, too, is a pretty description
of Ellen : "Terror had at first blanched her as white as a
lily. . . . . Shame next bore sway; and her blushing
countenance, covered by her slender white fingers, might
fantastically be compared to a variegated rose, with its
alternate stripes of white and red."   Its restraint is perhaps the most remarkable trait of the novel ; for though
this comes of timidity, it shows that Hawthorne, whether
this be to his advantage or not, was not of the order of
young genius which begins with tumid and excessive exhibition of power.   His early acquaintance with books,
breeding a respect for literary form, his shy, considerate
modes of dealing with any intellectual problem or question requiring judgment, and the formal taste of the
period in letters, probably conspired to this end.

IV.

TWILIGHT OF THE TWICE-TOLD TALES.

1828–1838.

E have now reached the point where the concealed foundations of Hawthorne's life terminate, and the final structure begins to appear above the surface, like the topmost portion of a coral island slowly rising from the depths of a solitary ocean.

When he left college, his friends Cilley and Pierce entered into law, the gateway to politics; Bridge returned to his father's estate at Bridgton, to engage later in a large enterprise there; and other classmates took up various activities in the midst of other men; but for Hawthorne no very clear path presented itself. Literature had not yet attained, in the United States, the rank of a distinct and powerful profession. Fifteen years before, Brockden Brown had died prematurely after a hapless struggle, worn out with overwork, — the first man who had undertaken to live by writing in this country since its colonization. "The North American Review," indeed, in Boston, was laying the corner-stone of a vigorous periodical literature; and in this year of 1825 William Cullen Bryant had gone to New York to edit "The New York Review," after publishing at Cambridge his first volume of poetry, "The Ages." Irving was an author of recent but established fame, who was drawing chiefly from the rich supplies of European manners, legend, and history; while Cooper, in his pleasant Pioneerland beside Otsego Lake, had begun to make clear his claim to a wide domain of native and national fiction. But to a young man of reserved temper, having few or no friends directly connected with publication, and living in a sombre, old-fashioned town, isolated as all like towns were before the era of railroads, the avenue to publicity and a definite literary career was dark and devious enough.

I suppose it was after his venture of "Fanshawe," that he set about the composition of some shorter stories which he called "Seven Tales of my Native Land." * His sister, to whom he read these, has told me that they were very beautiful, but no definite recollection of them remains to her, except that some of them related to witchcraft, and some to the sea, being stories of pirates and privateers. In one of these latter were certain verses, beginning, —

"The pirates of the sea, they were a fearful race."

Hawthorne has described in "The Devil in Manuscript," while depicting a young author about to destroy his manuscript, his own vexations in trying to find a publisher for these attempts. "They have been offered to some seventeen booksellers. It would make you stare to read their answers. . . . . One man publishes nothing but school-books; another has five novels already under examination; . . . . another gentleman is just giving up business on purpose, I verily believe, to escape publishing my book. . . . . In short, of all the seventeen booksellers, only one has vouchsafed even to read my tales;

* The motto prefixed to these was, "We are seven."

and he — a literary dabbler himself, I should judge — has the impertinence to criticise them, proposing what he calls vast improvements, and concluding . . . . that he will not be concerned on any terms. . . . . But there does seem to be one honest man among these seventeen unrighteous ones; and he tells me fairly that no American publisher will meddle with an American work, seldom if by a known writer, and never if by a new one, unless at the writer's risk." He indeed had the most discouraging sort of search for a publisher; but at last a young printer of Salem promised to undertake the work. His name was Ferdinand Andrews; and he was at one time half-owner with Caleb Cushing of an establishment from which they issued "The Salem Gazette," in 1822, the same journal in which Hawthorne published various papers at a later date, when Mr. Caleb Foote was its editor. Andrews was ambitious, and evidently appreciative of his young townsman's genius; but he delayed issuing the "Seven Tales" so long that the author, exasperated, recalled the manuscript. Andrews, waiting only for better business prospects, was loath to let them go; but Hawthorne insisted, and at last the publisher sent word, "Mr. Hawthorne's manuscript awaits his orders." The writer received it and burned it, to the chagrin of Andrews, who had hoped to bring out many works by the same hand.

This, at the time, must have been an incident of incalculable and depressing importance to Hawthorne, and the intense emotion it caused may be guessed from the utterances of the young writer in the sketch just alluded to, though he has there veiled the affair in a light film of sarcasm. The hero of that scene is called Oberon, one of the feigned names which Hawthorne himself used at times in contributing to periodicals. "'What is more potent than fire!' said he, in his gloomiest tone.

'Even thought, invisible and incorporeal as it is, cannot escape it. . . . . All that I had accomplished, all that I planned for future years, has perished by one common ruin, and left only this heap of embers ! The deed has been my fate. And what remains ? A weary and aimless life; a long repentance of this hour; and at last an obscure grave, where they will bury and forget me!'" There is also an allusion to the tales founded on witchcraft: "I could believe, if I chose," says Oberon, "that there is a devil in this pile of blotted papers. You have read them, and know what I mean, — that conception in which I endeavored to embody the character of a fiend, as represented in our traditions and the written records of witchcraft. O, I have a horror of what was created in my own brain, and shudder at the manuscripts in which I gave that dark idea a sort of material existence ! ' You remember how the hellish thing used to suck away the happiness of those who . . . . subjected themselves to his power." This is curious, as showing the point from which Hawthorne had resolved to treat the theme. He had instinctively perceived that the only way to make the witchcraft delusion available in fiction was to accept the witch as a fact, an actual being, and expend his art upon developing the abnormal character; while other writers, who have attempted to use the subject for romantic ends, have uniformly taken the historical view, and sought to extract their pathos from the effect of the delusion on innocent persons. The historical view is that of intelligent criticism; but Hawthorne's effort was the harbinger and token of an original imagination.

After the publication of "Fanshawe" and the destruction of his "Seven Tales," Hawthorne found himself advanced not so much as by a single footstep on the road to fame. " Fame ! " he exclaims, in meditation ; "some very humble persons in a town may be said to possess it, — as the penny-post, the town-crier, the constable, — and they are known to everybody ; while many richer, more intellectual, worthier persons are unknown by the majority of their fellow-citizens." But the fame that he desired was, I think, only that which is the recognition by the public that a man is on the way to truth. An outside acknowledgment of this is invaluable even to the least vain of authors, because it assures him that, in following his own inner impulse through every doubt and discouragement, he has not been pursuing a chimera, and gives him new heart for the highest enterprises of which he is capable. To attain this, amid the peculiar surroundings of his life, was difficult enough. At that time, Salem society was more peculiarly constituted than it has been in later years. A strong circle of wealthy families maintained rigorously the distinctions of class ; their entertainments were splendid, their manners magnificent, and the fame of the beautiful women born amongst them has been confirmed by a long succession reaching into the present day. They prescribed certain fashions, customs, punctilios, to disregard which was social exile for the offending party ; and they were divided even among themselves, I am told, by the most inveterate jealousies. It is said that certain people would almost have endured the thumb-screw rather than meet and speak to others. There seems to be good authority for believing that Hawthorne could have entered this circle, had he so chosen. He had relatives who took an active part within it ; and it appears that there was a disposition among some of the fashionable coterie to show him particular favor, and that advances were made by them with the wish to draw him out. But one can conceive that it would not be ac-

ceptable to him to meet them on any but terms of entire
equality. The want of ample supplies of money, which
was one of the results of the fallen fortunes of his family,
made this impossible; those who held sway were of older
date in the place than some of the Hawthornes, and, like
many another long-established stock, they had a conviction
that, whatever their outward circumstances might be, a
certain intrinsic superiority remained theirs. They were,
like the lady of Hawthorne blood mentioned in the "American Note-Books," "proud of being proud." The Hawthornes, it was said, were as unlike other people as the
Jews were to Gentiles; and the deep-rooted reserve which
enveloped Hawthorne himself was a distinct family trait.
So that, feeling himself to be in an unfair position, he
doubtless found in these facts enough to cause him acute
irritation of that sort which only very young or very
proud and shrinking men can know. Besides this, the altered circumstances of his line, and his years in Maine, had
brought him acquainted with humbler phases of life, and
had doubtless developed in him a sympathy with simpler
and less lofty people than these magnates. His father
had been a Democrat, and loyalty to his memory, as well
as the very pride just spoken of, conspired to lead him to
that unpopular side. This set up another barrier between
himself and the rich and powerful Whigs, for political feeling was almost inconceivably more bitter then than now.
Thus there arose within him an unquiet, ill-defined, com-
fortless antipathy that must have tortured him with weari-
some distress; and certainly shut him out from the sympathy and appreciation which, if all the conditions had
been different, might have been given him by sincere and
competent admirers. So little known among his own
townsfolk, it is not to be wondered at that no encouraging answer reached him from more distant communities.

In his own home there was the faith which only love can give, but outside of it a chill drove his hopes and ardors back upon himself and turned them into despairs. His relatives, having seen him educated by the aid of his uncle, and now arrived at maturity, expected him to take his share in practical affairs. But the very means adopted to train him for a career had settled his choice of one in a direction perhaps not wholly expected; all cares and gains of ordinary traffic seemed sordid and alien to him. Yet a young man just beginning his career, with no solid proof of his own ability acquired, cannot but be sensitive to criticism from those who have gained a right to comment by their own special successes. As he watched these slow and dreary years pass by, from his graduation in 1825 to the time when he first came fully before the public in 1837, he must often have been dragged down by terrible fears that perhaps the fairest period of life was being wasted, losing forever the chance of fruition. "I sat down by the wayside of life," he wrote, long after, "like a man under enchantment, and a shrubbery sprang up around me, and the bushes grew to be saplings, and the saplings became trees, until no exit appeared possible, through the entangling depths of my obscurity." Judge in what a silence and solitary self-communing the time must have passed, to leave a thought like this: "To think, as the sun goes down, what events have happened in the course of the day, — events of ordinary occurrence; as, the clocks have struck, the dead have been buried." Or this: "A recluse like myself, or a prisoner, to measure time by the progress of sunshine through his chamber." His Note-Books show how the sense of unreality vexed and pursued him; and how the sadness and solemnity of life returned upon him again and again; and how he clothed these dark visitants of his brain with the colors of imagination, and turned them away from him in the guise of miraculous fantasies. He talks with himself of writing " the journal of a human heart for a single day, in ordinary circumstances. The lights and shadows that flit across it, its internal vicissitudes." But this is almost precisely what his printed Note-Books have revealed to us. Only now and then do we get precisely the thought that is passing through his mind at the moment; it more often throws upon the page a reflected image, — some strange and subtle hint for a story, the germs of delicate fabrics long afterward matured, some merry or sad conceit, some tender yet piercing inference, — like the shadows of clouds passing quickly across a clear sky, and casting momentary glooms, and glances of light, on the ground below. These journals do not begin until a date seven years after " Fanshawe " was published; but it is safe to assume that they mirror pretty closely the general complexion of the intervening years.

His mode of life during this period was fitted to nurture his imagination, but must have put the endurance of his nerves to the severest test. The statement that for several years " he never saw the sun," is entirely an error; but it is true that he seldom chose to walk in the town except at night, and it is said that he was extremely fond of going to fires if they occurred after dark. In summer he was up shortly after sunrise, and would go down to bathe in the sea. The morning was chiefly given to study, the afternoon to writing, and in the evening he would take long walks, exploring the coast from Gloucester to Marblehead and Lynn, — a range of many miles. Or perhaps he would pace the streets of the town, unseen but observing, gathering material for something in the vein of his delicious " Night

Sketches." "After a time," he writes, "the visions vanish, and will not appear again at my bidding. Then, it being nightfall, a gloomy sense of unreality depresses my spirits, and impels me to venture out before the clock shall strike bedtime, to satisfy myself that the world is not made of such shadowy materials as have busied me throughout the day. A dreamer may dwell so long among fantasies, that the things without him will seem as unreal as those within." Or, if he chose a later hour, he might go abroad to people the deserted thoroughfares with wilder phantoms. Sometimes he took the day for his rambles, wandering perhaps over Endicott's ancient Orchard Farm and among the antique houses and grassy cellars of old Salem village, the witchcraft ground; or losing himself among the pines of Montserrat and in the silence of the Great Pastures, or strolling along the beaches to talk with old sailors and fishermen. His tramps along the Manchester and Beverly shores or from Marblehead to Nahant were productive of such delicate tracings as "Footprints by the Sea-shore," or the dream-autobiography of "The Village Uncle." "Grudge me not the day," he says, in the former sketch, "that has been spent in seclusion, which yet was not solitude, since the great sea has been my companion, and the little sea-birds my friends, and the wind has told me his secrets, and airy shapes have flitted around my hermitage. Such companionship works an effect upon a man's character, as if he had been admitted to the society of creatures that are not mortal." This touches the inmost secret of those lonely, youthful years, which moulded the pure-hearted muser with ethereal, unsuspected fingers. Elsewhere, Hawthorne has given another glimpse into his interior life at this time: "This scene came into my fancy as I walked along a hilly road, on a starlight October

evening; in the pure and bracing air I became all soul,
and felt as if I could climb the sky, and run a race
along the Milky Way.   Here is another tale in which
I wrapped myself during a dark and dreary night-ride
in the month of March, till the rattling of the wheels and
the voices of my companions seemed like faint sounds
of a dream, and my visions a bright reality.   That scrib-
bled page describes shadows which I summoned to my
bedside at midnight; they would not depart when I bade
them; the gray dawn came, and found me wide awake
and feverish, the victim of my own enchantments!"
Susan, the imaginary wife in "The Village Uncle," is
said to have had a prototype in the daughter of a Salem
fisherman, whose wit and charm gave Hawthorne frequent amusement; and I suppose that not seldom he
reaped delightful suggestions from his meetings with
frank, unconscious, and individual people of tastes and
life unlike his own.   I have heard it told with a polite,
self-satisfied scorn, that he was in the habit of visiting
now and then a tavern patronized by 'longshore-men
and nautical veterans, to listen to their talk.   I can
well believe it, for it is this sort of intercourse that a
person of manly genius, with a republican fellow-feeling
for the unrenowned, most covets.   How well he gives
the tone of these old sea-dogs, when he writes: "The
blast will put in its word among their hoarse voices, and
be understood by all of them!"   It was this constant
searching among the common types of men, and his ready
sympathy with them, refined as it was hearty, that stored
his mind with a variety of accurate impressions which
afterward surprised observers, in a man of habits so
retired.

His uncles, the Mannings, were connected with extensive stage-coach lines at this time, and Hawthorne seems

to have used these as antennæ to bring himself in contact with new and nutritive regions and people. A letter, probably written in 1830, which I do not feel at liberty to quote entire, tells something of a trip that he took with Samuel Manning through a part of Connecticut and the Connecticut valley. The extracts that follow give a glimpse of the fresh and alert interest he felt about everything; and I regard them as very important in showing the obverse of that impression of unhealthy solitude which has been so generally received from accounts of Hawthorne hitherto published.

" We did not leave New Haven till last Saturday . . . . and we were forced to halt for the night at Cheshire, a village about fifteen miles from New Haven. The next day being Sunday, we made a Sabbath day's journey of seventeen miles, and put up at Farmington. As we were wearied with rapid travelling, we found it impossible to attend divine service, which was (of course) very grievous to us both. In the evening, however, I went to a Bible class with a very polite and agreeable gentleman, whom I afterward discovered to be a strolling tailor of very questionable habits. . . . . We are now at Deerfield (though I believe my letter is dated Greenfield). . . . with our faces northward ; nor shall I marvel much if your Uncle Sam pushes on to Canada, unless we should meet with two or three bad taverns in succession. . . . .

" I meet with many marvellous adventures. At New Haven I observed a gentleman staring at me with great earnestness, after which he went into the bar-room, I suppose to inquire who I might be. Finally, he came up to me and said that as I bore a striking resemblance to a family of Stanburys, he was induced to inquire if I was connected with them. I was sorry to be obliged to answer in the negative. At another place they took me for a lawyer in search of a place to settle, and strongly recommended their own village. Moreover, I heard some of the students at Yale College conjecturing that

I was an Englishman, and to-day, as I was standing without my coat at the door of a tavern, a man came up to me, and asked me for some oats for his horse."

It was during this trip, I have small doubt, that he found the scenery, and perhaps the persons, for that pretty interlude, " The Seven Vagabonds." The story is placed not far from Stamford, and the conjurer in it says, " I am taking a trip northward, this warm weather, across the Connecticut first, and then up through Vermont, and may be into Canada before the fall." The narrator himself queries by what right he came among these wanderers, and furnishes himself an answer which suggests that side of his nature most apt to appear in these journeys: " The free mind that preferred its own folly to another's wisdom ; the open spirit that found companions everywhere ; above all, the restless impulse that had so often made me wretched in the midst of enjoyments : these were my claims to be of their society." " If there be a faculty," he also writes, " which I possess more perfectly than most men, it is that of throwing myself mentally into situations foreign to my own, and detecting with a cheerful eye the desirableness of each." There is also one letter of 1831, sent back during an expedition in New Hampshire, which supplies the genesis of another Twice-Told Tale, " The Canterbury Pilgrims."

" I walked to the Shaker village yesterday [he says], and was shown over the establishment, and dined there with a squire and a doctor, also of the world's people. On my arrival, the first thing I saw was a jolly old Shaker carrying an immense decanter of their superb cider ; and as soon as I told him my business, he turned out a tumblerful and gave me. It was as much as a common head could clearly carry. Our dining-room was well furnished, the dinner excellent, and the table attended by a middle-aged Shaker lady, good looking and cheerful. . . . . This establishment is immensely rich. Their land extends two or three miles along the road, and there are streets of great houses painted yellow and tipt with red. . . . . On the whole, they lead a good and comfortable life, and, if it were not for their ridiculous ceremonies, a man could not do a wiser thing than to join them. Those whom I conversed with were intelligent, and appeared happy. I spoke to them about becoming a member of their society, but have come to no decision on that point.

" We have had a pleasant journey enough. . . . . I make innumerable acquaintances, and sit down on the doorsteps with judges, generals, and all the potentates of the land, discoursing about the Salem murder [that of Mr. White], the cowskinning of Isaac Hill, the price of hay, and the value of horse-flesh. The country is very uneven, and your Uncle Sam groans bitterly whenever we come to the foot of a low hill; though this ought to make me groan rather than him, as I have to get out and trudge every one of them."

The " Chippings with a Chisel" point to some further wanderings, to Martha's Vineyard; and an uncollected sketch reveals the fact that he had been to Niagara. It was probably then that he visited Ticonderoga; * but not till some years later that he saw New York. With these exceptions, and a trip to Washington before going to Liverpool in 1853, every day of his life up to that date was passed within New England. In " The Toll-Gatherer's Day " one sees the young observer at work upon the details of an ordinary scene near home. The " small square edifice which stands between shore and shore in the midst of a long bridge," spanning an arm of the sea, refers undoubtedly to the bridge from Salem to Beverly. But how lightly his spirit hovers over the

---

* A brief sketch of the fortress is included in The Snow Image volume of the Works.

7 J

stream of actual life, scarcely touching it before springing up again, like a sea-bird on the crest of a wave!
Nothing could be more accurate and polished than his
descriptions and his presentation of the actual facts; but
his fancy rises resilient from these to some dreamy, far-
seeing perception or gentle moral inference. The visible
human pageant is only of value to him as it suggests the
viewless host of heavenly shapes that hang above it like
an idealizing mirage. His attitude at this time recalls
a suggestion of his own in "Sights from a Steeple":
"The most desirable mode of existence might be that of
a spiritualized Paul Pry, hovering invisible round man
and woman, witnessing their deeds, searching into their
hearts, borrowing brightness from their felicity, and shade
from their sorrow, and retaining no emotion peculiar to
himself." He had the longing which every creative
mind must feel, to mix with other beings and share to
the utmost the possibilities of human weal or woe, sup-
pressing his own experience so far as to make himself a
transparent medium for the emotions of mankind; but
he still lacked a definite connection with the multifarious drama of human fellowship; he could not catch
his cue and play his answering part, and therefore gave
voice to a constantly murmurous, moralizing "aside." He
delights to let the current of action flow around him and
beside him; he warms his heart in it; but when he again
withdraws by himself, it is with him as with the old toll-
gatherer at close of day, "mingling reveries of Heaven
with remembrances of earth, the whole procession of
mortal travellers, all the dusty pilgrimage which he has
witnessed, seems like a flitting show of phantoms for his
thoughtful soul to muse upon."

"What would a man do," he asks himself, in his journal, "if he were compelled to live always in the sultry

heat of society, and could never bathe himself in cool
solitude ? " As yet, this bracing influence of quietude,
so essential to his well-being, fascinates him, and he cannot shake off its influence so far as to enter actively and
for personal interests into any of the common pursuits
even of the man who makes a business of literature.
Yet nothing impresses him more than the fact that
every one carries a solitude with him, wherever he goes,
like a shadow. Twice, with an interval of three years between, this idea recurs in the form of a hint for romance.
" Two lovers or other persons, on the most private business, to appoint a meeting in what they supposed to be
a place of the utmost solitude, and to find it thronged
with people." The idea implied is, that this would in
fact be the completest privacy they could have wished.
" The situation of a man in the midst of a crowd, yet
as completely in the power of another, life and all, as
if they two were in the deepest solitude." This contradiction between the *apparent* openness that must rule
one's conduct among men, and the real secrecy that may
coexist with it, even when one is most exposed to the
gaze of others, excites in his mind a whole train of
thought based on the falsity of appearances. If a man
can be outwardly open and inwardly reserved in a good
sense, he can be so in a bad sense; so, too, he may have
the external air of great excellence and purity, while in-
ternally he is foul and unfaithful. This discovery strikes
our perfectly sincere and true-hearted recluse with intense and endless horror. He tests it, by turning it
innumerable ways, and imagining all sorts of situations in
which such contradictions of appearance and reality might
be illustrated. At one time, he conceives of a friend who
should be true by day, and false at night. At another he
suggests: "Our body to be possessed by two different

spirits, so that half the visage shall express one mood, and the other half another." "A man living a wicked life in one place and simultaneously a virtuous and religious one in another." Then he perceives that this same uncertainty and contradiction affects the lightest and seemingly most harmless things in the world. "The world is so sad and solemn," he muses, "that things meant in jest are liable, by an overpowering influence, to become dreadful earnest." And then he applies this, as in the following: "A virtuous but giddy girl to attempt to play a trick on a man. He sees what she is about, and contrives matters so that she throws herself completely into his power, and is ruined, — all in jest." Likewise, the most desirable things, by this same law of contradiction, often prove the least satisfactory. Thus: "A person or family long desires some particular good. At last it comes in such profusion as to be the great pest of their lives." And this is equally true, he finds, whether the desired thing be sought in order to gratify a pure instinct or a wrong and revengeful one. "As an instance, merely, suppose a woman sues her lover for breach of promise, and gets the money by instalments, through a long series of years. At last, when the miserable victim were utterly trodden down, the triumpher would have become a very devil of evil passions, — they having overgrown his whole nature; so that a far greater evil would have come upon himself than on his victim." This theme of self-punished revenge, as we know, was afterward thoroughly wrought out in "The Scarlet Letter." Another form in which the thought of this pervading falsehood in earthly affairs comes to him is the frightful fancy of people being poisoned by communion-wine. Thus does the insincerity and corruption of man, the lie that is hidden in nearly every life and almost every act, rise and thrust itself before him, which-

ever way he turns, like a serpent in his path. He is in
the position of the father confessor of whom he at one
time thinks, and of " his reflections on character, and the
contrast of the inward man with the outward, as he looks
around his congregation, all whose secret sins are known
to him." But Hawthorne does not let this hissing serpent either rout him or poison him. He is determined
to visit the ways of life, to find the exit of the maze, and
so tries every opening, unalarmed. The serpent is in all :
it proves to be a deathless, large-coiled hydra, encircling
the young explorer's virgin soul, as it does that of every
pure aspirer, and trying to drive him back on himself,
with a sting in his heart that shall curse him with a lifelong venom. It does, indeed, force him to recoil, but
not with any mortal wound. He retires in profound sorrow, acknowledging that earth holds nothing perfect, that
his dream of ideal beings leading an ideal life, which, in
spite of the knowledge of evil, he has been cherishing
for so many years, is a dream to be fulfilled in the hereafter alone. He confesses to himself that "there is evil
in every human heart, which may remain latent, perhaps,
through the whole of life; but circumstances may rouse
it to activity." It is not a new discovery; but from the
force with which it strikes him, we may guess the strength
of his aspiration, the fine temper of his faith in the good
and the beautiful. To be driven to this dismal conclusion is for him a source of inexpressible dismay, because
he had trusted so deeply in the possibility of reaching
some brighter truth. No; not a new discovery; — but
one who approaches it with so much sensibility *feels* it to
be new, with all the fervor which the most absolute novelty could rouse. This is the deepest and the true originality, to possess such intensity of feeling that the oldest
truth, when approached by our own methods, shall be full
of a primitive impressiveness.

But, in the midst of the depression born of his immense sorrow over sin, Hawthorne found compensations. First, in the query which he puts so briefly: "The good deeds in an evil life, — the generous, noble, and excellent actions done by people habitually wicked, — to ask what is to become of them." This is the motive which has furnished novelists for the last half-century with their most stirring and pathetic effects. It is a sort of escape, a safety-valve for the hot fire of controversy on the soul's fate, and offers in its pertinent indefiniteness a vast solace to those who are trying to balance the bewildering account of virtue with sin. Hawthorne found that here was a partial solution of the problem, and he enlarged upon it, toward the end of his life, in "The Marble Faun." But it was a second and deeper thought that furnished him the chief compensation. In one of the "Twice-Told Tales," "Fancy's Show-Box," he deals with the question, how far the mere thought of sin, the incipient desire to commit it, may injure the soul. After first strongly picturing the reality of certain sinful impulses in a man's mind, which had never been carried out, — "A scheme of guilt," he argues, taking up the other side, " till it be put in execution, greatly resembles a train of incidents in a projected tale. . . . . Thus a novel-writer, or a dramatist, in creating the villain of romance, and fitting him with evil deeds, and the villain of actual life in projecting crimes that will be perpetrated, may almost meet each other half-way between reality and fancy. It is not until the crime is accomplished that guilt clinches its gripe upon the heart, and claims it for its own. Then, and not before, sin is actually felt and acknowledged, and, if unaccompanied by repentance, grows a thousand-fold more virulent by its self-consciousness. Be it considered, also, that men often overestimate their capacity for evil. At a distance, while its attendant circumstances do not press upon their notice, its results are dimly seen, they can bear to contemplate it. . . . . In truth, there is no such thing in man's nature as a settled and full resolve, either for good or evil, except at the very moment of execution. Let us hope, therefore, that all the dreadful consequences of sin will not be incurred, unless the act have set its seal upon the thought. Yet . . . . *man must not disclaim his brotherhood, even with the guiltiest,* since, though his hand be clean, his heart has surely been polluted by the flitting phantoms of iniquity." That is, purity is too spotless a thing to exist in absolute perfection in a human being, who must often feel at least the dark flush of passionate thoughts falling upon him, however blameless of life he may be. From this lofty conception of purity comes that equally noble humility of always feeling " his brotherhood, even with the guiltiest." What more logical issue from the Christian idea, what more exquisitely tender rendering of it than this ? " Let the whole world be cleansed, or not a man or woman of us can be clean ! " was his exclamation, many years later, in that English workhouse which he describes in a heart-rending chapter of " Our Old Home " called " Outside Glimpses of English Poverty." And it was then that he revealed the vast depth and the reality of his human sympathy toward the wretched and loathsome little foundling child that silently sued to him for kindness, till he took it up and caressed it as tenderly as if he had been its father.

Armed with these two perceptions, of the good that still persists in evil persons, and the deep charity which every one must feel towards even the most abject fellow-being, Hawthorne moves forth again to trace the maze ; and lo, the serpent drops down, cowering. He has found a charm that robs sin and crime of their deadly hurt, and can handle them without danger. It is said by some that Hawthorne treats wrong and corruption too shrinkingly, and his mood of never-lessened and acute sensibility touching them is contrasted with that of " virile " writers like Balzac and George Sand. But these incline to make a menagerie of life, thrusting their heads into the very lion's mouth, or boldly embracing the snake of sin. They are indeed superior in strong dramatic and realistic effects; but, unvicious as may be their aim, they are not filled with a robust morality : they deliberately choose unclean elements to heighten the interest, — albeit using such elements with magnificent strength and skill. Let us be grateful that Hawthorne does not so covet the applause of the clever club-man or of the unconscious vulgarian, as to junket about in caravan, carrying the passions with him in gaudy cages, and feeding them with raw flesh ; grateful that he never loses the archangelic light of pure, divine, dispassionate wrath, in piercing the dragon!

We see now how, in this early term of probation, he was finding a philosophy and an unsectarian religiousness, which ever stirred below the clear surface of his language like the bubbling spring at bottom of a forest pool. It has been thought that Hawthorne developed late. But the most striking thing about the " Twice-Told Tales " and the first entries in the " American Note-Books " is their evidence of a calm and mellow maturity. These stories are like the simple but well-devised theme which a musician prepares as the basis of a whole composition : they show the several tendencies which underlie all the subsequent works. First, there are the scenes from New England history, — " Endicott and the Red Cross," " The Maypole of Merry Mount," " The Gray Champion," the " Tales of the Province House."

Then we have the psychological vein, in "The Prophetic Pictures," "The Minister's Black Veil," "Dr. Heidegger," "Fancy's Show-Box"; and along with this the current of delicate essay-writing, as in "The Haunted Mind," and "Sunday at Home." "Little Annie's Ramble," again, foreshadows his charming children's tales. It is rather remarkable that he should thus have sounded, though faintly, the whole diapason in his first works. Moreover, he had already at this time attained a style at once flowing and large in its outline, and masterly in its minuteness.

But this maturity was not won without deep suffering and long-deferred hope.

If actual contact with men resulted in such grave and sorrowful reflection as we have traced, how drearily trying must have been the climaxes of solitary thought after a long session of seclusion! And much the larger portion of his time was consumed amid an absolute silence, a privacy unbroken by intimate confidences and rife with exhausting and depressing reactions from intense imagination and other severe intellectual exercise. Not only must the repression of this period have amounted at times to positive anguish, but there was also the perplexing perception that his life's fairest possibilities were still barren. "Every individual has a place in the world, and is important to it in some respects, whether he chooses to be so or not." So runs one of the extracts from the "American Note-Books"; and now and then we get from the same source a glimpse of the haunting sense that he is missing his fit relation to the rest of the race, the question whether his pursuit was not in some way futile like all the human pursuits he had noticed, — whether it was not to be nipped by the same perversity and contradiction that seemed to affect all

7 *

things mundane. Here is one of his proposed plots, which turns an inner light upon his own frame of mind: "Various good and desirable things to be presented to a young man, and offered to his acceptance, — as a friend, a wife, a fortune; but he to refuse them all, suspecting that it is merely a delusion. Yet all to be real, and he to be told so when too late." Is this not, in brief, what he conceives may yet be the story of his own career? Another occurs, in the same relation: "A man tries to be happy in love; he cannot sincerely give his heart, and the affair seems all a dream. In domestic life the same; in politics, a seeming patriot: but still he is sincere, and all seems like a theatre." These items are the merest indicia of a whole history of complex emotions, which made this epoch one of continuous though silent and unseen struggle. In a Preface prefixed to the tales, in 1851, the author wrote: "They are the memorials of very tranquil and not unhappy years." Tranquil they of course were; and to the happy and successful man of forty-seven, the vexing moods and dragging loneliness of that earlier period would seem "not unhappy," because he could then see all the good it had contained. I cannot agree with Edwin Whipple, who says of them, "There was audible to the delicate ear a faint and muffled growl of personal discontent, which showed they were not mere exercises of penetrating imaginative analysis, but had in them the morbid vitality of a despondent mood." For this applies to only one of the number, "The Ambitious Guest." Nor do I find in them the "misanthropy" which he defines at some length. On the contrary, they are, as the author says, "his attempts to open an intercourse with the world," incited by an eager sympathy, but also restrained by a stern perception of right and wrong.

Yet I am inclined to adhere to the grave view of his inner life just sketched. When his friend Miss Peabody first penetrated his retirement, his pent-up sympathies flowed forth in a way that showed how they had longed for relief. He returned constantly to the discussion of his peculiar mode of living, as if there could be no understanding between himself and another, until this had been cleared up and set aside. Among other things, he spoke of a dream by which he was beset, that he was walking abroad, and that all the houses were mirrors which reflected him a thousand times and overwhelmed him with mortification. This gives a peculiar insight into his sensitive condition.

The noiseless, uneventful weeks slipped by, each day disguising itself in exact semblance of its fellow, like a file of mischievous maskers. Hawthorne sat in his little room under the eaves reading, studying, voicelessly communing with himself through his own journal, or — mastered by some wild suggestion or mysterious speculation — feeling his way through the twilight of dreams, into the dusky chambers of that house of thought whose haunted interior none but himself ever visited. He had little communication with even the members of his family. Frequently his meals were brought and left at his locked door, and it was not often that the four inmates of the old Herbert Street mansion met in family circle. He never read his stories aloud to his mother and sisters, as might be imagined from the picture which Mr. Fields draws of the young author reciting his new productions to his listening family; though, when they met, he sometimes read older literature to them. It was the custom in this household for the several members to remain very much by themselves; the three ladies were perhaps nearly as rigorous recluses as himself; and, speaking of the isolation which reigned among them, Hawthorne once said, "We do not even *live* at our house!" But still the presence of this near and gentle feminine element is not to be underrated as forming a very great compensation in the cold and difficult morning of Hawthorne's life.

If the week-day could not lure him from his sad retreat, neither could the Sunday. He had the right to a pew in the First Church, which his family had held since 1640, but he seldom went to service there after coming from college. His religion was supplied from sources not always opened to the common scrutiny, and it never chanced that he found it essential to join any church.

The chief resource against disappointment, the offset to the pain of so much lonely living and dark-veined meditation was, of course, the writing of tales. Never was a man's mind more truly a kingdom to him. This was the fascination that carried him through the weary waiting-time. Yet even that pleasure had a reverse side, to which the fictitious Oberon has no doubt given voice in these words: "You cannot conceive what an effect the composition of these tales has had upon me. I have become ambitious of a bubble, and careless of solid reputation. I am surrounding myself with shadows, which bewilder me by aping the realities of life. They have drawn me aside from the beaten path of the world, and led me into a strange sort of solitude . . . . where nobody wished for what I do, nor thinks or feels as I do." Alluding to this season of early obscurity to a friend who had done much to break it up, he once said, "I was like a person talking to himself in a dark room." To make his own reflection in a mirror the subject of a story was one of his projects then formed, which he carried out in the "Mosses." With that image of the dark room, and this suggested reflection in the mirror, we can rehabilitate the scene of which the broken lights and trembling shadows are strewn through the "Twice-Told Tales." Sober and weighty the penumbrous atmosphere in which the young creator sits; but how calm, thoughtful, and beautiful the dim vision of his face, lit by the sheltered radiance of ethereal fancies! Behind his own form we catch the movement of mysterious shapes, — men and women wearing aspects of joy or anger, calm or passionate, gentle and pitiable, or stern, splendid, and forbidding. It is not quite a natural twilight in which we behold these things; rather the awesome shadowiness of a partial eclipse; but gleams of the healthiest sunshine withal mingle in the prevailing tint, bringing reassurance, and receiving again a rarer value from the contrast. There are but few among the stories of this series afterward brought together by the author which are open to the charge of morbidness. In "The White Old Maid" an indefinable horror, giving the tale a certain shapelessness, crowds out the compensating brightness which in most cases is not wanting; perhaps, too, "The Ambitious Guest" leaves one with too hopeless a downfall at the end; and "The Wedding Knell" cannot escape a suspicion of disagreeable gloom. But these extremes are not frequent. The wonder is that Hawthorne's mind could so often and so airily soar above the shadows that at this time hung about him; that he should nearly always suggest a philosophy so complete, so gently wholesome, and so penetrating as that which he mixes with even the bitterest distillations of his dreams. Nor is the sadness of his tone disordered or destructive, more than it is selfish; he does not inculcate despair, nor protest against life and fate, nor indulge in

gloomy or weak self-pity. The only direct exposition of
his own case is contained in a sketch, "The Journal
of a Solitary Man," not reprinted during his life. One
extract from this I will make, because it sums up, though
more plaintively than was his wont, Hawthorne's view of
his own life at this epoch : —

"It is hard to die without one's happiness; to none more
so than myself, whose early resolution it had been to partake
largely of the joys of life, but never to be burdened with its
cares. Vain philosophy! The very hardships of the poorest
laborer, whose whole existence seems one long toil, has something preferable to my best pleasures. Merely skimming the
surface of life, I know nothing by my own experience of its
deep and warm realities, ... so that few mortals, even the
humblest and weakest, have been such ineffectual shadows in
the world, or die so utterly as I must. Even a young man's
bliss has not been mine. With a thousand vagrant fantasies,
I have never truly loved, and perhaps shall be doomed to loneliness throughout the eternal future, because, here on earth, my
soul has never married itself to the soul of woman."

The touch about avoiding the cares of life is no doubt
merely metaphorical ; but the self-imposed doom of eternal loneliness reveals the excess of sombreness in which
he clothed his condition to his own perception. One
may say that the adverse factors in his problem at this
time were purely imaginary ; that a little resolution and
determined activity would have shaken off the incubus :
but this is to lose sight of the gist of the matter. The
situation in itself, — the indeterminateness and repression
of it, and the denial of any satisfaction to his warm and
various sympathies, and his capacity for affection and
responsibility, — must be allowed to have been intensely
wearing. Hawthorne believed himself to possess a
strongly social nature, which was cramped, chilled, and to

some extent permanently restrained by this long seclusion at the beginning of his career. This alone might furnish just cause for bitterness against the fate that chained him. It was not a matter of option; for he knew that his battle must be fought through as he had begun it, and until 1836 no slightest loophole of escape into action presented itself. It lay before him to act out the tragedy of isolation which is the lot of every artist in America still, though greatly mitigated by the devotion of our first generation of national writers. If he had quitted his post sooner, and had tried by force to mould his genius according to theory, he might have utterly distorted or stunted its growth. All that he could as yet do for himself was to preserve a certain repose and harmony in the midst of uncertainty and delay; and for this he formed four wise precepts: "To break off customs; to shake off spirits ill disposed; to meditate on youth; to do nothing against one's genius." * Thus he kept himself fresh and flexible, hopeful, ready for emergency. But that I have not exaggerated the severity and import of his long vigil, let this revery of his show, written at Liverpool, in 1855: "I think I have been happier this Christmas than ever before, — by my own fireside, and with my wife and children about me; more content to enjoy what I have, less anxious for anything beyond it in this life. My early life was perhaps a good preparation for the declining half of life; it having been such a blank that any thereafter would compare favorably with it. For a long, long while I have been occasionally visited with a singular dream; and I have an impression that I have dreamed it ever since I have been in England. It is, that I am still at college, — or, sometimes, even at school, — and there is a sense that I have been there unconscionably

* American Note-Books, Vol. I.

long, and have quite failed to make such progress as my contemporaries have done; and I seem to meet some of them with a feeling of shame and depression that broods over me as I think of it, even when awake. This dream, recurring all through these twenty or thirty years, must be one of the effects of that heavy seclusion in which I shut myself up for twelve years after leaving college, when everybody moved onward, and left me behind." Experiences which leave effects like this must bite their way into the heart and soul with a fearful energy! This precursive solitude had tinged his very life-blood, and woven itself into the secret tissues of his brain. Yet, patiently absorbing it, he wrote late in life to a friend: "I am disposed to thank God for the gloom and chill of my early life, in the hope that my share of adversity came then, when I bore it alone." It was under such a guise that the test of his genius and character came to him. Every great mind meets once in life with a huge opposition that must somehow be made to succumb, before its own energies can know their full strength, gain a settled footing, and make a roadway to move forward upon. Often these obstacles are viewless to others, and the combat is unsuspected; the site of many a Penuel remains untraced; but none the less these are the pivots on which entire personal histories turn. Hawthorne's comparatively passive endurance was of infinitely greater worth than any active irruption into the outer world would have been. It is obvious that we owe to the innumerable devious wanderings and obscure sufferings of his mind, under the influences just reviewed, something of his sure and subtle touch in feeling out the details of morbid moods; for though his mind remained perfectly healthy, it had acquired acute sympathy with all hidden tragedies of heart and brain.

But another and larger purpose was not less well served by this probation. The ability of American life to produce a genius in some sense exactly responding to its most distinctive qualities had yet to be demonstrated; and this could only be done by some one who would stake life and success on the issue, for it needed that a soul and brain of the highest endowment should be set apart solely for the experiment, even to the ruin of it if required, before the truth could be ascertained. Hawthorne, the slowly produced and complex result of a line of New-Englanders who carried American history in their very limbs, seemed providentially offered for the trial. It was well that temperament and circumstance drew him into a charmed circle of reserve from the first; well, also, that he was further matured at a simple and rural college pervaded by a homely American tone; still more fortunate was it that nothing called him away to connect him with European culture, on graduating. To interpret this was the honorable office of his classmate Longfellow, who, with as much ease as dignity and charm, has filled the gap between the two half-worlds. The experiment to be tried was, simply, whether with books and men at his command, and isolated from the immediate influence of Europe, this American could evolve any new quality for the enrichment of literature. The conditions were strictly carried out; even after he began to come in contact with men, in the intervals of his retirement, he saw only pure American types. A foreigner must have been a rare bird in Salem, in those days; for the maritime element which might have brought him was still American. Hawthorne, as we have seen, and as his Note-Books show, pushed through the farming regions and made acquaintance with the men of the soil; and probably the first alien of whom he got at all a close view

K

was the Monsieur S—— whom he found at Bridge's, on his visit to the latter, in 1837, described at length in the Note-Books. So much did Hawthorne study from these types, and so closely, that he might, had his genius directed, have written the most homely and realistic novels of New England life from the material which he picked up quite by the way. But though he did not translate his observations thus, the originality which he was continuously ripening amid such influences was radically affected by them. They established a broad, irrepressible republican sentiment in his mind; they assisted his natural, manly independence and simplicity to assert themselves unaffectedly in letters; and they had not a little to do, I suspect, with fostering his strong turn for examining with perfect freedom and a certain refined shrewdness into everything that came before him, without accepting prescribed opinions. The most characteristic way, perhaps, in which this American nurture acted was by contrast; for the universal matter-of-fact tone which he found among his fellow-citizens was an incessant spur to him to maintain a counteracting idealism. Thus, singularly enough, the most salient feature of the new American product was its apparent denial of the national trait of practical sagacity. It is not to be supposed that Hawthorne adhered consciously to the aim of asserting the American nature in fiction. These things can be done only half consciously, at the most. Perhaps it is well that the mind on which so much depends should not be burdened with all the added anxiety of knowing how much is expected from it by the ages. Therefore, we owe the triumphant assertion of the American quality in this novel genius to Hawthorne's quiet, unfaltering, brave endurance of the weight that was laid upon him, unassisted by the certainty with which we now perceive that a great end was being served by it. But, although unaware of this end at the time, he afterward saw some of the significance of his youth. Writing in 1840, he speaks thus of his old room in Union Street : —

"This claims to be called a haunted chamber, for thousands upon thousands of visions have appeared to me in it ; and some few of them have become visible to the world. If ever I should have a biographer, he ought to make great mention of this chamber in my memoirs, because so much of my lonely youth was wasted here, and *here my mind and character were formed;* and here I have been glad and hopeful, and here I have been despondent. . . . . And now I begin to understand why I was imprisoned so many years in this lonely chamber, and why I could never break through the viewless bolts and bars ; for if I had sooner made my escape into the world, I should have grown hard and rough, and my heart might have become callous by rude encounters with the multitude. . . . . But living in solitude till the fulness of time, I still kept the dew of my youth and the freshness of my heart."

Yes, and more than this, Hawthorne ! It was a young nation's faith in its future which — unsuspected by any then, but always to be remembered henceforth — had found a worthy answer and after-type in this faithful and hopeful heart of yours ! Thus was it that the young poet who, in the sense we have observed, stood for old New England, absorbed into himself also the atmosphere of the United States. The plant that rooted in the past had put forth a flower which drew color and perfume from to-day. In such wise did Hawthorne prove to be the unique American in fiction.

I have examined the librarian's books at the Salem Athenæum, which indicate a part of the reading that the writer of the "Twice-Told Tales" went through.

The lists from the beginning of 1830 to 1838 include nearly four hundred volumes taken out by him, besides a quantity of bound magazines. This gives no account of his dealings with books in the previous five years, when he was not a shareholder in the Athenæum, nor does it, of course, let us know anything of what he obtained from other sources. When Miss E. P. Peabody made his acquaintance, in 1836 – 37, he had, for example, read all of Balzac that had then appeared; and there is no record of this in the library lists. These lists alone, then, giving four hundred volumes in seven years, supply him with one volume a week, — not, on the whole, a meagre rate, when we consider the volumes of magazines, the possible sources outside of the library, and the numberless hours required for literary experiment. I do not fancy that he plodded through books; but rather that he read with the easy energy of a vigorous, original mind, though he also knew the taste of severe study. "Bees," he observes in one place, "are sometimes drowned (or suffocated) in the honey which they collect. So some writers are lost in their collected learning." He did not find it necessary to mount upon a pyramid of all learning previous to his epoch, in order to get the highest standpoint for his own survey of mankind. Neither was he "a man of parts," precisely; being in himself a distinct whole. His choice of reading was ruled by a fastidious need. He was fond of travels for a rainy day, and knew Mandeville; but at other times he took up books which seem to lie quite aside from his known purposes.* Voltaire appears to have attracted him constantly; he read him in the original, together with Rousseau. At one time he examined Pascal, at another he read something

* See Appendix III.

of Corneille and a part of Raçine. Of the English dramatists, he seems at this time to have tried only Massinger; "Inchbald's Theatre" also occurs. The local American histories took his attention pretty often, and he perused a variety of biography, — "Lives of the Philosophers," "Plutarch's Lives," biographies of Mohammed, Pitt, Jefferson, Goldsmith, Coleridge, Shelley, and Keats, Baxter, Heber, Sir William Temple, and others. Brewster's "Natural Magic" and Sir Walter Scott's essay on "Demonology and Witchcraft" are books that one would naturally expect him to read; and he had already begun to make acquaintance with the English State Trials, for which he always had a great liking. "Colquhoun on the Police" would seem not entirely foreign to one who mentally pursued so many malefactors; but it is a little surprising that he should have found himself interested in "Babbage on the Economy of Machinery." He dipped, also, into botany and zoölogy; turned over several volumes of Bayle's "Critical Dictionary," read Mrs. Jameson, and the "London Encyclopædia of Architecture"; and was entertained by Dunlap's "History of the Arts of Design in America." It was from this last that he drew the plot of "The Prophetic Pictures," in the "Twice-Told Tales." Some Boston newspapers of the years 1739 to 1783 evidently furnished the material for an article called "Old News," reprinted in "The Snow Image." Hawthorne seems never to have talked much about reading: 't is imaginable that he was as shy in his choice of books and his discussion of them, as in his intercourse with men; and there is no more ground for believing that he did not like books, than that he cared nothing for men and women. Life is made up, for such a mind, of men, women, and books; Hawthorne accepted all three estates.

Gradually, from the midst of the young author's obscurity, there issued an attraction which made the world wish to know more of him. One by one, the quiet essays and mournful-seeming stories came forth, like drops from a slow-distilling spring. The public knew nothing of the internal movement which had opened this slight fountain, nor suspected the dark concamerations through which the current made its way to the surface. The smallest mountain rill often has a thunder-storm at its back; but the average reader of that day thought he had done quite enough, when he guessed that the new writer was a timid young man fabling under a feigned name, excellent in his limited way, who would be a great deal better if he could come out of seclusion and make himself more like other people.

The first contributions were made to the "Salem Gazette" and the "New England Magazine"; then his attempts extended to the "Boston Token and Atlantic Souvenir," edited by S. G. Goodrich; and later, to other periodicals. Mr. Goodrich wrote to his young contributor (October, 1831): "I am gratified to find that all whose opinion I have heard agree with me as to the merit of the various pieces from your pen." But for none of these early performances did Hawthorne receive any considerable sum of money. And though his writings began at once to attract an audience, he had slight knowledge of it. Three young ladies — of whom his future sister-in-law, Miss Peabody, was one — were among the first admirers; and though Hawthorne baffled his readers and perhaps retarded his own notoriety by assuming different names in print,* they traced his contributions assiduously, cut them

---

* Among these were "Oberon" and "Ashley Allen Royce," or "The Rev. A. A. Royce." The latter was used by him in the Democratic Review, so late as March, 1840.

out of magazines, and preserved them. But they could not discover his personal identity. One of them who lived in Salem used constantly to wonder, in driving about town, whether the author of her favorite tales could be living in this or in that house; for it was known that he was a Salem resident. Miss Peabody, who had in girlhood known something of the Hathorne family (the name was still written either way, I am told), was misled by the new spelling, and by the prevalent idea that Nathaniel Hawthorne was an assumed name. This trio were especially moved by "The Gentle Boy" when it appeared, and Miss Peabody was on the point of addressing "The Author of 'The Gentle Boy,'" at Salem, to tell him of the pleasure he had given. When afterward told of this, Hawthorne said, "I wish you had! It would have been an era in my life." Soon after, the Peabodys returned to Salem, and she learned from some one that the new romancer was the son of the Widow Hathorne. Now it so chanced that her family had long ago occupied a house on Union Street, looking off into the garden of the old Manning family mansion; and she remembered no son, though a vague image came back to her of a strong and graceful boy's form dancing across the garden, at play, years before. Her mind therefore fastened upon one of the sisters, who, she knew, had shown great facility in writing: indeed, Hawthorne used at one time to say that it was she who should have been the follower of literature. Full of this conception, she went to carry her burden of gratitude to the author, and after delays and difficulties, made her way into the retired and little-visited mansion. It was the other sister into whose presence she came, and to her she began pouring out the reason of her intrusion, delivering at once her praises of the elder Miss Hathorne's fictions.

"My brother's, you mean," was the response.

"It *is* your brother, then." And Miss Peabody added: "If your brother can write like that, he has no right to be idle."

"My brother never is idle," answered Miss Louisa, quietly.

Thus began an acquaintance which helped to free Hawthorne from the spell of solitude, and led directly to the richest experiences of his life. Old habits, however, were not immediately to be broken, and months passed without any response being made to the first call. Then at last came a copy of the "Twice-Told Tales," fresh from the press. But it was not until the establishment of the "Democratic Review," a year or two later, that occasion offered for a renewal of relations. Hawthorne was too shy to act upon the first invitation. Miss Peabody, finally, addressing him by letter, to inquire concerning the new periodical, for which he had been engaged as a contributor, asked him to come with both his sisters on the evening of the same day. Entirely to her surprise, they came. She herself opened the door, and there before her, between his sisters, stood a splendidly handsome youth, tall and strong, with no appearance whatever of timidity, but, instead, an almost fierce determination making his face stern. This was his resource for carrying off the extreme inward tremor which he really felt. His hostess brought out Flaxman's designs for Dante, just received from Professor Felton of Harvard,* and the party made an evening's entertainment out of them.

The news of this triumph, imparted to a friend of Miss

---

* The book may have been Felton's Homer with Flaxman's drawings, issued in 1833.

Peabody's, led to an immediate invitation of Hawthorne to dinner at another house, for the next day. He accepted this, also, and on returning homeward, stopped at the "Salem Gazette" office, full of the excitement of his new experiences, announcing to Mr. Foote, the editor, that he was getting dissipated. He told of the evening with Miss Peabody, where he said he had had a delightful time, and of the dinner just achieved. "And I 've had a delightful time there, too!" he added. Mr. Foote, perceiving an emergency, at once asked the young writer to come to his own house for an evening. Hawthorne, thoroughly aroused, consented. When the evening came, several ladies who had been invited assembled before the author arrived; and among them Miss Peabody. When he reached the place he stopped short at the drawing-room threshold, startled by the presence of strangers, and stood perfectly motionless, but with the look of a sylvan creature on the point of fleeing away. His assumed brusquerie no longer availed him; he was stricken with dismay; his face lost color, and took on a warm paleness. All this was in a moment; but the daughter of the house moved forward, and he was drawn within. Even then, though he assumed a calm demeanor, his agitation was very great: he stood by a table, and, taking up some small object that lay upon it, he found his hand trembling so that he was forced to put it down again.

While friends were slowly penetrating his reserve in this way, he was approached in another by Mr. Goodrich, who induced him to go to Boston, there to edit the "American Magazine of Useful and Entertaining Knowledge." This work, which only continued from 1834 to September, 1837, was managed by several gentlemen under the name of the Bewick Company. One of these was Bowen, of Charlestown, an engraver; another was

8

Goodrich, who also, I think, had some connection with the American Stationers' Company. The Bewick Company took its name from Thomas Bewick, the English restorer of the art of wood-engraving, and the magazine was to do his memory honor by its admirable illustrations. But, in fact, it never did any one honor, nor brought any one profit. It was a penny popular affair, containing condensed information about innumerable subjects, no fiction, and little poetry. The woodcuts were of the crudest and most frightful sort. It passed through the hands of several editors and several publishers. Hawthorne was engaged at a salary of five hundred dollars a year; but it appears that he got next to nothing, and that he did not stay in the position long. There is little in its pages to recall the identity of the editor; but in one place he quotes as follows from Lord Bacon : " The ointment which witches use is made of the fat of children digged from their graves, and of the juices of smallage, cinquefoil, and wolf's-bane, mingled with the meal of fine wheat," and hopes that none of his readers will try to compound it. In the tale of " Young Goodman Brown," when Goody Cloyse says, " I was all anointed with the juice of smallage and cinquefoil and wolf's-bane," and the Devil continues, " ' Mingled with fine wheat and the fat of a new-born babe,' — ' Ah, your worship knows the recipe,' cried the old lady, cackling aloud." A few scraps of correspondence, mostly undated, which I have looked over, give one a new view of him in the bustle and vexation of this brief editorial experience. He sends off frequent and hurried missives to one of his sisters, who did some of the condensing and compiling which was a part of the business. " I make nothing," he says, in one, " of writing a history or biography before dinner." At another time, he is in haste for a Life of Jefferson, but warns his correspondent to " see that it contains nothing heterodox." At the end of one of the briefest messages, he finds time to speak of the cat at home. Perhaps with a memory of the days when he built book-houses, he had taken two names of the deepest dye from Milton and Bunyan for two of his favorite cats, whom he called Beelzebub and Apollyon. "Pull Beelzebub's tail for me," he writes. But the following from Boston, February 15, 1836, gives the more serious side of the situation : —

" I came here trusting to Goodrich's positive promise to pay me forty-five dollars as soon as I arrived; and he has kept promising from one day to another, till I do not see that he means to pay at all. I have now broke off all intercourse with him, and never think of going near him. . . . . I don't feel at all obliged to him about the editorship, for he is a stockholder and director in the Bewick Company ; . . . . and I defy them to get another to do for a thousand dollars what I do for five hundred."

Goodrich afterward sent his editor a small sum ; and the relations between them were resumed. A letter of May 5, in the same year, contains these allusions : —

" I saw Mr. Goodrich yesterday. . . . . He wants me to undertake a Universal History, to contain about as much as fifty or sixty pages of the magazine. [These were large pages.] If you are willing to write any part of it, ... I shall agree to do it. If necessary I will come home by and by, and concoct the plan of it with you. It need not be superior in profundity and polish to the middling magazine articles. . . . . I shall have nearly a dozen articles in The Token, — mostly quite short."

The historical project is, of course, that which resulted in the famous " Peter Parley " work. " Our pay as his-

torians of the universe," says a letter written six days
later, "will be about one hundred dollars, the whole of
which you may have. It is a poor compensation, but
better than the Token; because the writing is so much
less difficult." He afterward carried out the design, or
a large part of it, and the book has since sold by millions,
for the benefit of others. There are various little partic-
ulars in this ingenious abridgment which recall Hawthorne, especially if one is familiar with his " Grandfather's
Chair " and " True Stories " for children ; though the
book has probably undergone some changes in successive
editions. This passage about George IV. is, however,
remembered as being his: "Even when he was quite
an old man, this king cared as much about dress as any
young coxcomb. He had a great deal of taste in such
matters, and it is a pity that he was a king, for he might
otherwise have been an excellent tailor."

Up to this time (May 12) he had received only twenty
dollars for four months' editorial labor. "And, as you
may well suppose," he says, "I have undergone very
grievous vexations. Unless they pay me the whole
amount shortly, I shall return to Salem, and stay there
till they do." It seems a currish fate that puts such men
into the grasp of paltry and sordid cares like these !
But there is something deeper to be felt than dissatisfaction at the author-publisher's feeble though annoying scheme of harnessing in this rare poet to be his unpaid
yet paying hack. This deeper something is the pathos of
such possibilities, and the spectacle of so renowned and
strong-winged a genius consenting thus to take his share
of worldly struggle ; perfectly conscious that it is wholly
beneath his plane, but accepting it as a proper part of
the mortal lot ; scornful, but industrious and enduring.
You who have conceived of Hawthorne as a soft-mar-

rowed dweller in the dusk, fostering his own shyness and fearing to take the rubs of common men, pray look well at all this. And you, also, who discourse about the conditions essential to the development of genius, about the *milieu* and the *moment,* and try to prove America a vacuum which the Muse abhors, will do well to consider the phenomenon. "It is a poor compensation, yet better than the Token"; so he wrote, knowing that his unmatched tales were being coined for even a less reward than mere daily bread. He took the conditions that were about him, and gave them a dignity by his own fine perseverance. It is this inspired industry, this calm facing of the worst and making it the best, which has formed the history of all art. You talk of the ages, and choose this or that era as the only fit one. You long for a cosey niche in the past; but genius crowds time and eternity into the present, and says to you, "Make your own century!"

Meanwhile, if he received no solid gain from his exertions, Hawthorne was winning a reputation. In January he had written home: "My worshipful self is a very famous man in London, the 'Athenæum' having noticed all my articles in the last Token, with long extracts." This refers to the 'Athenæum' for November 7, 1835, which mentioned "The Wedding Knell" and "The Minister's Black Veil" as being stories "each of which has singularity enough to recommend it to the reader," and gave three columns to a long extract from "The Maypole of Merry Mount"; the notice being no doubt the work of the critic Chorley, who afterward met Hawthorne in England. Thus encouraged, he thought of collecting his tales and publishing them in volume form, connected by the conception of a travelling story-teller, whose shiftings of fortune were to form the interludes and links between the separate stories. A portion of this, prefatory to "Dr. Heidegger's Experiment," has been published in the "Mosses," with the heading of "Passages from a Relinquished Work." Goodrich was not disposed to lavish upon his young beneficiary the expense of bringing out a book for him, and the plan of reprinting the tales with this framework around them was given up. The next year Bridge came to Goodrich and insisted on having a simple collection issued, himself taking the pecuniary risk. In this way the "Twice-Told Tales" were first brought collectively before the world; and for the second time this faithful comrade of Hawthorne laid posterity under obligation to himself. It was not till long afterward, however, that Hawthorne knew of his friend's interposition in the affair.

Mr. Bridge had not then entered the navy, and was engaged in a great enterprise on the Androscoggin; nothing less than an attempt to dam up that river and apply the water-power to some mills. In July of 1837, Hawthorne went to visit him at Bridgton, and has described his impressions fully in the Note-Books. It was probably his longest absence from Salem since graduating at Bowdoin. "My circumstances cannot long continue as they are," he writes; "and Bridge, too, stands between high prosperity and utter ruin."

The change in his own circumstances which Hawthorne looked for did not come through his book. It sold some six or seven hundred copies in a short time, but was received quietly,* though Longfellow, then lately

---

* Some of the sketches were reprinted in England; and "A Rill from the Town Pump" was circulated in pamphlet form by a London bookseller, without the author's name, as a temperance tract.

established in his Harvard professorship, and known as the author of "Outre-Mer," greeted it with enthusiasm in the "North American Review," which wielded a great influence in literary affairs.

On March 7, 1837, Hawthorne sent this note to his former classmate, to announce the new volume.

"The agent of the American Stationer's Company will send you a copy of a book entitled 'Twice-Told Tales,' — of which, as a classmate, I venture to request your acceptance. We were not, it is true, so well acquainted at college, that I can plead an absolute right to inflict my 'twice-told' tediousness upon you; but I have often regretted that we were not better known to each other, and have been glad of your success in literature and in more important matters." Returning to the tales, he adds: "I should like to flatter myself that they would repay you some part of the pleasure which I have derived from your own 'Outre-Mer.' Your obedient servant,

"NATH. HAWTHORNE."

Longfellow replied warmly, and in June Hawthorne wrote again, a long letter picturing his mood with a fulness that shows how keenly he had felt the honest sympathy of the poet.

"Not to burden you with my correspondence," he said, "I have delayed a rejoinder to your very kind and cordial letter, until now. It gratifies me that you have occasionally felt an interest in my situation; but your quotation from Jean Paul about the 'lark's nest' makes me smile. You would have been much nearer the truth if you had pictured me as dwelling in an owl's nest; for mine is about as dismal, and like the owl I seldom venture abroad till after dusk. By some witchcraft or other — for I really cannot assign any reasonable why and wherefore — I have been carried apart from the main current of life, and find it impossible to get back again. Since we last met, which you remember was in Sawtell's room, where you read a farewell poem to the relics of the class, — ever since that time I have secluded myself from society ; and yet I never meant any such thing, nor dreamed what sort of life I was going to lead. I have made a captive of myself, and put me into a dungeon, and now I cannot find the key to let myself out, — and if the door were open, I should be almost afraid to come out. You tell me that you have met with troubles and changes. I know not what these may have been, but I can assure you that trouble is the next best thing to enjoyment, and that there is no fate in this world so horrible as to have no share in either its joys or sorrows. For the last ten years, I have not lived, but only dreamed of living. It may be true that there have been some unsubstantial pleasures here in the shade, which I might have missed in the sunshine, but you cannot conceive how utterly devoid of satisfaction all my ret- rospects are. I have laid up no treasure of pleasant remem- brances against old age ; but there is some comfort in thinking that future years can hardly fail to be more varied and therefore more tolerable than the past.

" You give me more credit than I deserve, in supposing that I have led a studious life. I have indeed turned over a good many books, but in so desultory a way that it cannot be called study, nor has it left me the fruits of study. As to my literary efforts, I do not think much of them, neither is it worth while to be ashamed of them. They would have been better, I trust, if written under more favorable circumstances. I have had no external excitement, — no consciousness that the public would like what I wrote, nor much hope nor a passionate desire that they should do so. Nevertheless, having nothing else to be ambitious of, I have been considerably interested in literature ; and if my writings had made any decided impression, I should have been stimulated to greater exertions ; but there has been no warmth of approbation, so that I have always written with benumbed fingers. I have another great difficulty in the lack of materials ; for I have seen so little of the world that I have nothing but thin air to concoct my stories of, and it is not easy to give a lifelike semblance to such shadowy stuff. Sometimes through a peep-hole I have caught a glimpse of the real world, and the two or three articles in which I have portrayed these glimpses please me better than the others.

"I have now, or shall soon have, a sharper spur to exertion, which I lacked at an earlier period; for I see little prospect but that I shall have to scribble for a living. But this troubles me much less than you would suppose. I can turn my pen to all sorts of drudgery, such as children's books, etc., and by and by I shall get some editorship that will answer my purpose. Frank Pierce, who was with us at college, offered me his influence to obtain an office in the Exploring Expedition [Commodore Wilkes's]; but I believe that he was mistaken in supposing that a vacancy existed. If such a post were attainable, I should certainly accept it; for, though fixed so long to one spot, I have always had a desire to run round the world. . . . . I intend in a week or two to. come out of my owl's nest, and not return till late in the summer, — employing the interval in making a tour somewhere in New England. You who have the dust of distant countries on your ' sandal-shoon ' cannot imagine how much enjoyment I shall have in this little excursion. . . . .   Yours sincerely,

"NATH. HAWTHORNE."

A few days later the quarterly, containing Longfellow's review of the book, appeared; and the note of thanks which Hawthorne sent is full of an exultation strongly in contrast with the pensive tone of the letter just given.

SALEM, June 19th, 1837.

DEAR LONGFELLOW : — I have to-day received, and read with huge delight, your review of ' Hawthorne's Twice-Told Tales.' I frankly own that I was not without hopes that you would do this kind office for the book; though I could not have anticipated how very kindly it would be done. Whether or no the public will agree to the praise which you bestow on me, there are at least five persons who think you the most sagacious critic on earth, viz., my mother and two sisters, my old maiden aunt, and finally the strongest believer of the whole five, my own self. If I doubt the sincerity and correctness of any of my critics, it shall be of those who censure me. Hard would be the lot of a poor scribbler, if he may not have this privilege. . . . .

Very sincerely yours,
NATH. HAWTHORNE.

That "Evangeline" was written upon a theme suggested to Hawthorne (by a friend who had heard it from a French Canadian *) and by him made over to the poet, has already been made public. Hawthorne wrote, on its appearance : —

"I have read 'Evangeline' with more pleasure than it would be decorous to express. It cannot fail, I think, to prove the most triumphant of all your successes."

Nevertheless, he gave vent to some of his admiration in a notice of the work which he wrote for "The Salem Advertiser," a Democratic paper.

"The story of Evangeline and her lover," he there says, "is as poetical as the fable of the Odyssey, besides that it comes to the heart as a fact that has actually taken place in human life." He speaks of "its pathos all illuminated with beauty, — so that the impression of the poem is nowhere dismal nor despondent, and glows with the purest sunshine where we might the least expect it, on the pauper's death-bed. . . . . The story is told with the simplicity of high and exquisite art, which causes it to

* See American Note-Books, October 24, 1839.

flow onward as naturally as the current of a stream. Evangeline's wanderings give occasion to many pictures both of northern and southern scenery and life : but these do not appear as if brought in designedly, to adorn the tale ; they seem to throw their beauty inevitably into the calm mirror of its bosom as it flows past them. . . . . By this work of his maturity he has placed himself on a higher eminence than he had yet attained, and beyond the reach of envy. Let him stand, then, at the head of our list of native poets, until some one else shall break up the rude soil of our American life, as he has done, and produce from it a lovelier and nobler flower than this poem of Evangeline ! "

Longfellow's characteristic kindly reply was as follows : —

"MY DEAR HAWTHORNE : — I have been waiting and waiting in the hope of seeing you in Cambridge. . . . . I have been meditating upon your letter, and pondering with friendly admiration your review of ' Evangeline,' in connection with the subject of which, that is to say, the Acadians, a literary project arises in my mind for you to execute. Perhaps I can pay you back in part your own generous gift, by giving you a theme for story, in return for a theme for song. It is neither more nor less than the history of the Acadians, *after* their expulsion as well as before. Felton has been making some researches in the State archives, and offers to resign the documents into your hands.

"Pray come and see me about it without delay. Come so as to pass a night with us, if posssible, this week ; if not a day and night.

"Ever sincerely yours,

" HENRY W. LONGFELLOW."

There is nothing in our literary annals more unique and delightful than this history of Longfellow's warm recognition of his old classmate, and the mutual courtesies to which it led. One is reminded by it of the William Tell episode between Goethe and Schiller, though it was in this case only the theme and nothing of material that was transferred.

An author now almost forgotten, Charles Fenno Hoffman, also published in "The American Monthly Magazine," * which he was editing, a kindly review, which, however, underestimated the strength of the new genius, as it was at first the general habit to do. "Minds like Hawthorne's," he said, "seem to be the only ones suited to an American climate. . . . . Never can a nation be impregnated with the literary spirit by minor authors alone. . . . . Yet men like Hawthorne are not without their use." . . . . In this same number of the magazine, by the way, was printed Hawthorne's "Threefold Destiny," under the pseudonyme of Ashley Allen Royce; and the song of Faith Egerton, afterward omitted, is thus given: —

"O, man can seek the downward glance,
And each kind word, — affection's spell, —
Eye, voice, its value can enhance;
For eye may speak, and tongue can tell.

"But woman's love, it waits the while
To echo to another's tone;
To linger on another's smile,
Ere dare to answer with its own."

These versicles, though they might easily be passed over as commonplace, hold a peculiar inner radiance that perhaps issued from the dawn of a lifelong happiness for Hawthorne at this period.

* For March, 1838.

V.

AT BOSTON AND BROOK FARM.

1838–1842.

HAWTHORNE'S mood at this time was one of profound dissatisfaction at his elimination from the active life of the world. "I am tired of being an ornament," he said, with great emphasis, to a friend. "I want a little piece of land that I can call my own, big enough to stand upon, big enough to be buried in. I want to have something to do with this material world." And, striking his hand vigorously on a table that stood by: "If I could only make tables," he declared, "I should feel myself more of a man." He was now thirty-four, and the long restraint and aloofness of the last thirteen years, with the gathering consciousness that he labored under unjust reproach of inaction, and the sense of loss in being denied his share in affairs, had become intolerable. It was now, also, that a new phase of being was opened to him. He had become engaged to Miss Sophia Peabody, a sister of his friend.

President Van Buren had been two years in office, and Mr. Bancroft, the historian, was Collector of the port of Boston. One evening the latter was speaking, in a circle of Whig friends, of the splendid things which the Democratic administration was doing for literary men. "But there's Hawthorne," suggested a lady who was present.

"You've done nothing for him." "He won't take anything," was the answer: "he has been offered places." In fact, Hawthorne's friends in political life had urged him to enter politics, and he had at one time been tendered a post of some sort in the West Indies, but refused it because he would not live in a slaveholding community. "I happen to know," said the lady, "that he would be very glad of employment." The result was that a commission for a small post in the Boston Custom House came, soon after, to the young author. On going down from Salem to inquire further about it, he received another and a better appointment as weigher and gauger, with a salary, I think, of twelve hundred a year. Just before entering the Collector's office, he noticed a man leaving it who wore a very dejected air; and, connecting this with the change in his own appointment, he imagined this person to be the just-ejected weigher. Speaking of this afterward, he said: "I don't believe in rotation in office. It is not good for the human being." But he took his place, writing to Longfellow (January 12, 1839):

"I have no reason to doubt my capacity to fulfil the duties; for I don't know what they are. They tell me that a considerable portion of my time will be unoccupied, the which I mean to employ in sketches of my new experience, under some such titles as follows: 'Scenes in Dock,' 'Voyages at Anchor,' 'Nibblings of a Wharf Rat,' 'Trials of a Tide-Waiter,' 'Romance of the Revenue Service,' together with an ethical work in two volumes, on the subject of Duties, the first volume to treat of moral and religious duties, and the second of duties imposed by the Revenue Laws, which I begin to consider the most important class."

Two years later, when Harrison and Tyler carried the election for the Whigs, he suffered the fate of his predecessor.

And here I may offer an opinion as to Hawthorne's connection with the Democratic party. When asked why he belonged to it, he answered that he lived in a democratic country. "But we are all republicans alike," was the objection to his defence. "Well," he said, "I don't understand history till it's a hundred years old, and meantime it's safe to belong to the Democratic party." Still, Hawthorne was, so far as it comported with his less transient aims, a careful observer of public affairs; and mere badinage, like that just quoted, must not be taken as really covering the ground of his choice in politics. A man of such deep insight, accustomed to bring it to bear upon everything impartially, was not to be influenced by any blind and accidental preference in these questions; albeit his actual performance of political duties was slight. I think he recognized the human strength of the Democratic, as opposed to the theorizing and intellectual force of the Republican party. It is a curious fact, that with us the party of culture should be the radical party, upholding ideas even at the expense of personal liberty; and the party of ignorance that of order, the conservating force, careful of personal liberty even to a fault! Hawthorne, feeling perhaps that ideas work too rapidly here, ranged himself on the side that offered the greater resistance to them.

This term of service in Boston was of course irksome to Hawthorne, and entirely suspended literary endeavors for the time. Yet "my life only is a burden," he writes, "in the same way that it is to every toilsome man. . . . . But from henceforth forever I shall be entitled to call the sons of toil my brethren, and shall know how to sympathize with them, seeing that I likewise have risen at the dawn, and borne the fervor of the midday sun, nor turned my heavy footsteps homeward till eventide." He need not always have made the employment so severe, but the wages of the wharf laborers depended on the number of hours they worked in a day, and Hawthorne used to make it a point in all weathers, to get to the wharf at the earliest possible hour, solely for their benefit. For the rest, he felt a vast benefit from his new intercourse with men; there could not have been a better maturing agency for him at this time; and the interval served as an apt introduction to the Brook Farm episode.

That this least gregarious of men should have been drawn into a socialistic community, seems at first inexplicable enough; but in reality it was the most logical step he could have taken. He had thoroughly tried seclusion, and had met and conquered by himself the first realization of what the world actually is. Next, he entered into the performance of definite duties and the receipt of gain, and watched the operation of these two conditions on himself and those about him; an experiment that taught him the evils of the system, and the necessity of burying his better energies so long as he took part in affairs. This raised doubts, of course, as to how he was to fit himself into the frame of things; and while he mused upon some more generous arrangement of society, and its conflicting interests, a scheme was started which plainly proposed to settle the problem. Fourier had only just passed away; the spread of his ideas was in its highest momentum. On the other hand, the study of German philosophy, and the new dissent of Emerson, had carried men's thoughts to the very central springs of intellectual law, while in Boston the writing and preaching of Channing roused a practical radicalism, and called for a better application of Christianity to affairs. The era of the Transcendentalists had come. The

Chardon Street meetings — assemblages of ardent theorists and "come-outers" of every type, who, while their sessions lasted, held society in their hands and moulded it like clay — were a rude manifestation of the same deep current. In the midst of these influences, Mr. Ripley, an enthusiastic student of philosophy, received an inspiration to establish a modified socialistic community on our own soil. The Industrial Association which he proposed at West Roxbury was wisely planned with direct reference to the emergencies of American life; it had no affinity with the erratic views of Enfantin and the Saint Simonists, nor did it in the least tend toward the mistakes of Robert Owen regarding the relation of the sexes; though it agreed with Fourier and Owen both, as I understand, in respect of labor. In a better and freer sense than has usually been the case with such attempts, the design sprang out of one man's mind and fell properly under his control. His simple object was to distribute labor in such a way as to give all men time for culture, and to free their minds from the debasing influence of a merely selfish competition. It was a practical, orderly, noble effort to apply Christianity directly to human customs and institutions. " A few men and women of like views and feelings," one of his sympathizers has said, " grouped themselves around him, not as their master, but as their friend and brother, and the community at Brook Farm was instituted." At various times Charles Dana, Pratt, the young Brownson, Horace Sumner (a younger brother of Charles), George William Curtis, and his brother Burrill Curtis were there. The place was a kind of granary of true grit. People who found their own honesty too heavy a burden to carry successfully through the rough jostlings of society, flocked thither. "They were mostly individuals" says Hawthorne, " who had gone through such an experience as to disgust them with ordinary pursuits, but who were not yet so old, nor had suffered so deeply, as to lose their faith in the better time to come."

To men like Hawthorne, however little they may noise the fact abroad, the rotten but tenacious timbers of the social order shake beneath the lightest tread. But he knew that the only wise method is to begin repairing within the edifice, keeping the old associations, and losing nothing of value while gaining everything new that is desirable. Because Brook Farm seemed to adopt this principle, he went there. Some of the meetings of the associators were held at Miss E. P. Peabody's, in Boston, and the proceedings were related to him. Mr. Ripley did not at first know who was the " distinguished literary gentleman " announced as willing to join the company; and when told that it was Hawthorne, he felt as if a miracle had befallen, or "as if," he tells me, " the heavens would presently be filled with angels, and we should see Jacob's ladder before us. But we never came any nearer to having *that*, than our old ladder in the barn, from floor to hayloft." For his personal benefit, Hawthorne had two ends in view, connected with Brook Farm : one, to find a suitable and economical home after marriage; the other, to secure a mode of life thoroughly balanced and healthy, which should successfully distribute the sum of his life's labor between body and brain. He hoped to secure leisure for writing by perhaps six hours of daily service; but he found nearly sixteen needful. " He worked like a dragon," says Mr. Ripley.

The productive industry of the association was agriculture; the leading aim, teaching; and in some cases there were classes made up of men, women, children,

whom ignorance put on the same plane. Several buildings accommodated the members : the largest, in which
the public table was spread and the cooking done, being
called The Hive ; another, The Pilgrim House ; a smaller
one, The Nest; and still another was known as The Cottage. In The Eyrie, Mr. and Mrs. Ripley lived, and
here a great part of the associators would gather in the
evenings. Of a summer night, when the moon was full,
they lit no lamps, but sat grouped in the light and
shadow, while sundry of the younger men sang old bal-
lads, or joined Tom Moore's songs to operatic airs. On
other nights, there would be an original essay or poem
read aloud, or else a play of Shakespere, with the parts
distributed to different members ; and, these amusements
failing, some interesting discussion was likely to take
their place. Occasionally, in the dramatic season, large
delegations from the farm would drive into Boston in
carriages and wagons to the opera or the play. Sometimes, too, the young women sang as they washed the
dishes, in The Hive ; and the youthful yeomen of the
society came in and helped them with their work. The
men wore blouses of a checked or plaided stuff, belted
at the waist, with a broad collar folding down about
the throat, and rough straw hats ; the women, usually,
simple calico gowns, and hats, — which were then an
innovation in feminine attire. In the season of wood-
wanderings, they would trim their hats with wreaths of
barberry or hop-vine, ground-pine, or whatever offered,
— a suggestion of the future Priscilla of " Blithedale."
Some families and students came to the farm as boarders,
paying for their provision in household or field labor, or
by teaching ; a method which added nothing to the funds
of the establishment, and in this way rather embarrassed
it. A great deal of individual liberty was allowed. Peo-

ple could eat in private or public; and it has been said
by those who were there that the unconventional life
permitted absolute privacy at any time.   Every one was
quite unfettered, too, in the sphere of religious worship.
When a member wished to be absent, another would
generally contrive to take his work for the interval;
and a general good-will seems to have prevailed.   Still,
I imagine there must have been a temporary and uncertain air about the enterprise, much of the time; and the
more intimate unions of some among the members who
were congenial, gave rise to intermittent jealousies in those
who found no special circle.   "In this way it was very
much like any small town of the same number of inhabitants," says one of my informants.   Indeed, though every
one who shared in the Brook Farm attempt seems grateful for what it taught of the dignity and the real fellowship of labor, I find a general belief in such persons that
it could not long have continued at its best.   The system of compensating all kinds of service, skilled or otherwise, according to the time used, excited — as some have
thought — much dissatisfaction even among the generous
and enlightened people who made up the society.   " I
thought I could see some incipient difficulties working
in the system," writes a lady who was there in 1841.
"Questions already arose as to how much individual
freedom could be allowed, if it conflicted with the best
interests of the whole.   Those who came there were the
results of another system of things which still gave a
salutary check to the more radical tendencies; but the
second generation there could hardly have shown equal,
certainly not the same, character."   A confirmation of
this augury is the fact that the cast of the community
became decidedly more Fourieristic before it disbanded;
and it is not impossible that another generation might

have decolorized and seriously deformed human existence among them. Theories and opinions were very openly talked over, and practical details as well; and though this must have had its charm, yet it would also touch uncomfortably on a given temperament, or jar upon a peculiar mood. In such enterprises there must always be a slight inclination to establish a conformity to certain freedoms which really become oppressions. Shyness was not held essential to a regenerated state of things, and was perhaps too much disregarded; as also was illness, an emergency not clearly provided for, which had to be met by individual effort and self-sacrifice, after the selfish and old-established fashion of the world. How this atmosphere affected Hawthorne he has hinted in his romance founded on some aspects of community life: "Though fond of society, I was so constituted as to need these occasional retirements, even in a life like that of Blithedale, which was itself characterized by a remoteness from the world. Unless renewed by a yet further withdrawal towards the inner circle of self-communion, I lost the better part of my individuality. My thoughts became of little worth, and my sensibilities grew as arid as a tuft of moss . . . . crumbling in the sunshine, after long expectance of a shower." A fellow-toiler came upon him suddenly, one day, lying in a green hollow some distance from the farm, with his hands under his head and his face shaded by his hat. "How came you out here?" asked his friend. "Too much of a party up there," was his answer, as he pointed toward the community buildings. It has also been told that at leisure times he would sit silently, hour after hour, in the broad old-fashioned hall of The Hive, where he "could listen almost unseen to the chat and merriment of the young people," himself almost always holding a book before him, but seldom turning the leaves.

One sees in his letters of this time* how the life wore
upon him ; and his journal apparently ceased during the
whole bucolic experience. How joyously his mind begins
to disport itself again with fancies, the moment he leaves
the association, even temporarily ! And in 1842, as
soon as he is fairly quit of it, the old darkling or way-
wardly gleaming stream of thought and imagination flows
freshly, untamably forward. Hawthorne remained with
the Brook Farm community nearly a twelvemonth, a
small part of which time was spent in Boston. Some of
the letters which his sisters wrote him show a delightful
solicitude reigning at home, during the period of his
experiment.

" What is the use," says one, " of burning your brains out
in the sun, if you can do anything better with them ? . . . .
I am bent upon coming to see you, this summer. Do not you
remember how we used to go a-fishing together in Raymond ?
Your mention of wild flowers and pickerel has given me a longing for the woods and waters again."

Then, in August,

" C—— A——," writes his sister Louisa, " told me the
other day that he heard you were to do the travelling in Europe for the community."

This design, if it existed, might well have found a
place in the Dialogues of the Unborn which Hawthorne
once meant to write: for this was his only summer at
Brook Farm. " A summer of toil, of interest, of something that was not pleasure, but which went deep into my
heart, and there became a rich experience," he writes, in
" Blithedale." " I found myself looking forward to years,

* American Note-Books, Vol. I.

if not to a lifetime, to be spent on the same system."
This was, in fact, his attitude; for, after passing the
winter at the farm as a boarder, and then absenting himself a little while, he returned in the spring to look over
the ground and perhaps select a house-site, just before
his marriage, but came to an adverse decision.   This no
doubt accorded with perceptions which he was not called
upon to make public; but because he was a writer of
fiction there seems to have arisen a tacit agreement, in
some quarters, to call him insincere in his connection
with this socialistic enterprise.   He had not much to
gain by leaving the community; for he had put into its
treasury a thousand dollars, about the whole of his sav-
ings from the custom-house stipend, and had next to
nothing to establish a home with elsewhere, while a
niche in the temple of the reformers would have cost
him nothing but labor.   The length of his stay was by
no means uncommonly short, for there was always a transient contingent at Brook Farm, many of whom remained
but a few weeks.   A devoted but not a wealthy disciple,
who had given six thousand dollars for the building of the
Pilgrim House, and hoped to end his days within it, retired forever after a very short sojourn, not dissuaded
from the theory, but convinced that the practical application was foredoomed to disaster.   And, in truth, though
a manful effort was made, with good pecuniary success
for a time, ten years brought the final hour of failure to
this millennial plan.

Very few people who were at Brook Farm seem to
have known or even to have seen Hawthorne there,
though he was elected chairman of the Finance Committee just before leaving, and I am told that his handsome
presence, his quiet sympathy, his literary reputation, and
his hearty participation in labor commanded a kind of

reverence from some of the members. Next to his friend
George P. Bradford, one of the workers and teachers in
the community, his most frequent associates were a certain Rev. Warren Burton, author of a curious little book
called "Scenery-Shower," designed to develop a proper
taste for landscape; and one Frank Farley, who had been
a pioneer in the West, a man of singular experiences and
of an original turn, who was subject to mental derangement at times. The latter visited him at the Old Manse,
afterward, when Hawthorne was alone there, and entered
actively into his makeshift housekeeping.

President Pierce, on one occasion, speaking to an acquaintance about Hawthorne, said : " He is enthusiastic
when he speaks of the aims and self-sacrifice of some of
the Brook Farm people; but when I questioned him
whether he would like to live and die in a community
like that, he confessed he was not suited to it, but said
he had learned a great deal from it. 'What, for instance?' 'Why, marketing, for one thing.   I did n't
know anything about it practically, and I rode into Boston once or twice with the men who took in things to sell,
and saw how it was done.' "   The things of deepest moment which he learned were not to be stated fully in
conversation; but I suppose readers would draw the
same inference from this whimsical climax of Hawthorne's
as that which has been found in " The Blithedale Romance " ; namely, that he looked on his socialistic life as
the merest jesting matter. Such, I think, is the general
opinion; and a socialistic writer, Mr. Noyes, of the
Oneida Community, has indignantly cried out against the
book, as a " poetico-sneering romance." This study of
human character, which would keep its value in any state
of society that preserved its reflective faculty intact and
sane, to be belittled to the record of a brief experi-

ment! Hawthorne indeed, speaking in the prefatory third person of his own aim, says: "His whole treatment of the affair is altogether incidental to the main purpose of the romance; nor does he put forward the slightest pretensions to illustrate a theory, or elicit a conclusion, favorable or otherwise, in respect to socialism." And though he has told the story autobiographically, it is through a character whom we ought by no means to identify with Hawthorne in his whole mood. I have taken the liberty of applying to Hawthorne's own experience two passages from Coverdale's account, because they picture something known to be the case; and a careful sympathy will find no difficulty in distinguishing how much is real and how much assumed. Coverdale, being merely the medium for impressions of the other characters, is necessarily light and diaphanous, and Hawthorne, finding it more convenient, and an advantage to the lifelikeness of the story, does not attempt to hold him up in the air all the time, but lets him down now and then, and assumes the part himself. The allusions to the community scheme are few, and most of them are in the deepest way sympathetic. Precisely because the hopes of the socialists were so unduly high, he values them and still is glad of them, though they have fallen to ruin. " In my own behalf, I rejoice that I could once think better of the world than it deserved. It is a mistake into which men seldom fall twice in a lifetime; or, if so, the rarer and higher is the nature that can thus magnanimously persist in error." Where is the sneer concealed in this serious and comprehensive utterance? There is a class of two-pronged minds, which seize a pair of facts eagerly, and let the truth drop out of sight between them. For these it is enough that Hawthorne made some use of his Brook Farm memories in a romance, and then wrote that romance in the first person, with a few dashes of humor.

Another critic, acting on a conventional idea as to Hawthorne's "cold, self-removed observation," quotes to his disadvantage this paragraph in a letter from Brook Farm: "Nothing here is settled. . . . . My mind will not be abstracted. I must observe and think and feel, and content myself with catching glimpses of things which may be wrought out hereafter. Perhaps it will be quite as well that I find myself unable to set seriously about literary occupation for the present." This is offered as showing that Hawthorne went to the community — unconsciously, admits our critic, but still in obedience to some curious, chilly "dictate of his nature" — for the simple purpose of getting fresh impressions, to work up into fiction. But no one joined the society expecting to give up his entire individuality, and it was a special part of the design that each should take such share of the labor as was for his own and the general good, and follow his own tastes entirely as to ideal pursuits. A singular prerogative this, which every one who writes about Hawthorne lays claim to, that he may be construed as a man who, at bottom, had no other motive in life than to make himself uneasy by withdrawing from hearty communion with people, in order to pry upon them intellectually! He speaks of "that quality of the intellect and the heart which impelled me (often against my own will, and to the detriment of my own comfort) to live in other lives, and to endeavor — *by generous sympathies, by delicate intuitions*, by taking note of things too slight for record, and by bringing my human spirit into manifold accordance with the companions God had assigned me — to learn the secret which was hidden even from themselves"; and this is cited as evidence of "his cold in-

quisitiveness, his incredulity, his determination to worm
out the inmost secrets of all associated with him." Such
distortion is amazing. The few poets who search constantly for truth are certainly impelled to get at the inmost of everything. But what, in Heaven's name, is the
motive? Does any one seriously suppose it to be for the
amusement of making stories out of it? The holding up
to one's self the stern and secret realities of life is no such
pleasing pursuit. These men are driven to it by the divine impulse which has made them seers and recorders.

As for Hawthorne, he hoped and loved and planned
with the same rich human faith that fills the heart of
every manly genius; and if discouraging truth made him
suffer, it was all the more because his ideals — and at
first his trust in their realization — were so generous and
so high. Two of his observations as to Brook Farm,
transferred to the "The Blithedale Romance," show the
wisdom on which his withdrawal was based. The first
relates to himself: "No sagacious man will long retain
his sagacity, if he live exclusively among reformers and
progressive people, without periodically returning to the
settled system of things, to correct himself by a new observation from that old standpoint." He had too much
imagination to feel safe in giving free rein to it, in a special direction of theoretic conduct; he also remembered
that, as the old system of things was full of error, it was
possible that a new one might become so in new ways,
unless watched. The second observation touches the
real weakness of the Brook Farm institution: "It struck
me as rather odd, that one of the first questions raised,
after our separation from the greedy, struggling, self-
seeking world, should relate to the possibility of getting the advantage over the outside barbarians in their
own field of labor. But to own the truth, I very soon

became sensible that, *as regarded society at large, we stood in a position of new hostility rather than new brotherhood.*" And, in fact, the real good which Mr. Ripley's attempt did, was to implant the co-operative idea in the minds of men who have gone out into the world to effect its gradual application on a grander scale. It is by introducing it into one branch of social energy after another that the regenerative agency of to-day can alone be made effectual. The leaders of that community have been broad-minded, and recognize this truth. None of them, however, have ever taken the trouble to formulate it as Hawthorne did, on perceiving it some years in advance.

The jocose tone, it may be added, seems to have been a characteristic part of the Brook Farm experiment, despite the sober earnest and rapt enthusiasm that accompanied it. The members had their laughing allusions, and talked —in a strain of self-ridicule precisely similar to Coverdale's—of having bands of music to play for the field-laborers, who should plough in tune. This merely proves that they were people who kept their wits whole, and had the humor that comes with refinement; while it illustrates by the way the naturalness of the tone Hawthorne has given to Coverdale.

The Priscilla of Blithedale was evidently founded upon the little seamstress whom he describes in the Note-Books as coming out to the farm, and Old Moodie's spectre can be discerned in a brief memorandum of a man seen (at Parker's old bar-room in Court Square) in 1850. It has been thought that Zenobia was drawn from Margaret Fuller, or from a lady at Brook Farm, or perhaps from both: a gentleman who was there says that he traces in her a partial likeness to several women. It is as well to remember that Hawthorne distinctly negatived the idea that he wrote with any one that he knew before his mind ; and he illustrated it, to one of his most intimate friends, by saying that sometimes in the course of composition it would suddenly occur to him, that the character he was describing resembled in some point one or more persons of his acquaintance. Thus, I suppose that when the character of Priscilla had developed itself in his imagination, he found he could give her a greater reality by associating her with the seamstress alluded to ; and that the plaintive old man at Parker's offered himself as a good figure to prop up the web-work of pure invention which was the history of Zenobia's and Priscilla's father. There is a conviction in the minds of all readers, dearer to them than truth, that novelists simply sit down and describe their own acquaintances, using a few clumsy disguises to make the thing tolerable. When they do take a hint from real persons the character becomes quite a different thing to them from the actual prototype. It was not even so definite as this with Hawthorne. Yet no doubt, his own atmosphere being peculiar, the contrast between that and the atmosphere of those he met stimulated his imagination ; so that, without his actually seeing a given trait in another person, the meeting might have the effect of *suggesting* it. Then he would brood over this suggestion till it became a reality, a person, to his mind ; and thus his characters were conceived independently in a region somewhere between himself and the people who had awakened speculation in his mind.

He had a very sure instinct as to when a piece of reality might be transferred to his fiction with advantage. Mr. Curtis has told the story of a young woman of Concord, a farmer's daughter, who had had her aspirations roused by education until the conflict between these and the hard and barren life she was born to, made her thoroughly miserable and morbid ; and one summer's evening she sought relief in the quiet, homely stream that flowed by the Old Manse, and found the end of earthly troubles in its oozy depths.   Hawthorne was roused by Curtis himself coming beneath his window (precisely as Coverdale comes to summon Hollingsworth), and with one other they went out on the river, to find the poor girl's body.   "The man," writes his friend, "whom the villagers had only seen at morning as a musing spectre in the garden, now appeared among them at night to devote his strong arm and steady heart to their service."

By this dark memory is the powerful climax of "The Blithedale Romance" bound to the sphere of a reality as dread.

VI.

THE OLD MANSE.

1842-1846.

THERE is a Providence in the lives of men who act sincerely, which makes each step lead, with the best result, to the next phase of their careers. By his participation in the excellent endeavor at Brook Farm, Hawthorne had prepared himself to enjoy to the full his idyllic retirement at the Old Manse, in Concord. "For now, being happy," he says, "I felt as if there were no question to be put."

Hawthorne was married in July, 1842, and went at once to this his first home. Just before going to Brook Farm he had written "Grandfather's Chair," the first part of a series of sketches of New England history for children, which was published by Miss Peabody in Boston, and Wiley and Putnam in New York; but the continuation was interrupted by his stay at the farm. In 1842 he wrote a second portion, and also some biographical stories, all of which gained an immediate success. He also resumed his contributions to the "Democratic Review," the most brilliant periodical of the time, in which Whittier, Longfellow, Lowell, Poe, and other noted authors made their appearance. It was published at Washington, and afterward at New York, and made considerable pretensions to a national character. Hawthorne had been engaged as a contributor, at a fair rate, in 1838, and his articles had his name appended (not always the practice at that time) in a way that shows the high estimation into which he had already grown. "John Inglefield's Thanksgiving," "The Celestial Railroad," "The Procession of Life," "Fire Worship," "Buds and Bird Voices," and "Roger Malvin's Burial," all appeared in the "Democratic" in 1843. "Rappaccini's Daughter" and other tales followed in the next year; and in 1845 the second volume of "Twice-Told Tales" was brought out at Boston. During the same year Hawthorne edited the "African Journals" of his friend Bridge, then an officer in the navy, who had just completed a cruise. The editor's name evidently carried great weight, even then. "The mere announcement, 'edited by Nathaniel Hawthorne,'" said one of the critics, "is enough to entitle this book to a place among the American classics." I dwell upon this, because an attempt has been made to spread the idea that Hawthorne up to the time of writing "The Scarlet Letter" was still obscure and discouraged, and that only then, by a timely burst of appreciation in certain quarters, was he rescued from oblivion. The truth is, that he had won himself an excellent position, was popular, and was himself aware by this time of the honor in which he was held. Even when he found that the small profits of literature were forcing him into office again, he wrote to Bridge: "It is rather singular that I should need an office: for nobody's scribblings seem to be more acceptable than mine." The explanation of this lies in the wretchedly dependent state of native authorship at that time. The law of copyright had not then attained to even the refined injustice which it has now reached. "I continue," he wrote, in 1844, "to scribble tales with good success so far as re-

gards empty praise, some notes of which, pleasant enough
to my ears, have come from across the Atlantic. But the
pamphlet and piratical system has so broken up all regular literature, that I am forced to work hard for small
gains."

Besides the labors already enumerated, he edited for
the "Democratic" some "Papers of an old Dartmoor
Prisoner" (probably some one of his "sea-dog" acquaintance in Salem). He was in demand among the
publishers. A letter from Evert Duyckinck (New York,
October 2, 1845), who was then in the employ of Wiley
and Putnam, publishers of the "African Cruiser," says
of that book: "The English notices are bounteous in
praise. No American book in a long time has been
so well noticed." The same firm were now eager to
bring out his recent tales, and were also, as appears in
the following from Duyckinck, urging the prosecution
of another scheme: "I hope you will not think me a
troublesome fellow," he writes, "if I drop you another
line with the vociferous cry, MSS.! MSS.! Mr. Wiley's
American series is athirst for the volumes of tales; and
how stands the prospect for the History of Witchcraft,
I whilom spoke of?" The History Hawthorne wisely
eschewed; but early in 1846 the "Mosses from an Old
Manse" was issued at New York, in two volumes.

This attracted at once a great deal of praise, and it
certainly shows a wider range and fuller maturity than
the first book of "Twice-Told Tales"; yet I doubt
whether the stories of this group have taken such intimate
hold of any body of readers as those, although recom-
mending themselves to a larger audience. Hawthorne's
life at the Old Manse was assuredly one of the brightest
epochs of his career: an unalloyed happiness had come to
him, he was full of the delight of first possession in his

9 *

home, a new and ample companionship was his, and the quiet course of the days, with their openings into healthful outdoor exercise, made a perfect balance between creation and recreation. The house in which he dwelt was itself a little island of the past, standing intact above the flood of events; all around was a mild, cultivated country, broken into gentle variety of " hills to live with," and touched with just enough wildness to keep him from tiring of it: the stream that flowed by his orchard was for him an enchanted river. He renewed the pleasant sports of boyhood with it, fishing and boating in summer, and in winter whistling over its clear, black ice, on rapid skates. In the more genial months, the garden gave him pleasant employment; and in his journal-musings, the thought gratifies him that he has come into a primitive relation with nature, and that the two occupants of the Manse are in good faith a new Adam and Eve, so far as the happiness of that immemorial pair remained unbroken. The charm of these experiences has all been distilled into the descriptive chapter which prefaces the " Mosses "; and such more personal aspects of it as could not be mixed in that vintage have been gathered, like forgotten clusters of the harvest, into the Note-Books. It remains to comment, here, on the contrast between the peaceful character of these first years at Concord and the increased sombreness of some of the visions there recorded.

The reason of this is, that Hawthorne's genius had now waxed to a stature which made its emanations less immediately dependent on his actual mood. I am far from assuming an exact autobiographical value for the " Twice-Told Tales "; a theory which the writer himself condemned. But they, as he has also said, require " to be read in the clear brown twilight atmosphere in which they were written"; while the "Mosses" are the work of a man who has learned to know the world, and the atmosphere in which they were composed seems almost dissonant with the tone of some of them. "The Birth-mark," "The Bosom Serpent," "Rappaccini's Daughter," and that terrible and lurid parable of "Young Goodman Brown," are made up of such horror as Hawthorne has seldom expressed elsewhere. "The Procession of Life" is a fainter vibration of the same chord of awfulness. Such concentration of frightful truth do these most graceful and exquisitely wrought creations contain, that the intensity becomes almost poisonous. What is the meaning of this added revelation of evil? The genius of Hawthorne was one which used without stint that costliest of all elements in production, — time; the brooding propensity was indispensable to him; and, accordingly, as some of these conceptions had occurred to him a good while before the carrying out, they received great and almost excessive elaboration. The reality of sin, the pervasiveness of evil, had been but slightly insisted upon in the earlier tales: in this series, the idea bursts up like a long-buried fire, with earth-shaking strength, and the pits of Hell seem yawning beneath us. Dismal, too, is the story of "Roger Malvin's Burial," and dreary "The Christmas Banquet," with its assembly of the supremely wretched. In "Earth's Holocaust" we get the first result of Hawthorne's insight into the demonianism of reformatory schemers who forget that the centre of every true reform is the heart. And, incidentally, this marks out the way to "The Scarlet Letter" on the one hand, and "The Blithedale Romance" on the other, in which the same theme assumes two widely different phases. Thus we find the poet seeking more and more certainly the central fountain of moral suggestion from which he drew his best inspirations. The least pleasing quality of the work is, I think, its overcharged allegorical burden. Some of the most perfect of all his tales are here, but their very perfection makes one recoil the more at the supremacy of their purely intellectual interest. One feels a certain chagrin, too, on finishing them, as if the completeness of embodiment had given the central idea a shade of too great obviousness. Hawthorne is most enjoyable and most true to himself when he offers us the chalice of poetry filled to the very brim with the clear liquid of moral truth. But, at first, there seems to have been a conflict between his æsthetic and his ethical impulse. Coleridge distinguishes the symbolical from the allegorical, by calling it a part of some whole which it represents. "Allegory cannot be other than spoken consciously; whereas in the symbol it is very possible that the general truth represented may be working unconsciously in the writer's mind. . . . . The advantage of symbolical writing over allegory is that it presumes no disjunction of faculties, but simple predominance." Now in the "Allegories of the Heart," collected in the "Mosses," there is sometimes an extreme consciousness of the idea to be illustrated; and though the ideas are in a measure symbolical, yet they are on the whole too disintegrating in their effect to leave the artistic result quite generous and satisfying. Allegory itself, as an echo of one's thought, is often agreeable, and pleases through surprise; yet it is apt to be confusing, and smothers the poetic harmony. In his romances, Hawthorne escapes into a hugely significant, symbolic sphere which relieves the reader of this partial vexation. "The Celestial Railroad," of course, must be excepted from censure, being the sober parody of a famous work, and in itself a masterly satirical allegory. And in two cases, "Drowne's Wooden Image," and "The Artist of the Beautiful," we find the most perfect imaginable symbolism. In one, the story of Pygmalion compressed and Yankeefied, yet rendered additionally lovely by its homeliness; and the essence of all artistic life, in the other, presented in a form that cannot be surpassed. "Mrs. Bullfrog" is a sketch which is ludicrously puzzling, until one recalls Hawthorne's explanation: "The story was written as a mere experiment in that style; it did not come from any depth within me, — neither my heart nor mind had anything to do with it." * It is valuable, in this light, as a distinct boundary-mark in one direction. But the essay vein which had produced some of the clearest watered gems in the "Twice-Told Tales," begins in the "Mosses" to yield increase of brilliance and beauty; and we here find, with the gathering strength of imagination, — the enlarged power for bringing the most unreal things quite into the circle of realities, — a compensating richness in describing the simply natural, as in "Buds and Bird Voices," "Fire Worship," "The Old Apple-Dealer."

Everything in these two volumes illustrates forcibly the brevity, the absolutely right proportion of language to idea, which from the first had marked Hawthorne with one trait, at least, quite unlike any displayed by the writers with whom he was compared, and entirely foreign to the mood of the present century. This *sense of form*, the highest and last attribute of a creative writer, provided it comes as the result of a deep necessity of his genius, and not as a mere acquirement of art, is a quality that has not been enough noticed in him; doubtless because it is not enough looked for anywhere by the majority of critics and readers, in these days of adulteration

* American Note-Books, Vol. II.

and of rapid manufacture out of shoddy and short-fibred stuffs. We demand a given measure of reading, good or bad, and producers of it are in great part paid for length : so that with much using of thin and shapeless literature, we have forgotten how good is that which is solid and has form. But, having attained this perfection in the short story, Hawthorne thereafter abandoned it for a larger mould.

The "Mosses," as I have said, gained him many admirers. In them he for the first time touched somewhat upon the tendencies of the current epoch, and took an entirely independent stand among the philosophers of New England. Yet, for a while, there was the oddest misconception of his attitude by those at a distance. A Whig magazine, pleased by his manly and open conservatism, felt convinced that he must be a Whig, though he was, at the moment of the announcement, taking office under a Democratic President. On the other hand, a writer in "The Church Review" of New Haven, whom we shall presently see more of, was incited to a tilt against him as a rabid New England theorist, the outcome, of phalansteries, a subverter of marriage and of all other holy things. In like manner, while Hawthorne was casting now and then a keen dart at the Transcendentalists, and falling asleep over "The Dial" (as his journals betray), Edgar Poe, a literary *Erinaceus*, wellnigh exhausted his supply of quills upon the author, as belonging to a school toward which he felt peculiar acerbity. " Let him mend his pen," cried Poe, in his most high-pitched strain of personal abuse, " get a bottle of visible ink, hang (if possible) the editor of 'The Dial,' cut Mr. Alcott, and throw out of the window to the pigs all his odd numbers of the 'North American Review.' " This paper of Poe's is a laughable and pathetic case of his professedly punc-

tilious analysis covering the most bitter attacks, with
traces of what looks like envy, and others of a resistless
impulse to sympathize with a literary brother as against
the average mind.   He begins with a discussion of originality and peculiarity : " In one sense, to be peculiar is
to be original," he says, but the true originality is " not the
uniform but the continuous peculiarity, ... giving its own
hue to everything it touches," and touching everything.
From this flimsy and very uncertain principle, which
seems to make two different things out of the same thing,
he goes on to conclude that, " the fact is, if Mr. Hawthorne were really original, he could not fail of making
himself felt by the public.   But the fact is, he is *not*
original in any sense."   He then attempts to show that
Hawthorne's peculiarity is derivative, and selects Tieck
as the source of this idiosyncrasy.   Perhaps his insinu-
ation may be the origin of Hawthorne's effort to read
some of the German author, while at the Old Manse, —
an attempt given up in great fatigue.   Presently, the unhappy critic brings up his favorite charge of plagiarism ;
and it happens, as usual, that the writer borrowed from
is Poe himself !   The similarity which he discovers is between " Howe's Masquerade " and " William Wilson,"
and is based upon fancied resemblances of situation,
which have not the least foundation in the facts, and upon
the occurrence in both stories of the phrase, " Villain,
unmuffle yourself ! "   In the latter half of his review,
written a little later, Mr. Poe takes quite another tack : —

" Of Mr. Hawthorne's tales we would say emphatically that
they belong to the highest region of art, — an art subservient
to genius of a very lofty order.   We had supposed, with good
reason for so supposing, that he had been thrust into his present position by one of the impudent *cliques* who beset our

literature ; . . . . but we have been most agreeably mistaken.
. . . . Mr. Hawthorne's distinctive trait is invention, creation, imagination, originality, — a trait which, in the literature
of fiction, is positively worth all the rest. But the nature of
the originality . . . . is but imperfectly understood. . . . . The
inventive or original mind as frequently displays itself in novelty
of *tone* as in novelty of matter. Mr. Hawthorne is original
in *all* points."

This, certainly, is making generous amends; but before he leaves the subject, the assertion is repeated, that
" he is peculiar, and *not* original."

Though an extravagant instance, this tourney. of Poe's
represents pretty well the want of understanding with
which Hawthorne was still received by many readers.
His point of view once seized upon, nothing could be
more clear and simple than his own exposition of refined
and evasive truths; but the keen edge of his perception
remained quite invisible to some. Of the " Twice-Told
Tales " Hawthorne himself wrote : —

" The sketches are not, it is hardly necessary to say, profound; but it is rather more remarkable that they so seldom,
if ever, show any design on the writer's part to make them
so. . . . . Every sentence, so far as it embodies thought or
sensibility, may be understood and felt by anybody who will
give himself the trouble to read it, and will take up the book
in a proper mood."

But it was hard for people to find that mood, because
in fact the Tales *were* profound. Their language was
clear as crystal; but all the more dazzlingly shone through
the crystal that new light of Hawthorne's gaze.

After nearly four years, Hawthorne's tenancy of the
Manse came to an end, and he returned to Salem, with
some prospect of an office there from the new Democratic

government of Polk.   It is said that President Tyler had at one time actually appointed him to the Salem post-office, but was induced to withdraw his name.   There were local factions that kept the matter in abeyance. The choice, in any case, lay between the Naval Office and the surveyorship, and Bridge urged Hawthorne's appointment to the latter.   "Whichever it be," wrote Hawthorne, "it is to you that I shall owe it, among so many other solid kindnesses.   I have as true friends as any man has, but you have been the friend in need and the friend indeed."   At this time he was seriously in want of some profitable employment, for he had received almost nothing from the magazine.   It was the period of credit, and debts were hard to collect.   His journal at the Old Manse refers to the same trouble.   I have been told that, besides losing the value of many of his contributions to the "Democratic," through the failure of the magazine, he had advanced money to the publishers, which was never repaid ; but this has not been corroborated, and as he had lost nearly everything at Brook Farm, it is a little doubtful.   At length, he was installed as surveyor in the Salem Custom-House, where he hoped soon to begin writing at ease.

VII.

THE SCARLET LETTER.

1846–1850.

THE literary result of the four years which Hawthorne now, after long absence, spent in his native town, was the first romance which gave him world-wide fame. But the intention of beginning to write soon was not easy of fulfilment in the new surroundings.

"Literature, its exertions and objects, were now of little moment in my regard," he says, in "The Custom-House." "I cared not at this period for books; they were apart from me. . . . . A gift, a faculty, if it had not departed, was suspended and inanimate within me."

Readers of that charming sketch will remember the account of the author's finding a veritable Puritan scarlet letter in an unfinished upper room of the public building in which he labored at this time, and how he was urged by the ghost of a former surveyor, who had written an account of the badge and its wearer, to make the matter public. The discovery of these materials is narrated with such reassuring accuracy, that probably a large number of people still suppose this to have been the origin of "The Scarlet Letter." But there is no knowledge among

those immediately connected with Hawthorne of any actual relic having been found; nor, of course, is it likely
that anything besides the manuscript memorandum should
have been preserved. But I do not know that he saw
even this. The papers of Mr. Pue were probably a pure
invention of the author's.

A strange coincidence came to light the year after
the publication of the romance. A letter from Leutze,
the painter, was printed in the Art Union Bulletin, running thus: —

"I was struck, when some years ago in the Schwarzwald
(in an old castle), with one picture in the portrait-gallery; it
has haunted me ever since. It was not the beauty or finish
that charmed me; it was something strange in the figures, the
immense contrast between the child and what was supposed to
be her gouvernante in the garb of some severe order; the child,
a girl, was said to be the ancestress of the family, a princess of
some foreign land. No sooner had I read 'The Scarlet Letter'
than it burst clearly upon me that the picture could represent no
one else than Hester Prynne and little Pearl. I hurried to see
it again, and found my suppositions corroborated, for the formerly inexplicable embroidery on the breast of the woman, which
I supposed was the token of her order, assumed the form of the
letter; and though partially hidden by the locks of the girl and
the flowers in her hair, I set to work upon it at once, and made
as close a copy of it, with all its quaintness, as was possible to
me, which I shall send you soon. How Hester Prynne ever
came to be painted, I can't imagine; it must certainly have
been a freak of little Pearl. Strange enough, the castle is
named Perlenburg, the Castle of Pearls, or Pearl Castle, as
you please."

A more extraordinary incident in its way than this discovery, if it be trustworthy, could hardly be conceived;
but I am not aware that it has been verified.

The germ of the story in Hawthorne's mind is given below. The name Pearl, it will be remembered, occurs in the Note-Books, as an original and isolated suggestion "for a girl, in a story."

In "Endicott and the Red Cross," one of the twice-told series printed many years before, there is a description of "a young woman, with no mean share of beauty, whose doom it was to wear the letter A on the breast of her gown, in the eyes of all the world and her own children. Sporting with her infamy, the lost and desperate creature had embroidered the fatal token in scarlet cloth, with golden thread and the nicest art of needlework." A friend asked Hawthorne if he had documentary evidence for this particular punishment, and he replied that he had actually seen it mentioned in the town records of Boston, though with no attendant details.* This friend said to another at the time : "We shall hear of that letter again, for it evidently has made a profound impression on Hawthorne's mind." Returning to Salem, where his historical stories and sketches had mainly been written, he reverted naturally to the old themes; and this one

---

* I may here transcribe, as a further authority, which Hawthorne may or may not have seen, one of the laws of Plymouth Colony, enacted in 1658, about the period in which the events of "The Scarlet Letter" are placed. "It is enacted by the Court and the Authoritie thereof that whosoeuer shall committ Adultery shal bee seuerly Punished by whipping two seueral times viz : once whiles the Court is in being att which they are convicted of the fact, and the second time as the Court shall order, and likewise to were two Capitall letters viz : A D cut out in Cloth and sewed on their vpermost garments on their arme or backe ; and if at any time they shal bee taken without said letters, whiles they are in the Gou'ment soe worne, to be forthwith Taken and publicly whipt."

doubtless took possession of him soon after his entrance on his customs duties. But these disabled him from following it out at once. When the indefatigable Whigs got hold of the government again, Hawthorne's literary faculty came into power also, for he was turned out of office. In the winter of 1849, therefore, he got to work on his first regular romance. In his Preface to the "Mosses" he had formally renounced the short story; but "The Scarlet Letter" proved so highly wrought a tragedy that he had fears of its effect upon the public, if presented alone.

"In the present case I have some doubts about the expediency, [he wrote to Mr. Fields, the junior partner of his new publisher, Ticknor,] because, if the book is made up entirely of 'The Scarlet Letter,' it will be too sombre. I found it impossible to relieve the shadows of the story with so much light as I would gladly have thrown in. Keeping so close to its point as the tale does, and diversified no otherwise than by turning different sides of the same dark idea to the reader's eye, it will weary very many people, and disgust some. Is it safe, then, to stake the book entirely on this one chance?"

His plan was to add some of the pieces afterward printed with the "The Snow Image," and entitle the whole "Old Time Legends, together with Sketches Experimental and Ideal." But this was abandoned. On the 4th of February, 1850, he writes to Bridge: —

"I finished my book only yesterday: one end being in the press at Boston, while the other was in my head here at Salem; so that, as you see, the story is at least fourteen miles long. . . . .

"My book, the publisher tells me, will not be out before April. He speaks of it in tremendous terms of approbation; so does Mrs. Hawthorne, to whom I read the conclusion last night.* It broke her heart, and sent her to bed with a grievous headache, — which I look upon as a triumphant success. Judging from its effect on her and the publisher, I may calculate on what bowlers calls a 'ten-strike.' But I do not make any such calculation."

Now that the author had strongly taken hold of one of the most tangible and terrible of subjects, the public no longer held back. "The Scarlet Letter" met with instant acceptance, and the first edition of five thousand copies was exhausted in ten days. On the old ground of Salem and in the region of New England history where he had won his first triumphs, Hawthorne, no longer the centre of a small public, received the applause of a widespread audience throughout this country, and speedily in Europe too. His old friend, "The London Athenæum," received "The Scarlet Letter" with very high, though careful praise. But at the same time with this new and wide recognition, an assault was made on the author which it is quite worth while to record here. This was an article in "The Church Review" (an Episcopal quarterly published at New Haven),† written, I am told, by a then young man who has since reached a high place in the ecclesiastical body to which he belongs. The re-

---

* This recalls an allusion in the English Note-Books (September 14, 1855) : "Speaking of Thackeray, I cannot but wonder at his coolness in respect to his own pathos, and compare it with my emotions when I read the last scene of The Scarlet Letter to my wife just after writing it, — tried to read it, rather, for my voice swelled and heaved, as if I were tossed up and down on an ocean as it subsides after a storm. But I was in a very nervous state, then, having gone through a great diversity of emotion while writing it, for many months."

† In the number for January, 1851.

viewer, in this case, had in a previous article discussed the question of literary schools in America. Speaking of the origin of the term "Lake School," he pronounced the epithet *Lakers* "the mere blunder of superficial wit and raillery." But that did not prevent him from creating the absurd title of "Bay writers," which he applied to all the writers about Boston, baptizing them in the profane waters of Massachusetts Bay. "The Church Review" was in the habit of devoting a good deal of its attention to criticism of the Puritan movement which founded New England. Accordingly, "It is time," announced this logician, in opening his batteries on Hawthorne, "that the literary world should learn that Churchmen are, in a very large proportion, their readers and book-buyers, and that the tastes and principles of Churchmen have as good a right to be respected as those of Puritans and Socialists." Yet, inconsistently enough, he declared that Bay writers could not have grown to the stature of authors at all, unless they had first shaken off the Puritan religion, and adopted "a religion of indifference and unbelief." Thus, though attacking them as Puritans and Socialists (this phrase was aimed at Brook Farm), he denied that they were Puritans at all. Clear understanding of anything from a writer with so much of the boomerang in his mind was not to be expected. But neither would one easily guess the revolting vulgarity with which he was about to view "The Scarlet Letter." He could discover in it nothing but a deliberate attempt to attract readers by pandering to the basest taste. He imagines that Hawthorne "selects the intrigue of an adulterous minister, as the groundwork of his ideal" of Puritan times, and asks, "Is the French era actually begun in our literature?" Yet, being in some points, or professing to be, an admirer of the author, "We are glad," he says, "that 'The Scarlet Letter' is, after all, little more than an experiment, and need not be regarded as a step necessarily fatal." And in order to save Mr. Hawthorne, and stem the tide of corruption, he is willing to point out his error. Nevertheless, he is somewhat at a loss to know where to puncture the heart of the offence, for "there is a provoking concealment of the author's motive," he confesses, "from the beginning to the end of the story. We wonder what he would be at: whether he is making fun of all religion, or only giving a fair hint of the essential sensualism of enthusiasm. But, in short, we are astonished at the kind of incident he has selected for romance." The phraseology, he finds, is not offensive: but this is eminently diabolical, for "the romance never hints the shocking words that belong to its things, but, like Mephistopheles, hints that the arch-fiend himself is a very tolerable sort of person, if nobody would call him Mr. Devil." Where, within the covers of the book, could the deluded man have found this doctrine urged? Only once, faintly, and then in the words of one of the chief sinners.

"Shelley himself," says the austere critic, airing his literature, "never imagined a more dissolute conversation than that in which the polluted minister comforts himself with the thought, that the revenge of the injured husband is worse than his own sin in instigating it. 'Thou and I never did so, Hester,' he suggests; and she responds, 'Never, never! What we did had a consecration of its own.'"

And these wretched and distorted consolations of two erring and condemned souls, the righteous Churchman, with not very commendable taste, seizes upon as the moral of the book, leaving aside the terrible retribution which overtakes and blasts them so soon after their vain plan of flight and happiness. Not for a moment does Hawthorne defend their excuses for themselves. Of Hester : —

" Shame, Despair, Solitude ! These [he says] had been her teachers, — stern and wild ones, — and they had made her strong, but taught her much amiss."

And what she urges on behalf of herself and Dimmesdale must, of course, by any pure-minded reader, be included among the errors thus taken into her mind.

" The minister, on the other hand, had never gone through an experience calculated to lead him beyond the scope of generally received laws ; although, in a single instance, he had so fearfully transgressed one of the most sacred of them. . . . . Were such a man once more to fall, what plea could be urged in extenuation of his crime ? *None ;* unless it avail him somewhat, that he was broken down by long and exquisite suffering ; that his mind was darkened and confused by the very remorse which harrowed it."

But that these partial excuses are futile, the writer goes on to show, in this solemn declaration : —

" And be the stern and sad truth spoken, that the breach which guilt has once made into the human soul is never, in this mortal state, repaired. It may be watched and guarded. . . . . But there is still the ruined wall, and near it the stealthy tread of the foe that would win over again his unforgotten triumph."

How Mr. Dimmesdale yielded to this stealthy foe is then described; but it is also shown how Roger Chillingworth, the personified retribution of the two sinners, fastens himself to them in all their movements, and will be with them in any flight, however distant.

" ' Hadst thou sought the whole earth over,' said he, looking darkly at the clergyman, ' there was no one place so secret, no high place nor lowly place, where thou couldst have escaped me.' "

And it was precisely because Hawthorne would leave no specious turn of the hypocrisy of sin unrevealed, that he carried us through this delusive mutual consolation of the guilty pair, and showed us their empty hope, founded on wrong-doing, powdered to dust at the moment of fulfilment.

But the reverend critic, by some dark and prurient affinity of his imagination, saw nothing of the awful truths so clearly though briefly expressed, and finally came to the conclusion that the moral of the whole fiction was "that the Gospel has not set the relations of man and woman where they should be, and that a new gospel is needed to supersede the Seventh Commandment, and the bond of matrimony."

"The lady's frailty, [writes the reviewer,] is philosophized into a natural and necessary result of the Scriptural law of marriage, which by holding her irrevocably to her vows, as plighted to a dried-up old book-worm, ... is viewed as making her heart an easy victim. . . . . The sin of her seducer, too, seems to be considered as lying, not so much in the deed itself, as in his long concealment of it ; and in fact the whole moral of the tale is given in the words, ' Be true, be true ! ' as if sincerity in sin were a virtue, and as if ' Be clean, be clean ! ' were not the more fitting conclusion."

But this moral of cleanliness was one so obvious that Hawthorne probably never dreamed of any one's requiring it to be emphasized. In fact, it is the starting-point, the very foundation, of the tragedy. The tale is a massive argument for repentance, which is the flinging aside of concealment, and the open and truthful acknowledgment of sin. In the Puritan mode of dealing with sin, Hawthorne found the whole problem of repentance and confession presented in the most drastic, concentrated, and startling form; for the Puritans carried out in the severest style a practical illustration of the consequences of moral offence. Since men and women would not voluntarily continue in active remorse and public admission of wrong-doing, these governors and priests determined to try the effect of visible symbols in keeping the conscience alive. People were set before the public gaze, in the stocks, whipped in public at the whipping-post, and imprisoned in the pillory. Malefactors had their ears cropped; scolding women had to wear a forked twig on the tongue; other criminals to carry a halter constantly around the neck. But that this was only a hellish device, after all; that the inflictors of such punishment were arrogating too much to themselves, and shared the office of the fiend; that, moreover, this compulsion of a dumb outward truthfulness would never build up the real inner truth of the soul; — all this Hawthorne perceived and endeavored to portray in a form which should be as a parable, applying its morality to the men and women of to-day, all the more persuasively because of its indirectness. As a study of a system of social discipline never before so expounded, it claimed the deepest attention. And never was the capacity of sinning men and women for self-delusion more wonderfully illustrated than in this romance. The only avenue of escape from such delusion was shown to be self-analysis; that is, the conscientious view of one's self which keeps the right or wrong of one's conduct always clearly visible. Hester was on the whole the truest of the three persons in the drama,

and the advantages of this comparative trueness are
constantly made manifest. She in a measure conquers
evil and partly atones for her wrong, by the good which
she is able to do among her fellow-beings, — as much
compensation as can rightfully be hoped for a woman
who has once been so essentially corrupted as she.
Dimmesdale, too, retains so much of native truth that
he never allows his conscience to slumber for a moment, and plies the scourge of remorse upon himself
continually. To this extent he is better than Chillingworth, who, in order to take into his own hands the
retribution that belongs to Heaven, deliberately adopts
falsity for his guide, and becomes a monster of deceit,
taking a wicked joy in that which ought to have awakened an endless, piteous horror in him instead, and
have led to new contemplation and study of virtue. But
Dimmesdale, though not coolly and maliciously false,
stops short of open confession, and in this submits himself to the most occult and corrosive influence of his
own sin. For him, the single righteousness possible consisted in abject acknowledgment. Once announcing that
he had fallen, and was unworthy, he might have taken
his place on the lower moral plane ; and, equally resign-
ing the hope of public honor and of happiness with Hester, he could have lent his crippled energies to the doing
of some limited good. The shock to the general belief
in probity would have been great ; but the discovery that
the worst had been made known, that the minister was
strong enough to condemn himself, and descend from the
place he no longer was fit for, would have restored the
public mind again, by showing it that a deeper probity
is possible than that which it wanted to see sustained.
This is the lesson of the tragedy, that nothing is so destructive as the morality of mere appearances. Not that

sincerity in sin is a virtue, but that it is better than sin
and falsehood combined. And if anything were wanting,
at first, to make this clear, there certainly is not a par-
ticle of obscurity left by the glare of the catastrophe,
when the clergyman rejects Hester's hope that he and
she may meet after death, and spend their immortal life
together, and says that God has proved his mercy most
of all by the afflictions he has laid upon him.

As to the new truth which Hester hoped would be
revealed, it could have been no other than that ultimate
lifting up of the race into a plane of the utmost human
truthfulness, which every one who believes in the working
of all things for good, looks forward to with vague longing, but with most certain faith. How far the Puritan
organization was from this state of applied truth, the romance shows. Nearly every note in the range of Puritan
sympathies is touched by the poet, as he goes on. The
still unspoiled tenderness of the young matron who cannot but feel something of mercifulness toward Hester is
overruled by the harsh exultation of other women in her
open shame. We have the noble and spotless character
of Winthrop dimly suggested by the mention of his death
on the night of Dimmesdale's vigil at the pillory; but
much more distinct appears the mild and saintly Wilson,
who, nevertheless, is utterly incompetent to deal with the
problem of a woman's lost morality. Governor Belling-
ham is the stern, unflinching, manly upholder of the state
and its ferocious sanctions; yet in the very house with
him dwells Mistress Hibbins, the witch-lady, revelling in
the secret knowledge of widespread sin. Thus we are
led to a fuller comprehension of Chillingworth's attitude
as an exponent of the whole Puritan idea of spiritual government; and in his diabolical absorption and gloating
interest in sin, we behold an exaggerated — but logically

exaggerated — spectre of the Puritan attempt to precipi-
tate and personally supervise the punishments of eternity
on this side of death.

Dr. George B. Loring, of Salem, wrote at the time an
excellent reply to this article in "The Church Review,"
though he recognized, as all readers of general intelligence must, that the author of it did not by any means
represent the real enlightenment of the clergy and laity
for whom he undertook to be a mouthpiece.

Considered as a work of art, "The Scarlet Letter" is
perhaps not so excellent as the author's subsequent
books. It may not unjustly be called a novel without a
plot, so far as this touches the adroit succession of incidents and the interdependence of parts, which we call
"plot." Passion and motive and character, having been
brought together in given relations, begin to work toward a logical issue; but the individual chapters stand
before us rather as isolated pictures, with intervals between, than as the closely conjoined links of a drama
gathering momentum as it grows. There is succession
and acceleration, indeed, in the movement of the story,
but this is not quite so evident as is the hand which
checks each portion and holds it perfectly still, long
enough to describe it completely. The author does not,
like a playwright, reflect the action swiftly while it
passes, but rather arrests it and studies it, then lets it go
by. It may be that this is simply the distinction between the dramatist's and the novelist's method; but
probably we must allow it to be something more than
that, and must attribute it to the peculiar leisure which
qualifies all Hawthorne's fictions, at times enhancing their
effect, but also protracting the impression a little too
much, at times. Yet the general conception, and the
mode of drawing out the story and of illustrating the

characters, is dramatic in a high degree. The author's exegesis of the moods of his persons is brief, suggestive, restrained; and, notwithstanding the weight of moral meaning which the whole work carries, it is impossible to determine how much the movement of events is affected by his own will, or by that imperious perception of the necessary outcome of certain passions and temperaments, which influences novelists of the higher order.

As a demonstration of power, it seems to me that this first extended romance was not outdone by its successors; yet there is a harshness in its tone, a want of mitigation, which causes it to strike crudely on the æsthetic sense by comparison with those mellower productions. This was no doubt fortunate for its immediate success. Hawthorne's faith in pure beauty was so absolute as to erect at first a barrier between himself and the less devout reading public. If in his earlier tales he had not so transfused tragedy with the suave repleteness of his sense of beauty, he might have snatched a speedier popular recognition. It is curious to speculate what might have been the result, had he written "The House of the Seven Gables" before "The Scarlet Letter." Deep as is the tragic element in the former, it seems quite likely that its greater gentleness of incident and happier tone would have kept the world from discovering the writer's real measure, for a while longer. But "The Scarlet Letter" burst with such force close to its ears, that the indolent public awoke in good earnest, and never forgot, though it speedily forgave the shock.

There was another smaller but attendant explosion. Hawthorne's prefatory chapter on the Custom-House incensed some of his fellow-citizens of Salem, terribly. There seems to have been a general civic clamor against him, on account of it, though it would be hard to find any rational justification therefor. In reference to the affair, Hawthorne wrote at the time : —

"As to the Salem people, I really thought I had been exceedingly good-natured in my treatment of them. They certainly do not deserve good usage at my hands, after permitting me . . . . to be deliberately lied down, not merely once, but at two separate attacks, and on two false indictments, without hardly a voice being raised on my behalf."

This refers to political machinations of the party opposed to Hawthorne as an official: they had pledged themselves, it was understood, not to ask for his ejection, and afterward set to work to oust him without cause. There is reason to believe that Hawthorne felt acute exasperation at these unpleasant episodes for a time. But the annoyance came upon him when he was worn out with the excitement of composing "The Scarlet Letter"; and this ebullition of local hostility must moreover have been especially offensive at a moment when the public everywhere else was receiving him with acclaim as a person whose genius entitled him to enthusiastic recognition. Hawthorne had generous admirers and sincere friends in Salem, and his feeling was, I suppose, in great measure the culmination of that smouldering disagreement which had harassed him in earlier years, and had lurked in his heart in spite of the constant mild affection which he maintained toward the town.

But the connection between Hawthorne and Salem was now to be finally broken off. He longed for change, for the country, and for the recreation that the Old Manse garden had given him. "I should not long stand such a life of bodily inactivity and mental exertion as I have led for the last few months," he wrote to Bridge. "Here I hardly go out once a week." On this account, and because of his difficulty in writing while in office, he did not so much regret losing his place. One of the plans proposed at this time was that he should rent or buy the Sparhawk house, a famous old colonial mansion on Goose Creek, at Kittery, in Maine, which was then to be disposed of in some way. Hawthorne, I think, would have found much that was suggestive and agreeable in the neighborhood. After his return from abroad, he made a visit to the quaint and stately little city of Portsmouth, and dined at one of the most beautiful old houses in New England, the ancient residence of Governor Langdon, then occupied by the Rev. Dr. Burroughs. A memorial of that visit remains, in this bright note from his host : —

PORTSMOUTH, September, 1860.

MR. HAWTHORNE.

MY DEAR SIR : — There are no Mosses on our " Old Manse," there is no Romance at our Blithedale ; and this is no " Scarlet Letter." But you can give us a " Twice-Told Tale," if you will for the second time be our guest to-morrow at dinner, at half past two o'clock.

Very truly yours,

CHARLES BURROUGHS.

But, at present, Hawthorne's decision led him to Berkshire.

10 *   o

VIII.

LENOX AND CONCORD: PRODUCTIVE PERIOD.

1850-1853.

IN the early summer, after the publication of "The Scarlet Letter," Hawthorne removed from Salem to Lenox, in Berkshire, where himself and his family were ensconced in a small red house near the Stockbridge Bowl. It was far from a comfortable residence; but he had no means of obtaining a better one. Meantime, he could do what he was sent into the world to do, so long as he had the mere wherewithal to live.

He was much interested in Herman Melville, at this time living in Pittsfield. There was even talk of their writing something together, as I judge from some correspondence; though this was abandoned.

Between this summer of 1850 and June, 1853, Hawthorne wrote "The House of the Seven Gables," "The Blithedale Romance," "The Wonder-Book for Boys and Girls," and "Tanglewood Tales," besides the story of "The Snow Image" in the volume to which this supplies the title; and his short "Life of Franklin Pierce." The previous paucity of encouragements to literature, and the deterring effect of official duties and of the Brook Farm attempt, were now removed, and his pen showed that it could pour a full current if only left free to do so.

The industry and energy of this period are the more remarkable because he could seldom accomplish anything in the way of composition during the warm months. "The House of the Seven Gables" was under way by September, 1850.

"I sha' n't have the new story ready," he writes to his publisher on the 1st of October, "by November, for I am never good for anything in the literary way till after the first autumnal frost, which has somewhat such an effect on my imagination that it does on the foliage here about me, — multiplying and brightening its hues; though they are likely to be sober and shabby enough after all."

The strain of reflection upon the work in hand which he indulged one month later is so important as to merit dwelling upon.

"I write diligently, but not so rapidly as I had hoped. I find the book requires more care and thought than 'The Scarlet Letter'; also I have to wait oftener for a mood. 'The Scarlet Letter' being all in one tone, I had only to get my pitch, and could then go on interminably. Many passages of this book ought to be finished with the minuteness of a Dutch picture, in order to give them their proper effect. Sometimes, when tired of it, it strikes me that the whole is an absurdity, from beginning to end; but the fact is, in writing a romance, a man is always, or always ought to be, careering on the utmost verge of a precipitous absurdity, and the skill lies in coming as close as possible, without actually tumbling over. My prevailing idea is, that the book ought to succeed better than 'The Scarlet Letter,' though I have no idea that it will."

By the 12th of January, 1851, he was able to write: "My 'House of the Seven Gables' is, so to speak, finished; only I am hammering away a little at the roof, and doing up a few odd jobs that were left incomplete"; and at the end of that month, he despatched the manuscript to Boston, still retaining his preference for it over the preceding work.

"It has met with extraordinary success from that portion of the public to whose judgment it has been submitted, viz. from my wife.   I likewise prefer it to 'The Scarlet Letter'; but an author's opinion of his book just after completing it is worth little or nothing, he being then in the hot or cold fit of a fever, and certain to rate it too high or too low.

"It has undoubtedly one disadvantage, in being brought so close to the present time; whereby its romantic improbabilities become more glaring."

He also wrote to Bridge, in July, after listening to the critics, and giving his own opinion time to mature: —

"I think it a work more characteristic of my mind, and more proper and natural for me to write, than 'The Scarlet Letter,' — but, for that very reason, less likely to interest the public.   Nevertheless, it appears to have sold better than the former, and I think is more sure of retaining the ground that it acquires.   Mrs. Kemble writes that both works are popular in England, and advises me to take out my copyright there."

His opinion of the superiority of the fresh production to his first great romance is no doubt one that critics will coincide with as regards artistic completeness; though his fear that it would not succeed so well was not confirmed, because, as I have suggested, he had begun to acquire that momentum of public favor which sets in after its first immense inertia has once been overcome. Acting on the reports from England, he made a suggestion to his publisher; and though this at first met with discouragement, ten months later £200 were received from a London house for "The Blithedale Romance." English editions of his works had already become numerous. But Hawthorne began now to receive a more ethereal and not less welcome kind of tribute from abroad, that of praise from the makers and markers of literature. The critics welcomed him to a high place; authors wrote to him, urging him to cross the sea; and Miss Mitford — of whom he said, "Her sketches, long ago as I read them, are as sweet in my memory as the scent of new hay" — sent special messages expressive of her pleasure.

When the "Blithedale Romance" had come out, Mr. Hawthorne sent Miss Mitford a copy, and she wrote in reply this cordial and delightful note : —

SWALLOWFIELD, August 6, 1852.

At the risk of troubling you, dear Mr. Hawthorne, I write again to tell you how much I thank you for the precious volume enriched by your handwriting, which, for its own sake and for yours, I shall treasure carefully so long as I live. The story has your mark upon it, — the fine tragic construction unmatched amongst living authors, the passion of the concluding scenes, the subtle analysis of jealousy, the exquisite finish of style. I must tell you what one of the cleverest men whom I have ever known, an Irish barrister, the juvenile correspondent of Miss Edgeworth, says of your style : "His English is the richest and most intense essence of the language I know of ; his words conveying not only a meaning, but more than they appear to mean. They point onward or upward or downward, as the case may be, and we cannot help following them with the eyes of imagination, sometimes smiling, sometimes weeping, sometimes shuddering, as if we were victims of the mesmeric influence he is so fond of bringing to bear upon his characters. Three of the most perfect Englishmen of our day are Americans, — Irving, Prescott, and this great new writer, Mr. Hawthorne." So far my friend Mr. Hockey. I forget, dear Mr. Hawthorne, whether I told you that the writer of whose works you remind me, not by imitation, but by resemblance, is the great French novelist, Balzac. Do you know his books? He is untranslated and untranslatable, and it requires the greatest familiarity with French literature to relish him thoroughly. . . . . I doubt if he be much known amongst you; at least I have never seen him alluded to in American literature. He has, of course, the low morality of a Frenchman, but, being what he is, Mrs. Browning and I used to discuss his personages like living people, and regarded his death as a great personal calamity to both.

I am expecting Mrs. Browning here in a few days, not being well enough to meet her in London. . . . . How I wish, dear Mr. Hawthorne, that you were here to meet them! The day will come, I hope. It would be good for your books to look at Europe, and all of Europe that knows our tongue would rejoice to look at you.

Ever your obliged and affectionate friend,

M. R. MITFORD.

I must transcribe here, too, part of a letter from Herman Melville, who, in the midst of his epistle, suddenly assumes the tone of a reviewer, and discourses as follows, under the heading, "*The House of the Seven Gables: A Romance. By Nathaniel Hawthorne. 16mo. pp. 344.*"

"The contents of this book do not belie its clustering romantic title. With great enjoyment we spent almost an hour in each separate gable. This book is like a fine old chamber, abundantly but still judiciously furnished with precisely that sort of furniture best fitted to furnish it. There are rich hangings, whereon are braided scenes from tragedies. There is old china with rare devices, set about on the carved beaufet; there are long and indolent lounges to throw yourself upon; there is an admirable sideboard, plentifully stored with good viands ; there is a smell of old wine in the pantry ; and finally, in one corner, there is a dark little black-letter volume in golden clasps, entitled *Hawthorne: A Problem.* . . . .

"We think the book for pleasantness of running interest surpasses the other work of the author. The curtains are now drawn; the sun comes in more; genialities peep out more. Were we to particularize what has most struck us in the deeper passages, we should point out the scene where Clifford, for a minute, would fain throw himself from the window, to join the procession; or the scene where the Judge is left seated in his ancestral chair.

" Clifford is full of an awful truth throughout. He is conceived in the finest, truest spirit. He is no caricature. He is Clifford. And here we would say, that did the circumstances permit, we should like nothing better than to devote an elaborate and careful paper to the full consideration and analysis of the purpose and significance of what so strongly characterizes all of this author's writing. There is a certain tragic phase of humanity, which, in our opinion, was never more powerfully embodied than by Hawthorne : we mean the tragicalness of human thought in its own unbiased, native, and profound workings. We think that into no recorded mind has the intense feeling of the whole truth ever entered more deeply than into this man's. By whole truth, we mean the apprehension of the absolute condition of present things as they strike the eye of the man who fears them not, though they do their worst to him."

This really profound analysis, Mr. Mellville professes to extract from the " Pittsfield Secret Review," of which I wish further numbers could be found.

But chief among the prizes of this season were letters from his friends Lowell and Holmes. The latter's I insert, because it admirably illustrates the cordial relation which has always distinguished the famous writers of

New England, — no pleasant illusion of distance, but a notable and praiseworthy reality.

Boston, April 9, 1851.

My dear Sir : — I have been confined to my chamber and almost to my bed, for some days since I received your note ; and in the mean time I have received what was even more welcome, the new Romance "from the Author." While I was too ill to read, my wife read it to me, so that you have been playing physician to my heartaches and headaches at once, with the magnetism of your imagination.

I think we have no romancer but yourself, nor have had any for this long time. I had become so set in this feeling, that but for your last two stories I should have given up hoping, and believed that all we were to look for in the way of spontaneous growth were such languid, lifeless, sexless creations as in the view of certain people constitute the chief triumphs of a sister art as manifested among us.

But there is rich red blood in Hester, and the flavor of the sweet-fern and the bayberry are not truer to the soil than the native sweetness of our little Phœbe ! The Yankee mind has for the most part budded and flowered in pots of English earth, but you have fairly raised yours as a seedling in the natural soil. My criticism has to stop here ; the moment a fresh mind takes in the elements of the common life about us and transfigures them, I am contented to enjoy and admire, and let others analyze. Otherwise I should be tempted to display my appreciating sagacity in pointing out a hundred touches, transcriptions of nature, of character, of sentiment, true as the daguerreotype, free as crayon sketching, which arrested me even in the midst of the palpitating story. Only one word, then, this : that the solid reality and homely truthfulness of the actual and present part of the story are blended with its weird and ghostly shadows with consummate skill and effect ; this was perhaps the special difficulty of the story.

I don't want to refuse anything you ask me to do. I shall

come up, I trust, about the 1st of June. I would look over the MS. in question, as a duty, with as much pleasure as many other duties afford. To say the truth, I have as great a dread of the *Homo Caudatus* Linn., Anglicé, the Being with a Tale, male or female, as any can have.

> "If foes they write, if friends they read me dead,"

said poor Hepzibah's old exploded poet. Still, if it must be, I will stipulate to read a quantity not exceeding fifty-six pounds avoirdupois by weight or eighteen reams by measure or "tale," — provided there is no locomotion in the case. The idea of visiting Albany does not enter into my intentions. I do not know who would serve as a third or a second member of the committee ; Miss Sedgwick, if the Salic law does not prevail in Berkshire, is the most natural person to do it. But the real truth is, the little Albaneses want to see the author of "The Scarlet Letter," and don't care a sixpence who else is on the committee. That is what they are up to. So if you want two dummies, on the classical condition *not to leave the country except in case of invasion,* absentees, voters by proxy, potential but not personally present bottle-holders, I will add my name to those of Latimer, Ridley, and Co. as a Martyr in the cause of Human Progress.

Believe me, my dear sir,
Yours very sincerely,
O. W. HOLMES.

Hawthorne's interest in Dr. Holmes's works was also very great, and one of the last books which he read at all was "Elsie Venner," which he had taken up for a second time shortly before his death.

Amid all the variety of thoughtful and thoughtless praise, or of other comment on the new romance, he began to feel that necessity for abstracting his attention entirely from what was said of his work in current publications, which forces itself upon every creative mind attempting to secure some centre of repose in a chattering and unprivate age like the present. This feeling he imparted to Bridge, and it also appears in one or two published letters. At the same time, it must be remembered how careful a consideration he gave to criticism; and he wrote of Edwin Whipple's reviewing of the "Seven Gables" : —

"Whipple's notices have done more than pleased me, for they have helped me to see my book. Much of the censure I recognize as just ; I wish I could feel the praise to be so fully deserved. Being better (which I insist it is) than 'The Scarlet Letter,' I have never expected it to be so popular."

In this same letter occurs the following : —

" —— ——, Esq., of Boston, has written to me, complaining that I have made his grandfather infamous ! It seems there was actually a Pyncheon (or Pynchon, as he spells it) family resident in Salem, and that their representative, at the period of the Revolution, was a certain Judge Pynchon, a Tory and a refugee. This was Mr. ——'s grandfather, and (at least, so he dutifully describes him) the most exemplary old gentleman in the world. There are several touches in my account of the Pyncheons which, he says, make it probable that I had this actual family in my eye, and he considers himself infinitely wronged and aggrieved, and thinks it monstrous that the 'virtuous dead' cannot be suffered to rest quietly in their graves."

The matter here alluded to threatened to give Hawthorne almost as much inconvenience as the tribulation which followed the appearance of "The Custom-House." One of the complainants in this case, though objecting to the use of the name Pyncheon, "respectfully suggests," with an ill-timed passion for accuracy, that it should in future editions be printed with the *e* left out, because this was the proper mode in use by the family.

There has been some slight controversy as to the original of the visionary mansion described in this romance. Mr. Hawthorne himself said distinctly that he had no particular house in mind, and it is also a fact that none is recalled which fulfils all the conditions of that of the "Seven Gables." Nevertheless, one party has maintained that the old Philip English house, pulled down many years since, was the veritable model; and others support the Ingersoll house, which still stands. The Curwin, called the "Witch House," appears, by an antique painting from which photographs have been made, to have had the requisite number of peaks at a remote date; but one side of the structure being perforce left out of the picture, there is room for a doubt.*

In "The House of the Seven Gables" Hawthorne attained a connection of parts and a masterly gradation of tones which did not belong, in the same fulness, to "The Scarlet Letter." There is, besides, a larger range of character, in this second work, and a much more nicely detailed and reticulated portrayal of the individuals. Hepzibah is a painting on ivory, yet with all the warmth of a real being. Very noticeable is the delicate veneration and tenderness for her with which the author seems to inspire us, notwithstanding the fact that he has almost nothing definite to say of her except what tends to throw a light ridicule. She is continually contrasted with the exquisite freshness, ready grace, and beauty of Phœbe, and subjected to unfavorable comparisons in the mind of Clifford, whose half-obliterated but still exact æsthetic

---

* It is from one of these photographs that the cut in the new edition of Hawthorne's Works has been developed.

perception casts silent reproach upon her. Yet, in spite
of this, she becomes in a measure endeared to us. In
the grace, and agreeableness too, with which Hawthorne
manages to surround this ungifted spinster, we find a
unit of measure for the beauty with which he has invested the more frightful and tragic elements of the
story. It is this triumph of beauty without destroying
the unbeautiful, that gives the romance its peculiar artistic virtue. Judge Pyncheon is an almost unqualified
discomfort to the reader, yet he is entirely held within
bounds by the prevailing charm of the author's style, and
by the ingenious manner in which the pleasanter elements
of the other characters are applied. At times the strong
emphasis given to his evil nature makes one suspect that
the villain is too deeply dyed; but the question of equity
here involved is one of the most intricate with which
novelists have to deal at all. The well-defined opposition
between good and bad forces has always been a necessity
to man, in myths, religions, and drama. Real life furnishes the most absolute extremes of possession by the
angel or the fiend; and Shakespere has not scrupled
to use one of these ultimate possibilities in the person
of Iago. Yet Hawthorne was too acutely conscious of
the downward bent in every heart, to let the Judge's
pronounced iniquity stand without giving a glimpse of
incipient evil in another quarter. This occurs in the
temptation which besets Holgrave, when he finds that he
possesses the same mesmeric sway over Phœbe, the
latest Pyncheon offshoot, as that which his ancestor
Matthew Maule exercised over Alice Pyncheon. The
momentary mood which brings before him the absolute
power which might be his over this fair girl, opens a
whole new vista of wrong, in which the retribution would
have been transferred from the shoulders of the Pyn-

cheons to those of the Maules. Had Holgrave yielded then, he might have damned his own posterity, as Colonel Pyncheon had *his*. Thus, even in the hero of the piece, we are made aware of possibilities as malicious and destructive as those hereditary faults grown to such rank maturity in the Judge; and this may be said to offer a middle ground between the side of justice and attractiveness, and the side of injustice and repulsiveness, on which the personages are respectively ranged.

The conception of a misdeed operating through several generations, and righted at last solely by the over-toppling of unrestrained malevolence on the one hand, and on the other by the force of upright character in the wronged family, was a novel one at the time; this graphic depicture of the past at work upon the present has anticipated a great deal of the history and criticism of the following twenty-five years, in its close conjunction of antecedent influences and cumulative effects.

As a discovery of native sources of picturesque fiction, this second romance was not less remarkable than the one which preceded it. The theme furnished by the imaginary Pyncheon family ranges from the tragic in the Judge, through the picturesquely pathetic in Clifford, to a grotesque cast of pathos and humor in Hepzibah. Thence we are led to another vein of simple, fun-breeding characterization in Uncle Venner and Ned Higgins. The exquisite perception which draws old Uncle Venner in such wholesome colors, tones him up to just one degree of sunniness above the dubious light in which Hepzibah stands, so that he may soften the contrast of broad humor presented by little Ned Higgins, the "First Customer." I cannot but regret that Hawthorne did not give freer scope to his delicious faculty for the humorous, exemplified in the "Seven Gables." If he had let his genius career as forcibly in this direction as it does in another, when burdened with the black weight of the dead Judge Pyncheon, he might have secured as wide an acceptance for the book as Dickens, with so much more melodrama and so much less art, could gain for less perfect works. Hawthorne's concentration upon the tragic element, and comparative neglect of the other, was in one sense an advantage; but if in the case under discussion he had given more bulk and saliency to the humorous quality, he might also have been more likely to avoid a fault which creeps in, immediately after that marvellous chapter chanted like an unholy requiem over the lifeless Judge. This is the sudden culmination of the passion of Holgrave for Phœbe, just at the moment when he has admitted her to the house where Death and himself were keeping vigil. The revulsion, here, is too violent, and seems to throw a dank and deathly exhalation into the midst of the sweetness which the mutual disclosure of love should have spread around itself. There is need of an enharmonic change, at this point; and it might have been effected, perhaps, by a slower passage from gloom to gladness just here, and a more frequent play of the brighter mood throughout the book. But the tragic predilection seems ultimately to gain the day over the comic, in every great creative mind, and it was so strong with Hawthorne, that instead of giving greater play to humor in later fictions, it curtailed it more and more, from the production of the " Seven Gables " onward.

Mr. Curtis has shown me a letter written soon after the publication of the new book, which, as it gives another instance of the writer's keen enjoyment of other men's work, and ends with a glimpse of the life at Lenox, I will copy at length : —

LENOX, April 29, 1851.

MY DEAR HOWADJI: — I ought to be ashamed (and so I really am) of not having sooner responded to your note of more than a month ago, accompanied as it was by the admirable "Nile Notes." The fact is, I have been waiting to find myself in an eminently epistolary mood, so that I might pay my thanks and compliments in a style not unworthy of the occasion. But the moment has not yet come, and doubtless never will; and now I have delayed so long, that America and England seem to have anticipated me in their congratulations.

I read the book aloud to my wife, and both she and I have felt that we never knew anything of the Nile before. There is something beyond descriptive power in it. You make me feel almost as if we had been there ourselves. And then you are such a luxurious traveller. . . . . The fragrance of your chibouque was a marvellous blessing to me. It cannot be concealed that I felt a little alarm, as I penetrated the depths of those chapters about the dancing-girls, lest they might result in something not altogether accordant with our New England morality; and even now I hardly know whether we escaped the peril, or were utterly overwhelmed by it. But at any rate, those passages are gorgeous in the utmost degree. However, I suppose you are weary of praise; and as I have nothing else to inflict, I may as well stop here.

S—— and the children and I are plodding onward in good health, and in a fair medium state of prosperity; and on the whole, we are quite the happiest family to be found anywhere. We live in the ugliest little old red farm-house you ever saw. . . . .

What shall you write next? For of course you are an author forever. I am glad, for the sake of the public, but not particularly so for your own.

Very soon after the issue of the "Seven Gables," another lighter literary project was put into execution.

" I mean [he had announced on the 23d of May] to write within six weeks or two months next ensuing, a book of stories made up of classical myths. The subjects are: The Story of Midas, with his Golden Touch; Pandora's Box; The Adventure of Hercules in Quest of the Golden Apples; Bellerophon and the Chimera; Baucis and Philemon; Perseus and Medusa."

The " Wonder-Book " was begun on the first of June, and finished by the middle of July; so that the intention of writing it within six weeks was strictly carried out: certainly a rapid achievement, considering the excellent proportion and finish bestowed upon the book. It is a minor work, but a remarkable one; not its least important trait being the perfect simplicity of its style and scope, which, nevertheless, omits nothing essential, and preserves a thorough elegance. Its peculiar excellences come out still more distinctly when contrasted with Charles Kingsley's " The Heroes; or, Greek Fairy Tales," published in England five years after the appearance of the " Wonder-Book " here. The fresher play of Hawthorne's mind with those old subjects is seen in nothing more agreeably than in the graceful Introduction and interludes which he has thrown around the mythological tales, like the tendrils of a vine curling over a sculptured capital. This midsummer task — it was very uncommon for him to write in the hot season — perhaps had something to do with further unsettling Hawthorne's health, which at this time was not good. The somewhat sluggish atmosphere of the far inland valley did not suit his sea-braced temperament; and so, instead of renting Mrs. Kemble's country place, as he had thought of doing, he decided to leave Berkshire with the birds; but not to go southward. Moving to West Newton, near Boston, he remained there for the winter, writing " Blithedale," which was put forth in 1852.

The special characteristic of "The Blithedale Romance" seems to me to be its appearance of unlabored ease, and a consequent breeziness of effect distinguishing its atmosphere from that of any of the other romances. The style is admirably finished, and yet there is no part of the book that gives the same impression of almost unnecessary polish which occasionally intervenes between one's admiration and the "Seven Gables." On this score, "Blithedale" is certainly the most consummate of the four completed romances. And as Hawthorne has nowhere given us more robust and splendid characterization than that of Zenobia and Hollingsworth, the work also takes high rank on this ground. The shadows, which seemed partly dispersed in the "Seven Gables," gather again in this succeeding story; but, on the other hand, it is not so jarringly terrible as "The Scarlet Letter." From this it is saved partly by the sylvan surrounding and the pleasant changes of scene. In comparing it with the other works, I find that it lets itself be best defined as a mean between extremes; so that it ought to have the credit of being the most evenly attempered of all. The theme is certainly as deep as that of the earlier ones, and more tangible to the general reader than that of "The Marble Faun"; it is also more novel than that of "The Scarlet Letter" or even the "Seven Gables," and has an attractive air of growing simply and naturally out of a phenomenon extremely common in New England, namely, the man who is dominated and blinded by a theory. And the way in which Hollingsworth, through this very prepossession and absorption, is brought to the ruin of his own scheme, and has to concentrate his charity for criminals upon himself as the first criminal needing reformation, is very masterly. Yet, in discussing the relative positions of these four works, I

11   P

am not sure that we can reach any decision more stable than that of mere preference.

There is a train of thought suggested in " Blithedale " which receives only partial illustration in that story, touching the possible identity of love and hate. It had evidently engaged Hawthorne from a very early period, and would have made rich material for an entire romance, or for several treating different phases of it. Perhaps he would have followed out the suggestion, but for the intervention of so many years of unproductiveness in the height of his powers, and his subsequent too early death.

It was while at West Newton, just before coming to the Wayside, that he wrote a note in response to an invitation to attend the memorial meeting at New York, in honor of the novelist, Cooper, which should be read for its cordial admiration of a literary brother, and for the tender thought of the closing sentence.

To Rev. R. W. Griswold.

February 20, 1852.

DEAR SIR: — I greatly regret that circumstances render it impossible for me to be present on the occasion of Mr. Bryant's discourse in honor of James Fenimore Cooper. No man has a better right to be present than myself, if many years of most sincere and unwavering admiration of Mr. Cooper's writings can establish a claim. It is gratifying to observe the earnestness with which the literary men of our country unite in paying honor to the deceased; and it may not be too much to hope that, in the eyes of the public at large, American literature may henceforth acquire a weight and value which have not heretofore been conceded to it: time and death have begun to hallow it.   Very respectfully yours,

NATHANIEL HAWTHORNE.

Early in the summer of 1852 he went to Concord again, where he had bought a small house, there to establish his permanent home. Mr. Curtis was at this time writing some chapters for a book on "The Homes of American Authors," among which was to be included the new abode of Hawthorne. The project called forth from the romancer this letter : —

CONCORD, July 14, 1852.

MY DEAR HOWADJI : — I think (and am glad to think) that you will find it necessary to come hither in order to write your Concord Sketches ; and as for my old house, you will understand it better after spending a day or two in it. Before Mr. Alcott took it in hand, it was a mean-looking affair, with two peaked gables ; no suggestiveness about it and no venerableness, although from the style of its construction it seems to have survived beyond its first century. He added a porch in front, and a central peak, and a piazza at each end, and painted it a rusty olive hue, and invested the whole with a modest picturesqueness ; all which improvements, together with its situation at the foot of a wooded hill, make it a place that one notices and remembers for a few moments after passing it. Mr. Alcott expended a good deal of taste and some money (to no great purpose) in forming the hillside behind the house into terraces, and building arbors and summer-houses of rough stems and branches and trees, on a system of his own. They must have been very pretty in their day, and are so still, although much decayed, and shattered more and more by every breeze that blows. The hillside is covered chiefly with locust-trees, which come into luxuriant blossom in the month of June, and look and smell very sweetly, intermixed with a few young elms and some white-pines and infant oaks, — the whole forming rather a thicket than a wood. Nevertheless, there is some very good shade to be found there. I spend delectable hours there in the hottest part of the day, stretched out at my lazy length, with a book in my hand or an unwritten book in my thoughts. There is almost always a breeze stirring along the sides or brow of the hill.

From the hill-top there is a good view along the extensive level surfaces and gentle, hilly outlines, covered with wood, that characterize the scenery of Concord. We have not so much as a gleam of lake or river in the prospect; if there were, it would add greatly to the value of the place in my estimation.

The house stands within ten or fifteen feet of the old Boston road (along which the British marched and retreated), divided from it by a fence, and some trees and shrubbery of Mr. Alcott's setting out. Whereupon I have called it "The Wayside," which I think a better name and more morally suggestive than that which, as Mr. Alcott has since told me, he bestowed on it, — "The Hillside." In front of the house, on the opposite side of the road, I have eight acres of land, — the only valuable portion of the place in a farmer's eye, and which are capable of being made very fertile. On the hither side, my territory extends some little distance over the brow of the hill, and is absolutely good for nothing, in a productive point of view, though very good for many other purposes.

I know nothing of the history of the house, except Thoreau's telling me that it was inhabited a generation or two ago by a man who believed he should never die.* I believe, however, he is dead; at least, I hope so; else he may probably appear and dispute my title to his residence. . . . . .

I asked Ticknor to send a copy of "The Blithedale Romance" to you. Do not read it as if it had anything to do with Brook Farm (which essentially it has not), but merely for its own story and character. Truly yours,

NATHANIEL HAWTHORNE.

The Wayside was, perhaps, so named in remembrance of the time when its owner had "sat down by the wayside

---

* This is the first intimation of the story of Septimius Felton, so far as local setting is concerned. The scenery of that romance was obviously taken from the Wayside and its hill.

like a man under enchantment." It characterized well,
too, his mental attitude in maturity; though the spell
that held him now was charged with happiness.   The
house itself was small, but the proprietor might have
carved on his lintel the legend over Ariosto's door, *Par-
va, sed apta mihi.* In October, 1852, he wrote to Bridge
that he intended to begin a new romance within a day or
two, which he should make "more genial" than the last.
What design this was cannot now be even conjectured.
Hawthorne had written, in the preceding year, "I find
that my facility of labor increases with the demand for
it"; and he always felt that an unlimited reserve of invention and imagination awaited his drafts upon it, so
that he could produce as many books as he might have
time for writing.   But circumstances again called him
away from ideal occupations.   Just as he was preparing
to write the "Tanglewood Tales," as a sequel to the
"Wonder-Book," General Pierce, the Democratic nomi-
nee for President, urged him to write his biography, as a
"campaign" measure.   "I have consented to do so,"
wrote Hawthorne, to his publisher; "somewhat reluc-
tantly, however, for Pierce has now reached that altitude
where a man careful of his personal dignity will begin to
think of cutting his acquaintance.   But I seek nothing
from him, and therefore need not be ashamed to tell the
truth of an old friend."   To Bridge, after the book was
out, he wrote much more confidentially and strongly.
"I tried to persuade Pierce that I could not perform it
as well as many others; but he thought differently, and
of course, after a friendship of thirty years, it was impossible to refuse my best efforts in his behalf, at the great
pinch of his life."   In this letter, also, he states that
before undertaking the work, he resolved to "accept no
office" from Pierce; though he raises the query whether

this be not "rather folly than heroism." In discussing this point, he says, touching Pierce : —

"He certainly owes me something; for the biography has cost me hundreds of friends here at the North, who had a purer regard for me than Frank Pierce or any other politician ever gained, and who drop off from me like autumn leaves, in consequence of what I say on the slavery question. But they were my real sentiments, and I do not now regret that they are on record."

These have to do with Hawthorne's attitude during the war. Speaking of Pierce's indorsement of the Compromise, both as it bore hard on Northern views and exacted concessions from the South thought by it to be more than reciprocal, he says : —

"It was impossible for him not to take his stand as the unshaken advocate of Union, and of the mutual steps of compromise which that great object unquestionably demanded. The fiercest, the least scrupulous, and the most consistent of those who battle against slavery recognize the same fact that he does. They see that merely human wisdom and human efforts cannot subvert it, except by tearing to pieces the Constitution, breaking the pledges which it sanctions, and severing into distracted fragments that common country which Providence brought into one nation, through a continued miracle of almost two hundred years, from the first settlement of the American wilderness until the Revolution."

He predicted, too, the evils of forcible abolition being certain, and the good only a contingency, that the negroes would suffer aggravated injuries from the very process designed to better their state. It is useless here to enter into the question of degrees of right and wrong on either side, in the struggle which had already become formidable before Pierce's election; but one can see how sincerely, and with what generous motives, a man like Hawthorne would feel that the Union must be maintained peacefully. Without questioning the undoubted grandeur of achievement which we sanely fell upon through the insane fit of civil war, we may recognize a deep patriotism consistent with humanity which forced itself to dissent from the noble action of the fighters, because it could not share in any triumph, however glorious, that rested on the shedding of brothers' blood. It was this kind of humanity that found shelter in the heart of Hawthorne.

Unwelcome as was the task, he wrote the biography of Pierce, in friendship, but in good faith also, even seeing the elements of greatness in his old classmate, which might yet lead him to a career.* He had not much hope of his friend's election, but when that occurred, the question of office, which he had already mooted, was definitely brought before him. When Pierce learned that

* As a literary performance, the book is of course but slightly characteristic; and being distasteful to the author, it is even dry. Yet there is a great deal of simple dignity about it. The Whig journals belabored it manfully, and exhausted the resources of those formidable weapons, italics and small capitals, in the attempt to throw a ridiculous light on the facts most creditable to Pierce. Hawthorne came in for a share of the abuse too. One newspaper called the book his " new romance "; another made him out a worthy disciple of Simonides, who was the first poet to write for money. The other party, of course, took quite another view of the work. A letter to Hawthorne from his elder sister bears well upon his fidelity. " Mr. D—— has bought your Life of Pierce, but he will not be convinced that you have told the precise truth. I assure him that it is just what I have always heard you say."

he positively would not take an office, because to do so now might compromise him, he was extremely troubled. He had looked forward to giving Hawthorne some one of the prizes in his hand, if he should be elected. But the service he had exacted from his friend threatened to deprive Hawthorne of the very benefit which Pierce had been most anxious he should receive. At last, Mr. Ticknor, Hawthorne's publisher, was made the agent of Pierce's arguments, and to them he added personal considerations which were certainly not without weight. Literature gave but a bare subsistence, and Hawthorne was no longer young, having passed his forty-ninth year. His books were not likely, it seemed, to fill the breach that would be made in the fortunes of his family, were he to be suddenly removed. This, Mr. Ticknor urged, in addition to the friendly obligation which Pierce ought to be allowed to repay. Hawthorne, as we have seen, had always wished to travel, and the prospect of some years in Europe was an alluring one: the decision was made, to take the Liverpool consulship.

The appointment was well received, though many persons professed surprise that Hawthorne could accept it. One gentleman in public life, however, who knew how unjust current judgments may often be, was not of this number, as appears from his note below. —

SENATE CHAMBER, March 26, 1853.

MY DEAR HAWTHORNE: — "Good! good!" I exclaimed aloud on the floor of the Senate as your nomination was announced.

"Good! good!" I now write to you, on its confirmation. Nothing could be more grateful to me. Before you go, I hope to see you.

Ever yours,

CHARLES SUMNER.

ENGLAND AND ITALY.

1853-1860.

IT is very instructive to trace the contact of Hawthorne's mind with Europe, as exhibited in his "English Note-Books" and "French and Italian Note-Books." But in these records three things are especially observable. He goes to Europe as unperturbed, with an individual mood as easily sustained, as he would enter Boston or New York. He carries no preconception of what may be the most admirable way of looking at it. There has never been a more complete and charming presentment of a multitude of ingenuous impressions common to many travellers of widely differing endowment than here, at the same time that you have always before you the finished writer and the possible romancer, who suddenly and without warning flashes over his pages of quiet description a far, fleeting light of delicious imagination. It is as if two brothers, one a dreamer, and one a well-developed, intellectual, but slightly stoical and even shrewd American, dealing exclusively in common-sense, had gone abroad together, agreeing to write their opinions in the same book and in a style of perfect homogeneity. Sometimes one has the blank sheet to himself, sometimes the other; and occasionally they con each other's paragraphs, and the second modifies the ideas of the first. It is interesting to note their twofold inspection of Westminster Hall, for example. The understanding twin examines it methodically, finding its length to be eighty paces, and its effect "the ideal of an immense barn." The reasoning and imagining one interposes to this, "be it not irreverently spoken"; and also conjures up this splendid vision: "I wonder it does not occur to modern ingenuity to make a scenic representation, in this very hall, of the ancient trials for life or death, pomps, feasts, coronations, and every great historic incident . . . . that has occurred here. The whole world cannot show another hall such as this, so tapestried with recollections." But in any case it is always apparent that the thought is colored by a New World nurture. From this freshness of view there proceeded one result, the searching, unembarrassed, yet sympathetic and, as we may say, cordial criticism of England in "Our Old Home." But it also gave rise to the second notable quality, that exquisite apprehension of the real meaning of things European, both institutions and popular manners and the varied products of art. At times, Hawthorne seems to have been born for the one end of adding this final grace of definition which he so deftly attaches to the monuments of that older civilization. He brings a perception so keen and an innate sympathy so true for everything beautiful or significant, that the mere flowing out of this fine intellectual atmosphere upon the objects before him invests them with a quality which we feel to be theirs, even while we know that it could not have become *ours* without his aid. A breath of New England air touches the cathedral windows of the Old World, and — I had almost said — bedims them with a film of evanescent frost-work; yet, as that lingers, we suddenly discern through the veil a charm, a legendary fascination in their deep-gemmed gorgeousness, which, although we have felt it and read of it before, we never seized till now. I speak, of course, from the American point of view ; though in a great measure the effect upon foreign readers may be similar. But I fancy a special appropriateness for us in the peculiar mixture of estimation and enthusiasm which forms the medium through which Hawthorne looks at the spectacle of transatlantic life and its surroundings. He visits the British Museum, and encounters only disappointment at the mutilated sculptures of the Parthenon ; but out of th's confession, which is truth, slowly arises the higher truth of that airy yet profound response with which he greets the multiform mute company of marble or painted shapes that form the real population of Rome. Even there, he has much dissent to make, still ; and we may not find it at all essential or beneficial to follow each of his deviations ourselves. But however we may differ with him, it is impossible not to feel sure that within this circle of contradictions, of preference for new frames and of his friend Thompson's pictures to all but a very few of the old masters', somewhere within there is a perfectly trustworthy æsthetic sensibility which grasps the "unwritten rules of taste," the inmost truth of all art. This inmost secret is, however we may turn it, a matter of paradox, and the moment it professes to be explained, that moment are the gates of the penetralia shut upon us. The evasiveness and the protest, then, with which Hawthorne discourses to himself as he wanders through the galleries of Europe, are the trembling of the needle, perfectly steadfast to the polar opposites of truth, yet quivering as with a fear that it may be unsettled by some artificial influence from its deep office of inner constancy. And as if, in this singular world, all truth must turn to paradox at the touch of an

index finger, that almost faulty abstention from assuming
the European tone which has made Hawthorne the traveller appear to certain readers a little crude, — that very
air of being the uncritical and slightly puzzled American
is precisely the source of his most delightful accuracies of
interpretation.

The third greatest distinction of his foreign observation
is its entire freedom from specialism. Perhaps this cannot
be made to appear more clearly than in the contrast
presented by his "English Note-Books" and "Our Old
Home" to Emerson's "English Traits," and Taine's
"Notes on England." The latter writer is an acute,
alert, industrious, and picturesque comparer of his own
and a neighboring country, and is accompanied by a light
battery of literary and pictorial criticism, detached from
his heavier home armament. Emerson, on the other
hand, gives us probably the most masterly and startling
analysis of a people which has ever been offered in the
same slight bulk, unsurpassed, too, in brilliancy and pen-
etration of statement. But the "English Traits" is as
clear, fixed, and accurate as a machinist's plan, and perhaps a little too rigidly defined. Hawthorne's review of
England, though not comparable to Emerson's work for
analysis, has this advantage, that its outline is more flexible and leaves room for many individual discriminations
to which it supplies an easily harmonized groundwork.
Emerson and Taine give us their impressions of a foreign
land: Hawthorne causes us to inhale its very atmosphere,
and makes the country ours for the time being, rather
than an alien area which we scrutinize in passing.
Yet here and there he partakes of the very qualities
that are dominant with Emerson and Taine. "Every
Englishman runs to 'The Times' with his little grievance,
as a child runs to his mother," is as epigrammatic as

anything in "English Traits"; * and there is a tendency
in his pages to present the national character in a con-
crete form, as the French writer gives it. But, in addition, Hawthorne is an artist and a man of humor; and
renders human character with a force and fineness which
give it its true value as being, after all, far weightier and
dearer to us than the most important or famous of con-
gealed *results* of character. Withal a wide and keen observer and a hospitable entertainer of opinions, he does
not force these upon us as final. Coming and going at
ease, they leave a mysterious sense of greater wisdom
with us, an indefinable residue of refined truth.

It is a natural question, why did not Hawthorne write
an English romance, as well, or rather than an Italian
one? More than half his stay abroad was north of the
Channel, and one would infer that there could have been
no lack of suggestion there. "My ancestor left England," he wrote, "in 1630. I return in 1853. I sometimes feel as if I myself had been absent these two
hundred and twenty-three years, leaving England just
emerging from the feudal system, and finding it, on my
return, on the verge of republicanism." Herein lay a
source of romantic possibilities from which he certainly
meant to derive a story. But the greater part of his four
years in England was spent in Liverpool, where his con-

* No one, I think, has so well defined our relation to the
English as Hawthorne, in a casual phrase from one of his
printed letters: "We stand in the light of posterity to them,
and have the privileges of posterity." This, on London, ought
to become proverbial: "London is like the grave in one respect, — any man can make himself at home there; and whenever a man finds himself homeless elsewhere, he had better die,
or go to London."

sular duties suppressed fiction-making.*   Hawthorne's
genius was extremely susceptible to every influence about
it.   One might liken its quality to that of a violin which
owes its fine properties to the tempering of time and
atmosphere, and transmits through its strings the very
thrill of sunshine that has sunk into its wood.   His utterances are modulated by the very changes of the air.   In
one of his letters from Florence he wrote : —

"Speaking of romances, I have planned two, one or both of
which I could have ready for the press in a few months if I
were either in England or America.   But I find this Italian
atmosphere not favorable to the close toil of composition,
although it is a very good air to dream in.   I must breathe
the fogs of old England or the east-winds of Massachusetts,
in order to put me into working trim."

But though England might be his workshop for books
dreamed of in Italy, yet the aspect of English life seems
much more fittingly represented by his less excursively
imaginative side, as in "Our Old Home," than in a romance.   Perhaps this is too ingenious a consolation ; but
I believe we may much better spare the possible English romance, than we could have foregone the actual
Italian one.

In "The Marble Faun" Hawthorne's genius took

* And it was not till he reached the villa of Montauto at
Florence that he could write : —

"It is pleasant to feel at last that I am really away from America, —
a satisfaction that I never enjoyed as long as I stayed in Liverpool, where
it seemed to me that the quintessence of nasal and hand-shaking Yankee-
dom was continually filtered and sublimated through my consulate, on
the way outward and homeward.   I first got acquainted with my own
countrymen there.   At Rome, too, it was not much better.   But here in
Florence, and in the summer-time, and in this secluded villa, I have
escaped out of all my old tracks, and am really remote."

a more daring and impressive range than ever before, and showed conclusively — what, without this testimony, would most likely have been questioned, or even by some denied — that his previous works had given the arc of a circle which no English or American writer of prose fiction besides himself has even begun to span. It is not alone that he plucks from a prehistoric time — "a period when man's affinity with nature was more strict, and his fellowship with every living thing more intimate and dear" — this conception of Donatello, the fresh, free, sylvan man untouched by sin or crime. Donatello must rank with a class of poetic creations which has nearly become extinct among modern writers: he belongs to the world of Caliban, Puck, and Ariel. But besides this unique creation, the book reveals regions of thought wide, ruin-scarred, and verdurously fair as the Campagna itself, winning the mind back through history to the primitive purity of man and of Christianity. I recoil from any attempt at adequate analysis of this marvellous production, for it is one of those works of art which are also works of nature, and will present to each thoughtful reader a new set of meanings, according to his individuality, insight, or experience. The most obvious part of the theme is that which is represented in the title, the study of the Faun's nature; and this embraces the whole question of sin and crime, their origin and distinction. But it is not the case, as has been assumed, that in this study the author takes the position of advocate to a theory that sin was requisite to the development of soul in man. For, though he shows that remorse developed in Donatello "a more definite and nobler individuality," he also reminds us that "sometimes the instruction comes without the sorrow, and oftener the sorrow teaches no lesson that abides with us"; and he illustrates this in the exquisite height of spirituality to which Hilda has attained through sinlessness. He is not, I say, the advocate of a theory: this charge has been made by self-confident critics, who saw only the one idea, — that of a Beneficence which has so handled sin, that, instead of destroying man, "it has really become an instrument most effective in the education of intellect and soul." This idea is several times urged by Miriam and Kenyon, but quickly rejected each time; first by Kenyon, and then by Hilda; so that, while it is suggested, it is also shown to be one which human nature cannot trust itself to dwell upon. But the real function of the author is that of a profound religious teacher. The "Romance of Monte Beni" is, as Miriam plainly says, the story of the fall of man repeated. It takes us with fearless originality to the source of all religious problems, affirming, — as one interpreter * has said, — "the inherent freedom of man," and illustrating how he may choose the good or the evil. Donatello is the ideal of the childlike nature on the threshold of history who has lived without choosing either, up to the time when his love and defence of Miriam involve him in crime. Father Antonio, "the spectre of the catacombs," and Miriam's persecutor, is the outcome of a continual choice of evil and of utter degradation. These two extremes, more widely asunder than Prospero and Caliban, Hawthorne has linked together in his immense grasp of the inmost laws of life, and with a miraculous nicety of artistic skill. Then comes Donatello's fall, illustrating the genesis of sin from crime, in accordance with the Biblical story of Cain; and this precipitates an

* See an unsigned article, " The Genius of Hawthorne," in the Atlantic Monthly for September, 1868.

examination, not only of the result upon Donatello him-self, but of the degree in which others, even the most guiltless, are involved. There is first the reaction upon and inculpation of Miriam, whose glance had confirmed Donatello's murderous intent; only a glance, yet enough to involve her in the doom of change and separation — of sin in short — which falls upon the Faun. And in Hilda's case, it is the simple consciousness of another's guilt, which is "almost the same as if she had partici-pated" in it. The mutual relations of these persons, who are made to represent the whole of society, afford matter for infinite meditation, the artistic and moral abstract of which the author has given.

But with this main theme is joined a very marvellous and intricate study of the psychology of Beatrice Cenci's story, in a new form. Miriam is a different woman placed in the same circumstances which made the Cenci tragedy. In the "French and Italian Note-Books," Hawthorne describes the look he caught sight of in Guido's picture, — that "of a being unhumanized by some terrible fate, and gazing out of a remote and inac-cessible region, where she was frightened to be alone, but where no human sympathy could reach her." It was of this single insight that both Miriam and Hilda were born to his mind. He reproduces this description, slightly modified, in the romance (Vol. I. Chap. XXIII.): "It was the intimate consciousness of her father's guilt that threw its shadow over her, and frightened her into" this region. Now, in the chapter called "Beatrice," quite early in the story, he brings out between Miriam and Hilda a discussion of Beatrice and her history. It is evident, from the emphasis given by the chapter-title, that this subject is very deeply related to the theme of the romance ; and no theory can explain Miriam's pas-

Q

sionate utterances about the copy of Guido's portrait, except that which supposes her own situation to be that of Beatrice. This chapter is full of the strongest hints of the fact. Miriam's sudden resemblance to the picture, at the instant when she so yearns to grasp the secret of Beatrice's view of her own guilt or innocence; her ardent defence of Beatrice's course, as "the best virtue possible under the circumstances," when Hilda condemns it; her suggestion that, after all, only a woman could have painted the poor girl's thoughts upon her face, and that *she herself* has "a great mind to undertake a copy," giving it "what it lacks"; — all these things point clearly. But there is a mass of inferential evidence, besides; many veiled allusions and approaches to a revelation, as well as that very marked description of the sketches in which Miriam has portrayed in various moods a " woman acting the part of a revengeful mischief towards man," and the hint, in the description of her portrait of herself, that " she might ripen to be what Judith was, when she vanquished Holofernes with her beauty, and slew him for too much adoring it." There is no need to pursue the proof further: readers will easily find it on re-examining the book. But what is most interesting, is to observe how Hawthorne has imagined two women of natures so widely opposed as Hilda and Miriam under a similar pressure of questionable blood-guiltiness. With Miriam, it is a guilt which has for excuse that it was the only resort against an unnatural depravity in Father Antonio. But as if to emphasize the indelibleness of blood-stains, however justly inflicted, we have as a foil to Miriam the white sensitiveness of Hilda's conscience, which makes her — though perfectly free from even the indirect responsibility of Miriam — believe herself actually infected. In both cases, it is the shadow of crime

which weighs upon the soul; but Miriam, in exactly the
position of Beatrice Cenci, is a more complex and deep-
colored nature than she; and Hilda, differently affected
by the same question of conscience, is a vastly spiritualized image of the historic sufferer. Miriam, after the
avenging of her nameless wrong, doubts, as Beatrice must
have done, whether there be any guilt in such avenge-
ment; but being of so different a temperament, and having before her eyes the effect of this murder upon the
hitherto sinless Faun, the reality of her responsibility is
brought home to her. The clear conscience of Hilda
confirms it. Thus by taking two extremes on either side
of Beatrice, — one, a woman less simply and ethereally
organized, and the other one who is only indirectly connected with wrong or crime, — Hawthorne seems to extract from the problem of Beatrice all its most subtle significance. He does not coldly condemn Beatrice; but by
re-combining the elements of her case, he succeeds in
magnifying into startling distinctness the whole awful
knot of crime and its consequence, which lies inextricably
tangled up within it. How different from Shelley's use
of the theme! There is certainly nothing in the "Marble
Faun" to equal the impassioned expression of wrong,
and the piercing outcry against the shallow but awful
errors of human justice, which uplift Shelley's drama.
But Shelley stops, on the one side, with this climax : —

> "O plead
> With famine or wind-walking pestilence,
> Blind lightning or the deaf sea, not with man!"

And on the side of the moral question, he leaves us with
Beatrice's characterization of the parricide,

> "Which is, or is not, what men call a crime."

Hawthorne, on the contrary, starts from this latter
doubt. "The foremost result of a broken law," he says,
"is ever an ecstatic freedom." But instead of pausing
to give this his whole weight, as Shelley does, he distinctly pronounces the murder of Miriam's degraded
father to be crime, and proceeds to inquire how Miriam
and Donatello may work out their purification. So that
if the first part of the romance is the Fall of Man repeated, the second part is the proem to a new Paradise
Regained ; and the seclusion of the sculptor and the
Faun, and their journey together to Perugia, seasoned
with Kenyon's noble and pure-hearted advice, compose
a sort of seven-times-refined Pilgrim's Progress. Apt
culmination of a genius whose relations to Milton and
Bunyan we found to be so suggestive ! The chief means
which Kenyon offers for regeneration is that Miriam and
the Faun shall abandon any hope of mutual joy, and
consecrate themselves to the alleviation of misery in the
world. Having by violence and crime thrust one evil
out of life, they are now by patience and benevolence to
endeavor to exorcise others. At the same time, remark-
ing that Providence has infinitely varied ways of dealing
with any deed, Hawthorne leaves a possibility of happiness for the two penitents, which may become theirs as
"a wayside flower, springing along a path that leads
to higher ends." But he also shows, in Donatello's final
delivering of himself up to justice, the wisdom of some
definite judgment and perhaps punishment bestowed by
society. Thus, avenues of thought are opened to us on
every side, which we are at liberty to follow out ; but
we are not forced, as a mere theorist would compel us, to
pursue any particular one to the exclusion of the others.
In all we may find our way to some mystic monument of
eternal law, or pluck garlands from some new-budded

bough of moral truth. The romance is like a portal of ebony inlaid with ivory, — another gate of dreams, — swinging softly open into regions of illimitable wisdom. But some pause on the threshold, unused to such large liberty; and these cry out, in the words of a well-known critic, " It begins in mystery, and ends in mist."

Though the book was very successful, few readers grasped the profounder portions. It is a vast exemplar of the author's consummate charm as a simple story-teller, however, that he exercised a brilliant fascination over all readers, notwithstanding the heavy burden of uncomprehended truths which they were obliged to carry with them. Some critics complain of the extent to which Roman scenery and the artistic life in Rome have been introduced; but, to my mind, there is scarcely a word wasted in the two volumes. The "vague sense of ponderous remembrances" pressing down and crowding out the present moment till "our individual affairs are but half as real here as elsewhere," is essential to the perspective of the whole; and nothing but this rich picturesqueness and variety could avail to balance the depth of tragedy which has to be encountered; so that the nicety of art is unquestionable. It is strange, indeed, that this great modern religious romance should thus have become also the ideal representative of ruined Rome — the home of ruined religions — in its æsthetic aspects. But one instance of appreciation must be recorded here, as giving the highest pitch of that delightful literary fellowship which Hawthorne seems constantly to have enjoyed in England. His friend John Lothrop Motley, the historian, wrote thus of "The Marble Faun," from Walton-on-Thames, March 29, 1860 : —

" Everything that you have ever written, I believe, I have read many times, and I am particularly vain of having admired

'Sights from a Steeple,' when I first read it in the Boston
'Token,' several hundred years ago, when we were both
younger than we are now; of having detected and cherished, at
a later day, an old Apple-Dealer, whom, I believe, you have
unhandsomely thrust out of your presence, now that you are
grown so great.   But the 'Romance of Monte Beni' has the
additional charm for me, that it is the first book of yours that
I have read since I had the privilege of making your personal
acquaintance.   My memory goes back at once to those walks
(alas, not too frequent) we used to take along the Tiber, or in
the Campagna ; . . . . and it is delightful to get hold of the
book now, and know that it is impossible for you any longer,
after waving your wand as you occasionally did then, indicating
where the treasure was hidden, to sink it again beyond plum-
met's sound.

    " I admire the book exceedingly. . . . . It is one which, for
the first reading, at least, I did n't like to hear aloud. . . . . If
I were composing an article for a review, of course, I should
feel obliged to show cause for my admiration ; but I am only
obeying an impulse.   Permit me to say, however, that your
style seems, if possible, more perfect than ever.   Where, O
where is the godmother who gave you to talk pearls and dia-
monds ? . . . . Believe me, I don't say to you half what I say
behind your back ; and I have said a dozen times that nobody
can write English but you.   With regard to the story, which
has been somewhat criticised, I can only say that to me it is
quite satisfactory.   I like those shadowy, weird, fantastic, Hawthornesque shapes flitting through the golden gloom, which is
the atmosphere of the book.   I like the misty way in which
the story is indicated rather than revealed ; the outlines are
quite definite enough from the beginning to the end to those
who have imagination enough to follow you in your airy flights ;
and to those who complain, I suppose that nothing less than
an illustrated edition, with a large gallows on the last page,
with Donatello in the most pensile of attitudes, — his ears revealed through a white nightcap, — would be satisfactory.   I

beg your pardon for such profanation, but it really moves my spleen that people should wish to bring down the volatile figures of your romance to the level of an every-day romance. . . . . The way in which the two victims dance through the Carnival on the last day is very striking.   It is like a Greek tragedy in its effect, without being in the least Greek."

To this Hawthorne replied from Bath (April 1, 1860); and Mr. Motley has kindly sent me a copy of the letter.

MY DEAR MOTLEY : — You are certainly that Gentle Reader for whom all my books were exclusively written.   Nobody else (my wife excepted, who speaks so near me that I cannot tell her voice from my own) has ever said exactly what I loved to hear.   It is most satisfactory to be hit upon the raw, to be shot straight through the heart.   It is not the quantity of your praise that I care so much about (though I gather it all up most carefully, lavish as you are of it), but the kind, for you take the book precisely as I meant it; and if your note had come a few days sooner, J believe I would have printed it in a postscript which I have added to the second edition, because it explains better than I found possible to do the way in which my romance ought to be taken. . . . . Now don't suppose that I fancy the book to be a tenth part as good as you say it is.   You work out my imperfect efforts, and half make the book with your warm imagination; and see what I myself saw, but could only hint at.   Well, the romance is a success, even if it never finds another reader.

We spent the winter in Leamington, whither we had come from the sea-coast in October.   I am sorry to say that it was another winter of sorrow and anxiety . . . . [The allusion here is to illness in the family, of which there had also been a pro-tracted case in Rome].   I have engaged our passages for June 16th. . . . . Mrs. Hawthorne and the children will probably remain in Bath till the eve of our departure; but I intend to pay one more visit of a week or two to London, and shall certainly come and see you.   I wonder at your lack of recognition of my social propensities.   I take so much delight in my friends, that a little intercourse goes a great way, and illuminates my life before and after. . . . .

Your friend,

NATH. HAWTHORNE.

These seven years in Europe formed, outwardly, the most opulently happy part of Hawthorne's life.   Before he left America, although he had been writing — with several interruptions — for twenty-four years, he had only just reached a meagre prosperity.   I have touched upon the petty clamor which his Custom-House pictures aroused, and the offensive political attacks following the Life of Pierce.   These disagreeables, scattered along the way, added to the weary delay that had attended his first efforts, made the enthusiastic personal welcome with which he everywhere met in England, and the charm of highly organized society, with its powerful artistic classes centred upon great capitals there and in Italy, a very captivating contrast.   Still there were drawbacks.   The most serious one was the change in the consular service made during his term at Liverpool.   The consulate there was considered the most lucrative post in the President's gift, at the time of his appointment.   But, to begin with, Pierce allowed the previous incumbent to resign prospectively, so that Hawthorne lost entirely the first five months of his tenure.   These were very valuable months, and after the new consul came into office the dull season set in, reducing his fees materially.   Business continued bad so long, that even up to 1855 little more than a living could be made in the consulate.   In February of that year a bill was passed by Congress, remodelling the diplomatic and consular system, and fixing the salary of the Liverpool consul at $7,500, — less than

half the amount of the best annual income from it before
that time. The position was one of importance, and involved an expensive mode of life; so that even before
this bill went into operation, though practising "as stern
an economy," he wrote home, "as ever I did in my life,"
Hawthorne could save but little; and the effect of it
would have been not only to prevent his accomplishing
what he took the office for, but even to have imposed
loss upon him. For, in addition to social demands, the
mere necessary office expenses (including the pay of three
clerks) were very large, amounting to some thousands
yearly; and the needs of unfortunate fellow-citizens, to
whom Hawthorne could not bring himself to be indiffer-
ent, carried off a good portion of his income. As he
says, "If the government chooses to starve the consul, a
good many will starve with him." The most irritating
thing about the new law was that it merely cut down
the consular fees, without bringing the government anything; for the fees came from business that a notary-
public could perform, and the consul would naturally
decline to take it upon himself when his interest in it
was removed. Fortunately, the President was given
some discretion about the date of reappointment, and
allowed the old commission to continue for a time.
Meanwhile, Hawthorne was obliged, in anticipation of
the new rule, to alter his mode of life materially. He
now planned to give up the place in the autumn of
1855, and go to Italy; but this was not carried out till
two years later.

Italy charmed him wholly, and he longed to make it
his home. There had not been want of unjust criticism
of him in America, while at Liverpool. When some ship-
wrecked steamer passengers were thrown upon his hands,
for whom he provided extra-officially, on Mr. Buchanan's

(then minister) refusing to have anything to do with the matter, a newspaper rumor was started at home that Mr. Hawthorne would do nothing for them until ordered to by Mr. Buchanan.

"It sickens me," he wrote at that time, "to look back to America. I am sick to death of the continual fuss and tumult and excitement and bad blood which we keep up about political topics. If it were not for my children, I should probably never return."

And on the eve of sailing, he wrote to another friend : —

"I shall go home, I fear, with a heavy heart, not expecting to be very well contented there."

But his sense of duty, stronger than that of many Americans under similar circumstances, was rigorously obeyed. We shall see what sort of reward this fidelity to country won from public opinion at home.

X.

THE LAST ROMANCE.

1860-1863.

THERE are in the "English Note-Books" several dismal and pathetic records of tragic cases of brutality or murder on shipboard, which it was Hawthorne's duty as consul to investigate. These things, as one might have divined they would, made a very strong and deep impression upon him; and he tried strenuously to interest the United States government in bettering the state of the marine by new laws. But though this evil was and is still quite as monstrous as that of slavery, there was no means of mixing up prejudice and jealousy with the reform, to help it along, and he could effect nothing. He resolved, on returning home, to write some articles — perhaps a volume — exposing the horrors so calmly overlooked; but the slavery agitation, absorbing everybody, perhaps discouraged him : the scheme was never carried out. It is a pity; for, aside from the weight which so eminent a name might have given to a good cause, the work would have clearly proven the quick, responsive, practical nature of his humanity — a quality which some persons have seen fit to deny him — in a case where no question of conflicting rights divided his sense of duty.

He came to America in June, 1860.   For several years
the mutterings of rising war between the States had been
growing louder.   In June of 1856 he had written to
Bridge, expressing great hope that all would yet turn
out well.   But so rapidly did the horizon blacken, that
later in the same year he declared that "an actual
fissure" seemed to him to be opening between the two
sections of the country.   In January, 1857 : —

"I regret that you think so doubtfully of the prospects of
the Union ; for I should like well enough to hold on to the old
thing.   And yet I must confess that I sympathize to a large
extent with the Northern feeling, and think it is about time for
us to make a stand.   If compelled to choose, I go for the North.
New England is quite as large a lump of earth as my heart
can really take in. . . . . However, I have no kindred with nor
leaning toward the Abolitionists."

He felt, no doubt, that the vital principle of the Union
from the beginning had been compromise, mutual conces-
sion, and if it was to be severed, preferred that it should
be peacefully.   Still, his moods and wishes varied as did
those of many careful watchers at that time ; and he saw
too clearly the arguments on either side to hold fixedly
to one course.   In the December after his return, seces-
sion began ; and for more than a year following he could
not fix his attention upon literary matters.   He wrote
little, not even his journal, as Mrs. Hawthorne has told
us, until 1862.   Accustomed to respond accurately to
every influence about him, with that sensitized exterior
of receptive imagination which overlay the fixed substance of personal character, — so that, as we have seen,
even a change of climate left its impress on his productions, — it was not strange that the emotions of horror
and pain, the passion of hate, the splendid heroism which

charged the whole atmosphere about him, now, should absorb his whole sensibility, and paralyze his imagination. It was no time for quiet observation or creative revery. A new era had broken upon us, ushered by the wild din of trumpet and cannon, and battle-cry; an era which was to form new men, and shape a new generation. He must pause and listen to the agonies of this birth, striving vainly to absorb the commotion into himself and to let it subside into clear visions of the future. No hope! He could not pierce the war-smoke to any horizon of better things. He who had schooled himself so unceasingly to feel with utmost intensity the responsibility of each soul for any violence or crime of others, could not cancel the fact of multitudinous murder by any hypothesis of prospective benefit. Thus, in the midst of that magnificent turbulence, he was like the central quiet of a whirlpool: all the fierce currents met there, and seemed to pause, — but only seemed. Full of sympathy as he was for his fellows, and agitated at times by the same warlike impulses, he could not give himself rein as they did, nor dared to raise any encouraging strain in his writing, as others felt that they might freely do. His Puritan sense of justice, refined by descent and wedded to mercy, compelled him to weigh all carefully, to debate long and compassionately. But meantime the popular sense of justice — that same New England sentiment, of which his own was a development — cared nothing for these fine considerations, and Hawthorne was generally condemned by it as being warped by his old Democratic alliances into what was called treason. Nevertheless, he was glad to be in his native land, and suffer bitter criticism here, — if that were all that could be granted, — rather than to remain an unmolested exile.

An article which he contributed to the " Atlantic Monthly " in July, 1862, gives a faint inkling of his state of mind at this time; but nothing illustrates more clearly, either, the reserve which he always claimed lay behind his seemingly most frank expressions in print. For he there gives the idea of something like coldness in his attitude touching the whole great tragedy. But those who saw him daily, and knew his real mood, have remembered how deeply his heart was shaken by it. Fortunately, there are one or two epistolary proofs of the degree in which his sympathy with his own side of the struggle sometimes mastered him. He used to say that he only regretted that his son was too young and himself too old to admit of either of them entering the army; and just after the first battle of Bull Run he wrote to Mr. Lowell, at Cambridge, declining an invitation : —

The Wayside, Concord, July 23, 1861.

Dear Lowell : — I am to start, in two or three days, on an excursion with ——, who has something the matter with him, and seems to need sea-air and change. If I alone were concerned, ... I would most gladly put off my trip till after your dinner ; but, as the case stands, I am compelled to decline.

Speaking of dinner, last evening's news will dull the edge of many a Northern appetite ; but if it puts all of us into the same grim and bloody humor that it does me, the South had better have suffered ten defeats than won this victory.

Sincerely yours,

Nath. Hawthorne.

And to another friend, in October : —

" For my part, I don't hope (nor, indeed, wish) to see the Union restored as it was ; amputation seems to me much the better plan. . . . . I would fight to the death for the Northern slave States, and let the rest go. . . . . I have not found it possible to occupy my mind with its usual trash and nonsense during these anxious times; but as the autumn advances, I find myself sitting down at my desk and blotting successive sheets of paper as of yore."

He had now begun, I suppose, the "Romance of Immortality," or "Septimius Felton," which has been posthumously printed, but had been abandoned by him for another treatment of the same theme, called "The Dolliver Romance." This last, of which two chapters appeared, was left unfinished at his death. Of "Septimius" I shall not attempt an analysis: it contains several related and concentric circles of meaning, to survey which would require too much space. The subject had been one of the earliest themes of meditation with Hawthorne, and he wrote as with a fountain-pen in which was locked the fluid thought of a lifetime. One of the less obvious aspects of the book is the typification in Septimius's case of that endless struggle which is the lot of every man inspired by an ideal aim. The poet and the painter are, equally with Septimius, seekers after immortality, though of a more ethereal kind; and his morbidness and exaggeration serve to excite in us a tenderness and pity over him, assisting the reception of truth. These relate mainly to the temptation of the artist to effect a severance of ordinary, active human relations. (Sad to think what bitter cause the author had to brood upon this, the fault attributed to himself!) The poet, the creator in whatever art, must maintain his own circle of serene air, shutting out from it the flat reverberations of common life; but if he fail to live generously toward his fellows, — if he cannot make the light of every day supply the nimbus in which he hopes to appear shining to posterity, — then he will fall into the treacherous pit of selfishness where Septimius's soul lies smothered. But this set of meanings runs imperceptibly into others, for the book is much like the cabalistic manuscript described in its pages : now it is blurred over with deceptive sameness, and again it brims with multifarious beauties like those that swim within the golden depth of Tieck's enchanted goblet. The ultimate and most insistent moral is perhaps that which brings it into comparison with Goethe's "Faust" ; this, namely, that, in order to defraud Nature of her dues, we must enter into compact with the Devil. Both Faust and Septimius study magic in their separate ways, with the hope of securing results denied to their kind by a common destiny; but Faust proves infinitely the meaner of the two, since he desires only to restore his youth, that he may engage in the mere mad joy of a lusty existence for a few years, while Septimius seeks some mode, however austere and cheerless, of prolonging his life through centuries of world-wide beneficence. Yet the satanically refined egoism which lays hold of Septimius is the same spirit incarnated in Goethe's Mephistopheles, — *der Geist der stets verneint.* To Faust he denies the existence of good in anything, primarily the good of that universal knowledge to the acquisition of which he has devoted his life, but through this scepticism mining his faith in all besides. To Septimius he denies the worth of so brief a life as ours, and the good of living to whatever end seems for the hour most needful and noble. Septimius might perhaps be described as Faust at an earlier stage of development than that in which Goethe represents him.*

* Indeed, these words, applied by Mephistopheles to Faust, suit Septimius equally well : —

> " Ihm hat das Schicksal einen Geist gegeben
> Der ungebändigt immer vorwärts dringht
> Und dessen übereiltes Streben
> Der Erde Freuden überspringt."

As a further point of resemblance between the two cases, it may be noticed that the false dreams of both are dispelled by the exorcising touch of a woman. Both have fallen into error through perceiving only half of the truth which has hovered glimmering before them; these errors originate in the exclusively masculine mood, the asceticism, which has prevailed in their minds. It will be observed that, in the first relation of Rose to Septimius, Hawthorne takes pains to contrast with this mood, delicately but strongly, the woman's gentle conservatism and wisely practical tendency to be satisfied with life, which make her influence so admirable a poising force to man. The subsequent alteration of the situation, by which he makes her the half-sister of his hero, is owing, as Mr. Higginson has pointed out, to the fact "that a heroine must be supplied who corresponds to the idea in the lover's soul; like Helena in the second part of Faust." *

But there is a suitable difference between the working of the womanly element in "Faust" and in Hawthorne's romance. In the former instance it is through

---

* A phase of character rich in interest, but which I can only mention, in passing, is presented in the person of Sybil Dacy, who here occupies very much the same place, in some regards, as Roger Chillingworth in "The Scarlet Letter." The movement of the story largely depends on a subtle scheme of revenge undertaken by her, as that of "The Scarlet Letter" hangs upon the mode of retribution sought by the physician; but her malice is directed, characteristically, against the slayer of the young officer who had despoiled her of her honor, and, again characteristically, she is unable to consummate her plan, from the very tenderness of her feminine heart, which leads her first to half sympathize with his dreams, then pity him for the deceit she practised on him, and at last to rather love than hate him.

the gratification of his infernal desire that the hero is awakened from his trance of error and restored to remorse; while Septimius's failure to accomplish his intended destiny appears to be owing to the inability of his aspiring nature to accommodate itself to that code of "moral dietetics" which is to assist his strange project. "Kiss no woman if her lips be red; look not upon her if she be very fair," is the maxim taught him. "If thou love her, all is over, and thy whole past and remaining labor and pains will be in vain." How pathetic a situation this, how much more terrible than that of Faust, when he has reached the turning-point in his career! A nature which could accept an earthly immortality on these terms, for the sake of his fellows, must indeed have been a hard and chilly one. But there is still too much of the heart in it, to admit of being satisfied with so cruel an abstraction. On the verge of success, as he supposes, with the long-sought drink standing ready for his lips, Septimius nevertheless seeks a companion. Half unawares, he has fallen in love with Sybil, and thenceforth, though in a way he had not anticipated, "all is over." Yet, saved from death by the poison in which he had hoped to find the spring of endless life, his fate appears admirably fitting. There is no picture of Mephisto hurrying him off to an apparently irrevocable doom. The wrongs he has committed against himself, his friends, humanity, — these, indeed, remain, and are remembered. He has undoubtedly fallen from his first purity and earnestness, and must hereafter be content to live a life of mere conventional comfort, full of mere conventional goodness, conventional charities, in that substantial English home of his. Could anything be more perfectly compensatory?

Nothing is more noticeable than the way in which,

while so many symbolisms spring up out of the story, the hero's half-crazed and bewildered atmosphere is the one which we really accept, until the reading is ended. By this means we are enabled to live through the whole immortal future which he projects for himself, though he never in reality achieves any of it. This forcing of the infinite into the finite, we are again indebted to Mr. Higginson for emphasizing as "one of the very greatest triumphs in all literature." "A hundred separate tragedies," he says, "would be easier to depict than this which combines so many in one."

But notice the growth of the romance in Hawthorne's mind. "Dr. Heidegger's Experiment," in which several people are restored to youth for an hour by a life-elixir, was published before 1837. In 1840 we have this entry in the journal: "If a man were sure of living forever here, he would not care about his offspring." A few years afterward, in "A Virtuoso's Collection," the elixir vitæ is introduced, "in an antique sepulchral urn," but the narrator refuses to quaff it. "'No; I desire not an earthly immortality,' said I. 'Were man to live longer on the earth, the spiritual would die out of him. . . . . There is a celestial something within us, that requires, after a certain time, the atmosphere of heaven to preserve it from ruin.'" But the revolt against death, and then the reactionary meditation upon it, and final reverence for it, must, from the circumstances of his youngest years, have been very early familiar to Hawthorne; and in the course of these meditations, the conception of deathlessness must often have floated before him. The tradition as to the former owner of the Wayside, who had thought he should never die (alluded to in the letter to Curtis, in 1852*), brought it definitely home to him. He had

* See ante, p. 244.

in 1837 thought of this: "A person to spend all his life and splendid talents, in trying to achieve something totally impossible, — as, to make a conquest over nature"; but the knowledge of an actual person who had expected to live forever gave the scattered elements coherence. The way in which other suggestions came into the plan is exceedingly curious. The idea of a bloody footstep appears in the Note-Books in 1850: "The print in blood of a naked foot to be traced through the street of a town." By a singular corroboration, he encountered five years afterward in England an actual bloody footprint, or a mark held to be such, at Smithell's Hall in Lancashire. ("English Note-Books," Vol. I. April 7, and August 25, 1855.) The parting request of his hostess there was that he "should write a ghost-story for her house," and he observes that "the legend is a good one." Only five days after first hearing it he makes a note thus: "In my Romance, the original emigrant to America may have carried away with him a family secret, by which it was in his power, had he so chosen, to have brought about the ruin of the family. This secret he transmitted to his American progeny, by whom it is inherited throughout all the intermediate generations. At last the hero of my Romance comes to England, and finds that, by means of this secret, he still has it in his power to procure the downfall of the family." This clearly refers to something already rapidly taking shape in his mind, and recalls at once the antique chest containing family papers, and the estate in England waiting for an heir, of "Septimius." Could he have already connected the two things, the bloody footstep and this Anglo-American interest? The next piece of history comes in the shape of a manuscript book in journal form, written in 1858, after Hawthorne had left the consulate, and containing what must have been the earliest sketch of the story, as he then conceived it. It begins abruptly, and proceeds uncertainly, at the rate of a few pages each day, for about a month. Detached passages of narration alternate with abstracts of the proposed plot, and analysis of the characters. The chief interest seems to lie in the project which a young American has formed, during a visit to England, of tracing out and proving his inherited right to an old manor-house formerly the property of his ancestors. This old hall possesses the peculiarity of the bloody footstep, and with this some mystery is connected, which the writer himself does not yet seem to have discovered. He takes a characteristic pleasure in waiting for this suggestive footstep to track the lurking interest of his story to its lair, and lingers on the threshold of the tale, gazing upon it, indulging himself with that tantalizing pleasure of vague anticipation in which he hopes to envelop the good reader. The perusal of this singular journal, in which the transactions recorded are but day-dreams, is absorbing beyond description. But though at times he seems to be rapidly approaching the heart of the story, yet at every point the subtle darkness and coming terror of the theme seem to baffle the author, and he retires, to await a more favorable moment. At its conclusion, though he appears now to have formed a clear picture enough of what his persons are to do, there is still wanting the underlying thought, which he at moments dimly feels but cannot bring to light, and without which he is unable to fuse the materials into readiness for the mould.

Our only information as to the course of the story between April, 1858, and the time of writing "Septimius," must be gathered from a sketch found among the author's papers, the date of which it is not possible to determine with precision, though both its matter and form indicate that it must have been written subsequently to the journal above mentioned. Herein are curiously mingled certain features of both "Septimius" and the "Dolliver Romance." So far as is consistent with the essential privacy of the manuscript, I shall give a general outline of its contents. It consists of two sections, in the second of which a lapse of some years is implied. In the first of these chapters, for they hardly exceed that limit, the most prominent figure is that of a singular, morose old man, who inhabits a house overlooking a New England graveyard. But though his situation resembles in this particular that of Grandsir Dolliver, his characteristics resemble more those of Dr. Portsoaken. He is constantly accompanied, too, by brandy-and-water and a cloud-compelling pipe; and his study, like the doctor's chamber in "Septimius," is tapestried with spider-webs; a particularly virulent spider which dangles over his head, as he sits at his writing-desk, being made to assume the aspect of a devilish familiar. On the other hand, his is a far richer and less debased nature than that of Portsoaken. Hawthorne appears subsequently to have divided him, straining off from the rank sediments which settle into the character of Dr. Portsoaken the clear sweetness of good Grandsir Dolliver. This "grim doctor," as he is almost invariably styled in the manuscript, seems to have originated in Hawthorne's knowledge of a Mr. Kirkup, painter, spiritualist and antiquarian, of Florence,* who also probably stood as a model for Grandsir Dolliver. Not that either of these personages is copied from Mr. Kirkup; but the personality and surroundings of this quaint old gentleman had some sort of affinity with the author's idea, which led him to maintain a certain likeness between him and his

* French and Italian Note-Books, Vol. II.

own fictitious persons. As in the case of the Florentine antiquary, a little girl dwells in the house of the doctor, her chief playmate being, like that of Mr. Kirkup's adopted daughter, a very beautiful Persian kitten. There is much about her like Pansie, of the "Dolliver" fragment, but she is still only dimly brought out. The boy is described as of superior nature, but strangely addicted to revery. Though his traits are but slightly indicated, he suggests in general the character of Septimius, and may very easily have grown into him, at a later period. At first he is much neglected by the doctor, but afterwards, by resolute and manly behavior in questioning his mysterious guardian as to his own origin, and the connection subsisting between them, he secures greater consideration. The doctor gradually hints to him the fact of his descent from an old English family, and frequent mention is made of the ancestral hall, the threshold of which is stained by the imprint of a bloody footstep marking the scene of some dark tragedy, which, in the superstitious haze thrown over it by time, assumes various and uncertain forms. At different times two strangers are introduced, who appear to have some obscure knowledge of, and connection with, the ghastly footstep; and, finally, a headstone is discovered in the neighboring cemetery, marking the spot where an old man had been buried many years since, and engraved with the likeness of a foot. The grave has been recently opened to admit a new occupant, and the children, in playing about it, discover a little silver key, which the doctor, so soon as it is shown him, pockets, with the declaration that it is of no value. After this, the boy's education is taken in hand by his being sent to school; but presently the doctor sickens of life, and characteristically resolving to abandon brandy-drinking, and die, does so accordingly. Mention has previously been made of certain papers which he had kept in a secret place, and these the youth now secures. The second part describes his advent into England. He soon makes his way to the old hall, but just as his connection with it and its inmates begins, the manuscript terminates.

It will be noticed that in this fragment the scene is at first laid in New England, whereas the journalized sketch opened the drama in England. From this I infer that the former was written after the return to this country. "The Marble Faun" appropriated the author's attention, after the sketch of 1858; and in this, which was probably written just before the commencement of the war, he had not yet clearly struck the key-note of the story. When he recurred to it, in the autumn of 1861, on beginning to "blot successive sheets as of yore," it was at last with the definite design of uniting the legend of the deathless man with the legend of Smithell's Hall. It is as if, having left England, he could no longer write an English romance, but must give the book mainly an American coloring again. There is a pathetic interest, too, in his thus wavering between the two countries, which now so nearly equally divided his affections, and striving to unite the Wayside with the far-off English manor. Under the new design, everything began to fall into place. The deathless man was made the hero; the English inheritance became an inferior motive-power, on which, however, the romantic action depends; the family papers and the silver key came well to hand for the elucidation of the plot; the bloody footstep gained a new and deep significance; and a "purple everlasting flower," presented in 1854 to Mrs. Hawthorne by the gardener of Eaton Hall, blossomed out, with supernatural splendor, as a central point in the design. The scene being in

Concord, and the time of writing that of war, the Revolutionary association was natural. But the public phase of that epoch could not assume an important place : it was sunk into the background, forming merely a lurid field on which the figures of this most solemn and terrific of all Hawthorne's works stand out in portentous relief. One singular result of the historic location, however, is the use that was now made of that tradition which Lowell had told him at the Old Manse, concerning a boy who was chopping wood on the April morning of the famous fight, and found a wounded British soldier on the field, whom he killed with his axe. "Oftentimes, as an intellectual and moral exercise, I have sought to follow that poor youth through his subsequent career, and observe how his soul was tortured by the blood-stain. . . . . This one circumstance has borne more fruit for me than all that history tells us of the fight." Thus had he written, fourteen years before; and now that sombre study furnished him with the psychology of the death-scene in the beginning of " Septimius."

But the romance, even in this form, was again abandoned, as we learn from the prefatory note to Pierce in " Our Old Home," written in July, 1863. He there speaks of it as an "abortive project, utterly thrown aside," which "will never now be accomplished." In November of that year, "The Dolliver Romance" was announced for serial publication ; and in the first page of the isolated opening scene, published in July, 1864, occurs the mention of a certain potent cordial, from which the good doctor had received great invigoration, and which we may well suppose was destined to tincture the whole story. Another point from which a connection with " Septimius Felton " may perhaps be traced is the passing mention of Grandsir Dolliver's grandson Cornelius, by whom this cordial had been compounded, he having displayed a great efficiency with powerful drugs. Recalling that the author describes many nostrums as having been attributed to Septimius, which he had perhaps chanced upon in his unsuccessful attempts to distil the elixir of life, we may fairly conjecture this posthumous character of Cornelius, this mere memory, to be the remains of Septimius, who, it would seem, was to have been buried by the author under the splendid monument of a still more highly wrought and more aspiring form of the romance. The only remaining portions of this latest form have been printed, and are full of a silvery and resonant promise. Unquestionably it was to have been as much a "Romance of Immortality" as "Septimius"; and the exquisite contrast of the child Pansie — who promised to be the author's most captivating feminine creation — with the aged man, would no doubt have given us a theme of celestial loveliness, as compared with the forbidding and remorseless mournfulness of the preliminary work. In the manuscript sketch for "Septimius" there is a note referring to a description in the "English Note-Books" of two pine-trees at Lowood, on Windermere, "quite dead and dry, although they have the aspect of dark, rich life. But this is caused by the verdure of two great ivy-vines which have twisted round them like gigantic snakes, ... throttling the life out of them, ... and one feels that they have *stolen the life* that belonged to the pines." This does not seem to have been used; but the necessity of some life being stolen in order to add to any other life more than its share, is an idea that very clearly appears in the romance. In "Dolliver" the same strain of feeling would probably have reappeared; but it would there perhaps have been beautified, softened, expiated by the mutual love of Pansie and the grandsire;

each wishing to live forever, for the other. Even in "Septimius" we can discern Hawthorne standing upon the wayside hill-top, and, through the turbid medium of the unhappy hero, tenderly diffusing the essence of his own concluding thoughts on art and existence. Like Mozart, writing what he felt to be a requiem for his own death, like Mozart, too, throwing down the pen in midmost of the melody, leaving the strain unfinished, he labors on, prescient of the overhanging doom. Genial and tender at times, amidst their sadness, his reveries are nevertheless darkened by the shadow of coming death; and it is not until the opening of "The Dolliver Romance" that the darkness breaks away. Then, indeed, we feel once more the dewy freshness of the long-past prime, with a radiance unearthly fair, besides, of some new, undreamed-of morning. He who has gone down into the dark valley appears for a brief space with the light of the heavenly city on his countenance. Ah, prophet, who spoke but now so sadly, what is this new message that we see brightening on your lips? Will it solve the riddle of sin and beauty, at last? We listen intently; we seem to lean out a little way from earth.

Only an eddying silence! And yet the air seems even now alive with his last words.

XI.

PERSONALITY.

WHAT has thus far been developed in this essay, concerning Hawthorne's personality, though incidental, has, I hope, served the end in view, — that of suggesting a large, healthy nature, capable of the most profound thought and the most graceful and humorous mental play. The details of his early life already given show how soon the inborn honor of his nature began to shine. The small irregularities in his college course have seemed to me to bring him nearer and to endear him, without in any way impairing the dignity and beauty of character which prevailed in him from the beginning. It is good to know that he shared the average human history in these harmless peccadilloes; for they never hurt his integrity, and they are reminders of that old but welcome truth, that the greatest men do not need a constant diet of great circumstances. He had many difficulties to deal with, as unpicturesque and harassing as any we have to encounter in our daily courses, — a thing which people are curiously prone to forget in the case of eminent authors. The way in which he dealt with these throws back light on himself. We discover how well the high qualities of genius were matched by those of character.

Fragmentary anecdotes have a value, but so relative that to attempt to construct the subject's character out of them is hazardous. Conceptions of a man derived only from such matter remind one of Charles Lamb's ghosts, formed of the particles which, every seven years, are replaced throughout the body by new ones. Likewise, the grossest errors have been committed through the assumption that particular passages in Hawthorne's writings apply directly and unqualifiedly to himself. There is so much imagination interfused with them, that only a reverent and careful imagination can apply them aright. Nor are private letters to be interpreted in any other way than as the talk of the hour, very inadequately representative, and often — unless read in many lights — positively untrue, to the writer. It gives an entirely false notion, for example, to accept as a trait of character this modest covering up of a noble sentiment, which occurs in a letter refusing to withdraw the dedication of "Our Old Home" to Pierce, in the time of the latter's unpopularity : —

"Nevertheless, I have no fancy for making myself a martyr when it is honorably and conscientiously possible to avoid it ; and I always measure out my heroism very accurately according to the exigencies of the occasion, and should be the last man in the world to throw away a bit of it needlessly."

Such a passage ought never to have been printed without some modifying word ; for it has been execrably misused. "I have often felt," Hawthorne says, "that words may be a thick and darksome veil of mystery between the soul and the truth which it seeks." What injustice, then, that he should be judged by a literal construction of words quickly chosen for the transient embodiment of a mood !

The first and most common opinion about the man Hawthorne is, that he must have been extremely gloomy, because his mind nourished so many grave thoughts and solemn fancies. But this merely proves that, as he himself says, when people think he is pouring himself out in a tale or an essay, he is merely telling what is common to human nature, not what is peculiar to himself. "I sympathize with them, not they with me." He sympathizes in the special direction of our darker side. A creative mind of the higher order holds the thread which guides it surely through life's labyrinths; but all the more on this account its attention is called to the erratic movement of other travellers around it. The genius who has the clew begins, therefore, to study these errors and to describe them for our behoof. It is a great mistake to suppose that the abnormal or preposterous phases which he describes are the fruit of *self*-study, — personal traits disguised in fiction; yet this is what has often been affirmed of Hawthorne. We don't think of attributing to Dickens the multiform oddities which he pictures with such power, it being manifestly absurd to do so. As Dickens raises the laugh against them, we at once perceive that they are outside of himself. Hawthorne is so serious, that we are absorbed in the sober earnest of the thing, and forget to apply the rule in his case. Dickens's distinct aim is to excite us with something uncommon; Hawthorne's, to show us that the elements of all tragedies lie within our individual natures; therefore we begin to attribute in undue measure to *his* individual nature all the abnormal conditions that he has shown to be potential in any of us. But in truth he was a perfectly healthy person.

"You are, intellectually speaking, quite a puzzle to me," his friend George Hillard wrote to him, once. "How comes it that, with so thoroughly healthy an organization as you have, you have such a taste for the morbid anatomy of the human heart, and such a knowledge of it, too ? I should fancy, from your books, that you were burdened with some secret sorrow, that you had some blue chamber in your soul, into which you hardly dared to enter yourself; but when I see you, you give me the impression of a man as healthy as Adam in Paradise."

This very healthiness was his qualification for his office. By virtue of his mental integrity and absolute moral purity, he was able to handle unhurt all disintegrated and sinful forms of character; and when souls in trouble, persons with moral doubts to solve and criminals wrote to him for counsel, they recognized the healing touch of one whose pitying immaculateness could make them well.

She who knew best his habitual tone through a sympathy such as has rarely been given to any man, who lived with him a life so exquisitely fair and high, that to speak of it publicly is almost irreverent, has written : —

" He had the inevitable pensiveness and gravity of a person who possessed what a friend has called his ' awful power of insight'; but his mood was always cheerful and equal, and his mind peculiarly healthful, and the airy splendor of his wit and humor was the light of his home. He saw too far to be despondent, though his vivid sympathies and shaping imagination often made him sad in behalf of others. He also perceived morbidness wherever it existed instantly, as if by the illumination of his own steady cheer."

His closest friends, too, speak with delight of his genial warmth and ease in converse with them. He could seldom talk freely with more than two or three, however, on account of his constitutional shyness, and perhaps of a peculiarly concentrative cast of mind; though he possessed a ready adaptability. "I talk with everybody: to Mrs. T—— good sense; to Mary, good sense, with a mixture of fun; to Mrs. G——, sentiment, romance, and nonsense." * A gentleman who was with him at Brook Farm, and knew him well, tells me that his presence was very attractive, and that he inspired great esteem among all at the farm by his personal qualities. On a walking trip to Wachusett, which they once made together, Hawthorne showed a great interest in sitting in the bar-rooms of country taverns, to listen to the talk of the attendant farmers and villagers. The manner in which he was approached had a great deal to do with his response. If treated simply and wisely, he would answer cordially; but he was entirely dismayed, as a rule, by those who made demonstrations of admiration or awe. "Why do they treat me so?" he asked a friend, in one case of this sort. "Why, they're afraid of you." "But I tremble at *them*," he said. "They think," she explained, "that you're imagining all sorts of terrible things." "Heavens!" he answered; "if they only knew what I *do* think about." At one time, when he was visiting this same friend, he was obliged to return some calls, and his companion in the midst of conversation left him to continue it. He had previously asked his hostess, in assumed terror, what he should talk about, and she advised "climate." Accordingly, he turned to the naval officer whom he was calling upon, and asked him if he had ever been to the Sandwich Islands. "The man started," he said, on returning, "as if he had been struck. He had evidently been there and committed some terrible crime, which my allusion recalled. I had made a frightful mess of it. B—— led me away to the door." This

* American Note-Books, 1837.

woful account was, of course, an imaginary and symbolical representation of the terrors which enforced conversation caused him ; the good officer's surprise at the abrupt introduction of a new subject had supplied him with the ludicrous suggestion. Mr. Curtis has given an account of his demeanor on another occasion : —

"I had driven up with some friends to an æsthetic tea at Mr. Emerson's. It was in the winter, and a great wood-fire blazed upon the hospitable hearth. There were various men and women of note assembled ; and I, who listened attentively to all the fine things that were said, was for some time scarcely aware of a man who sat upon the edge of the circle, a little withdrawn, his head slightly thrown forward upon his breast, and his black eyes [' black ' is an error] clearly burning under his black brow. As I drifted down the stream of talk, this person, who sat silent as a shadow, looked to me as Webster might have looked had he been a poet, — a kind of poetic Webster. He rose and walked to the window, and stood there quietly for a long time, watching the dead-white landscape. No appeal was made to him, nobody looked after him ; the conversation flowed steadily on, as if every one understood that his silence was to be respected. It was the same thing at table. In vain the silent man imbibed æsthetic tea. Whatever fancies it inspired did not flower at his lips. But there was a light in his eye which assured me nothing was lost. So supreme was his silence, that it presently engrossed me, to the exclusion of everything else. There was very brilliant discourse, but this silence was much more poetic and fascinating. Fine things were said by the philosophers, but much finer things were implied by the dumbness of this gentleman with heavy brows and black hair. When he presently rose and went, Emerson, with the 'slow, wise smile' that breaks over his face like day over the sky, said, ' Hawthorne rides well his horse of the night.' "

He was not a lover of argumentation. " His principle

seemed to be, if a man cannot understand without talking to him, it is useless to talk, because it is immaterial
whether such a man understands or not."   And the same
writer says : —

> " His own sympathy was so broad and sure, that, although
> nothing had been said for hours, his companion knew that not a
> thing had escaped his eye, nor a single pulse of beauty in the
> day, or scene, or society, failed to thrill his heart.   In this way
> his silence was most social.   Everything seemed to have been
> said."

I am told that in his own home, though he was often
silent, it was never with sadness except in seasons of
great illness in the house, the prevailing effect of his manner being usually that of a cheerful and almost humorous
calm.   Mr. Curtis gives perhaps one of the best descriptions of his aspect, when he speaks of his " glimmering
smile " ; and of his atmosphere, when he says that at
Emerson's house it seemed always morning, but at
Hawthorne's you passed into

> " A land in which it seeméd always afternoon."

Hawthorne's personal appearance is said by those who
knew him to have been always very impressive.   He was
tall and strongly built, with beautiful and lustrous gray-
blue eyes, and luxuriant dark brown hair of great softness, which grew far back from his forehead, as in the
early engraved portrait of him.   His skin had a peculiar
fineness and delicacy, giving unusual softness to his
complexion.   After his Italian sojourn he altered much,
his hair having begun to whiten, and a thick dark mus-
tache being permitted to grow, so that a wit described
him as looking like a " boned pirate."   When it became imperative to shake off his reticence, he seems
to have had the power of impressing as much by

speech as he had before done by silence. It was the same abundant, ardent, but self-contained and perfectly balanced nature that informed either phase. How commanding was this nature may be judged from the fact related of him by an acquaintance, that rude people jostling him in a crowd would give way at once "at the sound of his low and almost irresolute voice." The occasions on which he gave full vent to his indignation at anything were very rare; but when these came, he manifested a strength of sway only to be described as regal. Without the least violence, he brought a searching sternness to bear that was utterly overwhelming, carrying as it did the weight of perfect self-control. Something even of the eloquent gift of old Colonel Hathorne seemed to be locked within him, like a precious heirloom rarely shown; for in England, where his position called for speech-making, he acquitted himself with brilliant honor. But the effort which this compelled was no doubt quite commensurate with the success. He never shrank, notwithstanding, from effort, when obligation to others put in a plea. A member of his family has told me that, when talking to any one not congenial to him, the effect of the contact was so strong as to cause an almost physical contraction of his whole stalwart frame, though so slight as to be perceptible only to eyes that knew his habitual and informal aspects; yet he would have sunk through the floor rather than betray his sensations to the person causing them. Mr. Curtis, too, records the amusement with which he watched Hawthorne paddling on the Concord River with a friend whose want of skill caused the boat continually to veer the wrong way, and the silent generosity with which he put forth his whole strength to neutralize the error, rather than mortify his companion by an explanation. His considerateness was always delicate and alert, and has left in his family a reverence for qualities that have certainly never been surpassed and not often equalled in sweetness.

He was simple in his habits, and fond of being out of doors, but not — after his college days — as a sportsman. While living beside the Concord, he rowed frequently, with a dreamy devotion to the pastime, and was fond of fishing; swimming, too, he enjoyed. But his chief exercise was walking; he had a vast capacity for it, and was, I think, never even seen upon horseback. At Brook Farm he "belabored the rugged furrows" with a will; and at the Old Manse he presided over his garden in a paradisiacal sort of way. Books in every form he was always eager for, sometimes, as has been reported, satisfying himself with an old almanac or newspaper, over which he would brood as deeply as over richly stored volumes of classic literature. At other times he was fastidious in his choice, and threw aside many books before he found the right one for the hour.* An impression has been set afloat that he cared nothing for books in themselves, but this is incorrect. He never had the

---

* He would attach himself to a book or a poem apparently by some law perceptible only to himself, perhaps often giving an interest by his own genius. A poem On Solitude, in Dryden's Miscellany, was at one time a special favorite with him. It begins : —

> " O Solitude, my sweetest choice,
> Places devoted to the Night,
> Remote from Tumult and from Noise,
> How you my restless thoughts delight ! "

And the last stanza has these lines : —

> " O, how I solitude adore,
> That element of noblest wit,
> Where I have learned Apollo's lore,
> Without the pains to study it."

means to accumulate a library of any size, but he had a passion for books.

"There yet lingers with me a superstitious reverence for literature of all kinds," he writes in "The Old Manse." "A bound volume has a charm in my eyes similar to what scraps of manuscript possess for the good Mussulman; . . . . every new book or antique one may contain the 'open sesame,' — the spell to disclose treasures hidden in some unsuspected cave of Truth."

When he lived at the Wayside, and would occasionally bring home a small package of books from Boston, these furnished him fresh pleasure for many days. He would carry some favorite of them with him everywhere, from room to room or to his hill-top. He was, as we have seen, a cordial admirer of other writers, seldom vexing himself with a critical review of their merits and defects, but applying to them instead the test of his own catholic capacity for enjoyment. The deliberate tone in which he judges his own works, in his letters, shows how little his mind was impressed by the greatness of their fame and of the genius found in them. There could not have been a more modest author, though he did not weakly underrate his work. "Recognition," he once said to Mr. Howells, "makes a man very modest."

An attempt has also been made to show that he had little interest in animals, partly based, ludicrous as it may seem, on his bringing them into only one of his books. In his American journals, however, there is abundant evidence of his acute sympathy in this direction; at the Old Manse he fried fish for his dog Leo, when he says he should not have done it for himself; and in the Trosachs he finds a moment for pitying some little lambs startled by the approach of his party.* I have already

* English Note-Books (May, 1856).

mentioned his fondness for cats. It has further been said that he did not enjoy wild nature, because in the "English Note-Books" there is no outgushing of ecstatic description. But in fact he had the keenest enjoyment of it. He could not enter into the spectacle when hurrying through strange regions. Among the English lakes he writes : —

"To say the truth, I was weary of fine scenery, and it seemed to me that I had eaten a score of mountains and quaffed as many lakes, all in the space of two or three days, and the natural consequence was a surfeit.

"I doubt if anybody ever does really see a mountain, who goes for the set and sole purpose of seeing it. Nature will not let herself be seen in such cases. You must patiently bide her time; and by and by, at some unforeseen moment, she will quietly and suddenly unveil herself and for a brief space allow you to look right into the heart of her mystery. But if you call out to her peremptorily, 'Nature! unveil yourself this very moment!' she only draws her veil the closer; and you may look with all your eyes, and imagine that you see all that she can show, and yet see nothing."

But this was because his sensibility was so great that he drew from little things a larger pleasure than many feel when excited by grand ones; and knowing this deeper phase, he could not be content with the hasty admiration on which tourists flatter themselves. The beauty of a scene which he could absorb in peace was never lost upon him. Every year the recurrent changes of season filled him with untold pleasure; and in the spring, Mrs. Hawthorne has been heard to say, he would walk with her in continuous silence, his heart full of the awe and delight with which the miracle of buds and new verdure inspired him. Nothing could be more accurate or sensi-

AT THE END

tive than the brief descriptions of nature in his works. But there is nothing sentimental about them; partly owing to the Anglo-Saxon instinct which caused him to seek precise and detailed statement first of all, and partly because of a certain classic, awe-inspired reserve, like that of Horace and Virgil.

There was a commendable indolence in his character. It was not a constitutional weakness, overcoming will, but the instinctive precaution of a man whose errand it was to rise to great emergencies of exertion. He always waited for an adequate mood, before writing. But these intervals, of course, were richly productive of revery which afterward entered into the creative moments. He would sometimes become deeply abstracted in imagination; and while he was writing "The Scarlet Letter" it is related by a trustworthy person that, sitting in the room where his wife was doing some sewing, he unconsciously took up a part of the work and cut it into minute fragments with the scissors, without being aware that he had done so. At some previous time, he had in the same way gradually chipped off with a knife portions of a table, until the entire folding-leaf was worn away by the process. The opinion was sometimes advanced by him that without a certain mixture of uncongenial labor he might not have done so much with the pen; but in this he perhaps underestimated the leisure in his blood, which was one of the elements of his power. Men of smaller calibre are hollowed out by the fire of ideas, and decay too quickly; but this trait preserved him from such a fate. Combined with his far-reaching foresight, it may have had something to do with his comparative withdrawal from practical affairs other than those which necessity connected him with. Of Holgrave he writes: —

"His error lay in supposing that this age more than any past or future one is destined to see the garments of antiquity exchanged for a new suit, instead of gradually renewing themselves by patchwork; .... and more than all, in fancying that it mattered anything to the great end in view whether he himself should contend for it or against it."

The implied opinion of the author, here, is not that of a fatalist, but of an optimist (if we must connect him with any "ism") who has a very profound faith in Providence; not in any "special providence," but in that operation of divine laws through unexpected agencies and conflicting events, which is very gradually approximating human affairs to a state of truthfulness. Hawthorne was one of the great believers of his generation; but his faith expressed itself in the negative way of showing how fragile are the ordinary objects of reverence in the world, how subject the best of us are to the undermining influence of very great sin; and, on the other hand, how many traits of good there are, by consequence, even in the worst of us. This, however, is a mere skeleton statement: the noblest element in his mood is that he believes with his heart. A good interpreter has said that he *feels* with his *brain*, and *thinks* with his *heart*, to show the completeness with which he mingled the two elements in his meditations on existence. A warm, pure, living sympathy pervaded all his analysis of mankind, without which that analysis would have taken no hold upon us. It is a crude view which reckons him to have been wanting in moral enthusiasm: he had not that kind which can crush out sympathy with suffering, for the sake of carrying out an idea. Perhaps in some cases this was a fault; but one cannot dwell on the mistaken side of such a phase, when it possesses another side so full of beneficent aid to humanity. And it must be remembered that with all this susceptibility, he was not a suffering poet, like Shelley, but distinctly an endurer. His moral enthusiasm was deeper than that of any scheme or system.

His distaste for society has been declared to proceed from the fact that, when he once became interested in people, he could no longer chemically resolve them into material for romance. But this assumption is also erroneous; for Hawthorne, if he felt it needful, could bring to bear upon his best friends the same qualitative measuring skill that he exercised on any one. I do not doubt that he knew where to place his friends and acquaintance in the scale of relative excellence. All of us who have not an equal analytic power with his own can at least reverence his discretion so far as to believe that he had stand-points not open to every one, from which he took views often more essentially just than if he had assumed a more sweeping estimate. In other cases, where he bestowed more friendship and confidence than the object of them especially deserved, he no doubt sought the simple pleasure of accepting what circumstances offered him. He was not a suspicious person; although, in fear of being fooled by his fancy, he cultivated what he often spoke of to a friend as "morose common-sense," deeming it a desirable alloy. There was even, in many relations, an unquestioning trust on his part; for he might well be called

> "As the greatest only are,
> In his simplicity sublime."

The connection between Pierce and himself involved too many considerations to make it possible to pass them with indifference; and he perhaps condemned certain public acts of the President, while feeling it to be utter disloyalty to an old friend to discuss these mis-

takes with any one.   As to other slighter connections, it
is very likely he did not take the trouble that might have
saved him from being imposed upon.

But it is impossible to define Hawthorne's personality
precisely.   A poet's whole effort is to indirectly express
this, by expressing the effect of things upon him; and
we may read much of Hawthorne in his books, if we
have the skill.   But it is very clear that he put only a
part of himself into them; that part which best served
the inexorable law of his genius for treating life in a given
light.   For the rest, his two chapters on "The Custom-
House" and "The Old Manse" show us something of
his mode of taking daily affairs.   But his real and inmost
character was a mystery even to himself, and this, because he felt so profoundly the impossibility of sounding
to the bottom any human heart.   "A cloudy veil stretches
over the abyss of my nature," he writes, at one time.
"I have, however, no love of secrecy or darkness."   At
another time: "Lights and shadows are continually flitting across my inward sky, and I know neither whence
they come nor whither they go; nor do I look too closely
into them."   A mind so conscious as his of the slight
reality of appearances would be dissatisfied with the few
tangible qualities which are all of himself that a man can
discern: at the same time he would hesitate to probe the
deeper self assiduously, for fear of turning his searching
gaze too intently within, and thus becoming morbid.   In
other persons, however, he could perceive a contour, and
pursue his study of investigation from without inward,
— a more healthy method.   His *instinctive* knowledge
of himself, being brought into play, would of course aid
him.   Incidentally, then, something of himself comes to
light in his investigation of others.   And it is perhaps
this inability to define their own natures, except by a

roundabout method, which is the creative impulse of all great novelists and dramatists. I doubt whether many of the famous delineators of character could give us a very distinct account of their own individualities; and if they did, it would probably make them out the most uninteresting of beings. It would certainly be divested of the special charm of their other writing. Imagine Dickens clearly accounting for himself and his peculiar traits: would he be able to excite even a smile? How much of his own delicious personality could Thackeray have described without losing the zest of his other portraitures? Hawthorne has given a kind of picture of himself in Coverdale, and was sometimes called after that character by his friends; but I suspect he has adroitly constructed Coverdale out of the *appearance* which he knew himself to make in the eyes of associates. I do not mean that Hawthorne had not a very decisive personality; for indeed he had. But the essence of the person cannot be compressed into a few brief paragraphs, and must be slowly drawn in as a pervasive elixir from his works, his letters, his note-books. In the latter he has given as much definition of his interior self as we are likely to get, for no one else can continue the broken jottings that he has left, and extend them into outlines. We shall not greatly err if we treat the hidden depths of his spirit with as much reverence as he himself used in scrutinizing them. Curiously enough, many of those who have studied this most careful and delicate of definers have embraced the madness of attempting to bind him down in unhesitating, absolute statements. He who mastered words so completely that he learned to despise their obscurity, has been made the victim of easy epithets and a few conventional phrases. But none can ever be said to know Hawthorne who do not leave large allowances for the unknowable.

XII.

POE, IRVING, HAWTHORNE.

THE names of Poe, Irving, and Hawthorne have been so often connected without due discrimination, that it is imperative to consider here the actual relation between the three men. Inquiry might naturally be roused by the circumstance that, although Hawthorne has freely been likened to Irving in some quarters, and in others to Poe, the latter two are never supposed to hold anything in common. Indeed, they might aptly be cited in illustration of the widely opposed tendencies already developed in our brief national literature. Two things equal to the same thing are equal to each other; and if Poe and Irving were each equal to Hawthorne, there would be some similarity between them. But it is evident that they are not like quantities; and we must conclude that they have been unconsciously used by critics, in trying to find a unit of measure to gauge the greatest of the triad with.

Undoubtedly there are resemblances in Hawthorne to both Poe and Irving. Hawthorne and Irving represent a dignity and roundedness of diction which is one of the old-fashioned merits in English writing; and because they especially, among eminent authors of the century, have stood for this quality, they have been supposed to stand close together. But Irving's speech is not so much an organic part of his genius as a preconceived method of expression which has a considerable share in modifying his thought. It is rather a manner than a style. On the other hand, it would be hard to find a style growing so naturally and strongly out of elemental attributes as Hawthorne's, so deftly waiting upon the slightest movement of idea, at once disclosing and lightly veiling the informing thought, — like the most delicate sculptured marble drapery. The radical differences of the two men were also obscured in the beginning by the fact that Hawthorne did not for some time exhibit that massive power of hewing out individual character which afterward had full swing in his romances, and by a certain kinship of fancy in his lighter efforts, with Irving's. "The Art of Book-Making" and "The Mutability of Literature" are not far removed from some of Hawthorne's conceits. And "The Vision of the Fountain" and "The Village Uncle" might have issued in their soft meditativeness from Geoffrey Crayon's own repertory, except that they are moulded with a so much more subtile art than his, and with an instinct of proportion so much more sure. But even in the earlier tales, taken all together, Hawthorne ranks higher than Irving in the heraldry of genius : he has more quarterings in his shield. Not only does he excel the other in brief essay, depending only on endogenous forces, whereas Irving is always adorning his paragraphs with that herb-o'-grace, quotation, but he also greatly surpasses him in the construction of his stories; and finally, his psychological analysis and symbolic imagination place him beyond rivalry. It is a brilliant instance of the more ideal mind asserting its commanding power, by admirable achievements in the in-

ferior styles, — so that even in those he was at once
ranked with the most famous practiser of them, — and
then quietly reaching out and grasping a higher order of
truths, which no one had even thought of competing for.
I suppose it is not assumed for a moment that "Wolfert's
Roost," the "Tales of a Traveller," the story of "Rip
Van Winkle," the "Legend of Sleepy Hollow," and the
picturesque but evanescent tales of "The Alhambra"
can be brought into discussion on the same terms with
Hawthorne's romances, as works of art; and they assuredly cannot be as studies of character, for of this
they have next to nothing.   The only phases of character which Irving has any success in dealing with are
those of credulity and prejudice.   The legendary tendency of the two men has perhaps confused some readers.
Both were lovers of association, and turned naturally
to the past for materials : the New-Yorker found delightful sources of tradition or of ludicrous invention
in the past of that city, where his family held a long-
established and estimable footing ; and the New-Englander, as we have seen, drew also through the channel
of descent from the dark tarn of Puritan experience.
But Irving turned his back upon everything else when
he entered the tapestried chamber of the past, while
Hawthorne sought that vantage-ground only to secure a
more impressive view of humanity.   There is one gift of
Irving's which won him an easier as well as a wider
triumph than that which awaited Hawthorne ; and this
is his ability to take the simple story-teller's tone, devoid
of double meanings.   Poe, also, had the passion for
narrative in and for itself, but in him it was disturbed by
a diseased mind, and resulted in a horrid fascination instead of cheerful attraction.   Hawthorne, to be sure,
possessed the gift of the *raconteur ;* but in general he

was at once seer and teller, and the higher exertions
of his imagination were always in the peculiarly symbolic
atmosphere we are wont to associate with him. Irving's
contented disposition in this regard is certainly very
charming; there are often moods in which it is a great
relief to turn to it; and he has in so far the advantage
over the other two. He pitches for us the tone of average cultured minds in his time and locality; and in reading him we have a comfortable sense of reality, than
which nothing in fiction is more reassuring. This is almost entirely absent from the spell with which Hawthorne holds us; and here, indeed, we touch the latter's
most decided limitation as a writer of fiction; for although
his magnificently portrayed characters do not want reality, an atmosphere of ghostliness surrounds them, warning us that we must not look to find life there as we see
it elsewhere. There is a Northern legend of a man who
lay down to sleep, and a thin smoke was seen to issue
from his nostrils, traverse the ground, cross a rivulet,
and journey on, finally returning to the place whence
it came. When he awoke, he described an imaginary
excursion of his own, following exactly the course which
the smoke had taken. This indirect contact might furnish a partially true type of Hawthorne's mysterious
intercourse with the world through his books.

It would be a mistake, however, to attribute this difference to the greater strength of Irving's humor,—a trait
always much lauded in him. It is without doubt a good
quality. This mild, sweet radiance of an uncontaminated
and well-bred spirit is not a common thing in literature.
But I cannot fall in with the judgment that calls it "freer
and far more joyous" than Addison's. Both in style and
in humor Irving has caught something of the grace of
"The Spectator"; but as in the style he frequently falls

short, writing feeble or jarring sentences, so in humor I
cannot see how he is to be brought at all on a level with
Addison, who is primarily a grave, stately, scholarly mind,
but all the deeper on that account in the lustre of his
humorous displays.   Addison, too, had somewhat of the
poet in him, and was capable of tragedy as well as of neat
satire and compact characterization.   But if we looked
for a pithy embodiment of the difference between Irving
and Hawthorne, we might call the former a "polite
writer," and the latter a profound poet : as, indeed, I
have called him in this essay, though with no intent to
confuse the term with that given to poets who speak
in verse.   Pathos is the great touchstone of humor,
and Irving's pathos is always a lamentable failure.   Is
it not very significant, that he should have made so
little of the story of Rip Van Winkle?   In his sketch,
which has won so wide a fame and given a lasting
association to the Kaatskills, there is not a suspicion
of the immense pathos which the skill of an industrious
playwright and the genius of that rare actor, Mr. Jefferson, have since developed from the tale.   The Dame Van
Winkle that we now know is the creation of Mr. Bouci-
cault; to him it is we owe that vigorous character, — a
scold, a tyrant to her husband, but nevertheless full of
relentful womanliness, and by the justice of her cause
exciting our sympathy almost as much as Rip himself
does.   In the story, she wears an aspect of singular
causelessness, and Rip's devotion to the drinking-can is
barely hinted : the marvellous tenderness, too, and joyful
sorrow of his return after the twenty years' sleep, are
apparently not even suspected by the writer.   It is the
simple wonder and picturesqueness of the situation that
charm him ; and while in the drama we are moved to the
bottom of our hearts by the humorous tragicalness it

casts over the spectacle of conflicting passions, the only outcome of the written tale is a passing reflection on the woe of being henpecked. "And it is a common wish of all henpecked husbands in the neighborhood, when life hangs heavy on their hands, that they might have a quieting draught out of Rip Van Winkle's flagon." To be sure, there is a hidden moral here, of the folly of driving men to drunkenness; but it is so much obscured as to suggest that this was of small moment in the writer's mind. Such a moral, in any case, must necessarily have been very delicately advanced, in order not to becloud the artistic atmosphere; but a person of searching dramatic genius would have found means to emphasize it without injury to art, just as it has been done on the stage. Imagine what divine vibrations of emotion Hawthorne would have smitten out of this theme, had he been the originator of it. Certainly we should, as the case stands, have missed the whole immortal figment, had not Irving given it to us in germ; the fact that our playwright and our master comedian have made it so much greater and more beautiful does not annul that primary service; but, looking at the matter historically, we must admit that Irving's share in the credit is that of the first projector of a scientific improvement, and the latter sort of person always has to forego a great part of his fame in favor of the one who consummates the discovery. I am willing to believe that there was a peculiar advantage in Irving's treatment; namely, that he secured for his story a quicker and more general acceptance than might have been granted to something more profound; but this does not alter the critical judgment that we have to pass upon it. If Irving had grasped the tragic sphere at all, he would have shone more splendidly in the comic. But the literary part of him, at least, never passed into the shade: it somehow contrived to be always on that side of the earth which was towards the sun. Observe, now, the vital office of humor in Hawthorne's thought. It gleams out upon us from behind many of the gravest of his conceptions, like the silver side of a dark leaf turning in the wind. Wherever the concretion of guilt is most adamantine, there he lets his fine slender jet of humor play like a lambent fire, until the dark mass crumbles, and the choragos of the tragedy begins his mournful yet hopeful chant among the ruins. This may be verified in the "Seven Gables," "Blithedale," and "The Marble Faun"; not in "The Scarlet Letter," for that does not present Hawthorne's genius in its widest action. In one place he speaks of "the tragic power of laughter," — a discrimination which involves the whole deep originality of his mind. It is not irrelevant here to remark that at the most affecting portions of the play "Rip Van Winkle," the majority of the audience always laugh; this, though irritating to a thoughtful listener, is really an involuntary tribute to the marvellous wisdom and perfection with which Jefferson mingles pathos and humor. Again Hawthorne : "Human destinies look *ominous* without some perceptible intermixture of the sable or the gray." And, elsewhere : "There is *something more awful in happiness than in sorrow*, the latter being earthly and finite, the former composed of the substance and texture of eternity, so that spirits still embodied may well tremble at it." These thoughts could never have occurred to Irving with the same intensity. Now, from all this we gather inference as to the deep sources of Hawthorne's humor. I sometimes think that Thalia was the daughter, and not the sister, of Melpomene. As to actual exhibition of humor, Hawthorne's is made a diffusive medium to temper the rays of tragedy with, and

never appears in such unmixed form as that of Irving.
So that even though we must confess a smaller mental
calibre in the latter, we may gladly grant him a superiority in his special mood of fun.

An excellent English critic, Leslie Stephen, lately
wrote: " Poe is a kind of Hawthorne and *delirium
tremens*." This announcement, however, betrays a singular misapprehension. When Hawthorne's tales first
appeared, they were almost invariably taken to bear an
intimate and direct relation to the author's own moods;
while Poe's were supposed to be daring flights of pure
imagination, or ingenious attempts to prove theories held
by the writer, but were not charged directly to his own
experience. Time has shown that the converse was the
case. The psychical conditions described by Hawthorne
had only the remotest connection with any mood of his
own; they were mainly translations, into the language
of genius, of certain impressions and observations drawn
from the world around him. After his death, the Note-
Books caused a general rustle of surprise, revealing as
they did the simple, wholesome nature of this strange
imaginer; yet though he there speaks — surely without prejudice, because without the least knowledge that
the world would ever hear him — of "the objectivity"
of his fictions, critics have not yet wholly learned how
far apart from himself these creations were. The observation of some mental habit in men, or law of intercourse between human beings, would strongly present
itself to him; and in order to get a concise embodiment,
his genius planned some powerful situation to illustrate it with; or, at another time it might be that a
strange incident, like that of Mr. Moody, suggesting
"The Minister's Black Veil," or a singular physiological
fact like that on which "The Bosom Serpent" is based,

would call out his imagination to run a race with reality and outstrip it in touching the goal of truth. But, the conception once formed, the whole fictitious fabric would become entirely removed from *himself*, except so far as it touched him very incidentally; and this expulsion of the idea from himself, so that it acquires a life and movement of its own, and can be contemplated by the artist from the outside, is the very distinction between deeply creative and merely inventive genius. Poe's was of the latter sort. He possessed a wild, arbitrary imagination, that sometimes leaped frantically high; but his impressiveness is always that of a nightmare, always completely morbid. What we know of Poe's life leads inevitably to the conclusion that this quality, if it did not spring from disease, was at least largely owing to it. For a time, it was the fashion to make a moral question of Poe's unfortunate obliquities; but a more humane tendency reduces it to a scientific problem. Poe suffered great disaster at the hands of his unjust biographer; yet he was a worse enemy to himself than any one else could be. The fine enamel of his genius is all corroded by the deadly acid of his passions. The imperfections of his temperament have pierced his poetry and prose, shattered their structure, and blurred their beauty. Only four or five of his poems — "The Raven," "Ligeia," the earlier of the two addressed "To Helen," and the sonnet to his wife — escape being flawed by some fit of haste, some ungovernable error of taste, some hopeless, unaccountable break in their beauty. In criticism, Poe initiated a fearless and agile movement; he had an acute instinct in questions of literary form, amounting to a passion, as all his instincts and perceptions did; he had also the knack of finding clever reasons, good or bad, for all his opinions. These things are essential to a critic's equipment, and it was good

service in Poe to exemplify them. Yet here, too, the
undermining processes of his thoroughly unsound mind
subverted the better qualities, vitiated his judgments
with incredible jealousies and conflicting impulses, and
withered the most that he wrote in this direction into
something very like rubbish. We have seen, for example, how his attempt to dispassionately examine Hawthorne resulted. Sooner or later, too, he ran his own
pen full against his rigid criteria for others. It is suggestive to find that the holder of such exacting doctrine about beauty, the man also of whom pre-eminently it may be said, as Baudelaire wrote of him,
"Chance and the incomprehensible were his two great
enemies," should so completely fail to reach even the
unmoral perfection which he assigned as the highest
attainable. Professing himself the special apostle of the
beautiful in art, he nevertheless forces upon us continually the most loathsome hideousness and the most debasing and unbeautiful horror. This passionate, unhelmed,
errant search for beauty was in fact not so much a normal and intelligent desire, as an attempt to escape from
interior discord; and it was the discord which found expression, accordingly, instead of the sense of beauty, —
except (as has been said) in fragments. Whatever the
cause, his brain had a rift of ruin in it, from the start, and
though his delicate touch often stole a new grace from
classic antiquity, it was the frangibility, the quick decay,
the fall of all lovely and noble things, that excited and
engaged him. "I have imbibed the shadows of fallen
columns," he says in one of his tales, "at Balbec, and
Tadmor, and Persepolis, until my very soul has become a
ruin." Always beauty and grace are with him most
poetic in their overthrow, and it is the shadow of ruined
grandeur that he receives, instead of the still living light

so fair upon them, or the green growth clinging around them. Hawthorne, too, wandered much amid human ruin, but it was not with delight in the mere fact of decay; rather with grieving over it, and the hope to learn how much of life was still left in the wreck, and how future structures might be made stronger by studying the sources of failure. One of the least thoughtful remarks which I have heard touching Hawthorne was this, that his books could not live because they dealt with the "sick side" of human nature. As if great poets ever refrained from dealing with it! The tenure of fame depends on whether the writer has himself become infected with sickness. With Hawthorne this is most certainly not the case, for the morbid phases which he studied were entirely outside of himself. Poe, on the other hand, pictured his own half-maniacal moods and diseased fancies. There is absolutely no study of character in his stories, no dramatic separateness of being. He looks only for fixed and inert human quantities, with which he may juggle at will. He did not possess insight; and the analytic quality of which he was so proud was merely a sort of mathematical ingenuity of calculation, in which, however, he was extraordinarily keen. As a mere potency, dissociated from qualities, Poe must be rated almost highest among American poets, and high among prosaists; no one else offers so much pungency, such impetuous and frightful energy crowded into such small compartments. Yet it would be difficult to find a poetic fury less allied to sane human life than that which informs his tales. It is not the *representation* of semi-insanity that he gives : he himself is its *representative*. Instead of commanding it, and bringing it into some sort of healthy relation with us, he is swayed and carried away by it. His genius flourished upon him like a destructive flame, and the ashes that it left are like a deadly powdered poison. Clifford Pyncheon in the "Seven Gables" is Poe himself, deprived of the ability to act: in both are found the same consummate fastidiousness, the same abnormal egotism. And it is worth attention that when Clifford is aroused to sudden action by Judge Pyncheon's death, the coruscating play of his intellect is almost precisely that brilliant but defective kind of ratiocination which Poe so delights to display. It is crazy wildness, with a surface appearance of accurate and refined logic. In this fact, that Hawthorne — the calm, ardent, healthy master of imagination — is able to create the disordered type that Poe *is*, we shall find by how much the former is greater than the latter.

A recent writer has raised distinctly the medical question as to Poe. He calls him "the mad man of letters *par excellence*," and by an ingenious investigation seems to establish it as probable that Poe was the victim of a form of epilepsy. But in demonstrating this, he attempts to make it part of a theory that all men of genius are more or less given over to this same "veiled epilepsy." And here he goes beyond the necessities of the case, and takes up an untenable position. There is a morbid and shattering susceptibility connected with some genius; but that tremulous, constantly readjusted sensitiveness which indicates the perfect equilibrium of health in other minds must not be confounded with it. Such is the condition of the highest genius alone; of men like Shakespere and Hawthorne, who, however dissimilar their temperaments, grasp the two spheres of mind and character, the sane and the insane, and hold them perfectly reconciled by their gentle yet unsparing insight. A case like Poe's, where actual mental decay exists in so advanced a stage and gives to his productions a sharper and more dazzling effect than would have been theirs without it, is probably more unique, but it is certainly less admirable, less original in the true sense, than an instance of healthier endowment like Hawthorne. On the side of art, it is impossible to bring Poe into any competition with Hawthorne: although we have ranked him high in poetry and prose, regarded simply as a dynamic substance, it must be confessed that his prose has nothing which can be called style, nor even a manner like Irving's very agreeable one. His feeling for form manifests itself in various ways, yet he constantly violates proportion for the sake of getting off one of his pseudo-philosophical disquisitions; and, notwithstanding many successful hits in expression, and a specious but misleading assumption of fervid accuracy in phraseology, his language is loose, promiscuous, and altogether tiresome.

Poe, Irving, and Hawthorne have one marked literary condition in common: each shows a double side. With Poe the antithesis is between poetry and criticism; Irving, having been brought up by Fiction as a foster-mother, is eventually turned over to his rightful guardian, History; and Hawthorne rests his hand from ideal design, in elaborating quiet pictures of reality. In each case there is more or less seeming irreconcilement between the two phases found in combination; but the opposition is rather more distinct in Hawthorne, and the grasp with which it is controlled by him is stronger than that of either Poe or Irving, — again a result pronouncing him the master.

There is still another issue on which comparison must be made. The question of nationality will for some time to come be an interesting one in any discussion of American authors. The American character is so relative, that it is only by a long series of contrasts, a careful study of the registering-plate of literature, that we shall come to the point of defining it. American quality in literature is not like Greek, German, French, English quality : those are each unified, and their component elements stoutly enough welded together to make what may be called a positive impression; but *our* distinctions are relative. The nearest and most important means that we have for measuring them is that of comparison with England; and anything strikingly original in American genius is found to be permanent in proportion as it maintains a certain relation to English literature, not quite easy to define. It is not one of hostility, for the best American minds thus far have had the sincerest kindliness toward the mother country; it involves, however, the claiming of separate standards of judgment. The primary division, both in the case of the New England Pilgrims and in that of our Revolutionary patriots, was based on clearer perceptions of certain truths on the part of the cisatlantic English; and this claiming of separate standards in literature is a continuation of that historic attitude. We are making a perpetual minority report on the rest of the world, sure that in time our voice will be an authoritative one. The attitude being a relative and not very positively predicable one, a singular integrity of judgment is required in sustaining it. Of this Poe exhibits nothing. It was a part of the ingrained rebellion in him, that he revolted against the moneyed mediocracy of this country, — a position in which he deserves much sympathy, — and perhaps this underlies his want of deep literary identification with the national character in general. But more probably his genius was a detonating agent which could have been convulsed into its meet activity anywhere, and had nothing to do with a soil. It is significant that he

14

was taken up by a group of men in Paris, headed by Baudelaire and assisted by Théophile Gautier, as a sort of
private demigod of art; and I believe he stands in high
esteem with the Rossetti-Morris family of English poets.
Irving, on the other hand, comes directly upon the
ground of difference between the American and the
English genius, but it is with the colors of a neutral.
Irving's position was peculiar. He went to Europe
young, and ripened his genius under other suns than
those that imbrowned the hills of his native Hudson.
He had won success enough through "Salmagundi" and
"Knickerbocker's History" to give him the importance
of an accredited literary ambassador from the Republic,
in treating with a foreign audience; and he really did us
excellent service abroad. This alone secures him an important place in our literary history. Particularly wise
and dignified is the tone of his short chapter called "English Writers on America"; and this sentence from it
might long have served in our days of fairer fame as a
popular motto: "We have but to live on, and every day
we live a whole volume of refutation." His friendship
with Scott, also, was a delightful addition to the ameni-
ties of literature, and shall remain a goodly and refreshing memory to us always. Yet what he accomplished in
this way for American literature at large, Irving compensated for with some loss of his own dignity. It cannot
be denied that the success of "The Sketch-Book" led to
an overdoing of his part in "Bracebridge Hall." "Salmagundi" was the first step in the path of palpable
imitation of Addison's "Spectator"; in "The Sketch-
Book," though taking some charming departures, the
writer made a more refined attempt to produce the same
order of effects so perfectly attained by the suave Queen
Anne master; and in "Bracebridge Hall" the recollec-

tion of the Sir Roger de Coverley papers becomes
positively annoying. It is not that the style of Addison is precisely reproduced, of course, but the general
resemblance in manner is as close as it could well have
been without direct and conscious copying, the memory
of Addisonian methods is too apparent. Irving's real
genius, which occasionally in his other writings emits
delicious flashes, does not often assert itself in this
work; and though he has the knack of using the dry
point of Addison's humor, he does n't achieve what
etchers call "the burr" that ought to result from its
use. Addison, too, stings his lines in with true aqua-
fortis precision, and Irving's sketches are to his as pen-
and-ink drawing to the real etching. But it was not only
this lack of literary independence that belittled Irving's
dignity. He had become so well satisfied with his post of
mediator between the writers of the two nations, that it
became paramount with him to preserve the good-will he
had won in England, and this appears in the cautious
and *almost* obsequious mien of "Bracebridge." One may
trace it also, with amused pain, in his correspondence
with Paulding, — honest, pathetic Paulding, a rabid miso-
Briton who burned to write something truly American,
and could n't; whom Drake laughingly hails as

> "The bard of the backwoods,
> The poet of cabbages, log-huts, and gin."

Irving was vexedly concerned at the violent outbreaks of
his old coadjutor, directed against the British; yet,
though they were foolish, they showed real pluck. But
if we need other proof of the attitude which Irving was
distinctly recognized to have taken up, we may turn to
a page on which "The Edinburgh Review," unusually
amiable toward him at first, thus vented its tyrannical

displeasure at his excessive complaisance: "He gasped for British popularity [it said]: he came, and found it. He was received, caressed, applauded, made giddy: natural politeness owed him some return, for he imitated, admired, deferred to us. . . . . It was plain he thought of nothing else, and was ready to sacrifice everything to obtain a smile or a look of approbation." In a less savage fashion we, too, may admit the not very pleasant truth here enunciated with such unjust extremeness. An interval of nearly forty years lies between the date of the "Sketch-Book" and "Bracebridge" and that of "Our Old Home"; the difference in tone fully corresponds to the lapse of time.

In the use of native material, of course, Irving was a pioneer, along with Cooper, and was in this quite different from Poe, who had no aptitude in that way. "Knickerbocker's History of New York" is too farcical to take a high position on this score, though it undoubtedly had a beneficial effect in stirring up pride and interest in local antiquities; but "Rip Van Winkle" and "The Legend of Sleepy Hollow" were valuable acquisitions so far as they went. Would that they had been wrought out with a more masterly touch; and would that Irving had penetrated further in this direction! But, though these Hudson legends will long keep his fame renewed, it will perhaps be chiefly as a historian that he will be prized. His pleasant compilation on Goldsmith, his "Mahomet," "Columbus," and "Conquest of Granada," though not too profound, fill an enviable niche in popular esteem; and his mellow and stately narrative of Washington's life is a work of enduring excellence. But these lie outside of our present discussion. Nor need we compare his achievements in native fiction with Hawthorne's, after the review we have been making of the latter's relation to New England.

Poe and Irving and Hawthorne have all met with acceptance in other countries, and their works have been translated into several languages. Irving has exercised no perceptible influence on literature at home or abroad; Poe has entered more or less into the workings of a school in England and a group in France. Hawthorne's position on the Continent has perhaps not been so much one of conquest as of receiving an abstract admiration; but he has taken much stronger hold of the Anglo-Saxon mind than either of the others, and it is probable that his share in inspiring noble literature in America will — as it has already begun to show itself an important one — become vastly greater in future. It is impossible, as we have seen, to fix an absolute ratio between these writers. Irving has a more human quality than Poe, but Poe is beyond dispute the more original of the two. Each, again, has something which Hawthorne does not possess. But, if we must attempt at all to reduce so intricate a problem to exact terms, the mutual position of the three may be stated in the equation, Poe *plus* Irving *plus* an unknown quantity equals Hawthorne.

XIII.

THE LOSS AND THE GAIN.

THE suddenness with which Hawthorne faded away and died, when at the zenith of his fame, is no less strange and sad and visionary now than it was a poignant anguish then. He returned from Europe somewhat lingeringly, as we have seen, knowing too well the difference between the regions he was quitting and the thinner, sharper, and more wasting atmosphere of a country where every one who has anything to give is constantly drawn upon from every side, and has less resource for intellectual replenishment than in other lands. His seven years in England and Italy had, on the whole, been a period of high prosperity, of warm and gratifying recognition, of varied and delightful literary encounter, in addition to the pleasure of sojourning among so many new and suggestive scenes. And when he found himself once more on the old ground, with the old struggle for subsistence staring him steadily in the face again, it is not difficult to conceive how a certain degree of depression would follow. Just as this reaction had set in, the breaking out of civil war threw upon Hawthorne, before he had time to brace himself for the shock, an immense burden of sorrowing sympathy. The

conflict of feelings which it excited on the public side has
been sketched; and that alone should have been enough
to make the years of strife a time of continuous gloom
and anxiety to him; but it would be losing sight of a
very large element in his distress, not to add that he
mourned over the multitude of private griefs which were
the harvest of battle as acutely as if they had all been
his own losses. His intense imagination burned them
too deeply into his heart. How can we call this weakness, which involved such strength of manly tenderness
and sympathy? "Hawthorne's life was shortened by
the war," Mr. Lowell says. Expressing this view once,
to a friend, who had served long in the Union army, I
was met with entire understanding. He told me that
his own father, a stanch Unionist, though not in military
service, was as certainly brought to his death by the war
as any of the thousands who fell in battle. In how
wide and touchingly humane a sense may one apply to
Hawthorne Marvell's line on Cromwell's death, —

"To Love and Grief the fatal writ was signed!"

His decline was gradual, and semi-conscious, as if from
the first he foresaw that he could not outlive these trials.
In April, 1862, he visited Washington, and wrote the
article "Chiefly about War Matters" already alluded to.
He has left this glimpse of himself at that time: —

"I stay here only while Leutze finishes a portrait, which
I think will be the best ever painted of the same unworthy
subject. One charm it must needs have, — an aspect of immortal jollity and well-to-do-ness; for Leutze, when the sitting
begins, gives me a first-rate cigar, and when he sees me getting
tired, he brings out a bottle of splendid champagne; and we
quaffed and smoked yesterday, in a blessed state of mutual
good-will, for three hours and a half, during which the picture

made a really miraculous progress. Leutze is the best of fellows."

The trip was taken to benefit his health, which had already begun to give way; and though he wrote thus cheerily, he was by no means well. In another published note there is this postscript: —

"My hair really is not so white as this photograph, which I enclose, makes me. The sun seems to take an infernal pleasure in making me venerable, — as if I were as old as himself."

He had already, as we know, begun to meditate upon "The Dolliver Romance," trudging to and fro upon his hill-top, which was called, at home, "the mount of vision." But before proceeding with that, he began the series of essays composing "Our Old Home," not yet feeling strong enough for the more trying exertion of fiction. But the preparation of these, charming as they are, brought no exhilaration to his mind.

"I am delighted," he writes to his publisher, "at what you tell me about the kind appreciation of my articles, for I feel rather gloomy about them myself. . . . . I cannot come to Boston to spend more than a day, just at present. It would suit me better to come for a visit when the spring of next year is a little advanced, and if you renew your hospitable proposition then, I shall probably be glad to accept it; though I have now been a hermit so long, that the thought affects me somewhat as it would to invite a lobster or a crab to step out of his shell."

His whole tone with regard to "Our Old Home" seems to have been one of fatigue and discouragement. He had, besides, to deal with the harassing question of the dedication to Franklin Pierce, which he solved in this manly and admirable letter to his publisher: —

"I thank you for your note of the 15th instant, and have delayed my reply thus long in order to ponder deeply on your advice, smoke cigars over it, and see what it might be possible for me to do towards taking it. I find that it would be a piece of poltroonery in me to withdraw either the dedication or the dedicatory letter. My long and intimate personal relations with Pierce render the dedication altogether proper, especially as regards this book, which would have had no existence without his kindness; and if he is so exceedingly unpopular that his name is enough to sink the volume, there is so much the more need that an old friend should stand by him. I cannot, merely on account of pecuniary profit or literary reputation, go back from what I have deliberately felt and thought it right to do; and if I were to tear out the dedication, I should never look at the volume again without remorse and shame. As for the literary public, it must accept my book precisely as I think fit to give it, or let it alone."

By this time, the energy requisite for carrying on the Romance had sunk still lower, so that he wrote:—

"I can't tell you when to expect an instalment of the Romance, if ever. There is something preternatural in my reluctance to begin. I linger at the threshold, and have a perception of very disagreeable phantasms to be encountered if I enter. I wish God had given me the faculty of writing a sunshiny book."

And, a little later:—

"I don't see much probability of my having the first chapter of the Romance ready so soon as you want it. There are two or three chapters ready to be written, but I am not yet robust enough to begin, and I feel as if I should never carry it through."

His inability to work has been illustrated in the numerous bulletins of this period published by Mr. Fields: they show him at times despondent, as in the extracts above, then again in a state of semi-resolution. At another time there is mixed presentiment and humor in his report.

"I am not quite up to writing yet, but shall make an effort as soon as I see any hope of success. You ought to be thankful that (like most other broken-down authors) I do not pester you with decrepit pages, and insist upon your accepting them as full of the old spirit and vigor. That trouble, perhaps, still awaits you, after I shall have reached a further stage of decay. Seriously, my mind has, for the present, lost its temper and its fine edge, and I have an instinct that I had better kept quiet. Perhaps I shall have a new spirit of vigor, if I wait quietly for it; perhaps not."

But over all these last notes there hangs a melancholy shadow that makes the flickering humor even sadder than the awesome conviction that he has done with writing. How singular the mingled mood of that last letter, in which he grimly jests upon the breaking-down of his literary faculty! Here he announces, finally: "I hardly know what to say to the public about this abortive Romance, though I know pretty well what the case will be. I shall never finish it." Yet the cause was not so much the loss of literary power, as the physical exhaustion that had already worn him away beyond recovery. He longed for England; and possibly if he could have gone thither, the voyage, the milder climate, and the sense of rest that he would have felt there, might have restored him. He had friends in this country, however, who made attempts to break up the disastrous condition into which he had so unexpectedly come. In May of 1863, when "Our Old Home" was printing, he received from his friend Mr. Lowell this most charming invitation to come to Cambridge: —

My dear Hawthorne : — I hope you have not forgotten that during "anniversary week" you were to make me a little anniversary by a visit? I have been looking forward to it *ever* so long. My plan is that you come on Friday, so as to attend the election-meeting of our club, and then stay over Sunday, and Monday, and Tuesday, which is the last day of my holidays. How will that do? I am glad to hear your book is going through the press, and you will be nearer your proofsheets here. I have pencils of all colors for correcting in all moods of mind, — red for sanguine moments when one thinks there is some use in writing at all, blue for a modest depression, and black for times when one is satisfied there is no longer an intelligent public nor one reader of taste left in the world. You shall have a room to yourself, nearly as high and quite as easy of access as your tower, and I pledge myself that my crows, cat-birds, orioles, chimbley-swallows, and squirrels shall present you with the freedom of their city in a hollow walnut, so soon as you arrive.

Now will you write and say when you are to be expected? I assure you I have looked forward to your coming as one of my chiefest spring pleasures, ranking it with the advent of the birds.

Always cordially yours,

J. R. LOWELL.

"I have smoked a cigar over your kind invitation," wrote Hawthorne, in answer, "and mean to come. There is a little bit of business weighing upon me (literary business of course, an article for the magazine and for my volume, which I ought to have begun and finished long ago), but I hope to smash it in a day or two, and will meet you at the club on Saturday. I shall have very great pleasure in the visit."

But, at the last moment, he was obliged to give it up, being detained by a cold. And there seemed indeed a fatality which interfered with all attempts to thwart the coming evil. At the beginning of April, 1864, completely broken down, yet without apparent cause, he set out southward with Mr. William Ticknor. On arriving at Philadelphia he began to improve; but Mr. Ticknor's sudden death overthrew the little he had gained, and caused him to sink still more. It is not my purpose here to dwell upon the sad and unbeautiful details of a last illness : these things would make but a harsh closing chord in the strain of meditation on Hawthorne's life which we have been following out, — a life so beautiful and noble that to surround its ending with the remembrance of mere mortal ailment has in it something of coarseness. But it was needful to show in what way this great spirit bowed beneath the weight of its own sympathy with a national woe. Even when Dr. Holmes saw him in Boston, though "his aspect, medically considered, was very unfavorable," and though "he spoke as if his work were done, and he should write no more," still "there was no failing noticeable in his conversational powers." "There was nothing in Mr. Hawthorne's aspect," wrote Dr. Holmes, "that gave warning of so sudden an end as that which startled us all." He passed on into the shadow as if of his own will; feeling that his country lay in ruins, that the human lot carried with it more hate and horror and sorrow than he could longer bear to look at; welcoming — except as those dear to him were concerned — the prospect of that death which he alone knew to be so near. It was on the 19th of May, 1864, that the news came from Plymouth, in New Hampshire, — whither he had gone with Ex-President Pierce, — that Hawthorne was dead. Afterward, it was recalled with a kind of awe that through many years of his life Hawthorne had been in the habit, when trying a pen or idly scribbling at any time, of writing the number sixty-four;

as if the foreknowledge of his death, which he showed in the final days, had already begun to manifest itself in this indirect way long before. Indeed, he had himself felt that the number was connected with his life in some fatal way. Five days later he was carried to Sleepy Hollow, the beautiful cemetery where he had been wont to walk among the pines, where once when living at the Manse he had lain upon the grass talking to Margaret Fuller, when Mr. Emerson came upon them, and smiled, and said the Muses were in the woods that day.

A simple stone, with the single word "Hawthorne" cut upon it, was placed above him. He had wished that there should be no monument. He liked Wordsworth's grave at Grasmere, and had written, "It is pleasant to think and know that he did not care for a stately monument." Longfellow and Lowell and Holmes, Emerson and Louis Agassiz, and his friends Pierce, and Hillard, with Ellery Channing, and other famous men, assembled on that peaceful morning to take their places in the funeral train. Some who had not known him in life came long distances to see him, now, and ever afterward bore about with them the memory of his aspect, strong and beautiful, in his last repose. The orchards were blossoming; the roadside-banks were blue with violets, and the lilies of the valley, which were Hawthorne's favorites among the flowers, had come forth in quiet companies, to look their last on his face, so white and quiet too. So, while the batteries that had murdered him roared sullenly in the distant South, the rites of burial were fulfilled over the dead poet. Like a clear voice beside the grave, as we look back and listen, Longfellow's simple, penetrating chant returns upon the ear.

In vain to sum up, here, the loss unspeakable suffered in Hawthorne's death; and no less vain the attempt to fix in a few words the incalculable gain his life has left with us. When one remembers the power that was unexhausted in him still, one is ready to impeach cold Time and Fate for their treason to the fair prospect that lay before us all, in the continuance of his career. We look upon these few great works, that may be numbered on the fingers of a hand, and wonder what good end was served by the silent shutting of those rich pages that had just begun to open. We remember the tardy recognition that kept the fountain of his spirit so long half concealed, and the necessities that forced him to give ten of his best years to the sterile industry of official duties. But there are great compensations. Without the youthful period of hopes deferred, Hawthorne, as we have seen, would not have been the unique force, the high, untrammelled thinker that he became through that fortunate isolation ; wanting the uncongenial contact of his terms at Boston and Salem and Liverpool, it may be that he could not have developed his genius with such balance of strength as it now shows ; and, finally, without the return to his native land, the national fibre in him would have missed its crowning grace of conscientiousness. He might in that case have written more books, but the very loss of these, implying as it does his pure love of country, is an acquisition much more positively valuable.

There is a fitness, too, in the abrupt breaking off of his activity, in so far as it gives emphasis to that incompleteness of any verbal statement of truth, which he was continually insisting upon with his readers.

Hawthorne, it is true, expanded so constantly, that however many works he might have produced, it seems unlikely that any one of them would have failed to record some large movement in his growth ; and therefore it is

perhaps to be regretted that his life could not have been
made to solely serve his genius, so that we might have
had the whole sweep of his imagination clearly exposed.
As it is, he has not given us a large variety of characters;
and Hester, Zenobia, and Miriam bear a certain general
likeness one to another. Phœbe, however, is quite at
the opposite pole of womanhood; Hilda is as unlike any
of them as it is easy to conceive of her being; and
Priscilla, again, is a feminine nature of unique calibre, as
weird but not so warm as Goethe's Mignon, and at the
same time a distinctly American type, in her nervous yet
captivating fragility. In Priscilla and Phœbe are embodied two widely opposed classes of New England
women. The male characters, with the exception of
Donatello and Hollingsworth, are not so remarkable as
the feminine ones: Coverdale and Kenyon come very
close together, both being artistic and both reflectors for
the persons that surround them; and Dimmesdale is to
some extent the same character, — with the artistic escape
closed upon his passions, so that they turn within and
ravage his heart, — arrested and altered by Puritan influences. Chillingworth is perhaps too devilish a shape
of revenge to be discussed as a human individual. Septimius, again, is distinct; and the characterization of
Westervelt, in "Blithedale," slight as it is, is very stimu-
lating. Perhaps, after all, what leads us to pronounce
upon the whole fictitious company a stricture of homogeneity is the fact that the author, though presenting us
each time with a set of persons sufficiently separate from
his previous ones, does not emphasize their differences
with the same amount of external description that we
habitually depend upon from a novelist. The similarity
is more in the author's mode of presentation than in the
creations themselves.

This monotone in which all the personages of his dramas share is nearly related with some special distinctions of his genius. He is so fastidious in his desire for perfection, that he can scarcely permit his actors to speak loosely or ungrammatically: though retaining their essential individuality, they are endowed with the author's own delightful power of expression. This outward phasis of his work separates it at once from that of the simple novelist, and leads us to consider the special applicability to it of the term "romance." He had not the realistic tendency, as we usually understand that, but he possessed the power to create a new species of fiction. For the kind of romance that he has left us differs from all compositions previously so called. It is not romance in the sense of D'Urfé's or Scudéri's; it is very far from coming within the scope of Fielding's "romances"; and it is entirely unconnected with the tales of the German Romantic school. It is not the romance of sentiment; nor that of incident, adventure, and character viewed under a wordly coloring: it has not the mystic and melodramatic bent belonging to Tieck and Novalis and Fouqué. There are two things which radically isolate it from all these. The first is its quality of revived belief. Hawthorne, as has been urged already, is a great believer, a man who has faith; his belief goes out toward what is most beautiful, and this he finds only in moral truth. With him, poetry and moral insight are sacredly and indivisibly wedded, and their progeny is perfect beauty. This unsparingly conscientious pursuit of the highest truth, this metaphysical instinct, found in conjunction with a varied and tender appreciation of all forms of human or other life, is what makes him so decidedly the representative of a wholly new order of novelists. Belief, however, is not what he has usually been credited with, so much as incredulity. But the appearance of doubt is superficial, and arises from his fondness for illuminating fine but only half-perceptible traces of truth with the torch of superstition. Speaking of the supernatural, he says in his English journal: "It is remarkable that Scott should have felt interested in such subjects, being such a worldly and earthly man as he was; but then, indeed, almost all forms of popular superstition do clothe the ethereal with earthly attributes, and so make it grossly perceptible." This observation has a still greater value when applied to Hawthorne himself. And out of this questioning belief and transmutation of superstition into truth — for such is more exactly his method — proceeds also that quality of value and rarity and awe-enriched significance, with which he irradiates real life until it is sublimed to a delicate cloud-image of the eternal verities.

If these things are limitations, they are also foundations of a vast originality. Every greatness must have an outline. So that, although he is removed from the list of novelists proper, although his spiritual inspiration scares away a large class of sympathies, and although his strictly New England atmosphere seems to chill and restrain his dramatic fervor, sometimes to his disadvantage, these facts, on the other hand, are so many trenches dug around him, fortifying his fair eminence. Isolation and a certain degree of limitation, in some such sense as this, belong peculiarly to American originality. But Hawthorne is the embodiment of the youth of this country; and though he will doubtless furnish inspiration to a long line of poets and novelists, it must be hoped that they, likewise, will stand for other phases of its development, to be illustrated in other ways. No tribute to Hawthorne is less in accord with the biddings of his genius

than that which would merely make a school of fol-
lowers.

It is too early to say what position Hawthorne will
take in the literature of the world; but as his influence
gains the ascendant in America, by prompting new and
un-Hawthornesque originalities, it is likely also that it
will be made manifest in England, according to some
unspecifiable ratio. Not that any period is to be distinctly colored by the peculiar dye in which his own
pages are dipped; but the renewed tradition of a highly
organized yet simple style, and still more the masculine
tenderness and delicacy of thought and the fine adjustment of æsthetic and ethical obligations, the omnipresent
truthfulness which he carries with him, may be expected to become a constituent part of very many minds
widely opposed among themselves. I believe there is
no fictionist who penetrates so far into individual con-
sciences as Hawthorne; that many persons will be found
who derive a profoundly religious aid from his unobtru-
sive but commanding sympathy. In the same way, his
sway over the literary mind is destined to be one of no
secondary degree. "Deeds are the offspring of words,"
says Heine; "Goethe's pretty words are childless." Not
so with Hawthorne's. Hawthorne's repose is the acme
of motion; and though turning on an axis of conservatism, the radicalism of his mind is irresistible; he is
one of the most powerful because most unsuspected
revolutionists of the world. Therefore, not only is he an
incalculable factor in private character, but in addition
his unnoticed leverage for the thought of the age is
prodigious. These great abilities, subsisting with a temper so modest and unaffected, and never unhumanized
by the abstract enthusiasm for art, place him on a plane
between Shakespere and Goethe. With the universality

of the first only just budding within his mind, he has not so clear a response to all the varying tones of lusty human life, and the individuality in his utterance amounts, at particular instants, to constraint. With less erudition than Goethe, but also less of the freezing pride of art, he is infinitely more humane, sympathetic, holy. His creations are statuesquely moulded like Goethe's, but they have the same quick music of heart-throbs that Shakespere's have. Hawthorne is at the same moment ancient and modern, plastic and picturesque. Another generation will see more of him than we do; different interpreters will reveal other sides. As a powerful blow suddenly descending may leave the surface it touches unmarked, and stamp its impress on the substance beneath, so his presence will more distinctly appear among those farther removed from him than we. A single mind may concentrate your vision upon him in a particular way; but the covers of any book must perforce shut out something of the whole, as the trees in a vista narrow the landscape.

Look well at these leaves I lay before you; but having read them throw the volume away, and contemplate the man himself.

APPENDIX.

I.

IN May, 1870, an article was published in the "Portland Transcript," giving some of the facts connected with Hawthorne's sojourn in Maine, as a boy. This called out a letter from Alexandria, Va., signed "W. S.," and purporting to come from a person who had lived at Raymond, in boyhood, and had been a companion of Hawthorne's. He gave some little reminiscences of that time, recalling the fact that Hawthorne had read him some poetry founded on the Tarbox disaster, already mentioned.* Himself he described as having gone to sea at twenty, and having been a wanderer ever since. In speaking of the date of the poetry, "We could not have been more than ten years old," he said. This, of course, is a mistake, the accident having happened in 1819, when Hawthorne was fourteen. And it is tolerably certain that he did not even visit Raymond until he was twelve.

The letter called out some reminiscences from Mr. Robinson Cook, of Bolster's Mills, in Maine, who had also known Hawthorne as a boy; some poetry on the Tarbox tragedy was also found, and printed, which afterward proved to have been written by another person; and one or two other letters were published, not especially relevant to Hawthorne, but concerning

---

* See *ante*, p. 89.

the Tarbox affair. After this, "W. S." wrote again from Alexandria (November 23, 1870), revealing the fact that he had come into possession, several years before, of the manuscript book from which he afterward sent extracts. The book, he explained, was found by a man named Small, who had assisted in moving a lot of furniture, among it a "large mahogany bookcase" full of old books, from the old Manning House. This was several years before the civil war, and "W. S." met Small in the army, in Virginia. He reported that the book — "originally a bound blank one not ruled," and "gnawed by mice or eaten by moths on the edges"—contained about two hundred and fifty pages, and was written throughout, "the first part in a boyish hand though legibly, and showing in its progress a marked improvement in penmanship." The passages reprinted in the present volume were sent by him, over the signature "W. Sims," to the "Transcript," and published at different dates (February 11, 1871 ; April 22, 1871). Their appearance called out various communications, all tending to establish their genuineness ; but, beyond the identification of localities and persons, and the approximate establishing of dates, no decisive proof was forthcoming. Sims himself, however, was recalled by former residents near Raymond ; and there seemed at least much inferential proof in favor of the notes. A long silence ensued upon the printing of the second portion ; and at the end of 1871 it was made known that Sims had died at Pensacola, Florida. The third and last supposed extract from Hawthorne's note-book was sent from Virginia again, in 1873 (published June 21 of that year), by a person professing to have charge of Sims's papers. This person was written to by the editors of the "Transcript," but no reply has ever been received. A relative of Hawthorne in Salem also wrote to the Pensacola journal in which Sims's death was announced, making inquiry as to its knowledge of him and as to the source of the mortuary notice. No reply was ever received from this quarter, either. Sims, it is said, had been in the secret service under Colonel Baker, of dreaded fame in war-days; and it may be that, having enemies, he feared the notoriety to which his contributions to journalism might expose him, and decided to die, — at least so far as printer's ink could kill him. All these circumstances are unfortunate, because they make the solution of doubts concerning the early notes quite impossible, for the present.

The fabrication of the journal by a person possessed of some literary skill and familiar with the localities mentioned, at dates so long ago as 1816 to 1819, might not be an impossible feat, but it is an extremely improbable one. It is not likely that an ordinary impostor would hit upon the sort of incident selected for mention in these extracts. Even if he drew upon circumstances of his own boyhood, transferring them to Hawthorne's, he must possess a singularly clear memory, to recall matters of this sort; and to invent them would require a nice imaginative faculty. One of the first passages, touching the " son of old Mrs. Shane" and the " son of the Widow Hawthorne," is of a sort to entirely evade the mind of an impostor. The whole method of observation, too, seems very characteristic. If the portion descriptive of a raft and of the manners of the lumbermen be compared with certain memoranda in the " American Note-Books " (July 13 and 15, 1837), derived from somewhat similar scenes, a general resemblance in the way of seizing characteristics will be observed. Of course, if the early notes are fabrications, it may be that the author of them drew carefully after passages of the maturer journal, and this among others. But the resemblance is crossed by a greater youthfulness in the early notes, it seems to me, which it would be hard to produce artificially. The cool and collected style of the early journal is not improbable in a boy like Hawthorne, who had read many books and lived much in the companionship of older persons. Indeed, it is very much like the style of " The Spectator " of 1820. A noticeable coincidence is, that the pedler, Dominicus Jordan, should be mentioned in both the journal and " The Spectator." The circumstance that the dates should all have been said to be missing from the manuscript book is sus-

picious.　Yet the last extract has the month and year appended,
August, 1819.　What is more important is, that the date of
the initial inscription is given as 1816; and at the time when
this was announced it had not been ascertained even by Hawthorne's own family and relatives that he had been at Raymond so early.　But since the publications in the " Transcript,"
some letters have come to light of which I have made use; and
one of these, bearing date July 21, 1818, to which I have alluded in another connection, speaks of Raymond from actual
recollection.　"Does the Pond look the same as when I was
there?　It is almost as pleasant at Nahant as at Raymond.　I
thought there was no place that I should say so much of."
The furnisher of the notes, if he was disingenuous, might indeed have remembered that Hawthorne was in Maine about
1816; he may also have relied on a statement in the " Transcript's " editorial, to the effect that Hawthorne was taken to
Raymond in 1814.　In that editorial, it is also observed:
" Hawthorne was then a lad of ten years."　I have already said
that Sims refers to the period of the verses on the Tarboxes
as being a time when he and Hawthorne were " not more than
ten years old."　This, at first, would seem to suggest that he
was relying still further upon the editorial.　But if he had been
taking the editorial statement as a basis for fabrication, it is
not likely that he would have failed to ascertain exactly the
date of the freezing of Mr. and Mrs. Tarbox, which was 1819.
The careless way in which he alludes to this may have been
the inadvertence of an impostor trying to make his account
agree with one already published; but it is more likely that the
sender of the notes did not remember the precise year in which
the accident occurred, and was confused by the statement of the
" Transcript."　An impostor must have taken more pains, one
would think.　It must also be noticed that " the Widow *Haw*-
thorne " is spoken of in the notes.　Sims, however, in his preliminary letter, refers to the fact that " the universal pronun-
ciation of the name in Raymond was Hathorn, — the first
syllable exactly as the word ' hearth ' was pronounced at that

time "; and the explanation of the spelling in the notes doubtless is that Sims, or whoever transcribed the passage, changed it as being out of keeping with the now historic form of the name. It is possible that further changes were also made by the transcriber; and a theory which has some color is, that the object in keeping the original manuscript out of the way may have been, to make it available for expansions and embellishments, using the actual record as a nucleus.

II.

THE theme referred to in Chapter III. is given in full below. After the earlier portion of the present essay had been stereotyped, an article by Professor G. T. Packard, on Bowdoin College, was published in "Scribner's Monthly," which contains this mention of Hawthorne: —

"The author's college life was prophetic of the after years, when he so dwelt apart from the mass of men, and yet stirred so deeply the world's sensibilities and delighted its fancy. His themes were written in the sustained, finished style that gives to his mature productions an inimitable charm. The late Professor Newman, his instructor in rhetoric, was so impressed with Hawthorne's powers as a writer, that he not infrequently summoned the family circle to share in the enjoyment of reading his compositions. The recollection is very distinct of Hawthorne's reluctant step and averted look, when he presented himself at the Professor's study, and with girlish diffidence submitted a composition which no man in his class could equal. . . . . When the class was graduated, Hawthorne could not be persuaded to join them in having their profiles cut in paper, the only class picture of the time; nor did he take part in the Commencement exercises. His classmates understood that he intended to be a writer of romance, but none anticipated his remarkable development and enduring fame. It seems strange that among his admirers no one has offered him a fitting tribute by founding the Hawthorne Professorship of English Literature in the college where, under the tutelage of the accomplished and appreciative Professor Newman, he was stimulated to cultivate his native gift."

DE PATRIS CONSCRIPTIS ROMANORUM.

SENATUM Romanorum jam primum institutum, simplicem simul atque præstantissimum fuisse sentiunt omnes. Imperium fuit, quod populo nec avaritia nec luxuria vitiato optimum videretur. Lecti fuerunt senatores, non qui ambitiose potestatem cupiere, sed qui senectute, qui sapientia, qui virtute bellica vel privata insignes, in republica plurimum pollebant. Hominum consiliis virtute tam singulari præditorum paruit populus libenter atque senatores ut patres civibus venerati. Studium illis paternum adhibuere. Nulla unquam respublica, quam tum Romana, nec sanctior nec beatior fuit; iis temporibus etenim solum in publicum commodum principes administrabant; fidemque principibus populi habebant. Sed virtute prisca reipublicæ perdita, inimicitiis mutuis patres plebesque flagrare cœperunt, alienaque prosequi. Senatus in populum tyrannice saeviit, atque hostem se monstravit potius quam custodem reipublicæ. Concitatur vulgus studio libertatis repetendæ, atque per multa secula patrum plebisque contentiones historia Romana memorat; patribus pristinam auctoritatem servare conatis, licentiaque plebis omnia jura spernante. Hoc modo usque ad Punicum bellum, res se habebant. Tum pericula externa discordiam domesticam superabant, reipublicæque studium priscam patribus sapientiam, priscam populis reverentiam reddidit. Hac ætate omnibus virtutibus enituit Roma. Senatus, jure omnium consensu facto, opes suas prope ad inopiam plebis æquavit; patriæque solum amore gloria quæsita, pecunia nihili habita est. Sed quum Carthaginem reformidavit non diutius Roma, rediit respublica ad vitia pristina. Patres luxuria solum populis præstiterunt, et vestigia eorum populi secuti sunt. Senatus auctoritatem, ex illo ipso tempore, annus unusquisque diminuit, donec in ætate Augusti interitus nobilium humiliumque delectus omnino fere dignitatem conficerunt. Augustus equidem antiquam magnificentiam patribus reddidit, sed fulgor tantum fuit sine fervore. Nunquam in republica senatoribus potestates recuperatae. Postremum species etiam amissa est.

HATHORNE.

THE ROMAN SENATE.

EVERY one perceives that the Roman Senate, as it was originally constituted, was a no less simple than illustrious body. It was a sovereignty which appeared most desirable to a populace vitiated neither by avarice nor luxury. The senators were chosen, not from those who were ambitious of power, but those who wielded the largest influence in the Republic through wisdom and warlike valor or private virtue. The citizens bowed willingly to the counsels of men endowed with such singular worth, and venerated the senators as fathers. The latter exercised a paternal care. No republic ever was holier or more blessed than that of

Rome at this time; for in those days the rulers administered for the public convenience alone, and the people had faith in their rulers. But, the pristine virtue of the Republic lost, the fathers and the commonalty began to blaze forth with mutual hostilities, and to seek after the possessions of others. The Senate vented its wrath savagely upon the people, and showed itself rather the enemy than the guardian of the Republic. The multitude was aroused by the desire of recovering liberty, and through a very long period Roman history recounts the contentions of the fathers and the commonalty; the fathers attempting to preserve their old authority, and the license of the commons scorning every law. Affairs remained in this condition until the Punic War. Then foreign perils prevailed over domestic discord, and love of the Republic restored to the fathers their early wisdom, to the people their reverence. At this period, Rome shone with every virtue. The Senate, through the rightfully obtained consent of all parties, nearly equalized its power with the powerlessness of the commonalty; and glory being sought solely through love of the fatherland, wealth was regarded as of no account. But when Rome no longer dreaded Carthage, the commonwealth returned to its former vices. The fathers were superior to the populace only in luxury, and the populace followed in their footsteps. From that very time, every year diminished the authority of the Senate, until in the age of Augustus the death of the nobles and the selection of insignificant men almost wholly destroyed its dignity. Augustus, to be sure, restored to the fathers their ancient magnificence, but, great as was the fire (so to speak), it was without real heat. Never was the power of the senators recovered. At last even the appearance of it vanished.

III.

The lists of books referred to in Chapter IV. were recorded by different hands, or in different ways at various dates, so that they have not been made out quite satisfactorily. Some of the authors named below were taken out a great many times, but the number of the volume is given in only a few cases. It would seem, for example, that Voltaire's complete works were examined by Hawthorne, if we judge by his frequent application for some part of them, and the considerable number of volumes actually mentioned. In this and in other cases, the same volume is sometimes called for more than once. To make the matter clearer here, I have reduced the entries to a simple list of the authors read, without attempting to show how often a particular one was taken up. Few or none of them were read consecutively, and the magazines placed together at the end of my list were taken out at short intervals throughout the different years.

1830.

Œuvres de Voltaire.
Mémoire de Litérature.
Liancourt.
Œuvres de Rousseau.
Mass. Historical Collections.
Trial and Triumph of Faith.
Œuvres de Pascal.
Varenius' Geography.
Mickle's Lucian.
Dictionnaire des Sciences.
Pamela. (Vols. I., II.)
Life of Baxter.
Tournefort's Voyage.
Swift's Works.
Hitt on Fruit-Trees.
Bibliotheca Americana.
Ames's Antiquities.
Hamilton's Works.
Gifford's Juvenal.

Allen's Biographical Dictionary.
Fénélon.
Académie Royale des Inscriptions.
Mather's Apology.
Vertol's History of Sweden.
Taylor's Sermons.
Life of Luckington.
L'an 2440.
Montague's Letters.
English Botany. (3 vols.)
Gay's Poems.
Inchbald's Theatre.
Sowerby's English Botany.
Crabbe's Borough.
Crabbe's Bibliographical Dictionary.
Collection of Voyages (Hakluyt's ?).
Lives of the Admirals.
British Zoölogy.

1831.

Los Eruditos.
Connoisseur.
Camilla.
Gifford's Persius.
Bartram's Travels.
Humphrey's Works.
Voltaire.
Pennant's British Zoölogy.
Mandeville's Travels.
Rehearsal Transposed.
Gay's Poems.
Pompey the Little.
Shaw's General Zoölogy.

Philip's Poems.
Sowerby's English Botany.
Racine.
Corneille.
Wilkinson's Memoirs and Atlas.
History of the Shakers.
The Confessional.
Calamy's Life of Baxter.
Académie Royale des Inscripts.
Essais de Montaigne. (Vols. I., II., III., IV.)
Cadell's Journey through Italy and Carniola.

Cobbet's Ride in France.
Temple's Works. (Vols. I., II., III.)
Asiatic Researches.
Cochran's Tour in Siberia.
Chardin's Travels.
Brandt's History of the Reformation.
Russell's Natural History.
Aleppo. (Vol. I.)
Answer to the Fable of the Bees.
Hanway's Travels.
Memoirs of C. J. Fox.
Bayle's Critical Dictionary. (Vols. II., V., VI.)
State Trials. (Vols. I., II., IV., V., VI.)

Tales of a Traveller.
Dictionnaire des Sciences. (Vol. XVII.)
Bacon's Works. (Vol. II.)
Gordon's Tacitus.
Colquhoun on the Police.
Cheyne on Health.
Pope's Homer. (Vol. I.)
Letters: De Maintenon. (Vol. IX.)
Reichard's Germany.
Œuvres de Rousseau.
Notes on the West Indies by Prichard.
Crishull's Travels in Turkey.

1832–33.

Clarendon's Tracts.
History of England.
Prose Works of Walter Scott. (Vols. III., V., VI.)
Feltham's Resolves.
Roscoe's Sovereigns.
Histoire de l'Académie.
South America.
Savages of New Zealand.
Stackhouse's History of the Bible.
Dryden's Poems.
Tucker's Light of Nature.
History of South Carolina.
Poinsett's Notes on Mexico.
Bruce's Travels.
Browne's Jamaica.
Collins's New South Wales.
Broughton's Dictionary.
Seminole War.
Shaw's Zoölogy.
Reverie.
Gifford's Pitt.
Curiosities of Literature.
Massinger.
Literary Recollections.
Coleridge's Aids to Reflection.
Coleridge, Shelley, and Keats.
Paris and Fonblanque.

Elia.
Gardens and Menagerie.
Medical Jurisprudence.
History of Paris.
Scott's Prose Works.
Kittell's Specimens American Poetry.
Lister's Journey.
Annals of Salem.
Library of Old English Prose Writers.
Memoirs of Canning.
Miscellaneous Works of Scott.
Jefferson's Writings.
History of Andover.
Good's Book of Nature.
History of Haverhill.
Madden's Travels. (Vols. I., II.)
Riedesel's Memoirs.
Boston Newspapers (1736, 1739, 1754, 1762, 1771, 1783).
Drake's Mornings in Spring.
Drake's Evenings in Autumn.
Anecdotes of Bowyer.
Gouverneur Morris. (Vols. I., II.)
Bryan Walton's Memoirs.
Moses Mendelssohn.
Collingwood.

Felt's Annals.
Strutt's Sports and Pastimes.
Schiller.
Mrs. Jameson. (2 vols.)
Thatcher's Medical Biography.
History of Plymouth.
Crabbe's Universal Dictionary.
Lewis's History of Lynn.
A Year in Spain, by a Young American. (Vols. I., II.)
Croker's Boswell.
Deane's History of Scituate.
Diplomatic Correspondence. (Vols. I., II.)
Temple's Travels. (Vol. II.)

Fuller's Holy State.
Remarkables of Increase Mather.
History of Portland. (Vols. I., II.)
Practical Tourist.
Elements of Technology.
Heber's Life, by Taylor.
Ductor Substantium.
Heber's Travels in India. (Vols. I., II.)
Byron's Works.
Travels in Brazil and Buenos Ayres.
History of Spain.
Franklin's Works.
Mental Cultivation.

1835.

Life of Gouverneur Morris.
Hamilton's Progress of Society.
Twiner's Sacred History.
Encyclopædia.
Life of Arthur Lee.
Life of Sir Humphry Davy.
Coleridge, Shelley, and Keats.
Prior's Poems. (Vol. I.)

Jefferson's Writings. (Vols. I., II.)
Memoirs of the Tower of London.
History of King's Chapel.
Memoirs of Dr. Burney.
Hone's Every Day Book. (Vols. I, II., III.)
Life of Livingstone.

1836.

Life of Hamilton. (Vol. I.)
Debates in Parliament. (Vol. I.)
Curiosities of Literature (Vol. I.)
Combe on the Constitution of Man.
Babbage on Economy of Machinery.
Eulogies on Jefferson and Adams.
Hone's Every Day Book. (Vols. I., III.)
Dunlap's History of the Arts of Design. (Vols. I., II.)
Mende's Guide to Observation of Nature.
Cobbett's Cottage Economy.
Douglas's Summary. (Vol. I.)
Practical Tourist. (Vols. I., II.)
Dick on Improvement of Society.
Bush's Life of Mohammed.

Temple's Travels in Peru. (Vol. I.)
Gay's Poems.
Pliny's Natural History.
Coleridge's Table-Talk.
Letters from Constantinople. (Vols. I., II.)
Reynolds's Voyages.
Adventures on Columbia River, by Ross Cox.
Baine's History of Cotton Manufacture.
History of Nantucket.
Travels in South America.
Müller's Universal History.
Antar. A Bedoueen Romance.
Lives of the Philosophers. (Vols. I., II.)

Description of Trades.
Colman's Visit to England.
Ludolph's History of Ethiopia.
Griffin's Remains.
McCree's Life of Knox.
Walker's Sufferings of the Clergy.
Voyage de la mer du Sud au Nord.
Biographia Literaria.
The Stranger in America.
Raumer's England in 1835.

Random Recollections of the House of Lords.
The German Student.
Sparks's American Biography.
Brewster's Natural Magic.
Prior's Life of Goldsmith.
Sparks's Washington.
Walter Scott's Demonology and Witchcraft.
Scott's Life of Bonaparte.   (3 vols.)

1837.

Washington's Writings.
Martineau's Miscellany.
Wraxall's Memoirs.
Bancroft's United States History.
Rush, on the Human Voice.
Drake's Indian Biography.
Wordsworth's Poetical Works.
Clarendon's History of the Rebellion.

Reliques of Ancient English Poetry.
Baylie's Historical Memoirs of Plymouth County.
Life of Jefferson, by Tucker.
Random Recollections of the House of Commons.
Specimens of American Poetry.

1838.

Life of Jefferson.
Brown's Novels.
Parr's Works.
Select Comedies.
Froissart's Ancient Chronology.
Byron's Works.
Plutarch's Lives.
London Encyclopædia of Architecture.
Gentleman's Magazine.
Monthly Magazine.
Monthly Review.
European Magazine.
Christian Examiner.
Edinburgh Magazine.
Annual Register.
Quarterly Review.

Southern Review.
Worcester's Magazine.
North American Review.
United States Service Journal.
Court Magazine.
Museum of Literature and Science.
Westminster Review.
London Monthly Magazine.
Eclectic Review.
Foreign Quarterly Review.
Blackwood's Magazine.
Metropolitan Magazine.
New England Magazine.
British Critic.
American Encyclopædia.
Rees's Cyclopædia.
Gifford's Juvenal.

INDEX.

15 *

Cambridge : Electrotyped and Printed by Welch, Bigelow, & Co.

WITHDRAWN